Consumer Reports®

EXPERT · INDEPENDENT · NONPROFIT

BUYING GUIDE

BEST BUYS FOR

2007

The editors of
CONSUMER REPORTS magazine

Consumers Union · Yonkers, NY

Contents

Shop Smart in 2007

Latest Buying Advice

Product Ratings and Reliability

More Useful Buying Information

CONSUMER REPORTS BUYING GUIDE 2007

CONSUMER REPORTS (ISSN 0010-7174) is published monthly, except twice in December, by Consumers Union of U.S., Inc., 101 Truman Avenue, Yonkers, NY 10703-1057. Periodicals postage paid at Yonkers, NY, and at other mailing offices. Canadian postage paid at Mississauga, Ontario, Canada. Canadian publications registration no. 2665247-98, agreement number 40015148. Title CONSUMER REPORTS registered in U.S. Patent Office. Contents of this issue copyright © 2006 by Consumers Union of U.S., Inc. All rights reserved under International and Pan-American copyright conventions. Reproduction in whole or in part is forbidden without prior written permission (and is never permitted for commercial purposes). CU is a member of Consumers International. Mailing lists: CU rents or exchanges its customer postal list so it can be provided to other publications, companies, and nonprofit organizations. If you wish your name deleted from lists and rentals, send your address label with a request for deletion to CONSUMER REPORTS, P.O. Box 2127, Harlan, IA 51593-0316. **U.S. Postmaster:** Send address changes to P.O. Box 2109, Harlan, IA 51593-0298. **Canada Post:** If copies are undeliverable, return to CONSUMER REPORTS, P.O. Box 1051, STN MAIN, Fort Erie, ON L2A 6C7. Back issues: Single copies of 12 preceding issues, $7.95 each; Buying Guide, $10 each. Write Back Issues, CONSUMER REPORTS, Customer Relations, 101 Truman Ave., Yonkers, N.Y. 10703. Consumer Reports Buying Guide 2007 (ISBN 1-933524-01-4 and 978-1-933524-01-6).

Buying Advice at Your Fingertips

The Consumer Reports Buying Guide 2007 is your handy one-stop source for making intelligent, informed, money-saving purchases for all your home and personal needs. Consult it before you shop and bring it to the store to help you compare brands. Here's how to make best use of this buying guide:

Whether you shop in stores, through catalogs, or online, arm yourself with time- and money-saving strategies by reading **Shopping Strategies to Get Best Value,** on page 7. This section includes two revealing surveys: **Appliance Retailers Compared** and **Computer Retailers Compared,** about the best places to go and methods to use when shopping for various products. It also includes a sidebar about the hooey you might be handed by a salesman trying to sell you an extended warranty you probably don't need.

You may not be stepping into an electronics store, appliance store, or car dealership this week, but we're pretty sure you'll be visiting a supermarket. Be sure to read **Shop Smart in the Supermarket** on page 15. Here you'll find simple strategies that can add up to big savings each year.

After you've brushed up on your shopping savvy, turn to the **Buying Advice** section, beginning on page 18, for guidance from the experts at CONSUMER REPORTS on more than 45 product categories. From air conditioners and microwave ovens to televisions and washing machines, you will get invaluable information on what's available, features that count, and

how to choose the model that's best for you.

Are you in the market for a car? The **Autos** section, starting on page 145, has the latest **Ratings** and information on new and used cars to help you make the right buying decision. In addition to reviews of the 2006-07 models, there's a section on the best and worst used cars, and reliability ratings for more than 225 models currently in the marketplace.

Ratings are given for more than 700 consumer products in 20 categories. Along with the Ratings, you'll find **Brand Reliability** information for some products that present survey results from thousands of readers on repairs and problems they've had with various brands.

Finally, there's the **Brand Locator**, with information about contacting manufacturers, and a list of recent **Product Recalls.**

For this 2007 edition, we have added buying advice for five new categories of products: air cleaners, flooring, hedge trimmers, coffeemakers, and countertops. So grab this handy little book whenever you shop. We hope it saves you money and helps you get the best value every time you take it out.

Consumer Reports®

WHO WE ARE

About the CONSUMER REPORTS family of products

Founded as a magazine in 1936, CONSUMER REPORTS now brings you its unbiased, trusted information in many formats. Products and publications include CONSUMER REPORTS magazine; buying guides and special issues from Consumer Reports Publications Development; two newsletters, Consumer Reports On Health and Consumer Reports Money Adviser; Consumer Reports TV News, a nationally syndicated consumer news service; and the new ShopSmart magazine.

ConsumerReports.org offers site subscribers a searchable version of our test findings and advice. Auto prices and custom reports are available through the **Consumer Reports New Car Buying Kit, Consumer Reports Used Car Buying Kit, Consumer Reports New Car Price Service,** and **Consumer Reports Used Car Price Service.** You can find prices, subscription rates, and more information on all these products and services at *www.ConsumerReports.org.* Go to "Bookstore" on the home page. **ConsumerReportsMedicalGuide.org** provides independent health information, including exclusive treatment Ratings and detailed data about prescription drugs, to help consumers with difficult medical decisions.

CONSUMER REPORTS magazine specializes in head-to-head, brand-name comparisons of autos and household products. It also provides informed, impartial advice on a broad range of topics from health and nutrition to personal finance and travel.

CONSUMER REPORTS buys all the products it tests and accepts no free samples. We accept no advertising from outside entities nor do we let any company use our information or Ratings for commercial purposes.

CONSUMER REPORTS is published by Consumers Union, an independent, nonprofit testing and information organization—the largest such organization anywhere in the world.

Since 1936, Consumers Union's mission has been to test products, inform the public, and protect consumers. Our income is derived solely from the sale of our publications and online information and services, and from nonrestrictive, noncommercial contributions, grants, and fees.

Shopping Strategies to Get Best Values

Are you a careful researcher, someone who takes the time to shop for the best price on whatever you're buying? Perhaps you're a time-saver, looking to get the best price as quickly as possible. Or do you window-shop? Whatever your shopping style, you have lots more choices these days.

While shopping alternatives have grown, the basic rules for smart shopping remain the same: Do your homework and determine the best value for your needs. In this chapter we give you strategies for shopping smart—in the store, online, and by catalog. As you plan your purchases, consult this guide for more than 700 product Ratings (page 226) plus brand reliability information for many products.

STORE STRATEGIES

Traditional retailers are still the principal shopping choice of most consumers. Brick-and-mortar stores allow what online or catalog shopping can't—an in-person judgment of overall appearance and important sensory qualities. Researching your purchase before you set off for the store can pay off in valuable product knowledge, time saved, and, maybe, a lower price.

Specialty stores, special service. Need help selecting a product in an unfamiliar category? Just want a real person to help you? Smaller stores, such as audio boutiques and Main Street shops, can provide a knowledgeable staff and personal service, including special ordering. These advantages may be offset by higher prices. Determine a fair price before you go, using this guide, the Web, or a retailer's catalog. Then decide how much the personal service is worth to you. Be aware that for some products, such as computers, you can better customize your purchase by buying online. A 2004 CONSUMER REPORTS survey found that people purchasing desktop computers via the Internet or a catalog were generally more satisfied than people who bought them at a brick-and-mortar store.

Bottom-line basics. Is finding the type of product you want at a good price more important than the latest technology and a large selection? Mass merchandisers such as Wal-Mart and Target cover many categories with a selection of moderately priced brands from well-known manufacturers, along with their own store brands. Though these stores usually have liberal return policies, returns may entail time and hassle.

Big stores, big selection. Specialty chains such as Circuit City and Best Buy account for about half of home-electronics sales. Home Depot and Lowe's control one-fourth of the home-improvement product market. CompUSA inhabits strip malls across the

Stores make big profits on warranties you don't need. Here's a look at some of the hooey you shouldn't heed.

Retailers want you to buy extended warranties, or service plans, because they're cash cows. Stores keep 50 percent or more of what they charge for warranties. That's more than they make selling actual products.

"You sell a $400 television set and maybe make $10," Eric Arnum, editor of Warranty Week, a trade newsletter, says of retailers. "But you sell a $100 warranty and make $50."

For the consumer, however, extended warranties are notoriously bad deals because products seldom break within the extended-warranty window (typically three years), and when they do, the repair often isn't much more than the cost of the warranty, our data show.

We have long advised against extended warranties, with the exception of treadmills, which require a house call to fix and are pricey, and three types of TVs. LCD and plasma TVs are expensive and we don't have enough data yet to determine their long-term reliability. The third type, microdisplay-projections, are also expensive and have been the most repair-prone type of TV in their first year of use.

Still, hardball sales tactics led consumers to spend $16 billion last year on extended warranties, and hardball sales tactics flourish. Don't be fooled by these lines, which our reporter heard in various stores.

1. "You'll be sorry."
Store: P.C. Richard & Son.
Product: Room air conditioner.
The scenario: When our reporter declined to pay $120 for a five-year service plan for a $160 air conditioner, the salesman cast a "you poor fool" look. He then summoned his colleagues. "You'll be sorry," a second salesman said. Our reporter noted that if the air conditioner broke, it would be nearly as cheap to buy another. The response? "So when something breaks you just throw it out? You either have plenty of money or don't care about being wasteful."
Reality check: The cost of the warranty is out of line with the replacement price. Room air conditioners have become inexpensive commodities. We don't collect reliability data for them anymore because we have found that all major brands have low repair rates.

---

country. Sears has a network of stores and a Web site with lots of product choices for major appliances and other home products.

These chains may also feature special services, such as viewing/listening rooms for home-theater demonstrations. And although sales-staff expertise may vary, your questions will usually be answered.

Join the club. If you're willing to be flexible on brand and model, check a warehouse club: Costco, BJ's Wholesale Club,

or Sam's Club (Wal-Mart's warehouse sibling). Since those stores emphasize value, not service or selection, expect long lines and little sales help. Prices are consistently low, though not necessarily the lowest.

Clubs charge an annual membership fee (generally $35 to $45). If you don't shop there frequently, that fee can undo much of your savings. But big savings on a single purchase can pay for your membership. Most clubs will issue a limited-time shop-

2. "Warranties are shorter."
Store: Sears.

Product: Gas range.

The scenario: "Do you recommend an extended warranty for a gas range?" our reporter asked. A salesman said: "People come back here all the time with their faces down, wishing they had. You get only one-year coverage from the manufacturer, and that only applies to defects. We cover everything. Plus, we come to your house once a year to inspect your range."

Reality check: Standard warranties are indeed getting skimpier. But the odds of your gas range breaking within the first three years is only 19 percent. When a breakdown occurred, readers we surveyed paid an average repair cost of $150 vs. $108 for the extended warranty. And ranges require minimal maintenance.

3. "These break all the time."
Store: Best Buy.

Product: Side-by-side refrigerator.

The scenario: When our reporter was on the fence about spending $150 on a three-year protection plan for a $1,500 refrigerator, the saleswoman went to work. "You see these electronic controls?" she said of digital touchpads on the door. "This is new tech-nology, and these things can go at any time. You never know when it's going to happen."

Reality check: Most refrigerators incorporate electronic controls. The product failure rate within three years ranges from 8 to 28 percent. Breakdowns probably have less to do with electronics than with whether a model has an icemaker. Side-by-side models that broke cost $150 on average to repair, close to the cost of the warranty.

4. "I can't vouch for imports."
Store: Lowe's.

Product: Dishwasher.

The scenario: "The quality isn't there anymore," a salesman told our reporter in a dual-edged pitch to sell a pricey, feature-laden dishwasher—and an extended warranty, just in case. "Manufacturers are cutting corners. Everything is being made in Mexico, and God only knows what they're doing down there."

Reality check: Only 13 percent of three-year-old dishwashers that readers have told us about in annual reliability surveys have been repaired. CONSUMER REPORTS has no data on whether dishwashers or any other large or small appliances are more or less reliable depending on the country where they are assembled.

ping pass, letting you browse without joining, but you may have to pay a surcharge if you buy goods as a nonmember.

CATALOG STRATEGIES
Catalogs offer selection and convenience, often from established, proven companies with top-notch customer service. And of course they offer 24/7 access. Most catalog merchants are also online.

The catalog-Web connection can give you the best of both venues. You can browse the catalog and then order online using a catalog's "quick search" feature, or call the toll-free number. Online catalogs typically feature more merchandise than expensive-to-mail paper catalogs. Web sites frequently feature lines not available in the paper catalog, online-only sales and bargains, even
Continued on page 14

APPLIANCE RETAILERS COMPARED

Shop independents for big stuff, online for small stuff

You have lots of choices when it's time to buy that new refrigerator, washing machine, or other large appliance. You can go to a big-box retailer, like Home Depot or Best Buy, or you can head downtown to your local mom-and-pop appliance store. When you're looking for a small appliance like a mixer or toaster, you also have the option of shopping online. To help you make the right choices, the Consumer Reports National Research Center in 2005 surveyed more than 13,000 subscribers to find out how satisfied they were with their experiences purchasing nearly 25,000 appliances in terms of price, selection, product quality and checkout ease.

What we found

• Don't assume you'll get a better price for large appliances at a big-box store. Our survey respondents found no meaningful differences in price or product quality regardless of where they shopped for large appliances. Despite their reputations for bargains, Home Depot and Wal-Mart were deemed merely average on price. Readers preferred the little guys to big boxes on the strength of their courteous, accessible, and helpful employees, and greater willingness to provide delivery and installation services.

• For small appliances, survey respondents found better prices at most big boxes than they did at independents. However, they were far more satisfied with Amazon.com and independents than they were with major merchants, including Sam's Club, Target, Best Buy, and Wal-Mart. Readers were much happier with Amazon's online shopping experience than with any of the big boxes. When it came to price, only Costco was competitive with Amazon, but it was at the bottom of the heap when it came to selection and service.

• The independents got top service scores for small and large appliances, though prices were higher than average for small appliances. Sears did especially well for small appliances.

• Of the major retailer in our Ratings that carry small and large appliances, Sears had a slight edge, scoring high for small appliance selection, service, and checkout, and better than average for large appliance checkout.

Appliance retailers

Better ← ⊖ ⊖ ○ ⊖ ● → Worse

Retailer	Reader score (0–100, P F G VG E)	Price	Selection	Product Quality	Service	Checkout ease
SMALL APPLIANCES						
Amazon.com	92	⊖	⊖	⊖	–	–
Independent stores	87	○	⊖	⊖	⊖	⊖
Costco	84	⊖	●	○	●	●
Sears	82	○	⊖	○	⊖	⊖
Lowe's	80	○	○	○	○	○
Home Depot	79	○	○	○	○	○
Sam's Club	78	○	●	○	●	●
Target	78	○	●	◐	●	⊖
Best Buy	76	●	○	◐	●	●
Wal-Mart	75	○	●	●	●	●
LARGE APPLIANCES						
Independent stores	87	○	○	○	⊖	⊖
P.C. Richard & Son	85	○	○	○	○	⊖
Sears	84	○	○	○	○	⊖
H.H. Gregg	84	○	○	○	○	○
Lowe's	83	○	○	○	○	○
Home Depot	80	○	●	○	⊖	○
Best Buy	78	○	◐	○	●	●

Guide to the Survey

The Ratings are based on 13,426 subscribers who reported on 24,956 appliance purchases in the 2005 Appliance Store Shopper Satisfaction Survey, conducted by the Consumer Reports National Research Center. Small appliances include air conditioners, gas grills, and vacuum cleaners. Large appliances include ranges, cooktops or wall ovens, dishwashers, over-the-range microwave ovens, refrigerators, washers, and dryers. Subscribers do not necessarily mirror the U.S. population. **Reader score** reflects readers' assessments of their overall buying experience. A score of 100 would mean all respondents had been completely satisfied; 80 would mean very satisfied, on average; 60, fairly well satisfied. Differences of less than 3 points aren't meaningful. **Price, selection, product quality, service,** and **checkout ease** scores reflect the percentage of respondents who rated the store as excellent or very good on each item. Higher scores mean that the store was rated more favorably, lower scores less favorably, compared with the median score for that attribute. Those attributes for small and large appliances are not comparable.

COMPUTER RETAILERS COMPARED

Web-based retailers offer better computer prices

It's now common to find fast, powerful, reasonably priced computers virtually everywhere in the marketplace. If you're looking to buy a desktop computer, be sure to check these survey results and Ratings on the best retailers for PCs to ensure that you get the model and service that match your personal computing needs.

What we found

Web-based retailers tended to score better overall on price in the latest Computer Shopping Survey, conducted by the Consumer Reports National Research Center. Amazon.com was the only vendor to get the highest rating for its prices in the survey, while PC/Mac Connection.com, PC/MacMall.com, and TigerDirect.com all rated better than average and were standouts for selection. Bear in mind, however, that most independent online retailers sell both new and refurbished systems, so make sure you know which you're getting.

• One limitation of independent online retailers is that you might not have a lot of flexibility in customizing. The best place to do that is at the manufacturer's own site. Among those, Apple rated tops in our survey, with superior selection and service. Lenovo (IBM) ranked among the highest overall for Windows PCs, though Dell earned top marks for selection.

• Our respondents were less satisfied overall with their buying experiences at retail stores. Most stores offered average prices at best and few earned high marks for their service or selection. Two exceptions were Apple's retail stores and Micro Center, both of which were highly rated for selection and service.

• For retailers with both online and brick-and-mortar stores, our survey respondents fared better by going the Web route. Costco and Circuit City's Web sites, for example, offered slightly better selection than their traditional stores, our respondents told us. One advantage of dealing with a retailer that has both: You can buy the system online, then pick it up almost immediately from the store (as did 61 percent of our respondents who bought computers on Circuit City's Web site). If you're dissatisfied with your computer, you can also return it to the store rather than having to ship it.

Guide to the Survey

Ratings are based on 81,941 responses from CONSUMER REPORTS subscribers who completed the Computer Shopping Survey conducted by the Consumer Reports National Research Center, covering home computers purchased new from January 2005 through June 2006. **Reader score** is based on the respondents' satisfaction with their purchase experience. A score of 100 would mean all respondents were completely satisfied; 80 would mean very satisfied, on average; 60, fairly well satisfied. Differences of less than 4 points are not meaningful. **Survey results** reflect how each vendor did in comparison with the average of all others. Respondents rated vendors on their **selection** of computers, **service** (including knowledge and helpfulness of staff), **prices**, and **Web site** usability. Service was rated only by those who bought computers in a store or phoned or e-mailed the vendor. Under **return policy**, **restock fee** indicates those stores that charge a percentage of the purchase price to return a computer; details vary. **Major brands sold** might not include all brands for sale. Subscribers may not be representative of the general population. A "–" indicates insufficient data or not applicable..

Computer retailers

Better ◖ ◖ ○ ◖ ● Worse

Key number	Computer store	Reader score	Selection	Service	Price	Web site	Days	Restock fees?	Apple	Averatec	Compaq	Dell	eMachines	Gateway	HP	Lenovo	Sony	Toshiba
	MANUFACTURER DIRECT *By web or phone. Allows configuration of models.*																	
1	Apple	93	◖	◖	○	◖	14	•	•									
2	Lenovo (IBM)	85	◖	◖	○	○	21	•								•		
3	Compaq/HP	84	◖	◖	○	○	21				•				•			
4	Dell	83	◖	○	○	○	21	•				•						
5	Sony	82	◖	○	●	○	30										•	
6	Toshiba	81	◖	○	○	○	15	•										•
7	Gateway	79	◖	◖	○	○	15	•						•				
	RETAIL WEB SITE/CATALOG *Some allow no configuration of models.*																	
8	Amazon.com	90	◖	–	◖	◖	30 [1]	•	•	•	•		•	•	•		•	•
9	PC/Mac Connection.com	90	◖	◖	◖	◖	30 [2]	•	•	•	•		•	•	•		•	•
10	Costco.com	87	◐	–	◖	○	6 mo.			•	•	•		•	•		•	
11	CDW.com	87	◖	–	○	○	30 [2]	•	•	•	•		•	•	•		•	•
12	TigerDirect.com	84	◖	–	◖	○	30 [2]	•	•	•		•	•	•	•		•	•
13	PC/MacMall.com	84	◖	◖	◖	○	15 [2]	•	•	•	•		•	•	•		•	•
14	Best Buy.com	81	○	–	○	◐	14	•	•	•	•		•	•	•		•	•
15	Circuit City.com	80	○	◐	○	◐	14	•	•	•	•		•	•	•		•	•
	RETAIL STORE *Some allow no configuration of models.*																	
16	Apple store	90	◖	◖	◐	–	14	•	•									
17	Micro Center	81	◖	◖	○	–	30/7 [3]	•	•	•	•		•	•	•	•	•	•
18	Dell kiosk	81	○	○	◖	–	21	•				•						
19	Costco	81	●	●	◖	–	6 mo.				•		•	•	•		•	
20	Sam's Club	79	●	●	○	–	6 mo.		•	•			•	•		•	•	
21	Office Depot	79	◐	○	○	–	14			•		•	•	•		•	•	•
22	Staples	78	●	○	○	–	14		•	•			•	•		•	•	•
23	OfficeMax	77	●	◐	◐	–	14		•	•			•	•		•	•	•
24	Circuit City	76	○	◐	◐	◐	14	•	•	•	•		•	•	•		•	•
25	Best Buy	76	○	○	○	◐	14	•	•	•	•		•	•	•		•	•
26	CompUSA	76	○	○	◐	–	14	•	•	•	•		•	•	•		•	•
27	Fry's Electronics	76	○	◐	○	–	30/15 [3]	•		•	•		•	•	•		•	•
28	Wal-Mart	71	●	●	○	–	15		•	•			•	•		•		•
	TV SHOPPING NETWORK *Allows no configuration of models.*																	
29	QVC	84	○	○	○	–	30		•		•			•				•
30	HSN	81	◐	○	○	–	30				•			•				•

[1] Policies of third-party vendors vary.   [2] Certain brands nonrefundable.   [3] Desktops/laptops.

product-selection tips and detailed enlargements of product photos. Readers of online catalogs can snap up specials and close-outs before items go out of stock.

Ordering from a catalog over the phone or the Web is usually quick, but popular items can still be on back-order, even if they seemed to be in stock when you placed the order. If you don't receive your purchase within the promised time, check back. And before you order, check shipping fees—they can vary widely and add significantly to the cost of the order.

WEB STRATEGIES

You can hunt down just about anything on the Web, from potato chips to vacation homes, but you'll find that some items are more compatible with e-commerce than others. Books, music, videos, DVDs, and computer software are big online successes because they're standardized products, and no bricks-and-mortar store is able to stock every title. Branded electronics items also lend themselves to online shopping because it's handy to select them by manufacturer and specific features. Shipping is another important factor: Small, lightweight purchases—books as opposed to, say, refrigerators—are top online sellers.

Perhaps even more than for buying, the Web is immensely useful for researching a purchase. Information that would previously have taken many hours and many phone calls to find (if it could be found at all) is now available with a few simple clicks of your mouse. Thus armed, you can make better decisions about where to buy, what to buy, and how much to pay.

BUYING THROUGH AUCTIONS

Internet auction sites deal in just about anything people want to sell. Though sellers provide descriptions (and often digital images), details about flaws and condition may be fuzzy. Except for sites operated by retailers or businesses, most auction sites do not verify the condition of an item—or whether it really exists. That's why you should read the seller's description for details about an item's condition and value, return policy, warranty information, and promised delivery date, plus an address and telephone number.

Buyers should consider insuring expensive items, and be sure that sellers ship packages in a traceable manner to help ensure a successful transaction. If a seller fails to deliver or misrepresents an item, eBay, the largest Internet auction site, will reimburse buyers for up to $175 of their loss. The site also offers links to third-party companies that provide authentication and grading services.

If you purchase something at an auction site, use a credit card (not a debit card) or work out terms with an online escrow service, such as Escrow.com, which processes transactions. (Fees are based on the amount of the transaction, method of payment, and sometimes shipping costs.)

At pick-your-own price sites, you name a price for, say, airline tickets, hotels, or a mortgage, and merchants come to you. Priceline originated this type of "reverse auction." The catch: You must provide a credit-card number up front. If Priceline finds the item at your price, your credit card is charged immediately, usually with no cancellation option. Nor can you request a specific brand.

For airline tickets, you are only allowed to make one bid within a seven-day period for the same itinerary; for hotel rooms, within a three-day period. Simply changing your bid amount is considered a duplicate bid and will be rejected automatically. If you want to bid again immediately, you must be willing to change, say, your departure date or hotel quality level.

Be a Smart Shopper In the Supermarket

It's easy to be casual in your approach to supermarket shopping. After all, we're not talking about SUVs or HDTVs here, just a bunch of small items you pick up every week that cost no more than a few dollars each. In reality though, you can save hundreds—even thousands—of dollars each year by following our supermarket money-saving strategies.

To see just how much you might save, CONSUMER REPORTS sent two shoppers to the same supermarket to buy similar groceries, asking one to use our tips and the other to shop without a care for savings. The smart shopper spent $56 on her groceries. And the other shopper? She spent $135—a difference of $79. If you saved that much each week, you'd be ahead by more than $4,000 a year.

MONEY-SAVING TIPS

Try store brands. They can yield big savings, often with quality similar to national brands. Also consider regional brands. Our thrifty shopper bought 2 pounds of Fireside Old-Fashioned fig bars for $2.49; 2 pounds of Fig Newtons were more than $7.

Buy big, but watch for "gotchas." Although bigger packages tend to be more economical, there are exceptions. At a Wal-Mart, we found cereal that cost 8 cents less per pound in a 14-ounce box than in a 20-ounce box. Comparing unit prices is especially important when one size is on sale.

Beware of sneaky price differences. At one store, Alpine Lace low-salt Muenster cheese was sold in two areas: sliced-to-order at the deli counter and prepackaged in a display 10 feet away. The smart shopper bought the cheese at the deli, where it cost $2 less per pound.

Weigh the cost of convenience. Prepped foods often cost more. For $1.49, our smart shopper got a 2¼-pound head of iceberg lettuce; for the same price, her colleague got just 1 pound of bagged salad consisting mostly of iceberg lettuce. Convenient packaging costs more, too. Our smart shopper chose a canister of store-brand quick-cooking oatmeal (13 servings) for $1.59, plus the cost of milk. That was much more economical than 10 single-serving cups of Quaker Instant Oatmeal Express, costing $9.90.

Compare prices of organics. Organics usually cost more, sometimes double what similar conventionally produced versions cost. But not always. With organics becoming more ubiquitous, you can find bargains. Our shoppers found organic and nonorganic carrots selling for the same price.

Look high and low. Companies can pay a premium to have products placed on eye-level shelves. You'll often find less expensive store brands placed on the top and bottom shelves.

Evaluate endcaps. Don't assume that items showcased in endcaps, those displays at the end of aisles, are bargains. They may not be discounted.

Resist checkout temptations. Candy, soda, and other snacks are apt to cost more at the checkout. That's where our shoppers found chilled, 20-ounce bottles of Coke for $1.09 each—about $22 for about 12 liters. In the aisles, six 2-liter bottles sold for $5.

Use coupons wisely. Our smart shopper saved $9.90 with coupons (it helped that the store doubled their value). But they won't save you money if they make you buy too much or entice you to buy products you don't need. Most coupons are distributed in newspaper inserts. You can also download them from Web sites like *www.CoolSavings.com* and *www.SmartSource.com*. However, you generally have to supply personal information to register. To safeguard your personal data and prevent unwanted e-mail, check the privacy policy of a site and be sure to opt out of any mailings you don't want to receive.

Consider a savings card. A shopper's club card is typically scanned at the checkout, and discounts are applied automatically. Our savvy shopper saved $6.49 with her card.

To get a card, you usually have to give at least your name and address, which means that the store can track your buying habits. Stores say the data are used for marketing purposes: they might send coupons to certain shoppers based on what they've bought. But critics contend that prices at stores with card programs tend to be higher than at stores without them. And they worry about where the data—which could reveal not just what kind of bologna you like but also, say, your alcohol-buying habits—might wind up.

Michael Sansolo of the Food Marketing Institute, a supermarket trade association whose members account for three-fourths of U.S. retail food sales, says that virtually all stores with card programs have privacy policies. "What we're being told across the board by stores that offer programs," he says, "is that privacy is paramount."

It makes sense to check a store's privacy policy before signing up for a card. Some stores, such as Albertsons and Food Lion, let you get a card without disclosing personal information. But if you pay by credit card at any store, your name could be linked to your purchases anyway.

Home Entertainment

Home Entertainment: Digital Dominates

Digital technology—the use of computer chips to create, store and play images and sounds—dominates more and more of today's home-entertainment choices. Traditional analog techniques of recording images on film or displaying them on a glass tube are fast becoming obsolete. The result: greater convenience, capability, and affordable prices. Consumers also face a fast-changing menu of home-entertainment options, with a technical vocabulary to match.

Two developments typify the digital trend. This year several manufacturers have announced their intention to discontinue production of film cameras, and sales of digital televisions are expected to surpass those of analog TVs. For some purists, digital photography will never offer the delicacy and range that film cameras do. And analog TV still has a huge installed base and brisk sales of low-priced smaller sets. Nonetheless, the digital direction is clear.

Where new and older-style home-entertainment technologies still coexist, consumers' attention is directed to digital. In video cameras, digital models far outnumber analog offerings. Digital audio players, with their MP3 files, have quickly replaced CD players as best-selling portable music sources. In televisions, with a cutoff date for all analog broadcasts looming in 2009, only digital models should be considered for purchase, unless low cost is of paramount importance. In fact, CONSUMER REPORTS now tests and rates only digital TVs.

Other notable trends in today's home entertainment and imaging marketplace echo previous waves of digital technology.

Specs keep rising. Home-entertainment gear's benchmark specifications, whether for resolution, capacity, or speed, continue to soar, especially in video and imaging. This year marks the debut of television models with the highest-quality HDTV picture currently possible, 1080p, displaying 1080 lines of resolution. They have also upped the ante in digital cameras, with entry-level models offering 5 megapixels of image resolution, instead of the 4-megapixel minimum last year. Audio- and video-player storage keeps growing, too, making huge multimedia libraries in the palm of one's hand a mundane occurrence.

Format wars flare up. Just when consumers could count on benefits in convenience and economies of scale from manufacturers agreeing to a single worldwide standard for new home-entertainment equipment, dueling formats are back to confuse and cost you more. The arrival of high-definition DVDs brings a rivalry between the incompatible formats HD-DVD and Blu-ray, with an array of manufacturers and movie studios supporting one or the other. Not since the Beta-VHS wars, which dampened the early adoption of VCRs, has there been such a standards brouhaha. (One possible solution: hardware that plays both formats, will only add to the prices consumers pay.)

How low can they go? Advances in digital technology mean prices keep trending down. Shrinking price tags are prompting the holdouts among consumers to shop for the latest in digital home entertainment.

CAMCORDERS

Fine picture quality and easy editing have improved the functionality of these moviemakers, especially for digital models.

You can do a lot more with videos shot on digital or analog camcorders than play them back, unedited, on your TV. You can edit and embellish them with music using your computer, then play your productions on your DVD or PC. Or even send them to friends or family via e-mail.

Digital camcorders, now the dominant type, generally offer very good to excellent picture quality, along with very good sound capability, compactness, and ease of handling. Making copies of a digital recording need not result in a loss of picture or sound quality. You can even take rudimentary still photos with most digital camcorders.

Analog camcorders, now a small part of the market, generally have good picture and sound quality and are less expensive. Some analog units are about as compact

and easy to handle as digital models, while others are a bit bigger and bulkier.

WHAT'S AVAILABLE

Sony dominates the camcorder market, with multiple models in a number of formats. Other top brands include Canon, JVC, Panasonic, and Samsung. Most digital models come in the MiniDV format, but there are also the disc-based DVD-RAM, DVD-R, and DVD+RW formats. Newer models record to flash memory or a hard drive. Some digital models weigh as little as one pound.

MiniDV. Don't let their small size deceive you. Although some models can be slipped into a large pocket, MiniDV camcorders can record very high-quality images. They use a unique tape cassette, and the typical recording time is 60 minutes at standard play (SP) speed. Expect to pay about $6.50 for a 60-minute tape. You must use the camcorder for playback—it converts its recording to an analog signal that can be played directly into a TV or VCR. If the TV or VCR has an S-video input jack, use it to get a high-quality picture. Price: $350 to more than $1,000.

Disc-based. Capitalizing on the popularity and capabilities of DVD movie discs, these formats offer benefits that tape can't provide: long-term durability, compactness, and random access to scenes as with a DVD. The 3¼-inch discs record standard MPEG-2 video, the same format used in commercial DVD videos. The amount of recording time varies according to the quality level you select, from 20 minutes per side at the highest-quality setting for DVD-RAM to about 60 minutes per side at the lowest setting. DVD-RAM discs are not compatible with most DVD players, but the discs can be reused. DVD-R is supposed to be compatible with most DVD players and computer DVD drives, but the discs are not rewriteable. DVD-RW and DVD+RW are reusable, rewriteable disc formats. Disc prices range from about $4 to $20. Price: $600 to $1,000.

Most analog camcorders now use the Hi8 format; VHS-C and Super VHS-C are fading from the market. Blank tapes range from $3.50 to $6.50. Analog camcorders usually weigh around 2 pounds. Picture quality is generally good, though a notch below digital. Price: $200 to $300.

FEATURES THAT COUNT

A flip-out liquid-crystal-display (LCD) monitor is common on all but the lowest-priced camcorders. And a wide-screen LCD monitor is becoming more common. You'll find it useful for reviewing footage you've shot and easier to use than the eyepiece viewfinder for certain shooting poses. Some LCD monitors are hard to use in sunlight, a drawback on models that have only a monitor and no eyepiece.

Screens vary from 2½ to 4 inches measured diagonally, with a larger screen offered as a step-up feature on higher-priced models. Since an LCD monitor uses batteries faster than an eyepiece viewfinder does, you don't have as much recording time when the LCD is in use.

An image stabilizer automatically reduces most of the shaking that occurs from holding the camcorder as you record a scene. Most stabilizers are electronic; a few are optical. Either type can be effective, though mounting the camcorder on a tripod is the surest way to get steady images. If you're not using a tripod, try holding the camcorder with both hands and bracing both elbows against your chest.

Full auto switch essentially lets you just point and shoot. The camcorder automatically adjusts the color balance, shutter speed, focus, and aperture (also called the "iris" or "f-stop" with camcorders).

Autofocus adjusts for maximum sharpness; manual focus override may be needed for problem situations, such as low light. (With some camcorders, you might have to tap buttons repeatedly to get the focus just right.) With many models, you can also control exposure, shutter speed, and white balance.

The zoom is typically a finger control—press one way to zoom in, the other to widen the view. The rate at which the zoom changes depends on how hard you press the switch. Typical optical zoom ratios range from 10:1 to 26:1. The zoom relies on optical lenses, just like a film camera (hence the term "optical zoom"). Many camcorders offer a digital zoom to extend the range to 400:1 or more, but at a lower picture quality.

For tape-based formats, analog or digital, every camcorder displays tape speeds the same way a VCR does. Every model, for example, includes an SP (standard play) speed. Digitals have a slower LP (long play) speed that adds 50 percent to the recording time. A few 8mm and Hi8 models have an LP speed that doubles the recording time. All VHS-C and S-VHS-C camcorders have an even slower EP (extended play) speed that triples the recording time.

With analog camcorders, slower speeds worsen picture quality. Slow speed usually doesn't reduce picture quality on digital camcorders. But using slow speed means sacrificing some seldom-used editing options and might restrict playback on other camcorders.

Disc-based formats have a variety of modes that trade recording time for image quality.

Quick review lets you view the last few seconds of a scene without having to press a lot of buttons.

For special lighting situations, **preset**

autoexposure settings can be helpful. A "snow and sand" setting, for example, adjusts shutter speed or aperture to accommodate high reflectivity.

A **light** provides some illumination for close shots when the image would otherwise be too dark. **Backlight** compensation increases the exposure slightly when your subject is lighted from behind and silhouetted. An **infrared-sensitive recording mode** (also known as night vision, zero lux, or MagicVu) allows shooting in very dim or dark situations, using infrared emitters. You can use it for nighttime shots, although colors won't register accurately in this mode.

Audio/video inputs let you record material from another camcorder or from a VCR, useful for copying part of another video onto your own. (A digital camcorder must have such an input jack if you want to record analog material digitally.) Unlike a built-in microphone, an external microphone that is plugged into a microphone jack won't pick up noises from the camcorder itself, and it typically improves audio performance.

A camcorder with **digital still capability** lets you take snapshots, which can be downloaded to your computer. The photo quality is generally inferior to that of a good still camera, although higher-cost camcorders typically offer better photo quality than lower-cost ones.

Features that might help editing include a **built-in title generator,** a **time-and-date stamp,** and a **time code,** which is a frame reference of exactly where you are on the recording media—the hour, minute, second, and frame. A **remote control** helps when you're using the camcorder as a playback device or when you're using a tripod. Programmed recording (a self-timer) starts the camcorder recording at a preset time.

HOW TO CHOOSE

Pick your price range and format. The least-expensive camcorders on the market are analog. All the rest are digital.

Once you've decided on price, you need to pick a specific recording format. That determines not only how much you'll be spending for tapes, discs, or memory, but also how much recording time you'll get. The tape-based digital formats are typically superior in picture quality to analog tape-based formats.

With analog, you can get 120 to 300 minutes of recording on a Hi8 cassette. With the SVHS-C or VHS-C formats, you can get only 30 to 120 minutes.

With digital formats that use MiniDV, Digital 8, or MicroMV tapes, you can get at least 60 minutes of recording on a standard cassette. MiniDV and D8 cassettes are the least expensive and easiest to find.

Tech tip

The recording format you select will determine how much you'll be spending for discs and how much recording time you'll get.

Digital DVD camcorders from Panasonic and Hitachi can accommodate DVD-RAM discs, which can be reused but aren't compatible with all DVD players. All brands also use DVD-R, one-use discs that work in most DVD players. The standard setting yields 60 minutes of recording; the "fine" setting, 20 to 30 minutes.

With digital formats using memory cards, the amount of video you can record at the highest-quality level can vary from 15 minutes to 1 hour on 256MB to 2GB cards. (To get a more precise estimate, check the camera's specifications.) Hard-drive-based camcorders are limited only by the capacity of the hard drive and the quality settings. On typical models, you can store several hours of video at the highest-quality setting or more than 10 hours at lower-quality settings.

If you're replacing an older camcorder, think about what you'll do with the tapes you've accumulated. If you don't stay with the same format you've been using, you will probably want to transfer the old tapes to an easily viewed medium, such as a DVD.

If you're buying your first camcorder, concentrate on finding the best one for your budget, regardless of format.

Check the size, weight, and controls. In the store, try different camcorders to make sure they fit your hand and are comfortable to use. Some models can feel disconcertingly tiny. You'll need to use a tripod if you want rock-steady video, no matter which camcorder you choose.

Most camcorders are designed so that the most frequently used controls—the switch to zoom in and out, the record button, and the button for still photos—are readily at hand. Make sure that the controls are convenient and that you can change the tape, DVD, or memory card and remove the battery easily.

Check the flip-out LCD viewer. Most measure 2.5 inches on the diagonal, but some are larger, adding about $100 to the price. If the viewer seems small and difficult to use or suffers from too much glare, consider trading up to a similar model or a different brand to get a better screen.

Think about the lighting. A camcorder isn't always used outdoors or in a brightly lighted room. You can shoot video in dim light, but don't expect miracles. In our tests, using the default mode, most camcorders produced only fair or poor images in very low light. Many camcorders have settings that can improve performance but can be a challenge to use.

Related CR report: November 2006
Ratings: page 233
Reliability: page 238

DIGITAL CAMERAS

Digital photography allows you to be more involved in creating prints without the darkroom that film photography requires.

Digital cameras give you extraordinary control over images. You can transfer them to your computer, then crop, adjust color and contrast, and add textures and other special effects. You can make prints at home on a color inkjet or snapshot printer, drop off the memory card at one of a growing number of photofinishers, use a self-service kiosk at your local drugstore to select, edit, and print pictures instantly, or upload images to an online photofinisher. Final results can be e-mailed, made into cards or T-shirts, or uploaded to a photo-sharing Web site for storage, viewing, and sharing with others.

Like camcorders, digital cameras have LCD monitors for composing shots or viewing those already taken. Many digital cameras can also shoot video with sound. While some camcorders can shoot still photos, a typical camcorder's resolution is no match for a good still camera's.

WHAT'S AVAILABLE

The leading brands are Canon, Fujifilm, HP, Kodak, Nikon, Olympus, and Sony. Other brands come from consumer-electronics, computer, and traditional camera and film companies.

It's easier than ever to go to extremes with a digital camera. Small is bountiful, and big is also booming. The smallest cameras we tested recently, subcompacts, weigh 5 to 8 ounces and can fit in a pocket. Price: $185 to $450.

Mainstream compacts are too big to pocket, but small enough for most handbags and glove boxes. The ones we tested recently weigh 7 to 14 ounces. Price: $140 to $480.

More serious cameras have the versatility and power to capture fast action or create photographic art under the most demanding light conditions. Advanced compact cameras are typically larger and heavier than compacts, with versatile controls and long zoom lenses. Price: $280 to $850.

Super-zoom cameras are characterized by a very long zoom range—10x or greater. While traditionally larger and heavier than compacts, a few new models are designed to be smaller and lighter than older models. Price: $250 to $700.

SLRs (single-lens reflex), the largest and heaviest type, offer the most versatility and power, including interchangeable lenses. Price: $600 to $1,700 for consumer models; professional models can cost thousands.

FEATURES THAT COUNT

Digital cameras are distinguished by their **resolution**—how many pixels, or picture elements, the image sensor contains. One megapixel equals 1 million picture elements. A 4-megapixel camera can make excellent 8x10s and pleasing 11x14s. There are also 5- to 10-megapixel models, including point-and-shoot ones. These are well-suited for making larger prints or for maintaining sharpness if you want to enlarge a portion of the original image. Professional digital cameras use as many as 16 megapixels. Price: $100 to $400 for 4 megapixels; $150 to $500 for 5 and 6 megapixels; $300 to $1,000 for 7- to 10-megapixel point-and-shoot models; and up to $1,700 for 10-megapixel SLRs.

Most digital cameras are highly automated, with features such as **automatic exposure control** (which manages the shutter speed, aperture, or both according to available light) and **autofocus.**

Instead of film, digital cameras record their shots on **flash-memory cards.** Compact Flash (CF) and SecureDigital (SD) are the most widely used. Once quite expensive, these cards have tumbled in price—a 256-megabyte card can now cost less than $20. Other types of memory cards used by cameras include MemoryStick Duo and xD.

To save images, you transfer them to a computer, typically by connecting the camera to the computer's USB or FireWire port, or inserting the memory card into a special reader. Some printers can take memory cards and make prints without putting the images on a computer first. Image-handling software, such as Adobe Photoshop Elements, Jasc Paint Shop, Microsoft Picture It, and ACDSee, lets you resize, touch up, and crop digital images using your computer. Most digital cameras work with both Windows and Macintosh machines.

The file format commonly used for photos is JPEG, which is a compressed format. Some cameras can save photos in the uncompressed TIFF format, but this setting yields enormous files. Other high-end cameras have a RAW file format, which yields the image data with no processing from the camera and can also be uncompressed.

The optical viewfinder is becoming increasingly rare, replaced by larger color LCD monitors. (Some are now as large as 3 inches.) Monitors are very accurate in framing the actual image you get—better than most optical viewfinders—but might be hard to view in bright sunlight. You can also view shots you've already taken on the LCD monitor. Many digital cameras provide a video output, so you can view your pictures on a TV set.

Many new models let you capture **video** and **sound.** Some let you record video in high-quality MPEG4 format, up to 30 frames per second, up to the memory card's capacity.

A **zoom lens** provides flexibility in framing shots and closes the distance between you and your subject—ideal if you want to quickly switch to a close shot. The typical 3x zoom on mainstream cameras goes from a moderately wide-angle view (35 mm) to moderate telephoto (105 mm). You can find cameras with extended zoom ranges between 8x and 15x, giving added versatility for outdoor photography. Other new cameras go down to 24 or 28 mm at the wide-angle end, making it easier to take in an entire scene in close quarters, such as a crowded party.

Shop smart

If you mainly want to shoot snapshots, a 4- or 5-megapixel camera is best for you.

Optical zooms are superior to digital zooms, which merely magnify the center of the frame without actually increasing picture detail, resulting in a somewhat coarser view.

Sensors in digital cameras are typically about as light sensitive as ISO 100 film, though many let you increase that setting. (At ISO 100, you'll probably need to use a flash indoors and in low outdoor light.) A camera's **flash range** tells you how far from the camera the flash will provide proper exposure. If the subject is out of range, you'll know to close the distance. But digital cameras can tolerate some underexposure before the image suffers noticeably.

Red-eye reduction shines a light toward your subject just before the main flash. (A camera whose flash unit is farther from the lens reduces the risk of red eye. Computer editing of the image may also correct red eye.) With **automatic flash**

mode, the camera fires the flash whenever the light entering the camera registers as insufficient. A few new cameras have built-in red-eye correction capability.

Some cameras with large LCDs, and some with powerful telephoto lenses, now come with some form of **image stabilizer.** (Optical-image stabilizers are the best type; some cameras use simulated stabilization to try to achieve the same effect.) Stabilizers compensate for handheld camera shake, letting you use a slower shutter speed than you otherwise could for following movement. But an image stabilizer won't compensate for the motion of subjects.

Most new 6- to 10-megapixel cameras come with **full manual controls,** including independent controls for shutter and aperture. That gives serious shutterbugs control over depth of field, shooting action, or shooting scenes with tricky lighting.

HOW TO CHOOSE

The first step is to determine how you will use the camera most of the time. Consider these two questions:

How much flexibility to enlarge images do you need? If you mainly want to make 4x6 snapshots, a camera with 4- or 5-megapixel resolution should be fine. It will also make an 8x10 print of an entire image without alteration that won't look much different than one from a 6- or 8-megapixel model. But to enlarge the image more or enlarge only part of it, you'll want a camera with resolution of 6 megapixels or greater.

How much control do you want over exposure and composition? Cameras meant for automatic point-and-shoot photos, with a 3x zoom lens, will serve casual shooters as well as dedicated hobbyists much of the time. The full-featured cameras in the advanced compact and superzoom categories offer capabilities that more-dedicated photographers will want to have. Two of the more important capabilities are a zoom range of 5x to 10x or more, which lets you bring distant outdoor subjects close and also lets you shoot candid portraits without getting right in your subject's face, and a full complement of manual controls that let you determine the shutter speed and lens opening.

Once you've established the performance priorities that you need from a camera, you can narrow your choices further by considering these convenience factors:

Size and weight. The smallest, lightest models aren't necessarily inexpensive 4-megapixel cameras. And the biggest and heaviest aren't necessarily found at the high end. If possible, try cameras at the store before you buy. That way, you'll know which one fits your hand best and which can be securely gripped. In our tests, we found that some of the smallest don't leave much room even for small fingers.

Battery type and life. All digital cameras run on rechargeable batteries, either an expensive battery pack or a set of AAs. In our tests, neither type had a clear performance advantage. The best-performing cameras offer at least 250 shots on a charge, while the worst manage under 100. We think it's more convenient to own a camera that accepts AA batteries. You can buy economical, rechargeable cells (plus a charger) and drop in a set of disposable lithium or alkaline batteries if the rechargeables run down in the middle of shooting.

Camera speed. With point-and-shoot cameras like the ones we tested, you must wait after each shot as the camera processes the image. Most models let you shoot an image every few seconds, but a few make you wait 5 seconds or more. They may frustrate you when you're taking photos of a subject that is very active, such as a child.

Your other cameras. If you own a film camera with interchangeable lenses, you can probably use those lenses on digital SLRs of the same brand. Some new Olympus digital SLRs require a special $100 adapter to use film lenses, but you'll only be able to focus those lenses manually.

Related CR report: July 2006
Ratings: page 244
Reliability: page 246

DVD PLAYERS

These devices offer high-quality playback of videos and CDs, and prices are lower than ever.

Great picture and sound quality, plus relatively low prices, have made digital videodisc, or DVD, players, among the most successful consumer-electronics products ever. The vast majority of U.S. households have one or more DVD players. Prices have dropped so low that they're now sold seemingly everywhere—even in supermarkets and drugstores.

But conventional DVDs may soon seem quaint as high-definition (HD) content becomes the norm. The first HD players are now on the market, following delays caused by technical issues and competition between the two incompatible formats, HD-DVD and Blu-ray. Toshiba has launched its HD-DVD players, Samsung has introduced a Blu-ray player, and Sony is due to follow with its Blu-ray players. But as with most new technologies, initial prices are high: $500 for Toshiba's low-end model and $1,000 for Samsung's first Blu-ray device. All but the most passionate videophiles might want to wait for prices to drop.

There's another even more compelling

reason to wait for the dust to settle: HD-DVD players won't be able to play movies that support the Blu-ray format, and vice versa. One of these formats might not survive, and if you back the losing candidate, you'll have paid a lot of money for obsolete technology.

WHAT'S AVAILABLE

Panasonic, Sony, and Toshiba are among the biggest-selling brands of DVD players. Virtually all new DVD players are progressive-scan models. When used with a conventional TV, these players provide the usual high DVD picture quality.

With a television that can display high-definition or enhanced-definition (ED) images, image quality is slightly better. (That's because HD and ED sets support the player's progressive-scan 480p mode, drawing 480 consecutive lines on the screen. By comparison, with a conventional TV, every other line is drawn and then interlaced or combined, a resolution referred to as 480i.) A player can be connected directly to your TV for viewing movies or routed through your receiver so you can listen to the movie soundtrack and audio CDs on your sound system.

Progressive-scan models come in single-disc and multidisc versions. The few non-progressive-scan players now on the market are mostly single-disc models; those tend to be the cheapest type.

Single-disc consoles. Even low-end models usually include all the video outputs you might want. Price: about $25 to more than $300.

Multidisc consoles. Like CD changers, these players accommodate more than one disc at a time, typically five. DVD jukeboxes that hold 400 or so discs are also available. Price: $100 to $400.

Portables. These DVD players generally come with a small, wide-screen format LCD screen and batteries that claim to provide three hours or more of playback. Some low-priced models don't come with a screen; they're intended for users who plan to connect the device to a television. You pay extra for portability either way. Price: about $100 to $800.

HD players. When used with HDTVs, HD players can potentially convey even better picture quality than you get with regular DVDs. Note that you might need to use an HDMI input on a TV to get HD resolution. High-def players may be able to output HD signals only through an HDMI connection; component-video connections, normally able to carry HD, may output only enhanced definition if the content on a particular disc was encoded that way by the producer. Price: $500 to $1,000.

FEATURES THAT COUNT

DVD-based movies often come in various formats. **Aspect-ratio control** lets you choose between the 4:3 viewing format of conventional TVs (4 inches wide for every 3 inches high) and the 16:9 ratio of newer wide-screen sets.

A DVD player gives you all sorts of control over the picture—control you might never have known you needed. **Picture zoom** lets you zoom in on a specific frame. **Black-level adjustment** brings out the detail in dark parts of the screen image. If you've ever wanted to see certain action scenes from different angles, **multiangle capability** gives you that opportunity. Note that this feature and some others work only with certain discs.

A DVD player enables you to navigate the disc in a number of ways. Unlike a VHS tape, most DVDs are sectioned. **Chapter preview** lets you scan the opening seconds of each section or chapter until you find what you want. A related feature, **chapter gallery,** shows thumbnails of section or chapter opening scenes. **Go-to by time** lets you enter how many hours and minutes into the disc you'd like to skip to. **Marker functions** allow easy indexing of specific sections.

To get the most from a DVD player, you need to hook it up to the TV with the best available connection. A **composite-video connection** can produce a very good picture, but there will be some loss of detail and some color artifacts such as adjacent colors bleeding into each other. Using the TV's **S-video input** can improve picture quality. It keeps the black-and-white and the color portions of the signal separated, producing more picture detail and fewer color defects.

Component-video, sometimes not provided on the lowest-end models, improves on S-video by splitting the color signal, resulting in a wider range of color. If you connect a DVD player via an S-video or component connection, don't be surprised if you have to adjust the television-picture setup when you switch to a picture coming from an antenna, a VCR, or a cable box that uses a radio-frequency (RF, also called antenna/cable) connection or a composite connection.

Two newer outputs found on some players, **Digital Video Interface (DVI)** and **High-Definition Multimedia Interface (HDMI),** are intended for use with digital TVs with corresponding inputs. They may be used to pass digital 480p, upconverted higher-resolution video signals, and HD signals. These connections potentially allow content providers to control your ability to record the content.

Another benefit of DVD players is the ability to enjoy movies with **multichannel surround sound.** To reap the full sound experience of the audio encoded into DVD titles, you'll need a Dolby Digital receiver and six speakers, including a subwoofer. (For 6.1 and 7.1 soundtracks, you'll need seven or eight speakers.) **Dolby Digital decoding built-in** refers to a DVD player that decodes the multichannel audio before the audio receiver. Without the built-in circuitry, you'd need to have the decoder built into the receiver or, in rare instances, use a separate decoder box to take advantage of the audio. (A Dolby Digital receiver will decode an older format, Dolby Pro Logic, as well.) Most players also support Digital Theater System (DTS) decoding for titles using 5.1-, 6.1- or 7.1-channel encoding format. When you're watching DVD-based movies, dynamic audio-range control helps keep explosions and other noisy sound effects from seeming too loud.

In addition to commercial DVD titles, DVD players often support playback or display of many other formats. They include CD-R/RW recordings of standard audio CDs; the recordable DVD formats DVD+R/RW, DVD-R/RW, and DVD-RAM; Video CD (VCD); and DVD-Audio and Super Audio CD (SACD). They can also play CD-R/RW discs containing MP3 and Windows Media Audio (WMA) files and JPEG picture files. Make sure the one you're considering plays the discs and formats you use now or might want to use in the future.

DVD players also provide features such as multilingual support, which lets you choose dialog or subtitles in different languages for a movie. Parental control lets parents "lock out" films by rating code.

HOW TO CHOOSE

Hold off on a high-def player. Given the current high prices of the first models

Shop smart

Wait until either HD-DVD or Blu-ray technology becomes dominant before buying a high-def DVD player.

and the incompatibility of the two rival formats, we strongly recommend that you wait awhile for things to shake out.

Buy a progressive-scan model unless the lowest price is your highest priority. Although you won't see progressive-scan picture quality on a conventional analog TV, it's worth spending a little extra for a progressive-scan player if you might get a digital (probably HD) TV at some point. You'll have a wider choice of products as well, since almost all new players are progressive-scan. It's definitely worth getting a progressive-scan player for use with a digital TV, which is capable of displaying the smoother picture these players can deliver.

Choose a multidisc model if you want continuous music. A single-disc player is fine for movies and CDs one at a time. But if you want this to be your main music player, consider a multidisc player. Note, though, that multidisc models are typically about 1 to 2 inches taller and 6 to 7 inches deeper than single-disc players.

Make sure there are enough connections. Virtually all DVD players now have outputs for optimal connection to most TV sets. A few players have DVI or HDMI connectors that are compatible with some new TVs, though these don't necessarily offer improved picture quality. If you want to use digital-audio connections from the DVD player to a receiver, make sure the DVD player's digital-audio outputs match the receiver's inputs. Some receivers use a coaxial input; others, an optical input. If you have an older receiver that lacks 5.1 surround-sound decoding, look for a player with a decoder for Dolby Digital.

Consider which, if any, special playback formats matter. All DVD players can play pre-recorded DVDs and CDs. Most models also play several types of

discs you record yourself, such as DVD-R, DVD+R, and CD-R/-RW. Most can read DVD+RW, but the ability to read DVD-RW discs depends on how they were recorded. Some can also play DVD-RAM discs. Most models play CD-audio and MP3 music recorded on discs you burn yourself. You'll need to shop around more if you want to play Windows Media Audio (WMA) files, video CD, and high-resolution SACD and DVD-Audio discs in their original format.

Do you want to present slide shows on your TV? Then choose a model that can read JPEG image files that you've captured with a digital camera and burned onto a disc. Some models have built-in card readers that accept various memory cards.

Related CR report: March 2006
Ratings: page 258

HD TELEVISIONS

HD sets can provide the best at-home viewing experience currently available, at ever-lower prices.

Today's gold standard for TV is high definition, or HD. This much-talked-about format offers images with lifelike detail and clarity. Digital programming, which includes HD, is available via cable, satellite, and over the air. To receive HD programming, you'll need an HD cable box, HD satellite receiver, or an antenna and HD decoder (either built into the TV or in a separate set-top box). And, of course, you'll need an HD-capable TV designed to display the sharp, fine detail contained in the HD signals. HD equipment can also accept standard definition (SD) and enhanced definition (ED) signals.

WHAT'S AVAILABLE

TV sets that are capable of displaying HD images are available in all TV types, from familiar picture-tube (direct-view) sets to the newest plasma, LCD, and rear-projection TVs. All these sets are capable of displaying the added detail in HD images. As of July 2006, all TVs with screens 25 inches and larger must have a built-in ATSC digital tuner, to comply with a government ruling. At this point, only LCD and picture-tube sets with smaller screens still don't have such tuners. By March 2007, all new TVs sold in the U.S., regardless of size and type, must include a digital tuner. Here's a rundown on the types of HD-capable TVs on the market:

HD monitors. Some manufacturers are getting around the government ruling by introducing sets called "monitors," which have no tuner of any type. These require a cable box or satellite receiver, or an external set-top box and antenna, to get any programming, not just HD content.

HD-ready sets. The few HD-ready sets still being sold have a tuner that enables them to display standard-definition programs (which still account for most non-prime-time TV broadcasts) on their own. To display digital programs, they require an external digital tuner that can decode those broadcasts. If you're getting your HD programming from cable or satellite, your digital cable box or satellite receiver will provide the necessary digital decoder. All you have to do is connect your HD-ready TV to the box and you're all set. Cable companies charge a small rental fee for digital or HD-capable boxes. To receive HD by satellite, you need an HD receiver and special dish antenna(e). Together, these cost about $300, but you might be able to get them from a satellite company at little or no charge as part of a promotion.

You can also get digital broadcasts, including HD, over the air, via an antenna. To do so, you'll have to buy a set-top box containing an ATSC tuner; these cost a few hundred dollars. You won't get the channels available only on cable or satellite, but there's no charge for service. To receive digital programming by antenna, you must be fairly close to a transmitter, with nothing blocking the signal. With digital signals, you'll either have a clear picture or none at all. Marginal reception will result in intermittent picture dropout.

Integrated HDTV sets. These have an ATSC digital tuner built in, which enables them to decode digital signals, including HD, with no equipment other than a roof antenna. As noted earlier, you may be able to receive the major networks' HD offerings transmitted over the air in your area, but you won't get the premium channels available on satellite and cable. To get HD via cable or satellite, integrated sets require an external HD-capable cable box or satellite receiver; their built-in digital tuner works only for off-air digital broadcasts.

Shop smart

There's no need to buy expensive cables to hook up your new HDTV. Resist the urge to splurge. Regular cables will work just fine.

Digital-cable-ready (DCR). Some integrated models, called digital-cable-ready (DCR) sets, can receive unscrambled digital-cable programming without using a set-top box. For HD and premium cable programming—and possibly for any digital programming—you must insert a CableCard into a slot on the set. You usually have to pay a few dollars a month to rent the card from the cable company. However, there's a downside to this setup: It doesn't provide the features offered by a cable box, such as an interactive program guide, video on demand, or pay-per-view ordering via remote. Second-generation DCR-TVs and CableCards are expected at some point, and they're likely to have two-way capability, allowing for interactive features. Integrated sets typically cost more than HD monitors, with digital-cable-ready models costing the most.

Price: Generally a few hundred dollars more than a comparable HD-ready set.

FEATURES THAT COUNT

Most features on HD sets are similar to those on conventional sets. ED and HD sets generally have a flat screen, which reduces reflections, and **picture-in-picture (PIP),** which lets you watch two shows simultaneously, or keep a program playing in a small box while exploring the onscreen program guide. A feature called **3:2 pulldown compensation** can improve the smoothness of movies played on interlaced (not usually progressive-scan) DVD players. It's sometimes referred to by brand-specific names such as CineMotion or Film mode.

Tech tip

Before you buy, make sure there is adequate HD programming in your area. Look for Web sites that list local content.

The **aspect ratio,** or width-to-height ratio, is of special importance when choosing an HD set. Some have a squarish 4:3 aspect ratio like that of a conventional TV. Widescreen sets have a rectangular 16:9 (or 15:9) shape that more closely resembles a movie-theater screen. TV programming is usually formatted for a 4:3 screen, but more programmers are adopting the 16:9 format. Most cinematic movies are close to 16:9. Content formatted for one type of screen has to be modified to fit the other, so you may see dark bars to the left and right or top and bottom. Most ED and HD sets are widescreen models. You'll find 4:3 screens only

on some picture-tube and LCD HD sets.

Stretch and zoom modes will expand or compress an image to better fill the screen shape. This helps to reduce the dark bands that can appear above, below, or on the sides of the image if you watch content formatted for one screen shape on a TV that has the other shape. (The picture may be distorted or cut off a bit in the process of stretching and zooming.) Those bars make the picture slightly smaller and over time may leave ghosted images on the screens of plasma and CRT-based rear-projection TVs. This "burn-in" is also a risk with any images left on the screen for long periods—say from a stock ticker.

In addition to the usual TV connections (antenna/cable, composite-video, S-video, and component-video) most HD-capable sets have a **Digital Visual Interface (DVI)** or **High-Definition Multimedia Input (HDMI).** These provide a high-quality digital connection to digital devices and may allow content providers to control your ability to record certain content. DVI inputs carry only video; HDMI inputs carry audio and video on one cable.

Audio outputs let you direct a TV's audio signal to a receiver or to self-powered speakers. Integrated digital TVs also include a Dolby Digital audio output for surround sound (available from some digital broadcasts). An automatic volume leveler compensates for the jarring volume jumps that often accompany commercials or changes in channel. Some plasma sets have a separate control unit—a video receiver, in effect, that accepts connections more easily than a panel you've had mounted onto a wall.

HOW TO CHOOSE

See HD images for yourself. Only first-hand experience will enable you to decide whether the quality is worth the extra cost.

Given a clean signal, some HD sets can make even standard-definition images look better than they do on a regular TV. With a poor signal, like the worst channels from cable, a digital set can make the images look worse, though. HD sets also provide a modest but noticeable upgrade in quality from most DVD movies. See if a local retailer can show you sets displaying various signals, and make sure you know exactly what you're watching. You may find it helpful to visit a friend or relative with an HD set and view different content of your own choosing.

Consider enhanced-definition models. An EDTV or an ED-ready plasma TV may cost little more than many standard-definition models and may cost significantly less than HD sets. Picture quality can approach that of an HD set when used with a DVD player or digital tuner. Some (but not all) of these sets can accept HD programming and display it at a lower quality. If you're willing to settle, such a set could give you some semblance of the HD experience for less.

Find out how much HD content is available where you live. Before you expend energy shopping for a set, find out about HD programming available in your area and how you'd get it. Most parts of the U.S. have access to a fair amount of HD content, but offerings vary by location and the reception method you use—antenna, cable, or satellite. To find out about digital and HD TV stations in your area, visit *www.HDTVpub.com*, *www.dtv.gov*, *www.DigitalTVzone.com*, or *CheckHD.com*.

Decide if today's price premium for HD is worth paying. The cost of HD sets is falling, but these TVs still cost more than conventional sets. It may be easier to justify the premium if you're shopping for your household's main set. With TVs that are pricey to begin with—such as plasma, LCD,

or rear-projection—you can make an especially strong case for getting an HD set. Why spend thousands for yesterday's television technology?

As with most electronics gear, there's also an argument to be made for waiting: Prices have fallen sharply already and are expected to keep moving downward over the near future as more HD sets are introduced and demand continues to rise.

Related CR report: March 2006

LCD TVs

Once available only with small screens, LCD (liquid-crystal display) TVs now come with bigger screens suitable for a household's primary set.

The introduction of 37- to 50-inch sets has positioned LCD TVs as strong competition for flat-panel plasma sets. In fact, Sony has stopped offering plasma TVs for the consumer market, instead focusing its flat-panel effort on LCD sets. That illustrates the growing importance of this category.

LCD TVs cost more than comparably sized plasma sets, but the gap is gradually narrowing. Differences in picture quality are narrowing as well. Recent improvements in LCDs address earlier weaknesses at displaying deep black levels, accurate colors, and fast motion. The introduction of some LCD sets with 1080p resolution—the highest currently available—has also raised the bar for picture quality.

Regardless of screen size, LCD TVs are only a few inches thick, giving them a small footprint. They're also relatively lightweight—30 pounds or less for mid-sized models, 60 pounds or so for big-screen sets—so they're easily moved or wall-mounted. But LCD technology, like plasma technology, is fairly new, so long-term reliability of these TVs is still a question. However, preliminary data are encouraging.

WHAT'S AVAILABLE

Top-selling brands include Sony, Sharp, Samsung, Panasonic, Magnavox, and Westinghouse. Prices have been dropping steadily, thanks in part to the arrival of low-priced brands from computer makers such as Dell and store brands from major retailers such as Best Buy, Circuit City, Wal-Mart, and Target.

Most LCD TVs with screens larger than 20 inches or so are high-definition (HD) models. HDTVs can display the sharpest, most detailed images. On most high-def sets, the resolution is 1024x768 or1366x768. Recently, some 1080p HDTVs have been introduced. With a native resolution of 1920x1080 pixels, the highest so far, 1080p TVs are the first with the potential to display all 1,080 lines in the most common high-definition format, called 1080i. The improvement is most noticeable on large screens, say, 50 inches and up.

In smaller sizes—screens of 20 inches or less—enhanced-definition LCD TVs are also available. ED sets, which are digital, have picture quality that's slightly better than standard definition but not as good as HD; these can accept 480p signals like those from a progressive-scan DVD player. Standard-definition TVs are analog models that can display only 480i signals like those used for most TV broadcasts. Analog TV broadcasts will cease on Feb. 17, 2009, when all broadcasters must switch to digital. An analog set you buy now will be able to receive digital programming when used with an external digital tuner, such as that in a cable or satellite box, or a set-top box and antenna.

Major-brand LCD HDTVs with 26-inch screens typically start at $1,000; $1,200 to $2,000 for a 32-inch set; and $2,000 to $2,500 for 37-inch set. In all size categories, you'll see less-familiar brands selling for hundreds less. A growing number of LCD TVs have even larger screens—up to 50 inches or more—and prices go up along with size.

FEATURES THAT COUNT

LCD TVs typically have all the usual features you expect on a TV. Other features are more specific to this type of set. The location of the **speakers** is one example. On some LCD models, the speakers are on both sides of the screen; on others they're below it. That affects the overall width of the set and could determine whether it will fit into a niche in an entertainment center, for example.

On some LCD TVs, speakers are detachable. That can be a plus if you want to fit the TV into a particular space or simply position the speakers away from the screen. The ability of a panel to tilt and swivel also varies, so see whether a given model can be adjusted as much as you'd like.

Some LCD sets have a **memory-card slot.** This enables you to view still photos or videos from a digital camera. You can also connect a camera or camcorder directly to the TV if it has a **USB** or **IEEE 1394/Firewire input**.

With more sources for video available all the time, it's handy to have a feature that allows you to customize settings for each source, such as the cable box or the DVD player. If you watch many DVD movies with your DVD player in non-progressive-scan mode, look for a **film-mode feature** on HD sets. This feature is also called **3:2 pull-down compensation,** or brand-specific names like **CineMotion** and **Film Mode.** This can make moving images that were converted from film to video look less jerky and jagged. On 16:9 sets, **stretch and zoom modes** will expand or compress an image to fill the screen shape better. This helps to reduce the dark bands that can appear on the sides or top and bottom of images if you watch content that isn't formatted for a wide screen. (The picture may be distorted or cut off a bit in the process of stretching or zooming.)

HOW TO CHOOSE

Consider what level of picture quality you're willing to pay for. The best LCD TVs are capable of excellent picture quality, although blacks may not be quite as deep as on a good plasma set. For a main TV or one you'll watch often, we'd strongly recommend an HD set with resolution of at least 1024x768. On screens larger than 30 inches or so, 1366x768 has the potential to offer better quality, though native screen resolution in and of itself doesn't guarantee a certain level of picture quality. Check our Ratings online to see which models make the most of their resolution.

It's probably not worth paying the premium for a 1080p set with 1920x1080 resolution for screens much smaller than 50 inches. The quality difference isn't as noticeable below that size. We'd recommend an ED or standard-definition LCD TV only for small sets used for casual viewing in the kitchen, for example, where you wouldn't want the cable or satellite box you generally need to receive HD signals. The picture quality almost certainly won't be as good as what you'll get with an HD set.

Check the viewing angle. Viewing angles have improved, so many new LCD TVs display a better image from off-center than older sets did—a must if the TV will be watched by several people at once. Some sets have wider viewing angles than others. Before buying one, see how the picture looks if you step off to the side or move up and down. With some, you'll see a dimmer, somewhat washed-out image as your viewing position angles away, particularly in a vertical direction.

Look for easy-to-use inputs. On many LCD televisions, the connections are on the side or rear of the panel and might be hard to reach. Some larger models have a separate control unit to which you connect all your external audio/video devices, such as a DVD player or cable box. You then have only one cable going from the control box to the panel itself. That's a plus for wall-mounting and can make the inputs easier to access. But it does give you another box to contend with.

Consider a set that doubles as a computer display. If you need a computer display as well as a TV, check connectivity options. An HD set with high native resolution is best for computer use. A standard VGA connection works with all computers; a Digital Visual Interface (DVI) input would be compatible with newer midrange computers.

Our preliminary survey data found few repair problems during the first year of use for LCD sets from Panasonic, Samsung, Sharp, Sony, and Toshiba, but it's too early to comment on other brands or on long-term reliability for any brand.

Related CR report: March 2006
Ratings: page 280

MP3 PLAYERS

The MP3 player continues its evolution from simple audio player to complex multimedia device.

More and more players come with color displays and the ability to show digital photos transferred from your computer, sometimes while the music is playing. Such models usually also play music videos, TV shows, and short films.

As digital players morph, one thing remains constant: The brand name that's on most of them. Apple's iPod players still account for more than three out of four MP3 players sold. Hardware alone doesn't explain Apple's dominance. While iPods score well in our tests, so do players from other manufacturers, many of which offer capabilities and features that iPods lack.

Apple's success rests in part on its creation of a self-contained digital-entertainment system. iTunes, its content-management software, works seamlessly—only with iPods—a fact that's prompted the French government to sue Apple for monopolistic practices. Its online iTunes store offers by far the largest library of online video content, supplementing its dominance over online music sales. Its content includes many exclusives and also offers comprehensive one-stop access to podcasts, the booming (and mostly free) online downloads that offer everything from National Public Radio broadcasts to music-preview shows to weekly self-help recordings.

And while you can play content obtained from the store (and use iTunes software) on virtually any computer, including Windows PCs and Macs, you need an iPod to enjoy it portably.

Not that all innovative content comes from Apple. Other legal online content sources include BuyMusic, MSN, MusicMatch, Napster, Real, Sony, Wal-Mart, and Yahoo. Unlike iTunes, some of these sites also offer subscription-based services, typically for less than $10 per month, that let you listen to music on your computer in real time (streaming). Downloaded songs from contemporary artists typically cost less than $1 per song, or $10 for an entire album; music videos, hit TV-show episodes, and short films cost $2 each.

Free online music-sharing, still the most popular way for acquiring MP3 music, has been driven underground by a flurry of record-industry lawsuits and a 2005 U.S. Supreme Court ruling. (The justices unanimously ruled that the popular music-sharing site Grokster, as well as similar operations, could be held liable if their networks were used to illegally distribute copyrighted music.) Napster, a pioneer of free peer-to-peer music-sharing, now allows you to stream music free from its (now legal) site, for up to five listens per song.

Before you buy any digital player, be sure your computer can handle it. New computers shouldn't be a problem, but make sure any player you're considering is compatible with your older Windows or Macintosh computer (including its operating system). Keep in mind that some operating-system upgrades can exceed the price of a player. And your computer must have a USB port.

Consider high-speed Internet access if you plan to download much of your music. Also keep in mind that getting started can be tricky with some players. Even if compatible with the player, an older computer might not recognize it easily, so you might have to seek help from the player manufacturer.

WHAT'S AVAILABLE

Major brands of MP3 players include Apple, Archos, Cowon, Creative Labs, iRiver, Philips, RCA, Samsung, SanDisk, Sony, and Toshiba. Brands from smaller companies are on the market as well. And MP3 playback has been incorporated into other handheld portable products, including CD players, cell phones, and personal digital assistants (PDAs).

Flash-memory players. These are the smallest and lightest players, often no bigger than a pack of gum, and they weigh no more than 2 or 3 ounces. They're solid-state, meaning they have no moving parts and tend to have longer audio playback time than players that use hard-disk storage. Storage capacities range from 128 megabytes to 6 gigabytes, or about 30 to 1,500 songs. (All capacities listed here are based on a standard CD-quality setting of 128 kilobits per second, which requires about 1 gigabyte per 250 songs. You can fit more music into memory if you compress songs into smaller files, but that may result in lower audio quality.) Some flash-memory players also have expansion slots to add more memory via card slots on the player.

Common expansion-memory formats include Compact Flash, MultiMedia, Secure Digital, and SmartMedia. Sony players may use a MagicGate MemoryStick, a copyright-protected version of Sony's existing MemoryStick media. Memory-card capacities range from about 32MB to 2GB. Memory costs have gradually dropped. Price: $40 to $280 for the player; $45 to $50 for a 1-GB memory card.

Hard-disk players. There are two types: microdrive and standard hard-disk. The palm-sized microdrive players have a tiny hard drive with a storage capacity of 3 to 8 GB (about 750 to 2,000 songs). They weigh about a quarter-pound. Standard hard-disk players are about the size of a deck of cards, and they have a storage capacity of 10 to 60 GB (about 2,500 to 15,000 songs). They typically weigh less than half a pound. Some hard-disk players with video capability have relatively larger displays, and as a result tend to be the bulkiest models. Price: $140 and up.

CD players with "MP3" compatibility.

Flash-memory and hard-disk portable players aren't the only way to enjoy digital music. Many of today's portable CD players can play digital music saved on discs and may support the copyright-protected formats from online music stores. Controls and displays are comparable to portable MP3 players, and you can group songs on each disc according to artist, genre, and other categories. A CD, with its 650- to 800-MB storage capacity, can hold more than 10 hours of MP3-formatted music at the standard CD-quality setting. You can create MP3 CDs using the proper software and your PC's CD burner. Price: $25 and up for the players; 15 to 75 cents or so for blank CDs.

Cell phones. An increasing number of phones have built-in MP3 players, some with controls and features that rival stand-alone players. Sprint, Verizon, and other cell-phone providers let subscribers download music over their networks. But music phones are pricey, and most can't store more than 150 songs. Price: 99 cents to $2.50 per song; $150 and up for a phone with a two-year contract, or $500 without one.

Tech tip

If you don't have high-speed Internet access, downloading songs to your new MP3 player might be frustrating.

Satellite radio. Some pocket-sized XM and Sirius receivers have built-in memory for recording up to 50 hours of satellite programming, and might also let you add your own MP3 songs to the mix. Not all models let you listen to live programming on the go; some must be docked at home. Price: $200 to $400 for the receiver; about $13 a month for satellite service.

FEATURES THAT COUNT

Software and hardware. Most MP3 players come with software to convert your

CDs into the audio playback format the player can handle. You can also organize your music collection according to artist, album, genre, and a variety of other categories, as well as create playlists to suit any mood or occasion. All come with software to help you shuttle content between your PC and the player via a Universal Serial Bus (USB) connection. All players work with a Windows PC, and some support the Macintosh platform.

Player upgradability. On most models, the firmware—the built-in operating instructions—can be upgraded so the player does not become obsolete. Upgrades can add or enhance features, fix bugs, and add support for other audio and video formats and operating systems. This is important for models with video playback because of the evolving nature of video formats.

Display. Most MP3 players have a display screen that allows you to view the song title, track number, amount of memory remaining, battery-life indicator, and other functions. Screens can be monochrome or color. Models with color displays also let you store and view pictures taken with your digital camera, and in some cases, video clips.

Some displays present a list of tracks from which you can easily make a selection, while others show only one track at a time, requiring you to advance through individual tracks to find the desired one. On some of the models you can access the player's function controls by a wired or infrared remote control. Most players have built-in management of songs that can be accessed via album, artist, or genre. Individual playlists of songs are usually created on a computer and transferred to the player, though many let you manage the music on the player, allowing you to edit playlists and delete files.

Photo playback. Virtually all players with color screens can display JPEGs, the default photo format of most digital cameras. Some can handle TIFFs, BMPs, and lesser-known formats as well. Many let you view your photos in slideshow fashion, complete with fade-outs, scrolls, and other transitions, as well as with music.

Video playback. A growing number of players with color displays can also store and play back video. The video is in a format that compresses about three hours of video into 1GB of memory space. Popular content sources include CinemaNow and iTunes, which let you download music videos, TV shows, and short films for $2 apiece. But iTunes works only with iPods, and CinemaNow supports only players that can handle copy-protected Windows formats. Virtually all video players come with software that converts non-protected movies into a format the player can handle.

As for the viewing experience, MP3-player screens are relatively tiny—even when compared with portable DVD players—and are hard to see in outdoor light. Players with the largest screens, up to 3 inches wide, are easier to watch for longer periods and some come with built-in speakers. But they can weigh as much a pound and are often too bulky to stuff into a hip pocket.

Sound enhancement. Expect some type of equalizer, which allows you to adjust the tone in various ways. A custom setting through separate bass and treble controls or adjustable equalizers gives you the most control over the tone. Some players have presets, such as "rock" or "jazz," as well as channel balance control.

Playback controls. Volume, track play/pause, and forward/reverse controls are standard. Most portable MP3 players let you set a play mode so you can repeat one or all music tracks, or play tracks in a random order, also referred to as "shuffle" mode. An A-B repeat feature allows you to set bookmarks and repeat a section of the music track.

Useful extras. In addition to playing music, most MP3 players can function as external hard drives, allowing you to shuttle files from one PC to another. Some players can act as a USB host, which lets you transfer images, data, or music directly from a memory-card reader, digital camera, or another MP3 player without using a computer. A few of these, however, won't let you play or view the files you transfer. Some allow you to view text files, photos, and videos on their display screens. Other convenient features include an FM radio tuner, a built-in microphone or line input for recording, and adapters or a line output for patching the player into your car's audio system.

HOW TO CHOOSE

New portable models with more features and greater capabilities are continually coming out. Decide how much you're willing to spend on a unit you may want to replace in a year or two. Here are some other considerations before you buy:

Decide whether to get an iPod. With Apple's family of players so ubiquitous, and so similar in many ways, it's worth considering the advantages and shortcomings of iPods before going further with your buying decision. iPods are easy to use, thanks to superb integration of the players and the company's iTunes software. The iTunes Store offers the largest selection of legal digital content on the Web, including virtually all the available downloads of major TV shows. And with the use of iTunes software so widespread, it's very likely that a friend or family member from whom you might want to borrow content already uses it—meaning you'll need an iPod to enjoy their songs or videos.

iPods also have a plethora of accessories to extend their use, from boom boxes and clock radios with iPod slots to iPod cases that come in many colors and fabrics. Few other brands of players have custom aftermarket equipment (although generic gear will, for example, allow you to pipe any player into a component sound system or a car stereo).

As for drawbacks, iPods typically cost a little more than non-Apple players with comparable capacity. They also lack some of the features and accessories that come with many other players, such as an FM radio, voice recorder, and an AC charger. Equipping a new iPod with some of these options can increase its price by more than $100. And iPods have some special limitations, such as the inability to easily transfer music to any other device. In addition, iPods require you to open iTunes to transfer music into the player; competing devices more conveniently let you drag and drop music files without opening music-management software.

Shop Smart

Because the technology is changing so quickly, look for a player that is upgradable.

Weigh capacity vs. size. Consider a flash-memory model (holding up to 1,500 songs) if a lower price, smaller size, lighter weight, and long playback time are more important to you than a vast selection of tunes. Look for flash models that can accept external memory cards if you want expanded song capacity. If you have a large music collection that you want to keep with you, a hard-disk player might make more sense. Those players can hold up to 15,000 songs and could serenade you for weeks without repeating a tune. However, a hard-disk player can be more complicated to manage than a flash-memory player. For some, navigating through the menus or directories (folders) of songs might also take longer.

Hard-disk players vary in size, generally in step with capacity. Microdrive players are about the size of a credit card, and a 4-GB model can hold about 1,000 songs, whereas models with 20-GB hard disks are about the size of a deck of cards and can hold about 5,000 songs.

Consider download choices. Be aware that online music copy-protected sources are limited with some models. For example, Sony players work only with one online music store, while iPods are compatible with iTunes and Real. Players that support the copy-protected WMA formats, like those from Archos, Creative, RCA, and Samsung, allow access to the greatest number of online stores, and, because of the competition, cheaper music. Another WMA-store benefit: BuyMusic, MSN, Real, and other sites offer songs at a higher bit rate than the standard 128 kbs, which has the potential to sound better.

Shop smart

Buying a charger and rechargeable batteries is more cost-effective in the long run than using disposable batteries.

Some players won't play music purchased from any online store. Downloading "free" music from such online sources as peer-to-peer Web sites is another option. But you risk a copyright-infringement lawsuit by the music industry. You'll also increase your exposure to a host of nasty computer viruses and spyware programs that tend to hitch rides on songs swapped on these sites.

Also, note that with most players, you have choices when it comes to software for recording (ripping) music. You can use the software that comes with your computer or player, such as Apple iTunes, MusicMatch, Napster, or Windows Media Player, or download other freeware or shareware applications. If the program has the software plug-in for your player, you can transfer the music to your player directly; otherwise you'll need to use the program that came with your player to perform the transfer. iPod owners, for example, need to use iTunes to transfer music to the player.

Ensure upgradability. Regardless of which player you choose, look for one with upgradable firmware for adding or enhancing player features, as well as accommodating newer encoding schemes or variations of compression. This is particularly important for models with video playback due to the evolving nature of video formats. However, note that upgrading firmware can be a time-consuming and sometimes risky process. MP3 players use several methods for upgrading; one method, which executes the upgrade file on the computer while the player is still attached, can cause permanent damage to the player if there's even a slight interruption during execution. Upgrades can be found at the manufacturer and music-management software application Web sites.

Consider headphone quality. While many players can produce near audio-CD quality music out of their headphone jacks, the headphones they come with can degrade the quality. Most perform respectably, and any performance differences might not be a bother you in typical, everyday use. If you're particular about listening quality, it would be worth buying better-quality after-market headphones for use with your player.

Consider power consumption and battery type. With any portable device, batteries are a consideration. Our tests found a wide variation in battery life among the players. Depending on the player settings, some will run out of power after only six hours of play, while others can play music for more than 50 hours before their batteries give out. Flash-memory players tend to have longer playback times than hard-disk players. Playing videos can run a battery down in just a few hours.

Many flash-memory players use AA or AAA batteries and can accept either standard or rechargeable batteries. You can expect a bit longer playback time using standard batteries, but purchasing a charger and using rechargeable batteries will be more cost effective in the long run as well as being more environmentally friendly. (For advice on recycling used batteries, call 800-822-8837 or go to the Rechargeable Battery Recycling Corp.'s site at *www.rbrc.org*. Our Web site *www.GreenerChoices.org*, also has advice on this topic.)

Other players use a rechargeable non-standard "block-" or "gumstick-" shaped nickel metal-hydride (Ni-MH) or lithium-ion (Li-ion) removable battery, which is both more expensive and harder to find. Many hard-drive players use a non-removable rechargeable battery. When the battery can no longer hold a charge, the player has to be sent back to the manufacturer for service—a costly procedure if the product is no longer under warranty.

Consider ergonomics and design. Whichever type of MP3 player you choose, make sure you'll be comfortable using the device. Look for a display and controls that are easy to read and that can be worked with one hand. Because sizes and shapes vary widely, check to see that the player fits comfortably in your pockets, and that it's easy to fish out when you need to access controls. Accessories that may be important to you may not be included, such as an AC charger, protector cases, or belt clips, a consideration to you in the overall cost of the player.

Related CR report: November 2005 Ratings: page 291

PLASMA TVs

Plasma TVs make a blockbuster first impression. A maximum of 6 inches thick, these sleek flat panels display bright images on screens measuring about 3 to 5 feet diagonally.

With more models 50 inches and larger now available, plasma sets have become an alternative to rear-projection sets for anyone seeking a jumbo screen.

A plasma screen is made up of thousands of pixels containing gas that's converted into "plasma" by an electrical charge. The plasma causes phosphors to glow red, green, or blue, as dictated by a video signal. Thanks to improvements in plasma technology, the best sets have excellent picture quality. They offer a wider viewing angle than most rear-projection sets and LCD TVs, along with deeper blacks and smoother motion than you get with LCD sets.

The picture isn't all rosy, however. Like projection TVs using CRT (cathode-ray tube) technology, plasma sets may be vulnerable to screen burn-in, although new screen-saving technologies minimize the risk. And because plasma sets are relatively new, their long-term reliability is still a question, although preliminary data are encouraging.

WHAT'S AVAILABLE

When buying a plasma TV, you'll face a choice between HD (high-definition) and ED (enhanced-definition) sets, which cost less. The two types differ in native resolution, meaning the fixed number of pixels on the screen. In a spec like 852x480, note the second number. If it's 480, the set is ED; 720 or higher, it's HD. Most 42-inch plasma HDTVs have resolution of 1024x768; 50-inch sets typically have 1366x768. Some new plasma TVs coming on the market have a still-higher resolution of 1920x1080. These so-called 1080p TVs have the potential to display all 1,080 lines in the most common high-definition format, called 1080i. The improvement is most noticeable on large screens, say 50 inches and up.

Both HD and ED sets should be capable of up- or down-converting signals to match their native resolution. ED sets can display the full detail of 480p signals, such as those output by a DVD player. When connected to an HD tuner, many can down-convert HD TV signals, which are 720p or 1080i, to suit their lower-resolution screens. The picture quality can be very good, even though it's not true HD. If you sit too close to an ED set, though, images may appear coarser than on an HD set, as if you were looking through a screen door. ED sets are likely to become less common as HD prices continue to fall.

As of 2006, all TVs with screens 25 inches and larger—a range encompassing all plasma TVs—must have a built-in ATSC digital tuner to comply with a government ruling. By March 2007, all new TVs sold in the U.S., regardless of size and type, must include a digital tuner. Some manufacturers are getting around that ruling, however, by introducing sets called "monitors," which have no tuner of any type. These require a cable box or satellite receiver to get any programming, not just HD content.

Among the leading brands in the plasma TV category are Panasonic, Hitachi, Philips, Pioneer, and Samsung. Sony recently stopped making plasma TVs to concentrate instead on LCD sets. Prices have dropped sharply over the past year or two. HD models with 40- to 44-inch screens, the best-selling size, cost $2,000 or more. TVs with screens 50 inches or larger cost $3,000 and up. Look for prices to fall further now that more brands of plasma TVs are available, many priced aggressively.

FEATURES THAT COUNT

Plasma TVs have all the usual features you expect on a higher-priced television, as well as others more specific to this type of TV. For example, some sets have screen-saver-type features to prevent burn-in from static images. On some models, the speakers are on both sides of the screen; on others they're below it. That affects the overall width of the set and could determine whether it will fit into a niche in an entertainment center, for example. Some plasma sets have a memory-card slot. This enables you to view still photos or videos from a digital camera. You can connect a camera or camcorder directly to the TV if it has a **USB** or **IEEE 1394/Firewire input.**

With more sources for video available all the time, it's handy to have a feature that allows you to customize settings for each source, such as the cable box or the DVD player. If you watch many DVD movies with your DVD player in nonprogressive-scan mode, look for a **film-mode feature** on HD sets. This feature is also called **3:2 pull-down compensation,** or brand-specific names like **CineMotion** and **Film Mode.** This can make moving images that were converted from film to video look less jerky, with less jaggedness around the edges. **Stretch and zoom modes** will expand or compress an image to better fill the screen shape. This helps to reduce the dark bands that can appear on the sides or top and bottom of images if you watch content that isn't formatted for a wide screen. (The picture may be distorted or cut off a bit by stretching or zooming.)

Picture-in-picture (PIP) lets you watch two channels at once, one in a small box, the other a full-screen image. It's useful if you want to browse the onscreen guide while keeping an eye on the program you're watching. A single-tuner TV requires another device with a tuner, such as a VCR or cable box, to display two programs at once; dual-tuner models can display two programs simultaneously on their own.

HOW TO CHOOSE

Decide whether you want true HD or the next best thing. HD sets generally perform better than ED sets with all types of signals. They're worth the higher cost if you're a purist who wants the best image quality. Most ED plasma sets can down-convert an HD signal to fit their lower resolution, so you can still enjoy HD programming. While it won't be true HD quality, it can be very good. For a main TV or one you'll watch often, we'd strongly recommend an HD set, which would have resolution of at least 1024x768. On screens 50 inches or so, 1366x768 has the potential to offer better quality, though native screen resolution in and of itself doesn't guarantee a certain level of picture quality. Note that the shiny surface of a plasma TV can produce annoying reflections, especially in brightly lighted rooms. Many of these sets look best in low light.

Weigh screen size against price. If you're buying a plasma TV, an important question is how much screen you can afford. All other things being equal, the bigger the screen, the bigger the price tag, and the greater the viewing distance you need to see optimal picture quality. You'll enjoy the best viewing experience if you sit at least 6 feet away from a 42-inch HD set, and a little farther from an ED set or larger screen.

Beware of burn-in and burnout. Plasma TVs may be prone to burn-in, much like CRT-based rear-projection TVs. Over time, static images displayed for long periods (such as a video game or a stock ticker) may leave permanent ghosted impressions onscreen, so minimize the risk as much as you can. New screen-saving technologies should help as well.

You may have seen reports, in print or online, suggesting that plasma TVs may not last as long as other types of TVs. Overall longevity and reliability are not yet proven because the technology is so new. Major manufacturers now tout 60,000 hours of use or more before a recent-model plasma screen loses half its brightness. Even in heavy use (40 hours a week), that's about 29 years.

Don't get hung up on specs. Ads touting high-contrast ratios and brightness (cd/m2, or candelas per square meter) may sway you to one set or another. But don't let this be the deciding factor. Manufacturers arrive at specs differently, so they may not be comparable. Try adjusting sets in the store yourself to compare contrast and brightness.

Determine what's included when comparing prices. Some plasmas are monitors only; they don't include speakers or a tuner for any type of TV signal. You won't have to pay for a tuner if you'll be using a cable box or satellite receiver, which will serve as the tuner for all programming. Otherwise, you'll need a set-top box to work with an antenna. If the plasma TV has no speakers, you'll have to buy them

> **Tech tip**
>
> Plasmas can be wall-mounted but they aren't lightweight, so consider hiring an installer to do the job right.

separately unless you plan to connect the set to your existing sound system.

Consider the logistics. Ads for plasma TVs might not show any wires, but you'll probably be connecting a cable box or satellite receiver and a DVD player, and possibly a DVR, DVD recorder, VCR and audio receiver. You can tuck wires behind the TV if you place it on a stand. With wall-mounting, you can run the wires behind the wall or through conduits, a task that might be best handled by a profes-sional. Often weighing 100 pounds or more, plasma TVs need adequate support and ample ventilation because of the heat they can generate. Ask the re-tailer to recommend an installer or con-tact the Custom Electronic Design & Installation Association (800-669-5329 or *www.cedia.net*). Figure on paying $300 to $1,000 for labor, plus a few hundred dollars for mounting brackets.

**Related CR report: March 2006
Ratings: page 296**

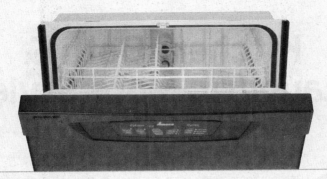

Kitchen, Bath, and Laundry

Kitchen, Bath & Laundry: More Style, Less Money

Slowing home sales have spawned a growing desire to make what you have work better and more stylishly. Home centers including Home Depot, Lowe's, and Sears are fueling this ongoing home-improvement boom by driving down prices on everything from ranges and refrigerators to dishwashers and flooring. As they scramble for your business, some retailers are also getting into the lending business with credit cards aimed squarely at remodelers.

Refrigerator and other appliance manufacturers are also pushing more options. Some refrigerators and ranges have even been super-sized along with some kitchens as major brands woo the upper end of the market. But as our tests and Ratings reveal, you needn't spring for a pricey behemoth to get space and style. Months evaluating thousands of products throughout the home confirm that big, expensive, pro-style appliances are often unimpressive and repair-prone. You may also want to steer clear of some of the trendier choices in floors and countertops.

Among our latest findings:

Cool trends heat up refrigerator sales. Many of the most stylish models are getting both cheaper and narrower to fit smaller spaces and budgets. Among these are French-door models, which meld a bottom-freezer with split refrigerator doors; several top performers now cost $1,800 or less. But some innovations come with a high price and a raft of compromises. Maytag is among the French-door models that now offer an on-the-door ice and water dispenser like the kind on side-by-sides. But the trade-off can be much less refrigerator space inside. We also tested a cabinet-depth model from Liebherr that towers 82 inches high, making its top shelf a stretch for many.

Real-wood warmth vs. longevity. If you want flooring that looks as if it spent years in a country kitchen, you'll be happy to see more genuine wood flooring available with that hand-scraped, distressed look. But our tests also show that solid wood flooring began showing wear from typical scrapes and scuffs twice as quickly as the best vinyl, linoleum, and laminate products.

Counters that can take it. Granite may get all the attention in home magazines and real-estate ads because of its many colors and variations. Lower prices are also moving this tony material downmarket. But if you want a tough-yet-stylish countertop without the hassle of periodic resealing, you'll probably prefer quartz. Also known as engineered stone, it proved especially durable under our barrage of typical kitchen wear and tear. We also tested ceramic tile, stainless steel, and other materials for stains, heat, and other everyday threats.

COFFEEMAKERS

Most models make a good cup of coffee. Higher-priced versions usually have more convenience features and fancier styling.

The popularity of Starbucks and other specialty coffee shops seems to be driving demand for a new generation of coffeemakers that seek to replicate the coffee-house experience at home. Customized brewing, integrated grinders, and thermal carafes are a few of the features manufacturers are hoping will encourage consumers to trade up. Truth is, virtually any model can make a good cup as long as you use decent coffee.

WHAT'S AVAILABLE

You'll find manual-drip systems, coffee presses, percolators, and "pod" coffeemakers that brew individual cups using ready-to-use packets of coffee. But consumers buy more automatic-drip coffeemakers than any other small kitchen appliance: about 14 million per year. Mr. Coffee and Black & Decker are the two largest brands, along with well-known names like Braun, Cuisinart, Delonghi, Krups, Melitta, and Proctor-Silex.

Coffeemakers come in sizes from single-cup models to machines capable of brewing up to 12 cups at a time. At the low end are bare-bones models with a single switch to start the brewing process and a plain metal hotplate. Pricier models can have pro-

grammable start and stop times, a water filter, frothing capability, an automatic shut-off, and a thermal carafe. Most consumers opt for the more basic models. Black and white remain the standard colors, but some brands have added other hues. Price: $10 to more than $200.

FEATURES THAT COUNT

A **removable filter** basket is the easiest for loading and removing the used filter; baskets that sit inside a pullout drawer can be messy. **Paper filters**—usually "cupcake" or cone-shaped—absorb oil and keep sediment from creeping through. Models with a **permanent mesh filter** need to be cleaned after each use, but can save you money over time. Neither type of filter detracted from coffee flavor in our tests. The simplest type of water **reservoir** is one with a big flip-top lid and lines that mark the number of cups in large, clearly visible numbers. Some reservoirs are removable—so you can fill up at the sink—and are dishwasher safe. **Transparent fill tubes** with **cup markings** let you check the water level while pouring.

A **thermal carafe** helps retain flavor and aroma longer than a glass pot on a hot-plate. Other niceties: a **small-batch setting,** which adjusts the flow of water through the coffee grounds to prevent you from getting a bitter or weak brew when making one to four cups; **temperature** and **brew-strength controls;** and a **pause and serve feature** that lets you pour a cup before the whole pot's done. A **programmable timer** lets you add ground coffee and water the night before so you can wake up to a freshly brewed pot in the morning. An **auto- shutoff** feature turns off the heating element, compensating for human forgetfulness. Most models have a preprogrammed time; others let you set the time. If you're pressed for space, you might appreciate a coffeemaker with **controls on the side.** This allows you to turn the machine sideways, making it less deep on the counter.

Full-sized coffeemakers can be full of features, but not all of them add much. Here are some features of dubious value.

There's little need for a **self-clean cycle.** Sending a mix of water and white vinegar through the machine usually cleans it effectively; a special cycle just holds the cleaning solution longer. A **water filter** is supposed to eliminate off-tastes and odors. But you must replace it after a specified number of pots (at about $5 per filter) to prevent bacteria buildup. If water quality is a worry, a whole-house or faucet filter may be a better choice than a coffeemaker filter.

A carafe **prewarm setting** heats the carafe before the coffee drips in. In theory, that helps keep coffee warmer longer. In practice, it doesn't make much difference. **Built-in bean grinders** can be annoying to use and clean. Grounds tend to spill, and you may need to upend the machine to empty residues. A separate burr-type grinder should work better. **Temperature adjustment** lets you set the temperature of some hot plates, from about 160 to 190 degrees. But we found that all plates kept coffee hot enough—about 175 degrees.

HOW TO CHOOSE

Consider how much you consume. If one cup of coffee is enough to jump-start your day, you'll like the convenience and compactness of a single-serve drip coffeemaker. You'll probably use (and waste) less coffee than with a full-sized machine. For coffee-to-go, consider a model that comes with an insulated mug.

"Pod" coffeemakers are the newest option for those who want just one cup at a time. They use pressurized water and individual packets of coffee with integral filters, called pods. But pod coffeemakers have significant shortcomings. Most pod machines made a relatively weak cup of coffee, though the three highest-rated models let you use two pods at a time to make stronger coffee. There's also little or no choice in the brands of coffee you can use, and coffee varieties within the brands can be limited. And you can expect to pay about 25 to 50 cents per pod. Double that if you like your coffee strong, which would require two pods per cup, about four times as much per cup as drip coffee using supermarket brands.

If you're a coffee lover, or if you entertain a lot, you'll need a bigger coffeemaker. Most large machines produce 10 to 12 cups, but be aware that a manufacturer's cup is usually 4 or 5 ounces, not the huge mug that may come to mind—and not the 6 ounces most coffee packages use as a basis for directions.

Consider how often you refill. If you wait an hour between cups, buy a full-sized coffeemaker with a thermal carafe. It will keep coffee hot and fresh-tasting for hours. The warming plates that accompany glass carafes keep coffee hot, but flavor suffers with constant heating.

Consider convenience. Certain basic design details apply to all coffeemakers, plain or fancy: The models rated highest for convenience have clearly marked water reservoirs, easy-to-use swing-out filter baskets, and simple, intuitive controls. The more annoying models have hard-to-read water gauges, filter baskets with a high fumble factor, and carafes that are as likely to spill coffee as pour it. Extra options to look for will depend on your coffee-drinking habits.

Consider counter space. Some machines need considerable space. Those with controls on the side instead of the front can be placed sideways on a countertop so they steal less depth.

Related CR report: December 2004

COOKTOPS AND WALL OVENS

Separate appliances give you the flexibility of two cooking areas, with burners and ovens placed just about anywhere you want. You also have the option of cooking with gas, electricity, or induction.

Like ranges, cooktops come in electric and gas versions. More consumers go for electric than gas, generally opting for glass ceramic smoothtops. There are fewer coil models from which to choose, but you may want to consider one if price is more important than style. Gas cooktops come in several types, including stainless-steel models with pro-style controls and hefty grates, and gas-on-glass models with burners on a glass ceramic surface. Cooktops with a porcelain enamel top are the lowest priced.

Gaggenau, Viking, Kenmore, and other brands are also introducing stand-alone induction cooktops, which cook with glass-covered magnetic coils that send nearly all of their heat to the pan, rather than the cooking surface. Besides heating faster than gas or electric cooktops, induction models respond instantly to the controls, but they require special cookware to work. (If a magnet sticks to the pot, it's OK.)

Because about one-third of cooktops and wall ovens are sold as part of a kitchen makeover, style sells. More and more of the appliances have sleek, flush surfaces that are easy to clean, or stainless-steel exteriors that let you easily mix and match brands.

Flexibility is the biggest reason to forgo the typical range and buy a separate cooktop and wall oven instead. But the two appliances usually cost more than a similar range. And you'll need to check the relia-bility of two appliances instead of one. Our tests show that you can bring home a pair of fine performers for about $1,300 for a 30-inch electric cooktop and electric oven. A smoothtop range with similar performance would cost about half that. But if you want more than four pots going at once, it won't cost you too much to upgrade from a 30-inch cooktop with four burners or elements to a 36-inch model with five or six. In most cases, the difference is $100 to $400.

WHAT'S AVAILABLE

Frigidaire, GE, Jenn-Air, Kenmore (sourced from others), KitchenAid, Maytag, and Whirlpool are the leading makers of cooktops and wall ovens. Mainstream brands have established high-end offshoots, such as Kenmore Elite, GE Profile, and Whirlpool Gold. High-end, pro-style brands include Bosch, Dacor, GE Monogram, KitchenAid Pro-Line, Thermador, Viking, and Wolf.

Cooktops. You can install a cooktop on a kitchen island or other location where counter space allows. Cooktops can be electric coil, electric smoothtop, gas, or induction. Cooktops add flexibility since they can be located separately from the oven. Most are 30 inches wide and are made of porcelain-coated steel or glass ceramic, with four elements or burners. Some are 24 or 36 inches wide, depending on the number of burners.

Modular cooktops let you mix and match parts—removing burners and adding a grill, say—but you pay a premium

Shop smart

If you want more than four pots going at once, it won't cost you much more to upgrade from a 30-inch cooktop with four burners or elements to a 36-inch model with five or six.

for that added flexibility. Preconfigured cooktops are less expensive. Price: electric cooktop, $250 to $1,500; gas cooktop, $250 to $2,500; induction cooktop, $1,800 and up.

Wall ovens. These can be single or double, electric or gas, self-cleaning or manual, with or without a convection setting. Width is typically 24, 27, or 30 inches. They allow you to eliminate bending by installing them at waist or eye level, though you can also nest them beneath a countertop to save space. Price: $500 to more than $2,500 for double-oven models; figure on about $300 extra for convection.

FEATURES THAT COUNT

On electric cooktops. Consider where the **controls** are located. On most electric cooktops, they take up room on the surface. Some models have electronic touchpads, however, allowing the cooktop to be flush with the counter.

Coil elements, the least expensive electric option, are easy to replace if they break. Spending $200 more will buy you a smoothtop model.

Most smoothtops have **expandable elements**—also called **dual elements**—that allow you to switch between a large, high-power element and a small, low-power element contained within it. Some smoothtops also include a low-wattage element for warming plates or keeping just-cooked food at the optimal temperature. Some have an elongated "bridge" element that spans two burners—a nicety for accommodating rectangular or odd-shaped cookware. And many have at least **one hot-surface light**—a key safety feature, since the surface can remain hot long after the elements have been turned off. The safest setup includes a dedicated "hot" light for each element.

Many electric cooktops have one large **higher-wattage element** in front and one in back. An **expanded simmer range** in some smoothtop models lets you fine-tune the simmer setting on one element for, say, melting chocolate or keeping a sauce from getting too hot.

On gas cooktops. Most gas cooktops have four burners in three sizes, measured in British thermal units per hour (Btu/hr.): one or two medium-power burners (about 9,000 Btu/hr.); a small burner (about 5,000 Btu/hr.); and one or two large ones (about 12,500 Btu/hr.). We recommend a model with one or more 12,000 Btu/hr. burners for quick cooktop heating. Some have a fifth burner instead of a center island. On a few models, the burners automatically re-ignite. Look for models that use larger burners for higher heat, so you can tell at a glance which burner is which.

For easier cleaning, look for **sealed burners.** Gas cooktops typically have **knob controls;** the best rotate 180 degrees or more. Try to avoid knobs that have adjacent off and low settings and that rotate no more than 90 degrees between high and low.

Spending more gets you either heavier **grates** made of porcelain-coated cast iron or a sleek **ceramic surface**—also called **gas-on-glass**—and **stainless-steel accents,** along with a low-power **simmer burner** with an extra-low setting for delicate sauces (though other burners are often capable of simmering).

On ovens. An oven's usable capacity may be less than what manufacturers claim because they don't take protruding broiler elements and other features into account.

A **self-cleaning cycle** uses high heat to burn off spills and splatters. An **automatic door lock,** found on most self-cleaning models, is activated during the cycle, then unlocks when the oven has cooled. Also useful is a **self-cleaning countdown** display, which shows the time left in the cycle.

Higher-priced wall ovens often include **convection,** which uses a fan and sometimes an electric element to circulate heated air. CONSUMER REPORTS tests have shown that this mode cuts cooking time for large roasts and in some cases bakes large cookie batches more evenly because of the circulating air. A few electric ovens have a low-power **microwave feature** that works with bake and broil elements to speed cooking time further. The GE Advantium over-the-range oven uses a **halogen heating bulb** as well as microwaves. Another cooking technology, Trivection, uses regular thermal heating, convection, and microwave energy to cut cooking time. Trivection is available in some top-of-the-line GE Profile and Monogram ovens. Though very good overall, it's very expensive.

A **variable-broil** feature in most electric ovens offers adjustable settings for foods such as fish or thick steaks that need slower or faster cooking. Ovens with **12-hour shutoff** turn off automatically if you leave the oven on for that long. But most models allow you to disable this feature. A **child lockout** allows you to disable oven controls for safety.

Manufacturers are also updating oven controls across the price spectrum. **Electronic touchpad controls** are common. A **digital display** makes it easier to set the precise temperature and keep track of it. A **cook time/delay start** lets you set a time for the oven to start and stop cooking. Remember, however, that you shouldn't leave most foods in a cold oven very long. An **automatic oven light** typically comes on when the door opens, although some ovens have a switch-operated light. A **temperature probe,** to be inserted into meat or poultry, indicates when you've obtained a precise internal temperature.

Oven windows come in various sizes. Those without a decorative grid usually offer the clearest view, although some cooks may welcome the grid to hide pots, pans, and other cooking utensils typically stored inside the oven.

HOW TO CHOOSE

Cooktop/wall oven or a range? With a cooktop/wall oven combo, you can put the appliances pretty much anywhere in the kitchen and mount the oven at a convenient height. Choose a range if you want it to be the centerpiece, as a professional-style model would be.

Installing separate appliances is more work. Electric wall ovens and cooktops each need their own electrical circuit and are best installed by a professional.

Gas, electric, or induction? If you have gas service, you might want to use both fuels. Electric wall ovens generally have a larger capacity than gas ones, and they're easier to install. With cooktops, the quick response of a gas flame might better suit your style of cooking. Gas performed very well in our tests. We have found, however, that electric cooktops tend to boil water faster and simmer sauces better. Induction offers faster heater, flawless simmering, and burners that shut off automatically when you remove the pot. But in addition to being more expensive, the reliability of the technology is unproven.

Consider cleanup and safety. To minimize the parts you need to clean around, look for a smooth-surface cooktop and an oven with a covered bottom-heating element and smooth touchpad controls.

Cooktops stay hot for a while after you turn off the heat. Since smoothtops blend

Tech tip

Trivection uses three kinds of technology: thermal, convection, and microwave. It's quite a pricey alternative to single-tech ovens.

into the surrounding counter, children and unwary adults could get burned. For safety, smoothtops have lights to signal which element is still hot.

Related CR report: August 2006

COUNTERTOPS

A countertop has to withstand considerable punishment over a long period of time. Fortunately, it's one product where beauty and practicality can coexist.

Falling prices for granite and other tony materials mean that you can now get a custom-look countertop for about what you'd pay for solid surfacing like Corian. You'll also see new products as high-end options hit the mainstream.

Retailers such as Home Depot and Lowe's now offer granite and quartz, also known as engineered stone, for as little as $40 per square foot. But even these luxury materials may not be distinctive enough for some design-conscious homeowners. Concrete, which is made to order, is one way to get a custom look. Another trend, stainless steel, appeals to homeowners who want to integrate their counters with pro-style appliances.

WHAT'S AVAILABLE

Butcher block. Butcher-block countertops are made of hardwoods; maple is the most common, though red oak and teak also are used. A slab of butcher block is useful for chopping and slicing, but it can become marred with everyday use. Butcher block is relatively easy to install and repair. The wood will almost certainly become scratched, nicked, burned, or stained as it's used; fortunately, it can be sanded

and resealed. Butcher block should either be treated regularly with mineral oil or beeswax, or be sealed with a varnish suitable for food-preparation surfaces. Wood is vulnerable to fluctuations in humidity, so butcher block is a poor choice for over a dishwasher or near a sink, where it can get wet frequently. Price: $40 to $65 per square foot, installed.

Ceramic tile. Ceramic tile comes in an almost limitless selection of colors, patterns, and styles. A professional or an adept do-it-yourselfer can install it easily. You can use tile to customize a countertop—on a backsplash or island top. Tile set into the counter near the range can serve as a built-in trivet. Glazed tiles are highly resistant to stains, scratches, and burns. And repairs are relatively easy and inexpensive. Grout can be tinted to match or contrast with the tiles, but the joints can trap crumbs and soak up unsightly stains. Cleaning it can be difficult even if the grout is sealed. Tile can be scratched by hard, sharp objects and chip or crack if hit hard enough. Price: $10 to $30 per square foot, installed.

Concrete. This still-exclusive countertop material can be tinted any color and include stone chips. Its exclusivity can be a drawback, however. Since concrete countertops typically are custom-formed by local fabricators, quality can vary. Concrete also cuts and chips easily and must be sealed. While topical sealers resist stains, they were susceptible to damage from hot pots in our tests. The reverse held for penetrating sealers. Concrete countertops are also expensive. Price: $80 to $120 per square foot, installed.

Laminate. Laminates such as Formica and Wilsonart are lightweight and relatively easy to install, although edge treatments add to installation cost and complexity. Laminate is the most popular countertop material, probably because it comes in hundreds of colors and patterns and the price is right. It usually consists of a colored top layer over a dark core. When laminate covers the top and edge of a countertop, part of that core shows as a dark line.

A prefabricated, seamless countertop and backsplash—known as a postformed counter—is also available. Laminate is not as durable as other materials. Solid colors and shiny finishes readily show scratches and nicks. Damaged areas can't be repaired. Water can seep through seams or between the countertop and backsplash, weakening the material underneath or causing the laminate to lift. Price: $10 to $30 per square foot, installed.

Natural stone. The most popular stones for kitchen countertops, granite and marble, come in a spectrum of colors. They also stand up to almost any type of physical abuse, resisting scratches, nicks, and scorching from hot pans. Granite is the tougher material. Marble is slightly softer and more prone to staining and etching from the acids in foods and cleaners. The stone's cold surface also makes it ideal for keeping pastry dough cool and firm while it's being rolled or kneaded. Both granite and marble should be sealed with a protective, penetrating sealer that's applied periodically.

Because these are natural materials, the grain you see in a display may not be the same in the stone delivered to your kitchen. But most suppliers will allow you to inspect and choose the stone slabs. Genuine stone is expensive, partly because it's heavy and difficult to install. Stone tiles are less expensive—and lighter weight—than thick slabs. Special equipment may be needed to move the slabs, which have to be arranged to match color and grain. Without sealing, stone counters can stain easily, and the stains may be difficult to remove. Limestone, slate, soapstone, and sandstone are also used as countertops, though they are softer than either granite or marble. Price: $40 to $100 per square foot, installed.

Quartz (engineered stone.) This material is a combination of small stone chips, resins, and pigments. Quartz can look much like granite but has a more uniform appearance. It's resistant to stains, heat, and abrasion, and never needs sealing. But engineered stone doesn't withstand impact—especially a blow to the edge—as well as real granite. Price: $45 to $90 per square foot, installed.

Solid surface. These materials, which imitate concrete, marble, and other types of stone, are sold under various brands: Avonite, DuPont Corian, Formica Surell, Nevamar Fountainhead, and Wilsonart Gibraltar. Solid-surface countertops are reasonably durable but expensive, and they're best installed by a contractor who has been certified by the manufacturer. Made of polyester or acrylic resins combined with mineral fillers, they come in various thicknesses and can be joined almost invisibly into one apparently seamless expanse. These materials can be sculpted to integrate the sink and backsplash, and routed to accept contrasting inlays.

Scratches and nicks don't show readily on solid surfaces and can be buffed out with an abrasive pad; some gouges can be filled. Repairing a solid-color surface tends to be less discernible than repairing a surface that mimics a granite pattern. Prolonged heat may cause a solid-surface material to discolor. Price: $35 to $80 per square foot, installed.

Stainless steel. Another emerging trend in countertops, stainless steel appeals to those who want to integrate their counters with pro-style and other stainless appliances. Major brands include John Boos and Elkay as well as local fabricators. Heat and stain resistance are a plus. But stainless tends to dent and scratch easily while showing fingerprints. It's also expensive. Price: $120 to $160 per square foot, installed.

HOW TO CHOOSE

See "What's Available," above, to match the look you want with how you'll use the counter. Then follow these tips:

Consider your lifestyle. If you have young children, a counter that needs TLC might not be worth the trouble.

Start with the sink. Most counters work with most sinks. But if you want an undermount sink, you'll need a waterproof material like solid surfacing, quartz, granite, or concrete. If you want a seamless sink made from the same material as the counter, you're limited to solid surfacing, stainless steel, and concrete.

Think about seams. The counter you choose could depend on whether you can live with visible joints. With solid surfacing, pieces are fused to get rid of seams. Stainless seams can be welded, ground, and buffed away. But think twice about other materials if seams are an issue.

Laminates typically require seams on the front edge and between the backsplash and counter. Post forming melds the backsplash, counter, and front edge into one laminate-wrapped unit, avoiding seams. But this option offers fewer color choices.

Use edges with discretion. Custom edges like bullnoses, ogees, and bevels can give low-priced counters added flair. But edges can cost up to $50 per linear foot—a concern if your budget is tight.

Consider the finish. Granite and engineered stone are sold polished or honed. Contrary to popular belief, our tests found that honed finishes resisted stains no better than glossy ones if the stains were allowed to dry overnight. Stainless offers brushed and random-grain finishes. These are better at hiding scratches, but if fingerprints

are an issue, consider fake-stainless laminate over the real stuff.

Combine more than one type. Using two or more materials can trim costs while adding functionality and variety.

Related CR report: August 2006

DISHWASHERS

Models selling for as little as $350 or so can excel at washing dishes, but they may not measure up to costlier models in quietness, water and energy use, or features.

Spend $300 to $400 and you can get a dishwasher that does a good job cleaning dirty dishes without prerinsing, but with a bit of noise. To get the best of everything—cleaning prowess plus the quietest operation, convenience features, water and energy efficiency, and designer styling—you'll have to spend $500 or more.

A dirt sensor, once a premium feature, is now becoming standard, even on lower-priced models. Sensors are designed to adjust the water used and the length of the cycle to the amount of soil on dishes.

WHAT'S AVAILABLE

Frigidaire, GE, Maytag, and Whirlpool make most dishwashers and sell them under their own names, associated brands, and sometimes the Sears Kenmore label. Whirlpool makes high-end KitchenAid, low-end Roper, and many Kenmore models. Maytag makes the high-end Jenn-Air, midpriced Amana, and low-priced Admiral dishwashers. GE offers a range of choices under the GE label and makes the value-priced Hotpoint. Asko, Bosch, and Miele are high-end European brands; Bosch also makes Siemens models. Haier is an import from China; LG and Samsung are Korean brands; Fisher & Paykel is from New Zealand.

Most models fit a 24-inch-wide space under a kitchen countertop and attach to a hot-water pipe, drain, and an electrical line. If you have the room, it's possible to get a wider dishwasher from Electrolux, although you'll pay a hefty premium. Portables in a finished cabinet can be rolled to the sink and connected to the faucet. A "dishwasher in a drawer" design from Fisher & Paykel and KitchenAid has two stacked drawers that can be used simultaneously or individually, depending on the number of dishes you need to wash. KitchenAid also sells a single-drawer dishwasher.

Price: $200 to $1,300 (domestic brands); $350 to $2,000 (foreign-made brands).

FEATURES THAT COUNT

Most models offer a choice of at least three wash cycles—Light, Normal, and Heavy (or Pots and Pans)—which should be enough for the typical dishwashing jobs. A few, including Kenmore, offer power-washing features designed to remove heavy soil such as baked-on brownie batter. Kenmore's Turbo Zone has a section that's exposed to high-pressure washing to handle extra-dirty dishes. It worked well in our tests.

Rinse/Hold lets you rinse dirty dishes before using the dishwasher on a full cycle. Other cycles offered on many models include **Pot Scrubber, Soak/Scrub,** and **China/Crystal,** none of which we consider crucial for most consumers. Dishwashers often spray water from multiple places, or "levels," in the machine. Most models typically offer a choice of **drying** with or without heat.

All dishwashers use **filters** to keep wash water free of food that can be redeposited on clean dishes. Most such models are self-cleaning: A spray arm cleans residue from the coarse filter during the rinse cycle, and a food-disposal **grinder** cuts up large food particles so they can be washed down the drain. Some of the more expensive dishwashers have a filter that you must pull out and clean manually; these are usually quieter than those with grinders. If noise is a concern, see if better **soundproofing**—often in the form of hard, rubbery insulation surrounded by a thick fiberglass blanket—is available as a step-up feature.

A **sanitizing wash** or **rinse option** that raises the water temperature above the typical 140° F doesn't necessarily mean improved cleaning. Remember, the moment you touch a dish while taking it out of the dishwasher, it's no longer sanitized.

Most dishwashers have **electronic touchpad controls.** On more expensive models, controls may be fully or partly hidden, (or integrated) in the top edge of the door. The least expensive models have mechanical controls, usually operated by a dial and push buttons. Touchpads are the easiest type of control to wipe clean. **Dials** indicate progress through a cycle. Some electronic models digitally display time left in the wash cycle. Others merely show a "clean" signal. A **delayed-start control** lets you set the dishwasher to start later, for example, at night when utility rates may be lower. Some models offer **child-safety features,** such as locks for the door and controls.

Most dishwashers hold cups and glasses on top, plates on the bottom, and silverware in a basket. **Racks** can sometimes be adjusted to better fit your dishes. On some units, the top rack can be adjusted enough to let you put 10-inch dinner plates on both the top and bottom racks simultaneously, or it can be removed entirely so very tall items will fit on the bottom.

Other features that enhance flexibility include **adjustable** and **removable tines,** which fold down to accommodate bigger dishes, pots, and pans; **slots for silverware** that prevent "nesting"; removable racks, which enable loading and unloading outside the dishwasher; stemware holders, which steady wine glasses; **clips** to keep light plastic cups from overturning; and **fold-down shelves,** which stack cups in a double-tiered arrangement.

Stainless-steel **tubs** should last virtually forever, but even plastic tubs generally have a warranty of 20 years, much longer than most people keep a dishwasher. Light-colored plastic may discolor, especially from tomato sauce, but there's otherwise no advantage to stainless. Dishwashers with stainless-steel tubs typically cost $500 and up.

> **Tech tip**
>
> Dishwashers with adjustable racks and fold-down tines are better if you want to wash oversized platters or odd-shaped serving pieces.

If you want a front panel that matches your cabinets, you can buy a kit compatible with many dishwashers. Some higher-priced models come without a front panel so you can choose your own, usually at a cost of several hundred dollars.

HOW TO CHOOSE

Our tests over the years have shown that most new dishwashers will do a great job cleaning even the dirtiest dishes without prerinsing, which wastes lots of water. But they differ in appearance, noise, loading, energy efficiency, and features. Here are points to consider when choosing a dishwasher:

Decide how many options you need. Adjustable racks and fold-down tines help dishwashers hold large bowls and other awkward items. But you may want to skip those features and pay less if you don't cook big meals or entertain often.

We also suggest thinking twice about half-load cycles, which allow you to wash just one rack. Running two half-load cycles can use more water and energy than one normal load. Half-load cycles that use only the top rack also limit your options, since some top racks can't accommodate dinner dishes or silverware.

Check quietness and energy use. New dishwasher models are probably quieter than the one you have now. But you might want the quietest models we tested if you have an open kitchen near a dining or family room, for example. You'll also hear a lot about Energy Star labels, which cite dishwashers that are 25 percent more energy-efficient than minimum government standards. We suggest using the energy scores in our Ratings, which are based on much dirtier loads. Most of the energy a dishwasher uses goes to heating the water. Water usage, and thus the operating costs, vary greatly from model to model. In our recent tests, water usage ranged from about 3½ to 12 gallons a load. Energy costs to heat the water and run the machine could vary by up to $65 a year for the tested models, depending on rates in your area. Over its lifetime, a more efficient model could be a better buy than a lower-priced model that is less energy-efficient.

Decide whether a self-cleaning filter is a must. Most dishwashers have self-cleaning filters, which can add to noise. The Asko, Bosch, Fisher & Paykel, Haier, Miele, and Siemens models we've tested have filters you clean yourself. That isn't a big deal: You simply remove the filter and rinse it off, usually every week or two. A clogged filter could affect wash performance.

Don't get hung up on dirt sensors. Dirt sensors, which adjust water use and cycle time to the soil on the dishes, are common. Some sensors don't distinguish well between slightly and very dirty dishes, however, increasing wash time and water use even if the load is lightly soiled.

Use rinse aids and enzyme-based detergents. Both tend to yield cleaner results. Rinse aids reduce spotting, while enzyme-based detergents help dissolve food starches and proteins.

Keep style in perspective. Most dishwashers have deleted the bottom panel below the door, adding space for taller items inside and allowing sleeker styling outside. You'll pay a premium for a stainless-steel tub, which doesn't spot and should last virtually forever. But plastic tubs should outlast most machines. Hidden controls are another stylish feature, though cycle progress isn't obvious at a glance. A good compromise: partly hidden controls, which show that the machine is running and often display remaining cycle time.

If speed matters, check cycle time. The normal cycle (including drying time) ranges from about 80 minutes to 150 minutes, but longer cycles don't necessarily clean better. In our tests, models with cycle times of about 100 minutes did just as thorough a job as others that took 145 minutes.

Consider the cost of delivery and installation. Installation can run $100 to $200 or more. Sears, which sells roughly 35 percent of all dishwashers, charges on average $105 to deliver and install a new unit.

Related CR report: August 2006
Ratings: page 248
Reliability: page 255

DRYERS

On the whole, clothes dryers do a good job. More sophisticated models dry your laundry with greater finesse.

Dryers are relatively simple. Their major differences are how they heat the air (gas or electricity) and how they're programmed to shut off once the load is dry (thermostat or moisture sensor). Gas models typically cost about $50 more than electric ones, but they're usually cheaper to operate.

CONSUMER REPORTS has found that dryers with a moisture sensor tend to recognize when laundry is dry more quickly than machines that use a traditional thermostat. Because they don't subject clothing to unnecessary heat, moisture-sensor models are easier on fabrics. And since they shut themselves off when laundry is dry, they use less energy. Sensors are now offered on many dryers, including some relatively low-priced ones. Thermostat-only dryers are generally the most basic models.

WHAT'S AVAILABLE

The top four brands—GE, Kenmore (Sears), Maytag, and Whirlpool—account for approximately 80 percent of dryer sales. Other brands include Frigidaire (made by Electrolux), Hotpoint (made by GE), and Admiral, Amana, KitchenAid, and Roper (made by Whirlpool). You may also run across smaller brands such as Crosley, Estate, and White-Westinghouse, all of which are made by the larger brands. Asko, Bosch, Miele, and Siemens are European brands. Fisher & Paykel is from New Zealand, LG and Samsung from Korea, and Haier from China.

Full-sized models. These models generally measure between 27 and 29 inches in width—the critical dimension for fitting in cabinetry and closets. Front-mounted controls on some models let you stack the dryer atop a front-loading washer, but shorter people may find it difficult to reach the dryer controls or the inside of the drum. Full-sized models vary in drum capacity from about 5 to 7½ cubic feet. Most have ample capacity for typical wash loads. A larger drum can more easily handle bulky items such as queen-size comforters. Buying a more expensive model may get you more capacity and a few extra conveniences. Price: electric, $200 to $1,000; gas, $250 to $1,100.

Space-saving models. Compacts, exclusively electric, are typically 24 inches wide, with a drum capacity roughly half that of full-sized models—about 3½ cubic feet. Aside from their smaller capacity, they perform much like full-sized machines. They can be stacked atop a companion washer. Some compact dryers operate on 120 volts, while others require a 240-volt outlet (as do full-sized electric dryers). Price: $200 to about $1,400.

Another space-saving option is a laundry center, which combines a washer and dryer in a single unit. Laundry centers come with either gas or electric dryers. There are full-sized (27 inches wide) or compact (24 inches wide) models available. The dryer component of a laundry center typically has a somewhat smaller capacity than a full-sized dryer. Laundry centers with electric dryers require a dedicated 240-volt power source. Price: $700 to $1,900.

Tech tip
Dryers with a moisture sensor tend to recognize when laundry is dry more quickly than machines that use a traditional thermostat.

FEATURES THAT COUNT

Full-sized dryers often have two or three **auto-dry cycles,** which shut off the unit when the clothes reach the desired dryness. Each cycle might have a **more dry** setting to dry clothes completely, and a **less dry** setting to leave clothes damp for ironing, plus gradations between those two extremes.

Most dryers have a separate **temperature control** that allows you to choose a lower heat for delicate fabrics, among other things. An **extended tumble** setting, sometimes called Press Care or Finish Guard, helps to prevent wrinkling when you don't remove clothes immediately. Some models continue to tumble without heat; others cycle on and off. An **express-dry cycle** is meant for drying small loads at high heat in less than a half hour. Large loads will take longer. **Touchpad electronic controls** found in higher-end models tend to be more versatile than mechanical dials and buttons—once you figure them out, that is. Some models allow you to save favorite settings that you use frequently. Some high-end dryers have a display with a progression of menus that enable you to program specific settings for recall at any time. These menus can be time-consuming (and sometimes confusing) to navigate, but they may allow custom programming or offer detailed help and information otherwise available only in the manual.

A **top-mounted lint filter** may be somewhat easier to clean than one inside the drum. Some models have a **warning light** that reminds you to clean the filter. It's important to clean it regularly to minimize any fire hazard and to maintain the dryer's efficiency. It's also advisable to use metal ducting (either rigid or flexible) instead of plastic or flexible foil. Plastic or foil ducts can create a fire hazard if they sag and clog with lint, causing lint to build up in the dryer, where it can ignite. You should clean the ducts out at least once a year.

Most full-sized models have a **drum light,** making it easy for you to spot stray items that may be hiding in the back. Some models allow you to raise or lower the volume of an **end-of-cycle signal** or shut it off. A **rack** included with many dryers attaches inside the drum to hold sneakers or other items that you want to dry without tumbling. Models with **drop-down doors** in front may fit better against a wall, but **side-opening doors** may make it easier to access the inside of the drum.

HOW TO CHOOSE

Consider gas if you can. Both gas and electric dryers perform comparably, our years of testing show. Gas dryers cost about $50 more than comparable electric models, but the savings in fuel costs should more than make up the difference in the long run. An electric dryer requires a 240-volt outlet, a gas dryer a gas hookup. If you have both, don't rule out the gas model simply because it costs more. (CONSUMER REPORTS now tests only electric dryers, which account for about 80 percent of the models sold, but equivalent gas models are listed in the Ratings.)

Insist on a moisture sensor. As noted earlier, overdrying can damage or shrink fabrics, and moisture sensors can minimize that possibility. Sensors are available on about half the dryers on the market, including most priced above $350. Whether a specific model has a sensor or thermostat may not be obvious from labeling or controls. Check the literature, visit the manufacturer's Web site, or pick a highly rated dryer that we've tested.

Don't get hung up on capacity. Manufacturers describe dryer capacity (as they do washer capacity) with such terms as extra large, super, and super plus. The differences aren't meaningful for everyday use. Most full-sized dryers can hold a typical wash load. If you want to dry big, bulky items, choose a model judged excellent for capacity in our Ratings.

Start in the middle. When using an automatic setting rather than a timed one (which we generally recommend), set the control to the midpoint and raise or lower it as needed. Using more dry routinely can overdry clothes and waste energy. Use less dry to leave clothing damp for ironing. Don't worry about knowing when an automatic cycle is done: If you don't hear the buzzer, an extended tumble without heat prevents wrinkles if you don't remove clothes immediately.

Don't pay for unnecessary extras. Higher-priced dryers may offer a dozen or so choices, including specialty cycles such as speed dry (15 minutes of high heat, for example). These can usually be replicated with standard settings. A choice of heat level—timed and autodry—and a few fabric types (regular/cotton and permanent press/delicate) is usually plenty. Touchpads look impressive and may allow you to save custom settings, but don't improve performance. Nor do stainless-steel tubs, unlike in washers.

Get a quiet dryer for living areas. If your dryer will be near the kitchen or a bedroom, look for a model judged very good or excellent for noise.

Related CR Report: March 2006
Ratings: page 256
Reliability: page 257

FOOD PROCESSORS & MIXERS

Match the machine to the way you prepare foods. But you may find you need more than one.

Which food-prep appliance best suits your style and the foods you prepare? Food processors are versatile machines that can chop, slice, shred, and purée. Mini-choppers are good for small jobs such as mincing garlic and chopping nuts. Hand mixers can handle light chores such as whipping cream or mixing cake batter. And powerful stand mixers are ideal for cooks who make bread and cookies from scratch.

WHAT'S AVAILABLE

Food processors. Several brands have introduced multifunction models designed to do the job of two or more machines—for instance, an interchangeable food-processor container and a glass blender jar and blade. Either attachment fits on a motorized base.

Another design trend is a mini-bowl insert that fits inside the main container for preparing smaller quantities of food. Newer designs tend to be sleek, with rounded corners. Dominant brands are Black & Decker, Cuisinart, Hamilton Beach, and KitchenAid. Mini-choppers such as the Magic Bullet have become popular due to infomercial advertising. Price: $20 to $400.

Shop smart

A midsized food processor model, around 7 cups, is probably fine for most tasks.

Stand and hand mixers. The big push in mixers is for more power, which is useful for handling heavy dough. You'll find everything from heavy-duty models offering the most power and the largest mixing bowls to light-service machines that are essentially detachable hand mixers resting on a stand. Models vary in power from about 200 to 800 watts. Sales of light-duty, convenient hand mixers have held their own in recent years.

KitchenAid owns over half the stand-mixer market; GE, Hamilton Beach and Sunbeam are the next best-selling brands. Price: $60 to $500.

Black & Decker, GE, Hamilton Beach, KitchenAid, Proctor Silex, and Sunbeam are the dominant brands among hand mixers. Price: $15 to $75.

FEATURES THAT COUNT

With food processors: All have a clear plastic **mixing bowl** and lid, an S-shaped metal **chopping blade** (and sometimes a duller version for kneading dough), and a **plastic food pusher** to safely prod food through the feed tube. Some have a wider tube so you don't have to cut up vegetables—such as potatoes—to fit the opening. One speed is the norm, plus a **pulse setting** to control processing precisely. Bowl capacity ranges from around 3 cups to 14 cups (dry), with most models holding 6 to 11 cups. A **shredding/slicing disk** is standard on full-sized processors. Some come with a juicer attachment. **Touchpad controls** are becoming more commonplace, too.

Mini-choppers look like little food processors, with a capacity of 2 to 3 cups, but they're for small jobs only, like chopping small quantities of nuts or half an onion.

With mixers: Stand mixers generally come with one **bowl** and either single or paired **beaters, whisks,** and **dough hooks.** Some offer options such as **splash guards** to prevent flour from spewing out of the bowl, plus **attachments** to make pasta, grind meat, and stuff sausage. Stand mixers generally have 5 to 16 speeds; we think five or six well-differentiated settings is enough. You should be able to lock a mixer's power head in the Up position so it won't crash into the bowl when the beaters are weighed down with dough. Conversely, it should lock in the Down position to keep the beaters from kicking back when tackling stiff dough.

Just about any hand mixer is good for nontaxing jobs such as beating egg whites, mashing potatoes, or whipping cream. The slow-start feature on some mixers prevents ingredients from spattering when you start up, but you can achieve the same result by manually stepping through three or so speeds. An indentation on the underside of the motor housing allows the mixer to sit on the edge of a bowl without taking the beaters out of the batter.

HOW TO CHOOSE
Food processors & choppers

Consider capacity. Food-processor capacity ranges from about 3 to 14 cups. (Those are manufacturers' figures; we've found that they typically hold a cup or two more or less than claimed.) Choppers, which are designed expressly for small jobs, hold from 1 to 3 cups.

If you regularly cook for a crowd or like to whip up multiple batches of a recipe, you might appreciate the bigger, 11- to 14-cup units. However, they tend to be pricier and heavier than smaller versions and take up more counter space. A midsized model (around 7 cups) is likely fine for most tasks.

Note that even big food processors can handle small jobs such as chopping half an onion. But using a chopper makes cleanup easier.

Don't focus on speeds. Food processors typically have two settings: on and pulse, which allows you to run the machine in brief bursts for more precise processing control. Choppers typically have one or two pulse settings (high and low). Those are really all the speeds you need. Some machines have a few extra speeds (a dough setting on some high-end processors, for example), but we haven't found that they perform much better.

Note feed-tube size. Some processors have wider feed tubes than others, which can save you the effort of having to cut potatoes, cucumbers, and other big items.

Expect to pay more for kneading prowess and quiet operation. The models we tested that cost $55 or less strained and jumped while kneading dough. They also made quite a racket, where most of the higher-end models we tested were quiet. Choppers can be noisy but are used only briefly.

Stand & hand mixers

Decide how much mixer you need. Just about any stand or hand mixer will do for all those simple mixing and whipping chores. But if you're a dedicated baker, you'll probably want to invest in a heavy, powerful stand mixer, because it can knead even two loaves' worth of bread dough with ease.

Downplay wattage and number of speed settings. Manufacturers stress wattage and number of speeds, but neither figure necessarily translates into better performance. For example, some stand mixers have as many as 16 speeds; some hand mixers have 9. We think five or six well-differentiated speeds are sufficient. The slower the lowest speed, the better; slow speeds prevent spattering.

Speeds should be clearly indicated. With some of the inexpensive hand mixers we tested, the switch you use to select speeds didn't line up well with the speed markings.

Consider size and weight. Hand mixers should feel well balanced and comfortable to hold; most that we tested did. Size and weight can be a concern with stand mixers—some weigh more than 20 pounds—but their heft gives them the stability to handle tough jobs.

Make sure that you will have enough clearance if you plan to keep the mixer on a counter below a cupboard.

Consider beater style and motion. Most of the top-performing hand mixers have wire beaters without the thick center post found on traditional-style beaters. The wire beaters performed well and were easier to clean.

Light-duty stand mixers typically have stationary beaters and a bowl that sits on a revolving turntable. The bowl sometimes needs a push to keep spinning.

Related CR report: July 2005

FREEZERS

Chest freezers cost the least to buy and run, but self-defrost uprights are the winners for convenience.

If you buy box-loads of burgers at a warehouse club or like to keep a few weeks' worth of dinner fixings on hand, the 4- to 6-cubic-foot freezer compartment in most refrigerators may seem positively Lilliputian. A separate freezer might be a good investment.

WHAT'S AVAILABLE

Most freezers sold in the U.S. are from one of three companies: Electrolux Home Products, which makes models sold under the Frigidaire, GE, and Kenmore labels; W.C. Wood, which makes models sold under its own name as well as Amana, Magic Chef, Maytag, and Whirlpool; and Haier, a Chinese manufacturer, which has become a major player in the freezer business in recent years. Haier is now the leading supplier of compact-sized freezers sold under its own name and some under the Amana, Kenmore, GE, and Maytag brands.

There are two types of freezers: chests, which are essentially horizontal boxes with a door that opens upward; and uprights, which resemble a single-door refrigerator. Both types are available in self-defrost and manual-defrost versions.

In recent tests, we found models of both types that failed to keep food frozen.

Manual-defrost chests. These freezers vary most in capacity, ranging from 4 to 25 cubic feet. Aside from a hanging basket or two, chests are wide open, letting you put in even large, bulky items. Nearly all the claimed cubic-foot space is usable. The design makes chests slightly more energy efficient and cheaper to operate than up-

rights. Cooling coils are built into the walls, so no fan is required to circulate the cold air. Because the door opens from the top, virtually no cold air escapes when you put in or take out food. A chest's open design, however, does make it hard to organize the contents. Finding something can require bending and often moving around piles of frozen goods. If you're short, you may find it difficult to extricate an item buried at the bottom (assuming you can remember it's stashed there). A chest also takes up more floor space than an upright. A 15-cubic-foot model is about 4 feet wide by 2½ feet deep; a comparable upright is just as deep but only about to 2½ feet wide.

Defrosting a chest can be a hassle, especially if it's fully loaded or has a thick coating of ice. You have to unload the food, keep it frozen somewhere until the ice encrusting the walls has melted, remove the water that accumulates at the drain, then put back the food. Price: $150 to $500.

Self-defrost chests. This type of freezer is relatively new to the marketplace and, except for defrosting, has the same advantages and disadvantages as a manual-defrost chest freezer. Self-defrosting involves heaters that turn on periodically to remove excess ice buildup, eliminating a tedious, messy chore but using extra energy. Because of the circulating fan, self-defrost models are somewhat noisier than manual-defrost chest freezers. Price: $250 to $700.

Manual-defrost uprights. These freezers have a capacity of 5 to 25 cubic feet, of which some 15 percent isn't usable. They cost less to buy and run than self-defrost models but aren't as economical as chests. Unlike their self-defrost counterparts, they don't have a fan to circulate cold air, which can result in uneven temperatures. Defrosting is quite a chore with some.

The metal shelves in the main space are filled with coolant, so if you're not careful scraping off the ice you can damage the shelves. What's more, ice tends to cling to the shelves, so defrosting can take up to 24 hours. Other models have a "flash" defrost system that heats the cooling coils to quickly melt any frost. There's no need to scrape, but as with any freezer, you must empty the contents before defrosting. Because a manual-defrost upright's shelves contain coolant, they can't be adjusted or removed to hold large items. Price: $170 to $700.

Self-defrost uprights. These models (sometimes called frost-free) have from 11 to 25 cubic feet of space. Like a refrigerator, they have shelves in the main compartment and on the door; some have pullout bins. This arrangement lets you organize and access contents, but reduces usable space by about 20 percent. Interior shelves can be removed or adjusted to fit large items. When you open the door of an upright, cold air spills out from the bottom while warm, humid air sneaks in at the top. That makes the freezer work harder and use more energy to stay cold, and temperatures may fluctuate a bit. These models compensate by using a fan to circulate cold air from the cooling coils, which are located in the back wall.

A self-defrost model costs about $20 a year more to run than a similar-sized manual-defrost model. For many people, the convenience may be worth the extra cost. Self-defrosting models are a bit noisier than other types, an issue only if they're located near a living area rather than in the basement or garage. While freezers of old weren't recommended for use in areas that got very hot or cold, current self-defrost models should work fine within a wide ambient temperature range—typically 32° F to 110° F. Price: $350 to $800.

FEATURES THAT COUNT

While freezers are simpler than some other major appliances, there are several features worth looking for. **Interior lighting** makes it easier to find things, especially if you place the freezer in a dimly lighted area. A **power-on light**, indicating that the freezer has power, is helpful. A **temperature alarm** lets you know when the freezer is too warm inside, such as after a prolonged power outage. (If you lose power, don't open the freezer door; food should remain frozen for about 24 to 48 hours.) A **quick-freeze feature** brings the freezer to its coldest setting faster by making it run continuously instead of cycling on and off, handy when you're adding a lot of food. The **flash-defrost feature** on some manual-defrost upright freezers can make defrosting easier and faster.

> **Tech tip**
>
> Self-defrosting freezers eliminate a tedious, messy chore but use extra energy.

HOW TO CHOOSE

Figure the capacity you need. This will depend on the size of your family and its fondness for frozen foods. Freezers are available in four general sizes: compact (5 cubic feet); small (6 to 9 cubic feet); medium (12 to 18 cubic feet); and large (more than 18 cubic feet). Aside from hanging baskets, chest freezers are wide open so that almost all of the claimed space is usable. Upright freezers have shelves and pull-out bins. These make it easier to organize and reach contents but reduce usable space by up to 20 percent.

Weigh manual vs. self-defrost. Manual-defrost freezers, either chest or upright, are generally quieter and more energy efficient than self-defrosting models of the same type. But manually defrosting a freezer is a lot of work and can take up to 24 hours.

Consider local power problems. If the area where you live is prone to brownouts or power failures, a chest freezer will be the better choice.

Check the controls and lights. Easy-to-reach controls make adjusting the temperature simple. An interior light makes it easier to find foods, especially if the freezer is in a dimly lighted area. A power-on light on the outside of the freezer lets you see at a glance that the freezer is on. That way you don't have to open the unit to check, letting cold air out. About half of the models we tested have this feature. We think all should have it.

Related CR Report: October 2005

MICROWAVE OVENS

You'll see larger capacity, sensors that detect doneness, and stylish designs to complement your kitchen.

Microwave ovens, which built their reputation on speed, are also showing some smarts. Many automatically shut off when a sensor determines that the food is cooked or sufficiently heated. The sensor is also used to automate an array of cooking chores, with buttons labeled for frozen entrées, baked potatoes, popcorn, beverages, and other common items. Design touches include softer edges for less boxy styling, hidden controls for a sleeker look, stainless steel, and for a few, a translucent finish.

WHAT'S AVAILABLE

GE leads the countertop microwave-oven market with approximately 30 percent of units sold, followed by Sharp. Other brands include Emerson, Kenmore, Panasonic, and many others. GE also sells the most over-the-range models.

Microwaves come in a variety of sizes, from compact to large. Most sit on the countertop, but a growing number sold—about 15 percent—are mounted over the range. Several brands offer speed-cooking via halogen bulbs or convection. Speed-cook models promise grilling and browning, though results can vary significantly depending on the food. Manufacturers are working to boost capacity without taking up more space by moving controls to the door and using recessed turntables and smaller electronic components.

Microwave ovens vary in the power of the magnetron, which generates the microwaves. Midsized and large ovens are rated at 850 to 1,650 watts, compact ovens at 600 to 800 watts. A higher wattage may heat food more quickly, but differences of 100 watts are probably inconsequential. Some microwave ovens have a convection feature—a fan and often a heating element—that lets you roast and bake, something you don't generally do in a regular microwave.

Price: $40 to $250 (countertop models); $100 to $700 (over-the-range); $250 to $1,000 (convection or halogen-bulb countertop or over-the-range).

FEATURES THAT COUNT

On most, a **turntable** rotates the food so it will heat more uniformly, but the center of the dish still tends to be cooler than the rest. With some models, you can turn off the rotation when, for instance, you're using a dish that's too large to rotate. The results won't be as good, however. Some models have replaced the turntable with a rectangular tray that slides from side to side to accept larger dishes. Most turntables are removable for cleaning.

You'll find similarities in **controls** from model to model. A **numeric keypad** is used to set cooking times and power levels. Most ovens have shortcut keys for particular foods and for reheating or defrosting. Some microwaves start immediately when you hit the shortcut key, others make you enter the food quantity or weight. Some models have an **automatic popcorn feature** that takes just one press of a button. Pressing a **1-minute** or **30-second key** runs the oven at full power or extends the current cooking time. Microwave ovens typically have a number of **power levels.** We've found six to be more than adequate. A **child lock** renders controls inoperable.

A **sensor** helps prevent over- or under-cooking by determining when the food is done based on infrared light or the steam emitted by the food. The small premium you pay for a sensor is worth it. A **convection mode** maximizes browning and crisping with heated air circulated by a fan. A few ovens have a **crisper pan** for making bacon or crisping pizza crust.

Over-the-range microwave ovens vent themselves and the range with a **fan** that usually has several speed settings. Typically, the fan will turn on automatically if it senses excessive heat coming from the range below. Over-the-range microwaves can be vented to the outside or they can recirculate air in the kitchen. If the oven is venting inside, you'll need a **charcoal filter** (sometimes included). An over-the-range microwave generally doesn't handle ventilation as well as a hood-and-blower ventilation system because it doesn't extend over the front burners.

HOW TO CHOOSE

Decide which type meets your needs. Countertop microwave ovens cost the least and are best for kitchens with lots of counter space. Compact models can cost very little. Midsized and large models have more capacity and features, although most eat up 2.8 to 3.2 square feet of counter space. You can hang some countertop models below a cabinet, though doing so often leaves little working space below the microwave oven.

You're likely to consider an over-the-range oven only if you're replacing one or remodeling your kitchen. While they save counter space, installation is an added expense and may require an electrician. What's more, they can't vent steam and smoke from a range's front burners as well as the range hoods they replace.

Choose convenience, not clutter. There's little reason to buy a microwave without a sensor, which shuts off power when it senses the food is hot; sensor models begin at about $85. Our tests have found that sensor models generally perform better than those without them. But you may want to avoid ovens with an array of shortcut and defrost settings for foods you don't eat.

Consider convection. Paying extra for a convection mode is worth it if you use your microwave as a second oven, but it might not be necessary otherwise. Combination convection and microwave cooking saves time, although these units seldom brown and crisp food as well as conventional ovens and toaster ovens, which you probably own already.

Be skeptical about capacity. Manufacturers, we found, sometimes exaggerate the capacity of their ovens by counting wasted space in the corners. The ovens' actual cooking space can be as much as 50 to 60 percent less than claimed. Check whether a large platter fits inside an oven you're considering.

Related CR Report: February 2006
Ratings: page 283
Reliability report: page 290

RANGES

You don't have to spend top dollar for impressive performance with high-end cooking features and stainless- steel styling.

If you're in the market for a range, you're faced with several choices. You can buy a freestanding one that combines a cooktop and oven, or you can buy a separate cooktop and wall oven. The oven can be equipped with a convection feature. If you have access to a gas hookup, you need to decide whether you want gas, electricity, or a combination of the two.

All of these choices bring innovations and upgrades as competition among manufacturers heats up. Smoothtop electric ranges where the heating elements are below a ceramic glass surface now outnumber traditional coiltop models. Both offer quick heating and the ability to maintain low heat levels. Gas ranges use burners, which typically don't heat as quickly as electric elements, despite increasingly higher power—measured in British thermal units per hour (Btu/hr.). Even the highest-powered burners tend to heat more slowly than the fastest electric coil elements, sometimes because the heavy cast-iron grates that typically come with them slow the process by absorbing some of that heat. But you can see how high or low you are adjusting the flame. Several electric and gas ranges offer the flexibility of two ovens—either one regular-sized oven plus a smaller one or one regular oven and a microwave oven drawer.

You'll also see more high-end or professional-style gas ranges with beefy knobs, heavy cast-iron grates, thick, stainless-steel construction, and four or more high-powered burners. These high-heat behemoths can easily cost $2,000 or more and typically require a special range hood and blower system, along with special shielding and a reinforced floor in some applications. But because the look is so popular, you'll find a growing number of stoves that include stainless trim and other pro-style perks for far less.

Shared characteristics between electric and gas ranges are also a growing trend. Some gas models have electric warming zones. Convection features are available on both gas and electric ranges. More and more manufacturers are offering dual-fuel gas ranges, which pair a gas cooktop with an electric oven. These cost about $1,400 and up.

WHAT'S AVAILABLE

GE, Kenmore (sourced from others), Frigidaire, Maytag, and Whirlpool are the leading makers of ranges, cooktops, and wall ovens. Other major brands include Amana, Bosch, Electrolux, Hotpoint, Jenn-Air, KitchenAid, and LG. Mainstream brands have established high-end offshoots, such as Kenmore Elite, GE Profile, and Whirlpool Gold. High-end, pro-style brands include Dacor, GE Monogram, KitchenAid Pro-Line, Thermador, Viking, and Wolf.

Freestanding range. These ranges can fit in the middle of a kitchen counter or at the end. Widths are usually 24 to 48 inches, although most are 30 inches wide. They typically have oven controls on the backsplash. Slide-in models eliminate the backsplash and side panels to blend into the countertop, while drop-ins rest atop toe-kick-level cabinetry and typically lack a storage drawer. Nearly all mainstream ranges now include a self-cleaning feature and—for gas models—sealed burners, which keep crumbs from falling beneath the cooktop. On the higher end of the scale, electric models have one or more expandable electric elements; gas models have two or more high-powered burners, a convection oven, and warming drawers. Price: $400 to $1,600.

Pro-style range. Bulkier than freestanding ranges, these gas models can be anywhere from 30 to 60 inches wide. Larger ones include six or eight burners, a grill or griddle, and a double oven. Many have a convection feature, and some have an infrared gas broiler. While you usually don't get a storage drawer, more pro-style stoves now include a self-cleaning oven and sealed burners. Price: $2,000 to $5,000.

FEATURES THAT COUNT

On all ranges. Look for easy-cleaning features such as a **glass** or **porcelain backguard,** instead of a painted one; **seamless corners and edges,** especially where the cooktop joins the backguard; a **warming drawer** for convenience; **six or more oven-rack positions** for flexibility; and a **raised edge** around the cooktop to contain spills. Note, though, that a range's usable capacity may be less than what manufacturers claim, because they don't take protruding broiler elements and other features into account.

On electric ranges. Consider where the **controls** are located. Slide-in ranges have the dials to the front panel, while freestanding models have them on the backguard. Some models put controls to the left and right, with oven controls in between, giving you a quick sense of which control operates which element. But controls clustered in the center stay visible when tall pots sit on rear heating elements.

Coil elements, the least expensive electric option, are easy to replace if they break. On an electric range with coil elements, look for a **prop-up top** for easier cleaning, and deep **drip pans** made of porcelain to better contain spills and ease cleaning.

Spending $200 more will buy you a **smoothtop** model; most use radiant heat. Some smoothtops have **expandable ele-ments**—also called **dual elements**—which allow you to switch between a large, high-power element and a small, low-power element contained within it. Some smoothtops also include a **low-wattage element** for warming plates or keeping just-cooked food at the optimal temperature. Some have an elongated "bridge" element that spans two burners—a nicety for accommodating rectangular or odd-shaped cookware. And many have at least **one hot-surface light**—a key safety feature, since the surface can remain hot long after the elements have been turned off. The safest setup includes a dedicated "hot" light for each element.

Most electric ranges have one large, **higher-wattage element** in front and one in back. An **expanded simmer range** in some electric models lets you fine-tune the simmer setting on one element for, say, melting chocolate or keeping a sauce from getting too hot.

On gas ranges. Most gas ranges have four burners in three sizes, measured in British thermal units per hour (Btu/hr.): one or two medium-power burners (about 9,000 Btu/hr.); a small burner (about 5,000 Btu/hr.); and one or two large ones (about 12,500 Btu/hr.). We recommend a model with one or more 12,000 Btu/hr. burners for quick cooktop heating. Some have a fifth burner instead of a center island. On a few models, the burners automatically re-ignite. Look for models that use larger burners for higher heat, so you can tell at a glance which burner is which.

For easier cleaning, look for **sealed burners.** Gas ranges typically have **knob controls;** the best rotate 180 degrees or more. Try to avoid knobs that have adjacent off

Shop smart

More and more manufacturers are offering dual-fuel gas ranges, which pair a gas cooktop with an electric oven.

and low settings and that rotate no more than 90 degrees between high and low.

Spending more gets you either heavier **grates** made of porcelain-coated cast iron or a sleek **ceramic surface**—also called **gas-on-glass**—and **stainless-steel accents,** along with a low-power **simmer burner** with an extra-low setting for delicate sauces (though other burners often are capable of simmering).

On pro-style ranges. These models have four or more brass or cast-iron burners, all of which offer very high output (usually about 15,000 Btu/hr.). The burners may be non-sealed, with hard-to-clean crevices, though sealed burners are appearing on some models. Large knobs are another typical pro-style feature, as are **continuous grates** designed for heavy-duty use. The latter, however, can be unwieldy to remove for cleaning.

A **self-cleaning cycle** uses high heat to burn off spills and splatters. Most ranges have it, although some pro-style gas models still don't. **An automatic door lock,** found on most self-cleaning models, is activated during the cycle, then unlocks when the oven has cooled. Also useful is a **self-cleaning countdown** display, which shows the time left in the cycle.

Higher-priced ranges often include **convection,** which uses a fan and, sometimes, an electric element to circulate heated air. CONSUMER REPORTS tests have shown that this mode cut cooking time for a large roast and, in some cases, baked large cookie batches more evenly because of the circulating air. A few electric ovens have a low-power **microwave feature** that works with bake and broil elements to speed cooking time further. Another cooking technology, called Trivection, uses regular thermal heating, convection, and microwave energy to cut cooking time. Trivection is available in some top-of-the-line GE Profile and Monogram ranges. Though very good overall, Trivection is very pricey.

A **variable-broil** feature in some ranges offers adjustable settings for foods such as fish or thick steaks that need slower or faster cooking. Ranges with **12-hour shutoff** turn off automatically if you leave the oven on for that long. But most models allow you to disable this feature. A **child lockout** allows you to disable oven controls for safety.

Manufacturers are also updating oven controls across the price spectrum. **Electronic touchpad controls** are common. A **digital display** makes it easier to set the precise temperature and keep track of it. A **cook time/delay start** lets you set a time for the oven to start and stop cooking. But remember that you shouldn't leave most foods in a cold oven very long. An **automatic oven light** typically comes on when the door opens, although some ovens have a switch-operated light. A **temperature probe,** to be inserted into meat or poultry, indicates when you've reached the optimal internal temperature.

Oven windows come in various sizes. Those without a decorative grid usually offer the clearest view, although some cooks may welcome the grid to hide pots, pans, and other cooking utensils typically stored inside the oven.

HOW TO CHOOSE

Think about your cooking. If you often cook for a crowd, look for at least one high-powered element or burner and a large oven. Indeed, you'll find more mid-priced gas ranges with the ultrahigh heat once exclusive to professional-style stoves. High-heat burners can be useful for searing, stir-frying, or heating large quantities. Ranges with convection can speed roasting a little. Models that excelled in broiling produced burgers seared on the outside and cooked quickly and evenly.

Think hard before buying a pro-style range. For most consumers, they aren't the best choice. In our tests, they did no better than conventional ranges. Some pro-style models lack common features, and some brands have had higher repair rates.

Consider the fuel. Electric surface elements tend to heat faster and maintain low heat better. But a gas flame makes it easier to see the heat level. Either type is capable of very good performance. A dual-fuel range combines an electric oven and gas cooktop. But our tests don't support the claim that an electric oven cooks more evenly than a gas one. On average, dual-fuel ranges scored lower than top-performing gas or electric models and cost more.

Balance convenience and durability. Electric smoothtops are pretty easy to clean, but they require a special cleaner. They can be damaged by a dropped pot or sugary liquids. Coil tops aren't as susceptible to such harm, but they require more cleaning time.

Keep high-tech in perspective. Ranges with special baking modes may not outperform conventional models. Touchpad oven controls are more precise than knobs. But front-mounted touchpads can be bumped and reset by accident, so see if the controls are logically placed and visible while you're cooking.

Related CR report: August 2006
Ratings: page 306
Reliability: page 315

REFRIGERATORS

The trend is toward bigger and better as manufacturers add more space, more doors, and more options.

If you're shopping for a new refrigerator, you're probably considering models that are fancier and more energy-efficient than your current fridge. Spacious models with flexible, more efficient storage space abound, and useful features that were once found only in expensive refrigerators, such as spillproof, slide-out glass shelves; temperature-controlled compartments; and through-the-door ice and water are now practically standard in midpriced models. Stainless-steel doors are stylish, but they add to the cost. Bottom freezer, French-door models offer the convenience of a full-width refrigerator at eye level with the style and narrow door swing of a side-by-side. Built-in refrigerators appeal to people who want to customize their kitchens and are willing to pay thousands of dollars for the custom look. Some mainstream cabinet-depth models offer a built-in-style look for less.

Style and convenience might not be the only reasons to replace an aging refrigerator. Doing so could also reduce your utility bill, since refrigerators are more energy efficient today. The U.S. Department of Energy toughened its rules in the early 1990s and imposed even stricter requirements in July 2001 for this appliance, which is among the top electricity users in the house. A new standard is currently in the works.

WHAT'S AVAILABLE

Only a handful of companies actually manufacture refrigerators. The same or very similar units may be sold under several brand names. Frigidaire, General Electric, Kenmore, and Whirlpool account for about three-quarters of top-freezer sales. For side-by-side models, these brands and Maytag account for more than 80 percent of sales.

Brands offering bottom-freezers include Amana, Frigidaire, GE, Jenn-Air, Kenmore, KitchenAid, LG, Maytag, Samsung, Sub-Zero, Thermador, and Whirlpool.

Mainstream companies have introduced high-end brand lines such as Electrolux Icon, Frigidaire Gallery, GE Monogram and Profile, Kenmore Elite, and Whirlpool Gold. These brands cover built-ins: GE (Monogram and Profile), Jenn-Air, KitchenAid, Sub-Zero, Thermador, and Viking. You can get built-in-style or cabinet-depth models from Amana, Bosch, Electrolux, Frigidaire, GE, Jenn-Air, Kenmore, KitchenAid, LG, Maytag, and Whirlpool.

Top-freezers. These models are generally less expensive and more space efficient than comparably sized side-by-side models. Widths typically range from about 30 to 33 inches. The eye-level freezer offers easy access. Fairly wide refrigerator shelves make it easy to reach the back, but you have to bend to reach the bottom shelves and drawers. Claimed labeled capacity typically ranges from about 10 to 25 cubic feet. With top-freezers, the usable capacity is typically about 80 percent of its nominal capacity, according to our measurements. Price: $400 to $1,200.

Bottom-freezers. These units put frequently used items at eye level. Fairly wide refrigerator shelves provide easy access. Although you must bend to find items in the freezer, even with models that have a pull-out drawer, you will probably do less bending overall because the main refrigerated compartment is at eye level. Bottom-freezers are a bit pricier than top-freezers and offer less capacity relative to their external dimensions because of the inefficiency of the pull-out bin. Widths typically range from 30 to 36 inches. Claimed capacity is up to 25 cubic feet, nominally, and usable space is a bit less than with top-freezers, but more than offered by side-by-

Shop smart

Usable space is always less than claimed capacity.

sides. French-door models are increasingly available. Price: $700 to $1,500; French-door type, $1,500 to $2,000.

Side-by-sides. These are by far the most fully featured fridges, most often equipped with through-the-door ice and water dispensers—among the most requested consumer features—as well as temperature-controlled bins and rapid ice-making cycles. Their narrow doors are handy in tight spaces. High, narrow compartments make finding stray items easy in front (harder in the back), but they may not hold wide items such as a sheet cake or a large turkey. Compared with top- and bottom-freezer models, a higher proportion of capacity goes to freezer space. Side-by-sides are typically large—32 to 36 inches wide, with claimed capacity of 20 to 30 cubic feet. About 65 percent of that space is usable. They're much more expensive than similar-sized top-freezer models and are less efficient in terms of energy use, as well as space. Price: $800 to $2,000.

Built-ins. These refrigerators are generally side-by-side and bottom-freezer models. They show their commercial heritage, often having fewer standard amenities and less soundproofing than lower-priced "home" models. Usually 25 to 26 inches front to back, they fit nearly flush with cabinets and counters. Their compressor is on top, making them about a foot taller than regular refrigerators—an issue if you have overhead cabinets. Most can accept extra-cost front panels that match the décor of your kitchen. Side-by-side models in this style are available in 42-inch and 48-inch widths (vs. the more typical 36-inch width). You can even obtain a built-in pair: a separate refrigerator and freezer mounted together in a 72-inch opening. Price: $4,000 to $7,000.

Cabinet-depths. These freestanding refrigerators offer the look of a built-in for less money. They are available mostly in side-by-side styles, with some top- and bottom-freezers available. Many accept extra-cost panels for a custom look. Cabinet-depth models have less usable space than deeper freestanding models and cost more. Price: $1,500 to $3,200.

Under-cabinet refrigerator drawers. These are among the latest luxuries for kitchens where even the most massive refrigerator simply isn't enough. But these models tend to be large on price and small on space. What's more, while refrigerator drawers cost little to run, their limited capacity makes them energy inefficient.

FEATURES THAT COUNT

Interiors are ever more flexible. **Adjustable door bins** and **shelves** can be moved to fit tall items. Elevator shelves can be cranked up and down without removing the contents. Some **split shelves** can be adjusted to different heights independently. With other shelves, the front half of the shelf slides under the rear portion to provide clearance.

Shelf snuggers—sliding brackets on door shelves—secure bottles and jars. A few models have a wine rack that stores a bottle horizontally.

Glass shelves are easier to clean than wire racks. Most glass shelves have a raised, sealed rim to keep spills from dripping over. Some slide out. **Pull-out freezer shelves** or **bins** improve access. An alternative is a bottom-freezer with a sliding drawer.

More models have replaced mechanical controls with **electronic touchpads.** Some have a digital display that shows the temperature setting; a few show the actual temperature, which is more useful.

A **temperature-controlled drawer** can be set to be several degrees cooler than the rest of the interior, useful for storing meat

or fish. Crispers have controls to maintain humidity. Our tests have shown that, in general, temperature-controlled drawers work better than plain drawers; results for humidity controls are less clear-cut. See-through drawers let you see at a glance what's inside.

Curved doors give the refrigerator a distinctive profile and retro look. Most manufacturers have at least one curved-door model in their lineups.

Step-up features include a **variety of finishes and colors.** Every major manufacturer has a stainless-steel model that typically costs significantly more than one with a standard pebbled finish. Some brands offer fingerprint-resistant stainless with clear coatings, while other brands have fake stainless that resists prints. Another alternative is a smooth, glass-like finish.

Most models have an **icemaker** in the freezer or give you the option of installing one yourself. Typically producing several pounds of ice per day (although some produce 10 pounds or more), an icemaker reduces freezer space by about a cubic foot. The ice bin is generally located below the icemaker, but some new models have it on the inside of the freezer door, providing a bit more usable volume. **Through-the-door ice-and-water dispensers,** a side-by-side staple, have been hard to come by on top- and bottom-freezers (these features are starting to appear on French-door models). More of those models have added water dispensers inside the fridge in recent years, and some now have through-the-door water dispensers—icemakers are usually still in the freezer.

With many models, the icemaker and/or water dispenser includes **a water filter,** designed to reduce lead, chlorine, and other impurities in ice and/or drinking water. An icemaker or water dispenser will work without one. You can also have a filter installed in the tubing that supplies water to the refrigerator.

Once the **controls** are set, there should be little need to adjust temperature. Still, accessible controls are an added convenience.

HOW TO CHOOSE

Size is likely to be more important than style or price, since most new refrigerators must fit in the same space as the old one. So begin by measuring the available space. If there's a wall on the hinge side of the door, don't forget to factor in the space you'll need to open the door wide enough to pull out bins and drawers. Also measure doorways and halls through which the refrigerator must pass upon delivery.

Then choose a type that fits your space, needs, and budget. Once you've decided on a type, keep these shopping tips in mind:

Look for space-stretching features. For a refrigerator, claimed capacity lists raw volume, including space taken up by lights, hardware, and unreachable nooks. Top- and bottom-freezers give you more storage for their size than side-by-sides. Some 30-inch-wide, 18-cubic-foot top-freezers we tested have about 15 cubic feet of usable space—nearly as much as some 36-inch-wide, 25-cubic-foot side-by-sides. With any fridge, look for features that maximize space, such as split shelves and cranks for adjusting shelf height. Pull-out shelves provide access to the back of the fridge and freezer. In bottom-freezers, full-extension drawers help you find items in the rear.

Consider costs and efficiency. Most new refrigerators cost about $40 to $70 a year to run, based on average energy rates, but up to twice as much in the priciest markets. Top- and bottom-freezers are typically more efficient than side-by-sides. To get the most bang for the buck, pick a model that scored well for energy efficiency in our tests.

Weigh the likelihood of repairs. Some brands have been more reliable than others, and an icemaker and ice-and-water dispenser increase the chance that a fridge will need repair. Built-in bottom-freezers appear to have had higher repair rates than freestanding bottom-freezers.

Listen up. Any new refrigerator will probably be quieter than an older one. If your kitchen is a gathering spot, look for a model that did very well in our noise tests.

Keep styles coordinated. If you want the fridge to blend in with cabinetry, consider a built-in or cabinet-depth model that accepts custom panels. If you're mixing stainless-steel and metallic look-alikes, make sure different finishes don't bother you.

Don't jump at package deals. Buying a refrigerator with other appliances from the same brand can save you money and help coordinate styling. But you'll have less choice, and you could sacrifice refrigerator performance and reliability.

Skip extended warranties. Our repair survey data show that most refrigerators don't fail during the extended-warranty period. In general, we suggest skipping the extra $100 to $400 or so that you'll pay for an extended warranty.

Related CR report: August 2006
Ratings: page 316
Reliability: page 324

SHOWERHEADS

For a quick rinse, any showerhead will do the job. But if you want a pounding stream of water to jump-start your morning or a gentle spray to help you unwind at day's end, the right showerhead is a must.

With literally hundreds of models on the market, from old-fashioned wall-mounted showerheads to oversized rainshower styles to shower towers, there's bound to be a fixture to suit your style. Most sell for less than $100, though you can spend $1,000 for elaborate fixtures in expensive finishes. Considering the low cost and easy installation of most, getting a new showerhead is a great way to rev up a bathroom.

WHAT'S AVAILABLE

The big names include Delta, Moen, Peerless, Pollenex, and Waterpik. Other manufacturers include American Standard, Kohler, and Price Pfister.

Adjustable showerheads. These give you multiple settings so you can choose the strength of flow, from nice and easy to a vigorous massage. Levers, push buttons, and dials are designed to make it easy to change spray settings on adjustable models. Most are low-priced and easy to install. But style isn't their strong suit, and sometimes the most forceful settings can be noisy and too intense. Some can be hard to adjust, especially with wet hands. Price: $25 to $175.

Rainshower. These stylish showerheads are best for those who want a soft, soothing shower. These fixtures have diameters of 6 to 12 inches or more, so they deliver a wider spray that covers more of the body at once. They're very quiet when in use, but most have only one setting, which may not be strong enough to quickly rinse off soap or shampoo or to provide an invigorating feel. You might need more room for one if it needs to be mounted directly overhead to function properly. Some may require additional plumbing parts or special installation. Price: $30 to $500.

Shower towers. These elaborate models are best for creating a spa-like experience without the cost and mess of behind-the-wall plumbing work, but they're pricier than showerheads and more complex to install. They use lots of water—up to 2.5 gallons per nozzle per minute, requiring a larger hot-water heater or a separate, dedicated unit. And the volume of water could overwhelm a septic system. Lower-cost models don't offer much. Price: $200 to $2,500.

FEATURES THAT COUNT

Some improvements in showerheads include dozens of **spray channels** for wide water distribution and **anticlog nozzles** to combat hard-water deposits. Some models come in **handheld** versions, which adds flexibility.

Today's shower fixtures come in a range of styles, from traditional to contemporary. Chrome remains the best-selling finish, but brass, brushed nickel, and other trendy finishes are often available at higher prices.

HOW TO CHOOSE

While style may sway you, be sure to consider these performance factors:

Choose an adjustable fixture for spray options and oomph. Adjustable showerheads generally have three or more settings, ranging from a gentle mist to a needle-like spray and a pulsating massage. Continuously variable settings let you choose anything in between. Many of these models can deliver a forceful water flow.

Consider a rainshower fixture if you want a soft shower and stylish design. The eye-catching design of rainshower heads may appeal to style-conscious users. Most rainshower heads have only one setting that's described as a "cascade" or "downpour" by marketers. But on all but a few, we found the flow to be gentle and not very forceful—"wimpy" in the words of our testers. That can be relaxing, but it takes effort to rinse off soap and shampoo. Because many rainshower models are mounted directly above you, they extend farther from the wall and aren't suited to small areas. Also, the overhead position makes it hard to keep your hair dry.

Beware of water pressure. Almost all the adjustable and rainshower models we tested can deliver the government-mandated maximum of 2.5 gallons per minute when the water pressure is 80 pounds per square inch (psi). However, many homes with a municipal water supply have lower pressure, so the stream from the showerhead will be weaker. Also ask a plumber whether adjusting or replacing your pressure regulator might help.

Look for easy-to-use adjustments. With wet, soapy hands and water dripping into your eyes, you don't want to fumble with adjustments. Try setting the showerheads in the store to see how easy it is to change the spray setting and to adjust the height or angle of the showerhead. For maximum flexibility, consider a handheld model that can be set in a wall bracket or removed to focus the spray.

Consider installation. Even if you are only slightly handy, adjustable showerheads and most rainshowers are a do-it-yourself project. Think twice about heavy rainshower heads that require additional support or extra hardware for proper installation.

Choose a model that works with your water hardness. Many U.S. households have hard water, which contains a high percentage of calcium carbonate. This leaves a chalky buildup on fixtures, tiles, and doors, and can clog a showerhead's nozzles. Many had a plastic face or rubbery nozzles that were easier to clean and less likely to clog than all-metal showerheads.

Be choosy if you like it hot. Some showerheads aerate the spray to make it feel more substantial, but that cools the water by about 15 degrees before it hits your back. To compensate, you have to adjust the mix of hot and cold water using the shower controls.

Related CR report: August 2005

TOASTERS

Toaster or toaster oven? The decision will depend on how picky you are about that morning toast.

If you want perfectly browned bread, opt for the straightforwardness of a basic toaster. Toaster ovens generally don't toast bread as well. They leave tiger stripes on one side, and they take longer to do the job—4 to 6 minutes compared with 2 to 3 minutes for toasters, on a medium setting. But if you prefer a multifunction appliance that can not only toast but also bake muffins, heat frozen entrées, or broil a small batch of burgers or a small chicken—and the space savings that result from having one machine that can do the work of two—choose a toaster oven.

Either way, you can get good performance without spending a lot. For $20 or less, you can buy a competent product that will make decent toast with all the basics: a darkness control to adjust doneness, a push-down lever to raise or lower the bread, and cool-touch housing to keep you from burning your fingers. For $60 or less, you can get a toaster that's stylish as well as functional. Spend $80 or less for one of our highly rated toaster ovens.

WHAT'S AVAILABLE

Toastmaster invented the pop-up toaster in the 1920s and now shares shelf space with other venerable brands of toasters and toaster ovens such as Black & Decker, Hamilton Beach, and Sunbeam, plus players like Cuisinart, DeLonghi, Kenmore

(Sears), KitchenAid, Krups, Rival, T-Fal, and West Bend. Dualit makes old-fashioned, commercial-style, heavy-gauge stainless-steel toasters.

Toasters come in a variety of exterior finishes, like chrome, copper, brushed metal, and colors. Of the 12 million toasters sold annually, two-slice models outsell four-slicers by about 3 to 1. Over 90 percent of toaster ovens sold are equipped with a broiler function. Most toaster ovens are countertop models, though a few under-the-cabinet models are sold.

Price: $10 to $100 and up (toasters); $20 to $100 and up (toaster ovens and broilers).

FEATURES THAT COUNT

Electronic touchpads are a good choice, as are the numbered dials found on many toasters. Less-convenient models have a **shade dial** with no numbers or unlabeled symbols you might need instructions to decipher. If you favor oblong slices of bread, look for **deep slots.** Some slots are less than 5 inches deep; others are about 5½ inches. A **bread lift** lets you raise smaller items such as English muffins above the slots so there's no need to fish around with a fork, a potentially dangerous exercise if you don't unplug the toaster. Another safety note: In late 2001, Underwriters Laboratories, a safety watchdog, called for an automatic shutoff of toaster heating elements when toast sticks in slots.

Recent toaster-oven innovations include various ways to speed up the cooking process, including use of a **convection fan** or **infrared heat.**

A **slide-out crumb tray** is easier to clean than one that's hinged. More and more models incorporate a control that automatically defrosts and toasts in a single step, nice if you regularly prepare items such as frozen hash-brown patties. With toaster ovens, a **nonstick** or **porcelain interior** makes cleaning easier.

HOW TO CHOOSE
Toasters

If you want mainly to toast bread, bagels, and English muffins, a toaster is the right choice.

Consider the features. Find a toaster with the features that suit your needs. A bread lift is handy as are warm/reheat and defrost settings, and easy-to-use controls. Some toasters (and toaster ovens) have a way to wrap the cord to keep it from wriggling over countertops, an added convenience.

Consider space and capacity. If you're buying a two-slice model it may have two side-by-side slots or one long slot for two slices. Four-slice toasters tend to be bulky, but they save time when everyone's trying to be out the door by 8 a.m. All the toasters can fit a split bagel. Those with a bagel setting can toast on one side, such as the cut side of a bagel.

Consider safety. Toasters that have a plastic housing are less likely to retain heat and feel hot to fingers than those made of metal. It's important never to operate a toaster or toaster oven and leave the room. While we've had no problems in the lab with tested models, it's probably a good idea to unplug your toaster or toaster oven when you're not using it—just like your mother told you.

Toaster ovens

To toast and cook, pick a toaster oven.

Consider the features. If you'll be cooking burgers, be sure the toaster oven can broil. If speed is of the essence, consider a toaster oven that uses convection cooking, which speeds roasting and baking, or infrared heating, which speeds toasting. For ease of use, select a model with an electronic touchpad and a porcelain interior. Some toaster ovens come with nonstick pans. Citing health concerns, the Environmental Protection Agency has asked manufacturers to reduce the use of perfluorooctanic acid, or PFOA, in non-stick products. While the EPA says the routine use of these products is safe, if you're concerned don't use the toaster oven's nonstick pan.

Consider counter space and capacity. Some toaster ovens are slightly bigger than others. The smallest we tested is about 16x8x11 (WHD); the biggest, about 20x10x15 (WHD).

Related CR Report: June 2006

TOILETS

Even the utilitarian commode is getting a revamp as toilet manufacturers strive to make this most basic of bathroom fixtures more accommodating and efficient.

Some of the first low-flush toilets on the market earned a reputation for being problematic because they required two or more flushes to do their job—and often clogged in the process. Many of the newer models that were tested work quite well on a single flush. But there are large differences in performance—even within a given brand.

Trends include more comfort-height models, which raise the rim from the usual 14 inches to as much as 17 inches above the floor. The added height makes getting on and off easier, especially for aging boomers, who have helped boost sales to roughly twice what they were in 2001. But their added comfort is likely to appeal to younger buyers, too. Added efficiency is another selling point as major brands attempt to improve upon the 1.6 gallons per flush that has been the legal threshold since 1994. A growing number of models with dual-flush technology use a mere 0.8 gallons for liquid-waste removal.

WHAT'S AVAILABLE

Most major manufacturers offer an extensive array of models in different designs and colors and in a range of prices. Within types, more money does not buy better performance, just more upscale design.

Pressure-assist. These toilets create the most flushing power, as pressure created when water displaces air within a sealed tank causes the water to thrust waste forcefully out through the bowl. They work very well as long as household water pressure is at least 25 pounds per square inch. They're best for large families, kids, and heavy use, where clogs are likeliest. But they tend to be pricey and noisy. Their raucous whoosh can be disconcerting, especially near bedrooms. Price: $225 to $300 for most.

Vacuum-assist. A vacuum chamber inside the tank works like a siphon to pull air out of the trap below the bowl so it can quickly fill with water to clear waste. These toilets are best for close quarters where quietness counts. But while some vacuum models performed well in past tests, the latest we tested had far less flushing power than pressure-assisted toilets, yet typically cost as much. Fewer vacuum models sold also means fewer choices. Price: $225 to $300 for most.

Gravity. The most common type, these rely on water dropping from the tank into the bowl and trap to move waste down the drain. Pressure as low as 10 pounds per square inch is adequate, since gravity does all the work. They're best for those who want a quiet, proven design or have low water pressure. But models that approach pressure-assisted performance typically cost just as much, while lower-priced models often aren't up to the job. Price: $150 to $300 for most.

FEATURES THAT COUNT

Bathroom remodeling is the most common reason to buy a new toilet. Depending on the configuration of the new bathroom, you may want a round-front or elongated **bowl.** A round-front style is generally a better choice for a small bathroom than an elongated one. Two-piece designs, with a tank that bolts onto the bowl, are less expensive than one-piece designs. Toilets are available in several different "rough-in" dimensions—the clearance to the back wall needed to connect to the water line. The most common rough-in is 12 inches.

HOW TO CHOOSE

If you're simply replacing a broken gravity toilet, consider having it fixed, especially if you bought it after 1994. A new flapper valve (about $5) or new fill valve (about $15) solves most problems and is easy to install. Once you've decided to buy a new toilet, begin by considering the bathroom's location. If it's near a kitchen or other living area, or your home is small, you're likelier to prefer a quieter toilet.

After you've chosen the type you want, pressure-assisted, vacuum-assisted, or gravity, keep these shopping tips in mind:

Check your water pressure. Before buying a pressure-assisted toilet, be sure that your home has the water pressure it requires. You can check your pressure yourself with a $10 gauge that connects to an outdoor spigot. You'll need at least 25 pounds per square inch for the toilet; allow a little extra to compensate for pressure drops from the spigot to the toilet. If you need to adjust your water pressure, don't go above 80 psi, which can harm toilets and other fixtures.

Consider your cleaning. Most toilets use a two-piece design with a separate tank and bowl; the seam between the two tends to trap grime. One-piece models from Eljer, Kohler, Toto, and others add style while eliminating the seam. But most we tested cost $400 or more.

Choose colors with caution. More models now are available in glacier blue, peach bisque, and other hues. But as with the avocado green and harvest gold that graced '70s kitchens, some could make your bathroom look dated over time.

Decide on a shape. Toilets with a round bowl take the least room and accept the widest variety of seats. If you have space, consider elongated bowls, which are stylish and allow a longer seat that provides more room and support for a variety of users.

Check the date. Manufacturers often change a toilet's design without changing the model name. An example is the Briggs Classic Vacuity 4200, a top-scoring vacuum model in 2002. A revised version of that model performed much worse in our current tests. Toilets typically have a date stamped inside the tank.

Check the specs on gravity models. Gravity toilets rely on a flush valve to discharge water from the tank and into the bowl. Beefier valves 3 to 3¼ inches wide deliver more thrust in our tests than gravity models with 2-inch valves. Ask to see the manufacturer's specifications for the flush valve when considering a gravity toilet.

Related CR report: August 2005

WASHING MACHINES

Top loaders are getting more energy-efficient, but front-loaders still tend to provide the best of everything when it comes to efficient washing.

You'll find more variety in the washing-machine aisle when you visit an appliance store these days. Tougher new energy standards due for 2007 have led to the manufacture of more energy-efficient washers.

While traditional top-loaders with agitators are still going strong, front-loading washers are gaining ground, due to their very good washing performance, large capacity, water and energy efficiency, and quiet operation.

You'll also find a growing number of high-efficiency top-loaders that meet the newest standard using a unique wash action and a faster-spinning drum. The design increases capacity and reduces water and energy usage. Models include the Oasis from Kenmore, the Harmony from GE, the Cabrio from Whirlpool, and Fisher and Paykel's IWL16.

WHAT'S AVAILABLE

The top four brands—GE, Kenmore (Sears), Maytag, and Whirlpool—account for approximately 80 percent of washing-machine sales. Other brands include Frigidaire (made by Electrolux), Hotpoint (made by GE), and Admiral, Amana, KitchenAid, and Roper (made by Whirlpool). You may also run across smaller brands such as Crosley, Estate, and White-Westinghouse, all of which are made by the larger brands. Asko and Miele are European brands. Fisher & Paykel is imported from New Zealand, LG and Samsung from Korea, and Haier from China.

Traditional top-loaders. These fill the tub with water, then agitate the clothing. They use more water than other types of washers, and thus consume more energy to heat it. They also extract less water from laundry during the spin cycle, which results in longer drying time and higher energy costs. Because they need to move the laundry around to ensure thorough cleaning, these machines hold about 12 to 16 pounds, which is less than large front-loaders and top-loaders without agitators in the center of the tub.

On the plus side, they make it easier to load laundry and to add items midcycle.

You can also soak laundry easily. This type of machine has the shortest cycle times and is the only one that gives the best results with regular detergent. They also cost the least overall. But most top-loaders are noisier than front-loaders, and there's a risk of loads becoming unbalanced. Price: $300 to $650.

High-efficiency top-loaders. These newer designs incorporate wash plates—discs that lift and tumble laundry—and other replacements for the traditional agitator. Washing performance is usually better than with regular top-loaders, and capacity is generally greater as well. These top-loaders work somewhat like front-loaders, filling partly with water and spinning at very high speeds. Most are more efficient with water and energy than regular top-loaders, but the high spin speeds that reduce drying time (and energy consumption) can make clothing more tangled and wrinkled. These machines work best with low-foaming, high-efficiency detergent. What's more, they aren't cheap. Price: $800 to $1,200.

Front-loaders. Front-loaders get clothes clean by tumbling them in the water. Clothes are lifted to the top of the tub, then dropped into the water below. They fill only partly with water and then spin at high speed to extract it, which makes them more efficient than regular top-loaders. Most handle between 12 and 20 pounds of laundry. Like high-efficiency top-loaders, front-loaders wash best with low-sudsing detergent. But the best still outperformed the best high-efficiency top-loaders overall. Many front-loaders can be stacked with a dryer to save floor space. Price: $700 to $1,600.

Space-saving options. Compact models are typically 24 inches wide or less (compared with about 27 inches for full-sized washers of all types) and they can wash 8 to 12 pounds of laundry. A compact front-loading washer can be stacked with a compact dryer. Some compact washers can be stored in a closet and rolled out to be hooked up to the kitchen sink. Price: $450 to $1,700.

Washer-dryer laundry centers combine a washer and dryer in one unit, with the dryer located above the washer. These can be full-sized (27 inches wide) or compact (24 inches wide). The full-sized models hold about 12 to 14 pounds, the compacts a few pounds less. Performance is generally comparable to that of full-sized machines. Price: $700 to $1,900.

FEATURES THAT COUNT

A porcelain-coated steel **inner tub** can rust if the porcelain is chipped. Stainless-steel or plastic tubs won't rust. A stainless-steel tub can withstand higher spin speeds, which extract more water from laundry and speed drying. A porcelain top/lid resists scratching better than a painted metal one.

Controls should be legible, easy to push or turn, and logically arranged. High-end models often have **touchpad controls;** others have traditional **dials.** Touchpad controls tend to be more versatile; for instance, you may be able to save favorite settings that you use frequently. Some high-end models have a display with a progression of menus. Such menus can be time-consuming to navigate, but they may allow custom programming or offer detailed help information otherwise available only in the manual. A plus: **lights** or **signals** that indicate the cycle.

On some top-loaders, an **automatic lock** during the spin cycle keeps children from opening the lid. Front-loaders lock at the beginning of a cycle but can usually be opened by interrupting the cycle, although some doors remain locked briefly after the machine stops.

Front-loaders and some top-loaders set water levels automatically, ensuring effi-cient use of water. Some top-loaders can be manually set for four or more levels; three or four are probably as many as you would need.

Most machines establish wash and rinse temperatures by mixing hot and cold water in preset proportions. For incoming cold water that's especially cold, an **automatic temperature control** adjusts the flow for the correct wash temperature. This feature is useful if your incoming water is very cold or if your washer is a long way from the water heater.

Some models allow an extra rinse, which can help for those sensitive to detergent residue, or an extended spin to remove more water from laundry. A **time-delay feature** lets you program the washer to start at a later time, such as at night, when your utility rates are low. **Automatic dispensers** for bleach, detergent, and fabric-softener release powder or liquid at the appropriate time in the cycle so they work effectively. Bleach dispensers also prevent spattering.

HOW TO CHOOSE

For best high-end performance, go with a front-loader. If you're willing to spend at least $700 or so, at this point we'd steer you to a front-loader. The best offer very good washing, ample capacity, and quiet operation. The front-loading design has been around for awhile, and GE, Kenmore, Frigidaire, and Whirlpool front-loaders have a better track record for reliability than Maytag front-loaders, the most repair-prone of all washers. Note that numerous readers have reported that front-loading washers developed mold or a musty smell. Leaving the door ajar between uses and using chlorine bleach occasionally should help. Vibration can also be an issue if the front-loader is not leveled properly when installed.

Think twice about new-technology top-loaders. Even though some top-loaders have done well in our tests, they haven't been among our top picks. The Whirlpool Calypso and Kenmore Calypso were the more repair-prone top-loaders and left garments tangled and wrinkled in our tests. The GE Profile Harmony models we've tested weren't very gentle on clothes.

Get a conventional top-loader for good performance at a modest price. If you want a less expensive machine that's decent across the board, consider a familiar top-loader. Even though these machines aren't as exciting as newer types, they offer decent washing for $500 or less and include a large selection of reliable brands. A model judged good or very good for washing should be fine for all but very soiled laundry and should satisfy most consumers.

Consider energy usage. Our tests for energy efficiency differ from those used to determine the government's Energy Star eligibility, giving more weight to performance with maximum loads. As a result, some Energy Star models haven't scored that well for energy efficiency in our Ratings.

Decide if noise is an issue. If you plan to install a washer in a laundry room near the kitchen or a bedroom, we strongly recommend one judged very good or excellent for noise. Front-loaders as a group tend to be very quiet; some top-loaders are as well.

For sets, choose the washer first. Even the best dryer is only as good as the washer's ability to remove moisture, since less moisture means shorter drying times and less energy use per load. Remember, too,

that unless you insist on the same style, there's no need to match a washer and a dryer. If your old dryer still works fine, don't think you have to replace it when you buy a new washer.

Weigh the value of pricey extras. The more features a washer has, the more it usually costs. Don't buy an expensive model just to get four or more water levels, dozens of cycle and setting combinations, or dedicated cycles for fabrics such as silk. The basic cycles and settings can handle most washing needs, and you can replicate most special cycles with buttons or dials. An electronic touchpad may allow custom programming, but it can also be more confusing to use, especially at first.

Use the proper detergent. Any washing machine will do a better job if you use a good detergent. For traditional top-loaders, regular detergent is fine, and that's what we used. With front-loaders and high-efficiency top-loaders, you'll get the cleanest clothes with special low-sudsing detergent; that's what we used for these machines. In fact, using regular detergent can cause excessive sudsing in high-efficiency washers. Not only is it hard to rinse clothing, but the foam can cause problems with the washer. There are fewer high-efficiency products to choose from than with regular detergent, and they cost about 5 to 10 cents more per load than regular detergent. Consider the cost and convenience of ongoing detergent purchases when you're buying a washer.

Related CR report: March 2006
Ratings: page 337
Reliability: page 342

Home and Yard

Home & Yard:
More Value for Less

Growing competition among retailers and independent dealers has made this an ideal time to upgrade your arsenal of indoor and outdoor home products. Besides driving down prices on an array of items, big-box home centers such as Home Depot and Lowe's have dialed up pressure on manufacturers to move high-end features down to the mainstream.

Months of testing have shown that newer isn't necessarily better, however. Some manufacturers are delivering more features for less by taking shortcuts that could affect performance. Here's what to look for—and watch out for—as you shop:

Vacuums get new pet-hair test. We've taken our upright and canister tests beyond just dust and dirt and have begun evaluating how well they pick up what pets leave behind. Using fur from coon and other long-haired cats, we measure how much pet hair stays in the rug and how much sticks to the rotating brush without reaching the bag or bin. Bagless vacs proved especially vexing when emptying because of their static electricity from their plastic bins.

Among the vacs that are leading the pet-hair competition so far: Models from Dirt Devil, Hoover, Kenmore, and Panasonic.

Cool prices on room air conditioners. At prices as low as $100, room ACs cost less than ever and they have more features such as remote controls and relatively precise electronic temperature controls. The latest also save energy; all models met or exceeded the 10.7 Energy Efficiency Rating needed for

Energy Star certification in our latest tests.

Easier, lower-cost mowing. You don't have to buy a $700 mower to get a showcase lawn. Self-propelled, walk-behind models now offer better cuts and more features for hundreds less as big-box stores and home centers battle it out for your business. Step up to a lawn tractor, and you'll find $1,400 models from John Deere that mow as well as much pricier Deere models we tested last year.

Gas grills dish out more for less. While you can easily pay more than $1,000 for a gas grill, you needn't spend even half that much for good grilling. Our CR Best Buys begin at as little as $200.

Balance selection, service, and price. Larger chains such as Sears and Wal-Mart usually include a wide array of lower-priced brands. Home centers such as Home Depot and Lowe's offer a mix of low-priced, mid-priced, and upscale brands. Meanwhile, local hardware stores and other independents tend to carry mid- and higher-priced brands while traditionally offering more personal service and tips on using tractors and other power equipment.

Home and yard products are also sold on the Internet through sites such as Amazon.com, Homedepot.com, Lowes.com, and Sears.com. These sites can be useful for research as well as promotions, rebates, close-outs, and other limited-time offers. Still, it's hard to beat a trip to the store so you can try out the products for yourself.

AIR CLEANERS

Even the best air cleaner may be a questionable investment, since there's little medical evidence that air cleaners alone reduce the effects of indoor pollutants for those with asthma and allergies.

The air inside your home is more polluted than the air outside, according to estimates by the U.S. Environmental Protection Agency. But that doesn't mean it's unhealthy and needs to be cleaned—or that you need an air cleaner.

Before you buy one, try some common-sense solutions to eliminating and controlling pollutants and ensuring proper ventilation. If these aren't enough, an air cleaner may help. But only people with respiratory problems are likely to benefit.

For homes with forced-air heating and cooling, a competent, professionally installed whole-house air cleaner is likely to outperform most slide-in filters. (Two filters we tested, the American Air Filter Dirt Demon Ultra High Efficiency and the 3M Filtrete Ultra Allergen Reduction 1250, performed well.) Otherwise, your only option is a room air cleaner.

WHAT'S AVAILABLE

Whole-house air cleaners. Major brands include 3M, American Air Filter, Aprilaire, Carrier, Honeywell, Lennox, Precisionaire, Purolator, and Trane. Models range from low-cost fiberglass furnace filters to electronic precipitators, which must be installed professionally in the duct system.

Furnace filters range from plain matted-fiberglass (about $1), meant to trap large particles of dust and lint, to electrostatically charged pleated filters ($10 to $30), which are designed to attract pollen, lint, pet dander, and dust.

Electronic-precipitator air cleaners impart an electrical charge to particles flowing through them, then collect the particles on oppositely charged metal plates or filters. These more-elaborate systems must be fitted into ductwork and wired into the house's current. Most have a collector-plate assembly that must be removed and washed every one or two months. Price: about $600, plus $200 or more for installation.

Room air cleaners. Major brands include Bionaire, Friedrich, Holmes, Honeywell, Hunter, Kenmore, Ionic Pro, Oreck, Sharper Image, and Whirlpool. Most weigh between 10 and 20 pounds. They can be round or boxy, and can stand on the floor or on a table.

Some room air cleaners can work well, even on dust and cigarette-smoke particles, which are much smaller and harder to trap than pollen and mold spores. But they aren't good at trapping viruses and gases such as carbon monoxide or radon.

Two technologies predominate. The most common uses a high-efficiency particulate air (HEPA) filter to strain the air of fine particles. The other uses an electronic precipitator that works like those in some whole-house systems, with a fan to move air through them. Several small, quiet ionizing models use the same basic technology, but have been ineffective in our tests.

Price: $50 to $600 for most. Annual filter cost: $20 to $230.

FEATURES THAT COUNT

Whole-house air filters generally include a range of standard sizes, with some adaptable to fit a range of filter box or return air openings. Some brands say their filters are treated with a special antimicrobial agent, presumably to prevent bacterial growth on the filter. We haven't evaluated those claims.

Room air cleaners typically use a **fan** to pull air into the unit for filtration. Some with an electronic precipitator or a HEPA filter include ionizing circuitry that uses powered needles or wires to charge particles so that they are more easily trapped by the oppositely charged filter. But this ionization may also make the particles stick to walls or furnishings, possibly soiling them. An **indicator** in most models let you know when to change or clean the filter.

HEPA filters are typically supposed to be replaced annually and can cost more than $100—sometimes as much as the room air cleaner itself. **Prefilters,** which are designed to remove larger particles, are generally changed quarterly, while washable prefilters should be cleaned monthly. An electronic precipitator's **collector-plate assembly** must be removed and washed every month or so; it slides out of the cabinet and can be put in a dishwasher or rinsed in a sink. be sure it's completely dry before reinstalling it in the air cleaner.

Most room models have a **handle,** while some heavier models have **wheels. Fan speeds** are usually low, medium, and high. A few use a **dust sensor** and an **air-quality monitor** designed to raise or lower the fan speed automatically, depending on conditions. But in our tests these sensors didn't kick in until levels were high, then shut off before levels dropped sufficiently.

HOW TO CHOOSE

Don't assume health benefits. Medical experts and the federal Environmental Protection Agency agree that an air cleaner won't alleviate carbon monoxide, viruses, and dust mites. While capable air cleaners can trap dust, smoke particles, pollen, and pet dander, you can reduce all of those allergens for little or no money:

Remove or reduce pollution sources. Ban indoor smoking. Avoid candles, incense, air fresheners, and scented cleaners. Vacuum often, using a low-emission machine. Keep dust-sensitive people out of the area when vacuuming. Don't get pets if you're allergic; if you already have them, keep them out of the bedroom.

Minimize dust mites. Encase pillows, mattresses, and box springs in mite-proof covers. Wash laundry in the hottest water you can. Avoid carpeting and other furnishings that attract dust and harbor mites.

Control harmful gases. Test for radon with a kit (about $15). Minimize carbon-monoxide risks; don't idle cars or fuel-burning power equipment in garages. Don't store or use chemicals, solvents, glues, or pesticides in the house. Also maintain heating equipment, wood stoves, fireplaces, chimneys, and vents to properly remove combustion gases such as carbon monoxide from indoors. And install carbon-monoxide alarms.

Open windows and doors. Do both based on weather and outdoor air quality.

Use outdoor-venting fans. Putting these fans in the kitchen, bath, and laundry areas helps expel odors and excessive moisture, which can breed mold.

If you decide to buy an air cleaner:

Decide on whole-house or room. Whole-house models are the only sensible choice for forced-air heating or cooling. For room models, the best performed at least as well on low as most others did on high, minimizing noise and energy use.

Choose a type. Electronic-precipitator air cleaners worked best overall and restricted airflow least among whole-house models. But we suggest avoiding room versions without a fan, which have cleaned poorly and can emit significant amounts of ozone. Also avoid dedicated ozone generators. Unlike electrostatic precipitators, which emit ozone as a byproduct, these niche products produce large amounts of it by design. Ozone is a concern, especially for people with asthma and respiratory allergies, which ozone can aggravate. Whole-house filters tend to cost the least up front, but can be pricey over time, since you usually must replace filters frequently.

Check efficiency. Most room air cleaners are certified by the Association of Home Appliance Manufacturers as part of a voluntary program that includes appropriate room size and clean-air delivery rate (CADR), a measure of cleaning speed on High. We judge CADR above 350 excellent and below 100 poor. Choose a model certified for a larger area than you require for better cleaning at a quieter speed. Many whole-house filters have a minimum efficiency reporting value (MERV). Top performers typically had MERV of 11 to 13.

Related CR report: October 2005

AIR CONDITIONERS

Low prices and high efficiency make individual room air conditioners an inexpensive alternative to central air for cooling one or two rooms.

Room air conditioners now cost as little as $100 and often include controls with digital temperature readouts instead of vague "warmer" and "cooler" settings.

Added efficiency is also a plus. All models we tested meet the 9.7 Energy Efficiency Rating (EER) now required for air conditioners below 8,000 British thermal units per hour (Btu/hr.) and 9.8 EER for those with 8,000 to 13,999 Btu/hr. Most also meet or exceed the 10.7 EER needed to qualify for the federal Energy Star designation, a voluntary program that helps identify models at least 10 percent more efficient than the minimum allowed.

WHAT'S AVAILABLE

Fedders, Frigidaire, GE, Haier, Kenmore (Sears), and LG are the leading brands of room air conditioners. You'll find cooling capacities that range from 5,000 British thermal units per hour (Btu/hr.) to more than 30,000 Btu/hr., though most are small and midsized models from 5,000 to 9,000 Btu/hr. You'll also find large models (9,800 to 12,500 Btu/hr.) in stores.

Price: about $100 to $600 for small to midsized models based mostly on capacity, and $200 to $700 for larger models.

FEATURES THAT COUNT

An air conditioner's exterior-facing portion contains a **compressor, fan,** and **condenser,** while the part facing a home's interior contains a **fan** and an **evaporator.** Most room models are designed to fit **double-hung windows,** though some are built for **casement** and **slider windows** and others for **in-wall installation.**

Most models have **adjustable vertical** and **horizontal louvers** to direct airflow. Many offer a fresh-air intake or **exhaust setting** for ventilation, although this feature moves a relatively small amount of air. An **energy-saver setting** on many stops the fan when the compressor cycles off and monitors the temperature. **Electronic controls** and **digital temperature readouts** are also common. A timer lets you program the unit to switch on or off at a given time.

Many models include a **remote control.** Some models install with a **slide-out chassis**—an outer cabinet that anchors in the window, into which you slide the unit.

All models built after July 2004 also have **safer plugs** that help prevent fires by shutting down power if they sense the power cord is damaged. The plugs include test and reset buttons like those on bathroom and outdoor outlets. Some Frigidaire models include **infinitely variable fan speeds,** while some Haier and LG units have a **dehumidifying-only mode** that's useful on humid but cool days in spring and fall.

HOW TO CHOOSE

Here are some tips for choosing an appropriately sized air conditioner that combines performance, efficiency, and value:

Determine how much cooling you need. A general rule: 5,000 to 6,000 Btu/hr. models cool rooms 100 to 300 square feet; 7,000 to 8,200 Btu/hr. models cool rooms 250 to 550 square feet; and 9,800 to 12,500 Btu/hr. models cool rooms 350 to 950 square feet. Room construction, climate, and other factors also affect your choice, however.

Consider window location. Does the air conditioner need to blow air to the left or right to direct air to the room's center for uniform cooling? Most models do a better job directing air in one direction or the other, in part because of the design of their internal fan. Our Ratings show which models are more directionally biased than others.

Look for third-party certification. When assessing Energy Efficiency Ratings, you should look for a certification sticker from the Association of Home Appliance Manufacturers (AHAM) or the Canadian Standards Association (CSA). An energy-efficient unit will not only help the environment, but it may also qualify for rebates in some areas; see the Energy Star Web site, at *www.energystar.gov,* for details.

Skip features you don't need. Low-profile models take less space and can also direct air upward but tend to be pricier.

Clean it periodically. With any model, clean the filter biweekly or as needed. Where possible, hose off the back of the unit if debris has clogged cooling coils.

Related CR report: July 2006
Ratings: page 227

CIRCULAR SAWS

Circular saws are a mainstay for quickly cutting the two-by-fours and plywood used in many popular home-improvement projects.

Indeed, circular saws are the most common home power tool after drills. Battery-powered saws offer go-anywhere convenience, but plug-ins are far more capable.

WHAT'S AVAILABLE

Black & Decker, Bosch, Craftsman (Sears), DeWalt, Hitachi, Makita, Milwaukee, Ridgid, Ryobi, and Skil brands account for most of the circular saws sold.

Corded models. These offer up to seven times the speed and power of cordless saws and run on an electric motor that can range from 10 to 15 amps. The higher the amps, the more power you can expect. Most models have the motor perpendicular to the blade. Price range: $30 to $175.

High-torque worm/hypoid-geared models have the motor parallel to the blade. That provides more twisting power, or torque, making the blade less likely to bind in dense or thick wood. But sawing tends to be slower, since blade speed is reduced. They're also relatively heavy. Price: $150 to $175.

Cordless models. These range from 18 to 28 volts. The blade is usually smaller than corded models' and run time is limited by the battery. Price: $60 to $300.

FEATURES THAT COUNT

Every saw has a large main **handle** and a stubby **auxiliary handle**; the main handle incorporates the saw's **on/off switch.** Some saws include a **safety interlock**, a second switch you must press to turn on the motor. While it helps prevent accidental startups, it can make the saw awkward to use.

Inexpensive saws have a stamped-steel base and thin housing; pricier models use thicker, more rugged material such as reinforced steel for harder use. A blade with two dozen large teeth cuts quickly but can splinter the wood; a blade with 40 or more **smaller teeth** gives a cleaner cut.

Bevel adjustment is used to change the angle of the cut from 0 to 45 degrees or more for some saws. **Depth adjustment** changes the blade's cutting depth. A circular saw works best when the teeth just clear the bottom of the wood.

A **visible blade** located to the left of the motor or a **notch** in the upper blade guard helps you see the blade and your cutting mark without leaning over the saw. Because the motor on worm-drive saws is parallel to the blade, it's easier to see your cutting mark—a reason pros like them. Many models include a **laser guide** but you must still draw a line and use a steady hand. It's also useless outdoors in bright sunlight.

A **spindle lock** keeps the blade from spinning while you change blades. A **blade brake** stops the blade quickly when you release the trigger. The **dust chute** directs sawdust away so you can see what you're doing. A **long power cord** (9 or 10 feet) often makes an extension cord unnecessary or helps keep the extension-cord connection away from your work.

HOW TO CHOOSE

Decide the kind of work you'll do. For occasional light cutting, most any saw is fine. For heavy use or for cutting hard or thick wood, choose a saw with speed and power, such as the top-rated models. Speed also affects safety; you're more likely to push a slow saw, dulling the blade quickly and overheating the motor as well as raising the risk of jamming and kickback.

Try it out. Look for easy blade changes and adjustments for depth and angle, good balance, a comfortable handle, and a handy on/off switch. Also look for easily accessible motor brushes, a heavy-duty base, and rugged hardware for blade-depth and cutting-angle-adjustments.

Check the blade. Most saws now have carbide-tipped blades, which cut quicker and last longer than steel blades. (You can retrofit them to older saws.) Match the number of teeth with the material you want to cut; blades for plywood, say, have more teeth than those for rough cutting.

Safety counts. All saws are loud enough to warrant hearing protection. They also kick up lots of chips and dust, so wear a mask and safety glasses or goggles.

Related CR report: August 2005

CORDLESS DRILLS

Many 14.4-volt drill/drivers pack all the power you need for a variety of chores. You'll also find higher-voltage drills that cost little more than less-capable, lower-voltage models.

Battery packs with higher efficiency allow today's cordless models to run longer and more powerfully per charge. The best can outperform corded drills and handle decks and other big jobs with minimum recharging. Recent tests show that you needn't spend $200 or more to get fine performance. Models in the 14.4- to 18-volt range that cost as little as $100 or so perform nearly as well as pricier drills.

You'll also see more impact drivers. While similar to conventional drill/drivers, these emphasize added tightening and loosening power, courtesy of a spinning internal hammer that strikes an anvil attached to the chuck to boost twisting force. Besides being lighter and smaller (most use 12- or 14.4-volt batteries), they don't twist in your hands under load. But they tend to be slower at drilling and require special drill bits. All those we've tested have also been loud enough to require hearing protection.

> **Shop smart**
>
> Buy a midrange drill instead of a lower voltage one. You'll get better performance for about the same price.

WHAT'S AVAILABLE

Black & Decker and Craftsman (Sears) are the major brands. Along with Ryobi and Skil, they're aimed primarily at homeowners. Bosch, DeWalt, Hitachi, Makita, Milwaukee, Ridgid, and Porter-Cable offer pricier drills designed for professionals. Most 9.6-volt models cost less than $100. At about 3 pounds, they weigh half as much as some 18-volt models. But unless you value their low weight and low cost over performance, you're likely to be disappointed.

Price: about $40 to $100 for 9.6-volt drills, $50 to $130 for 12-volt drills, $60 to $200 for 14.4-volt models, and $100 to $300 for 18-volt models.

Cordless impact drills are offered by the same brands who sell conventional drill/drivers. Many cost $200 or more.

FEATURES THAT COUNT

A **"smart" charger** recharges a drill's battery in an hour or less, compared with three to five hours or more for conventional chargers. They also extend battery life by adjusting the charge as needed. Most switch into a **maintenance** or **"trickle-charge" mode** as the battery approaches full charge. Some models have a **dual charger** that charges two batteries at once.

Most cordless drills 12 volts and more have **two speed ranges:** Low for driving screws, high for drilling. Low speed provides more torque, or turning power, than the high-speed setting, which is better for drilling holes. Most models also have a **variable speed trigger,** which can make starting a hole easier, and an **adjustable clutch,** which lowers maximum torque to avoid driving a screw too far into softwood or wallboard or mangling its head.

Most drills have a ⅜-inch chuck, but some higher-voltage models have a ½-inch chuck for drill bits up to ½ inch. (Large-diameter bits with a reduced shank will fit smaller chucks.) Today's models are also **reversible,** letting you more easily remove a screw or back a drill bit out of a hole.

Some models have a **second handle** that attaches onto the side of the drill so you can use two hands for better control when driving large screws. All but the least-expensive drills come with **two batteries,** letting you use one while the other charges.

Most cordless drills run on **nickel-cadmium (NiCad) batteries,** which can be recharged hundreds of times. Once they're depleted, though, NiCads must be recycled, since cadmium is toxic and can leach out of landfills to contaminate groundwater if disposed of improperly. Incineration can release the substance into the air and pose an even greater hazard.

A few models run on **nickel-metal-hydride (NiMH)** or **lithium-ion batter-**

ies. Both battery types are free of cadmium and are friendlier to the environment. In recent tests, Consumer Reports found that models with these batteries tend to run longer yet weigh the same as or less than typical NiCad-powered models.

Some drills are bundled with other cordless tools and sold as **kits.** The package typically includes a circular saw, a reciprocating saw, and often a flashlight and carrying case. Some kits are a relatively good deal. But as our reports have shown, cordless circular saws tend to be far weaker than corded models. And some kits are merely a collection of mediocre tools.

HOW TO CHOOSE

High value in the 14.4- to 18-volt category means there's little reason to buy a conventional 12- or 9.6-volt drill/driver. You'll save little money, and power and run time are lower. You'll also find lower-voltage drills that combine ample power for your larger household projects without being too heavy for smaller ones.

Determine how much voltage you're going to need for the drilling and screwdriving tasks you do most. Then ask yourself these questions while you're shopping:

Are high-end brands worth it? You can buy an 18-volt drill with a ½-inch chuck for thicker bits vs. the usual ⅜-inch chuck, letting you drill larger holes. But you may not want to pay the $200 or more typical of most cordless drills with that feature if your home to-do list doesn't include larger projects or heavier-duty drilling.

How much are replacement batteries? A cordless drill's battery can typically be recharged roughly 500 times before it must be replaced. While batteries can last five years or more, frequent use can deplete them sooner. At $20 to $80 each for many of the batteries that power drills, replacing them can cost as much as buying a new drill.

Battery replacement may be less of a concern if you're buying a $250 drill you plan to keep for awhile. And for models that cost less than $100, simply replacing the drill may make more sense than buying a new pair of batteries. Otherwise, consider battery cost along with the drill.

Are you buying other cordless tools? You might be tempted to purchase one of the multitool kits, which cost far less than you'd pay for the tools separately, since the tools in each kit are powered by the same batteries and charger. But some of those tools have delivered mediocre performance. Ryobi is one manufacturer that lets you buy separate tools without batteries, letting you use the ones you have for multiple tools.

Related CR report: December 2005

DECK TREATMENTS

Deck treatments that look good longest are the ones that are most like paint. Clear finishes don't provide long-term protection.

Unprotected lumber doesn't fare well. Rain and sun crack and split wood by swelling and drying it, while moisture promotes mold and mildew. Even redwood, cedar, and pressure-treated wood can benefit from a protective coat. Our tests show that clear deck treatments usually don't offer more than a year of protection before their appearance has visibly degraded.

WHAT'S AVAILABLE

Major brands include Ace, Behr, Benjamin Moore, Cabot, Flood, Glidden, Olympic, Sherwin-Williams, Sikkens,

Thompson's, and Wolman. You'll also find many smaller, specialized brands.

Opaque: These finishes hide the wood grain like a coat of paint and last longest. They're best for the typical deck made of pressure-treated pine, where grain isn't important. Usually solid-color stains, they hold up for at least three years.

On the downside, some decks look better with their wood grain exposed. Opaque finishes can also build up a film, especially after several coats, which can peel, chip, and crack like a paint film. What's more, refinishing with opaque is generally more extensive and lengthy than with semitransparent and clear treatments.

Semitransparent: These finishes usually contain a small amount of pigment but let the wood grain show. They're best for cedar, redwood, or other expensive woods you want to show off. Choices range from little pigment to nearly opaque. On the downside, you may need to reapply them every two to three years.

Clear: These contain water repellents but no pigment. They may also have UV inhibitors and wood preservatives to help protect the wood. They're ideal for people who value the natural look of wood over the treatment's longevity, especially for decks built of premium wood. But our years of testing have shown that most clear deck finishes don't last more than one year, making deck refinishing an annual chore.

Price range for all deck treatments: $15 to over $40 per gallon.

FEATURES THAT COUNT

Deck treatments may be alkyd-based (solvent) or latex-based (water). Most alkyd-based products require cleaning with mineral spirits, but a few can be cleaned with water like latex. Linseed oil and tung oil have largely been replaced by synthetic resins. These are described as preservatives, protectors, stabilizers, repellents, sealers, cleaners, restorers, or rejuvenators.

HOW TO CHOOSE

Opaque treatments are your first choice for longevity. Consider semitransparent if you want the wood grain to show. While clear shows even more of the grain, you'll probably have to do the job over again within a year. Also remember that you'll need goggles, gloves, and respirators when scraping or sanding pressure-treated wood because of its toxic ingredients.

Related CR report: July 2006

FLOORING, WOOD AND WOOD ALTERNATIVES

Natural-wood flooring offers warmth and the ability to be refinished more than once. But tougher copycats could be better for active families.

Real solid hardwood remains the premium choice for flooring and figures prominently on the list of talking points when homes are sold. More of it is sold with hand-scraped and other distressed finishes. But when it comes to real-world scrapes, scuffs, and other wear and tear, you may want to consider the fake stuff, especially for high-traffic areas.

WHAT'S AVAILABLE

You'll find wood and wood-look flooring at flooring suppliers and lumberyards as well as at home centers such as Home Depot, Lowe's, and Menards. Flooring suppliers tend to have the widest selection, particularly for exotic woods, while home centers usually offer better prices.

Oak is the most popular and readily

available choice among the hardwoods; others include maple, cherry, and hickory. (Pine, a softwood, costs less.) All can typically be sanded and refinished more than once. Major brands include Anderson, Armstrong, Bruce, Tarkett, and Shaw, among others. Price: about $7 to $12 per square foot installed for prefinished wood flooring.

Plastic laminates are the fastest-growing wood-floor alternative. Essentially dense fiberboard with a photo of the real thing beneath a clear protective layer, they can mimic nearly anything from oak to marble. Installation is easier than wood, since most can be clicked together and laid in place—called floating—rather than being nailed like solid wood. The best also withstood wear and other damage much better than wood in our tests.

On the downside, while you may be able to do minor touchups on plastic laminate, it can't be refinished and must be replaced when its outer layer wears through. Some versions can have a repetitive pattern that compromises realism. Brands include Armstrong, Mannington, Mohawk, Pergo, Wilsonart, and others. Price: about $4 to $8 per square foot installed.

Engineered wood, which uses a thin veneer of real wood or bamboo over structural plywood, is another option. Both kinds can typically be floated, nailed, or glued, and be refinished once. But engineered wood didn't wear as well as plastic laminate or even solid wood in our tests, while bamboo can darken under the sun's UV rays. Brands include the same as for solid and engineered wood. Price: about $5 to $10 per square foot installed.

Vinyl and linoleum are also popular choices with added style. Premium vinyl flooring is designed to more closely match stone, tile, and even oak, and can be especially good at fending off wear, dents,

scratches, and other abuse. You'll also find more styles and colors for linoleum, which is mostly linseed oil and wood. But even the best vinyl still looks like vinyl, while linoleum can be vulnerable to wear and scratches. Brands include Armstrong, Congoleum, Mannington, NAFCO, Tarket, and others. Price: about $3 to $7 per square foot installed for vinyl, $4 to $9 per square foot installed for linoleum.

Ceramic tile is another popular choice. It tends to resist wear, moisture, scratches, and other abuse. But its hard surface can break dropped cups and dishes more easily. It's also relatively hard to install and can be expensive. Price: about $8 to $15 per square foot installed.

FEATURES THAT COUNT

With prefinished solid wood. Narrow boards are called **strips**; wide ones, **planks**. Most are ¾-inch thick or less. An outer **finish layer** protects the flooring from spills, stains, and wear. Flooring is usually nailed or stapled to a plywood subfloor and can also cover above-ground concrete using a vapor barrier. For nailing into wood, you'll need a manual or pneumatic nailer.

With plastic laminate. A clear outer **wear layer** protects against spills, stains, and wear, and covers the pattern layers. A **fiberboard core** supports the top layers, while a **foam layer** goes between the laminate and the subfloor. A **vapor barrier** is recommended between the subfloor and the foam layer if moisture is a concern.

With engineered wood. Here, too, a clear **wear layer** protects the wood veneer—usually ⅛-inch thick or less—which goes above **construction-grade plywood.** Engineered wood is usually stapled down (the most secure method) or glued to the subfloor, though sometimes it can be floated like plastic laminate. You may be able to refinish engineered wood, by lightly sanding and varnishing it, at least once depending on the thickness of its veneer.

With vinyl flooring. For easier installation, **peel-and-self-stick tiles** are clearly the easiest to install and repair. But **sheet vinyl** offers a seamless look.

Among sheet vinyl products, you'll find **perimeter-bonded** floors, which are glued down only around the edge of the room and along any seams, and **fully adhered** floors, which are laid in a coat of mastic spread over the entire subfloor. Both are similar in cost and performance. Perimeter-bonded floors do a better job of hiding small surface imperfections in the subfloor since they're not stuck down. Fully adhered vinyl lies flatter and is less likely to bubble up; it's installed mostly by pros.

> **Shop smart**
>
> Unfinished wood might cost less but you'll still need to sand and finish it, which might wipe out your savings.

HOW TO CHOOSE

Determine where the flooring will go and how much traffic, sun exposure, and other wear and tear it will encounter. Also determine whether you'll install it yourself or hire a pro. Then keep these tips in mind:

For solid wood, consider the finish. More solid-wood flooring is factory-finished like the kind we tested. While unfinished wood costs roughly 40 percent less, installation can offset that savings, since the floor must be sanded and finished over several days to seal it from moisture. Prefinished floors should also hold up better than site-finished floors in wear resistance, and their warranty comes from the manufacturer, rather than the installer. But the beveled board edges on many examples many not be for everyone.

Consider spills. Vinyl proved tops in our moisture tests, with linoleum, plastic laminate, and solid wood nearly as good. But some engineered-wood products buckled, warped, or separated after 24 hours, even with little moisture.

Related CR report: August 2006

GAS GRILLS

Many people are choosing high-end models that do more than just grill. But you needn't spend a fortune for great grilling at your next barbecue.

Getting a good grill has become both easier and cheaper; some of the best we tested cost $200 or less. You'll also find $500 grills with the added style, space, and convenience of models that cost far more.

Stainless steel tops the list of high-end features moving down the price spectrum. Many lower-priced models now have at least some stainless trim, while midpriced models typically have more as manufacturers find ways to offer it for less.

You'll also find a greater number of grills that cost $1,000-plus as kitchen-appliance brands such as Frigidaire, Jenn-Air, and Viking move out onto the patio. While we did not test any new-for-this-year small and portable grills, manufacturers continue to target the tailgating set with them.

WHAT'S AVAILABLE

Char-Broil, Coleman, Kenmore (Sears), and Weber account for more than 60 percent of gas-grill sales overall.

Basic grills. These are ideal for those who want a good small or medium-sized grill that serves four to six without the frills. Features include a painted cart and cast-aluminum firebox and hood; thin porcelain-steel grates; a side burner for some; more stainless trim as you spend more. But most of these grills lack premium, coated cast-iron or thick stainless grates; burners with long warranties; rotisseries; and trays that hold wood chips for smoking. Many carts have only two wheels and lack drawers and other features. Price: about $100 to $300.

Midpriced grills. These are the best choice for most outdoor cooks. Options include medium-sized grills with more features and, increasingly, large models that can cook enough for 15 people. Features include higher-heat, recessed side burners; an electronic igniter; a rotisserie or smoker tray; more stainless steel; and double doors. Some carts have only two wheels. Many midpriced models have premium grates or burners with long warranties, but few have both. Price: $300 to $500

High-end grills. These are best for those who want a more-stylish medium-sized or large grill that can serve up to 15 people. Features include those on midpriced grills plus mostly or all-stainless construction; lifetime burner warranties; more burners with more heat; a fully rolling cart; and better storage space. Paying $1,000 or more often buys a toe-kick that hides the wheels. But based on our tests, paying more than $1,000 usually doesn't buy you better grilling. Price: $500 to $1,000-plus.

FEATURES THAT COUNT

Most cooking **grates** are made of porcelain-coated steel, with others made of the somewhat sturdier porcelain-coated cast iron, bare cast iron, or stainless steel. A porcelain-coated grate is rustproof and easy to clean, but it can chip. Bare cast iron is sturdy and sears beautifully, but you have to season it with cooking oil to fend off rust.

The best of both worlds: Stainless steel, which is sturdy and resists rust without a porcelain coating. Cooking grates with **wide bars that are closely spaced** tend to provide better searing than grates with thin, round rods, which may allow more food to fall to the bottom of the grill. Grills are mounted on a **cart,** usually made of painted steel tubing assembled with nuts and bolts. Higher-priced grills have welded joints, and some have a stainless-steel cart.

Then there's the stainless itself. Pricier grills often use **300-series stainless steel,** which includes nickel and has more corrosion-fighting chromium than less-expensive, 400-series stainless. Manufacturers often use the cheaper stuff to cut costs. A stainless grill that is magnetic is made of the less-expensive material. Carts with two wheels and two feet must be lifted at one end to move; better are **two large wheels** and **two casters** or **four casters,** which make moving easier. Wheels with a **full axle** are better than those bolted to the frame, which can bend over time.

Gas grills generally have one or more **exterior shelves,** which flip up from the front or side or are fixed on the side. Shelves are usually made of plastic, though cast-aluminum or stainless shelves tend to be more durable. (Wood shelves are the least sturdy and tend to deteriorate.) Most grills have **interior racks** for keeping food warm without further cooking. A **stainless or porcelain-coated-steel lid** and **firebox** are more durable than cast aluminum.

Battery-powered igniters tend to work better than pushbutton or knobs. Also look for **lighting holes** on the side of or beneath the grill—handy if the igniter fails and you need to use a wooden match or propane lighter to start the fire.

Most gas grills have **steel burners,** though some premium burners are **stainless steel, cast iron,** or **cast brass.** Premium versions typically last longer and carry warranties of 10 years or more. Many grills have **three or more burners,** which can add cooking flexibility. A **side burner,** which resembles a gas-stove burner and has its own heat control, is handy for cooking vegetables or sauce without leaving the grill. Other step-up features include an **electric rotisserie**, a **fuel gauge**, a **smoker drawer**, a **wok**, a **griddle pan**, a **steamer pan**, a **deep fryer**, a **nonstick grill basket**, and one or more high-heat **infrared burners** in place of the conventional type.

Most grills also use a **cooking medium**— a metal plate or metal bars, ceramic or charcoal-like briquettes, or lava rocks—between the burner and grates to distribute heat and vaporize juices, flavoring the food. Our tests have shown that no one type is better at ensuring even heating.

Gas grills sometimes include a **propane tank;** buying a tank separately costs about $25. Some grills can be converted to run on natural gas or offer a **natural-gas version**. The tank usually sits next to or on the base of the grill and attaches to its gas line with a handwheel. All tanks must now comply with upgraded National Fire Protection Association standards for overfill protection. Noncompliant tanks have a circular or five-lobed valve and aren't refillable, although they can be retrofitted with a three-lobed valve or swapped for a new tank at a hardware store or other refilling facility.

HOW TO CHOOSE

Most gas grills should perform at least adequately at your next alfresco feast. As with indoor ranges, some models do so with more style and panache.

Consider your cooking. Grills with wide or thick stainless or cast-iron grates tend to be best at searing and browning quickly to seal in juices—essential for meats and fish. Wide grates also leave the wide grill marks barbecue buffs crave. But heavy grates can take longer to heat up.

Take a head count. If you often entertain large crowds, look for a large grill with lots

of grilling, shelf, and storage space. You'll find several capable choices.

Inspect the burners. These distribute the gas and flames and are a grill's most-replaced part. Main burners with warranties for 10 years or more should last longest. Recessed side burners are also a plus, since some can accept a griddle and others include one. If you don't cover your grill, look for a side burner with its own cover.

Check the construction. Make sure the rolling cart that supports the firebox and lid doesn't rattle when shaken. If you want a stainless-steel grill and you're picky about stains, look for stainless fasteners and better, 300-series stainless (bring a magnet to the store). Or, consider buying a grill made with the cheaper, 400-series stainless and protecting it with a cover (about $40 to $50).

Related CR report: June 2006
Ratings: page 261

HEDGE TRIMMERS

A gas or electric hedge trimmer can enhance your tool arsenal if your property includes lots of shrubs. Both types tend to be easier than hand clippers, since an engine or motor powers their blades.

But using any powered hedge trimmer can still be hard work, since you're holding these devices in midair, often with arms out, for extended periods. That means your buying decision needs to factor in weight, balance, and vibration along with power.

WHAT'S AVAILABLE

Black & Decker and Craftsman (Sears) dominate the electric-powered (corded and cordless) market. (Craftsman also sells gas-powered models.) Other brands include Echo, Homelite, Husqvarna, Little Wonder, Remington, Ryobi, Stihl, and Weed Eater.

Corded electric hedge trimmers. Most homeowners prefer plug-in electric trimmers because they are relatively light and quiet, start with the push of a button, produce no exhaust emissions, require little maintenance, and are inexpensive. The best can also perform comparably to gasoline-powered models—provided you're within range of a power outlet (the longest extensions cords are about 100 feet). Price: about $30 to $100.

Cordless electric hedge trimmers. Battery-powered trimmers combine the mobility of gas models with the convenience, clean running, and easy maintenance of plug-ins, courtesy of an onboard battery (14.4 volt to 24 volt). On the downside, they offer relatively little power and run time per charge (no more than about 45 minutes). They can also cost as much as some gas-powered models. Price range:$70 to $120.

Gasoline-powered hedge trimmers. Commercial landscapers favor gas-powered models for their power and mobility. Indeed, a gas-powered, long-reach trimmer can provide access to remote spots a corded electric trimmer can't reach. But their two-stroke engines entail fuel mixing, pull starting, and maintenance, and pollute more than four-stroke engines. Gas trimmers can also be expensive. Price: about $130 to $450.

FEATURES THAT COUNT

The blades on a hedge trimmer consist of two flat metal plates with tooth-lined edges. **Blade length** typically ranges from 13 to 30 inches, although most are between 16 and 24 inches long. **Blade gap**—the distance between teeth—is also important, since it

helps determine how large a branch you can cut. In general, the wider the gap, the larger the branch a trimmer can handle and the easier it is to push through a hedge.

Gasoline-powered, professional-grade trimmers have blade gaps of 1 inch or more, while homeowner-grade models typically have ⅜- to ¾-inch gaps—typically narrow enough to help keep fingers out.

Double-sided blades allow cutting in both directions, letting you stand in one position longer than you can with single-sided blades, which cut in one direction only. **Dual-reciprocating blades,** where both the top and bottom blade plates move back and forth, tend to cut faster and reduce vibration compared with single-action blades, where only the top blade moves.

Trimmers with a **wrap-around front handle** let you keep your hands in a comfortable position as you pivot the trimmer to cut vertically or at odd angles. Safety features include **tooth extensions,** which are designed to prevent thighs and other body parts from contacting the blade teeth. Some are part of the blades and move with them; separate, stationary tooth extensions tend to provide better protection. Trimmers also have a **front-handle shield** designed to keep your forward hand from the blade.

HOW TO CHOOSE

Any powered hedge trimmer should be able to handle light-duty trimming. The strongest can cut branches roughly ⅝ inches in diameter, while dense ¼-inch-thick branches were enough to stop battery-powered trimmers we tested.

Decide on a trimmer type. Electric corded models are relatively quiet and inexpensive. They also deliver the best combination of cutting power, maneuverability, and ease provided you're within range of a power outlet. Battery-powered trimmers offer cord-free convenience, but their lack of cutting power and limited run time between charges makes them best suited to touch-ups and other light-duty work. In either case, look for an Underwriters Laboratories (UL) seal, which means that the trimmers have crucial safety features. Gasoline-powered models are for heavier-duty trimming beyond the range of a cord.

Trim safely. Make sure you wear protective work gloves, safety glasses or goggles, and nonskid shoes when using any powered trimmer. And wear hearing protection when working with gas-powered trimmers—they can be loud (more than 100 decibels at ear level, well above the dBA at which we recommend hearing protection). Also do your trimming on firm footing or on a steady ladder. Don't try to work beyond your reach. If you're using an electric trimmer, use a GFCI outlet or extension cord. And be sure the cord trails away from the blades so you don't slice it (tuck a loop of the cord up under your belt at toward your back).

Related CR report: June 2006

HUMIDIFIERS

Using a humidifier can help ease dry skin and other problems associated with dry air. But choosing one involves trade-offs in efficiency, cost, noise, and convenience.

Who needs a humidifier? Anyone who suffers from uncomfortably dry or itchy eyes, throat, or skin, or whose asthma is a problem indoors during the heating season. Ideally, the indoor relative humidity should be 30 to 50 percent. But that level can drop significantly in winter, since cold air holds less moisture, and heating it makes it even drier.

Humidifiers have improved over some earlier models, which spewed white dust in our tests. But that doesn't mean they all work equally well. What's more, CONSUMER REPORTS tests show that manufacturer claims can be a poor guide to how well a humidifier will work. Several small tabletop models fell well short of their claimed output and may not raise the humidity to the desired level.

WHAT'S AVAILABLE

Major humidifier brands include Holmes, Honeywell, Hunter, Kaz, and Reli-On (Wal-Mart). Other brands include Bemis, Bionaire, Crane, Sears, Slant Fin, and Sunbeam.

Humidifiers come in three major configurations:

Tabletop. These cost the least and are fine for one room. Tabletop humidifiers include evaporative models, which use a fan to blow air over a wet wick, and warm-mist models, which use a heating unit to boil water before cooling the steam. However, smaller tanks need to be refilled more frequently. Evaporative models are noisy; warm-mist models are costly to run. Price: $20 to $100.

Console. With larger tanks that require less refilling, console models are a suitable choice for humidifying multiple rooms. They're are also efficient and can be placed unobtrusively. But all use evaporative technology and are relatively noisy. The larger the tank, the more difficult it will be to handle. Price: $80 to $140.

In-duct. These whole-house humidifiers are convenient, quiet, and efficient, making them the least expensive to operate. Most are evaporative bypass units, which tap into the air supply and return ducts. Some are warm-mist; others are nebulizers, which use a spray technology. Using a nebulizer can result in white dust. In-duct humidifiers can be used only with forced-air heat. While inexpensive to operate, they're the most expensive to buy and often require professional installation. Price: $100 to $300, plus another $100 to $200 to install.

FEATURES THAT COUNT

A good portable model should offer relatively easy carrying, filling, cleaning, and wick replacement. Also look for easy-to-use controls and tanks that fit beneath faucets. Some portable models can be programmed to turn on automatically.

HOW TO CHOOSE

Choose a size based on how many rooms you need to humidify. Before buying a portable model, be sure you're willing to clean and disinfect it regularly to prevent mold and mildew. Otherwise, consider an in-duct humidifier, which is plumbed into the water supply and drainpipes, needn't be refilled, and has an easy-change filter that needs attention only once or twice a year.

Then keep these considerations in mind:

Be sure it has a humidistat. Whether it's dial or digital, a humidistat controls humidity levels and shuts the humidifier off when the set level is reached. Models without a humidistat can allow humidity levels to rise high enough to form condensation on windows and other cold surfaces. Overhumidification can also lead to mold and bacteria. Those that display room humidity levels and settings are best.

Also be aware that some humidistats aren't accurate or reliable. And most portable humidifiers won't let you set humidity levels below 30 percent. When outside temperatures drop below 20° F, even a 30-percent indoor humidity level can lead to window condensation. Be sure to lower humidity levels as outdoor temperatures drop.

Noise level. Consider a warm-mist tabletop if quietness counts. All of these were quieter than evaporative models; some make little or no noise beyond mild boiling and hissing sounds. Comparably sized evaporative humidifiers generated 45 to 50 decibels on low settings—as much noise as a small air conditioner—and emitted more than 50 decibels on high. At 80 decibels on its high setting, one model proved as raucous as a loud vacuum cleaner.

For larger areas, consider buying a noisier console model and placing it away from sleeping areas; the water vapor travels quickly through the home air and will still benefit remote bedrooms if doors remain open for air exchange. While you could alternatively buy several warm-mist tabletop models, doing so costs more.

Factor in running costs. In-duct systems and other evaporative models are the most energy-efficient. While initially pricey, in-duct humidifiers are likely to cost the least over time; you can easily spend $350 yearly to run four tabletop models compared with $28 for one in-duct model.

Consider your water. Some humidifiers have lower output with hard water and require more frequent maintenance. Nonetheless, you'll find tabletop, console, evaporative, and warm-mist humidifiers that perform well under those conditions.

Related CR report: October 2004

LAWN MOWERS

Practically any mower cuts grass. But you'll get better results if you choose one based on your lawn size, mowing preferences, and budget.

Mowing options range from $100 manual-reel mowers to tractors that cost $4,000 or more. If you have a small, level yard, a manual-reel or electric walk-behind mower is probably fine. Gasoline-powered walk-behind mowers are appropriate for most lawns up to about a half-acre. For larger lawns, you might want the ease and speed of a lawn tractor.

Compared with cars, gasoline-powered lawn mowers produce a disproportionate amount of air pollution. While mowers are run far less than cars, federal emissions rules have made today's gas-powered mowers cleaner than older ones—something to consider if you're using an older mower.

WHAT'S AVAILABLE

Manual-reel mowers are still made by only a few companies. Major brands of electric mowers include Black & Decker and Craftsman (Sears)—a brand that also sells the most gasoline-powered walk-behind mowers. Other less-expensive, mass-market brands include Poulan, Weed Eater, Yard Machines, and Yard-Man. Pricier brands traditionally sold at outdoor power-equipment dealers include Ariens, Bolens, Honda, Husqvarna, John Deere, Lawn-Boy, Poulan, Snapper, Toro, Troy-Bilt, and Yard Machines. Several of those brands are now available at large retailers, including Home Depot and Lowe's.

> **Tech tip**
>
> An overhead-valve engine creates less pollution than a side-valve engine.

Which type is best for your lawn? Here are the basics about each to help you decide:

Manual-reel mowers. Pushing these simple mowers turns a series of curved blades that spin with the wheels. Reel mowers are quiet, inexpensive, and non-polluting. They're also relatively safe to operate and require little maintenance other than periodic blade adjustments and sharpening. On the downside, cutting performance is typically mediocre, and most can't cut grass higher than 1½ inches or trim closer than 3 inches around obstacles. Models have cutting swaths just 14 to 18 inches wide—another drawback. Consider them for small, flat lawns a quarter-acre or less. Price: $100 to about $400.

Electric mowers. These push-type, walk-behind mowers use an electric motor to drive a rotating blade. Both corded and cordless versions start with the push of a button, produce no exhaust emissions, and, like reel mowers, require little maintenance aside from sharpening. Most offer a side or rear grass catcher, and many can mulch—a process where clippings are recut until they're small enough to hide unobtrusively within the lawn. But electrics are less powerful than gas mowers and less adept cutting tall or thick grass and weeds. And their narrow, 18- to 19-inch swaths take a smaller bite than the 21-inch swath on most gasoline mowers.

Corded mowers limit your mowing to within 100 feet of a power outlet—the typical maximum length for extension cords. Cordless versions weigh up to 30 pounds more than plug-ins and typically mow just one-quarter to one-third acre before their batteries need recharging. Both types are suitable mainly for small, flat lawns of a quarter-acre or less. Price: corded, $125 to $250; cordless, $400 or more.

Gas-powered walk-behind mowers. These include push mowers and self-propelled models with driven wheels. Most have a 4.5- to 6.5-hp four-stroke engine and a cutting swath 21 or 22 inches wide, allowing you to cover more ground with each pass, and handle long or thick grass and weeds. All can mow as long as there's fuel in the tank. But gas mowers are relatively noisy and require regular maintenance.

Most gas mowers provide three cutting modes: bagging, which gathers clippings in a removable catcher; side-discharging, which spews clippings onto the lawn; and mulching, which cuts and recuts clippings until they're small enough to settle and decompose within the lawn.

Consider a push-type model for mowing relatively flat lawns of about a quarter-acre or for trimming larger lawns. Choose a self-propelled model for hilly lawns or lawns of a half-acre or more. You might also choose a self-propelled mower if you mostly bag clippings; a full bag can add 20 or 30 pounds to the mower's weight. Price: push-type, $150 to $400; self-propelled, $200 to $900.

FEATURES THAT COUNT

For electric mowers. A **sliding clip** electric cord keeper (holder) helps ease turns when using corded mowers by allowing the cord to move from side to side. Some have a **flip-over handle** you move from one end of the mower to the other as you reverse direction, say, at the end of a row.

For gas-powered mowers. Some models have a **blade-brake clutch system** that stops the blade but allows the engine to keep running when you release the handlebar safety bail. This is more convenient than the usual **engine-kill system,** which stops the engine and blade and requires that you restart the engine. An **overhead-valve engine** tends to generate less pollution than a traditional side-valve engine and is often quieter.

With most gas mowers, you press a small rubber bulb called a **primer** to supply extra fuel for cold starting. Some now use a choke that automatically shuts off after the engine starts, while some from Craftsman, John Deere, and Troy-Bilt ease starting further by eliminating the need to fiddle with a primer or choke. An **electric starter** is easier to use than a recoil starter, though it typically adds $75 to the price. Most mowers with a **recoil starter** are easier to start than they once were, however.

Some self-propelled mowers have just one

speed, usually about 2½ mph; others have **several speeds** or a **continuous range,** typically from 1 to 3½ mph. Driven mowers also include **front-drive** and **rear-drive** models. Rear-wheel-drive models tend to have better traction on hills and with a full grass-collection bag. Mowers with **swivel front wheels** offer the most maneuverability by allowing easy 180-degree turns. But on some, each front casterlike wheel must be removed to adjust cutting height.

You'll also find several different deck choices. Most are steel, although some mowers offer **aluminum** or **plastic** decks, which are rustproof; plastic decks also resist dents and cracks. Many mowers have **tools-free cutting-height adjusters,** which raise and lower the deck with wheel-mounted levers. Some let you adjust cut height with only one or two levers, rather than having to adjust each wheel. Most models also allow you to change mowing modes without tools, although a few still require wrenches and, rarely, a blade change. One model has a **variable-mode lever** that lets you mulch some of the clippings and bag the rest. Some models use a **side-bagging deck design,** where a side-exit chute routes clippings into a side-mounted bag or out onto the lawn—or is blocked with a plate or plug for mulching.

Mowers with a **rear-bagging deck** tend to cost more, but their rear-mounted bag holds more than side bags and eases maneuvering by hanging beneath the handlebar rather than out to the side. The rearward opening is fitted with a chute for side discharging or a plug for mulching.

HOW TO CHOOSE

You'll see lots of competent choices for mowing the typical quarter- to half-acre lawn. Here are the most critical points to consider as you shop:

Pick your power. Gasoline-powered mowers continue to perform best overall, especially in long or dense grass. Self-propelled models are best for larger or hillier terrain, while lighter push models are fine for smaller, flatter lawns or for trimming. On the downside, gas models of both types are relatively noisy, create exhaust emissions, and require periodic tune-ups. Most also require pull-starting.

Electric mowers are quieter and create no exhaust emissions. They also free you from fueling and engine maintenance, and start with just the push of a button. But even the best corded electric mowers aren't as powerful as gas models. Cordless models free you from the tether and tangles of a power cord. But they're pricey and have limited run time before their batteries need recharging.

Manual reel mowers are another clean and quiet option, since they rely solely on people power to move their spiral-shaped mowing blades. Most models are relatively inexpensive (about $130 to $200). But some can be hard to push. And those in past tests couldn't match a power mower's cut quality.

Pick your mowing mode. Most walk-behind mowers can mulch, bag, or side-discharge clippings. But not all mowers handle all three modes equally well. Choose a model that scored well in the mowing mode you use most. If you bag most clippings, you'll probably prefer a self-propelled mower, since a full bag can make push types a handful, especially uphill.

Check the drive control. Most self-propelled mowers have two controls: a blade-engagement bail you must hold against the handlebar and a bail for adjusting the speed. Some new models now use a short lever that allows you to engage and vary ground speed by squeezing it with the right hand.

Those we tested worked well. But some levers can be stiffer than others—a poten-tial problem for some users, since all require constant pressure to keep the machine moving. As with all controls, see if you can try such levers before buying.

Don't get bowled over by big names. You'll find a Honda engine on even more non-Honda walk-behind lawn mowers as Craftsman, Lawn-Boy, Yard-Man, and other brands use Honda's premium image to give their machines some added cachet. These newer engines aren't the commercial-grade versions that made Honda's reputation for durability, however. While those we tested performed well, so did the more-plebeian Briggs & Stratton and Tecumseh engines on many other machines.

Don't count horses. High horsepower is another rallying cry at the store and online. Many of the mowers we tested now have up to 7 hp on tap. But mowers with at least 5.5 hp performed just as well overall as models with higher horsepower.

Related CR report: May 2006
Ratings: page 268
Reliability: page 273

LAWN TRACTORS

If your lawn is larger than a half-acre, a ride-on lawn tractor could be your best option.

Heated competition among the big-box stores has lowered the price of a well-equipped automatic-drive tractor to as little as $1,000 or so. That's several hundred dollars less than comparable machines from only a few years ago.

Big-name brands are also piling on premium features as they trade some of the profit margins they enjoyed at the corner mower shop for the added volume of home centers and large retailers like Sears, which together sell nearly 70 percent of lawn tractors.

WHAT'S AVAILABLE

Lawn tractors now dominate the ride-on marketplace, with some models available for less than the cost of a rear-engine riding mower. (Keep in mind, though, that a bagging kit will typically add another $250 to $400 to the total cost). Tractors can accept light-duty attachments to plow, tow a cart, or clear snow. Lower prices and versatility help explain why lawn tractors have become far more popular than riding mowers.

Tight-turning riders are a growing alternative. Also known as zero-turn-radius models, these let you steer by pushing or pulling levers, each controlling a driven rear wheel. The advantage is added maneuverability in tight spots and around obstacles. But you pay a premium for agility and faster cutting.

Price: lawn tractors, $1,000 to $2,500; tight-turning riders (ZTR), $2,500 to $7,000 and beyond.

FEATURES THAT COUNT

Lower-priced models are **gear-driven** and require a shift lever and combination brake/clutch to change speed. Spending more will buy you a model with a **clutchless automatic drive,** which allows even more convenient, continuously variable speed changes via a **hydrostatic transmission** or a continuously variable transmission (CVT). Most models have a **translucent fuel tank,** making it easy to check fuel level. Some have a **fuel gauge** and **cupholders.** Still others provide **cruise control** to rest your foot on long runs and an electric **power takeoff (PTO) switch** to engage the cutting blades, instead of a manual lever.

HOW TO CHOOSE

Wide-swath mowing at a reasonable price makes lawn tractors an appealing choice if you have a half-acre or more of lawn. Falling prices for tractors also help explain why small, rear-engine riders are nearly extinct.

Keep these points in mind as you shop:

Determine the mowing you'll do. All tractors can side-discharge clippings, the mode most people use. Many include a mulching plate that seals the deck so clippings are cut finely and deposited into the lawn rather than on it. But a kit for bagging clippings typically costs hundreds of dollars extra. Before paying more for that bagging, be sure that the model you're considering did well in that mode and that you will use it.

Pick your retailer. Most of the brands we tested are now at major retailers as well as dealers. Big-box stores tend to have the lowest prices. But dealers typically offer more personalized service, setup, and instruction. Cub Cadet, John Deere, Poulan, Toro, and Yard Machines are at Home Depot. Bolens, Husqvarna, John Deere, and Troy-Bilt are sold at Lowe's. Sears sells Craftsman and Husqvarna, and Wal-Mart has Yard Machines and Yard-Man.

Don't count horses. Some models now pack 20 hp or more. Higher horsepower doesn't guarantee more performance, however; models with as little as 17 hp mowed as well as brawnier models.

Play it safe. Use common sense when mowing. Wear earplugs or muffs; all of the machines we tested emitted more than the 85 decibels at which we recommend hearing protection. Don't mow on grades steeper than 15 percent. Look behind you when you mow in reverse.

Related CR report: June 2006
Ratings: page 274
Reliability: page 279

MATTRESSES

Once you've settled on the size you need, shop around for the firmness and feel you like. Try each top choice for 15 minutes in the store.

Shopping for a mattress can be a nightmare. The reason is that shoppers are flying blind. It's hard to tell one box of metal, foam, fuzz, and fabric from another, making you vulnerable to a sales pitch. Model names differ from store to store, making it impossible to comparison shop. And prices vary so much that the $1,300 mattress set you look at one day can cost $2,600 the next.

From years of bashing and dissecting, we know that all but the cheapest mattresses are apt to be sturdy, but there are no reliability data for specific models or even brands. The bottom line is that despite the claims you'll hear, there is no best bed for everyone. You'll need to spend time finding the mattress that's most comfortable and supportive for you. The good news is that trying a mattress for 15 minutes in a store can predict long-term satisfaction.

WHAT'S AVAILABLE

Innerspring mattresses are the most widely sold type. Sealy, Serta, Simmons, and Spring Air are the top-selling brands. Highly hyped alternatives to conventional innerspring mattresses include Duxiana (springs galore, in layers); Select Comfort (air-filled, with adjustable firmness for each partner); and Tempur-Pedic (polyurethane "memory foam"). Price: $500 to more than $5,000.

FEATURES THAT COUNT

Most stores have a cutaway or cross-section of at least some of the mattress sets on display. Here's what matters:

Ticking, the outermost layer, is typically polyester or cotton-polyester. On fancier mattresses, you'll see plush fabrics like fancy damask, jersey knit, microsuede, wool, cashmere, and silk. None of this matters. What does? The stitching that binds the ticking to the top padding can affect feel. If you like a deep, cushiony sensation, look for a large quilt pattern. A smaller pattern tends to squeeze down top padding, creating a slightly firmer feel. Some ticking includes silk, which adds to the price but provides no real benefit.

Top padding generally consists of one or more types of polyurethane foam, with or without polyester batting. Polyester batting provides a soft feel and makes a mattress more breathable, allowing perspiration to dissipate quickly. Look for a mattress with polyester; more than an inch, and it's apt to sag eventually. In foam layers, look for latex, which is soft, supportive, and resilient, and visco-elastic "memory foam," which conforms to your body and can help keep you from feeling motion on the other side of the bed. Convoluted foam ("egg crate") feels softer than a straight slab of the same type of foam.

Coils provide the main support, and all the hyped types—whether Bonnell (in an hourglass shape), continuous wire, or individually pocketed—are up to the task. The wire's gauge is what counts. Heavier-gauge coils can provide a stiffer suspension. Lighter-gauge coils usually lend a springier feel.

For **extra support,** some manufacturers beef up certain areas by using more closely spaced coils, slabs of stiff foam around edges and between coils, or thicker wire. Stiffer edges make for a solid place to sit and tie your shoes, and keep you from feeling as if you'll roll off. Salespeople are also quick to point out extra support at the mattress's head, foot, or center. Among big-name mattresses with extra-support zones: Simmons BackCare and Sealy BackSaver.

There's nothing springy about box springs; they simply provide support. Manufacturers often deliver the same box spring with various models within their lines, regardless of price. If you buy an ultrathick mattress, consider pairing it with a "low profile" box spring, 4 to 6 inches thick, instead of the usual 10 inches or so. That way, you won't need a stepladder to climb into bed.

HOW TO CHOOSE

Consider an innerspring first. A conventional innerspring mattress is the most common choice and often the least expensive. Memory foam, which was developed to protect astronauts against g-forces, is heat-sensitive and conforms to your body. Tempur-Pedic is the big name, but there are other brands. Not all memory foam feels the same, and it can take time to get used to. A third option: an inflatable mattress that lets you choose a different firmness for each half of the bed. Select Comfort is the major brand.

Decide where to shop. Buy at a store, not online or over the phone, unless you've already tried the identical mattress in a store. Department stores have frequent sales and lots of brands, but can be somewhat crowded, cluttered, and short on sales help. Bedding stores like Sleepy's and 1-800-Mattres, and furniture stores offer plenty of variety and are often less crowded.

Understand the name game. Manufacturers usually modify any innerspring mattress they make for different sellers, changing the color, padding, quilting pattern, and so forth. Then each seller can call the mattress by a different name. Consumers are the losers. Since such mattresses are at least somewhat different, and the names vary, you can't comparison-shop. (A big chain such as Sears or Bloomingdale's has the same model names for the same beds at all of its stores, usually at the same price.)

Some bedmakers do provide helpful information on their Web sites. Go to *www.simmons.com*, for example, and you'll uncover basics about the company's flagship Beautyrest lines, the Classic, World Class, and Exceptionale. You'll see those names wherever you find Beautyrest, and all beds in each line share attributes.

Choose the right firmness. Don't rely on names: Levels are described differently. One company's ultraplush might be another's supersoft. Orthopedists once recommended sleeping on an extremely firm mattress, but there's little evidence to support that view.

Do the 15-minute in-store test. Don't be embarrassed to lie down on lots of mattresses in the store. Salespeople expect it. Wear loose clothes and shoes that you can slip off. Spend at least five minutes on each side and your back (your stomach, too, if that's a preferred position).

Assess your need for a new box spring. Foundations can sell for as much as the mattress they're sold with, even though they're generally just a wood frame enclosing stiff wire and covered with fabric matching the mattress's.

We found that companies frequently pair the same foundation with mattresses in different price ranges. You might save by buying a higher-priced mattress with a lower-priced foundation. Once the bed is made, no one will know. If your current foundation is only a few years old, with no rips, warps, creaks, or "give," consider using it with a new mattress. If the old box has bouncy springs instead of stiff wire, it needs to be replaced.

Be wary of "comparables." If you like a mattress at one store and ask elsewhere for something similar, you'll probably be steered toward a same-brand mattress that's supposed to have the same construction, components, and firmness. It's unlikely. Manufacturers don't publish a directory of comparables.

Don't count on warranties. They cover defects in materials and workmanship, not comfort or normal wear. They typically cover 10 years; Duxiana, Select Comfort, and Tempur-Pedic are in effect for 20. Some warranties don't cover full replacement value; an annual usage charge is deducted from the current retail price.

When you make a claim, the store or manufacturer sends an inspector to your house. You'll need to show your receipt. If you say the bed has sagged, the inspector checks whether the dip is below the allowable limit, 1½ inches. A company will void a warranty if you remove the "do not remove" tag, if the mattress is soiled, or if it has uneven support from foundation or frame.

Wait for a sale, and bargain. Specialty mattresses usually have a set price, but you can save at least 50 percent off list price for an innerspring type. Ads for "blowout" sales make such events seem rare. They aren't. If the price is good, buy; if not, wait. An advertised "bargain" may not be all it seems, so read the fine print.

Related CR report: June 2005

MINI-TILLERS

Mini-tillers aren't just for ardent gardeners. The best of these machines can handle more pedestrian chores such as tearing away crabgrass and whisking away weeds far more quickly and easily than a spade or hoe.

Several new models add faster starts and more digging power, courtesy of a four-stroke engine like the kind on mowers. They also run cleaner, since four-stroke tillers produce fewer exhaust emissions than two-stroke models—a prime reason most two-stroke tillers are not certified for stricter California emissions standards. Yet at about $300, most of these cleaner machines cost only slightly more than two-stroke models.

You'll also find plug-in electric tillers, along with tiller attachments that replace the bottom half of the shaft on some string trimmers.

WHAT'S AVAILABLE

Half of all tillers are sold by Home Depot (Honda, Ryobi, Yard Machines), Lowe's (Troy-Bilt), and Sears (Craftsman). Other brands include Mantis and Yard-Man.

Gas mini-tillers. Gas models are best for planting shrubs, reseeding lawn patches, and tending areas smaller than 300 square feet. Most four-stroke models are easier to start and handle, and most have a swath 9 to 10 inches wide. Gas models do require maintenance, though, and tend to be louder and heavier than electrics. Two-stroke models require mixing gas and oil. All gas-powered tillers are noisy. All the gasoline-powered tillers and trimmer-driven machines we tested produced noise levels at or above the 85 decibels at which we recommend hearing protection. Price: $150 to $400.

Electric mini-tillers. If you're near an outlet and have lighter-duty tasks, this kind should do the trick. Most are lighter and quieter than gas tillers, and all free you from fueling, pull-starting, and engine tune-ups, and produce no exhaust emissions. Most have a swath 9 to 10 inches wide. Most, however, just don't perform as well as gas models. Be careful of the power cord, which can get caught in the tines or damage fragile plants. Electric tillers are quiet by comparison; the quietest emitted just 68 decibels at ear level, making it quieter than many vacuum cleaners. Price: $150 to $300.

Trimmer-based tillers. This model is right if you already own a string trimmer and care mostly about light-duty weeding. These replace the line head on trimmers that take attachments. Most swaths are 9 to 10 inches wide. On the downside, it does tend to be heavy, poorly balanced, and short on performance. Dedicated tillers are a better bet. Price: about $90 for the tiller; $80 to $200 for the trimmer.

Larger tillers. These are the bigger machines, best for reseeding a large lawn, deeper tilling jobs in harder or rockier soil, and tending areas that are larger than 300 square feet. Most have a swath 14 to 21 inches wide. But size can also be a drawback: they're heavy, bulky, and pricey. The largest can also be hard to handle. Consider renting as an option if you're only going to use it occasionally. Price: $600 to $2,000; about $60 per day to rent one.

FEATURES THAT COUNT

A **four-stroke engine** typically starts with fewer pulls and delivers more power at lower speeds. It also produces fewer emissions than a two-stroke and requires no fuel-mixing. Tillers with **clevis pins** at the outsides of the tines, rather than within, make it easier to remove tines to clear a jam or narrow the tilling width. A **handle-mounted switch** lets you stop the engine or motor quickly from the operator's position. Models with an effective **drag stake** help keep the moving tines from pulling the tiller forward too fiercely as you work. Good ones are long enough to penetrate the soil. Some tillers use a relatively short stake or a roller. **Transport wheels** let you roll, rather than carry, a tiller to and from the garage or shed. If the ground is too rough for wheels, look for a **lift handle,** which makes carrying easier. **Angled tines** tend to be better for mixing soil. **Pointed tines** reduce pulling effort and are often better at sod-busting.

HOW TO CHOOSE

Mini-tillers have grown in sales as lot sizes and gardens have shrunk. But they aren't for everyone. You'll probably prefer renting or even buying a larger tiller for yard projects beyond 300 square feet or for rocky soil. You may also prefer the added control of hand tools for jobs smaller than 100 square feet.

If you've decided advantages outweigh disadvantages, keep these points in mind as you shop:

Determine how you'll use it. The best of these machines excel at tilling, sod-busting, and weeding. But you may be willing to trade some performance in one or more of those areas for a lower price or an electric's push-button starting.

> **Shop smart**
> Be sure that your mini-tiller is reasonably easy to lift and rolls smoothly on its wheels.

Look for convenience. Features that make some tillers easier to use include a four-stroke engine for gas models, along with easy tine removal and wheels for all tillers. Also be sure that any tiller is reasonably easy to lift and rolls smoothly on its wheels. Check, too, that the handlebar is wide enough to allow both elbows to clear your sides when you pull back on the machine—something you'll do often while working as the tines pull the tiller ahead.

Consider repairs down the road. Some of these retailers have service agreements with local dealers, as do brands such as Hoffco, which are sold by manufacturers. Before buying, ask which dealer will provide your service. Then call or visit the dealer to get a sense of whether you'll be treated as well as customers who bought their machines at that dealer.

Think twice about add-ons. With some tillers, you can buy de-thatchers, edgers, aerators, and other attachments for roughly $40 to $100 each. As with tiller attachments for trimmers, however, we've typically found these add-ons less effective than dedicated machines.

Keep it safe. Wear goggles, boots, and hearing protection when using a gas tiller. And keep children and pets away while you work.

Related CR report: March 2005

PAINT, EXTERIOR

The best paint can improve your home's appearance and protect it from the weather for about nine years.

While a fresh coat of paint on the siding and trim will give your house curb appeal, exterior paint isn't just for show. It provides an important layer of protection against moisture, mildew, and the effects of the sun.

WHAT'S AVAILABLE

Major brands include Ace, Behr (sold at Home Depot), Benjamin Moore, Dutch Boy, Glidden, Sears, Sherwin-Williams, True Value, and Valspar (sold at Lowe's). You'll also see many brands of paint sold regionally.

Exterior paints come in a variety of sheens. The dullest is flat, followed by low-luster (often called eggshell or satin), semigloss, and gloss. The flatter finishes are best for siding, with the lowest-sheen variety the best choice if you need to mask imperfections. Glossy paint is most often used for trim because it highlights the details of the woodwork and the paint is easy to clean. Price: $15 to $40 a gallon.

HOW TO CHOOSE

Our tests of exterior paints are very severe, exposing painted panels on outdoor racks angled to catch the maximum amount of sun. One year of testing is equal to approximately three years of real-life exposure. Generally, most paints will look good for at least three years; some should look good for about six, and top-rated products about nine years. Most also do a good job of resisting the buildup of mildew and preventing the wood from cracking. To determine the best paint for your home, consider the following tips:

Buy the best. Our tests have found that the grade of paint matters. "Good" or "economy" grades don't weather as well as top-of-the-line products. Using a cheaper grade of paint means you'll spend more time and money in the long run because you'll need to repaint more often. "Contractor" grades of paint that we've tested in the past also tended to be mediocre.

Consider where you live. Paints of any color accumulate dirt over time. The top-rated ones tended to resist it better than the others and darker colors hide it better. Good dirt resistance is important in urban areas. Mildew can be a problem in damp areas, from rainy Seattle to steamy Tampa, or on any house that gets more shade than sun. Baking in bright sun can change even the best-quality pigments. Blues and yellows are the most likely to change.

Don't overlook the prep work. Be sure you scrape, sand, and clean the siding thoroughly before applying the paint. Good preparation makes any paint last longer. And plan to apply two coats.

Tailor your prep work. Our tests are based on applying one primer coat and two top coats to new pine siding. If you're painting over other materials, different steps may be necessary. Stucco and masonry may need sealing beforehand. Vinyl siding can fade before it fails. But to avoid the possibility of warping, don't use a darker color than the original.

If you plan to sand or scrape paint on a house built before 1978, be warned: The older coats of paint may contain lead, so you'll need to take extra precautions.

Related CR report: June 2006

PAINT, INTERIOR

Plenty of high-quality, durable wall paints are available to brighten your rooms. And you won't need to endure as many fumes as in years past.

A fresh coat of paint is an easy, inexpensive way to freshen a room. Today's paints are significantly better than their predecessors in several important respects: They spatter less, keep stains at bay, and have ample tolerance for scrubbing. They also resist the buildup of mildew (important if you're painting a kitchen, a bath, or a basement room that tends to be damp). Some are labeled low-VOC (volatile organic compounds).

WHAT'S AVAILABLE

Major brands include Ace, Behr (sold at Home Depot), Benjamin Moore, Dutch Boy, Glidden, Kilz (sold at Wal-Mart), Olympic, Sears, Sherwin-Williams, and American Tradition by Valspar (sold at Lowe's). You'll also see designer names such as Martha Stewart and Ralph Lauren, as well as many brands of paint sold regionally.

You'll find several types of paints for interior use. Wall paints can be used in just about any room. Glossier trim enamels are used for windowsills, woodwork, and the like. Kitchen and bath paints are usually fairly glossy and formulated to hold up to water and scrubbing and to release stains. Price: $15 to $45 per gallon.

FEATURES THAT COUNT

Paint typically comes in a variety of sheens—**flat, low luster,** and **semigloss.** The degree of glossiness can be different from one manufacturer to another. Flat paint, with the dullest finish, is the best at hiding surface imperfections, but it also tends to pick up stains. It's well suited for formal living rooms, dining rooms, and other spaces that don't see heavy use.

A low-luster finish (often called eggshell or satin) has a slight sheen and is good for family rooms, kids' rooms, hallways, and the like. Semigloss, shinier still, usually works best on kitchen and bathroom walls and on trim because it's generally easier to clean. Low-luster and semigloss paints look best on smooth, well-prepared surfaces, since the paint's shine can accentuate imperfections on the wall.

Most brands come in several tint bases—the uncolored paint that forms the foundation for the specific color you choose. The tint base largely determines the paint's toughness, resistance to dirt and stains, and ability to withstand scrubbing. The colorant determines how much the paint will fade. Whites and browns tend not to fade; reds and blues fade somewhat; bright greens and yellows tend to fade a lot.

HOW TO CHOOSE

Begin with the gloss. The gloss level will affect your perception of the color. Flat paints and textured walls absorb light, so colors seem darker. Glossy paints and smooth surfaces reflect, so colors look brighter.

Then choose a color. Take advantage of the various color-sampling products and computer programs to get the color you think you want. Most manufacturers now sell small samples of many paint colors, so you can test a paint without having to buy large quantities. Manufacturers also offer large color chips or coupons, which are easier to use than the conventional small swatches. Sunlight and room light can affect your perceptions, so check samples on different walls or at different times of day.

Fluorescent light enhances blues and greens but makes warm reds, oranges, and yellows appear dull. Incandescent light works with warm colors, but might not do much for cool ones. Even natural light changes from day to day, room to room, and morning to night.

Many aspects of paint performance depend on the quality of the base and not on the particular color. We test each brand's pastel and medium bases as well as white. So if you want a medium or dark color, it won't matter whether it's red or blue or something in between. Its performance should track with our findings.

Buy the top of the line. The paints we test represent the top of each manufacturer's line. Over the years, we have found that lower grades—typically dubbed good, better, or contractor grade—do not perform as well. If a top-line paint will cover all but the darkest colors in two coats, lower-quality paints might need three or four coats. That makes them a poor value. But plan on two coats even with a top-rated paint for best coverage.

Match a paint's strong points to the room's use. Here are the most important considerations:

• Stains are more of a problem with flat paints.

• Heavily used rooms need a paint that can stand up to scrubbing. Our tests show that paints in every gloss level can perform well in this regard. Some low-luster and semigloss paints may change sheen when scrubbed.

• Mildew can grow in any warm, humid room, not just a bathroom or kitchen. A paint with high mildew resistance won't kill existing mildew (you must clean it off with a

bleach solution), but it will slow new growth.

• Sticking can occur with glossier paints long after they've dried. Books seem glued to shelves, and windows become hard to open. Most of the glossy paints we tested did not have that problem.

Related CR report: September 2005

POWER BLOWERS

The best electric handheld blowers outperform their gas counterparts and cost less. But they aren't any quieter, and the power cord can be a hassle.

These miniature wind machines take some of the effort out of sweeping and cleaning fallen leaves and other small yard and driveway debris. Many can also vacuum and shred what they pick up. But practically all available models still make enough noise to annoy the neighbors and require the use of hearing protection. Indeed, some localities have ordinances restricting their use.

WHAT'S AVAILABLE

Mainstream brands include Black & Decker, Craftsman (Sears), Homelite, Poulan, Toro, and Weed Eater. Pricier brands of gas-powered blowers include Echo, Husqvarna, John Deere, and Stihl. As with other outdoor power tools, gas and electric blowers have their pros and cons. You'll also find variations among gas-powered models. Here are your choices:

Electric handheld blowers. Designed for one-handed maneuvering, these are light (about 7 pounds or less). Many are also relatively quiet, produce no exhaust emissions, and can vacuum and shred. Some perform better than handheld gas-powered models, although mobility and range are limited by the power cord. Price: $30 to $100.

Gasoline handheld blowers. These perform like the best electrics but aren't restricted by a cord. As with other gas-powered equipment, tougher regulations have reduced emissions. Manufacturers have also quieted some models in response to noise ordinances. But all are still loud enough to warrant hearing protection. Other drawbacks include added weight (most weigh 7 to 12 pounds) and the fuel-and-oil mixing required by the two-stroke engines most gas models use. A few blowers have a four-stroke engine that burns gasoline only, though they tend to be heavy for this group. Price: $75 to $160.

Gasoline backpack blowers. At 16 to 25 pounds, these are double the weight of handheld blowers, which is why you wear rather than carry them. But the payoff with most is added power and ease of use for extended periods, since your shoulders support their weight. Hearing protection is strongly recommended. Backpack blowers don't vacuum, and they can be expensive. Price: $170 to $420.

Gasoline wheeled blowers. These offer enough oomph to sweep sizable areas quickly. All use a four-stroke engine that requires no fuel mixing. But these machines are large and heavy, and require some effort to push around. They also cost the most and tend to be hard to maneuver, which can make it difficult to precisely direct leaves and other yard waste. These are the blowers that most professionals use to get the job done quickly. Count on using hearing protection. Price: $400 to $800.

FEATURES THAT COUNT

Look for an easy-to-use **on-off switch** and **multiple speeds** on electric blowers, a **variable throttle** you can preset on gasoline-powered models, and a convenient **choke** on gas-powered units. Varying the speed lets you use maximum force for sweeping and minimum force around plants. Blowers that excel at cleaning or loosening debris usually have **round-nozzle blower tubes; oblong** and **rectangular nozzles** are better for moving or sweeping leaves. A bottom-mounted **air intake** is less likely to pull at clothing.

A **control stalk** attached to the blower tube of backpack models improves handling, while an **auxiliary handle** on the engine or motor housing of a handheld blower makes it easier to use—provided the handle is comfortable. Other useful features on gas-powered models include a **wide fuel fill** and a **translucent fuel tank,** which shows the level inside. An **adjustable air deflector,** found on most wheeled blowers, lets you direct airflow forward or to the side.

HOW TO CHOOSE

For sheer power, you can't go wrong with any of the backpack or wheeled blowers and several of the handheld models we tested. There's more to blowers than air power, however. The best in each group also proved easier to handle and control. And some are less noisy than others. Here's what else to think about:

Consider what you'll clear. If it's mostly fallen leaves or grass clippings, choose a model judged very good or excellent in our sweeping tests.

Handheld models that vacuum are also handy for cleaning between shrubs, though their small reduction ratios and bags are impractical for vacuuming larger areas or leaf piles. If embedded leaf fragments are a frequent problem, look for a machine that did well at freeing tenacious debris in our loosening tests.

Consider what you can handle. High performance and low weight at a relatively low price make electric blowers your first choice if arm fatigue or weak arm strength is a factor. Backpack blowers put their added weight on your back, not your arms, and provide more air power, though at a much higher price.

Wheeled blowers deliver the most air power, thanks to their larger fans and higher-horsepower engines. But because they lack the drive systems available on mowers, moving these 100-plus-pound machines requires plenty of push, especially uphill. Wheeled blowers also require about 8 square feet of storage space.

Consider your neighbors. While none of these blowers is quiet, several can move lots of debris with a bit less noise. Regulations typically limit blowers to 65 decibels at 50 feet. About a third of the tested models should meet that standard and were judged very good or excellent in that performance category.

Related CR report: September 2003

POWER SANDERS

These smooth operators save time and effort. More convenience and safety features for less money help account for their growing popularity.

Some of the latest power sanders can skim off as much wood in 5 minutes as you could in 30 minutes of continuous sanding by hand. Many are easier to use than older models. And nearly all have a dust bag—important considering the health risks of inhaling wood dust.

WHAT'S AVAILABLE

Major brands include Black & Decker, Bosch, Craftsman, Dewalt, Makita, Porter

Cable, Ryobi, and Skil. You'll find four major types of power sanders at the store:

Random-orbit. Best for versatility, these can do some rough sanding and most finish sanding, which helps explain their large share of the market. The round pad moves in a random ellipse to help prevent gouges. Price: about $20 to $100.

Finishing. Best for small to moderate-sized tasks, finishing sanders have squared-off pads that reach in corners. The most popular type along with random-orbit models, finishing sanders handle a variety of homeowner tasks. Price: about $20 to $70.

Belt. Best for smoothing doors, tabletops, and other large or uneven areas, a belt sander has a pulley-driven loop that removes more wood in less time than other sanders. But it isn't meant for small-area or finish sanding. Price: about $50 to $200.

Detail. Best for sanding around tight spots, most detail sanders have triangular pads that are good for corners. Some also come with finger-shaped pads for sanding around slots and grooves. But none are meant for rough sanding or large areas. Price: $30 to $50.

FEATURES THAT COUNT

An attached **dust bag** captures dust routed into it through holes in the pad, but requires frequent emptying. A **vacuum connection** lets you attach a wet/dry vac for more thorough dust-collecting, though the hose may hamper maneuverability and handling.

Random-orbit and detail sanders use a **hook-and-loop system** to attach the sanding pad. Many finishing sanders have a **lever-and-clip system.** And all finishing sanders can be converted to pressure-sensitive adhesive pads. All belt sanders use a **flip-out lever** and **tracking control** to lock the sandpaper loop in place.

Many models of all types can be gripped

securely with one or both hands for added ease and stability. A **two-handed grip** is especially important for a belt sander's heavier-duty rough sanding, as is a large front grip that keeps hands well spaced to ease larger jobs. Some belt sanders can be secured to a bench with the belt facing upward—convenient for two-handed shaping where you hold the wood against the spinning belt, rather than the belt against the work piece.

Many belt sanders allow you to adjust tracking with a **knob** or **thumbscrew** instead of a screwdriver to move the paper nearer to one edge or the other. Many also have a **trigger lock** that can be locked in the On position with one hand.

Most finishing sanders with a dust bag or vacuum connection include a **template** for punching the pattern for the dust-routing holes in replacement sandpaper.

Variable speed adds control by letting you sand more slowly and carefully.

A **long cord** lets you dispense with an extension cord near an electrical outlet. A **carrying case** makes storage easier and neater.

HOW TO CHOOSE

Lots of choices for power sanders mean more considerations when shopping. Here are some of the major features you should be thinking about:

Decide how you'll use it. Determine which of the four types of power sanders meets your needs. If you're buying just one sander, you'll probably prefer a random-orbit or a finishing sander, which offer the most versatility.

If you're buying a finishing sander, choose a one-quarter-sheet model for mostly small jobs and a larger, one-third-sheet model for the occasional tabletop.

Consider your strength. A heavier sander tends to remove more wood in less time, since more weight helps the sander contact the wood more effectively. While the added heft isn't an issue with most types of sanders, it could be with belt sanders, some of which weigh 11 pounds or more. Particularly for belt-type sanders, try lifting and holding the sander at the store. Then choose the heaviest model you can handle comfortably.

Check the grip. For added control, especially with larger, harder-working models, make sure the sander is easy to grasp with one or both hands.

Look for a bag and a vac connection. Many sanders now include at least one of these features. But most of the low-cost models lack an attached dust-collection bag, a port for connecting a wet/dry vacuum hose, or both. A vacuum connection is especially important. Besides capturing dust more thoroughly than a bag, attaching a wet/dry vacuum helped speed sanding with several models we tested.

Look for easy paper changes. Even small projects may require that you replace the sandpaper several times. The hook-and-loop pads now common on random-orbit and detail sanders are the easiest to change. Some sanders of other types also make changing the sandpaper relatively convenient.

Related CR report: January 2004

PRESSURE WASHERS

Professional cleaning at a do-it-your-self price has helped move pressure washers beyond the tool-rental shop and into your local home center.

Pressure washers use a gas engine or electric motor, pump, and concentrating nozzle to boost water pressure from your garden hose as much as 60 times. That lets them blast away deck mildew, driveway stains, and other grunge a hose can't touch while cleaning chairs, siding, and other items more quickly and easily than you could with a scrub brush.

For as little as $90 for electric machines and $300 for gas, owning one is a tempting alternative to renting one for $50 to $90 per day.

Lower prices and less upkeep explain why 60 percent of buyers choose an electric pressure washer. But gas machines have roughly twice the cleaning power, which is the main reason you'll see fewer plug-in models at the big-box stores where half of pressure washers are sold.

WHAT'S AVAILABLE

Models from Black & Decker, Campbell Hausfeld, Craftsman, Excell, Honda, Husky, Karcher, and Troy-Bilt are among the brands you'll find.

Gas-powered washers. If you need to quickly clean large areas, such as decks or siding, or want to whisk away gum, tree sap, and other tough stains, a gas-powered model is right for you. Water pressure is typically measured in pounds per square inch (psi). Gas-powered models typically put out 2,000 to 2,800 psi of pressure compared with 1,000 to 1,800 psi for electric models. Much higher pressure allowed the top-performing gas machines to clean a grimy concrete patio three times faster than the fastest electrics.

Gas models are relatively noisy and heavy, though, and they require tune-ups. Pumps must be winterized with antifreeze in colder areas, since gas machines should not be stored inside a home. Remember that more power raises damage and injury risks. Gas models require more caution and control than

the electrics to avoid splintering and etching wood and other soft surfaces. Price: $200 to $500.

Electric washers. Electrics are best for small decks and patios, furniture, and other smaller jobs that emphasize cleaning over stain removal. They're relatively light and quiet, require little upkeep, and create no exhaust emissions. They start and stop with a trigger and are small enough to be stored indoors without winterizing. But less pressure means slower cleaning compared with gas models. Wands and nozzles are less-sturdy plastic, rather than metal. And you need to be near an outlet. Price: $90 to $180.

FEATURES THAT COUNT

A **soap tank** saves you the hassle of using separate containers. **Tool and cord storage** is a plus, as are **wheels** for heavier models. **Adjustable nozzles** are more convenient than replaceable nozzles; a twist is all it takes to change spray width or pressure. But replaceable nozzles let you customize the spray pattern with specific spray angles.

HOW TO CHOOSE

Any of these pressure washers can handle decks, walks, and other typical cleaning tasks. They're also forceful enough to harm a car's paint, which is why we suggest using a hose for cars.

If you decide that a pressure washer's benefits outweigh its risks, then keep these shopping tips in mind:

Don't buy solely on specs. Retailers and manufacturers often push lofty numbers for water pressure and volume. Some talk about "cleaning units," which are simply the pressure multiplied by the volume.

Faster is noisier. All the gas pressure washers produced at least 85 decibels (dBA), the threshold at which we recommend hearing protection. Electric models averaged 78 dBA when running and are silent with their triggers released, since doing so stops the motor.

Related CR report: July 2005

SNOW THROWERS

Bigger, better, and easier to use describe the latest imachines.

Some of the newest snow throwers are larger and more capable, yet easier to control. Many also cost less, thanks to price pressure from major retailers such as Home Depot, Lowe's, and Sears, which now account for about 60 percent of sales.

Two-stage models are the largest of these machines. Unlike smaller, single-stage models, which rely solely on a rubber-edged auger to move and disperse snow and provide some pulling power, two-stage models add drive wheels and a fanlike impeller to help disperse what they pick up.

You needn't buy the biggest snow thrower to get competent clearing. Honda and Toro are among the brands with single-stage models that rival some larger machines, yet weigh far less and require less storage space. Manufacturers are designing more-capable models for homeowners with smaller driveways as well as for women, who make at least part of the buying decisions in more than 30 percent of snow-thrower purchases.

Other advances in snow throwers include easier steering and chute controls. You'll also find easy-handling electric models for smaller driveways.

WHAT'S AVAILABLE

Major brands include Ariens, Craftsman (Sears), Honda, Husqvarna, John Deere,

Simplicity, Toro, Troy-Bilt, Yard Machines, and Yard-Man. While two-stage snow throwers all have a gas engine, single-stage models are sold in both gas and electric versions. Here are the pros and cons of each type:

Two-stage gas. Best for long, wide, or hilly driveways, with a typical snowfall over 8 inches. They're essential for gravel driveways, since the auger doesn't contact the ground. All offer electric starting and have driven wheels, an auger that gathers snow, and an impeller to throw it. Some clear a swath 28 to 30 inches wide. But two-stage gas models are relatively heavy, can take as much space as some lawn tractors, and require regular maintenance. And those without trigger-drive releases can be hard to maneuver. Price: $600 to $2,100.

Single-stage gas. Best for flat, midsize paved driveways and walks, with typical snowfall less than 8 inches. They're lighter and easier to handle, and take up about as much storage space as a mower. Most offer electric starting. But they're a poor choice for gravel, since the auger contacts the surface and can throw stones. Most clear a 20- to 22-inch swath. All lack drive wheels and require regular maintenance. The auger's limited drive action isn't enough for steep hills and can pull from side to side. Price: $300 to $900.

Single-stage electric. Best for short, flat driveways or decks and walks, with snowfall 4 inches or so. Single-stage electric models are lightest, smallest, and easiest to handle and store. They're also less noisy than gas-powered models, and their electric motors free you from fueling and other engine maintenance. But they're as unsuited to gravel driveways as single-stage gas snow throwers. Their small, 11- to 18-inch swath slows clearing. Electric machines also trade engine fueling and maintenance for the hassle of a power cord. Price: $100 to $300.

FEATURES THAT COUNT

A **one-handed drive/auger control** on two-stage models lets you engage the drive-wheel and auger-control levers with one hand, leaving the other free to control the chute. A growing number of new two-stage machines use **handlebar-mounted trigger releases** that ease steering by letting you quickly disconnect either or both wheels from the transmission on the fly, rather than having to stop and move a pin or lever at a wheel.

A **dead-man control** is an especially critical safety feature. It stops the spinning auger and, on two-stage models, the impeller when the handlebar-grip controls are released. Also look for a **clearing tool**—typically a plastic stick that is attached to the machine so it's handy for safely clearing clogs in the discharge chute or auger housing. Use a wooden broom handle, never hands or feet, on models without the tool.

Shop smart

Always use a fuel stabilizer in snow throwers. It will help them start after long periods of sitting idle.

Some snow throwers let you quickly change the chute direction and height of thrown snow via a **single-lever joystick** on two-stage machines or a long handle you can reach from the operator's position on single-stage models. That's easier than wrestling with two separate controls on many two-stage snow throwers, or the stiff, awkward discharge-chute handle on many single-stage models.

All electric models turn on with a switch, though most gas-powered models now offer **plug-in starting**—handy if you're near an outlet. All two-stage snow throwers have a four-stroke engine that requires periodic oil changes. Some single-stage models use a two-stroke engine that requires no oil changes, but entails mixing oil with the fuel. All gas snow throwers must meet the same emissions standards. **Headlights** for night use are an added nicety you'll now find on many two-stage machines.

HOW TO CHOOSE

Snow-throwing may be easier than shoveling, but it's harder than using a self-propelled mower. Consult a doctor before buying a snow thrower if you have hypertension, diabetes, or heart disease. Also consider having your driveway plowed if it's especially long and two or more cars wide. But if a snow thrower meets your needs, match the type to your space and climate and then consider these tips:

Try the controls. Independent dealers and even big-box stores typically have floor samples. Along with trigger releases on two-stage models, look for electric starting. Also be sure you're comfortable with the handle height and the chute adjustment, which you'll use frequently.

Don't get hung up on power claims. You'll find two-stage snow throwers with engines that boast 11 hp or more. But higher power claims don't necessarily mean more performance; some less-powerful machines in our most recent tests cleared snow on a par with the highest-horsepower models.

Some manufacturers and retailers are also pushing Briggs & Stratton engines vs. the usual Tecumseh powerplants. We found that the Tecumseh engines on most of these machines performed competently.

Don't get dazzled by drive speeds. Most two-stage machines have five or six forward speeds—useful for going slowly through heavy snow to prevent clogs, or quickly when returning to the garage. While the seven forward speeds on some two-stage models sound like a plus, we found them within the typical range for six-speed models.

Related CR report: October 2004

STRING TRIMMERS

Some of the latest electric trimmers perform better than ever. But gas models are still tops overall for tall grass and weeds.

A string trimmer can pick up where a lawn mower leaves off. It provides the finishing touches, slicing through tufts of grass around trees and flowerbeds, straightening uneven edges along a driveway, and trimming stretches of lawn your mower or tractor can't reach. While capable trimming and edging has required spending $100 or more for a gasoline-powered model, several plug-in trimmers provide both for less.

Edging is an especially demanding job that involves slicing vertically into the ground. Dual cutting lines like the ones on most gas-powered trimmers helped the best electrics edge and trim shorter grass about as well as the best gas models. But even the best plug-in trimmers can't match the best gas models in tall grass and weeds.

Faster starts, fewer tangles, and easier handling are among the string-trimmer features you'll find as manufacturers improve these tools. Some gas models from Echo, Stihl, and Troy-Bilt use a spring-assist system that makes pulling easier. More gas models also offer simplified 1-2-3 starting: Push the primer bulb, flip the choke lever, and pull the cord. Models that use it typically started with just one or two pulls. You can also avoid cutting-line jam-ups with a fixed-line head

that uses two precut pieces of cutting line. Lighter weight for electric and gas trimmers is another plus.

WHAT'S AVAILABLE

Black & Decker, Craftsman (Sears), Toro, and Weed Eater are the major brands of electric string trimmers, while Craftsman, Homelite, McCulloch, Ryobi, Troy-Bilt, and Weed Eater are the big names in gas-powered models. Leading high-end gas-trimmer brands include Bolens, Echo, Husqvarna, John Deere, and Stihl.

Gasoline-powered trimmers. These are better than electrics at cutting heavy weeds and brush, and are often better at edging. They also go anywhere, so they're the best choice if you'll be trimming far from a power outlet. On the downside, gas trimmers are heavier than electrics, weighing about 10 to 14 pounds. Most have a two-stroke engine that requires a mixture of gas and oil. These tend to pollute more than four-stroke engines, which burn gasoline only, and entail pull-starting and regular maintenance. Gas-powered trimmers are also noisy enough to make hearing protection necessary. Price: $50 to $200; $70 to $150 for most.

Corded electric trimmers. These are the least expensive and usually the lightest; many weigh only about 5 pounds. Some work about as well as gas trimmers for most trimming. All are quieter and easier to start than gas trimmers—you simply push a button rather than pulling a starter cord. The power cord limits your range to about 100 feet from an outlet, however. Models with the engine at the bottom of the shaft can be more difficult to manage than those with the engine at the top, near the handle. Corded electric trimmers are noisy enough to make hearing protection a necessity. And even the most powerful models are unlikely to handle the tall grass and weeds that the best gas-powered trimmers can tackle. Price: $20 to $100.

Electric battery-powered trimmers. Cordless trimmers combine the free range of gas trimmers with the convenience of corded electrics: Easy starting and stopping, no fueling, and no exhaust emissions. They're also the quietest overall. But they're weak at cutting and run only about 15 to 20 minutes before the onboard battery needs recharging, which can take up to a day. They also tend to be pricey and heavy for their performance (about 10 pounds). Some models have the motor at the bottom of the shaft, where it can be even harder to handle than it is on lighter, corded versions. Price: $30 to $100 or more.

> **Shop smart**
>
> Before you buy, adjust the front handle for comfort and hold the trimmer in the cutting position with both hands to gauge weight and balance.

FEATURES THAT COUNT

All trimmers have a **shaft** that connects the engine or motor and controls to the trimmer head, where the plastic lines revolve. **Curved shafts** are the most common and can be easier to handle when trimming up close. **Straight shafts** tend to be better for reaching beneath bushes and other shrubs, or if you are taller. Some models have a **split shaft** that comes apart so you can replace the trimmer head with a leaf blower, edging blade, or other yard tool, though we've found that most of these attachments aren't very effective.

Gas-powered trimmers have their engine on top, which helps balance the load in your hands. Many electric models have their motor on the bottom, down at the cutting head, though some have a **top-mounted motor.**

Most gas-powered trimmers and a growing number of electrics have two **cutting lines,** rather than one, which cuts less with each revolution. Most gas and electric trimmers have a **bump-feed line advance** that feeds out more line when you bump the trimmer head on the ground; a blade on the safety shield cuts it to the right length. Models with a **fixed-line head** use two strips of line instead of a spool, which isn't as convenient but eliminates tangles and jammed line.

Most gasoline models use **two-stroke engines,** which burn lubricating oil with the gasoline. A few trimmers use inherently cleaner **four-stroke engines,** but these tend to weigh and cost more. Corded and battery models typically use a 1.8- to 5-amp motor.

To start most gas trimmers, you set a **choke** and push a **primer bulb,** then pull a starter rope. On most models, you have to pull, prime, and adjust the choke several times before the engine starts. But some models use **spring-assisted starting** or have an easy **three-step starting system** that reduces the hassles and starts quicker.

On most gas trimmers, a **centrifugal clutch** allows the engine to idle without spinning the line—safer and more convenient than models where the line continues to turn. On trimmers without a clutch (usually less-expensive models), the string is spinning while the engine is running. Electric-trimmer lines don't spin until you press the switch.

Some models make edging more convenient with a **rotating head** that puts the trimmer head in the vertical position. Heavier-duty models often offer a **shoulder harness,** which can ease handling and reduce fatigue. Other convenient features include easy-to-reach and easy-to-adjust switches, comfortable handles, and—on gas models—a **translucent fuel tank.**

HOW TO CHOOSE

You don't have to invest in a pricey, professional-grade trimmer unless you need its metal-blade capability for cutting saplings and other woody waste. Most of the gas trimmers and even some electrics we tested can handle the grass and tall weeds that account for most trimming.

Determine whether a gas-powered or electric trimmer fits your needs. Then keep these points in mind while shopping at the store:

Consider the landscape. Trimmers with a straight shaft can reach beneath shrubs more easily and are less likely than curved-shaft ones to spatter you with clippings. Curved-shaft trimmers trade those benefits for easier maneuvering and, often, less weight—a plus for shorter users and those with less arm strength.

See how it feels. While a lighter trimmer tends to reduce fatigue, weight isn't the whole story. Good balance can be just as critical. To check it, adjust the front handle for comfort and hold the trimmer in the cutting position with both hands. Its weight should feel evenly distributed or slightly heavier at the top.

Also check that all the controls are smooth and easy to reach. If you're left-handed, make sure a gasoline-powered trimmer you're considering has a deflector that routes the hot exhaust gases rearward. Most now include one.

Check the gap. Tall grass and weeds can slow a trimmer by wrapping around the top of its cutting head, especially if there's a gap between it and the mounting for the grass-debris guard. Models with a smaller gap or a protective sleeve around the shaft avoided that problem in our tests.

Consider your neighbors. If they're close by, you may want to choose a corded or cordless electric trimmer. Nearly all the ones we tested are significantly less noisy than gasoline-powered models. If you opt for gas, protect your ears with earmuffs or plugs.

Related CR report: May 2006

VACUUM CLEANERS

High-priced, feature-laden machines don't necessarily deliver better cleaning. You'll find plenty of strong performers at a reasonable price.

Which type of vacuum cleaner to buy used to be a no-brainer. Uprights were clearly better for carpets, while canisters were the obvious choice for bare floors. That distinction has blurred somewhat as more upright models clean floors without scattering dust and more canisters do a very good job with carpeting. Central vacuum systems, a third option, add a measure of convenience but at higher prices.

You'll also see a growing number of features such as dirt sensors and bagless dirt bins, but some of those features may contribute more to price than to function, while other, more essential features may be missing from the least-expensive models. And while cordless and even robotic vacuums have joined your list of choices, neither have been top performers so far.

WHAT'S AVAILABLE

Hoover, the oldest and largest vacuum manufacturer, has experienced declining sales of late. Other players include Dirt Devil, which sells uprights and canisters as well as stick brooms and hand vacuums; Bissell, a mostly mass-marketed brand; Eureka, which offers low-priced models, central vacs, and high-end Electrolux-branded models; Dyson, a high-priced British brand with a brightly colored lineup; Oreck models, which are sold in their own stores and directly by the company; and Kenmore, the biggest name in canister models, accounting for about 20 percent of U.S. sales.

Additional brands such as Miele, Panasonic, and Riccar are likely to be sold at specialty stores. Higher-priced Aerus (which also makes central vacs) is sold in its own stores and by direct mail; upscale Kirby is still sold door-to-door. You'll also find Roomba, the robotic vac, and Euro-Pro stick vacs.

Along with the brand of vacuum, your choices include several types:

Uprights. These models, which account for the majority of vacuum sales, tend to be the least expensive. Their one-piece design also makes them easier to store than canister vacs. A top-of-the-line upright might provide a wider cleaning path, be self-propelled, and have a HEPA filter, dirt sensor, and full-bag indicator. Price range for most: $50 to $400, with the highest-priced models priced at more than $1,300.

Canister vacuums. These types tend to do well on bare floors because they allow you to turn off the brush or use a specialized tool to avoid scattering dirt. Most are quieter than uprights, and their long, flexible hose tends to make them better at cleaning stairs and in hard-to-reach areas. The added clutter of the loose hose and wand makes canisters somewhat harder to store, however. While canister vacs still tend to cost the most, you'll find a growing number of lower-priced models. Price range for most: $150 to $500, with the most-expensive ones costing $1,000 to $1,500.

Central vac systems. These models clean like a canister vac without your having to push, pull, or carry the motor and body around. They're also relatively quiet and require less-frequent emptying. But they're the most expensive option, and generally require professional installation. The typical 35-foot-long hose can be cumbersome, and you don't have a place to carry tools while you work. Price range: $500 to $1,250 for the unit including tools, plus $300 to $750 to install.

Stick vacs and hand vacs. Whether corded or cordless, these miniature vacuums typically lack the power of a full-sized unit. But they can be handy for small, quick jobs. Price: $20 to $100.

FEATURES THAT COUNT

Typical attachments include **crevice** and **upholstery tools.** Most vacuums also include **extension wands** for reaching high places. A **full-bag alert** can be handy, since an overstuffed bag impairs the cleaning ability of a vacuum.

Many uprights now feature a **bagless** configuration with a **see-through dirt bin** that replaces the usual bag. Performance has improved for bagless vacs, though emptying their bins can raise enough dust to cause concern even if you don't have allergies. You'll also find dirt-collection bins on most stick vacs and hand vacs. Some of these have a **revolving brush,** which might help remove surface debris from a carpet. Stick vacs can hang on a hook or, if they're cordless, on a wall-mounted charger base.

Canister vacuums we've tested have a **power nozzle** that cleans carpets more thoroughly than a simple suction nozzle. Look for a **suction-control feature.** Found on most canisters and some uprights, it allows you to reduce airflow for drapes and other delicate fabrics. On uprights, also look for an **on/off switch for the brush** if you plan to use attachments. Stopping the brush protects you from injury, the power cord from damage, and your furnishings from undue wear. Some uprights automatically stop the brush when the handle is in the up position.

Most canisters and a few uprights have a **retractable cord** that rewinds with a tug or push of a button—a plus, considering the 20- to 30-foot length for most. Another worthwhile feature is **manual pile-height adjustment,** which can improve cleaning by letting you match the height of the vacuum to the carpet pile more effectively than machines that adjust automatically. While a self-propelled mode takes the push out of more and more uprights, it can make them heavier and harder to transport.

Midpriced **accessory kits for central vacs** typically include an electrically powered cleaning head—a must for carpets— as well as a floor brush, crevice tool, upholstery brush, dusting brush, and extension wands. Spending more gets you more tools, a premium powerhead, and a longer hose. A sound-deadening **muffler,** installed in the exhaust air pipe near the central-vac base unit, comes on some models; it can be added to any model for about $10 to $25. Most central vacs have a **suction switch** at the wand handle so you can turn the vacuum unit on and off where you're standing.

Some vacuums have a **dirt sensor** that triggers a light indicator when the concentration of dirt particles in the machine's air stream reaches a certain level. But the sensor signals only that the vacuum is no longer picking up dirt, not whether there's dirt left in your rug. That can result in your vacuuming longer and working harder with little or no more cleanliness.

You'll also hear lots of claims about **microfiltration,** which typically uses a bag with smaller pores or a second electrostatic filter that supplements the standard motor filter in an attempt to capture fine particles that may pass through the bag or filter and escape into the air through the exhaust.

Some vacuums have a **HEPA filter,** which may benefit someone with asthma. But many models without a HEPA filter have performed just as well in CONSUMER REPORTS emissions tests, since the amount of dust emitted depends as much on the design of the entire machine as on its filter.

The design of a vacuum can also affect how long it lasts. With some uprights, for example, dirt sucked into the machine passes through the blower fan before entering the bag—a potential problem because most fans are plastic and vulnerable to damage from hard objects. Better systems filter dirt through the bag before it reaches the fan. While hard objects can lodge in the motorized brush, they probably won't break the fan.

HOW TO CHOOSE

Some of the best vacuums cost $350 or less. But you might be willing to spend more for models with other strengths. Here's what to think about at the store:

Match the vacuum to your cleaning. Most uprights are still better than canisters for carpets. They also cost less and are easier to store. Canisters tend to be better for cleaning drapes, upholstery, and under furniture, are more stable on stairs.

Consider suction. Look for models that performed well in our airflow tests if you often clean with tools. These vacuums maintained more suction through the hose as they filled with dust, reducing the need to change bags and empty bins.

Pick your features. Models with bags tend to hold more than bagless vacs and create less dust when emptying. A brush on/off switch allows you to turn off the brush on floors and delicate rugs, and reduces dust and the risk of thrown objects when using tools. Manual pile-height adjustment can improve carpet cleaning by letting you raise or lower the powerhead.

Don't be dazzled by gadgets. Most vacuums include a narrow crevice tool, a small brush for upholstery, and a round one for dusting—enough for most users. Hand tools with powered brushes tend to add little over nonpowered tools when removing pet hair from upholstery.

Try before buying. Weight can be critical if your arms aren't strong or your home has more than one level. Self-propelled uprights ease pushing and pulling, though their added heft makes lifting and storing more challenging.

Protect your ears and lungs. Vacuums that scored a poor in our noise tests produced 85 decibels or more, the level at which we recommend ear protection. If you're sensitive to dust, choose a model that scored well in emissions. You also might want to avoid buying a bagless model. If you do, purchase a bagless type, wear a dust mask when emptying the bin.

Related CR report: October 2006
Ratings: page 325
Reliability: page 336

Computers, Phones, and Peripherals

Computers, Phones, & Peripherals: Portable and Versatile

Faster. Lighter. More powerful. These are the constant imperatives for computing and mobile communications gear makers and users alike. The latest laptops and cell phones offer unprecedented connectedness that even James Bond would admire. Chip speeds, network improvements, and design innovation are driving spectacular growth in digital capabilities. Where the smallest devices once commanded premium pricing, now smaller is often cheaper, too.

A sign of the times: more laptops are being bought by consumers than ever before. Desktop computers are becoming commodity products, with prices as low as $300 for speedy models. Starting at $400, laptops at all price points can challenge their desktop counterparts on speed and capability. And why remain tethered to a power cord and network cabling when Wi-Fi wireless connectivity beckons? (For those who prefer the heft and expandability of desktop computers, larger, thinner monitors with widescreen proportions are changing the look of home offices and living rooms.)

Among other trends shaping computing and communications hardware, you'll find:

Cell phones sizzle. Mobile telephony is no longer just a matter of voice and text messaging. Most new cell phones allow you to check e-mail, browse the Web, play games, and take photos. Wireless video and TV can use improvement, but models that double as MP3 players are handy hybrids. Top-of-the-line models called smart phones combine personal digital assistant (PDA) capabilities with mobile phoning so you can make voice calls or directly connect to the Internet at near wired broadband speeds.

Cordless phones go cell-like. Some cordless phones can tap into cell-phone service as well as resemble a cell phone. For greater security, new cordless phones use higher frequency bands. A growing number can handle multiple handsets from a single base, even if phone jacks are scarce. Some cordless models connect directly to VoIP (Voice over Internet Protocol) telephone service, for added savings.

A new vista on computing. The latest version of Microsoft's PC operating system software, Windows Vista, is to be released in early 2007. A new version of Mac OSX (Leopard) is also expected around that time. Computer shoppers in 2006 will want to consider their new systems' compatibility with either Vista's basic or enhanced capabilities. Most computers sold today can run elementary Vista, but the graphics technology necessary for Vista Home Premium is available only on higher end machines.

Practice safe cyber. CONSUMER REPORTS' latest look at the State of the Net found that your odds of becoming a cybervictim are about 1 in 3, the same as a year ago. Because of viruses and spyware, American consumers spent at least $7.8 billion for computer repairs, parts, and replacements over the past two years, according to the third annual survey of online activity and threats conducted by the Consumer Reports National Research Center. If you go online, always run updated firewall, antivirus, and antispyware software.

CELL PHONES

Complex pricing schemes and incompatible technologies can make it hard to find the right calling plan to go with the right handset.

There are now more than 200 million cell-phone subscribers, an average of more than one per household. Of those, close to 10 percent use a cell phone (aka a mobile phone) as their only phone, and that number is steadily growing. Phone manufacturers and wireless-service providers are promoting new generations of equipment that let users do much more than merely make phone calls.

Despite its popularity, wireless service has a reputation for problems: dead zones, where you can't get service; calls that inexplicably end in midconversation; inadequate capacity, so you can't put a call through when you want; hard-to-fathom calling plans; and errors in bills. Problems like those are why one-third of the cell-phone users we surveyed said they're seriously considering switching carriers.

Switching is now easier than ever, thanks to the government mandate on local number portability. Keep in mind, though, that the phones themselves aren't portable. If you switch carriers, expect to buy a new phone.

WHAT'S AVAILABLE

You can find cell phones in many outlets, including carrier stores, independent wireless retailers, electronics stores, and Web sites. But the cell phone itself is only part of what you need. You also have to sign up for service with a wireless provider and choose a calling plan.

The providers. The major national companies are Cingular (which merged with AT&T Wireless), Sprint Nextel (two major carriers whose merger became final in 2005), T-Mobile, and Verizon Wireless. There are also many local or regional providers.

You'll often find phones described as trimode, dual-band, quad- or tri-band, or multinetwork. Those terms describe the ways a phone can connect to one or more wireless networks, which affects the coverage your phone provides. Here are the specifics:

• Tri-mode phones can access a digital network in two frequency bands and older analog wireless networks, giving you the best potential coverage in most areas of the U.S.

• Dual-band phones can connect to a digital network in two different frequency bands. GSM (global system for mobile) providers often use the term 850/1900 MHz instead of dual-band. Dual-band phones work as well as tri-mode as long as you are in range of your home network.

• Multinetwork phones are compatible with more than one digital network, often in two frequency bands. Some can also access analog networks. These are best for people who travel frequently overseas and who are customers of Sprint Nextel or Verizon. Both Sprint Nextel and Verizon offer multinetwork phones that operate on GSM networks internationally. They also work domestically on their CDMA (code division multiple access) networks (for the Sprint and Verizon phones) or iDEN (integrated digital enhanced network) networks for the Nextel phones.

• Tri-band, quad-band, or "world phones" operate on GSM networks in both the U.S. and abroad. Tri-band phones with 850/1800/1900MHz capability can operate on two bands domestically and one internationally. Tri-band phones with 900/1800/1900MHz capability operate on one band in the U.S. (1900MHz) and two bands internationally. Quad-band phones can operate on all four bands for maximum potential coverage.

The calling plans. Most providers offer a range of plans based around a "bucket" of calling time minutes. The more minutes in the bucket, the more the plan costs you each month. However, the total number of minutes isn't the most important figure. Some of those minutes may be good anytime, others available only on nights and weekends. If you exceed the allotment of minutes, you'll be charged 20 to 50 cents per minute, depending on the plan. Cingular and Sprint Nextel let you avoid wasting unused minutes by either rolling them over to the next month or adjusting your monthly quota. Most plans require you to sign a one- or two-year contract and will levy a hefty fee if you want to cancel before the contract expires.

Prepaid plans can be a good choice if you're averse to a long-term contract. Many wireless providers, as well as Liberty Wireless, Metro PCS, TracFone, and Virgin Mobile, offer prepaid calling. You pay in advance for airtime minutes, which typically last 45 to 60 days before they expire.

The phones. The major phone manufacturers are Kyocera, LG, Motorola, Nokia, Samsung, Sanyo, Sony-Ericsson, and UTS-Starcom (formerly Audiovox). Some phones are simple rectangles with a display window and keypad on the front. Most have a flip-open cover to protect the keys. Light weight is pretty much standard. All the newer phones can send and receive text messages up to 160 characters long to or from any other cell-phone user, and most phones now come with a full-color display. Phones equipped with cameras allow you to send and receive picture messages from other people, even if they're not on your network. You'll also see phones that can play games, offer wireless Internet access, or are combined with a personal digital assistant (PDA). Music and video programming from cell carriers are becoming increasingly common, and live TV via cell phone has also been launched, with more services coming.

FEATURES THAT COUNT

Most service providers now offer Internet access and multimedia services using new high-speed data networks and selected phones. Sprint's Power Vision network and Verizon's V CAST network use an advanced CDMA format known as EV-DO (Evolution, Data Only) to boost transmission speeds. These networks comprise what is commonly known as 3G. Cingular uses an enhancement to its GSM network known as EDGE (Enhanced Data for Global Evolution). Some services, such as Verizon's V CAST video and Sprint's Music Store, are only available through the enhanced networks. Other services, such as e-mail and

> **Tech tip**
>
> Most cell phones have a vibrating alert or a flashing light-emitting diode to let you know about an incoming call, which is useful when you're in a meeting or at the movies.

Internet access, are available without having to access the enhanced networks, but tasks like Web browsing are much slower. One caveat: The newer networks aren't available in all areas of the country, so check your carrier's coverage maps before you upgrade your phone and plan.

Among basic cell-phone features, look for a **display** that is readable in both low- and bright-light conditions. Be sure it's easy to see the battery-life and signal-strength indicators and the number you're dialing. The **keypad** should be clearly marked and easy to use. **Single-key last-number redial** is useful for dropped calls or when you're having trouble connecting. Most phones these days have voice dial, which lets you dial someone's phone number by speaking their name. But the number and name have to be in your phone's contact list, and you have to program each voice-dial name—a time-consuming process. **Voice command-enabled phones** don't require training. You can dial anyone's number in your contact list, and even dial a number not in the list by speaking the digits.

In addition to ringing, most handsets have a **vibrating alert** or a flashing, light-emitting diode to let you know about an incoming call, useful when you're in a meeting or at the movies. Handiest is an **easy-to-mute ringer,** which switches from ring to vibrate when you press and hold one key. **Volume controls** on the side let you change the earpiece volume level without moving the phone too far from your ear. You can't do that if the volume controls are on the keypad. A **speaker phone** boosts the earpiece volume and microphone sensitivity, so you can carry on a conversation without having the phone against your ear.

Some cell-phone models include a **headset.** That capability is sometimes required by local laws for drivers using cell phones. A **standard headset connector** (also known as

a 2.5-mm jack) is the most common type. Phones with this connector are compatible with a wider variety of wired headsets. If you frequently use a headset but hate fussing with cords, consider a phone with Bluetooth voice capability, which allows you to use a cordless headset. Not all phones with Bluetooth are equal. **Bluetooth data** lets you transfer items like pictures and contacts to other Bluetooth-enabled devices like printers, PDAs, and computers. Bluetooth data capability is found on GSM phones but not always on CDMA phones.

Many CDMA phones have **analog back-up** capability, which may be important if you travel through rural areas or places where your digital carrier doesn't provide service. Phones with analog capability can sometimes connect in places where digital-only phones cannot.

Phones vary widely in keypad design, readability of screen displays, and ease of using the function menu or performing basic tasks like one-button redial and storage of frequently called numbers for speed-dialing later. It's important to handle a phone in the store before you buy, to be sure that its design and your fingers are well matched.

HOW TO CHOOSE

Begin by selecting a service. Finding good service where you want it can be a challenge. The best way is to ask your friends and business associates—people who literally travel the same roads you do—how satisfied they are with their cell-phone service. In addition, keep in mind that Verizon Wireless has consistently come in first in CONSUMER REPORTS satisfaction surveys and is worth considering first if it's offered in your area.

Choose a calling plan. You need to determine when and where you'll be using a cell phone most in order to select a plan that's right for you. As a rule, a national calling plan (which typically eliminates extra long-distance charges or fees for "roaming" from your home calling area) is worth considering first, even if you don't travel often. With a regional plan, roaming charges can add up if you make calls too far away from your home. No matter which carrier you choose, take advantage of any trial period to test the service and sign up for the shortest contract available, usually one year.

If two or more family members use cell phones, consider a plan that lets up to four people share a large monthly pool of minutes for a smaller additional monthly charge. If you aren't sure how many minutes of phone time you'll use in a month, choose a plan with more minutes than you think you will use. It's often better to let minutes go unused than to have to pay stiff per-minute charges if you exceed your allotment.

Select a phone. You can spend as little as $20 or as much as $600 on a cell phone. Once you've settled on a price range, follow these steps:

• First look for practical features. Cameras, games, music players, and the like are appealing, fun, and even useful for some people. But features such as a folding case, volume controls on the side, and an easy-to-mute ringer will prove useful every day.

• Hold the phone. In the store, take the phone in your hand and make sure you can comfortably access most keys with one hand. Try to make a test call and access the menu items on a working demo. We've found that phones with unconventional shapes can be difficult to use. So are keys that are small, oddly shaped, or arranged in unusual patterns, especially if you're trying to dial a number in dim light.

• Check the display. Most color screens perform well in dim light, but some are hard to see in daylight. Try the phone outside or under bright light. In our tests, phones that display incoming and outgoing numbers with large black type against a white background were the easiest to read under most conditions. Also make sure indicators for battery life and signal strength are clearly visible.

• Check the return policy. Make sure you can return the phone if you're not happy with it. Some stores attach stiff service-cancellation fees on top of what a carrier may charge.

• Don't buy phone insurance. All major cell carriers provide insurance policies that cover lost, stolen, or damaged phones, typically for about $4 to $6 a month, with a $35 to $100 deductible. But we don't think those are worth buying. Besides charging for premiums and deductibles, some insurance plans require you to fill out a police report. And damaged phones are often replaced with a refurbished phone, perhaps not even the same model as the original.

Related CR report: January 2006
Ratings: Page 239

CORDLESS PHONES

Two noteworthy trends: Phones use higher frequency bands, and a growing number can handle multiple handsets from a single base.

It's easier than ever to have a phone where you want one. The newest breed of cordless phone lets you put a handset in any room in the house, even if no phone jack is nearby.

WHAT'S AVAILABLE

AT&T, GE, Panasonic, Uniden, and VTech account for most of the market. VTech owns the AT&T Consumer Products

Division and now makes phones under the AT&T brand as well as its own name.

Current trends include phones that support two or more handsets with one base, less expensive 2.4- and 5.8-GHz analog phones, and full-featured 2.4- and 5.8-GHz digital phones. More than a third of the cordless phones sold include a digital answering machine. Price: $15 and up for single-handset phones, $50 and up with built-in answering machine; $25 and up for multiple-handset phones, $80 and up with built-in answering machine.

The newest phones, called DECT, short for Digitally Enhanced Cordless Telecommunication, use the 1.9-GHz band that the Federal Communications Commission reserved in 2005 for voice-only applications. By using this exclusive frequency band, DECT phones avoid interference problems caused by home networks and other wireless devices. Other phones use wireless Bluetooth technology to tap into your mobile phone service, allowing you to make and take calls over either service.

FEATURES THAT COUNT

Standard features on most cordless phones include a handset earpiece volume control, handset ringer, last-number redial, a pager to locate the handset, a flash button to answer call waiting, and a low-battery indicator. Some phones let you support two or more handsets with just one base without the need for extra phone jacks. Additional handsets, including the charging cradle, can be sold separately, although more phones are being bundled with an additional handset and charging cradle.

An **LCD screen**, found on many handsets and on some bases, can display a personal phone directory and useful information such as the name and/or number dialed, caller ID, battery strength, or how long you've been connected. **Caller ID** displays the name and number of a caller and the date and time of the call if you use your phone company's caller ID service. If you have caller ID with **call waiting**, the phone will display data on a second caller when you're already on the phone.

A phone that supports **two lines** can receive calls for two phone numbers—useful if you have, say, a business line and a personal line that you'd like to use from a single phone. Some of the phones have **two ringers**, each with a distinctive pitch to let you know which line is ringing. The two-line feature also facilitates **conferencing** two callers in three-way connections. Some two-line phones have an **auxiliary jack data port** to plug in a fax, modem, or other phone device that can also be useful.

A **speaker phone** offers a hands-free way to converse or wait on hold and lets others chime in as well. A **base speaker phone** lets you answer a call without the handset; a **handset speaker phone** lets you chat hands-free anywhere in the house as long as you stay within a few feet of the handset.

A **base keypad** supplements the keypad on the handset. It's handy for navigating menu-driven systems, since you don't have to take the phone away from your ear to punch the keys. Some phones have a **lighted keypad** that either glows in the dark or lights up when you press a key, or when the phone rings. All phones have a **handset ringer**, and many phones have a **base ringer**. Some let you turn them on or off, adjust the volume, or change the auditory tone.

Many cordless phones have a **headset jack** on the handset and include a **belt clip** for carrying the phone. This allows hands-free conversation anywhere in the house. Some phones have a headset jack on the base, which allows hands-free conversation without any drain on the handset battery. Headsets are usually sold separately for about $20.

Other convenient features include **auto-talk**, which lets you lift the handset off the base for an incoming call and start talking without having to press a button, and any key answer. Some phones have a **side-volume control** on the handset conveniently placing the control for adjusting volume while you're on a call.

Some phones provide a **battery holder for battery backup**—a compartment in the base to charge a spare handset battery pack or to hold alkaline batteries for base-power backup, either of which can enable the phone to work if you lose household AC power. Still, it's wise to keep a corded phone somewhere in your home.

Some multiple-handset capable phones allow conversation between handsets in an **intercom** mode and facilitate conferencing handsets with an outside party. In intercom mode, the handsets have to be within range of the base for handset-to-handset use. Others lack this handset-to-handset talk capability; they allow you to transfer calls from handset to handset but not to use the handsets to conference with an outside caller. Still other phones allow direct communication between handsets, so you can take them with you to use like walkie-talkies.

Some phones have **Caller ID alerts**. A phone with **distinctive ring capability** allows you to hear who is calling by associating the calling number with a specific ring tone. Some are visual, so you can tell who's calling by the handset display or the antenna flashing a particular color. Phones with **talking Caller ID**, or also referred to as Caller ID announce, speak the name of the caller, useful since you don't have to view the display to know who's calling.

Most phone-answerers have one **mailbox**. Some answerers have several mailboxes where a caller can direct a voice message to an individual family member, or to separate business and personal calls, for instance. This allows the convenience of listening to messages meant just for you.

Most answerers can skip to the next message, skip back to a previous message, and repeat a message. Some also have advanced playback controls such as fast playback (to listen to messages more quickly), slow playback (to slow down a part of the message, say to understand a phone number), and rewind (to go back to part of a message).

Some have an audible message alert, typically a beep, which lets you know you have new messages without having to look at the answerers' visual new message indicator.

Some have **remote handset** that allows you to listen to messages from the handset and may allow access to other answerer functions, such as recording your greeting; this offers more privacy and convenience.

HOW TO CHOOSE

Choose analog or digital technology. A main distinction among cordless phones is the way they transmit their signals. Here are some terms that you may see while shopping and what they mean for you.

Analog phones are the least expensive type and tend to have better voice quality than digital models, though their range is somewhat shorter. They are also unlikely to cause interference with other wireless products. But analog transmission isn't very secure; anyone with an RF scanner or comparable wireless device might be able to listen in. Analog phones are also more likely than digital phones to suffer occasional static and RF interference from other wireless products. Also, multiple-handset capable phones can't conference handsets with an outside party, and the number of handsets that can be supported by the base unit is typically limited to two.

Digital phones provide an added measure of security and more immunity to RF interference. Their range may be slightly better than that of analog phones. Some digital models support up to 10 handsets from one base and allow conferencing of handsets.

To be sure you're actually getting a digital model, check the packaging carefully. Look for wording such as "digital phone," "digital spread spectrum (DSS)," "frequency-hopping spread spectrum (FHSS)," or digitally enhanced cordless telecommunication or telephone (DECT). Phrases such as "phone with digital security code," "phone with all-digital answerer," or "spread spectrum technology" (not digital spread spectrum) all denote phones that are less secure.

Pick a frequency. Cordless phones use one or two of the four available frequency bands: 1.9, 2.4, or 5.8GHz, and 900MHz. Most phones are dual-band, which means they transmit between base and handset in one frequency band and receive in another; you can't switch to or choose one band or another. Most phones use the 5.8- and 2.4-GHz frequency bands. Since 1.9-GHz phones are new, only a few are currently available. A few manufacturers still make inexpensive, 900-MHz phones, usually analog. They are fine for many households, but they are dwindling. This band is now mainly used along with 5.8- or 2.4-GHz analog transmission dual-band phones.

Phones that use the 2.4-GHz band, unfortunately, share their frequency with many other wireless products, including baby monitors, wireless computer networks, home security monitors, wireless speakers, and microwaves ovens. Analog phones that use the 2.4-GHz band are inherently susceptible to RF interference from these devices, while their digital counterparts may actually interfere with them. Some digital phones use portions of the 2.4-GHz band that are less likely to interfere or be interfered with by wireless home networks. These are billed as "wireless network friendly" or "802.11-friendly."

Decide on number of extensions. A single-handset phone is best suited for smaller homes where you're never far from the phone. If your home is too large for that, give first consideration to multiple-handset phones, which support (and usually include) multiple handsets from one base; each extra handset sits in its own charging cradle, without the need of a phone jack, making it easier to station the handset where you want it.

Settle on the features you want. You can expect caller ID, a headset jack, and a base that can be wall-mounted. As a rule, the more feature-laden the phone, the higher its price.

Decide which performance nuances matter most to you. Our tests show that most new cordless phones have very good overall voice quality. Some are excellent, approaching the voice quality of the best corded phones. In our latest tests, most fully charged batteries provided an ample eight hours or more of continuous conversation before they needed recharging. Most manufacturers claim that a fully charged battery will hold its charge at least a week in standby mode. When the battery can no longer hold a charge, a replacement battery, usually proprietary, costs about $10 to $25. Some phones use less-expensive AA or AAA rechargeable batteries. (To find stores that recycle used cordless phone batteries, call 800-822-8837 or go to the Rechargeable Battery Recycling Corp.'s site at *www.rbrc.org*. Our Web site *www.GreenerChoices.org* also has advice on this topic.)

Decide whether you want an answerer. Many people still do, despite the ubiquity of cell phones with voice-mail capability. Both single- and multiple-handset phones come in versions with a built-in answerer. Such phones often cost little more than comparable phone-only models and take up about the same space. If you're considering an answerer, you need to make these two additional decisions:

Consider voice-quality differences. In our tests, most answerers delivered very good voice quality for recorded messages and good quality for the greeting. Phones that let you record your greeting through the handset (using the remote handset access) usually sounded better. Some let you listen to your greeting through the handset, as opposed to listening through the base speaker; that gives you a better indication of how the greeting will sound to the calling party.

Choose features. Answerers usually have standard features and capabilities such as a selectable number of rings and a toll-saver, answerer on/off control, call screening, remote access, speaker-volume control, and a variety of ways to navigate through your messages. Most have one mailbox, a message day/time stamp, a message-counter display that indicates the number of messages received, and a visual indicator that lets you know you have new messages. During a momentary power outage, most will retain messages and the greeting.

Don't discard your corded phones. It's a good idea to keep at least one corded phone in your home, if only for emergencies. A cordless phone may not work if you lose electrical power, and a cell phone won't work if you can't get a signal or the circuits are full. A corded phone draws its power from the phone system and can function without household AC power.

Make sure you can return it. Before buying, check the return policy in case you encounter unexpected problems at home that you can't resolve, like wireless interference.

Related CR report: October 2005

DESKTOP COMPUTERS

Even the least-expensive desktops can deliver impressive performance.

For most users, the desktop computer has become just another appliance you use every day. Replacement sales—not first-time purchases—now drive the desktop computer market. Fully loaded desktops selling for less than $700 are common, even among established brands. When choosing a model, it's hard to go too far wrong; the performance of today's computers are uniformly high.

That is why differences in reliability and technical support matter more than ever. Repair rates for computers are higher than for most products we track, based on respondents to our Annual Questionnaire. You increase your chances of getting a reliable computer by choosing brands that have proven reliable in the past.

Technical support might be a deciding factor in which manufacturer gets your business. Tech support remains a hot-button issue judging from our latest subscriber survey of computer users. Apple has maintained its lead in tech support, while other brands continue to show only so-so performance and face some chronic support woes.

Our subscribers still say that tech support is dismal. The most serious complaint from our questionnaire is that the support people simply can't solve the problem. Major complaints about phone support included being kept on hold too long, being bounced around among support staff, and communication problems. Support via e-mail or the manufacturer's Web site was also lacking.

WHAT'S AVAILABLE

There are eight major brands to choose from. Computers from Dell, Compaq, eMachines, Gateway (which owns eMachines), Hewlett-Packard (which owns Compaq), Lenovo (formerly branded as IBM), and Sony all use Microsoft's Windows operating system. Apple is the sole maker of Macintosh models. (A new generation of Macs released in 2006 can run Windows as well as Apple's own OS X operating system). Many small mail-order and store brands also cater to budget-minded buyers. Price: $300 to $3,000.

FEATURES THAT COUNT

The **processor** houses the "brains" of a computer. Its clock speed, measured in gigahertz (GHz), and the chip's design, termed "architecture," determine how fast it can process information. Within a processor family, the higher the clock speed, the faster the computer.

But different processor families attain different efficiencies. Pentium 4 processors have the higher speed ratings; other desktop single-processor families, such as Celeron D, Athlon 64, and Sempron, have a slower-rated speed but actually perform on a par with Pentium 4 processors. Dual-core processor families have been introduced recently by Intel (Core Duo) and AMD (Athlon 64 X2). These represent the newest technologies developed to increase processing power beyond what a single-chip processor can achieve.

Macs have transitioned to Intel core-series processors. In short, the different types of processors make direct speed comparisons difficult, but any type of processor is likely to deliver all the speed you'll need.

All brand-name computers sold today have at least 256 megabytes (MB) of RAM, or **random-access memory,** the memory the computer uses while in operation.

Memory upgrades are not expensive. For most users, 512MB is plenty, but 1024MB can speed things up for advanced users or those who want to be ready for the Windows Vista operating system due out in early 2007. Video RAM, also measured in megabytes, is secondary RAM that works with the graphics processor to provide smooth video imaging and game play. Gamers may want 128MB or even 256MB.

The **hard drive** is your computer's long-term data storage system. Given the disk-space requirements of today's multimedia games, digital photos, and video files, bigger is better. Sizes range from 40 to 500 gigabytes (GB).

Commonly supplied is a **CD-RW (CD-rewriteable) drive,** also known as a "burner," that lets you create backup files or make music compilations on a compact disc. A DVD-ROM drive brings full-length movies or action-packed multimedia games with full-motion video to the desktop. It complements the burner on midline and higher-end systems, allowing you to copy CDs directly between the two drives.

A **DVD drive** will also play CDs and CD-ROMs. Combo drives combine CD-writing and DVD-playing in a single drive, saving money and space. The newest in this family, rapidly becoming a common choice, is the DVD writer, which lets you transfer home-video footage to a DVD disc, or store as much data as six CDs.

There are three competing, incompatible DVD formats—DVD-RW, DVD+RW, and DVD-RAM—as well as drives that can create dual-layer DVDs that store twice as much. Some drives can write in more than one format, but all can create a disk that

> **Shop smart**
>
> The bigger the hard drive, the better for the long term. You'll find hard drives ranging from 40 to 300 gigabytes.

will play on stand-alone DVD players. Just arriving: DVD burners with new technology designed for high-definition video, which will allow storing 25GB or more on a disk. We recommend waiting until the two competing versions—Blu-ray and HD DVD—sort out their differences.

Many PCs now come with a memory-card reader that can also serve for file transfer. You can also get external drives or use a USB memory module to copy files from the hard drive.

The computer's flat-panel **liquid-crystal display (LCD)** or **cathode-ray tube (CRT) monitor** contains the display screen and renders the images sent from the graphics processor—internal circuitry that creates the images. Monitors come in sizes (measured diagonally) ranging from 15 to 21 inches and larger. Seventeen-inch LCD monitors are the most common.

Apple's iMac comes with a built-in monitor, while its Mac Mini doesn't have one. LCD displays are now the most popular, taking up less space and using less power than CRTs. Better LCD displays can use a Digital Video Interface (DVI) connection, found on many newer PCs. You might obtain a substantial discount on an LCD monitor by buying it bundled with a new computer at a manufacturer's Web site.

All computers have a **graphics adapter**, which might be integrated on the motherboard or on a separate, internal plug-in card. In addition to feeding the computer's display with an analog (VGA) or sometimes a digital (DVI) connection, a graphics adapter may have an additional output to feed video to an external TV (common), or accept video from an external analog source (less common). But it can always display video from whatever source it comes: a file, a DVD, an external analog feed, or a TV tuner.

At minimum, all desktops and laptops come with integrated graphics suitable for watching videos or playing simple games like Solitaire. If you want to run Windows Vista's new 3D user interface or play more challenging 3D intensive games, like the Sims or World of Warcraft, we recommend the ATI Radeon X1600, the Nvidia GeForce 7600, or higher.

The critical components of a desktop computer are usually housed in a case called a **tower.** A minitower is the typical configuration and can fit either on top of or under a desk. More expensive machines have a midtower, which has extra room for upgrades. A microtower is a space-saving alternative but has less room inside for upgrading. All-in-one computers, such as the Apple iMac, have no tower; everything but the keyboard and mouse is built into the monitor. Apple's Power Mac line of computers has a tower. Apple's least-costly desktop model, the Mac Mini, has a space-saving design that puts everything but the monitor, keyboard, and mouse in a case about the size of a hardcover book. Macs are more user-friendly than comparable Windows PCs, and some versions include a DVD writer.

An **"entertainment PC"**—one with a TV tuner built in—comes in a case that is more like an audio or video component, made to fit with other home-entertainment devices. Some computer makers, including Dell and HP, offer Microsoft's Windows Media Center Edition (MCE) as a standard operating system (or for a small fee) on desktops priced about $500 and above. Media Center's main advantage over other versions of Windows is its simpler interface for playing DVDs, CDs, and MP3s and for viewing photos and video. It can also "serve" this content to an Xbox 360 game system. One of MCE's features, a TiVo-like onscreen guide that can find and record TV programs, is useful only if your PC is equipped for TV broadcasts. A TV tuner and remote are typically a $100 option.

A **mouse,** a small device that fits under your hand and has a "tail" of wire that connects to the computer, moves the cursor (the pointer on the screen) via a rolling ball or a light sensor on its underside. Alternative input devices include a trackball, which is rolled with the fingers in the direction you want the cursor to go; a pad, which lets you move the cursor by sliding a finger; a tablet, which uses a penlike stylus for input; and a game pad, used to play computer games.

Most computers come with a **standard keyboard,** although you can also buy one separately. Many keyboards have CD (or DVD) controls to pause, playback, change tracks, and so on. Many also have keys to facilitate getting online, starting a search, launching programs, or retrieving e-mail. There are also **wireless keyboards** and mice that give you flexibility in how you work.

Computers for home use feature a high-fidelity **sound system** that plays music from CDs or downloaded music files, synthesized music, game sounds, and DVD-movie soundtracks. Some have a subwoofer for deeper, more powerful bass. Surround-sound systems can turn a PC into a home theater. Some computers come with a microphone for recording, or one can be added.

PCs usually come with a **modem** to allow a dial-up Internet connection, as well as an Ethernet port or wireless network adapter that lets you link several computers in the household to share files, a printer, or a broadband Internet connection. Parallel and serial ports, the traditional connections for printers and scanners, are being replaced by universal serial bus (USB) ports. FireWire or IEEE 1394 ports are used to capture video from digital camcorders and connect to other peripheral devices. An S-video output jack lets you run a video cable from the computer to a television, so you can use the computer's DVD drive to view a movie on a TV instead of on the computer monitor. Media center PCs that are equipped with TV tuners can capture video from a VCR and allow you to copy tapes to DVDs.

HOW TO CHOOSE

First, decide whether to upgrade your current computer. Upgrading rather than replacing it might make sense if your additional needs are modest—a second hard drive, say, because you're running out of room for digital photos. Adding memory or a CD burner is usually more cost-effective than buying a whole new machine. If your PC has become unreliable, your wish list is more demanding, or if there's software you must run that your system is not up to, a new PC is the logical answer.

Consider a laptop. A desktop computer typically costs less for equivalent performance and is easier to upgrade, expand, and repair. It usually offers better ergonomics, such as a more comfortable keyboard, bigger eye-level display, and enhanced audio. But a laptop merits consideration if portability and compactness are priorities.

Pick the right type of desktop. Most manufacturers offer several lines at different prices. Budget computers are the least expensive, and they are suitable for routine work, like e-mail, word processing, and Web surfing. You can also do photo editing. Workhorse computers cost a few hundred dollars more but are faster, more versatile, and upgradable. They can run complex 3D games and edit video. All-in-one models have most of the components in a single case. And entertainment or media PCs can include TV tuners, a remote control, and software that give them the functions of a DVR.

Choose by brand. Our surveys have consistently shown differences in reliability and technical support among computer brands. And some brands are generally more expensive than others. Those factors could help you decide which of two similarly equipped computers is the better buy.

Choose between preconfigured and custom-built. You can buy a PC off the shelf in a store or via the Web configured with features and options the manufacturer pitches to average consumers. Or consider purchasing a desktop that you configure to order, either online or in a store. When you configure a computer to order online, onscreen menus typically show you the options and let you see how a change in one affects the overall price. Be sure to double-check your choices before ordering and look for unwanted items that some manufacturers include by default.

Decide between Windows and Mac. More home and entertainment software is available for Windows computers than for Macs. The Apple brand, however, repeatedly scores best in tech support and has been reliable. The newest Macs let you install Windows as an alternative operating system. In early 2007, Microsoft plans to release a major new version of its flagship Windows operating system called Vista. It promises simpler networking, fewer crashes, better security, and visual features similar to the ones Apple put into Mac OS X a couple of years ago. Apple also plans to release a new version of Mac OSX, with new features, in early 2007.

Plan for software. At first glance, virtually any computer you buy will seem filled with useful software for virus scanning, managing finances, and working with audio or image files. But much of it is "teaserware" that works for a limited period or needs an upgrade for full capacity. Especially with Windows computers, check before buying that the selected model includes antivirus and antispyware software that will work (and can be updated) for at least a year. When comparing computer prices, consider any other necessary software as adding to the true cost.

Consider security. Security might not be foremost in your mind, but it should play a part in your decision. Your choice of hardware and software can affect your ability to deflect intruders and defend your data. Viruses and spyware are far more likely to target Windows PCs than Macs. It's too soon to know, however, whether new Intel-based Macs that Apple has begun shipping are more vulnerable to attack.

Whether you opt for a Windows PC or a Mac, you should use antivirus, firewall, and antispyware programs. Many computers include software such as Norton Internet Security or McAfee Security Center, but those are often limited to 30 to 90 days of use. Upgrade and update these starter packages as necessary or replace them to maintain protection over the long haul.

Skip the extended warranty. A recent subscriber survey found that the average cost of a service contract was not substantially less than the average repair cost. That means you might be better off paying for repairs yourself rather than buying a service contract that you might never use.

Related CR report: June 2006
Ratings: Page 242

LAPTOP COMPUTERS

A longtime companion at work, school, and on the road, the laptop has finally come home.

Bigger, crisper displays and more usable key layouts have replaced small screens and cramped keyboards. Processors have caught up in speed, and innovative new processors provide some real advantages. Fast CD and

DVD recording drives are common, as are ample hard drives. As computers become a repository for digital photos, music, and video, manufacturers are making laptops and the peripherals to which they connect increasingly compatible with home-entertainment systems. And a growing interest in wireless computing plays to the laptop's main strength: its portability. A laptop is the most convenient way to take full advantage of the growing availability of high-speed wireless Internet access at airports, schools, hotels, restaurants, and coffee shops.

Most laptops now have wireless networking capability built in and deliver commendably long battery life. The thinnest laptops on the market are less than an inch thick and weigh just 3 to 5 pounds. To get these light, sleek models, however, you'll have to pay a premium and make a few sacrifices in performance and screen size.

WHAT'S AVAILABLE

Dell, Gateway, Hewlett-Packard (which also makes Compaq), Lenovo (formerly branded as IBM), Sony, and Toshiba are the leading Windows laptop brands. Apple makes Mac OS MacBook and MacBook Pro models. Laptops can be grouped into several basic configurations:

Budget models. These have slower processors, fewer features, and lower screen quality but are suitable for routine office work and home software. Price: $1,000 or less.

Workhorse/multimedia models. These have faster processors and more built-in devices, so there's less need for external attachments. They also have larger screens and enhanced sound and video components. They're not lightweight or battery-efficient enough for frequent travelers. Price: $1,000 and up.

Slim-and-light models. These are for travelers. They are about an inch thick and weigh about 3 to 4 pounds. Some require an external drive to read DVDs or burn CDs. Price: $1,000 and up.

Tablet-style. These sit in your hand like a clipboard and have handwriting-recognition software. Some convert to a "normal" laptop with a keyboard. Price: $1,600 and up.

FEATURES THAT COUNT

Windows laptops generally have a 1.2- to 3.5-GHz processor. Popular processors include Intel Core Solo and Duo and AMD Turion 64. Apple laptops have made the transition to Intel processors and use Intel's Core Duo. The different types of processors make direct speed comparisons difficult, but any type of processor will probably deliver all the speed you'll need.

Laptops come with a 40- to 160-gigabyte hard drive and 256 megabytes or more of **random-access memory (RAM)**. We recommend at least 512MB.

Laptops use a **rechargeable lithium-ion battery.** In CONSUMER REPORTS tests, a normal battery provided two to five hours of continuous use when running office applications. (Laptops go into sleep mode when used intermittently, extending the time between charges.) You can extend battery life somewhat by dimming the display as you work, turning off wireless devices when they aren't needed, or only using basic applications. Playing a DVD movie uses more battery power than usual, but most laptops should be able to play one through to the end. Many laptops can accept an "extended" battery, adding size and weight but giving as much as twice the battery life.

A laptop's **keyboard** can be quite different from that of a desktop computer. The keys themselves may be full-sized (generally only lightweight models pare them down), but they may not feel as solid. Some laptops have extra buttons to expedite your access to e-mail or a Web browser, or to control DVD playback. You can attach a USB keyboard, which you may find easier to use.

A 14- to 15-inch **display,** measured diagonally, should suit most people. Displays that are 17-inches are becoming more common. A resolution of 1280x800 (WXGA) pixels (picture elements) or more is better than 1024x768 (XGA) for viewing the fine detail in photographs or video but may shrink objects on the screen. You can use settings in Windows to make them larger. Many models are now offered with a display that has a glossy surface instead of a matte one. Those look better in bright ambient light, as long as you avoid direct reflections. A "wide-aspect" display (WXGA or WSX-GA) fits wide-screen DVD movies better.

Most laptops use a small **touchpad** in place of a mouse—you slide your finger across the pad to move the cursor. You can also program the pad to respond to a "tap" as a "click," or to scroll as you sweep your index finger along the pad's right edge (or use two fingers). An alternative system uses a pencil-eraser-sized pointing stick in the middle of the keyboard. You can attach a USB mouse or trackball if you prefer.

Laptops usually include at least one **PC-card** or **Expresscard slot** for expansion. You might add a wireless-network card or a cellular modem, for example, if those are not built in. Many laptops offer a connection for a **docking station,** a $100 to $200 base that makes it easy to connect an external monitor, keyboard, mouse, printer, network and power in one step. Most laptops let you attach these devices anyway, without the docking station. An external display lets you set up your workspace more ergonomically. At least two **USB ports,** for easy hookup of, say, a printer, digital camera, or scanner, is standard. A **wired network (Ethernet) port** is common, as is a **FireWire port** for digital-video transfer. Many models have a standard **internal wireless-network (Wi-Fi) adapter.** An increasingly common option is an internal **Bluetooth** wireless adapter to link to a cell phone, PDA, or another laptop.

For backing up files or transferring them to other computers, you can use a **USB memory drive** (about $20 and up), which fits on a keychain and holds up to 8GB. Or save files on a writeable CD or camera-memory card. The small speakers built into laptops often sound tinny, with little bass. **Headphones** or **external speakers** deliver much better sound.

HOW TO CHOOSE

Decide if a laptop is right for you. If you're on a tight budget and aren't cramped for space, a comparably equipped desktop computer may be preferable because it costs a few hundred dollars less. It's also a better choice for heavy users who spend hours at the computer each day. Otherwise, consider a laptop. If you'll use it mostly at home, built-in wireless networking lets you use it throughout the house and easily store it.

Windows vs. Macintosh. Many people choose laptops using the Windows operating system because it's what they've always used, but Apple's Mac OSX is a fine alternative. In recent subscriber surveys, CONSUMER REPORTS found Apple technical support to be top-notch, and Lenovo (IBM) was better for tech support among Windows systems. According to a recent survey, we also found that Apple computers have been less susceptible to most viruses and spyware than Windows-based computers. Apple's MacBook is good for basic photo editing, music, video, and office applications, but the 13.3-inch screen is small. The MacBook Pro is suited to more intensive tasks but is relatively expensive.

Buy à la carte. Dell and Gateway pioneered the notion that every computer can be tailored to an individual's needs, much like choosing the options for a car. This configure-to-order model is now common practice for laptops as well as desktops.

Menus show you all the options and let you see how a change in one affects the overall price. You might decide to use a less-expensive processor, for example, but spend more for wireless capability or better graphics. Configure-to-order will often give you choices you won't get if you buy an off-the-shelf model. Be sure to double-check your choices before ordering, and look for unwanted items that some manufacturers include by default.

You can also purchase a computer off the shelf. (You can do the same online if you opt for the default choices of equipment the manufacturer offers.) That's fine if you don't have very strict requirements for how a laptop is outfitted or if you want to take advantage of an attractive sale.

Downplay the processor speed. Speed is no longer the be-all and end-all of personal computers. Current processors deliver all the speed most people need. Spend the money on more memory instead.

Look closely at warranties and insurance. Since the average cost of repair is usually not much more than the average cost of an extended warranty, we don't recommend buying a service you might not use. If you intend to travel a lot, consider buying screen insurance from the manufacturer.

Related CR report: June 2006
Ratings: Page 265

MONITORS

Prices are dropping for larger CRT monitors and for flat-panel LCD displays that free up desk space.

Deciding whether to buy a flat-panel LCD or a standard, fairly fat CRT monitor comes down to this: Do you need more space on the surface of your desk or on the screen? If freeing up space on your desk is a priority, an LCD is the clear choice. But since LCDs are more costly, you might opt for a CRT. And a CRT still has some other advantages. Desktop computers and monitors are often sold as a package, with some manufacturers offering attractive discounts for monitors bundled with PCs sold online.

WHAT'S AVAILABLE

Apple, Dell, eMachines (which merged with Gateway in 2004), Gateway, Hewlett-Packard (which merged with Compaq in 2002), Lenovo, and Sony all market their own monitors for their computers. Other brands of monitors, such as Acer, Envision, KDS, LG, NEC, Samsung, and ViewSonic, are sold separately. Many brands are manufactured on an outsource basis.

Flat-panel LCD monitors. These have been outselling CRTs for years. Because the monitors have a liquid-crystal display rather than a TV-style picture tube, they take up much less desktop space than CRTs. They operate with analog or digital input, or both. Unlike a CRT, the nominal and the viewable-image size (VIS) of a flat-panel LCD are the same. Desktop models typically measure 17 or 19 inches diagonally and just a few inches deep, and they weigh around 15 pounds, compared with 30 to 50 pounds for a CRT. LCDs with a screen 20 inches or larger are available, but they are still somewhat pricey. Wide-screen LCDs with a 17-inch VIS, specially designed for watching wide-format videos, are also available. These screens have an aspect ratio of 16:9, like those found on most digital TVs, and they're also fairly expensive.

Flat-panel displays deliver a very clear image, but they have some inherent quirks.

Their range of color is a bit narrower than a CRT's. And you have to view a flat-panel screen straight on; except for wide-screen models, the picture loses contrast as you move off-center, and fine lines might appear grainy. In analog mode you have to tweak the controls in order to get the best picture, but we have seen some improvements lately regarding the narrow angle. Price: $150 to $300 (15-inch); $175 to $500 (17-inch); $200 to $600 (19-inch); and $250 to $1,500 (20-inch).

CRT monitors. These typically range from 17 to 22 inches. To reduce glare, some CRTs have flattened, squared-off screens (not to be confused with flat-panel LCD screens). The nominal image size—the screen size touted in ads—is generally based on the diagonal measurement of the picture tube. The image you see, the viewable-image size, is usually an inch smaller. Thus a 17-inch CRT has a 16-inch VIS. As a result of a class-action lawsuit, ads must state a CRT's VIS as well as its nominal image, but you might have to squint at the fine print to find it.

Generally, the bigger the screen, the more room a CRT takes up on your desk, with depth roughly matching nominal screen size. "Short-depth" models shave an inch or more off the depth.

A 17-inch monitor, the most frequent choice these days, has almost one-third more viewable area than the 15-inch version now vanishing from the market. The larger size is especially useful when you're using the Internet, playing video games, watching DVD movies, editing photos, or working in several windows.

If you regularly work with graphics or sprawling spreadsheets, consider a 19-inch monitor. Its viewable area is one-fourth larger than a 17-inch model's. A short-depth 19-inch model doesn't take up much more desktop space than a standard 17-inch.

Aimed at graphics professionals, 21- and 22-inch models provide ample viewing area but they gobble up desktop space. Price: $50 to $500 (17-inch); $150 to $650 (19-inch); and $400 to $800 (21- to 22-inch).

FEATURES THAT COUNT

A monitor's resolution refers to the number of picture elements, or pixels, that make up an image. More pixels mean finer detail. Most monitors can display at several resolutions, generally ranging from 640x480 to 1600x1200 depending on the monitor and the graphics card. An LCD usually displays a sharper image than a CRT of comparable size when both are viewed at identical resolutions. But that's only if the LCD is set to its "native" resolution—1024x768 pixels for a 15-inch screen; 1280x1024, 1400x1050, or 1440x900 wide-screen for a 17-, 18-, or 19-inch model.

On both types of monitor, the higher the resolution the smaller the text and images, so more content fits on the screen. Bigger CRT screens can handle higher resolutions and display more information.

Dot pitch, measured in millimeters, refers to the spacing between a CRT's pixels. All else being equal, a smaller dot pitch produces a more detailed image, though that's no guarantee of an excellent picture. In general, avoid models with a dot pitch larger than 0.28 mm.

A CRT requires a high **refresh rate** (the number of times per second an image is redrawn on the screen) to avoid annoying image flicker. In general, you'll be more comfortable with a 17-inch monitor with a refresh rate of at least 75 hertz (Hz) at the resolution you want. For a 19-inch monitor, you might need an 85-Hz rate to avoid eyestrain, especially at higher resolutions. The refresh rate isn't an issue with flat-panel displays.

Monitors have controls for **brightness** and **contrast.** Most of them also have controls for color balance (usually called color temperature), distortion, and such. Buttons activate onscreen controls and menus.

Bigger CRTs use a considerable amount of juice: about 80 watts for a typical 19-inch model, 65 to 70 watts for a 17-inch model, and about 20 watts for a 15-inch flat-panel LCD, for example. Most monitors have a sleep mode when the computer is on but not in use that uses less than 3 watts.

Some monitors include a microphone, integrated or separate speakers, or composite-video inputs for viewing the output of a VCR or camcorder. Plug-and-play capability makes it fairly simple to add a new monitor to an existing computer.

HOW TO CHOOSE

Decide between LCD and CRT monitors. If your computer's monitor is hogging the top of your desk, you can reclaim much of that space by replacing it with an LCD. But doing so will cost you about $100 to $300 more than if you bought a new CRT monitor. And LCD screens have an inherent shortcoming: The image appears to fade as you move left, right, up, or down. However, most LCD monitors in our recent tests had a wider viewing angle than we've seen in the past. If space isn't an issue but budget is, a CRT monitor is a good choice. Because they deliver truer color and render fast-moving objects better, they are a superior choice for photographers, designers, and gamers.

Settle on size. For most people, a 17-inch CRT is big enough. Larger monitors are best suited for people who need to show photo enlargements or who regularly display multiple windows on the screen.

Consider helpful features. A monitor you can raise or lower can compensate for a desk that's too high or low. It's a feature found on some LCD monitors, but not on CRTs because they're so heavy. Some monitors can be rotated 90 degrees, from a landscape to portrait orientation, with the image automatically adjusting itself. That can be handy for viewing photos and Web pages. Also look for conveniently placed controls that adjust contrast, brightness, and other settings that affect images.

Look for a long warranty. Many monitors, both LCDs and CRTs, come with a three-year warranty on parts and labor. A warranty that long is worth looking for, especially when purchasing a more-expensive model.

Convergence with TV isn't here yet. Manufacturers offer monitors with TV tuners and LCD TVs with computer connections.

Related CR report: June 2006

PDAs

Besides serving as an address book, calendar, and to-do list, many personal digital assistants offer multimedia functions.

PDAs can store thousands of phone numbers, appointments, tasks, and notes. All models can exchange, or synchronize, information with a full-sized computer. To do this, you connect the PDA to your computer via a cradle or cable. For models that run on rechargeable batteries, the cradle doubles as a charger. Infrared, Bluetooth, and Wi-Fi (wireless) let you synchronize with a computer without wires or a cradle.

Most PDAs can be made to work with both Windows and Macintosh computers, but PDAs with the Pocket PC operating system usually require third-party software for Macs. PDAs with Wi-Fi (wireless) capability can access the Internet. Those without can with the addition of a separately purchased modem. Most PDAs can record your voice, play videos, display digital photos, and hold maps, city guides, and books.

WHAT'S AVAILABLE

Most PDAs on the market are the familiar tablet-with-stylus type that feature a squarish display screen, a design pioneered by Palm Inc. Today the main choices are models that use the Palm operating system (OS)—mostly Palm models—and Pocket PC devices from companies like Dell and Hewlett-Packard. The latter use a stripped-down version of Microsoft Windows. A few PDAs use a proprietary operating system. Hewlett-Packard, Nokia, Palm, Samsung, and Sony Ericsson offer units that combine a cell phone and a PDA, often referred to as smartphones.

Palm OS systems. Equipped with software to link with Windows and (for Palm-brand units) Macintosh computers, Palm units and their clones have a simple user interface. You use a stylus to enter data by tapping an onscreen keyboard or writing in shorthand known as Graffiti. Some models have a tiny tactile keyboard. Or you can download data from your computer.

Most Palm OS-based PDAs can synchronize with a variety of desktop e-mail programs, such as Outlook Express and Eudora. (Palm models with VersaMail software are good at handling e-mail with attachments.) And all include a basic personal information management (PIM) application. Palm OS units are easy to use, although navigation between different programs is cumbersome because of the operating system's "single tasking" nature.

Most models make it difficult or impossible to replace the battery yourself. And beyond the warranty period, you can't be sure the manufacturer will do it for you.

Most Palm OS-based models have expansion slots that let you add memory or attach separately purchased accessories. All Palm OS-based PDAs can be enhanced by adding third-party software applications—the more free memory that a model comes with, the more software it can accommodate. There is a large body of Palm OS-compatible freeware, shareware, and commercial software available for download at such sites as www.palmgear.com. Many Palm models come with Documents To Go—word-processing and spreadsheet software similar to that used in Pocket PCs but more versatile. Price: $100 to $400.

Palm's top-of-the-line model, the LifeDrive, combines a 3.7-GB hard drive with many of the best features of the Pocket PC and Palm OS operating systems. When it's connected to a Windows PC, you can drag and drop files to the LifeDrive's hard drive, even on PCs that don't have Palm's desktop software installed. It's also handy for storing photos from a digital camera that uses a MMC/SD (MultiMedia/ SecureDigital) memory card and for listening to MP3 music.

Pocket PC systems. These resemble Palm OS-based models but are more like miniature computers. They have a processor with extra horsepower and come with familiar applications such as a word processor and a spreadsheet. Included is a scaled-down version of Internet Explorer, plus voice recording and perhaps some financial functions. The included e-mail program handles Word and Excel attachments easily. Also standard is an application that plays MP3 music files, as well as Microsoft Reader, an eBook application.

As you might expect, all the application software included in a Pocket PC integrates well with the Windows computer environment. You need to purchase third-party software to use a Mac. And you'll need Microsoft Office programs such as Word, Excel, and Outlook on your computer to exchange data with a PDA. Pocket

PCs have a color display and rechargeable lithium-ion batteries. Unlike most Palm OS-based PDAs, replacing the battery of most Pocket PCs is usually straightforward. Price: $200 to $600.

Ultra Mobile PCs (UMPCs). These are small, fully functional computers that run a version of Microsoft's Windows XP. An early model, the Samsung Q1, released in early 2006, has a 7-inch display, measuring 5½ inches x 9 inches x 1 inch and weighing 1.7 pounds. It lacks a built-in keyboard and costs about $1,100.

FEATURES THAT COUNT

Whichever operating system your PDA uses, you might need to install programs in your computer to enable the PDA to synchronize with it. This software lets you swap data with leading PIM programs such as Lotus Organizer or Microsoft Outlook.

All PDAs have the tools for basic tasks: a calendar to keep track of your appointments, **contact/address software** for addresses and phone numbers, **tasks/to-do lists** for reminders and keeping track of errands, and a **calculator.** A **notes/memo function** lets you make quick notes to yourself. Other capabilities include **word-processing, spreadsheet,** and **e-mail functions.** A **voice recorder,** which uses a built-in microphone and speaker, works like a tape recorder. **MP3 playback** lets you listen to digital-music files stored in that format, and a picture viewer lets you look at digital photos. A few models also include a **built-in digital camera** and **keyboard.**

A PDA's **processor** is the system's brain. In general, the higher the processing speed of this chip, the faster the PDA will execute tasks—and the more expensive it will be. But higher-speed processors may require more battery power and thus deplete batteries more quickly. Processing speeds are 200 to 624 megahertz (MHz), and models

typically have 16 to 256 megabytes (MB) of user memory. Even the smallest amount in that range should be more than enough for most people.

Nearly every PDA offers an **expansion slot** for some form of removable memory card: CompactFlash, MultiMedia card (slots also accept SecureDigital cards), or Memory Stick. Models with two expansion slots can accommodate a peripheral device, such as a Wi-Fi wireless networking card and removable memory.

If you plan to transfer photos from a digital camera to your PDA, make sure the two devices use the same type of card. Some PDAs offer **wireless connectivity.** Models with a capability known as **Bluetooth** can connect wirelessly over short distances to a properly equipped computer or peripheral such as a printer or modem. Models with **Wi-Fi** can connect over medium distances to a Wi-Fi-enabled home network or to the Internet at "hot spots" in certain airports, coffee shops, and hotels. A PDA combined with a cell phone can make voice calls or directly connect to the Internet via a wireless Internet service provider. It's possible for a single PDA to have more than one of these types of wireless connectivity.

HOW TO CHOOSE

Consider your ties to a computer. Pocket PCs provide a Windows-like interface that allows simple PC-to-PDA file transfer with drag-and-drop capability. They're also more convenient than Palm OS models for setting up a Wi-Fi (wireless) e-mail connection. Most have replaceable batteries along with accessible flash memory to which you can back up data.

Palm OS models run a wider range of third-party software applications than do Pocket PCs. For the basics, they're still easier to use. While most PDAs can sync with Macs, only Palm models do so out of the box. Programs like Missing Sync (*www.markspace.com*) and PocketMac (*www.pocketmac.net*) support Palm OS PDAs from Garmin and others, as well as Pocket PCs that run older versions of that operating system, such as the Asus A730W. Currently, neither Missing Sync nor PocketMac support PDAs that run Microsoft Windows Mobile 5.0. Both are priced under $50.

Small size vs. extra features. As a rule, a model with a larger display or physical keyboard won't be the lightest or smallest. A PDA with two slots for memory and peripherals is more expandable but will tend to be larger.

Related CR report: October 2005

PRINTERS

Inexpensive inkjets print color superbly, and they do it faster than ever. Laser printers excel at printing black-and-white text.

Inkjet printers have become the standard for home-computer use. They can turn out color photos nearly indistinguishable from lab-processed photos, along with banners, stickers, transparencies, T-shirt transfers, and greeting cards. Many produce excellent black-and-white text. With some very good models selling for less than $200, it's no surprise that inkjets account for the vast majority of printers sold for home use.

Laser printers still have their place in home offices. If you print reams of black-and-white text documents, you probably need the quality, speed, and low per-copy cost of a laser printer. Printers use a computer's microprocessor and memory to process data. The latest inkjets and lasers are so fast partly because computers themselves have become more powerful and contain much more memory than before.

WHAT'S AVAILABLE

The printer market is dominated by a handful of well-established brands. Hewlett-Packard is the market leader. Other major brands include Brother, Canon, Dell, Epson, and Lexmark. Printers designed for printing 4x6-inch snapshots are also sold by Kodak, Olympus, Samsung, and Sony.

The type of computer a printer can serve depends on its ports. The most common by far, a Universal Serial Bus (USB) port, lets a printer connect to Windows or Macintosh computers. A few models also have a parallel port, which allows connections to older Windows computers. All these printers lack a serial port, which means they won't work with older Macs.

Inkjet printers. Inkjets use droplets of ink to form letters, graphics, and photos. Some printers have one cartridge that holds the cyan (greenish-blue), magenta, and yellow inks, and a second for the black ink. Others have an individual cartridge for each color. For photos, many inkjets also have additional cartridges for lighter shades of cyan and magenta inks, or gray ink.

Most inkjet printers output black-and-white text at a speed of 2 to 10 pages per minute (ppm) but are much slower for color photos. Various models we tested took 2 to 11 minutes to print a single 8x10, depending on the complexity of the image. The cost of printing a black-and-white text page with an inkjet varies considerably from model to model, from 2 to 12 cents. The cost of printing a color 8x10 photo can range from 90 cents to $1.60. Printer price: $60 to $700. You can also get them with scanning, copying, and sometimes fax capability. These all-in-one models typically cost more than stand-alone inkjets. Price: $100 and up.

Specialty snapshot printers. For printing photos at home, a speedy snapshot printer can be more convenient than a full-sized model. Most are limited to 4x6-inch snapshots, but a few models can also print on 5x7 paper. These models use either inkjet or dye-sublimation technology. Like most full-sized inkjet printers, most of these models can hook up directly via cable to a digital camera through the PictBridge connection, so you can print without using a computer. This is the simplest and quickest way to print at home, provided you don't want to edit the photos. Many also have slots for camera memory cards. Price: $80 to $300.

Laser printers. These work much like plain-paper copiers, forming images by transferring toner (powdered ink) to paper passing over an electrically charged drum. The process yields sharp black-and-white text and graphics. Laser printers usually outrun inkjets, cranking out black-and-white text at a rate of 12 to 18 ppm. Black-and-white laser printers generally cost about as much as midpriced inkjets, but they're cheaper to operate. Laser cartridges, about $50 to $100, can print thousands of black-and-white pages for a per-page cost of 2 to 4 cents. Price: $100 and up. All-in-one laser printers add scanning, copying, and sometimes fax capability. Price: $200 and up. Color laser printers are also available, but those now on the market can't print on glossy photo paper, so they're not a good choice for printing photos. Price: $300 and up.

FEATURES THAT COUNT

Printers differ in the fineness of detail they can produce. **Resolution,** expressed in dots per inch (dpi), is often touted as the main measure of print quality. But other factors, such as the way dot patterns are formed by software instructions from the printer driver, count, too. At their default settings—where they're usually expected to run—inkjets currently on the market typically have a resolution of 600x600 dpi. The dpi can be increased for color photos. Some printers go up to 5760x1440 dpi. Laser printers for home use typically offer 600 or 1200 dpi. Printing color inkjet photos on photo paper at a higher dpi setting can produce smoother shading of colors but can slow printing significantly.

Most inkjet printers have an **ink monitor** to warn when you're running low, but they vary in accuracy. Generic ink cartridges usually cost less but most produce fewer prints than the brand-name inks, so per-print costs may not be lower. And print quality and fade-resistance may not be as good.

For double-sided printing, you can print the odd-numbered pages of a document first, then flip those pages over to print the even-numbered pages on a second pass. A few printers can automatically print on both sides, but it slows down printing.

HOW TO CHOOSE

Be skeptical about advertised speeds. Print speed varies depending on what you're printing and at what quality, but the speeds you see in ads are generally higher than you're likely to achieve in normal use. You can't reliably compare speeds for different brands because each company uses its own methods to measure speed. We run the same tests on all models, printing text pages and photos that are similar to what you might print. As a result, our print times are realistic and can be compared across brands.

Don't get hung up on resolution. A printer's resolution, expressed in dots per inch, is another potential source of confusion. All things being equal, the more ink dots a printer puts on the paper, the more detailed the image. But dot size, shape, and placement also affect quality, so don't base your choice solely on resolution.

Consider supply costs as well as a printer's price. High ink-cartridge costs can make a bargain-priced printer a bad deal in the long run. Shop around for the best cartridge prices, but be wary of off-brands. We have found that brand-name cartridges overall have better print quality and fade-resistance, and per-page costs are often comparable. Glossy photo paper costs about 25 to 75 cents a sheet, so use plain paper for works in progress and save the good stuff for the final results. We've gotten the best results using the recommended brand of paper. You might be tempted to buy a cheaper brand, but bear in mind that lower-grade paper can reduce photo quality and might not be as fade resistant.

Decide if you want to print photos without using a computer. Printing without a computer saves you an extra step and a little time. Features such as memory-card support, PictBridge support (a standard that allows a compatible camera to be connected directly to the printer), or a wireless interface are convenient. But when you print directly from camera to printer, you compromise on what may have attracted you to digital photography in the first place—the ability to tweak size, color, brightness, and other image attributes. And with a snapshot printer, you give up the ability to print on larger media.

Weigh convenience features. Most printers can make borderless prints like those from a photo developer. This matters most if you're printing to the full size of the paper, as you might with 4x6-inch sheets. Otherwise, you can trim the edges off. If you plan to use 4x6-inch paper regularly, look for a printer with a 4x6-inch tray or a second paper tray, which makes it easier to feed paper of this size. With these small sheets, though, the cost per photo might be higher than ganging up a few

images on 8½ x11-inch paper. With some models, if you want to use the photo inks to get the best picture quality, you have to remove the black-ink cartridge and replace it with the photo-ink cartridge. Then, to print text or graphics, you have to swap the black cartridge back in. This process can get tedious. The models that hold all the ink tanks simultaneously eliminate that hassle.

Consider connections. All new computers and printers have USB 2.0 ports, which are compatible with plain USB. Computers more than seven years old may have only a parallel port.

Decide whether you need scanning and copying. An all-in-one inkjet unit provides scanning and color copying (and sometimes faxing) while saving space. The downside is that the scanners in all-in-one units might be slower and have fewer features than the latest stand-alone scanners. Stand-alone scanners are best for handling negatives and slides, although some all-in-one printers now include a light in the lid and a holder to keep negatives and slides in place. And if one part of the unit breaks, the whole unit must be repaired or replaced.

Related CR report: May 2006
Ratings: Page 298

SCANNERS

A scanner is a simple, cheap way to digitize images for printing, editing on your computer, or sending via e-mail.

You don't need a digital camera to take advantage of the computer's ability to edit photos. Continuing improvements in scanners have made it cheaper and easier to turn photos into digital images that you can enhance, resize, and share. And flatbed scanners are no longer restricted to printed originals. Our tests show that the best flatbeds are now a match for pricey film scanners when it comes to digitizing slides and negatives. That's no small accomplishment, reflecting improvements to the resolution that new scanners deliver and better accessories to hold film strips or slides securely for sharp, accurate scans.

WHAT'S AVAILABLE

A number of scanners come from companies, including Microtek and Visioneer, that made their name in scanning technology. Other brands include computer makers and photo specialists such as Canon, Epson, Hewlett-Packard, and Nikon.

Which type of scanner you should consider—flatbed or film—depends largely on how you will use it. If you're short on space, consider a multifunction device.

Flatbed scanners. More than 90 percent of the scanners on the market are flatbeds. They work well for text, graphics, photos, and anything else that is flat, including a kindergartner's latest drawing. Flatbeds include optical-character-recognition (OCR) software, which converts words on a printed page into a word-processing file in your computer. They also include basic image-editing software. Some stores may throw in a flatbed scanner for free, or for a few dollars extra, when you purchase a desktop computer.

A key specification for a scanner is its maximum optical resolution, measured in dots per inch (dpi). You'll pay more for greater resolution. Price: less than $100 for 600x1,200 dpi; $100 to $500 for models with greater resolution.

Film scanners. Serious photographers may want a film-only scanner that scans directly from an original slide (transparency) or negative. Some can accept small prints as well. Price: $400 to $800.

FEATURES THAT COUNT

While the quality of images a scanner produces depends in part on the software included with it, there are several hardware features to consider.

You start scanning by running **driver software** that comes with the scanner or by pressing a preprogrammed button. Models with buttons automate routine tasks to let you operate your scanner as you would other office equipment. On some models you can customize the functions of the buttons. Any of these tasks can also be performed through the scanner's software without using buttons. A **copy/print button** initiates a scan and sends a command to print the results on your printer, effectively making the two devices act as a copier. Other button functions found on some models include **scan to a file, scan to a fax modem, scan to e-mail, scan to Web, scan to OCR, cancel scan, power save, start scanner software,** and **power on/off.**

You can also start the driver software from within an application, such as a word processor, that adheres to an industry standard known as TWAIN. A scanner's driver software allows you to **preview** a scan onscreen and crop it or adjust **contrast** and **brightness.** Once you're satisfied with the edited image, you can perform a final scan and pass the image to a running program or save it on your computer. You can make more extensive changes to an image with specialized **image-editing software.** And to scan text from a book or letter into a word-processing file in your computer, you run **OCR software.**

Many documents combine text with graphic elements, such as photographs and drawings. A handy software feature that's found on many scanners, called multiple-scan mode, lets you break down such hybrids into different sections that can be processed separately in a single scan. You can designate, for example, that the sections of a magazine article that are pure text go to the OCR software independently of the article's graphic elements. Other scanners would require a separate scan for each section of the document.

Some flatbed models come with film adapters designed to scan film or slides, but if you need to scan from film or slides often, you're better off getting a separate film scanner.

HOW TO CHOOSE

Consider how much resolution you need. If you want to scan only printed originals, you can buy a basic scanner with 1200-dpi resolution for less than $100. That's all you need for most same-size scans of photos, graphics, and text.

If there's any chance you might want to scan transparent material or blow up portions of an image, you're better off spending a little more for higher resolution. Models with 2400 dpi or higher were priced at $100 to $250. You can always lower a scanner's setting to the resolution required—and you should, to keep scan times short and file sizes small.

For scanning film and slides, 2400 dpi is the minimum you'll need, but you'll get better results with 3200 or 4800 dpi. In our tests, the 4800-dpi models produced the best scan quality with transparent originals. The higher resolution allows you to capture more detail when enlarging a 35-mm original or zooming in on a portion of an image. When comparing specs, focus on native optical resolution. "Interpolated" or "enhanced" resolution comes in handy only for scanning line art.

Consider color-bit depth for film. For enlarging prints or scanning negatives or slides, the greater the color-bit depth, the better the scanner can differentiate among subtle gradations of shading: 24-bit (8 bits per color channel) is basic; 48-bit (16 bits per channel) is better.

Choose quality and speed that suit your needs. Most of the tested scanners did very well at reproducing a color photo at 300 dpi. Those judged good produced decent but less crisp scans, with less accurate colors. Fewer models did well with film.

Speed matters if you expect to be scanning regularly. In our tests, the fastest took about 11 seconds to scan an 8x10-inch photo at 300 dpi, while the slowest took about 30 seconds.

Don't sweat the software. All the scanners we tested came with software for scanning, image editing, and optical character recognition for scanning text into a word-processing program. Some have software for making digital photo albums or other projects.

Related CR report: May 2006

Autos

Your Inside Track for New and Used Vehicles

To get the right car at the best price you need to do your research. But how do you determine the quality of your information? More people turn to CONSUMER REPORTS for car-buying advice than any other publication or Web site. That's because CONSUMER REPORTS, published by the nonprofit, independent Consumers Union, holds a special place in the world of auto information.

• CR is the only publication that buys its own test vehicles anonymously. We put them through the most comprehensive auto-testing program of any U.S. publication or Web site at our 327-acre Auto Test Center. More than 50 tests and evaluations are performed on every vehicle.

• CR does not accept advertising, so we don't have to pull punches in our Ratings, reviews, and safety reporting. Unlike other publications that must placate advertisers, we tell you which vehicles are the best and which are the worst.

This 80-page section is structured to be your all-in-one guide to buying a vehicle. Starting off on page 147, we detail our 5 Steps to Get the Right Car at the Best Price. Buying a car can be thrilling and terrifying at the same time, but following these five easy steps can take the advantage out of the salesperson's hands and put you in charge of the buying and negotiating process.

Turn to page 157 to see which vehicles, among the 228 we recently tested, did best and worst in our Ratings. Here you can see how each ranks among its competitors in overall test score, real-world fuel economy, Ratings for predicted reliability, accident avoidance, and crash tests.

The vehicle profiles, starting on page 167, are our summary reviews of 260 vehicles, including our recommendations and Predicted Reliability Ratings.

Consumers considering a used vehicle should turn to the Best & Worst Used Cars, on page 191. You'll find our CR Good Bets, models that have performed well in our road tests and reliability surveys, as well as the CR Bad Bets, vehicles with poor reliability that you should avoid.

We close the section with our Predicted Reliability charts, starting on page 196. These charts are based on responses from our annual survey, when we ask our approximately six million magazine and Web site subscribers about any serious problems they have had with their vehicles in the preceding 12 months.

This edition's reliability data are based on more than one million vehicles. They provide you with information on more than 216 vehicles, showing you how models from 1998 through 2005 are holding up in 15 trouble spots. These are comprehensive reliability data you can't get from other publications.

5 STEPS TO GET THE RIGHT CAR AND BEST PRICE

Buying a new car can be an exciting time. But many people are intimidated by the dealership experience, including the price negotiations and the high-pressure sales tactics that can be used to manipulate you into spending more than you need to. Others find it confusing and frustrating to try to pick the right vehicle from the more than 300 models on the market.

To ensure that you get the right vehicle at the best price, you need to be an informed buyer. That means investing time in research and preparation. The car-buying process can be boiled down to five steps:

• **Get the right information** to narrow your choices and make a smart decision.

• **Check out the cars** by doing a thorough test drive.

• **Set a target price** and learn the value of your trade-in.

• **Shop for financing before you deal** by comparing terms and interest rates, and getting preapproved for a loan.

• **Get the best deal** by contacting dealerships, comparing offers, and using a proven negotiating strategy.

Step 1: Get the right info

To accurately compare vehicles and determine the best one for your needs, gather as much information as you can about any models you're considering. Fortunately, the Internet makes that easy to do. But just as cars can vary greatly in quality, so can sources of information. The key is knowing what to look for and finding the best sources of information. Here, we list some of the major areas in which you should consider when comparing models.

AUTOMAKER WEB SITES

Use these sites to get basic information, such as which models and trim levels the manufacturer offers, available features and options, specifications, retail pricing, warranties, and the locations of dealerships. Most sites also let you compare vehicles and "build your own car," giving you a retail price for your individual configuration. That doesn't guarantee, however, that you'll find a vehicle configured the way you want it on a dealership's lot. Keep in mind, too, that the main purpose of these sites is to promote their own products, so the model information is the same as advertising.

VEHICLE RATINGS

CONSUMER REPORTS' Ratings (see page 157) can help you narrow your list by giving you a quick look at how tested vehicles compare with their competitors in several areas. The Ratings chart also shows you which vehicles meet our stringent requirements to be recommended.

MODEL REVIEWS

Reviews give you an in-depth perspective on a vehicle's performance, comfort and convenience, and overall driving character, as well as insight into deficiencies that might not be apparent on a test drive. Because different sources have varying points of view, we recommend reading a variety. But keep in mind that most are in publications or on Web sites that are supported by automaker advertising, and no company wants to bite the hand that feeds it. So you might not find hard-hitting analysis or insight into safety or reliability issues. Only a few do their own instrumented testing, which allows more accurate comparisons between different vehicles.

CONSUMER REPORTS conducts the most comprehensive auto-testing program of any U.S. publication or Web site. We differ from other reviewers in several significant ways, including the fact that we don't accept advertising, we buy all of our test vehicles from dealerships, just like you do, and we conduct more than 50 tests and evaluations on each vehicle over several months and thousands of miles.

Summary reviews of all models are included in the model profiles that begin on page 167. Full road-test reports and test results are included in CONSUMER REPORTS magazine and are available to subscribers of ConsumerReports.org.

RELIABILITY

A vehicle's reliability can have a huge effect on how satisfied you'll be with it over the years, and it can significantly affect its resale value. Reliability, however, is a difficult and expensive quality to evaluate because the information has to come from vehicle owners; the more, the better. CR provides the most comprehensive reliability information available to consumers. Our 2005 subscriber survey, for instance, drew responses on more than one million vehicles, the most ever.

FUEL ECONOMY

The fuel-economy figures printed on a vehicle's window sticker and in automaker advertising and brochures are estimates based on a test created by the U.S. Environmental Protection Agency (EPA). You can find a list of these figures at *www.fueleconomy.gov*. In CR's extensive real-world fuel economy testing, however, we've found that EPA estimates are often much higher than you're likely to get in normal driving. You can get a more accurate figure for vehicles that we tested by referring to the Vehicle Ratings chart (see page 157).

SAFETY RATINGS

Several different elements affect a vehicle's overall safety capability:

Crash tests: Frontal- and side-impact crash tests are conducted by the Insurance Institute for Highway Safety (IIHS; *www.iihs.org*) and the National Highway Traffic Safety Administration (NHTSA; *www.safercar.gov*). CR provides a single overall crash protection Rating for many models, based on our assessment of government and insurance-industry tests. See the Vehicle Ratings chart on page 157.

Accident avoidance: A vehicle's ability to help you avoid an accident is just as important as its ability to protect you in a crash. For every accident there are numerous near misses that statistics don't reflect. Several factors contribute to a vehicle's accident-avoidance capability, with the two most important being braking and emergency handling. To see CR's accident-avoidance rating on all tested vehicles, see the Vehicle Ratings chart on page 157.

Rollover resistance: Rollover accidents account for about 33 percent of all vehicle-occupant deaths, and are of particular concern with taller vehicles, such as SUVs and pickups. To help consumers compare vehicles, NHTSA provides a five-star rating system called the Rollover Resistance Rating (RRR). The RRR is calculated from two factors: a vehicle's static stability factor (SSF) and a dynamic rollover test. The SSF, which is determined from static measurements of the vehicle, essentially indicates how top-heavy it is. The dynamic test simulates a driver having to make a series of sharp steering maneuvers, as can happen in an emergency. Vehicles that tip-up at any speed fail the test. We believe that a vehicle that tips-up in this type of situation has serious stability problems, and we will not recommend it. RRR ratings are available at *www.safercar.gov*. To see if a vehicle tipped-up in the dynamic test, however, you need to click on the model's name or star ratings to get more information, then scroll down to "Rollover."

Rear-impact protection: Although rear-enders are usually not life-threatening, they have a high injury rate, especially for whiplash neck injuries. The design of a car's head restraints and seats are critical factors in how severe a whiplash injury will be. CONSUMER REPORTS evaluates head restraints for all seating positions in every tested vehicle. Any problems are noted in our road-test reports. Another good source for information on rear-impact protection is the IIHS Web site, *www.iihs.org*. The institute conducts evaluations of head restraints and performs dynamic rear-impact tests that measure how well the seat/head-restraint combinations in different models protect against whiplash.

Blind zones: Every year, children are injured and killed because drivers don't see them while backing up. A contributing factor is that some larger vehicles, such as SUVs and pickups, have larger blind zones—the area behind a vehicle that the driver can't see. CONSUMER REPORTS measures the blind zone of every vehicle we test and publishes the information free at *www.Consumer Reports.org*.

Power-window switches: Some vehicles have rocker- or toggle-type power-window switches that raise the window when pressed down or forward. This is a risky design because a child who is leaning out of an open window can accidentally kneel on the switch and close the window, possibly causing injury or death. A better design is a lever switch, which only raises the window when it's pulled upward. Vehicles with the riskier switches are noted in our road-test reports.

RECOMMENDED SAFETY FEATURES

Buyers often overlook important safety features because they aren't aware of them or don't understand their benefit. The following are ones that we recommend you consider for your vehicle:

Antilock brake system (ABS). Without antilock brakes, a vehicle's wheels can lock up (stop turning) during hard braking, particularly on slippery surfaces. When that happens, the vehicle tends to keep plowing ahead in whatever direction it is going. You can't steer, and locked wheels can cause a vehicle to slide sideways or even spin. ABS prevents the wheels from locking up. This, in turn, allows the driver to retain steering control while braking, so that the car can be maneuvered around an obstacle, if necessary. It also helps keep the vehicle from sliding and often stops it in a shorter distance on most surfaces.

Electronic stability control (ESC). CONSUMER REPORTS highly recommends you get ESC on your vehicle. ESC helps keep the vehicle on its intended path during a turn to avoid sliding or skidding out of control. It is especially helpful in slippery conditions and accident-avoidance situations. With tall, top-heavy vehicles like SUVs and pickups, it can also help keep the vehicle from getting into a situation where it could roll over. Each automaker tends to have a proprietary name for its ESC system, making it confusing for buyers to know what's what. If in doubt whether a car has it, find out before you buy.

Head-protecting side air bags. IIHS side-impact crash tests clearly show the benefit of this feature. To date, no vehicle that was tested without head-protecting side air bags has scored higher than poor. There are two types of side bags. A standard side air bag deploys from the seat or door trim. It typically protects a person's torso, but many don't do an adequate job of protecting the head. We recommend that you look for a dedicated head-protection bag that deploys from above the side windows. The most common type is a side-curtain air bag that covers the side windows in both the front and rear, preventing occupants from hitting their heads and shielding them from flying debris. A curtain bag can also keep people from being ejected during a rollover.

Safety-belt features. While the safety belt is arguably the single most important piece of safety equipment, enhanced features are helping safety belts do their job more effectively. Adjustable upper anchors help position the belt across the chest instead of the neck to prevent neck injuries. They also can help keep the belt from pulling down on a tall person's shoulder, making it more comfortable.

Safety-belt pretensioners instantly retract the belts to take up slack during a frontal impact. This helps position occupants properly to take full advantage of a deploying air bag. Force limiters, a companion feature to pretensioners, manage the force that the shoulder belt builds up on the occupant's chest. After the pretensioners tighten it, force limiters let the belt pay back out a little.

'Smart' frontal air bags. Front air bags are now standard in all new vehicles, but some models offer an advanced, multistage system that tailors their deployment to the front occupants. Depending on the model, a "smart" systems can detect the presence and weight of the person in the front passenger seat, the driver's seat position, and whether their safety belts are fastened. It can then adjust the deployment of the air bags to minimize the chance of injury to occupants or children in a crash.

Step 2: Conduct a test drive

A lot of vehicles look good on paper, but the test drive is the moment of truth. This is your best chance to see how a vehicle measures up to expectations, to see how well it "fits" you, and to evaluate its driving character, performance, and comfort. After all, you don't want any surprises after you've bought it.

You should make a separate visit to the dealership just for a test drive and walk-around inspection. Don't wait until the day you're ready to buy; that won't give you enough time to thoroughly evaluate the cars you're considering.

It's important that you spend as much time with the vehicle as possible, with an eye on what it will be like to live with over the long haul. Here are some tips to make your dealership test drive count:

BE ORGANIZED AND THOROUGH

• Before you go to the dealership, list what you like and dislike about your current car so you can compare this with the vehicle you'll be driving. Take along a notebook so you can jot down impressions.

• If you're considering different models, test drive them all before you make a final decision. If more than one person will be driving the vehicle on a regular basis, make sure all have a chance to test drive it before you buy.

• Before you drive, evaluate the driving position and interior. Set the seat in a comfortable driving position and attach the safety belt. Make sure that you're at least 10 inches away from the steering wheel and that you can fully depress all the pedals. Make sure that you can reach all the controls without straining and that they're easy to use and the displays are easy to see.

• Don't be rushed; take at least 30 minutes. Try to drive along a route that includes different types of road surfaces and driving conditions. If the dealership is in an unfamiliar place, scout out a route ahead of time. Take someone along to give you the passenger's viewpoint. If possible, take the test drive without a salesperson, so you can better concentrate on the vehicle.

• As you drive, make sure that you can see out well, that you can judge the ends of the vehicle, and that there are no serious blind spots. Pay attention to all of the vehicles' characteristics—how it rides, handles, accelerates, and stops, as well as how quiet it is. Take notes so you can compare the model with others that you test drive, and record your impressions of the vehicle's comfort, handling, and responsiveness.

• If you use child-safety seats, bring them with you and take the time to install them properly so you can see how easy or difficult it is.

Step 3: Crunch the numbers

In many ways, negotiating a good deal on a new vehicle is a game of numbers. The best way to ensure that you aren't manipulated is to go in armed with accurate pricing information, which lets you assess how good a salesperson's offer really is. Two key figures you need are a target price on the new vehicle and the value of your current vehicle.

SET A TARGET PRICE

The figure on a car's window sticker is only a suggested retail price set by the auto manufacturer. Dealerships are free to sell vehicles at whatever price they want.

An informed buyer, prepared with accurate price information, can often buy a vehicle for hundreds or thousands of dollars below the sticker price.

That's why it's important to calculate a reasonable target price before you go to the dealership to buy. To get the lowest price, you have to start with a figure that's based on how much the dealer actually paid for the vehicle. By knowing this, you'll know how much profit margin the dealership has to work with.

To figure out the dealer's real cost you need to find the dealer-invoice price, any current behind-the-scenes dealer sales incentives, and the dealer's holdback amount. Dealer-invoice prices are now so common that you can find them on many Web sites and pricing guides, but you'll have to do a little more digging to find dealer incentives and the holdback.

To point you in the right direction, Consumer Reports' New Car Price Reports do this work for you. Each report shows you all three factors: the dealer-invoice price, the amount of any national or regional dealer sales incentives, and the holdback amount. It also includes the CR Wholesale Price, which takes all of these figures into consideration to give a close approximation of the dealer's cost. Or, you can look up current sales incentives and holdback amounts yourself at some auto-pricing Web sites.

A reasonable price for a vehicle is about 4 to 8 percent over the CR Wholesale Price or dealer's cost, depending on how popular the model is.

It can also be helpful to check your target price against those offered by dealerships affiliated with autobuying Web sites. On these sites, you can ask for a price quote on a vehicle that's configured the way you want it, and one or more dealerships will reply by e-mail. The services are free and you aren't under any obligation to buy. CarsDirect.com will also give you a no-haggle price that their contracted dealerships have agreed to honor.

You can compare these quotes against the target price range you calculated based on the dealer's cost. Usually, the quotes will be higher. But if, by chance, a quote is lower than your figure, this gives you more leverage with which to bargain.

Another point of comparison could be so-called transaction prices posted on some auto-buying Web sites. These are intended to reflect the average of what other buyers are actually paying for new vehicles. These prices are available on sites such as Autobytel and Edmunds, which posts its True Market Value price.

Since these transaction prices are an average of nationwide sales prices, keep in mind that some actual prices were higher and some were lower. These prices also might not be accurate for your area. By having a target price based on the dealer's cost, you might be able to do better than those transaction prices. At the very least, during your negotiating process, it's comforting to know approximately how much you should be paying.

Step 4: Find the best financing options

You might be a whiz at getting a low price on a new car, but if you don't choose your financing carefully, you could lose everything you saved on the vehicle's purchase price and more. It's critical that you comparison shop and get preapproved for an auto loan before you go to the dealership to buy the vehicle. Otherwise, not only is your choice of loans restricted to what the dealership can offer you, but many dealers do what's called "interest-rate bumping," in which they mark up the interest rate over

what you actually qualify for. Overall, this can cost you hundreds or even thousands of dollars more over the term of the loan.

SHOP FOR THE RIGHT TERMS

Compare interest rates at various financial institutions, such as banks, thrifts, and credit unions, as well as the dealership. Getting preapproved for a loan allows you to keep the financial arrangements out of the vehicle-price negotiations at the dealership. The figure to focus on is the annual percentage rate (APR). You can get a quick read on the terms that various banks are offering at *www.bankrate.com*.

Try to keep the length of the loan as short as possible. A three-year loan costs you far less overall than a four- or five-year loan at the same interest rate. But you need to balance the total cost of the loan against a monthly payment you can afford.

PLAYING THE INCENTIVE GAME

Some automakers have been regularly offering aggressive, low-interest financing incentives on many models, but there are catches:

• Some low rates are available only for 36-month loans, meaning the payments will be quite high.

• Without a stellar credit record, you might not qualify. Always phone the dealership before you visit to find out what credit score qualifies a borrower for the lowest financing rate and, if you don't qualify, what the next best rate would be.

• You often have to make a choice between a low interest rate and a cash rebate. You will have to run the numbers both ways to see which offer saves you the most money. You'll find an autofinancing calculator that lets you make these types of comparisons in the Wheeling and Dealing section of ConsumerReports.org.

• Low-interest rates are no bargain if they

lead you to buy a car you're not happy with. It might make better financial sense over the long term, for instance, to buy a consistently reliable model at a little higher interest than an unreliable model at 0 percent. Likewise, saving a few dollars each month on your payments might not seem worthwhile over the long run if you don't like the vehicle's performance, comfort, or other details.

Even if a dealership is offering a special financing incentive, you should still do your homework by carefully shopping around for the best loan offers. This lets you accurately evaluate the dealership's terms so you can make the best decision.

Step 5: The best deal for you, not the salesperson

When you go to the dealership, the salesperson will probably want to focus on the

---

Know the pros and cons before you lease

Whether leasing is right for you depends on your lifestyle, expectations, and budget. When leasing a vehicle, you usually get lower monthly payments and a lower down payment, and you avoid any resale or trade-in hassles. Leasing can also let you drive a higher-priced, better-equipped vehicle for the same monthly payment you'd be making to buy a less-expensive model. But leasing makes sense only if you stay within the annual mileage limit (typically 12,000 miles), keep the car until the end of the lease (to avoid early-termination penalties), maintain the car well to avoid excess wear-and-tear charges, and plan to trade in your car every two or three years.

Many people who lease end up paying more than they have to because they aren't familiar with the process and don't try to negotiate the vehicle's price. Here are some tips:

1. Negotiate the purchase price of the vehicle as if you were going to buy it. Once you have a firm price, then bring up your desire to lease.

2. Other negotiable elements include the mileage limit, the down payment, and the purchase-option price, or how much you'll have to pay if you want to buy the vehicle at the end of the lease.

3. Avoid lease terms that extend past the vehicle's basic warranty.

4. The four-digit "money factor" is roughly equivalent to a loan's annual percentage rate. To translate this into a percentage rate, multiply the money factor by 2,400.

5. Buy extra miles up front if there's a risk of running over the standard allotment. Excessive mileage at the lease's end is typically charged at a higher rate.

6. Protect yourself with gap insurance. In case you have an accident that totals the car, this covers the difference between an insurance settlement and the actual payoff for the car. In some cases, gap insurance is included in the lease. If it's extra, we recommend that you shop around. Prices can vary dramatically, so get a number of quotes. If your own insurance company provides it, that could be your best bet.

7. Understand your end-of-lease options, such as turning in the vehicle and walking away, purchasing the car, or rolling into another lease.

vehicle's MSRP or on how much of a monthly payment you can afford.

Don't go down this road. Using the monthly payment as the focus, the salesperson will lump the whole process together, including the price for the new vehicle, the trade-in, and financing, if appropriate. This gives him or her more latitude to give you a "good price" in one area while making up for it in another. In the end, this could cost you more overall.

Instead, insist on negotiating one thing at a time. Your first priority is to settle on the lowest price you can get on the new vehicle. Only after you've locked that in should you begin to discuss a trade-in or financing.

ESTABLISH THE GROUND RULES

When you first meet the salesperson, you should set the tone of your negotiations by politely explaining the following:

• You have carefully researched the vehicle you want and have taken a test drive.

• You know exactly what trim level and options you want, have researched the price for that configuration, and know what the dealership paid for it.

• You have already calculated what you are prepared to pay. Reassure him that your offer will include a fair profit.

• If he or she can meet your target price you'll be ready to buy today; if not, you intend to visit other dealerships.

If the salesperson asks about a trade-in, say that you have investigated various options for selling your old car and that you might be open to a trade-in—but only after you've agreed on the new vehicle's price.

When asked, let the salesperson know that you are preapproved for a loan, but that you might be willing to consider financing through the dealership—provided the rate is competitive and you can come to terms on the purchase price of the new car.

SET YOUR SIGHTS ON THE PRICE

When negotiating a vehicle's price, you've got two arrows in your quill:

• Your target price, based on what the dealer paid for the vehicle.

• Competing bids from other local dealerships or car-buying Web sites.

The price you end up with will likely be somewhere between the two. You can start by showing the salesperson your rock-bottom target price. But don't disclose your competitive bids, which are the upper range of what's acceptable. Otherwise, the salesperson will focus on undercutting that higher figure by a token amount instead of working off the lower figure.

For example, the CR Bottom Line for a 2006 Chevrolet Tahoe LS 4x4 is $30,205. Add a 4 to 8 percent markup to that ($31,413 to $32,621), and that's where you begin your negotiations. Tell the salesperson your 4 percent figure and that you want the lowest markup over that price you can get. Inch up if necessary, but don't go over the lowest competing bid.

Only if the negotiations have stalled, and the salesperson is willing to let you walk out the door, should you tell him your lowest competing price as a way of letting him know that he isn't yet in the ballpark. If tyou can agree on an acceptable price, you can proceed to wrap up the deal. If not, you can go to another dealership, now armed with the price that the first dealership gave you.

Never negotiate under pressure. Salespeople's favorite customers are those who seem to be in a rush, since they tend to be the ones who buy a more expensive car than they set out to, or don't negotiate the price down. In addition, a salesperson might tell you that someone else is very interested in the same car and is coming by later to look at it—a common sales tactic.

How to get top dollar for your current car

Whether you trade in your current vehicle or sell it yourself, it's important to know its current cash value. This depends on a number of factors, including the vehicle's age, mileage, condition, trim level, optional equipment, and the region in which it's being sold.

For any used car there are two prices to consider: retail and wholesale. The retail price is what you would expect to pay for the car if you were buying it at a dealership, and is probably the most you should expect to get if you sold it yourself. The wholesale price is essentially its trade-in value. It is notably lower than the retail price.

Find the book value

You can get a basic idea of a vehicle's value from printed pricing guides and Web sites that provide used-car prices. The first figure you'll see when you look up a vehicle in these pricing guides is the car's base value. To get a more accurate figure, you must factor in any options as well as the vehicle's mileage and condition. Some Web sites let you do this online and then give you adjusted figures.

To help, CR offers Used Car Price Reports that are tailored to specific models. Each report gives you the retail and wholesale/trade-in value of the model and walks you through the process of adjusting the value according to options, mileage, and condition.

What are others asking?

You can often get a better fix on how much a vehicle is worth in your region by checking the classified ads and dealer ads in local newspapers, classified-ad publications, and Web sites that specialize in used-car sales. Look for vehicles that are similar to yours in terms of model year, mileage, trim level, options, and condition. But remember that the listed prices are only the asking prices, not necessarily what people are paying. You should assume that all such prices are negotiable.

Even if it is true, you should never feel that you have to make any deal immediately. There are always other cars out there.

TIME TO TALK TRADE-IN

Once you've settled on a price, discuss financing and any trade-in separately. This makes it easier to get the best deal at every step of the transaction.

When discussing a trade-in, you should get the full wholesale value for your current car in a trade-in allowance. To help shore up your case, you should have printouts from several pricing sources. This diffuses any attempt by the salesperson to pull out a used-car pricing book to "prove" that

your figures are too high.

Remember, if the trade-in negotiations become too burdensome, you can always take the car elsewhere or sell it yourself, which will probably get you a higher price anyway. If, however, you're dependent on the trade-in to make the downpayment you want, these alternatives will mean that you'll have to sell your current car before you can sign the contract for your new one.

WEIGH EXTENDED WARRANTIES

An extended warranty is one that takes effect after your factory warranty expires, and can cost hundreds of dollars. Most new cars today come with at least a three-year/36,000-mile, bumper-to-bumper factory warranty. So if you trade in your vehicle every five years or so, or if you lease your new vehicle under a typical 3-year lease with a 12,000-mile-per-year mileage allowance, buying an extended warranty would be a waste of money.

As a general rule, if the model you're buying has an above-average reliability record—earning a very good or excellent CONSUMER REPORTS' Predicted Reliability Rating (see the vehicle reviews on page 167)—it's probably not worth spending the money for an extended warranty. If the model has a below-average record, and you plan to keep it well past the factory warranty period, it may be worth buying the coverage.

If you do decide that an extended warranty is for you, don't feel pressured to buy one the same day you buy the vehicle. You can usually buy a plan any time before the basic warranty expires. We suggest sticking to a plan offered by the automaker. Third-party coverage varies enormously in quality, coverage, and price.

Review any service plan carefully to find out what is and isn't covered, who must perform repairs, and how to file a claim. If you're buying from a dealer, always negotiate the price. And make sure the plan is transferable if you sell the car.

Don't waste money on unnecessary extras

Dealerships often try to get you to buy extra services that are usually overpriced. Don't waste your money. What could cost the dealer about $90 can cost you $1,000 or more. These can include:

Rustproofing and undercoating. Today's vehicles are manufactured with good corrosion protection. In fact, according to CR's reliability surveys, rust problems have almost vanished in modern vehicles.

Fabric protection. If you buy a vehicle with cloth seats, you might want to spend a few bucks for a can of fabric protector and apply it yourself.

Paint sealant. This is little more than vastly overpriced wax. You can easily purchase a good protectant from any autoparts store and apply it yourself.

VIN etching. This is a service in which the vehicle identification number is etched into the windows to deter theft. Some states require that a dealer offer it to you, but none require that you buy it. It's not unusual to find a charge for VIN etching already printed on the purchase agreement, as if it's assumed that you will pay for this service. This has been the case for several vehicles that we've bought for testing. We recommend that you refuse this charge. Even if you decide you want VIN etching, you can have it done less expensively elsewhere, or even do it yourself with a kit that costs about $25.

Dealer prep fees. Inquire about any fees that the dealership is charging you for preparing the vehicle. The manufacturer pays the dealership to prepare the vehicle for you; you shouldn't be charged for this service.

Don't accept those unnecessary services and fees. If the items are on the bill of sale, put a line through them.

RATING THE 2007 MODELS

ncluded here are Ratings on more than 200 vehicles that CR has recently tested. Within each category, they are ranked by their overall road-test score. Recommended models (✓) not only tested well, but have shown average or better reliability and, if crash-tested or included in a government rollover test, provided good crash protection based on our combination of insurance-industry and government crash tests. Recommended models that provide very good or excellent crash protection are designated with a ✓.

Predicted reliability is our forecast of how well a new car will likely hold up based on

data from our 2005 subscriber survey. Owner satisfaction comes from our annual survey where we ask subscribers whether they would buy their vehicle again.

Accident avoidance reflects how capable a vehicle is in helping you avoid an accident through braking, emergency handling, or accelerating out of harm's way. The crash protection Rating is given only to vehicles that have been in both IIHS frontal offset and side-crash tests. Split results indicate whether the vehicle was tested in the IIHS side-crash test with or without side and/or curtain air bags. Overall fuel economy is based on CR's real-world tests.

Better ⟵ ⟶ Worse
⊖ ⊖ ○ ⊖ ●

Make and model	Version tested	Price as tested	Overall road-test score	Survey results		Safety		Fuel economy
				Predicted reliability	Owner satisfaction	Accident avoidance	Crash protection w/wo side air bags	Overall MPG

SMALL CARS (MANUAL TRANSMISSION)

Make and model	Version tested	Price as tested	Overall road-test score	Predicted reliability	Owner satisfaction	Accident avoidance	Crash protection w/wo side air bags	Overall MPG
Honda Civic	EX	$18,810	81	⊖	⊖	⊖	⊖	31
Mazda3	i	17,290	78	⊖	⊖	⊖	-/○	30
Ford Focus	ZX4 ST	19,145	73	○	⊖	⊖	-/○	26
Kia Spectra	EX	15,185	61	NA	NA	○	⊖	28
Scion xB	-	14,245	55	⊖	⊖	⊖	-	32
Scion xA	-	13,045	42	⊖	⊖	⊖	-	31
Suzuki Forenza	Base	13,994	39	NA	NA	○	⊖	27
Chevrolet Aveo	LS	12,925	30	○	○	○	-	27

	Make and model	Version tested	Price as tested	Overall road-test score	Predicted reliability	Owner satisfaction	Accident avoidance	Crash protection w/wo side air bags	Overall MPG

SMALL CARS (AUTOMATIC TRANSMISSION)

	Make and model	Version tested	Price as tested	Overall road-test score	Predicted reliability	Owner satisfaction	Accident avoidance	Crash protection	Overall MPG
✅	Honda Civic	EX	$19,610	78	⊖	⊖	⊖	⊖	28
✓	Ford Focus	ZX4 SES	19,080	77	○	◓	⊖	-/○	24
	Volkswagen Jetta	TDI	24,580	75	NA	NA	⊖	⊖	34
	Volkswagen Jetta	2.5	23,580	72	NA	NA	⊖	⊖	24
✅	Honda Civic	Hybrid	22,400	72	⊖	⊖	⊖	⊖	37
✓	Mazda3	i	18,190	72	⊖	⊖	⊖	-/○	27
✅	Toyota Prius	-	23,780	68	⊖	⊖	○	⊖/○	44
✅	Toyota Corolla	LE	17,910	67	⊖	⊖	○	⊖/○	29
✅	Subaru Impreza	2.5i	19,720	60	⊖	○	⊖	⊖	23
	Kia Spectra	EX	16,185	57	NA	NA	○	◓	25
✓	Scion xB	-	14,995	50	⊖	⊖	⊖	-	30
	Chevrolet Cobalt	LS	16,350	49	●	NA	○	⊖/○	23
	Mitsubishi Lancer	ES	16,574	39	⊖	●	○	-/○	26
	Saturn Ion	3	18,415	38	○	●	⊖	◓/●	25
	Scion xA	-	14,445	37	⊖	⊖	⊖	-	30
	Suzuki Forenza	Base	14,794	35	NA	NA	○	◓	24
	Chevrolet Aveo	LS	13,885	32	○	◓	○	-	28

CONVERTIBLES

	Make and model	Version tested	Price as tested	Overall road-test score	Predicted reliability	Owner satisfaction	Accident avoidance	Crash protection	Overall MPG
✓	Mini Cooper	S (MT)	$29,820	72	○	⊖	⊖	-	25
✓	Toyota Camry Solara	XLE (V6, AT)	31,087	69	⊖	⊖	⊖	-	21
✓	Chrysler PT Cruiser	GT turbo (MT)	29,305	58	○	⊖	⊖	-	22
	Ford Mustang	Premium (V6, AT)	28,070	55	●	⊖	⊖	-	20

Make and model	Version tested	Price as tested	Overall road-test score	Predicted reliability	Owner satisfaction	Accident avoidance	Crash protection w/wo side air bags	Overall MPG
ROADSTERS								
Porsche Boxster	2.7	$49,075	90	NA	◒	◒	-	22
Mazda MX-5 Miata	Grand Touring	27,095	89	◒	◒	◒	-	27
Mercedes-Benz SLK350	-	53,950	84	◖	◒	◒	-	21
Chevrolet Corvette	Base	57,020	81	●	◒	◒	-	21
Nissan 350Z	Grand Touring	42,800	80	○	◒	◒	-	20
Honda S2000	-	33,665	80	◒	◒	◒	-	25
BMW Z4	3.0i	46,070	79	○	◒	◒	-	26
Lotus Elise	-	45,545	55	NA	NA	◒	-	29
Pontiac Solstice	Base	25,895	50	New	New	◒	-	23
Saturn Sky	Base	26,274	50	New	New	◒	-	23
PERFORMANCE/LUXURY SPORTS CARS								
Porsche 911	Carrera S	$87,520	96	NA	◒	◒	-	20
Chevrolet Corvette	Z06	64,890	93	●	◒	◒	-	19
Audi S4	-	50,870	88	●	◒	◒	◒	20
Mercedes-Benz SL550	-	105,855	86	●	◒	◒	-	17
BMW 650i Coupe	-	77,440	85	NA	NA	◒	-	19
Cadillac CTS-V	(V8)	52,685	83	○	◒	◒	-	17
Jaguar XK Convertible	-	85,635	74	New	New	◒	-	19
Lexus SC430	-	67,084	73	◒	◒	◒	-	21
Cadillac XLR	Base	77,290	72	NA	NA	◒	-	17
Dodge Viper	SRT10	91,990	67	NA	NA	◒	-	15

Make and model	Version tested	Price as tested	Overall road-test score	Predicted reliability	Owner satisfaction	Accident avoidance	Crash protection w/wo side air bags	Overall MPG
SPORTS/SPORTY CARS								
✓ Volkswagen GTi	-	$23,975	91	New	New	⊖	-	25
✓ Subaru Impreza	WRX STi	32,870	90	⊖	⊜	⊜	-	20
✓ Mazda RX-8	-	31,305	86	○	○	⊜	-	18
✓ Honda Civic	Si	20,540	85	⊜	⊜	⊜	-	27
Mitsubishi Lancer	Evolution	29,094	81	NA	NA	⊜	-	20
✓ Subaru Impreza	WRX TR	24,620	79	⊜	⊜	⊜	-	22
Chevrolet Cobalt	SS	22,635	73	NA	NA	⊜	-	23
✓ Scion tC	TRD	20,665	73	○	⊜	⊜	-	26
✓ Ford Mustang	GT (V8)	29,020	72	○	⊜	⊜	-	20
✓ Scion tC	Base	17,115	69	○	⊜	⊜	-	26
✓ Chevrolet Monte Carlo	SS (AT)	30,300	54	⊜	New	⊜	-	17
✓ Chrysler Crossfire	Coupe	29,920	54	○	○	⊜	-	22
✓ Hyundai Tiburon	GT (V6)	21,389	48	○	◒	⊜	-	22
Mitsubishi Eclipse	GS (4-cyl.)	21,764	41	New	New	○	-	23
UPSCALE SEDANS								
✓ Acura TL	-	$33,670	90	⊖	⊜	⊜	⊜	23
✓ Lexus IS250	-	33,734	84	⊜	⊜	⊜	⊜	24
BMW 325i	-	36,720	78	New	⊜	⊜	⊜	24
✓ Acura TSX	-	29,760	77	⊜	⊜	⊜	⊜	23
✓ Audi A4	2.0T	35,855	77	○	⊜	⊜	⊜	23
Lincoln Zephyr	-	32,250	77	New	New	⊜	○	20
✓ Cadillac CTS	2.8	35,275	74	○	⊜	⊜	-	19
Mercedes-Benz C230	-	34,225	73	◒	○	⊜	⊜	22
✓ Infiniti G35	-	36,760	71	⊜	⊜	⊜	⊜	20
Jaguar X-Type	3.0	39,120	71	◒	◒	⊜	⊜	19
Saab 9-3	2.0T	31,615	65	●	◒	⊜	⊜	23
✓ Volvo S60	2.5T	34,980	58	⊖	○	○	⊜	22

Make and model	Version tested	Price as tested	Overall road-test score	Predicted reliability	Owner satisfaction	Accident avoidance	Crash protection w/wo side air bags	Overall MPG
LUXURY SEDANS								
Infiniti M35	X (V6,AWD)	$50,980	97	⊖	⊖	⊖	⊖	18
BMW 530i*	-	55,370	85	○	○	⊖	-	20
Audi A6	3.2 Quattro	50,820	83	◑	⊖	⊖	⊖	21
Cadillac STS	(V6)	50,335	78	○	○	⊖	-	19
Audi A8	L	76,470	77	●	⊖	⊖	-	17
Acura RL	-	49,670	76	○	⊖	○	-	18
Jaguar S-Type	4.2	54,795	76	●	⊖	⊖	-	19
Jaguar XJ8	Vanden Plas	73,295	76	◑	⊖	⊖	-	19
Lexus GS300	AWD	51,859	75	⊖	⊖	⊖	⊖	20
Mercedes-Benz CLS500*	-	76,784	73	New	New	⊖	-	18
BMW 745Li*	-	84,145	70	●	○	⊖	-	18
LARGE SEDANS								
Toyota Avalon	XLS	$33,070	89	○	⊖	⊖	⊖	22
Hyundai Azera	Limited	30,075	83	New	New	⊖	⊖	19
Ford Five Hundred	SEL (FWD)	27,510	70	○	⊖	○	⊖/○	21
Mercury Montego	Luxury (FWD)	27,710	70	○	⊖	○	⊖/○	21
Cadillac DTS	Luxury II	47,395	69	New	New	○	⊖	17
Ford Five Hundred	SEL (AWD)	29,115	68	○	⊖	○	⊖/○	20
Mercury Montego	Luxury (AWD)	29,080	68	○	⊖	○	⊖/○	20
Chrysler 300	C (V8)	37,480	64	●	⊖	⊖	⊖/○	16
Chrysler 300	Touring (V6)	30,255	60	○	⊖	⊖	⊖/○	19
Dodge Charger	R/T (V8)	36,295	59	New	New	⊖	⊖/○	17
Dodge Charger	SXT (V6)	28,860	58	New	New	⊖	⊖/○	19
Buick Lucerne	CXL (V6)	30,680	56	New	New	○	⊖	19
Kia Amanti	-	29,740	55	⊖	⊖	○	-	18
Lincoln Town Car	Signature	42,715	54	○	⊖	○	-	17
Ford Crown Victoria	LX	30,900	43	○	○	○	-/○	16
Mercury Grand Marquis	LSE	32,765	43	○	○	○	-/○	16

Overall road-test score scale: 0 P F G VG E 100

* Powertrain changes since last test

Make and model	Version tested	Price as tested	Overall road-test score	Predicted reliability	Owner satisfaction	Accident avoidance	Crash protection w/wo side air bags	Overall MPG

FAMILY SEDANS

Make and model	Version tested	Price as tested	Overall road-test score	Predicted reliability	Owner satisfaction	Accident avoidance	Crash protection w/wo side air bags	Overall MPG
✓ Honda Accord	EX (V6)	$27,850	89	⊖	⊖	⊖	⊖	23
Volkswagen Passat	3.6 (V6)	33,315	89	New	New	⊖	⊖	22
✓ Honda Accord	Hybrid (V6)	31,540	87	⊖	⊖	⊖	⊖	25
✓ Toyota Camry	XLE (V6)	29,839	87	⊖	⊖	⊖	-	23
Volkswagen Passat	2.0T (4-cyl.)	27,440	86	New	New	⊖	⊖	24
✓ Toyota Camry	Hybrid (4-cyl.)	30,667	84	⊖	⊖	⊖	-	34
✓ Honda Accord	EX (4-cyl.)	23,515	78	⊖	⊖	⊖	⊖	24
✓ Toyota Camry	LE (4-cyl.)	21,080	77	⊖	⊖	⊖	-	24
Ford Fusion	SEL (V6)	26,025	77	New	New	⊖	-/◑	20
Mercury Milan	Premier (V6)	25,870	77	New	New	⊖	-/◑	20
Hyundai Sonata	GLS (V6)	22,995	76	New	New	⊖	⊖	21
✓ Subaru Legacy	2.5 GT (4-cyl.)	30,370	75	⊖	⊖	⊖	⊖	18
Hyundai Sonata	GLS (4-cyl.)	21,345	74	New	New	⊖	⊖	23
✓ Mazda6	i (4-cyl.)	21,930	69	○	◔	⊖	-/○	23
Ford Fusion	SE (4-cyl.)	19,976	69	New	New	⊖	-/◑	23
Mercury Milan	Base (4-cyl.)	20,415	69	New	New	⊖	-/◑	23
Mazda6	s (V6)	27,790	69	◑	○	⊖	-/○	20
✓ Toyota Prius	-	23,780	68	⊖	⊖	○	⊖/○	44
Chevrolet Malibu	LS (4-cyl.)	20,125	66	◑	◑	⊖	⊖/○	24
Chevrolet Malibu	LT (V6)	22,460	66	◑	◑	⊖	⊖/○	23
✓ Mitsubishi Galant	GTS (V6)	27,094	64	⊖	◔	⊖	⊖	20
✓ Chevrolet Impala	3LT (3.9)	26,840	63	⊖	New	○	⊖	20
✓ Volvo S40	2.4i (5-cyl.)	29,145	59	○	⊖	⊖	⊖	23
✓ Mitsubishi Galant	ES (4-cyl.)	20,944	58	⊖	⊖	⊖	⊖	23
✓ Buick LaCrosse	CXL	31,450	55	⊖	○	○	⊖	18
✓ Pontiac G6	Base (V6)	23,080	51	○	⊖	○	⊖/○	21
Pontiac Grand Prix	GT (V6)	28,255	38	⊖	●	○	⊖/-	20

Make and model	Version tested	Price as tested	Overall road-test score	Predicted reliability	Owner satisfaction	Accident avoidance	Crash protection w/wo side air bags	Overall MPG
MINIVANS								
Honda Odyssey	EX	$32,610	91	○	⊖	⊖	⊖	19
Toyota Sienna	XLE *	34,909	89	⊖	⊖	○	⊖	19
Hyundai Entourage	SE	30,595	78	New	New	⊖	⊖	17
Kia Sedona	EX	31,365	78	New	New	⊖	⊖	17
Nissan Quest	3.5 SL	26,580	70	●	⊖	○	⊖	18
Chrysler Town & Country	Limited	37,115	59	⊖	⊖	○	⊖/○	17
Dodge Grand Caravan	SXT	34,140	59	⊖	⊖	○	⊖/○	17
Ford Freestar	SEL	33,285	58	○	⊖	○	⊖/○	17
Chevrolet Uplander	LS*	25,725	56	●	⊖	○	⊖/○	17
Saturn Relay	3*	30,895	56	●	⊖	○	⊖/○	17
WAGONS AND HATCHBACKS								
Mazda5	Touring	$22,615	86	New	New	⊖	-	23
Volkswagen Passat	3.6 4Motion	36,480	80	New	New	⊖	-	20
Mazda3	s Grand Touring	22,095	79	⊖	⊖	⊖	-	25
Audi A3	2.0T	27,990	76	New	New	⊖	⊖	25
Subaru Outback	2.5i	28,670	73	⊖	⊖	○	-	21
BMW 325xi	(AWD)	40,520	72	New	New	⊖	-	22
Mazda6	s	25,840	72	⊖	○	⊖	-	19
Volvo XC70	-	43,205	71	○	⊖	○	-	19
Subaru Outback	3.0 R VDC	36,538	71	⊖	⊖	○	-	19
Toyota Matrix	Standard	19,260	66	⊖	○	○	-	27
Pontiac Vibe	Base	19,960	66	⊖	○	○	-	27
Ford Focus	ZX5 S	18,750	65	○	○	⊖	-	24
Chevrolet Malibu Maxx	LT (V6)	23,225	65	○	○	○	-	21
Volvo V50	T5 (AWD)	35,270	61	●	○	⊖	-	20
Saab 9-2X	2.5i	25,560	61	⊖	NA	⊖	⊖	22
Subaru Impreza	2.5i	19,720	61	⊖	○	⊖	⊖	22

Powertrain changes since last test

	Make and model	Version tested	Price as tested	Overall road-test score	Predicted reliability	Owner satisfaction	Accident avoidance	Crash protection w/wo side air bags	Overall MPG

WAGONS AND HATCHBACKS *continued*

	Make and model	Version tested	Price as tested	Overall road-test score	Predicted reliability	Owner satisfaction	Accident avoidance	Crash protection w/wo side air bags	Overall MPG
✓	Chrysler PT Cruiser	Limited (turbo)	23,485	61	○	◑	○	-	20
✓	Dodge Magnum	SXT (V6)	29,630	55	○	○	○	-	19
	Chevrolet HHR	LT (2.4)	21,045	55	New	New	○	-	23
	Dodge Caliber	R/T (AWD)	23,860	51	New	New	○	◑	22
✓	Scion xB	-	14,995	50	◑	◑	○	-	30
	Dodge Caliber	SXT (FWD)	19,015	49	New	New	○	◑	24

COMPACT PICKUPS

	Make and model	Version tested	Price as tested	Overall road-test score	Predicted reliability	Owner satisfaction	Accident avoidance	Crash protection w/wo side air bags	Overall MPG
✓	Nissan Frontier	LE (V6)	$30,110	67	○	◑	○	-	15
✓	Toyota Tacoma	TRD (V6)	29,210	63	○	◑	◑	-	17
	Dodge Dakota	SLT (4.7)	29,970	58	◑	○	○	-	14
	Ford Explorer Sport Trac	XLT (V6)	30,395	54	New	New	○	-	14
	Chevrolet Colorado	LS Z71 (5-cyl.)*	29,315	40	●	◑	◑	-	16
	GMC Canyon	SLE Z71 (5-cyl.)*	30,080	40	●	◑	◑	-	16

FULL-SIZED PICKUPS

	Make and model	Version tested	Price as tested	Overall road-test score	Predicted reliability	Owner satisfaction	Accident avoidance	Crash protection w/wo side air bags	Overall MPG
✓	Honda Ridgeline	RTS	$30,825	79	◑	◑	○	-	15
✓	Toyota Tundra	SR5 (4.7)*	33,459	67	◑	◑	○	-	14
	Chevrolet Avalanche	LT (5.3)	46,560	73	New	New	○	-	13
	Ford F-150	XLT (5.4)	35,940	65	◑	◑	○	-	14
	Nissan Titan	SE (5.6)	36,520	62	●	◑	○	-	13
	Dodge Ram 1500	SLT (5.7)	36,015	44	○	○	○	-	11
	Dodge Ram 1500	SLT (4.7)	33,995	39	○	○	◑	-	12

SMALL SPORT-UTILITY VEHICLES

	Make and model	Version tested	Price as tested	Overall road-test score	Predicted reliability	Owner satisfaction	Accident avoidance	Crash protection w/wo side air bags	Overall MPG
✅	Toyota RAV4	Limited (V6)	$30,328	83	◑	◑	◑	◑	22
✅	Toyota RAV4	Base (4-cyl.)	23,163	77	◑	◑	◑	◑	23
✅	Subaru Forester	2.5 X	23,420	71	◑	◑	◑	◑	22
	Hyundai Tucson	GLS (V6)	22,610	67	●	○	◑	○	18

Powertrain changes since last test

Make and model	Version tested	Price as tested	Overall road-test score	Predicted reliability	Owner satisfaction	Accident avoidance	Crash protection w/wo side air bags	Overall MPG

SMALL SPORT-UTILITY VEHICLES *continued*

Make and model	Version tested	Price as tested	Score	Predicted reliability	Owner satisfaction	Accident avoidance	Crash protection w/wo side air bags	Overall MPG
Kia Sportage	EX (V6)	22,290	67	●	NA	◒	○	18
Ford Escape Hybrid	(AWD)	31,210	66	◒	◒	○	◒/◖	26
Mercury Mariner Hybrid	(AWD)	31,910	66	◒	○	○	◒/◖	26
Subaru Baja	-	23,920	64	◒	◒	◒	-	20
Ford Escape	XLT (V6)	26,745	61	○	◖	○	◒/◖	18
Mazda Tribute	s (V6)	27,020	61	○	◖	○	◒/◖	18
Mercury Mariner	Luxury (V6)	26,445	61	◒	○	○	◒/◖	18
Honda Element	EX	22,240	59	◒	◒			20
Nissan Xterra	S	28,000	59	NA	NA	○	-	17
Suzuki Grand Vitara	Premium	22,894	56	New	New	○	-	18
Saturn Vue	(V6)	26,810	49	●	◖	○	-/○	19
Chevrolet Equinox	LT	25,385	47	◖	●	○	-	17
Pontiac Torrent	(AWD)	26,360	47	New	New	○	-	17
Kia Sorento	LX	24,865	43	◖	○	○	-	15
Jeep Liberty	Sport (V6)	24,310	42	○	◖	○	-	15

MIDSIZED SPORT-UTILITY VEHICLES

Make and model	Version tested	Price as tested	Score	Predicted reliability	Owner satisfaction	Accident avoidance	Crash protection w/wo side air bags	Overall MPG
Toyota Highlander Hybrid	Limited	$39,885	86	◒	◒	○	-	22
Lexus RX400h	-	49,883	84	◒	◒	◒	-	23
Lexus RX330	*	44,833	79	◒	◒	◒	-	18
Honda Pilot	EX-L	34,835	79	◒	◒	◒	-	17
Mercedez-Benz GL450	-	67,820	76	New	New	○	-	15
Mercedez-Benz R500	-	62,055	76	New	New	○	-	15
Toyota Highlander	Limited (V6)	35,155	75	◒	◒	◒	-	19
Nissan Murano	SL	36,390	75	◒	◒	◒	-	19
Volvo XC90	(V8)	47,685	74	●	○	◒	-	16
Cadillac SRX	(V8)	53,730	74	●	○	◒	-	16
Ford Freestyle	SEL (AWD)	32,675	73	●	○	○	-	18

Powertrain changes since last test

Make and model	Version tested	Price as tested	Overall road-test score		Survey results		Safety		Fuel economy
			0 ... 100 P F G VG E		Predicted reliability	Owner satisfaction	Accident avoidance	Crash protection w/o side air bags	Overall MPG
MIDSIZED SPORT-UTILITY VEHICLES Continued									
✓ Infiniti FX35	(V6)	39,960	71		⊖	⊖	⊖	-	18
Audi Q7	4.2	57,920	69		New	New	○	-	15
Mercedes-Benz ML350	-	48,880	69		New	New	⊖	-	16
✓ BMW X3	2.5i*	40,195	68		○	○	⊖	-	17
✓ Lexus GX470	-	51,787	68		⊖	⊖	⊖	-	15
✓ Mitsubishi Endeavor	LS	32,394	66		⊖	○	○	-	17
✓ Toyota 4Runner	SR5 (V6)	33,330	65		⊖	○	⊖	-	16
✓ Subaru B9 Tribeca	Limited	36,550	65		⊖	New	⊖	-	16
✓ Nissan Pathfinder	LE	36,310	62		○	○	○	-	15
Land Rover LR3	SE (V8)	50,150	61		●	⊖	○	-	13
Ford Explorer	Eddie Bauer (V8)	39,025	57		●	New	○	-	14
Ford Explorer	XLT (V6)	35,520	53		●	New	○	-	15
Dodge Durango	Limited 5.7 (V8)	39,620	52		⊖	○	○	-	12
Jeep Commander	Limited (5.7)	33,085	51		New	New	○	-	13
Jeep Grand Cherokee	Laredo 4.7 (V8)	35,500	50		●	⊖	○	-	14
Chevrolet TrailBlazer	LT (V6)	35,625	43		⊖	⊖	○	-	15
GMC Envoy	SLT (V6)	35,125	43		⊖	⊖	○	-	15
LARGE SPORT-UTILITY VEHICLES									
Mercedes-Benz GL450	-	67,820	76		New	New	○	-	15
✓ Toyota Land Cruiser	*	$55,590	67		⊖	⊖	○	-	14
Nissan Armada	LE	43,570	64		●	⊖	○	-	13
✓ Toyota Sequoia	Limited*	46,705	62		⊖	⊖	○	-	15
Cadillac Escalade	Base	64,905	61		New	New	○	-	13
Chevrolet Tahoe	LT (5.3)	42,849	53		New	New	○	-	14
GMC Yukon	SLT (5.3)	43,169	53		New	New	○	-	14
Dodge Durango	Limited 5.7 (V8)	39,620	52		⊖	○	○	-	12

Powertrain changes since last test

REVIEWS OF THE 2006-07 MODELS

This rundown of all the major 2007 models can start you on your search for a new car, minivan, SUV, or pickup. You'll find a summary of each model, often based on recent road tests that are applicable to this year's models.

Most models include CONSUMER REPORTS' predicted reliability rating, an indication of how problematic we expect a model to be. It is based on our annual subscriber surveys, where we ask owners about any serious problems they've had with their vehicles in the previous 12 months. This data allows us to predict how this year's models are likely to hold up.

Recommended models (✔) not only tested well, but showed average reliability or better and performed at least adequately if crash-tested or included in a government rollover test. Recommended models that have performed especially well in both IIHS crash tests and at least one government crash test are designated with a ✔ .

Entries include, where available, the date of the last road test for that model published in CONSUMER REPORTS magazine. These road-test reports are also available to subscribers of our Web site, at *www .ConsumerReports.org*.

The 2007 cars, trucks, SUVs & minivans

Predicted reliability is a judgment based on our annual reliability survey data. New or recently redesigned models are marked "New." NA means data not available.

Better ◄—————————► Worse
⊖   ⊖   ○   ⊖   ●

Model	Predicted reliability	Description/with last road-test date
Acura MDX	⊖	One of our top-rated SUVs, the MDX is a well-designed car-based SUV that can hold seven passengers. Ride and handling are competent. The interior is flexible, with a third-row seat that folds flat into the cargo floor. A redesign arrives for 2007. **To be tested**
Acura RDX	NEW	This car-based SUV shares the same platform as the redesigned Honda CR-V and uses a turbocharged 2.3-liter, four-cylinder engine that is not as smooth or responsive as a V6. **To be tested**
✔ **Acura RL**	○	The AWD RL is powered by a V6. The powertrain is polished, but ride and handling don't stand out. The less-expensive TL has similar interior room, and the RL's driver interaction system isn't particularly intuitive. **Sept. 2005**
✔ **Acura TL**	⊖	The TL provides a near-ideal blend of comfort, convenience, and sportiness. Handling is taut and agile, and the engine delivers quick acceleration. The ride is firm yet comfortable and quiet. **Feb. 2004**
✔ **Acura TSX**	⊖	The TSX four-door features a smooth-revving engine and slick transmission. Handling is agile, but the ride is a bit stiff and rear seat room is tight. Good crash results and reliability round out the package. **Nov. 2004**

Model	Predicted reliability	Description/with last road-test date
Audi A3	NEW	The sporty A3 four-door hatchback has a tasteful interior. It uses a quick turbocharged 2.0-liter, four-cylinder engine, and the optional DSG transmission works well. An AWD version with a 3.2-liter V6 is also available. Crash-test results are impressive. **Sept. 2006**
✓ Audi A4	○	The A4 handles nimbly. The 2.0T is noisy and the 3.2 V6 is refined. The low-speed ride is a bit firm. The comfortable interior is cramped in the rear. AWD is available, as are wagon and convertible models. **May 2006**
Audi A6	◒	The A6 sedan offers a V6 and V8 engines with optional all-wheel drive. The ride is firm yet comfortable, but is no match for the Mercedes-Benz E-Class. Handling is responsive and secure. Crash-test results are impressive, but reliability is disappointing. **Sept. 2005**
Audi A8	●	Audi's flagship features a strong V8, AWD, and an aluminum body. The roomy interior is well-crafted. It is quiet and agile, but the ride is too ordinary for a luxury car. A V12 engine is optional. The MMI driver interaction system is cumbersome to use. **Nov. 2003**
Audi Q7	NEW	Audi's first SUV uses a 4.2-liter V8 mated to a six-speed automatic. The Q7 lacks off-road gearing but has three-row seating to accommodate seven passengers. It is fairly nimble, but the low speed ride is stiff. A V6 engine arrives in 2007. **Nov. 2006**
Audi S4	●	The high-performance version of the A4 uses a 4.2-liter V8. AWD is standard. It has very capable handling but lacks finesse. Wagon and convertible versions, and a super high performance RS4, are available. Unlike the A4, reliability has been poor. **Sept. 2004**
Audi TT	◒	This coupe has a nicely detailed interior. Four-cylinder and V6 engines are available, with optional AWD. The ride is stiff and handling is less sporty than a Porsche Boxster's. The 2007 redesign uses the turbocharged 2.0-liter four-cylinder and the 3.2-liter V6. **To be tested**
BMW 3 Series	NEW	The 3 Series has agile, a supple ride, and smooth, six-cylinder engines. The interior is comfortable and luxurious. Redesigned coupe and convertible models arrive for 2007, and an all-wheel-drive wagon is available. **May 2006**
✓ BMW 5 Series	○	The 5 Series is impressive and frustrating. We found the iDrive control system tedious to use. Handling is agile, and the ride is comfortable and quiet. The automatic transmission and engine are smooth. Reliability has been average. **June 2004**
BMW 6 Series	NA	The 6 Series coupe is based on the 5 Series platform. The standard engine is a smooth and punchy 4.8-liter V8. A convertible version and a limited-production, high-performance V10-powered M6 are available. **Oct. 2006**
BMW 7 Series	●	The 7 Series is quiet, quick, and agile. The iDrive control system and other ergonomic quirks add stress instead of making the driving experience comforting and luxurious. The ride is steady, and the seats are comfortable. **Nov. 2003**
✓ BMW X3	○	The X3 is loosely based on the previous-generation 3 Series, but with a roomier rear seat. The ride is firm and handling is agile. A

Model	Predicted reliability	Description/with last road-test date
		2007 freshening brings more power and improved interior fit and finish. **Dec. 2004**
BMW X5	NEW	The X5 delivers an impressive drivetrain and comfortable front seats. The ride is choppy. All engines deliver spirited acceleration. Reliability, has been average. A redesign, with a third-row seat, arrives for 2007. **To be tested**
BMW Z4	O	The Z4 is a sporty two-seater available as a coupe or convertible. Our tested convertible lacked agility. The cabin is roomy, and the 3.0-liter six-cylinder is strong. The power-operated top is simple to use. The M-badged versions offer 330 horsepower. **Oct. 2005**
Buick Enclave	NEW	This car-based three-row SUV shares a new platform with the Saturn Outlook and GMC Acadia. All three vehicles use GM's smooth 3.6-liter, V6 engine. The Enclave goes on sale next spring. **To be tested**
Buick LaCrosse	⊖	The LaCrosse is quiet and comfortable yet offers fairly responsive handling. The interior is well-constructed. Rear-seat room is tight. The 3.8-liter V6 engine is thirsty and sounds coarse. The 3.6-liter V6 is more refined and stronger. **March 2005**
Buick Lucerne	NEW	The Lucerne comes with a standard 3.8-liter V6; a 4.6-liter V8 is optional. The V6 is thirsty and coarse-sounding. Braking and handling are below par, but the ride is comfortable. Rear seat room is better than in the LaCrosse. **Aug. 2006**
Buick Rainier	O	The Rainier is the upscale version of the Chevrolet TrailBlazer. It comes with a 4.2-liter six-cylinder or a 5.3-liter V8. The permanently engaged AWD system has no low range, making it more suited for slippery roads than for off-roading.
Buick Rendezvous	O	This minivan-based SUV features an independent suspension, optional all-wheel drive, and room for seven. Handling is secure, but reluctant. Acceleration is so-so and the interior feels cheap.
Buick Terraza	●	The Terraza uses a standard 3.9-liter V6 for 2007. Removing the second-row seats is cumbersome. The third-row seat only folds flat on the floor. Handling is reluctant, interior fit and finish is insubstantial, and the ride is stiff and noisy.
Cadillac CTS	O	This sports sedan feels agile and taut but has pesky oversights. A 2.8-liter V6 and a smooth 3.6-liter V6 are offered. Acceleration is quick and the transmission is very smooth. The ESC is too slow to intervene, allowing too much tail slide. Reliability is average. **May 2006**
Cadillac CTS-V	O	This is a sports car with the practicality of a sedan. Acceleration from the Corvette V8 engine is quick, and the six-speed manual transmission works well. Handling is very agile and precise, but the electronic stability control intervenes too late. **Sept. 2004**
Cadillac DTS	NEW	The DTS is a freshening of the DeVille. It offers two versions of the smooth and powerful 4.6-liter Northstar V8. Accommodations are ample and luxurious, and the rear seat roomy and comfortable. The ride is quiet and comfortable, but handling is clumsy. **Aug. 2006**

Model	Predicted reliability	Description/with last road-test date
Cadillac Escalade	NEW	The redesigned Escalade is an upscale version of the Chevrolet Tahoe, and available in three versions: the standard Escalade, extra-long ESV, and EXT pickup. A 6.2-liter V8, six-speed automatic, and electronic stability control are standard. **Nov. 2006**
Cadillac SRX	●	The upscale SRX is the first car-based SUV from Cadillac. This tall wagon is powered by a smooth V8 or a V6. Handling is agile and secure. The ride is taut yet supple. The optional power-folding third-row seat operates slowly. **March 2004**
✓ **Cadillac STS**	○	The rear-drive STS uses a 3.6-liter V6 or the 4.6-liter Northstar V8. All-wheel drive is optional. The ride is firm yet supple. Handling is taut and agile, and the cabin is quiet, but the rear seat isn't as large as the class leaders. **Sept. 2005**
Cadillac XLR	NA	The XLR is based on the Corvette, but uses the smooth Northstar V8 and a five-speed automatic. It is quick and elegant, but not sporty. The more powerful XLR-V uses a supercharged V8 and six-speed automatic. **Oct. 2006**
Chevrolet Avalanche	NEW	This redesigned crew-cab pickup has a unified bed and cab. The midgate at the back of the cab can be folded down to extend the cargo bed into the rear of the cabin. The 5.3-liter V8 provides adequate acceleration but was thirsty. **Nov. 2006**
Chevrolet Aveo	○	The Aveo sedan and hatchback are Daewoos rebadged as Chevrolets. They handle clumsily but are ultimately secure. Acceleration and fuel economy are unimpressive for an economy car. Fit and finish is adequate. **Aug. 2004**
Chevrolet Cobalt SS	●	The Cobalt's 2.2-liter four-cylinder is a bit noisy and not fuel-efficient. A more powerful 2.4-liter and a supercharged 2.0-liter are available. Overall this sedan is not competitive with the best in the class. Without the optional side-curtain air bags, the Cobalt scored poor in the IIHS side-crash test. **May 2005**
Chevrolet Cobalt	NA	The supercharged 2.0-liter engine makes the Cobalt SS coupe quick and fun. Handling is nimble and the firm ride isn't too stiff. The trunk is roomy, but the SS isn't as versatile as some hatchbacks. **Dec. 2005**
Chevrolet Colorado	●	The Colorado's five-cylinder engine is unrefined, lacks punch, and has worse fuel-economy than competing V6s. Handling is sound but unexceptional. The ride is unsettled, and the body constantly quivers. Overall, it trails the competition. **July 2005**
Chevrolet Corvette	●	The Corvette is powered by a 6.0-liter V8 that delivers impressive performance. The ride is comfortable, and handling is capable but less agile than other sports cars. The sportier Z06 has a 7.0-liter V8 that produces 505 hp and has much better handling. **Oct. 2005**
Chevrolet Equinox	◐	The Equinox has a roomy rear seat that can move fore and aft to increase passenger or cargo room. Interior quality is subpar, and the V6 is noisy and unrefined. Handling is clumsy. Tip-ups in the government rollover tests are a negative. **Oct. 2004**

Model	Predicted reliability	Description/with last road-test date
Chevrolet HHR	NEW	The HHR is a raised wagon based on the same platform as the Chevrolet Cobalt. Both the 2.2- and 2.4-liter, four-cylinder engines lack punch, and the steering is too light. Visibility is compromised by the retro styling cues. **Jan. 2006**
✓ **Chevrolet Impala**	⊖	The Impala is freshened for 2006. The 3.9-liter V6 delivers responsive performance. The 5.3-liter V8 is quick, but spins the front tires easily. Handling is sound, but body lean is noticeable. The ride is absorbent but unsettled. Side curtain air bags are standard. **March 2006**
Chevrolet Malibu	⊖	This sedan offers easy interior access and a comfortable ride. The V6 delivers quick acceleration and 23 mpg overall in the sedan. Side-curtain air bags are a must for crash protection. Reliability of the sedan is below average. **May 2004**
✓ **Chevrolet Malibu Maxx**	○	This is a hatchback version of the Malibu four-door sedan. The Maxx's extended wheelbase and movable second-row seats provide more rear-seat room and the interior flexibility of a wagon or small SUV. We recommend the optional curtain air bags. **Feb. 2005**
✓ **Chevrolet Monte Carlo**	⊖	This long-standing model was freshened for the 2006 model year. The 5.3-liter V8 has a lot of power and spins the front tires easily. The base engine is a 3.5-liter V6. The SS model has a stiff and busy ride. **March 2006**
Chevrolet Silverado 1500 (new)	NEW	The new Silverado is now on sale. We expect improved handling and better fit and finish, as in the redesigned Tahoe and Avalanche we tested. The optional four-wheel drive is a selectable full-time system, a plus. Extended-cab versions have a usable rear seat, a rarity in this class. **To be tested**
Chevrolet Suburban	NEW	The redesigned Suburban is a longer version of the Tahoe. Handling is more agile, steering and brakes are better, and the ride is more controlled. Interior quality is much improved. The Suburban can seat eight with cargo space left over and tow a heavy trailer.
Chevrolet Tahoe	NEW	The redesigned Tahoe has better handling, braking, ride, and interior materials than its predecessor. 4WD models have a selectable full-time system that can remain engaged indefinitely. ESC is standard. A rear-view camera system is optional. **July 2006**
Chevrolet TrailBlazer	⊖	A compliant low-speed ride is the TrailBlazer's only real asset. Otherwise, it has sloppy handling, uncomfortable seats, ill-fitting trim, and too much wind noise. The EXT model with a third-row seat has been dropped. **July 2006**
Chevrolet Uplander	●	For 2007 the Uplander received a standard 3.9-liter V6. Removing the second-row seats is cumbersome. The folding third-row seat only folds flat on the floor. Handling is reluctant, interior fit and finish is insubstantial, and the ride is stiff and noisy. **March 2005**
✓ **Chrysler 300**	○	The RWD 300 offers two V6 engines in base trims and a powerful V8 in the 300C and SRT8. Interior materials are OK, but don't stand out in this class. The claustrophobic cabin and limited outward visibility are detractions. Reliability has been average. **Jan. 2005**

Model	Predicted reliability	Description/with last road-test date
Chrysler Aspen	NEW	The Aspen is a twin of the Dodge Durango. The interior has fake wood trim and an analog clock. The Durango we tested was fairly quiet but thirsty. Handling was secure although less responsive than some competing models.
✓ **Chrysler Crossfire**	○	Based on the old Mercedes-Benz SLK, this rear-drive two-seater has a strong engine, but handling lacks finesse. The ride is stiff, visibility is poor, and there's too much wind noise. A convertible and a supercharged SRT6 are available. **Dec. 2003**
✓ **Chrysler PT Cruiser**	○	This tall wagon has a versatile interior and secure, predictable handling. Acceleration with the two turbocharged engines is quick. The ride is somewhat stiff, and the cabin is a bit noisy, with wind noise particularly evident in the convertible version. **Jan. 2006**
Chrysler Pacifica	◐	The Pacifica combines the characteristics of an SUV, a minivan, and a wagon. Ride and handling are capable, and the powertrain gets a needed upgrade for 2007. Access is easy, and the third row folds flat when not needed. A five-passenger version is available. **To be tested**
Chrysler Sebring	NEW	A new, much improved Sebring arrives for 2007, replacing the unpleasant current model. The new convertible will be offered with a folding hard top as well as a soft top. **To be tested**
Chrysler Town & Country	◐	The Town & Country has a roomy interior and optional flat-folding seats. It is pleasant to drive, but the 3.8-liter V6 isn't very smooth or fuel-efficient. The minivan rides well enough with a light load and handles securely. Reliability is below average. **March 2005**
Dodge Caliber	NEW	The Caliber four-door hatchback replaced the Dodge Neon sedan, and has a raised seating position similar to a small SUV. The engine is a bit noisy and fit and finish is mediocre, but the ride and handling are sound. Fuel economy wasn't impressive. **Sept. 2006**
Dodge Caravan/ Grand Caravan	◐	The Grand Caravan has a roomy interior and optional flat-folding seats. It is pleasant to drive, but the 3.8-liter V6 isn't very smooth or fuel-efficient. The minivan rides well enough with a light load and handles securely. Reliability is below average. **March 2005**
Dodge Charger	NEW	The sedan version of the Magnum wagon has a very powerful 5.7-liter Hemi V8, but the 3.5-liter V6 is adequate. The ride is stiff, and the steering feels darty. Rear seat headroom is marginal. IIHS crash-test results were Poor without the optional side air bags. **March 2006**
Dodge Dakota	◐	Our Dakota with the 4.7-liter V8 accelerated slower than many V6 pickups and returned just 14 mpg. The ride is buoyant, the truck lacks agility, and body roll is pronounced. Interior quality could be better. Reliability is below average. **July 2005**
Dodge Durango	◐	The Durango handles soundly and securely, and the ride is compliant. The cabin is fairly quiet, but the engine is a bit noisy. The third-row seat is usable. Fit and finish falls short. Reliability is below average. ESC is standard for 2007. **March 2004**
✓ **Dodge Magnum**	○	The Magnum wagon is powered by two V6 engines in the lower-priced trims, or a V8 in the RT model. Stability control and all-wheel drive are optional. Outward visibility is compromised by the styling. Reliability is average. **Dec. 2004**

Model	Predicted reliability	Description/with last road-test date
Dodge Nitro	NEW	The Nitro is based on the Jeep Liberty, but with better controls and a roomier rear seat. An optional sliding cargo floor extends rearward to ease loading. Dodge will offer both two- and four-wheel-drive versions. **To be tested**
Dodge Ram 1500	○	The Ram has a jittery ride and cumbersome handling. The engines are strong but noisy and thirsty, particularly the 11-mpg Hemi V8. The cargo bed in the crew-cab is longer than competitors, and the Mega Cab has a larger cabin. **July 2004**
Dodge Viper	NA	The Viper coupe and convertible feature a V10 engine with explosive acceleration. The noise from the V10 engine is loud and not quite invigorating, and the clutch is heavy. Handling is capable but lacks finesse. **Oct. 2006**
Ford Crown Victoria	○	This big, old-fashioned sedan has a jiggly ride and too much engine noise, revealing how dated the car is. Braking and emergency handling are fairly good. Rear leg room is less generous than expected, but the trunk is cavernous. **Feb. 2003**
Ford Edge	NEW	The Ford Edge car-based SUV is based on the Mazda6 platform. Its styling is similar to the Ford Fusion sedan and it shares the basic platform with the new Mazda CX-7. The powertrain will feature a 3.5-liter V6 engine and a six-speed automatic transmission. **To be tested**
Ford Escape	⊖	The Escape has a roomy interior and a spacious rear bench. Handling is relatively nimble, and the brakes are strong. Fuel economy is disappointing. The hybrid returned 26 mpg in our tests and has above-average reliability; the regular version is average. Because of a tip-up in the government rollover test, we do not recommend the Escape. **Aug. 2005**
Ford Expedition	NEW	The freshened Expedition offers a standard version and a 15 inch longer EL with increased cargo space. Standard safety equipment includes three-row curtain air bags and electronic stability control. Reliability has been much worse than average. **To be tested**
Ford Explorer	●	The Explorer's 2006 freshening brought quieter V6 and V8 engines. Fit and finish and design of the controls did not improve much. Handling is secure thanks to standard ESC but the ride is stiff. The 4WD system is permanently engaged. **July 2006**
Ford Explorer Sport Trac	NEW	The redesigned Sport Track is based on the Explorer, and features a switch to an independent rear suspension. The ride is stiff and handling is just so-so. The rust-proof composite bed is now slightly larger. Stability control with a rollover mitigation system is standard. **Nov. 2006**
Ford F-150	⊖	The redesigned F-150 has improved towing and payload capacities and better crashworthiness. It is now quieter, steers better, and rides more comfortably than the old model, but the engine is noisy. Reliability has been below average. **July 2004**
Ford Five Hundred	○	The Five Hundred (and its Mercury Montego twin) is a large sedan with elevated seating positions to improve outward vision and access. The lackluster V6 engine is mated to either a six-speed automatic or a continuously variable transmission (CVT). Front-wheel drive is standard, with AWD optional. **Jan. 2005**

Model	Predicted reliability	Description/with last road-test date
✓ **Ford Focus**	○	All versions of the Focus tested very well. It's agile, spacious, and fun to drive. It is also available in wagon and hatchback models. Overall crash protection is good. We recommend only the Focus with side air bags. **May 2005**
Ford Freestar	○	The Freestar is a freshened Windstar minivan. Like its competitors, it features a flat-folding third-row seat. The two V6 engines are still noisy and road noise is pronounced. Handling is more responsive, but the ride is unsettled. Crash-test results are impressive. **March 2004**
Ford Freestyle	●	This wagon version of the Five Hundred is available with front- or all-wheel drive. The ride is comfortable, but handling suffers because of the lack of electronic stability control. Reliability has been average. **Jan. 2006**
Ford Fusion	NEW	This sibling of the Lincoln Zephyr and Mercury Milan has a four-cylinder engine that delivers adequate performance, but is noisy; the V6 offers more zip and refinement. The ride is firm and controlled, and handling is alert and responsive. **March 2006**
✓ **Ford Mustang**	○	The Mustang offers a coarse V6 or a muscular V8. The live rear axle results in a stiff ride. Handling is nimble but lacks finesse. Interior materials are unimpressive. The convertible is free of body shake. Reliability of the V8 is average; the V6 is below average. **April 2005**
Ford Ranger	○	The Ranger and similar Mazda B-Series are long in the tooth. The ride is stiff and choppy. The seats are thin and low, and the rear of the SuperCab is suitable for cargo only.
GMC Acadia	NEW	The Acadia is a car-based SUV that shares a platform with the Buick Enclave and the Saturn Outlook. Power comes from a 3.6-liter V6 engine mated to a six-speed automatic transmission. It will offer seating for seven and goes on sale in January. **To be tested**
GMC Canyon	●	The Canyon's five-cylinder engine is unrefined, lacks punch, and has worse fuel-economy than competing V6s. Handling is sound but unexceptional. The ride is unsettled, and the body constantly quivers. Overall, it trails the competition. **July 2005**
GMC Envoy	◒	This midsized SUV, twin of the Chevrolet TrailBlazer, has a compliant low-speed ride. But handling is sloppy, the seats are uncomfortable, and wind noise is excessive. The XL model with a third-row seat has been dropped. **July 2006**
GMC Sierra 1500 (new)	NEW	The new Sierra (a twin of the Silverado) is now on sale. We expect improved handling and better fit and finish, as in the redesigned Tahoe and Avalanche we tested. The optional four-wheel drive is a selectable full-time system, a plus. Extended-cab versions have a usable rear seat, a rarity in this class. **To be tested**
GMC Yukon	NEW	The redesigned Yukon has improved handling, braking, ride, and interior materials, based on our tests of its Chevrolet Tahoe twin. The selectable full-time 4WD system can remain engaged indefinitely. ESC is standard. A rear-view camera system is optional. **July 2006**
GMC Yukon XL	NEW	This twin of the Chevrolet Suburban has improved handling, the steering and brakes are better, and the ride is more controlled.

Model	Predicted reliability	Description/with last road-test date
		Interior quality is much improved. The Yukon XL can seat eight with cargo space left over and tow a heavy trailer.
Honda Accord	⊖	The Accord features agile handling and a steady, compliant ride. The cabin is roomy, and controls are intuitive. The four-cylinder is smooth, and the V6 is relatively fuel efficient. The hybrid V6 returned only 25 mpg in our testing. **Aug. 2006**
Honda CR-V	⊖	One of the better car-based SUVs, the CR-V will be redesigned for 2007. The outgoing model has a supple and controlled ride. The rear seat is roomy. Road noise is pronounced. Crash-test results are impressive. **To be tested**
Honda Civic	⊖	The Civic is our top-rated small sedan. The base 1.8-liter, four-cylinder engine and smooth five-speed automatic provide an impressive 28 mpg overall. Ride and handling are good, but road noise is pronounced. Crash-test results are impressive. **Feb. 2006**
Honda Civic Hybrid	⊖	The Civic hybrid delivers 37 mpg overall. It can't drive solely on battery power, instead using battery power to assist the engine. Standard safety gear includes ABS and curtain air bags. Crash-test results are impressive. **Feb. 2006**
Honda Civic Si	⊖	The Civic Si coupe is sportier than the model it replaces. The 197-hp, 2.0-liter engine revs easily, and the six-speed manual has ideal gear spacing. Handling is nimble, but the steering feels vague. A four-door version arrives for 2007. **June 2006**
Honda Element	⊖	This small SUV is based on the CR-V. Styling is boxy, with rear doors that are hinged at the rear and no middle roof pillar, creating a huge loading port. Curtain air bags are standard for 2007. Antilock brakes are now standard. **June 2003**
Honda Fit	NEW	The Fit is a small four-door hatchback with impressive interior room and versatility. Cabin access is easy and visibility is good. The 1.5-liter engine is smooth. The ride is choppy, but supple enough. ABS and curtain air bags are standard. **Dec. 2006**
Honda Odyssey	○	The Odyssey has good interior flexibility and impressive fit and finish. The third row folds into the floor. Handling is agile and precise, and the ride is steady. The V6 is smooth and quiet. First-year reliability has been average. Crash-test results are impressive. **March 2005**
Honda Pilot	⊖	This car-based SUV can hold eight passengers with its flat-folding third-row seat. Ride and handling are competent. Road noise is pronounced. A two-wheel-drive model is available. All trim levels have standard stability control and curtain air bags. **April 2005**
Honda Ridgeline	⊖	This crew-cab pickup has a supple and steady ride. Its 5-foot-long composite cargo bed features an all-weather, lockable trunk. The 3.5-liter, V6 engine is quiet, smooth, and responsive. Stability control is standard. First-year reliability has been outstanding. **July 2005**
Honda S2000	⊖	This uncompromising rear-drive roadster has a small four-cylinder engine that delivers impressive power, complemented by a crisp-shifting six-speed manual. Handling is precise and predictable at its limits. The ride is hard and noisy. ESC is standard. **Oct. 2005**

Model	Predicted reliability	Description/with last road-test date
Hummer H2	●	The H2 is based on the previous-generation Chevrolet Tahoe. Ride and handling are fairly civilized, with exceptional off-road ability. The short windshield and wide roof pillars make the view out difficult. The H2 SUT is a pickup version.
Hummer H3	NEW	The H3 is based on the Chevrolet Colorado/GMC Canyon. The coarse engine provides tepid acceleration and so-so fuel economy. A 3.7-liter version arrives 2007. Off-roading is terrific, but access, visibility, and ride comfort come up short. **Nov. 2005**
Hyundai Accent	NEW	The Accent offers basic transportation in sedan or a two-door hatchback. The ride is relatively quiet and compliant, but isn't very agile. It is powered by a 1.6-liter, four-cylinder engine. Curtain air bags is a positive, but ABS may be hard to find. **Dec. 2006**
Hyundai Azera	NEW	The Azera has a smooth 3.8-liter, V6. The roomy interior is well finished and quiet, with straightforward controls. The ride is comfortable and steady, and handling is fairly responsive. IIHS side-crash-test results were merely acceptable. **Aug. 2006**
Hyundai Elantra	NEW	The Elantra rides quietly and handles securely but lacks agility. A four-door hatchback is also available. IIHS offset-crash results are good, but side-crash scores are poor. ABS can be difficult to find. Reliability has been average. A redesign arrives for 2007. **To be tested**
Hyundai Entourage	NEW	This is a version of the redesigned Kia Sedona minivan. Standard safety features include electronic stability control and three-row side-curtain air bags. Power comes from a 3.8-liter V6 mated to a five-speed automatic transmission, but fuel economy is not great. **Sept. 2006**
Hyundai Santa Fe	NEW	The 2007 Santa Fe is larger than the outgoing model, adding more power and an available third-row seat. Comprehensive safety equipment will be standard, including stability control and curtain air bags. **To be tested**
Hyundai Sonata	NEW	The redesigned Sonata is bigger, more powerful, and more refined than the old one. The four-cylinder engine delivers adequate performance; the 3.3-liter V6 is more responsive. Standard safety gear includes stability control and side-curtain air bags. **March 2006**
✓ Hyundai Tiburon	○	The GT V6 version of this sporty coupe delivers refined power. The ride is stiff, but handling is not so agile. The car feels nose-heavy, and the steering isn't particularly quick. Even average-height drivers will have to duck under the low roof. **Oct. 2002**
Hyundai Tucson	●	The Tucson is powered by a 2.0-liter four-cylinder. The optional 2.7-liter V6 delivers unimpressive fuel economy. Handling is not very agile, but standard ESC makes it secure. The ride is comfortable. First-year reliability has been much worse than average. **Aug. 2005**
✓ Infiniti FX	⊖	The FX drives like a sports sedan. The FX45 has a V8, but even the V6-powered FX35 is quick. Handling is nimble, but the stiff ride transmits bumps and pavement flaws to the passengers. The cabin feels snug, partly because of the high doorsills and low roof. **Sept. 2003**

Model	Predicted reliability	Description/with last road-test date
Infiniti G	◒	The G35's 3.5-liter V6 provides abundant power, and the firm, supple suspension provides capable handling and a comfortable ride. The sedan offers AWD. Interior materials were improved, but the seat controls are annoying. An updated model arrives for 2007. **July 2003**
Infiniti M	◒	The 2006 M35 is a roomy, contemporary design that is competitive in its class. The 3.5-liter V6 is strong. Ride and handling are quite capable, and the plush interior is well-constructed. The audio and navigation functions are relatively easy to master. **Sept. 2005**
Infiniti QX	●	This is Infiniti's version of the Nissan Armada. The V8 in our tested Armada was smooth and powerful, linked to a slick five-speed automatic. Handling was quite responsive. The ride was stiff, and engine noise is pronounced. Reliability has been much worse than average.
Isuzu Ascender	NA	This midsized SUV is essentially a rebadged Chevrolet TrailBlazer. The TrailBlazer we tested was spacious, with a comfortable low-speed ride and a spirited, inline six-cylinder, but emergency handling was sloppy and braking mediocre.
Isuzu i-Series	NEW	These pickup trucks are rebadged versions of the Chevrolet Colorado and GMC Canyon. The base extended-cab truck has a 2.8-liter four-cylinder. The 4WD i-350 is similar to the Colorado crew-cab we tested. Both engines grow in displacement and horsepower for 2007.
Jaguar S-Type	●	The S-Type lacks the interior quality and quiet of its competitors, and the rear seat is snug. The 3.0-liter V6 doesn't feel very responsive. The 4.2-liter V8 is strong. The ride is supple and well controlled. Handling is sound. Reliability continues to be subpar. **June 2004**
Jaguar X-Type	◐	Based on the European Ford Mondeo, this entry-level Jag comes with standard all-wheel drive and a 3.0-liter, V6 engine. It targets the Audi A4 and BMW 3 Series but lacks their refinement and driving enjoyment. **March 2002**
Jaguar XJ	◐	The XJ8 features an aluminum body and offers a bit more interior room. The classy styling remains. The powertrain is strong, but the ride isn't luxurious. Handling is nimble, but steering is light. A long-wheelbase model is available. **Nov. 2003**
Jaguar XK	NEW	The redesigned 2007 XK has a 4.2-liter V8 and six-speed automatic transmission, which make a powertrain that's smooth and powerful. Handling is athletic and capable. The ride is very supple and controlled. Two children can fit in the very small rear seats **Oct. 2006**
Jeep Commander	NEW	This is a three-row Grand Cherokee, but the second and third rows are cramped. Rear visibility is compromised. The 3.7-liter V6 is lackluster and the powerful 5.7-liter Hemi is thirsty. A 6.7-liter is also available. Handling is secure but not agile. The ride is absorbent but unsettled over undulations. **July 2006**
Jeep Compass	NEW	This is Jeep's first small car-based SUV. The Compass shares its platform with the Dodge Caliber and the new Jeep Patriot. Front-wheel drive is standard; all-wheel drive is optional, but this isn't a true off-road Jeep. Interior quality is on the cheap side. **To be tested**

Model	Predicted reliability	Description/with last road-test date
Jeep Grand Cherokee	●	This SUV features sound handling and a good ride. The 3.7-liter V6 is lackluster; our tested 4.7-liter is a better choice. Fit and finish isn't good, and rear-seat comfort is just so-so. ESC is standard. Reliability has been well below average. **Nov. 2005**
Jeep Liberty	○	The Liberty has independent front suspension and a modern rack-and-pinion steering setup for more precise handling on and off road, but the ride is still jittery. The cockpit is narrow, and access is awkward. Stability control and ABS are standard. **May 2002**
Jeep Patriot	NEW	This is Jeep's second small SUV based on the Compass and Dodge Caliber. Front- and all-wheel-drive versions are available. It should be capable for the occasional trail excursion. An optional off-road package with low-range gearing will be offered. **To be tested**
Jeep Wrangler	NEW	The old Wrangler was small and crude, with a hard, noisy ride. Handling is primitive, but off-road performance wa very good. The long-wheelbase Unlimited model improves rear-seating room. A redesigned Wrangler will include a four-door version. **To be tested**
✓ **Kia Amanti**	◒	The Amanti has a soft, buoyant ride but has clumsy handling, although its optional ESC keeps it secure. The V6 delivers only adequate performance, and its 18-mpg fuel economy is unexceptional. The interior boasts impressive fit and finish. **Jan. 2005**
Kia Optima	NEW	The redesigned Optima is longer and wider than the car it replaces. Curtain air bags are now standard, but ABS and electronic stability control are optional. While the old Optima was an also-ran in its class, the new one is a step forward. **To be tested**
Kia Rio	NEW	The redesigned Rio sedan and hatchback are some of the lowest-priced cars sold in the U.S. The 10-year/100,000-mile powertrain warranty is one of the few selling points. A 1.6-liter engine from the Hyundai Accent is standard. ABS is very hard to find. **Dec. 2006**
Kia Sedona	NEW	The redesigned Sedona is larger, with greater interior flexibility than before. It is competitive in its class and affordable. The 3.8-liter V6 and five-speed automatic are a refined powertrain, but fuel economy is unimpressive. **Sept. 2006**
Kia Sorento	◓	This small SUV is larger than most competitors. Acceleration is spirited but fuel economy is abysmal. The roomy interior has good fit and finish. The ride is stiff, and handling is clumsy though ultimately secure. Reliability is below average. **June 2004**
✓ **Kia Spectra**	NA	The Spectra is available as a sedan or a hatchback. It is relatively comfortable and quiet but lacks agility and has mediocre fuel economy. The Spectra scored a Poor in the IIHS side-crash test despite standard side and curtain air bags. ABS may be difficult to find. **Aug. 2004**
Kia Sportage	●	This Hyundai Tucson sibling has a standard four-cylinder engine with front-wheel drive. It is relatively roomy and comfortable but lacks agility. ABS, stability control, and head-protection air bags are standard. First-year reliability is much worse than average. **Aug. 2005**
Land Rover LR3	●	The LR3's smooth V8 struggles to move this heavy vehicle and returns poor fuel economy. Cabin access and interior quality have been

Model	Predicted reliability	Description/with last road-test date
		improved. The ride is comfortable but handling is lumbering. Off-road capability is terrific. Reliability is below average. **Nov. 2005**
Land Rover Range Rover	●	The Range Rover delivers smooth, strong acceleration and a very comfortable ride, but isn't agile. It features a height-adjustable air suspension and luxury amenities. The seats are very comfortable, and the wood and leather interior is upscale, but reliability has been poor.
Land Rover Range Rover Sport	NEW	Despite the name, this luxury midsized SUV is really based on the new LR3. Power comes from standard 4.4-liter V8. A supercharged 4.2-liter V8 is optional. Off-road capability should be acceptable with the proper tires, but the Sport is geared more for on-road performance.
Lexus ES	⊖	The Lexus ES has always been a solid and sedate sedan, and the re-designed 2007 ES350 has excellent fit and finish, more room, and increased horsepower. Power comes from a 3.5-liter V6 mated to a six-speed automatic. **To be tested**
Lexus GS	⊖	The redesigned GS features a new V6 engine and optional AWD. The 4.3-liter V8 is quick. Both have a six-speed automatic transmission and a host of safety and high-tech features. The cockpit is tight, and handling isn't sporty. **Sept. 2005**
Lexus GX	⊖	The GX is based on the Toyota 4Runner and combines comfort, luxury, and off-road capability. It is a bit smaller than the LX but also offers a third seat. The ride is comfortable and quiet, but it becomes unsettled. Cornering isn't very agile, but is ultimately secure. **March 2004**
Lexus IS	⊖	The redesigned IS offers two V6 engines and rear-wheel drive, with optional AWD. The interior is well-constructed, but cramped. The 2.5-liter, V6 is refined and gets good fuel economy, while the 3.5 is very quick. We found the ride jittery, and handling isn't very sporty. **May 2006**
Lexus LS	⊖	Lexus's flagship is one of the world's finest luxury sedans. The engine and transmission are extremely smooth, and passengers are pampered with every imaginable convenience. The ride is smooth, supple, and quiet. A redesigned LS arrives this fall, and a hybrid version will follow. **To be tested**
Lexus LX	⊖	This luxury SUV, based on the Toyota Land Cruiser, features a height-adjustable suspension and a well-equipped interior. The engine and transmission are smooth, and the ride is comfortable and quiet. It's capable off-road and civilized on pavement. ESC is standard.
Lexus RX	⊖	This well-rounded upscale SUV balances a refined powertrain and comfortable ride with well-planned details and a very quiet interior. For 2007 the RX350 will use a 3.5-liter V6. The RX400h hybrid is very quick and gets good mileage for an SUV. **Sept. 2003**
Lexus RX400h	⊖	The RX400h combines gas and electric engines to produce 268 hp. Acceleration is impressive and seamless, while returning 23 mpg overall. Typical Lexus characteristics include a beautifully finished interior, a quiet cabin, and a comfortable ride. **Nov. 2005**

Model	Predicted reliability	Description/with last road-test date
✓ Lexus SC	⊖	This luxury car features a metal roof that retracts into the trunk at the touch of a button. The rear seat is tiny. The 4.3-liter V8 is smooth and fit and finish is impressive. Handling is not sporty and the ride is jittery. **Oct. 2006**
Lincoln MKX	NEW	The new Lincoln MKX is based on the Mazda6 platform used in the new Ford Edge and Mazda CX-7. This car-based architecture is a departure from the original truck-based Aviator. Power comes from a 3.5-liter, V6 engine that is mated to a six-speed automatic.
Lincoln MKZ	NEW	This renamed Zephyr is the upscale sibling of the Ford Fusion and Mercury Milan. A 3.5-liter V6 arrives this fall. The ride is firm and controlled, and handling is responsive. Electronic stability control is not offered, a surprising omission in this class. **May 2006**
Lincoln Mark LT	NEW	The Mark LT is based on the new Ford F-150 pickup, which we found to ride more comfortably, handle more nimbly, and have a quieter, better-trimmed interior than the previous version. The Mark LT sports a luxurious interior, but the 4WD system is part-time only.
Lincoln Navigator	●	The freshened 2007 Navigator includes the L version, which is about 15 inches longer than the regular model. Standard safety equipment includes three-row curtain air bags and electronic stability control. Reliability has been much worse than average.
✓ Lincoln Town Car	○	The Town Car is outdated, with an unrefined engine, clumsy handling, and a jiggly ride. The front seats are soft and poorly shaped. The rear fits three with ease, and the trunk is very large. Crash-test results are impressive. **Feb. 2003**
Lotus Elise	NA	This lightweight, midengined roadster is super-quick. Power comes from a high-revving four-cylinder from Toyota. Details include a very spartan interior, difficult cabin access, race-car agility, and an unforgiving tendency to spin at its high cornering limits. **Oct. 2005**
Mazda B-Series	○	The Mazda B-Series and the similar Ford Ranger are long in the tooth. The ride is stiff and choppy. The seats are thin and low, and the rear of the SuperCab is suitable for cargo only. The V6 engines are adequate, but trail the competition.
Mazda CX-7	NEW	The CX-7 SUV is based on the Mazda6 platform. Handling is responsive, but the ride is so-so. There's too much hesitation from the turbocharged four-cylinder at launch. Well-equipped all-wheel-drive versions are priced in the low-$30,000 range. **To be tested**
Mazda CX-9	NEW	The car-based CX-9 will offer three rows of seats and uses a different platform than the similar-looking CX-7. The 3.5-liter V6 is paired with a six-speed automatic. Side-curtain air bags and stability control will be available when the CX-9 arrives in early 2007 **To be tested**
✓ Mazda MX-5 Miata	⊖	The redesigned MX-5 fun and agile, yet fairly civilized and affordable. The 2.0-liter four-cylinder and standard six-speed manual are a joy to use. A paddle-shifting six-speed automatic is optional. A power retractable hard top arrives for 2007. **June 2006**
✓ Mazda RX-8	○	This agile and fun coupe revs exceptionally smoothly, and the ride is impressive for a sports car. The Rotary engine is smooth, but fu-

Model	Predicted reliability	Description/with last road-test date
		el economy is disappointing. The rear-hinged rear doors ease back seat access. Reliability has improved to average. **Dec. 2003**
Mazda Tribute	○	The Tribute's interior is roomy, and the rear seat is spacious. The base engine is a 2.3-liter four-cylinder. The 3.0-liter V6 has unimpressive fuel economy. Handling is quite nimble, but the ride is stiff. We do not recommend the Escape and its siblings because of a tip-up in the government rollover test. **Oct. 2004**
✓ **Mazda3**	⊖	The Mazda 3's standard 2.0-liter, four-cylinder engine is relatively quick and sparing with fuel; the 2.3-liter is strong and refined. Handling is precise and sporty. Interior quality is very good. Without the curtain air bags, the Mazda3 received a poor rating in the IIHS side-crash test. **Aug. 2004**
Mazda5	NEW	This six-passenger small minivan is based on the Mazda3 and provides the utility of a minivan with easy maneuverability, all at an affordable price and with good fuel economy. It is agile, quiet, and comfortable, but not very powerful. **Jan. 2006**
✓ **Mazda6**	○	The Mazda6 has nimble handling and a firm ride. The four-cylinder doesn't feel punchy or refined. Wagon and hatchback versions are available. IIHS side-crash results were poor without the optional side air bags. Reliability of the wagon is above average; the V6 sedan is below average. **May 2003**
Mercedes-Benz C-Class	⊖	The C-Class comes with a variety of V6 engines and optional all-wheel drive. It has quick acceleration, a quiet, comfortable ride, and agile, secure handling. The seats are comfortable and supportive, but the rear is tight. Reliability has been below average. **May 2006**
Mercedes-Benz CL	NA	This coupe version of the S-Class luxury sedan is just as fast, comfortable and luxurious. The ride is comfortable, yet handling is agile with restrained body roll. There is room in the back for two adults to sit comfortably. The V8 supplies abundant acceleration.
Mercedes-Benz CLK	●	The C-Class coupe accelerates quickly, handles well, and rides comfortably. The available engines are powerful. Rear seating is reasonably hospitable. A convertible is available. Handling is agile. The V6 is nice, and the V8 is muscular.
Mercedes-Benz CLS	NEW	The CLS is a four-door sedan with a swoopy, streamlined roof and seating for just four passengers. Even so, rear-seat room is tight, and the angle of the roof cuts into head room. The luxurious and comfortable CLS delivers powerful performance and agile handling. **Oct. 2006**
Mercedes-Benz E-Class	NEW	The E-Class blends spirited acceleration and respectable fuel economy. The strong 3.5-liter V6 is mated to a seven-speed automatic. Seat comfort and driving position are first class. Wagon, diesel, and AWD models are available. Reliability has been poor. **To be tested**
Mercedes-Benz GL-Class	NEW	This unibody seven-passenger luxury SUV uses the same platform as the new M-Class. It is very quiet, with a comfortable ride and responsive handling. The third-row seat is roomy enough for adults. **Nov. 2006**

Model	Predicted reliability	Description/with last road-test date
Mercedes-Benz M-Class	NEW	The redesigned M-Class has improved interior fit and finish. Handling is responsive and the ride is firm, yet supple. The smooth V6 returned only 16 mpg overall. The seven-speed automatic doesn't always shift at the appropriate moment. Some controls can be confusing. **Nov. 2005**
Mercedes-Benz R-Class	NEW	The three-row R-Class shares the same AWD platform with the redesigned M-Class. Access is easy and room for six is very good, but the long rear doors easily bump into adjacent vehicles. The ride is comfortable and quiet, but handling is not sporty. **Nov. 2006**
Mercedes-Benz S-Class	NEW	Early impressions of the redesigned S-Class indicate it is still comfortable, agile, and powerful. However, the new iDrive-like control system is awkward. A night-vision system is also new. Reliability of the old model was below average. **To be tested**
Mercedes-Benz SL	●	This coupe/convertible employs a retractable metal roof. The V8 is smooth and powerful, and the AMG model is even more so. The SL is sporty and agile, yet luxurious and comfortable. **Oct. 2006**
Mercedes-Benz SLK	◒	This roadster features a folding hard top and a strong 3.5-liter V6. The manual shifter and clutch are more user-friendly than in the first-generation SLK. Handling is more agile than the previous version, and the ride is relatively comfortable. **Oct. 2005**
✓ **Mercury Grand Marquis**	○	A big, old-fashioned sedan, the Grand Marquis' ride is jiggly, and engine noise is pronounced. Braking and emergency handling are fairly good. Rear leg room is less generous than you might expect. Crash-test results are impressive. **Feb. 2003**
Mercury Mariner	◓	This is a twin of the Ford Escape. The Escape's handling is relatively nimble, and the rear seat is roomy. Interior trim was upgraded, and it is now quieter and more comfortable. Because of a tip-up in the government rollover test, we do not recommend the Escape and its siblings. **Oct. 2004**
Mercury Milan	NEW	This sibling of the Ford Fusion has a noisy four-cylinder engine that delivers adequate performance. The V6 offers more zip. The ride is firm and controlled, and handling is responsive. IIHS side-crash-test results were poor without the optional curtain air bags. **March 2006**
Mercury Montego	○	The Montego (and its Ford Five Hundred twin) is a large sedan with elevated seating positions to improve outward vision and access. The lackluster V6 engine has to work hard to move the Montego. Front-wheel drive is standard, with AWD optional. **Jan. 2005**
Mercury Monterey	○	This upscale version of the Ford Freestar uses a noisy 4.2-liter V6 and features a flat-folding third-row seat. Handling is more responsive, but the ride is unsettled. Fit and finish is poor. Crash-test results are impressive. **March 2004**
Mercury Mountaineer	●	The Mercury version of the Ford Explorer has a coarse 4.0-liter V6 that performs adequately. Our tested 4.6-liter V8 was more powerful but noisy and thirsty. The ride is unremarkable, and handling is secure. The third-row seat is relatively roomy. ESC is standard. **July 2006**

Model	Predicted reliability	Description/with last road-test date
✔ **Mini Cooper**	○	The Mini features extremely agile handling and is fun to drive, but the ride is choppy. The rear is very tight, and some controls are confusing. The convertible top is easy to use. The base engine lacks oomph, but the supercharged Cooper S is strong. Reliability has improved to average. **June 2005**
Mitsubishi Eclipse	NEW	A powerful engine in the GT trim is this coupe's major appeal. The cockpit is very cramped, and the rear seat is unusable. Handling lacks agility. The four-cylinder engine is noisy and the manual transmission is clunky. The ride is stiff and busy. **Dec. 2005**
✔ **Mitsubishi Endeavor**	⊖	The Endeavor is a midsized, car-based SUV. The refined 3.8-liter V6 delivers strong acceleration. Front- and all-wheel-drive versions are available. The Endeavor rides reasonably well, but cornering isn't particularly agile. **Aug. 2003**
✔ **Mitsubishi Galant**	⊖	The redesigned Galant arrived for 2004. Engine choices include a weak four-cylinder and a powerful V6 that overwhelms the front wheels. The ride is not very comfortable. Handling is secure but not particularly agile. The interior is roomy but bland, with disappointing fit and finish. **May 2004**
Mitsubishi Lancer	⊖	Mitsubishi's small sedan falls short of the competition-and offers no price advantage, either. Handling is clumsy, the ride unsettled, and the interior noisy. The Lancer received a Poor in the IIHS side-crash test. The redesigned Lancer will share a platform with the 2007 Outlander SUV. **July 2002**
Mitsubishi Lancer Evolution	NA	This turbocharged, all-wheel-drive version of the Lancer sedan competes well with the Subaru Impreza WRX STi. The car is super-fast, agile, and fun, but it has a harsh ride. For 2006 horsepower has been increased and the suspension is revised slightly. **Dec. 2003**
Mitsubishi Outlander	NEW	The Outlander is available with either front- or all-wheel drive, powered by a 2.4-liter four-cylinder. The ride is reasonably comfortable and secure but with pronounced body lean. Cargo volume is relatively small. A redesign with a V6 arrives for 2007. **To be tested**
Mitsubishi Raider	NEW	This reskinned Dodge Dakota offers two Dodge engines, a 3.7-liter V6 or a 4.7-liter V8. Extended- and crew-cab body styles will be offered. We found the Dakota's ride buoyant and front head room limited, and it suffered from excessive body roll and lacked agility.
✔ **Nissan 350Z**	○	The 350Z is a two-seater powered by a smooth-revving 3.5-liter V6. The manual gearbox feels slightly notchy. Handling is agile, and the stiff ride has been improved. The seat controls are awkward to use. The convertible has a power-operated top. **Oct. 2005**
Nissan Altima	NEW	The Altima is roomy, with strong engines and secure handling but a stiff and jittery ride. Interior fit and finish has improved from the previous model. The front seats are comfortable, but the rear seat lacks support. It scored Poor in the IIHS side-crash test without the optional curtain air bags. A redesign arrives for 2007. **To be tested**
Nissan Armada	●	This large SUV has seating for eight. Power comes from a 5.6-liter, V8 engine mated to a five-speed automatic. Two- and four-wheel drive versions are available, and it features an independent rear suspension. Reliability has been poor. **March 2004**

Model	Predicted reliability	Description/with last road-test date
✓ **Nissan Frontier**	○	The Frontier is quick and nimble, with a stiff but tolerable ride. The V6 revs smoothly and feels like a V8. A 2.5-liter four-cylinder is standard. It's easy to find models with the optional stability control. Rear-seat room is tight. Reliability has been average. **July 2005**
Nissan Maxima	○	The Maxima's powerful V6 is quick but produces torque steer. The CVT transmission is smooth. Handling is secure, but not particularly agile, and the ride is stiff and jiggly. The interior is roomy. The wide turning circle is a nuisance. **To be tested**
✓ **Nissan Murano**	◔	This sporty, car-based SUV offers roomy seating for five. The rear seat can be folded by flipping a lever. The V6 delivers strong performance but requires premium fuel. Handling is fairly nimble, but the ride is stiff. Reliability has been above average. **April 2005**
✓ **Nissan Pathfinder**	○	The Pathfinder features a strong 4.0-liter V6, independent-rear suspension, and third-row seat. The ride is stiff, though handing is responsive. The third-row seat is tolerable for short trips. Stability control is standard. First-year reliability has been average. **Nov. 2005**
Nissan Quest	●	The freshened Quest has a more conventional dashboard. The powerful V6 engine is refined. Both the second- and third-row seats fold flat when not in use. Reliability has been poor, but crash-test results are impressive. **Oct. 2003**
Nissan Sentra	NEW	A new Sentra goes on sale in September 2006. The 2.0-liter, four-cylinder engine produces 135 horsepower and comes with an optional continuously variable transmission (CVT), which might improve fuel economy. The rear seat appears to be roomier than in the outgoing model. **To be tested**
Nissan Titan	●	The Titan has a comfortable ride, but the engine is loud. The cargo bed is smaller than competing trucks, and the 1,105-pound payload capacity is meager. Safety features include optional ESC and curtain air bags. Reliability has dropped to well below average. **July 2004**
Nissan Versa	NEW	The Versa hatchback and sedan pack a relatively spacious interior in a short body. The engine is civilized but not overly powerful. The ride is comfortable and the rear seat is roomy. Handling isn't particularly nimble. Side curtain air bags will be optional. **To be tested**
Nissan Xterra	NA	The Xterra has good off-road capability but is also civilized. The 4.0-liter V6 delivers quick acceleration but just 17 mpg. The four-wheel-drive system is still part-time. The spartan interior looks rugged and is well-assembled. ESC is standard and head-protection air bags are optional. **Aug. 2005**
Pontiac G5	NEW	The G5 is a coupe version of the Chevrolet Cobalt, and is available in both base and GT trim. A 2.2-liter, 148-hp four-cylinder engine powers the base model, and the 2.4-liter in the GT makes 173 hp. First-year reliability of the Cobalt was poor.
✓ **Pontiac G6**	○	The G6 has a coarse-sounding V6 that provides ample power and acceptable fuel economy. Base models lack agility and tire grip, and the ride is stiff. The styling impedes rear access and visibility. IIHS side-crash-test results were Poor without the optional side-curtain air bags. First-year reliability has been average. **Feb. 2005**

Model	Predicted reliability	Description/with last road-test date
Pontiac Grand Prix	⊖	The Grand Prix's ride, rear-seat comfort, and 20 mpg fuel economy trail the competition. The V6 is fairly quick but noisy. Taller drivers wished for more head room. The rear seats are very cramped. **Jan. 2004**
Pontiac Solstice	NEW	This two-seat roadster is meant to compete with the Mazda MX-5, but is no match. It's powered by a noisy 2.4-liter, four-cylinder engine. Wide spacing between the gears in the manual is a detraction. The GXP turbo is more powerful. Raising and lowering the top is a nuisance. **June 2006**
Pontiac Torrent	NEW	This is Pontiac's version of the Chevrolet Equinox. We found the Equinox's movable rear seat roomy. Interior quality is subpar, and the V6 is noisy and unrefined. Handling is clumsy and a tip-up by the Equinox in the government rollover test is another negative. **Oct. 2004**
✓ **Pontiac Vibe**	⊖	The Vibe is a roomy small wagon with good cabin and cargo access. Handling and ride are OK, but the engine is noisy. All-wheel drive is optional. This is a sensible alternative to a small SUV. Stability control is optional for 2005. **Jan. 2006**
Porsche 911	NA	The 911 is among the very few true sports cars that can serve as a daily driver. It is exceptionally agile and the ride is fairly civilized. Coupe and a convertible are offered. Both the 3.6- and 3.8-liter engines are powerful and sound good. **Oct. 2006**
Porsche Boxster	NA	This roadster's handling and braking are superb, and the ride is firm but not punishing. It is relatively quick and fun to drive. The two trunks give it a bit of practicality. The power top can be operated at low speeds. **Oct. 2005**
Porsche Cayenne	●	The Cayenne is a midsized, luxury car-based SUV with all-wheel drive. Low-range gearing and advanced electronics promise some off-road capability. It comes with a choice of engines and available adjustable ride height. Poor reliability is a disappointment.
Porsche Cayman	NEW	This coupe is based on the Boxster. Power comes from a midmounted, flat-six engine. It is positioned between the Boxster and 911. A six-speed manual is standard, and the five-speed Tiptronic is optional. Base and S models are offered.
☑ **Saab 9-2X**	⊖	This thinly disguised Subaru Impreza wagon has a traditional Saab nose, but the rest of the vehicle is virtually identical to the Impreza. All-wheel drive and the Subaru's adequate four-cylinder are standard. The WRX's turbo engine comes in the Aero trim line. 2006 is the final year for the 9-2X. **Sept. 2006**
Saab 9-3	●	The 9-3 sedan is available with two turbocharged engines. Handling is fairly nimble and secure. The rear seat is cramped and the ride is stiff. A convertible and wagon are available. Reliability is well below average. **May 2006**
Saab 9-5	NEW	The 9-5 has unimpressive ride and handling. The front seats are comfortable, and the rear is relatively roomy. The wagon is competent and well-designed. Crash-test results are excellent. A mild face-lift and more horsepower arrived for 2006. **To be tested**

Model	Predicted reliability	Description/with last road-test date
Saab 9-7X	NA	Saab's SUV is a Chevrolet TrailBlazer with upgraded interior and exterior appointments, and a revised suspension. The AWD system is permanent and lacks a low range. Reliability of the TrailBlazer has been subpar, and offset crash-test results are unimpressive.
Saturn Aura	NEW	The Aura, a replacement for the lackluster midsized Saturn L-series sedan, is based on the Pontiac G6 and Chevrolet Malibu. The base engine is a 3.5-liter V6 paired with a four-speed automatic transmission. A smooth, responsive 3.6-liter V6 with a six-speed automatic transmission is optional. **To be tested**
Saturn Ion	O	The Ion has an acceptable ride and capable handling, but steering feel is inconsistent. The noisy engine returned less-than-exceptional fuel economy. The cramped interior feels cheap. The Ion received a Poor rating in the IIHS side-crash test. **May 2005**
Saturn Outlook	NEW	The Outlook is a car-based SUV with three rows of seats. It shares a platform with the Buick Enclave and the GMC Acadia. It uses GM's smooth 3.6-liter, V6 engine mated to a six-speed automatic transmission. It goes on sale in January. **To be tested**
Saturn Relay	●	The Relay is powered by a 3.9-liter, V6 engine for 2007. Removing the second-row seat is cumbersome. The folding third-row seat only folds flat on the floor. Handling is reluctant, interior trim is insubstantial, and the ride is stiff and noisy. **March 2005**
Saturn Sky	NEW	The Sky is Saturn's version of the Pontiac Solstice roadster. The rear-drive, two-seat Sky is powered by a 2.4-liter, four-cylinder engine. The Vue Red Line gets a turbocharged engine. A five-speed automatic is optional. **June 2006**
Saturn Vue	●	The Vue has light steering and the AWD system is slow to engage. Interior fit and finish are subpar, and the front and rear seats lack support. A Poor in the IIHS side-crash test without the optional curtain air bags and tip-ups in government rollover tests are negatives. **Oct. 2004**
✓ Scion tC	O	The tC coupe is the third Scion model. Power comes from a 2.4-liter, four-cylinder engine. It drives nicely but isn't particularly sporty. Rear seat room is generous for a coupe, and there is a lot of standard equipment for the money. **Dec. 2005**
Scion xA	⊖	The xA is a small, four-door hatchback powered by a 1.5-liter four-cylinder. Handling is nimble, but the ride is stiff and choppy. Acceleration is so-so and the engine is buzzy, but the xA is affordable and gets good mileage. The cargo area is small. **Aug. 2004**
✓ Scion xB	⊖	The xB is a small, tall, slab-sided wagon powered by a 1.5-liter four-cylinder. It is very space-efficient. Antilock brakes and stability control are standard. High levels of wind and engine noise, and the stiff, choppy ride make the xB fatiguing on long drives. **Aug. 2004**
✓ Subaru B9 Tribeca	⊖	Subaru's first SUV is designed to carry seven people, but the second and third rows are cramped. The standard 3.0-liter engine struggles to pull the Tribeca, and the transmission doesn't downshift readily. Interior appointments are impressive. **Nov. 2005**

Model	Predicted reliability	Description/with last road-test date
Subaru Baja	⊜	The Baja is a small pickup with four full-sized doors. A removable partition between cabin and cargo bed adds to its versatility. Acceleration is not brisk with the standard engine, but a turbocharged model is available. Reliability is above average. **June 2003**
Subaru Forester	⊜	The Forester has a tall and roomy cargo area and a controlled, compliant ride. Handling is relatively responsive, and acceleration and rear-seat room have improved. For mid-2005 Subaru revised some styling cues and boosted engine power. **July 2006**
Subaru Impreza	⊜	The Impreza delivers good handling and a comfortable ride. The well-assembled interior feels cheap and the tight rear seat doesn't fold in the sedan. The Outback Sport wagon rides more stiffly and doesn't handle as well. The sedan scored Good in the IIHS offset-crash test. **Feb. 2006**
Subaru Impreza WRX/STi	⊜	The WRX/WRX STi has race-car-like handling and a relatively good ride. The WRX's engine provides quick and effortless acceleration. The ferociously quick WRX STi has performance numbers the same as vehicles costing twice as much. **Feb. 2006**
Subaru Legacy	⊜	The Legacy has a supple ride, agile handling, and precise steering. The standard engine is sluggish with the automatic. The GT's turbocharged engine is quick but thirsty. Stability control is not available on the Legacy. Reliability has been above average. **Nov. 2004**
Subaru Outback	⊜	This raised wagon has good steering feel and a supple ride, but isn't quick with the standard engine and automatic. The XT uses a strong turbocharged engine, but fuel economy suffers. Interior quality is improved. ESC is available only in the Outback 3.0 VDC, and is slow to react. **Dec. 2004**
Suzuki Aerio	○	The Aerio features a tall roofline designed to increase head room and improve outward visibility. It's available in sedan and four-door wagon/hatchback versions. The Aerio received a Poor rating in the IIHS side-crash test even with standard side air bags.
Suzuki Forenza	NA	The Forenza does not compete well in its class. Acceleration is slow and fuel economy just so-so. The ride is stiff and not well-controlled. Interior fit and finish is good, and the rear seat of the hatchback is roomy. A wagon version is also available. It received a Poor in the IIHS side-crash test. **Aug. 2004**
Suzuki Grand Vitara	NEW	The redesigned Grand Vitara became a car-based SUV for 2006. It is designed for on-road refinement and light off-roading. The interior is roomy, but the ride is jittery. Side- and head-protection air bags and stability control are standard. **July 2006**
Suzuki SX4	NEW	The SX4 is a new small raised hatchback developed with Fiat. It is available in front- or all-wheel drive. Power comes from a 130-hp, 2.0-liter, four-cylinder engine. Curtain air bags are standard, and electronic stability control is optional. **To be tested**
Suzuki XL-7	NEW	This small SUV offers three-row seating and part-time four-wheel drive. The standard 2.7-liter V6 and five-speed automatic provide adequate acceleration. The ride is crude, and handling is vague, though secure. Reliability has been average. The 2007 XL-7 will be based on the Chevrolet Equinox. **To be tested**

Model	Predicted reliability	Description/with last road-test date
✓ **Toyota 4Runner**	⊖	The 4Runner is roomy and has an optional third-row seat. This credible off-roader offers hill-descent control and a system that prevents roll-back on slow, steep ascents. Fuel economy was unimpressive at 16 mpg. Electronic Stability Control is standard. **Aug. 2003**
⨀ **Toyota Avalon**	○	The Avalon has a roomy rear seat, an impressive interior, and a comfortable ride. It tends to float on the highway, but the Touring model isn't as bad. Handling is responsive but not sporty. The V6 is smooth and punchy. First-year reliability has been average. **Sept. 2005**
✓ **Toyota Camry**	⊖	The redesigned Camry is quiet, comfortable, and refined. The telescoping steering column is a plus. The V6 returns 23 mpg overall; the four-cylinder returned 24 mpg. The interior is spacious. Curtain air bags are standard, but stability control is optional. **Aug. 2006**
✓ **Toyota Camry Hybrid**	⊖	The Camry hybrid returned 34 mpg overall and has a 600-mile cruising range. It is a bit slow off the line, but accelerates well. The interior is quiet and spacious. Curtain air bags are standard, but stability control is optional. **Aug. 2006**
✓ **Toyota Camry Solara**	⊖	The Solara coupe and convertible are based on the previous Toyota Camry and have a relatively roomy back seat. The ride is comfortable, but handling is not sporty. The convertible suffered from body shake, but the top is well-insulated. **June 2005**
⨀ **Toyota Corolla**	⊖	This small car has a roomy, high-quality interior. The engine delivers responsive performance and excellent fuel economy, but is a bit boomy. ESC is optional. Without the optional curtain air bags, the Corolla rated Poor in the IIHS side-crash test. **July 2002**
Toyota FJ Cruiser	NEW	This off-road-oriented SUV is based on the 4Runner. Power comes from a 4.0-liter V6. Visibility is awful, compromised by the thick roof pillars and small windows. The rear doors are awkward to use. Electronic stability control is standard. **To be tested**
✓ **Toyota Highlander**	⊖	This car-based SUV is roomy, quiet, comfortable, and well designed. It uses the same platform as the Lexus RX330 but less expensive. Excellent offset-crash results as well as outstanding reliability round out this highly rated SUV. **Nov. 2005**
✓ **Toyota Highlander Hybrid**	⊖	This SUV is roomy, quiet, and comfortable. Not only was the Hybrid quicker than the conventional model, it also returned 22 mpg overall in our tests. Excellent offset-crash results as well as outstanding reliability round out this highly rated SUV. **Nov. 2005**
✓ **Toyota Land Cruiser**	⊖	This big, expensive SUV uses a quiet 4.7-liter V8 and has a smooth ride. The interior offers lots of room and a third seat. It combines plushness and quality with off-road ability. Standard ESC and a permanently engaged 4WD system are major advantages.
Toyota Matrix	⊖	This roomy small wagon has good cabin and cargo access. The driving position is compromised for some drivers. Handling and ride are OK, but the engine is noisy. Stability control and AWD are optional. This is a sensible alternative to a small SUV. **Aug. 2002**
⨀ **Toyota Prius**	⊖	Toyota's hybrid returned 44 mpg in our tests. Ride and handing are competent, though the steering feels vague. Access is easy.

Model	Predicted reliability	Description/with last road-test date
		Reliability is outstanding. The Prius earned a Poor in IIHS side-crash tests without its optional side curtain air bags. **May 2004**
Toyota RAV4	⊖	The redesigned RAV4 has a flexible, well-designed interior. Handling is agile and secure with standard stability control. The rear seat is roomy. A third-row seat is optional. The optional 3.5-liter V6 is quick and returns good fuel economy. Curtain air bags are standard for 2007. **July 2006**
Toyota Sequoia	⊖	The Sequoia as a refined 4.7-liter V8. Rear-wheel and selectable full-time four-wheel drive are available. The ride is stiff, and handling is ungainly but ultimately secure with the standard stability control. More power and a five-speed automatic were added in 2005. **Nov. 2002**
Toyota Sienna	⊖	The Sienna rides very comfortably and quietly. The third seat folds flat into the floor. The 3.3-liter, V6 engine is smooth and strong. Handling is secure, predictable, and responsive. Crash-test results are impressive. AWD is available. We've heard many complaints about fast tire wear with the run-flat tires. **March 2005**
Toyota Tacoma	○	The Tacoma has a 4.0-liter V6 that provides strong performance. The ride trails some competitors and the driving position is too low. Payload capacity is small. We recommend the optional ESC. Reliability has been average for the V6 and above average for the four-cylinder. **July 2005**
Toyota Tundra	⊖	The Tundra's V8 is smooth and quiet. 2005 brought a new 4.0-liter V6. The ride is civilized, the cabin is quiet and roomy in the crew cab, and fit and finish is top-notch. Extended-cab models have a cramped rear seat. ESC can be very difficult to find. A 2007 redesign is around the corner. **July 2004**
Toyota Yaris	NEW	The Yaris replaced the Echo. It is available as a two-door hatchback or a four-door sedan. The 1.5-liter four-cylinder engine is not especially powerful, but it is economical. Road noise is pronounced and some drivers found the center-mounted gauges annoying. **Dec. 2006**
Volkswagen Eos	NEW	The Eos is equipped with a folding metal hard top. Head-protection curtain air bags are housed in the doors. Power comes from the same 2.0-liter, turbocharged four-cylinder engine or 3.2-liter V6 found in other Audis and Volkswagens. **To be tested**
Volkswagen GTI	NEW	The GTI, a sporty version of the new Rabbit (Golf), is one of the better affordable performance cars. It is quick and agile with a gutsy turbocharged 2.0-liter four-cylinder that sounds good, all of which make it fun to drive. A four-door version is available as well. **June 2006**
Volkswagen Jetta	NA	The new Jetta uses a noisy 2.5-liter, five-cylinder engine. A 2.0-liter turbo and a diesel are also available. The new Jetta rides comfortably and handles better than the previous generation. The interior is considerably roomier. **Feb. 2006**
Volkswagen New Beetle	●	The New Beetle rides and handles well. The front seats are supportive, but the rear is cramped. The power-operated convertible top is well-insulated from wind noise. Reliability is below average and the Beetle scored a Poor in the IIHS side-crash test.

Model	Predicted reliability	Description/with last road-test date
Volkswagen Passat	NEW	The Passat is roomier and more powerful than the previous model. The turbocharged four-cylinder engine has excellent performance; the 3.6-liter V6 is even quicker. AWD is available. Handling is agile and responsive. The front seats are comfortable and supportive. IIHS crash-test results are impressive. **March 2006**
Volkswagen Rabbit	NEW	The Rabbit is really a hatchback version of the Jetta. The standard engine is a 2.5-liter five-cylinder that is noisy and not very fuel efficient. Handling is responsive and forgiving with standard electronic stability control, and the ride is compliant. **To be tested**
Volkswagen Touareg	●	Volkswagen's car-based SUV has features such as low-range gearing and a locking center differential, making capable off road. The V6 is thirsty and underpowered; the V8 is stronger but expensive. The interior is elegant but not so roomy. Reliability has been below average. The V10 turbodiesel returns for 2007. **To be tested**
Volvo C70	NEW	The C70 is a convertible version of the S40 with a power-folding metal folding top. It features a 2.5-liter turbocharged five-cylinder engine. AWD is not offered. Expect the C70 to have standard safety features, including curtain air bags. **To be tested**
✓ **Volvo S40**	○	The S40 sedan corners fairly nimbly but has a stiff ride. The standard 2.4-liter engine sounds raspy. A stronger turbocharged engine powers the T5. The interior is well-finished. The front seats are supportive, but the rear seat is very tight. Reliability has been average. **Nov. 2004**
✓ **Volvo S60**	⊖	The S60 is neither luxurious nor sporty. It has a quiet interior and the front seats are comfortable. Handling is secure but not particularly agile, and the ride is stiff. The rear seat is cramped. Volvo improved the confusing radio controls. All-wheel drive is available. **Feb. 2004**
Volvo S80	NEW	Volvo's front- or all-wheel-drive flagship performs well. It's roomy, quiet, and comfortable. A turbocharged five-cylinder is the only available engine for 2006. Crash-test results are outstanding. A wide turning circle hampers parking maneuvers. Reliability has improved to average. A redesign arrives for 2007. **To be tested**
Volvo V50	●	The wagon version of the S40 corners fairly nimbly but has a stiff ride. The standard 2.4-liter engine sounds raspy. A stronger turbocharged engine powers the T5. The front seats are supportive, but the rear seat is very tight. All-wheel drive is available. Reliability is below average. **Dec. 2004**
✓ **Volvo V70/XC70**	○	The V70 is spacious, with comfortable seats. The all-wheel-drive XC70 Cross Country model is an SUV alternative. Its ride and handling isn't as good as that of the V70. AWD is also available on the fast V70R. **Nov. 2006**
Volvo XC90	●	This seven-seat SUV has a flat-folding third row. The stability-control system can react to an impending rollover. The ride is more comfortable than in the XC70. The V8 engine is strong and smooth, and a new six-cylinder is available. Reliability is much worse than average. **Nov. 2006**

THE BEST AND WORST USED CARS

These lists guide you to the most reliable vehicles from model years 1998 to 2005 and alert you to those that have been problematic. **Reliable Used Cars** and **Used Cars to Avoid** include all models that showed above- or below-average overall reliability in our 2005 subscriber survey, which drew responses for just over 1 million vehicles.

Pay particular attention to the **CR Good Bets** and **Bad Bets**. Compiled from the longer lists, these are models for which we have sufficient data for at least three years. They have either performed notably well or have been especially troublesome. CR weighs problems with the engine, engine cooling, transmission, and drive system more heavily than other areas. For the detailed reliability Ratings for all the vehicles on which these lists are based, turn to pages 196 to 224

KEY: The abbreviations 2WD, 4WD, and AWD stand for two-, four-, and all-wheel drive.

Reliable used cars

This list features all models from 1998 through 2005 that exhibited better-than-average Used Car Verdicts in our latest survey (see page 196). They are grouped by price range and listed alphabetically within groups. Price ranges (rounded to the nearest $1,000) are approximately what you should expect for a typically equipped car with average mileage.

LESS THAN $6,000
Chevrolet Prizm '98-00
Ford Escort '99, '01-02,
   Mustang (V6) '98,
   Ranger (2WD) '98-99
Honda Civic '98
Hyundai Accent '03
Mazda B-Series (2WD)
   '98-00, **Protegé** 98-00
Mercury Tracer '99
Nissan Altima (4-cyl.) '98,
   Frontier (4-cyl.) '98,
   Sentra '99
Saturn SL '99, '01, **SW** '98
Subaru Legacy '98
Toyota Corolla '98-99,
   Echo '00

$6,000-$8,000
Acura CL '98, **Integra** '98
Buick Regal '00
Chevrolet Prizm '01-02

Ford Crown Victoria '98-99,
   F-150 (2WD) '98-99,
   Mustang (V6) '99-00,
   Ranger (2WD) '00
Honda Accord (4-cyl.) '98-
   99, **Civic** '99, **Odyssey** '98
Hyundai Accent '04,
   Elantra '02
Infiniti G20 '99, **I30** '98
Mazda 626 '00, **Millenia** '99
Mercury Grand Marquis
   '98-99
Mitsubishi Galant '00-01
Nissan Altima (4-cyl.) '99-
   00, **Frontier** '99, **Frontier
   (4-cyl.)** '01, **Maxima** '98-
   99, **Pathfinder** '98,
   Sentra '01
Saturn SL '02
Subaru Impreza '99
Toyota Avalon '98, **Camry**
   '98, **Camry (4-cyl.)** '99,

   Camry Solara (4-cyl.)
   '99, **Corolla** '00-01, **Echo**
   '01-02, **RAV4** '98-99,
   Sienna '98, **T100** '98

$8,000-$10,000
Acura CL '99, **Integra** '99,
   TL '98
Buick Century '02, **Regal** '01
Ford Crown Victoria '00-01,
   F-150 (2WD) '00, **F-150
   (4WD)** '98-99, **Mustang
   (V6)** '01, **Mustang (V8)**
   '99 **Ranger (2WD)** '01
Honda Accord (4-cyl.) '00,
   Accord (V6) '98-99, **Civic**
   '00-01, **CR-V** '00, **Insight**
   '00, **Prelude** '98
Hyundai Elantra '03
Infiniti G20 '00, **I30** '99,
   QX '98
Lincoln Continental '00,

Town Car '98-99
Mazda B-Series (2WD) '01,
  Millenia '00, **MPV** '00,
  MX-5 Miata '99, **Protegé**
  '01-02
Mercury Grand Marquis '00
Mitsubishi Galant '02,
  Lancer '03
Nissan Altima (4-cyl.) '01,
  Frontier '00, Pathfinder '99
Subaru Impreza '00
Toyota 4Runner (4-cyl.)
  '98, **Avalon** '99, **Camry
  (4-cyl.)** '00, **Camry (V6)**
  '99, **Camry Solara (V6)**
  '99, **Celica** '99, **Corolla**
  '02, **Echo** '03, **RAV4** '00,
  Sienna '99, **Tacoma** '98,
  Tacoma (4-cyl.) '99

$10,000-$12,000

Acura RL '98, **TL** '99
Buick Century '03, **Regal** '02
**Chevrolet Silverado 1500
  (2WD)** '00
Chrysler PT Cruiser '02
Ford Crown Victoria '02,
  F-150 (2WD) '01, **Mustang
  (V6)** '02, **(V8)** '00
GMC Sierra 1500 (2WD) '00
Honda Accord (4-cyl.) '01,
  Accord (V6) '00, **Civic**
  '02, **CR-V** '00, **Prelude** '99
Hyundai Elantra '04,
  Sonata '03
Infiniti Q '98, **QX** '99
Kia Optima '04
Lexus ES '98
Mazda 626 '02, **MPV** '01,
  MX-5 Miata '00,
  Protegé '03
Mercury Grand Marquis
  '01-02
Mitsubishi Eclipse '01,
  Galant '03
Nissan Frontier (4-cyl.)
  '02-03, **Frontier (V6)** '01,
  Maxima '00, Pathfinder
  '00, Xterra '02
Subaru Impreza '01, **Legacy**
  '00, **Outback (4-cyl.)** '00
Toyota 4Runner (4-cyl.)

'99, **4Runner (V6)** '98,
  Camry (4-cyl.) '01, Camry
  (V6) '00, **Camry Solara
  (4-cyl.)** '00, **Celica** '00-
  01, **Corolla** '03, **Echo** '04,
  Sienna '00, **Tacoma
  (4-cyl.)** '00, **Tacoma
  (V6)** '99

$12,000-$14,000

Acura Integra '00-01, **TL** '00
Buick Century '04,
  LeSabre '02, Regal '03
Chevrolet Impala '03,
  Monte Carlo '03,
  Silverado 1500 (2WD) '01
Ford F-150 (2WD) '02,
  F-150 (4WD) '01
  Mustang (V8) '01
GMC Sierra 1500 (2WD) '01
Honda Accord (4-cyl.) '02,
  Accord (V6) '01, Civic
  '03, CR-V '01, Odyssey
  '00
Hyundai Santa Fe '02,
  Sonata '04
Infiniti G20 '02, **I30** '00, **Q** '99
Lexus ES '99
Lincoln Town Car '00
Mazda Millenia '01,
  MX-5 Miata '01
Mitsubishi Eclipse '02,
  Outlander '03
Nissan Maxima '01,
  Sentra '05
Pontiac Vibe '03-04
Scion xA '05, xB '04-05
Subaru Forester '01,
  Impreza '03, Outback
  (4-cyl.) '01
Toyota 4Runner (4-cyl.)
  '00, **4Runner (V6)** '99,
  Avalon '00, Camry (4-
  cyl.) '02, Camry (V6) '01,
  Camry Solara (4-cyl.)
  '01, Camry Solara (V6)
  '00, Corolla '04, Echo
  '05, Matrix '03, MR2
  '01,Prius '01, Sienna '01,
  Tacoma (4-cyl.) '01-02,
  Tacoma (V6) '00, Tundra
  (V6) '00-01

$14,000-$16,000

Acura RL '99, **RSX** '02
Buick LeSabre '03
Chevrolet Impala '04,
  Monte Carlo '04
Ford Crown Victoria '04,
  Escape '03, F-150 (2WD)
  '03, F-150 (4WD) '02,
  F-150 Heritage (2WD)
  '04, Mustang (V6) '04,
  Mustang (V8) '02,
  Ranger (2WD) '05
Honda Accord (4-cyl.) '03,
  Accord (V6) '02, Civic
  '04, CR-V '02, Element
  '03, Prelude '01
Hyundai Santa Fe '03
Infiniti I30 '01, **QX** '00
Kia Amanti '04
Lexus ES '00, **GS** '98, **RX**
  '99
Lincoln Continental '02,
  Town Car '01
Mazda B-Series (2WD) '05,
  Millenia '02, MX-5 Miata
  '02-03, Tribute '03, 3 '04
Mitsubishi Galant '04,
  Outlander '04
Nissan Altima (4-cyl.) '03,
  Altima (V6) '02, Frontier
  (V6) '02, Maxima '02,
  Pathfinder '01, Xterra '02
Pontiac Grand Prix '04,
  Vibe '05
Saturn Ion '05
Subaru Baja '03, **Forester**
  '02, **Impreza** '04, **Legacy**
  '01
Toyota 4Runner (V6) '00,
  Avalon '01, Camry (4-
  cyl.) '03, Camry (V6) '02,
  Camry Solara (4-cyl.) 02,
  Camry Solara (V6) '01,
  Celica '02-03, Corolla '05,
  Highlander (4-cyl.) '01,
  Matrix '04, MR2 '02,
  Prius '02, RAV4 '01-02,
  Sienna '02, Tacoma (4-
  cyl.) '03-05, Tacoma (V6)
  '01, Tundra (V6) '02,
  Tundra (V8) '00

$16,000-$18,000

Acura RL '00, **RSX** '03
BMW M3 '98, **Z3** '99
Buick LeSabre '04,
    Regal '04
Ford Escape '04, **F-150**
    Heritage (4WD) '04
Honda Accord (4-cyl.) '04,
    Accord (V6) '03, **Civic**
    '05, **Civic Hybrid** '03,
    CR-V '03, **Element** '04,
    S2000 '00
Infiniti I30 '02, **QX** '01
Lexus ES '01, **GS** '99, **LS**
    '98, **RX** '00
Mazda MX-5 Miata '04,
    Tribute '04, **3** '05
Mercedes-Benz SLK '98
Mercury Grand Marquis
    '04, **Mariner** '05
Nissan Altima (4-cyl.) '04,
    Altima (V6) '03-04,
    Frontier (V6) '03,
    Maxima '03, **Pathfinder**
    '02, **Xterra** '03
Pontiac Grand Prix '05
Subaru Forester '03,
    Impreza '05, **Impreza**
    WRX '03, **Legacy** '02,
    Outback (6-cyl.) '01
Toyota Avalon '02,
    Camry (4-cyl.) '04-05,
    Camry (V6) '03, **Camry**
    Solara (4-cyl.) '03-04,
    Camry Solara (V6) '02,
    Highlander (V6) '01,
    Matrix '05, **Prius** '03,
    RAV4 '03, **Tacoma (V6)**
    '02, **Tundra (V6)** '03-04,
    Tundra (V8) '01
Volvo S60 (FWD) '02

$18,000-$20,000

Acura RSX '04
BMW Z3 '00
Buick Rendezvous '04
Chevrolet Impala '05
Chrysler PT Cruiser
    Turbo '05
Ford Mustang V8 '04
Honda Accord (4-cyl.) '05,

Civic Hybrid '04-05,
    CR-V '04, **Element** '05,
    S2000 '01
Lexus GS '00, **IS** '01, **LS** '99
Lincoln Town Car '02
Mercedes-Benz SLK '99
Nissan Pathfinder '03
Subaru Forester '04,
    Legacy '03-05, **Outback**
    (4-cyl.) '03-04,
    Outback (6-cyl.) '02-03
Toyota 4Runner (V6) '01,
    Camry (V6) '04, **Camry**
    Solara (4-cyl.) '05,
    Camry Solara (V6) '03,
    Highlander (4-cyl.) '02,
    Land Cruiser '98-99,
    RAV4 '04, **Sienna** '03,
    Tacoma (V6) '03-04,
    Tundra (V6) '05,
    Tundra (V8) '02

$20,000-$24,000

Acura MDX '01, **RL** '02, **TL**
    '03, **TSX** '04
Audi A4 sedan (4-cyl.) '04
BMW 3 Series (AWD) '02,
    5 Series (6-cyl.) '01-02,
    M3 '99
Buick LaCrosse '05,
    Rendezvous '05
Ford Thunderbird '02
Honda Accord (V6) '04-05,
    CR-V '05, **Odyssey** '03-
    04, **Pilot** '03, **S2000** '02-
    03
Infiniti I30 '03-04, **QX**
    '02-03
Lexus ES '02, **GS** '01, **IS** '02-
    03, **LS** '00, **LX** '99, **RX**
    '01-02
Nissan Altima (V6) '05,
    Pathfinder '04
Subaru Forester '05,
    Impreza WRX, STi '04,
    Legacy Turbo '05,
    Outback (4-cyl) '05,
    Outback (6-cyl) '04
Toyota 4Runner (V6) '02,
    Avalon '03-04, **Camry**
    (V6) '05, **Camry Solara**

(V6) '05, **Highlander**
    4-cyl '03-05, **(V6)** '02-
    03, **Land Cruiser** '00,
    Prius '04-05, **RAV4** '05,
    Sequoia '01, **Tundra**
    (V8) '03-04
Volvo S60 (FWD) '04, **S60**
    (FWD) '04, **S80 (AWD)** '04

$24,000-$28,000

Acura MDX '02, **RL** '03, **TSX**
    '05
Audi A4 sedan (4-cyl.) '05
BMW Z3 '02
Honda Pilot '04, **S2000** '04
Infiniti G '04, **Q** '02
Lexus ES '03, **GS** '02, **IS** '04,
    LX '00, **RX** '03
Lincoln Town Car '04
Nissan Murano '04
Porsche Boxster '00
Subaru Impreza WRX, STi
    '05
Toyota 4Runner '03,
    4Runner (V6) '04-05,
    Highlander (V6) '04-05,
    Land Cruiser '01, **Sequoia**
    '02, **Tundra (V8)** '05
Volvo S60 (AWD) '04, **S60**
    (FWD) '05, **S80 (FWD)**
    '04

$28,000 AND UP

Acura MDX '03-05, **RL** '04,
    TL '04-05
BMW X3 '05
Ford Escape Hybrid '05
Honda Accord Hybrid '05,
    Pilot '05, **S2000** '05
Infiniti FX (V6) '03-05, **G**
    '05, **M** '03
Lexus ES '04-05, **GS** '03-05,
    GX '03-04, **LS** '01-03, '05,
    LX '01-05, **RX** '04-05, **SC**
    '02-04
Mercedes-Benz SLK '03
Nissan Murano '05
Toyota 4Runner (V8) '04-
    05,**Land Cruiser** '02-04,
    Sequoia '04-05, **Sienna**
    '05

CR Good Bets & Bad Bets

CR Good Bets are reliable models that have consistently performed well in CONSUMER REPORTS road tests over the years and have several or more years of better-than-average Used Car Verdicts, with fewer problems than most models each year. **CR Bad Bets** are models from the Used Cars to Avoid list. They have shown multiple years of Used Car Verdicts that are much worse than average. They have regularly shown more problems than most models each production year. All are listed alphabetically within groups.

GOOD BETS

Acura Integra
Acura MDX
Acura RL
Acura RSX
Acura TL
BMW Z3, Z4
Buick Regal
Chevrolet Prizm
Ford Crown Victoria
Ford Escort
Ford Mustang (V8)
Honda Accord
Honda Civic
Honda Civic Hybrid
Honda CR-V
Honda Element
Honda Odyssey
Honda Pilot
Honda Prelude
Honda S2000
Infiniti FX (V6)
Infiniti G
Infiniti I
Infiniti QX
Lexus ES
Lexus GS

Lexus IS
Lexus GX
Lexus LS
Lexus RX
Lincoln Town Car
Mazda Millenia
Mazda MX-5 Miata
Mazda Protegé
Mercury Grand Marquis
Mitsubishi Galant
Nissan Altima
Nissan Maxima
Nissan Murano
Nissan Pathfinder
Pontiac Vibe
Subaru Forester
Subaru Impreza
Subaru Impreza WRX
Subaru Legacy
Subaru Outback
Toyota 4Runner
Toyota Avalon
Toyota Camry
Toyota Camry Solara
Toyota Celica
Toyota Corolla
Toyota Echo

Toyota Highlander
Toyota Land Cruiser
Toyota Matrix
Toyota Prius
Toyota RAV4
Toyota Sequoia
Toyota Sienna
Toyota Tundra

BAD BETS

BMW 7 Series
BMW X5 (V8)
Chevrolet Astro
Chevrolet Blazer
Chevrolet Express
  1500
Chevrolet S-10 (4WD)
Chevrolet TrailBlazer
Chevrolet Venture
Chrysler Town &
  Country (AWD)
Dodge Grand
  Caravan (AWD)
GMC Envoy
GMC Jimmy
GMC Safari
GMC Savana 1500

GMC Sonoma (4WD)
Jaguar S-Type
Jaguar X-Type
Kia Sedona
Land Rover
  Discovery
Lincoln LS
Lincoln Navigator
Mercedes-Benz CLK
Mercedes-Benz
  E-Class (V8)
Oldsmobile Alero
Oldsmobile
  Bravada
Oldsmobile
  Silhouette
Pontiac Aztek
Pontiac Trans
  Sport/Montana
Saturn Vue (AWD)
Volkswagen Cabrio
Volkswagen Jetta
Volkswagen New
  Beetle
Volkswagen Passat
  Wagon (V6)
Volvo XC90

Used cars to avoid

Here are all the models that had below-average Used Car Verdicts in our survey covering 1998 to 2005. They are listed alphabetically, by make, model, and year.

Audi A4 Avant '99, 01; **A4 sedan** '98-00, '02; **A4 sedan (4-cyl.)** '01; **A4 sedan (V6)** '05; **A6 Avant** '99-00; **A6 sedan (V6)** '98-00, '02-05;

A6 sedan (V6, Turbo) '00-01, '03; **A8** '04; **Allroad** '01-03; **S4** '00, '04-05; **TT** '03 **BMW 3 Series** '04; **5 Series (6-cyl.)** '04; **5 Series (V8)**

'98-00, '04; **7 Series** '98-04; **M3** '02-03; **X5 (V8)** '01-02, '05 **Buick LeSabre** '05; **Park Ave.** '98; **Rendezvous** '02; **Terraza** '05

adillac Catera '98; CTS '03;
DeVille '00-03, '05;
Escalade '03; Seville '98-
03; SRX '04-05

hevrolet Astro '98-03;
Avalanche '03; Blazer 98-
04; Camaro '00-02;
Cavalier Coupe/Conv. '03-
04; Cavalier Sedan '03;
Cobalt '05; Colorado (2WD)
'04; Colorado (4WD) '04-
05; Corvette '05; Equinox
'05; Express '98-04; Impala
'01; Malibu '98-01, '04;
Malibu Maxx '04; Monte
Carlo '00-01; S-10 (2WD)
'98-99, '02-03; S-10 (4WD)
'98, '00-03; K1500 '98;
Silverado 1500 (4WD) '03;
Suburban '98-99, '03;
Tahoe '98-99, '03; Trail-
Blazer '02-04; Uplander
'05; Venture '98-02;
Venture (ext.) '03

hrysler 300 (V8) '05; 300M
'99, '03; Concorde '99; LHS
'99; Pacifica '04-05; PT
Cruiser Turbo '03; Sebring
Convertible '01-02, '04;
Sebring Sedan '02-03; Town
& Country '00-03; Town &
Country (ext., AWD) '99,
Town & Country (ext.,
FWD) '04; Town & Country
(reg.) '98; Voyager (4-cyl.)
'01-03; Voyager (V6) '01-03

odge Caravan (4-cyl.) '98,
'01-03; Caravan (V6) '98,
'00-03; Grand Caravan '00-
03; Grand Caravan (FWD)
'04; Grand Caravan (AWD)
'99; Dakota (2WD) '98, '05;
Dakota (4WD) '98-00, '02,
'05; Durango '98-01, '03-04;
Intrepid '98-99, '03-04;
Neon '98-99; Ram 1500
(2WD) '99; Ram 1500
(4WD) '98; RamVan/
Wagon '99; Stratus Sedan
(4-cyl.) '98-99; Stratus
Sedan (V6) '02-03

Ford Contour '98; Econoline

'01; Excursion '03-04;
Expedition '03-05; Explorer
'02-05, (4WD) '00; Explorer
Sport Trac '04; F-150 '04-
05; Focus Sedan '00, Focus
Wagon '00, '05; Freestyle
(AWD) '05; Mustang (V6)
'05; Ranger (2WD) '04,
(4WD) '01; Taurus Sedan
'05; Windstar '98-01

GMC Canyon (2WD) '04;
Canyon (4WD) '04-05;
Envoy '02-04; Jimmy '98-
01; Safari '98-04; Savana
'98-04; Sierra 1500
(4WD)'98, '03; S-15
Sonoma (2WD) '98-99, '02-
03; S-15 Sonoma (4WD)
'98, '00-03; Suburban '98-
99; Yukon XL '03; Yukon
'98-99, '03

Honda Passport '99-02

Hummer H2 '03-04

Hyundai Accent '00; Sonata
'00-01; Tiburon '03; Tuscon
'05; XG300 '01

Infiniti QX56 '04-05

Isuzu Rodeo '99-02

Jaguar S-Type '00-04; XJ '98-
00, '04; X-Type '02-04

Jeep Grand Cherokee '98-03,
'05

Kia Sedona '02-03; Sorento
'05; Sportage '01, '05

Land Rover Discovery '99-01;
'03-04; LR3 '05; Freelander
'02; Range Rover '03

Lincoln Aviator '03-04; LS '00-
01, '03-04; Navigator '01-05

Mazda B-Series (2WD) '04; B-
Series (4WD) '01; MPV '03-
04; 6 Hatchback '04; 6
Sedan (V6) '03, '05

Mercedes-Benz C-Class (4-
cyl.) '02-03, '05; C-Class
(V6) '01-04; CLK '01-05; E-
Class Sedan '01-05; E-Class
(V8) '98; E-Class Wagon
'01-02, '04; M-Class '98-03;
S-Class '00, '02-04; SL '04;
SLK '02, '05

Mercury Cougar '99;

Mountaineer '02-05; (4WD)
'00; Mystique '98; Sable
Sedan '05

Mini Cooper Base '02-03; S '02

Nissan 350Z '03; Armada
'04-05; Quest '04-05; Titan
'04-05

Oldsmobile Alero '99-02;
Aurora '98, '01; Bravada
'98-00, '02-03; Cutlass '98-
99; Silhouette '98-03

Plymouth Breeze '98-99;
Grand Voyager '00; Neon
'98-99; Voyager (4-cyl.)
'98; Voyager (V6) '98, '00

Pontiac Aztek '01-03;
Bonneville '98, '00-03;
Firebird '00-02; Grand Am
'98-02; Grand Prix '98, '01;
Grand Prix SC '00; GTO
'04; Trans Sport Montana
'98; Montana '99-02;
Montana (ext) '03; Montana
SV6 '05; Sunfire '03-04

Porsche 911 '02, '04; Cayenne
'04-05

Saab 9-3 '03-05; 9-5 Sedan
'99-00; 9-5 Wagon '99, '01

Saturn Ion '04; L-Series (V6)
'00-02; Relay '05; Vue '02-
03; Vue (AWD) '04

Volkswagen Cabrio '99, '01-02;
EuroVan '02-03; Golf (4-
cyl.) '98, '03-04; Golf (4-
cyl. turbo) '01; Jetta (4-
cyl.) '98-02, '05; Jetta (4-
cyl., turbo) '01-03; Jetta
(4-cyl., turbo-diesel) '02;
Jetta (V6) '99-03; New
Beetle '98-04; New Beetle
Convertible '05; Passat (4-
cyl.) '98-02, '05; Passat
(V6) '99-01; '04; Passat
Wagon '03; Passat W8
'03; Touareg '04-05

Volvo C70 '00, '04; Cross
Country '98-01; S60 (AWD)
'03, '05; S80 '99-02;
S90/V90 '98; V40 '00;
V50 '05; V70 (FWD) '01,
'03; V70 (AWD) '98; XC90
'03-05

DETAILED RELIABILITY

The charts on the following pages give you a model's complete reliability picture for both its used versions (1998 through 2005) and the new one currently on sale. These detailed reliability Ratings are based on our 2005 Annual Car Reliability Survey, for which we received responses for just over 1 million vehicles.

If the reliability charts on these pages were a car, we'd say that they underwent a major redesign for 2006.

They don't look much different from previous years (that's intentional), but they have been completely revised to make them easier to use.

Previously, to get an accurate assessment of how well a model held up in each of the individual trouble spots, compared with other vehicles of the same age, you needed to compare the Ratings in its chart with those of an "average model" chart, usually on a different page. That is because the trouble-spot Ratings were calculated on an absolute

How to use the charts

MAJOR REDESIGNS

A model year in **bold** identifies the year the model was introduced or underwent a major redesign.

TROUBLE SPOTS

To assess a used car in more detail, look at the individual Ratings for each of the 15 trouble spots. They will pinpoint a model's strengths and weaknesses. Ratings are based on the percentage of survey respondents who reported problems for that trouble spot, compared with the average of

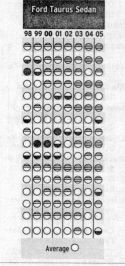

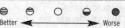

all vehicles for that year. Models that score a ● are not necessarily unreliable, but they have a higher problem rate than the average model. Similarly, models that score a ⊖ are not necessarily problem-free, but they had relatively few problems compared with other models.

Because problem rates in some trouble spots are very low, we do not assign a ● or ◐ unless the model's problem rate exceeds 3 percent. If a problem rate is below 2 percent, it will be assigned a ⊖; below 1 percent, it will be assigned a ⊖.

scale; the problem rate dictated the Rating regardless of how it compared with other models.

That's why some Ratings that appeared to be good, such as a ⊖ for a newer car, could have been below average when compared with the average model. Similarly, a ○ rating on an older car might not look impressive, but it could have been notably better than the average model.

Our new relative method of calculation factors the average problem rate into the Ratings, so you get an accurate assessment within a single chart. It also brings the trouble-spot Ratings in line with the Used Car Verdicts, which have always been calculated on a relative scale.

The Annual Car Reliability Survey is sent to subscribers of CONSUMER REPORTS and ConsumerReports.org. In the 2005 survey, respondents reported on any serious problems they had with their vehicles in any of the trouble spots included in the chart below during the previous year (April 1, 2004, through March 31, 2005) that they considered serious because of cost, failure, safety, or downtime. Because high-mileage vehicles tend to have more problems than low-mileage ones, problem rates are standardized to minimize differences related to mileage. The 2005 models were generally less than six months old at the time of the survey and had been driven an average of about 3,000 miles.

USED CAR VERDICTS

To check the overall reliability of a used car, look at the Used Car Verdict for the appropriate model year. This Rating shows whether the model had more or fewer problems overall than did the average model of that year.

The verdict is calculated from the total number of problems reported by subscribers in all trouble spots. Because problems with the engine, cooling system, transmission, and drive system can be serious and expensive to repair, our calculations give extra weight to them.

NEW CAR PREDICTIONS

To see how a 2006 or 2007 model that's currently on sale is likely to hold up, look at the New Car Prediction Rating at the bottom of each chart. The Predicted Reliability Ratings are also shown in the Vehicle Ratings chart (page 157) and vehicle profiles (page 167). For this, we averaged a model's Used Car Verdict for the most recent three years, provided the vehicle did not change significantly in that time and hasn't been redesigned for 2006/2007. We have

found that several model years' data are a better predictor than the single most recent model year.

One or two years' data may be used if the model was redesigned in 2005 or 2004, or if there were insufficient data for more years. Sometimes we include a prediction for a model that is new or has been redesigned, provided its reliability history or the manufacturer's track record has been consistently above average. "NA" means there were insufficient data to make a New Car Prediction.

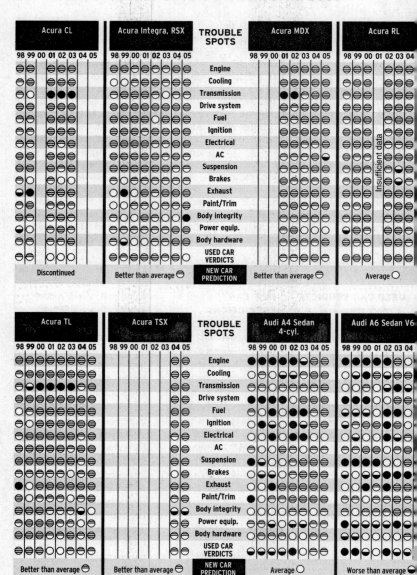

Acura CL	Acura Integra, RSX	TROUBLE SPOTS	Acura MDX	Acura RL
98 99 00 01 02 03 04 05	98 99 00 01 02 03 04 05		98 99 00 01 02 03 04 05	98 99 00 01 02 03 04
		Engine		
		Cooling		
		Transmission		
		Drive system		
		Fuel		
		Ignition		
		Electrical		
		AC		
		Suspension		Insufficient data
		Brakes		
		Exhaust		
		Paint/Trim		
		Body integrity		
		Power equip.		
		Body hardware		
		USED CAR VERDICTS		
Discontinued	Better than average ⊖	NEW CAR PREDICTION	Better than average ⊖	Average ○

Acura TL	Acura TSX	TROUBLE SPOTS	Audi A4 Sedan 4-cyl.	Audi A6 Sedan V6
98 99 00 01 02 03 04 05	98 99 00 01 02 03 04 05		98 99 00 01 02 03 04 05	98 99 00 01 02 03 04
		Engine		
		Cooling		
		Transmission		
		Drive system		
		Fuel		
		Ignition		
		Electrical		
		AC		
		Suspension		
		Brakes		
		Exhaust		
		Paint/Trim		
		Body integrity		
		Power equip.		
		Body hardware		
		USED CAR VERDICTS		
Better than average ⊖	Better than average ⊖	NEW CAR PREDICTION	Average ○	Worse than average ⊖

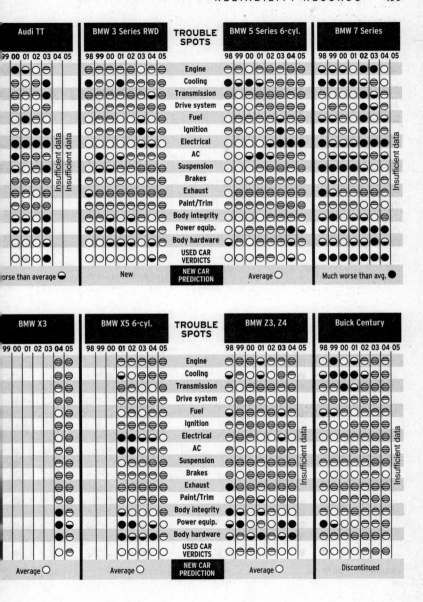

Top row models: Audi TT | BMW 3 Series RWD | TROUBLE SPOTS | BMW 5 Series 6-cyl. | BMW 7 Series

Years: 99 00 01 02 03 04 05 | 98 99 00 01 02 03 04 05 | | 98 99 00 01 02 03 04 05 | 98 99 00 01 02 03 04 05

Trouble Spots: Engine, Cooling, Transmission, Drive system, Fuel, Ignition, Electrical, AC, Suspension, Brakes, Exhaust, Paint/Trim, Body integrity, Power equip., Body hardware, USED CAR VERDICTS

Audi TT: Insufficient data (later years)
BMW 3 Series RWD — NEW CAR PREDICTION: New
BMW 5 Series 6-cyl. — Average ○
BMW 7 Series: Insufficient data (later years); Much worse than avg. ●

Legend: worse than average ◒ | New | NEW CAR PREDICTION | Average ○ | Much worse than avg. ●

Bottom row models: BMW X3 | BMW X5 6-cyl. | TROUBLE SPOTS | BMW Z3, Z4 | Buick Century

Years: 99 00 01 02 03 04 05 | 98 99 00 01 02 03 04 05 | | 98 99 00 01 02 03 04 05 | 98 99 00 01 02 03 04 05

BMW X3 — Average ○
BMW X5 6-cyl. — NEW CAR PREDICTION: Average ○
BMW Z3, Z4 — Average ○; Insufficient data (later years)
Buick Century — Discontinued; Insufficient data (later years)

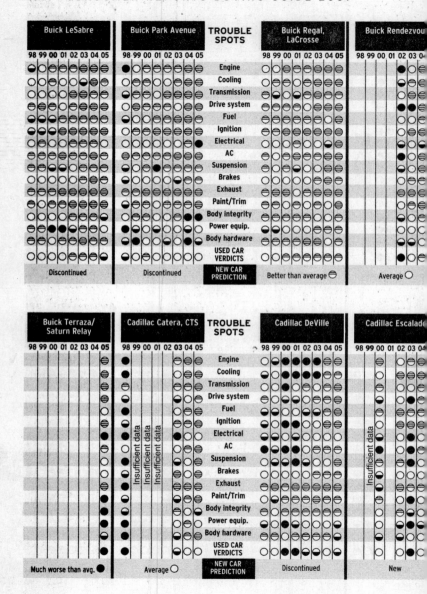

	Buick LeSabre	Buick Park Avenue	TROUBLE SPOTS	Buick Regal, LaCrosse	Buick Rendezvous
	98 99 00 01 02 03 04 05	98 99 00 01 02 03 04 05		98 99 00 01 02 03 04 05	98 99 00 01 02 03 04
Engine					
Cooling					
Transmission					
Drive system					
Fuel					
Ignition					
Electrical					
AC					
Suspension					
Brakes					
Exhaust					
Paint/Trim					
Body integrity					
Power equip.					
Body hardware					
USED CAR VERDICTS					
NEW CAR PREDICTION	Discontinued	Discontinued		Better than average ⊖	Average ○

	Buick Terraza/ Saturn Relay	Cadillac Catera, CTS	TROUBLE SPOTS	Cadillac DeVille	Cadillac Escalade
	98 99 00 01 02 03 04 05	98 99 00 01 02 03 04 05		98 99 00 01 02 03 04 05	98 99 00 01 02 03 04
Engine					
Cooling					
Transmission					
Drive system					
Fuel					
Ignition					
Electrical		Insufficient data			Insufficient data
AC					
Suspension					
Brakes					
Exhaust					
Paint/Trim					
Body integrity					
Power equip.					
Body hardware					
USED CAR VERDICTS					
NEW CAR PREDICTION	Much worse than avg. ●	Average ○		Discontinued	New

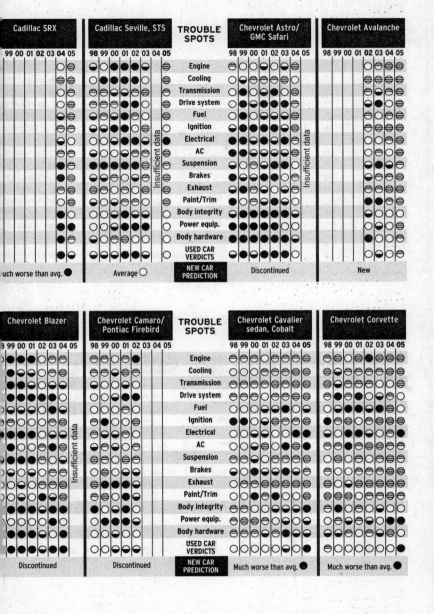

Top section

TROUBLE SPOTS	Cadillac SRX	Cadillac Seville, STS	Chevrolet Astro/ GMC Safari	Chevrolet Avalanche
	99 00 01 02 03 04 05	98 99 00 01 02 03 04 05	98 99 00 01 02 03 04 05	98 99 00 01 02 03 04 05
Engine				
Cooling				
Transmission				
Drive system				
Fuel				
Ignition				
Electrical				
AC				
Suspension				
Brakes				
Exhaust				
Paint/Trim				
Body integrity				
Power equip.				
Body hardware				
USED CAR VERDICTS				
NEW CAR PREDICTION	Much worse than avg. ●	Average ○	Discontinued	New

Cadillac Astro/GMC Safari: Insufficient data. Cadillac Seville/STS: Insufficient data.

Bottom section

TROUBLE SPOTS	Chevrolet Blazer	Chevrolet Camaro/ Pontiac Firebird	Chevrolet Cavalier sedan, Cobalt	Chevrolet Corvette
	99 00 01 02 03 04 05	98 99 00 01 02 03 04 05	98 99 00 01 02 03 04 05	98 99 00 01 02 03 04 05
Engine				
Cooling				
Transmission				
Drive system				
Fuel				
Ignition				
Electrical				
AC				
Suspension				
Brakes				
Exhaust				
Paint/Trim				
Body integrity				
Power equip.				
Body hardware				
USED CAR VERDICTS				
NEW CAR PREDICTION	Discontinued	Discontinued	Much worse than avg. ●	Much worse than avg. ●

Chevrolet Blazer: Insufficient data.

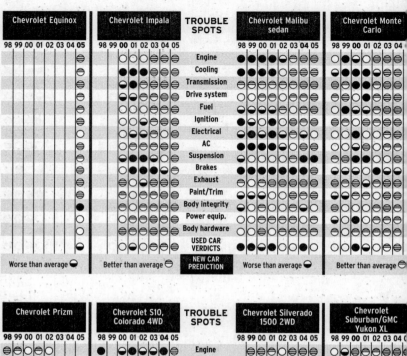

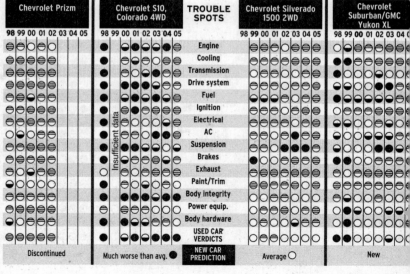

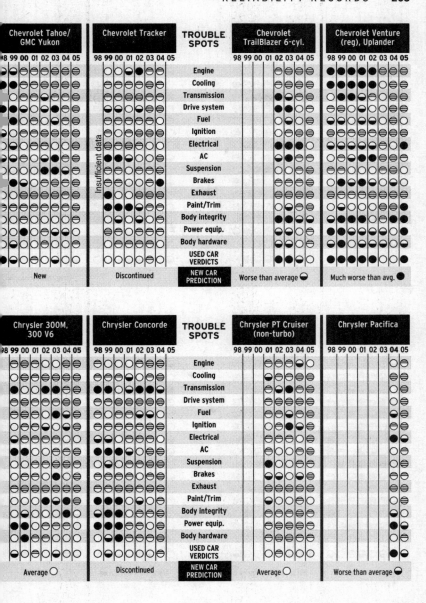

Top section

	Chevrolet Tahoe/ GMC Yukon	Chevrolet Tracker	TROUBLE SPOTS	Chevrolet TrailBlazer 6-cyl.	Chevrolet Venture (reg), Uplander
Years	98 99 00 01 02 03 04 05	98 99 00 01 02 03 04 05		98 99 00 01 02 03 04 05	98 99 00 01 02 03 04 05
			Engine		
			Cooling		
			Transmission		
			Drive system		
			Fuel		
			Ignition		
		Insufficient data	Electrical		
			AC		
			Suspension		
			Brakes		
			Exhaust		
			Paint/Trim		
			Body integrity		
			Power equip.		
			Body hardware		
			USED CAR VERDICTS		
	New	Discontinued	NEW CAR PREDICTION	Worse than average	Much worse than avg.

Bottom section

	Chrysler 300M, 300 V6	Chrysler Concorde	TROUBLE SPOTS	Chrysler PT Cruiser (non-turbo)	Chrysler Pacifica
Years	98 99 00 01 02 03 04 05	98 99 00 01 02 03 04 05		98 99 00 01 02 03 04 05	98 99 00 01 02 03 04 05
			Engine		
			Cooling		
			Transmission		
			Drive system		
			Fuel		
			Ignition		
			Electrical		
			AC		
			Suspension		
			Brakes		
			Exhaust		
			Paint/Trim		
			Body integrity		
			Power equip.		
			Body hardware		
			USED CAR VERDICTS		
	Average	Discontinued	NEW CAR PREDICTION	Average	Worse than average

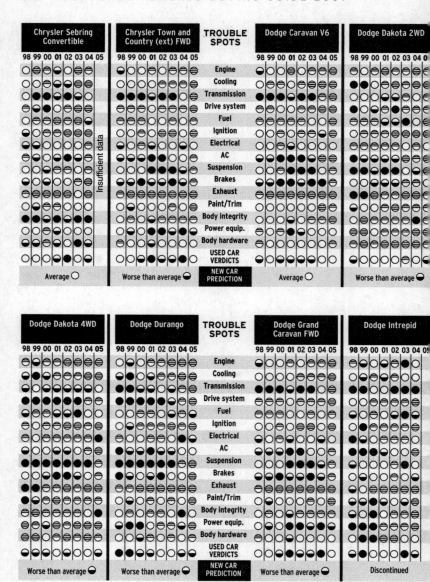

TROUBLE SPOTS	Chrysler Sebring Convertible	Chrysler Town and Country (ext) FWD	Dodge Caravan V6	Dodge Dakota 2WD
	98 99 00 01 02 03 04 05	98 99 00 01 02 03 04 05	98 99 00 01 02 03 04 05	98 99 00 01 02 03 04 05
Engine				
Cooling				
Transmission				
Drive system				
Fuel				
Ignition				
Electrical				
AC				
Suspension				
Brakes				
Exhaust				
Paint/Trim				
Body integrity				
Power equip.				
Body hardware				
USED CAR VERDICTS				
NEW CAR PREDICTION	Average ○	Worse than average ◒	Average ○	Worse than average ◒

(Chrysler Sebring Convertible column marked "Insufficient data")

TROUBLE SPOTS	Dodge Dakota 4WD	Dodge Durango	Dodge Grand Caravan FWD	Dodge Intrepid
	98 99 00 01 02 03 04 05	98 99 00 01 02 03 04 05	98 99 00 01 02 03 04 05	98 99 00 01 02 03 04 05
Engine				
Cooling				
Transmission				
Drive system				
Fuel				
Ignition				
Electrical				
AC				
Suspension				
Brakes				
Exhaust				
Paint/Trim				
Body integrity				
Power equip.				
Body hardware				
USED CAR VERDICTS				
NEW CAR PREDICTION	Worse than average ◒	Worse than average ◒	Worse than average ◒	Discontinued

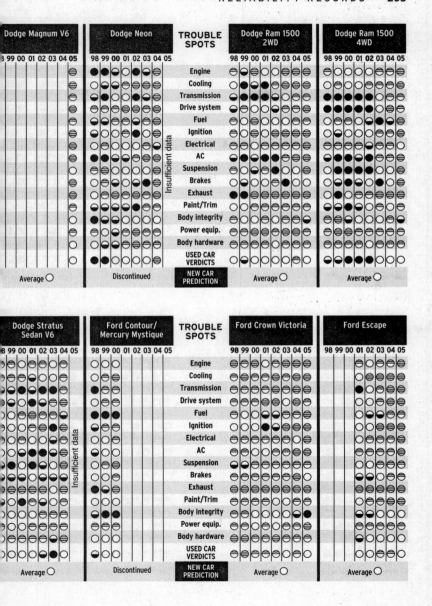

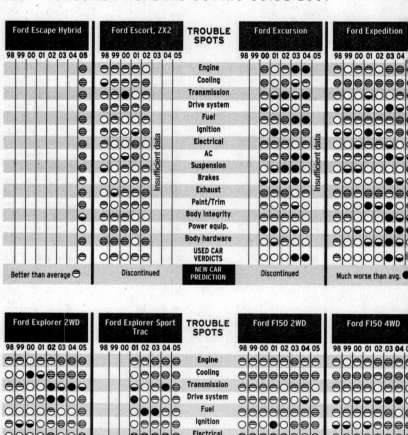

Ford Escape Hybrid	Ford Escort, ZX2	TROUBLE SPOTS	Ford Excursion	Ford Expedition
98 99 00 01 02 03 04 05	98 99 00 01 02 03 04 05		98 99 00 01 02 03 04 05	98 99 00 01 02 03 04 05
		Engine		
		Cooling		
		Transmission		
		Drive system		
		Fuel		
		Ignition		
		Electrical		
		AC		
		Suspension		
		Brakes		
		Exhaust		
		Paint/Trim		
		Body integrity		
		Power equip.		
		Body hardware		
		USED CAR VERDICTS		
Better than average ⊖	Discontinued	NEW CAR PREDICTION	Discontinued	Much worse than avg. ●

Ford Explorer 2WD	Ford Explorer Sport Trac	TROUBLE SPOTS	Ford F150 2WD	Ford F150 4WD
98 99 00 01 02 03 04 05	98 99 00 01 02 03 04 05		98 99 00 01 02 03 04 05	98 99 00 01 02 03 04
		Engine		
		Cooling		
		Transmission		
		Drive system		
		Fuel		
		Ignition		
		Electrical		
		AC		
		Suspension		
		Brakes		
		Exhaust		
		Paint/Trim		
		Body integrity		
		Power equip.		
		Body hardware		
		USED CAR VERDICTS		
Worse than average ⊖	New	NEW CAR PREDICTION	Worse than average ⊖	Worse than average ⊖

Insufficient data

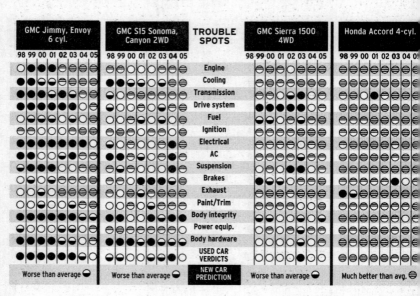

| | GMC Jimmy, Envoy 6 cyl. | GMC S15 Sonoma, Canyon 2WD | TROUBLE SPOTS | GMC Sierra 1500 4WD | Honda Accord 4-cyl. |

Worse than average ⊖ | Worse than average ⊖ | NEW CAR PREDICTION | Worse than average ⊖ | Much better than avg. ⊜

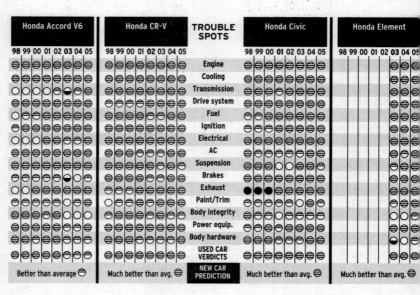

| | Honda Accord V6 | Honda CR-V | TROUBLE SPOTS | Honda Civic | Honda Element |

Better than average ⊜ | Much better than avg. ⊜ | NEW CAR PREDICTION | Much better than avg. ⊜ | Much better than avg. ⊜

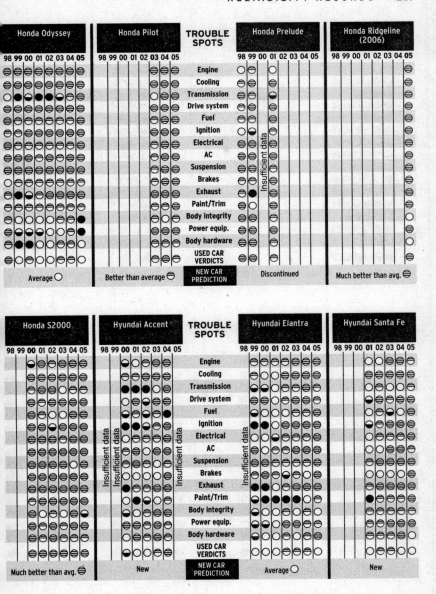

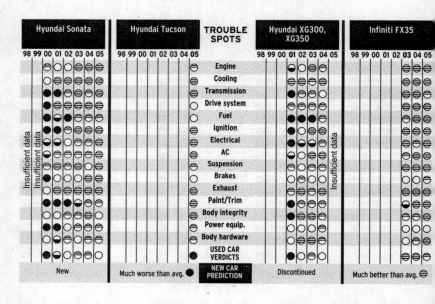

	Hyundai Sonata	Hyundai Tucson	TROUBLE SPOTS	Hyundai XG300, XG350	Infiniti FX35
	98 99 00 01 02 03 04 05	98 99 00 01 02 03 04 05		98 99 00 01 02 03 04 05	98 99 00 01 02 03 04 05
			Engine		
			Cooling		
			Transmission		
			Drive system		
			Fuel		
			Ignition		
			Electrical		
			AC		
			Suspension		
			Brakes		
			Exhaust		
			Paint/Trim		
			Body integrity		
			Power equip.		
			Body hardware		
			USED CAR VERDICTS		
	New	Much worse than avg. ●	NEW CAR PREDICTION	Discontinued	Much better than avg. ⊖

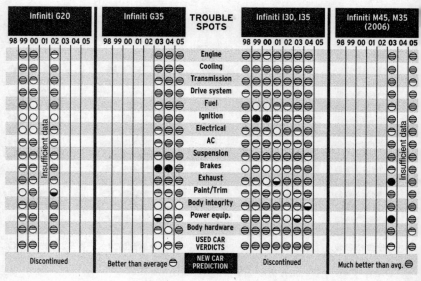

	Infiniti G20	Infiniti G35	TROUBLE SPOTS	Infiniti I30, I35	Infiniti M45, M35 (2006)
	98 99 00 01 02 03 04 05	98 99 00 01 02 03 04 05		98 99 00 01 02 03 04 05	98 99 00 01 02 03 04 05
			Engine		
			Cooling		
			Transmission		
			Drive system		
			Fuel		
			Ignition		
			Electrical		
			AC		
			Suspension		
			Brakes		
			Exhaust		
			Paint/Trim		
			Body integrity		
			Power equip.		
			Body hardware		
			USED CAR VERDICTS		
	Discontinued	Better than average ⊖	NEW CAR PREDICTION	Discontinued	Much better than avg. ⊖

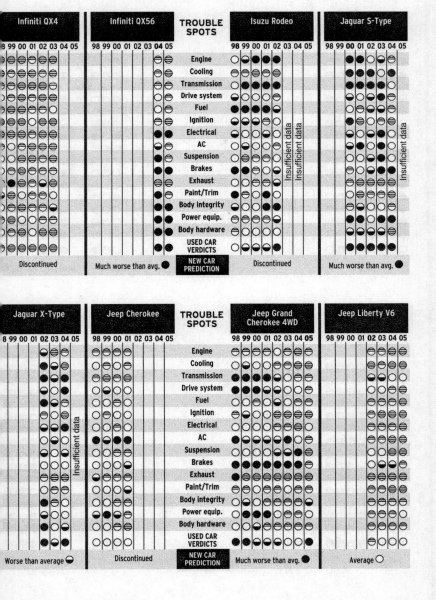

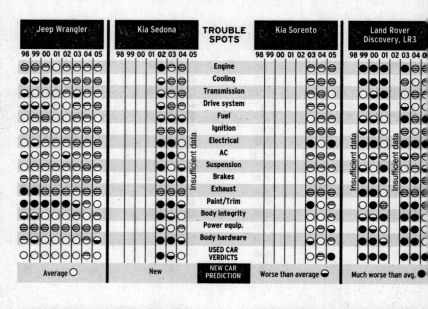

	Jeep Wrangler	Kia Sedona	TROUBLE SPOTS	Kia Sorento	Land Rover Discovery, LR3
	98 99 00 01 02 03 04 05	98 99 00 01 02 03 04 05		98 99 00 01 02 03 04 05	98 99 00 01 02 03 04 05
Engine					
Cooling					
Transmission					
Drive system					
Fuel					
Ignition					
Electrical					
AC					
Suspension					
Brakes					
Exhaust					
Paint/Trim					
Body integrity					
Power equip.					
Body hardware					
USED CAR VERDICTS					

Average ○   New   NEW CAR PREDICTION   Worse than average ⊖   Much worse than avg. ●

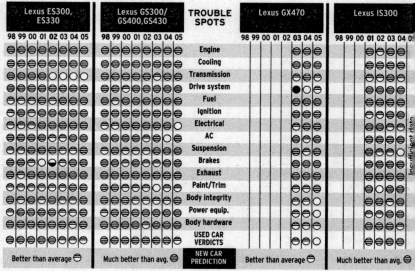

	Lexus ES300, ES330	Lexus GS300/ GS400, GS430	TROUBLE SPOTS	Lexus GX470	Lexus IS300
	98 99 00 01 02 03 04 05	98 99 00 01 02 03 04 05		98 99 00 01 02 03 04 05	98 99 00 01 02 03 04 05
Engine					
Cooling					
Transmission					
Drive system					
Fuel					
Ignition					
Electrical					
AC					
Suspension					
Brakes					
Exhaust					
Paint/Trim					
Body integrity					
Power equip.					
Body hardware					
USED CAR VERDICTS					

Better than average ⊖   Much better than avg. ⊖   NEW CAR PREDICTION   Better than average ⊖   Much better than avg. ⊖

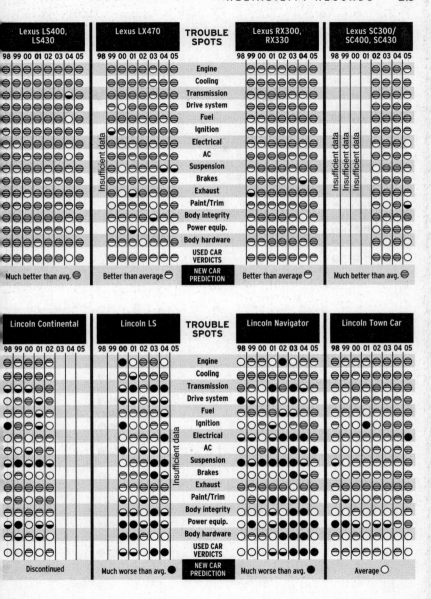

TROUBLE SPOTS

	Lexus LS400, LS430	Lexus LX470	Lexus RX300, RX330	Lexus SC300/ SC400, SC430
	98 99 00 01 02 03 04 05	98 99 00 01 02 03 04 05	98 99 00 01 02 03 04 05	98 99 00 01 02 03 04 05
Engine				
Cooling				
Transmission				
Drive system				
Fuel				
Ignition				
Electrical				
AC				
Suspension				
Brakes				
Exhaust				
Paint/Trim				
Body integrity				
Power equip.				
Body hardware				
USED CAR VERDICTS				
NEW CAR PREDICTION	Much better than avg. ⊖	Better than average ⊖	Better than average ⊖	Much better than avg. ⊖

	Lincoln Continental	Lincoln LS	Lincoln Navigator	Lincoln Town Car
	98 99 00 01 02 03 04 05	98 99 00 01 02 03 04 05	98 99 00 01 02 03 04 05	98 99 00 01 02 03 04 05
Engine				
Cooling				
Transmission				
Drive system				
Fuel				
Ignition				
Electrical				
AC				
Suspension				
Brakes				
Exhaust				
Paint/Trim				
Body integrity				
Power equip.				
Body hardware				
USED CAR VERDICTS				
NEW CAR PREDICTION	Discontinued	Much worse than avg. ●	Much worse than avg. ●	Average ○

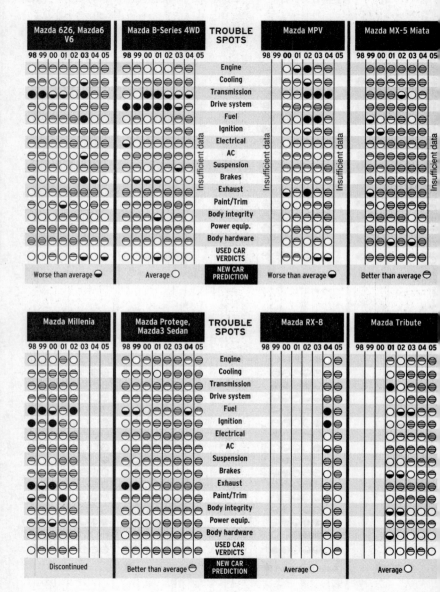

Top row models: Mazda 626, Mazda6 V6 | Mazda B-Series 4WD | TROUBLE SPOTS | Mazda MPV | Mazda MX-5 Miata

Years: 98 99 00 01 02 03 04 05

Trouble Spots:
- Engine
- Cooling
- Transmission
- Drive system
- Fuel
- Ignition
- Electrical
- AC
- Suspension
- Brakes
- Exhaust
- Paint/Trim
- Body integrity
- Power equip.
- Body hardware
- USED CAR VERDICTS

NEW CAR PREDICTION

- Mazda 626, Mazda6 V6: Worse than average ◒
- Mazda B-Series 4WD: Average ○ (Insufficient data)
- Mazda MPV: Worse than average ◒
- Mazda MX-5 Miata: Better than average ◐ (Insufficient data)

Bottom row models: Mazda Millenia | Mazda Protege, Mazda3 Sedan | TROUBLE SPOTS | Mazda RX-8 | Mazda Tribute

Years: 98 99 00 01 02 03 04 05

Trouble Spots:
- Engine
- Cooling
- Transmission
- Drive system
- Fuel
- Ignition
- Electrical
- AC
- Suspension
- Brakes
- Exhaust
- Paint/Trim
- Body integrity
- Power equip.
- Body hardware
- USED CAR VERDICTS

NEW CAR PREDICTION

- Mazda Millenia: Discontinued
- Mazda Protege, Mazda3 Sedan: Better than average ◐
- Mazda RX-8: Average ○
- Mazda Tribute: Average ○

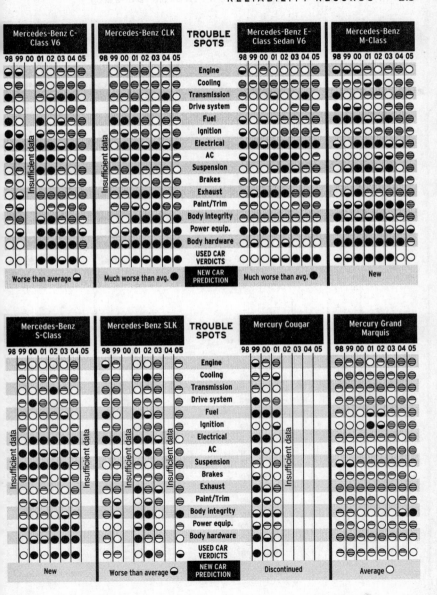

	Mercedes-Benz C-Class V6	Mercedes-Benz CLK	TROUBLE SPOTS	Mercedes-Benz E-Class Sedan V6	Mercedes-Benz M-Class
	98 99 00 01 02 03 04 05	98 99 00 01 02 03 04 05		98 99 00 01 02 03 04 05	98 99 00 01 02 03 04 05
Engine					
Cooling					
Transmission					
Drive system					
Fuel					
Ignition					
Electrical					
AC					
Suspension					
Brakes					
Exhaust					
Paint/Trim					
Body integrity					
Power equip.					
Body hardware					
USED CAR VERDICTS					
	Worse than average ⊖	Much worse than avg. ●	NEW CAR PREDICTION	Much worse than avg. ●	New

	Mercedes-Benz S-Class	Mercedes-Benz SLK	TROUBLE SPOTS	Mercury Cougar	Mercury Grand Marquis
	98 99 00 01 02 03 04 05	98 99 00 01 02 03 04 05		98 99 00 01 02 03 04 05	98 99 00 01 02 03 04 05
Engine					
Cooling					
Transmission					
Drive system					
Fuel					
Ignition					
Electrical					
AC					
Suspension					
Brakes					
Exhaust					
Paint/Trim					
Body integrity					
Power equip.					
Body hardware					
USED CAR VERDICTS					
	New	Worse than average ⊖	NEW CAR PREDICTION	Discontinued	Average ○

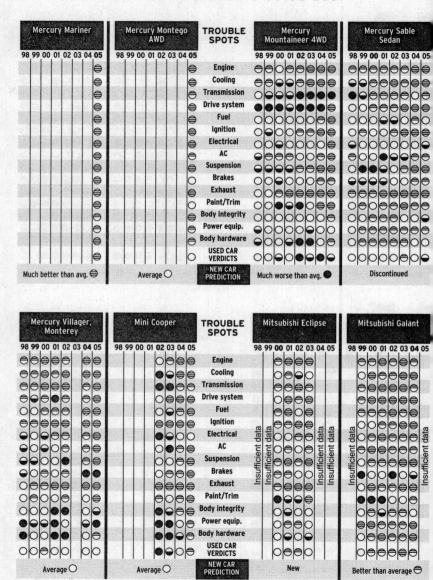

Mercury Mariner — 98 99 00 01 02 03 04 05

Mercury Montego AWD — 98 99 00 01 02 03 04 05

Mercury Mountaineer 4WD — 98 99 00 01 02 03 04 05

Mercury Sable Sedan — 98 99 00 01 02 03 04 05

TROUBLE SPOTS

- Engine
- Cooling
- Transmission
- Drive system
- Fuel
- Ignition
- Electrical
- AC
- Suspension
- Brakes
- Exhaust
- Paint/Trim
- Body integrity
- Power equip.
- Body hardware
- USED CAR VERDICTS

Much better than avg. ⊜   Average ○   **NEW CAR PREDICTION**   Much worse than avg. ●   Discontinued

Mercury Villager, Monterey — 98 99 00 01 02 03 04 05

Mini Cooper — 98 99 00 01 02 03 04 05

Mitsubishi Eclipse — 98 99 00 01 02 03 04 05 (Insufficient data)

Mitsubishi Galant — 98 99 00 01 02 03 04 05 (Insufficient data)

TROUBLE SPOTS

- Engine
- Cooling
- Transmission
- Drive system
- Fuel
- Ignition
- Electrical
- AC
- Suspension
- Brakes
- Exhaust
- Paint/Trim
- Body integrity
- Power equip.
- Body hardware
- USED CAR VERDICTS

Average ○   Average ○   **NEW CAR PREDICTION**   New   Better than average ⊜

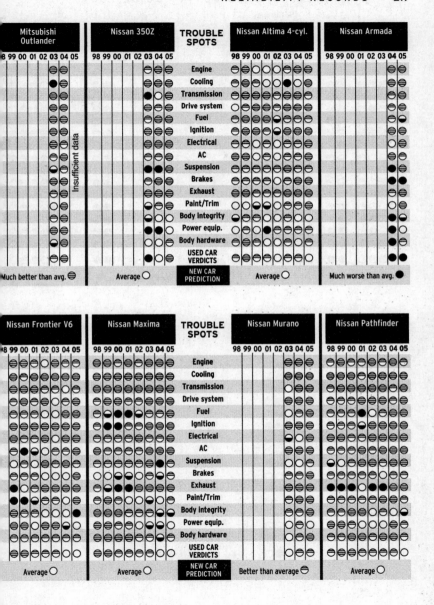

	Mitsubishi Outlander	Nissan 350Z	TROUBLE SPOTS	Nissan Altima 4-cyl.	Nissan Armada

Top panel columns (years): 98 99 00 01 02 03 04 05

TROUBLE SPOTS: Engine, Cooling, Transmission, Drive system, Fuel, Ignition, Electrical, AC, Suspension, Brakes, Exhaust, Paint/Trim, Body integrity, Power equip., Body hardware, USED CAR VERDICTS

Mitsubishi Outlander: Insufficient data

NEW CAR PREDICTION — Nissan 350Z: Average ○
NEW CAR PREDICTION — Nissan Altima 4-cyl.: Average ○

Much better than avg. ⊖   Average ○   Much worse than avg. ●

	Nissan Frontier V6	Nissan Maxima	TROUBLE SPOTS	Nissan Murano	Nissan Pathfinder

Bottom panel columns (years): 98 99 00 01 02 03 04 05

TROUBLE SPOTS: Engine, Cooling, Transmission, Drive system, Fuel, Ignition, Electrical, AC, Suspension, Brakes, Exhaust, Paint/Trim, Body integrity, Power equip., Body hardware, USED CAR VERDICTS

Nissan Frontier V6: Average ○
Nissan Maxima: Average ○
NEW CAR PREDICTION — Nissan Murano: Better than average ⊖
Nissan Pathfinder: Average ○

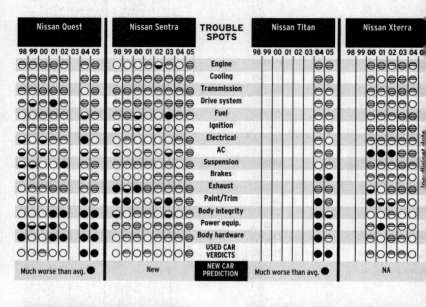

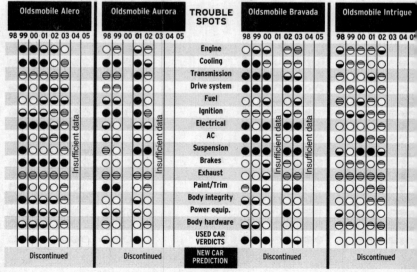

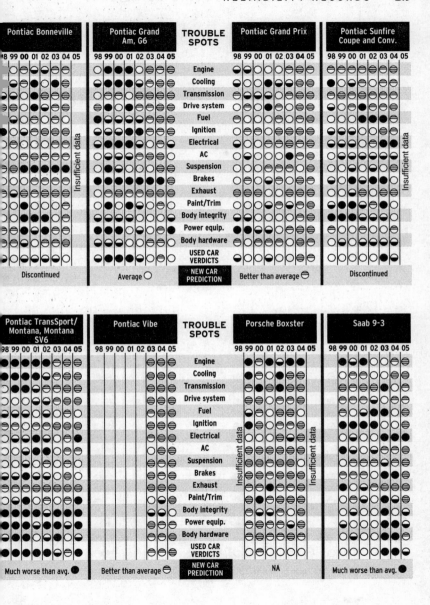

	Pontiac Bonneville 98 99 00 01 02 03 04 05	Pontiac Grand Am, G6 98 99 00 01 02 03 04 05	TROUBLE SPOTS	Pontiac Grand Prix 98 99 00 01 02 03 04 05	Pontiac Sunfire Coupe and Conv. 98 99 00 01 02 03 04 05
Engine					
Cooling					
Transmission					
Drive system					
Fuel					
Ignition					
Electrical					
AC					
Suspension					
Brakes					
Exhaust					
Paint/Trim					
Body integrity					
Power equip.					
Body hardware					
USED CAR VERDICTS					
	Discontinued (Insufficient data)	Average ○	NEW CAR PREDICTION	Better than average ⊖	Discontinued (Insufficient data)

	Pontiac TransSport/ Montana, Montana SV6 98 99 00 01 02 03 04 05	Pontiac Vibe 98 99 00 01 02 03 04 05	TROUBLE SPOTS	Porsche Boxster 98 99 00 01 02 03 04 05	Saab 9-3 98 99 00 01 02 03 04 05
Engine					
Cooling					
Transmission					
Drive system					
Fuel					
Ignition					
Electrical					
AC					
Suspension					
Brakes					
Exhaust					
Paint/Trim					
Body integrity					
Power equip.					
Body hardware					
USED CAR VERDICTS					
	Much worse than avg. ●	Better than average ⊖	NEW CAR PREDICTION	NA (Insufficient data)	Much worse than avg. ●

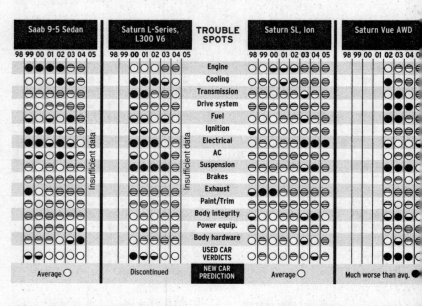

TROUBLE SPOTS

Trouble Spot	Saab 9-5 Sedan 98 99 00 01 02 03 04 05	Saturn L-Series, L300 V6 98 99 00 01 02 03 04 05	Saturn SL, Ion 98 99 00 01 02 03 04 05	Saturn Vue AWD 98 99 00 01 02 03 04 0
Engine				
Cooling				
Transmission				
Drive system				
Fuel				
Ignition				
Electrical				
AC				
Suspension				
Brakes				
Exhaust				
Paint/Trim				
Body integrity				
Power equip.				
Body hardware				
USED CAR VERDICTS				

Saab 9-5 Sedan: Average ○
Saturn L-Series, L300 V6: Discontinued
Saturn SL, Ion: Average ○
Saturn Vue AWD: Much worse than avg. ●

NEW CAR PREDICTION

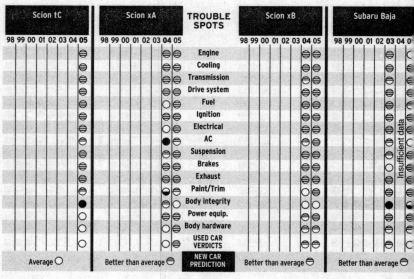

TROUBLE SPOTS

Trouble Spot	Scion tC 98 99 00 01 02 03 04 05	Scion xA 98 99 00 01 02 03 04 05	Scion xB 98 99 00 01 02 03 04 05	Subaru Baja 98 99 00 01 02 03 04 0
Engine				
Cooling				
Transmission				
Drive system				
Fuel				
Ignition				
Electrical				
AC				
Suspension				
Brakes				
Exhaust				
Paint/Trim				
Body integrity				
Power equip.				
Body hardware				
USED CAR VERDICTS				

Scion tC: Average ○
Scion xA: Better than average ⊖
Scion xB: Better than average ⊖
Subaru Baja: Better than average ⊖

NEW CAR PREDICTION

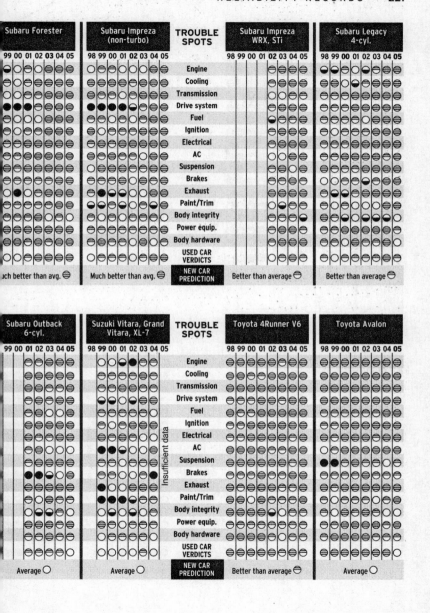

TROUBLE SPOTS

Top row of models:

Subaru Forester	Subaru Impreza (non-turbo)	Subaru Impreza WRX, STi	Subaru Legacy 4-cyl.
99 00 01 02 03 04 05	98 99 00 01 02 03 04 05	98 99 00 01 02 03 04 05	98 99 00 01 02 03 04 05

Trouble Spots: Engine, Cooling, Transmission, Drive system, Fuel, Ignition, Electrical, AC, Suspension, Brakes, Exhaust, Paint/Trim, Body integrity, Power equip., Body hardware, USED CAR VERDICTS

- Subaru Forester — uch better than avg. ⊖
- Subaru Impreza (non-turbo) — Much better than avg. ⊖
- NEW CAR PREDICTION
- Subaru Impreza WRX, STi — Better than average ⊖
- Subaru Legacy 4-cyl. — Better than average ⊖

Bottom row of models:

Subaru Outback 6-cyl.	Suzuki Vitara, Grand Vitara, XL-7	Toyota 4Runner V6	Toyota Avalon
99 00 01 02 03 04 05	98 99 00 01 02 03 04 05	98 99 00 01 02 03 04 05	98 99 00 01 02 03 04 05

Trouble Spots: Engine, Cooling, Transmission, Drive system, Fuel, Ignition, Electrical, AC, Suspension, Brakes, Exhaust, Paint/Trim, Body integrity, Power equip., Body hardware, USED CAR VERDICTS

(Suzuki Vitara column marked "Insufficient data")

- Subaru Outback 6-cyl. — Average ○
- Suzuki Vitara, Grand Vitara, XL-7 — Average ○
- NEW CAR PREDICTION
- Toyota 4Runner V6 — Better than average ⊖
- Toyota Avalon — Average ○

Toyota Camry 4-cyl.

Trouble Spots	98	99	00	01	02	03	04	05
Engine	⊖	⊖	⊖	⊖	⊖	⊖	⊖	⊖
Cooling	⊖	⊖	⊖	⊖	⊖	⊖	⊖	⊖
Transmission	⊖	⊖	⊖	⊖	⊖	⊖	⊖	⊖
Drive system	⊖	⊖	⊖	⊖	⊖	⊖	⊖	⊖
Fuel	⊖	⊖	⊖	⊖	⊖	⊖	⊖	⊖
Ignition	⊖	⊖	⊖	⊖	⊖	⊖	⊖	⊖
Electrical	⊖	⊖	⊖	⊖	⊖	⊖	⊖	⊖
AC	⊖	⊖	⊖	⊖	⊖	⊖	⊖	⊖
Suspension	○	○	⊖	⊖	⊖	⊖	⊖	⊖
Brakes	⊖	⊖	⊖	⊖	⊖	⊖	⊖	⊖
Exhaust	⊖	⊖	⊖	⊖	⊖	⊖	⊖	⊖
Paint/Trim	⊖	⊖	⊖	○	⊖	⊖	⊖	⊖
Body integrity	⊖	⊖	⊖	⊖	⊖	⊖	⊖	⊖
Power equip.	⊖	⊖	⊖	⊖	⊖	⊖	⊖	⊖
Body hardware	⊖	⊖	⊖	⊖	⊖	⊖	⊖	⊖
USED CAR VERDICTS	⊖	⊖	⊖	⊖	⊖	⊖	⊖	⊖

Better than average ⊖

Toyota Camry Solara V6

Trouble Spots	98	99	00	01	02	03	04	05
Engine			⊖	⊖	⊖	⊖	⊖	⊖
Cooling			⊖	⊖	⊖	⊖	⊖	⊖
Transmission			⊖	⊖	⊖	⊖	⊖	⊖
Drive system			⊖	⊖	⊖	⊖	⊖	⊖
Fuel			⊖	○	○	⊖	⊖	⊖
Ignition			⊖	⊖	⊖	⊖	⊖	⊖
Electrical			⊖	⊖	⊖	⊖	⊖	⊖
AC			⊖	⊖	⊖	⊖	⊖	⊖
Suspension			○	⊖	⊖	⊖	●	⊖
Brakes			⊖	⊖	⊖	⊖	⊖	⊖
Exhaust			⊖	⊖	⊖	⊖	⊖	⊖
Paint/Trim			⊖	⊖	⊖	⊖	⊖	⊖
Body integrity			⊖	⊖	○	⊖	●	○
Power equip.			⊖	⊖	⊖	⊖	⊖	⊖
Body hardware			⊖	⊖	⊖	⊖	○	○
USED CAR VERDICTS			⊖	⊖	⊖	⊖	○	○

Better than average ⊖

Toyota Camry V6

Trouble Spots	98	99	00	01	02	03	04	05
Engine	⊖	⊖	⊖	⊖	⊖	⊖	⊖	⊖
Cooling	⊖	⊖	⊖	⊖	⊖	⊖	⊖	⊖
Transmission	⊖	⊖	⊖	⊖	⊖	⊖	⊖	⊖
Drive system	⊖	⊖	⊖	⊖	⊖	⊖	⊖	⊖
Fuel	○	○	⊖	○	⊖	⊖	⊖	⊖
Ignition	⊖	⊖	⊖	⊖	⊖	⊖	⊖	⊖
Electrical	⊖	⊖	⊖	⊖	⊖	⊖	⊖	⊖
AC	⊖	⊖	⊖	⊖	⊖	⊖	⊖	⊖
Suspension	○	⊖	⊖	⊖	○	⊖	⊖	⊖
Brakes	⊖	⊖	⊖	⊖	○	⊖	⊖	⊖
Exhaust	⊖	⊖	⊖	⊖	⊖	⊖	⊖	⊖
Paint/Trim	⊖	⊖	⊖	⊖	○	⊖	⊖	⊖
Body integrity	⊖	⊖	⊖	⊖	⊖	⊖	⊖	○
Power equip.	⊖	⊖	⊖	⊖	⊖	⊖	⊖	⊖
Body hardware	⊖	⊖	⊖	⊖	⊖	⊖	⊖	⊖
USED CAR VERDICTS	⊖	⊖	⊖	⊖	⊖	⊖	⊖	⊖

Better than average ⊖

Toyota Corolla

Trouble Spots	98	99	00	01	02	03	04
Engine	⊖	⊖	○	⊖	⊖	⊖	⊖
Cooling	⊖	⊖	⊖	⊖	⊖	⊖	⊖
Transmission	⊖	⊖	⊖	⊖	⊖	⊖	⊖
Drive system	⊖	⊖	⊖	⊖	⊖	⊖	⊖
Fuel	⊖	⊖	⊖	⊖	⊖	⊖	⊖
Ignition	⊖	⊖	⊖	⊖	⊖	⊖	⊖
Electrical	⊖	⊖	⊖	⊖	⊖	⊖	⊖
AC	⊖	⊖	⊖	⊖	⊖	⊖	⊖
Suspension	⊖	⊖	⊖	⊖	⊖	⊖	⊖
Brakes	⊖	⊖	⊖	⊖	⊖	⊖	⊖
Exhaust	⊖	⊖	⊖	⊖	⊖	⊖	⊖
Paint/Trim	○	⊖	⊖	⊖	⊖	⊖	⊖
Body integrity	⊖	⊖	⊖	⊖	⊖	⊖	○
Power equip.	⊖	⊖	⊖	⊖	⊖	⊖	⊖
Body hardware	○	⊖	⊖	⊖	⊖	⊖	⊖
USED CAR VERDICTS	⊖	⊖	⊖	⊖	⊖	⊖	⊖

Much better than avg. ⊖

Toyota Echo

Trouble Spots	98	99	00	01	02	03	04	05
Engine			⊖	⊖	⊖	⊖	⊖	
Cooling			⊖	⊖	⊖	⊖	⊖	
Transmission			⊖	⊖	⊖	⊖	⊖	
Drive system			⊖	⊖	⊖	⊖	⊖	
Fuel			⊖	⊖	⊖	⊖	⊖	
Ignition			⊖	⊖	⊖	⊖	⊖	
Electrical			⊖	⊖	⊖	⊖	⊖	
AC			⊖	⊖	⊖	⊖	⊖	
Suspension			⊖	⊖	⊖	⊖	⊖	
Brakes			⊖	⊖	⊖	⊖	⊖	
Exhaust			⊖	⊖	⊖	⊖	⊖	
Paint/Trim			⊖	⊖	⊖	⊖	○	
Body integrity			⊖	⊖	⊖	⊖	○	
Power equip.			⊖	⊖	⊖	⊖	⊖	
Body hardware			⊖	⊖	⊖	⊖	○	
USED CAR VERDICTS			⊖	⊖	⊖	⊖	⊖	

Discontinued

Toyota Highlander V6

Trouble Spots	98	99	00	01	02	03	04	05
Engine				⊖	⊖	⊖	⊖	⊖
Cooling				⊖	⊖	⊖	⊖	⊖
Transmission				⊖	⊖	⊖	⊖	⊖
Drive system				⊖	⊖	⊖	⊖	⊖
Fuel				⊖	⊖	⊖	⊖	⊖
Ignition				⊖	⊖	⊖	⊖	⊖
Electrical				⊖	⊖	⊖	⊖	⊖
AC				⊖	⊖	⊖	⊖	⊖
Suspension				⊖	⊖	⊖	⊖	⊖
Brakes				○	⊖	⊖	⊖	⊖
Exhaust				⊖	⊖	⊖	⊖	⊖
Paint/Trim				⊖	⊖	⊖	⊖	⊖
Body integrity				⊖	⊖	⊖	⊖	⊖
Power equip.				⊖	⊖	⊖	⊖	⊖
Body hardware				⊖	⊖	⊖	⊖	⊖
USED CAR VERDICTS				⊖	⊖	⊖	⊖	

Much better than avg. ⊖

Toyota Land Cruiser

Trouble Spots	98	99	00	01	02	03	04	05
Engine	⊖	⊖	⊖	⊖	⊖	⊖	⊖	
Cooling	⊖	⊖	⊖	⊖	⊖	⊖	⊖	
Transmission	⊖	⊖	⊖	⊖	⊖	⊖	⊖	
Drive system	⊖	⊖	⊖	⊖	⊖	⊖	⊖	
Fuel	⊖	⊖	⊖	⊖	⊖	⊖	⊖	
Ignition	⊖	⊖	⊖	⊖	⊖	⊖	⊖	
Electrical	⊖	⊖	⊖	⊖	⊖	⊖	⊖	
AC	⊖	⊖	⊖	⊖	⊖	⊖	⊖	
Suspension	⊖	⊖	⊖	⊖	⊖	⊖	⊖	
Brakes	⊖	⊖	○	⊖	⊖	⊖	⊖	
Exhaust	⊖	⊖	●	⊖	⊖	⊖	⊖	
Paint/Trim	○	⊖	⊖	⊖	⊖	⊖	⊖	
Body integrity	○	⊖	⊖	○	⊖	⊖	⊖	
Power equip.	○	⊖	⊖	○	⊖	⊖	●	
Body hardware	○	⊖	⊖	⊖	⊖	⊖	⊖	
USED CAR VERDICTS	⊖	⊖	⊖	⊖	⊖	⊖	⊖	

Insufficient data

Much better than avg. ⊖

Toyota Matrix

Trouble Spots	98	99	00	01	02	03	04
Engine						⊖	⊖
Cooling						⊖	⊖
Transmission						⊖	⊖
Drive system						⊖	⊖
Fuel						⊖	⊖
Ignition						⊖	⊖
Electrical						⊖	⊖
AC						⊖	⊖
Suspension						⊖	⊖
Brakes						⊖	⊖
Exhaust						⊖	⊖
Paint/Trim						○	○
Body integrity						○	○
Power equip.						⊖	⊖
Body hardware						⊖	○
USED CAR VERDICTS						⊖	⊖

Much better than avg. ⊖

TROUBLE SPOTS

NEW CAR PREDICTION

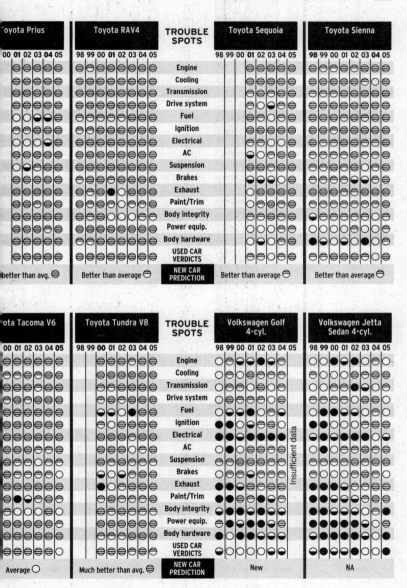

	Toyota Prius	Toyota RAV4	TROUBLE SPOTS	Toyota Sequoia	Toyota Sienna
	00 01 02 03 04 05	98 99 00 01 02 03 04 05	Engine	98 99 00 01 02 03 04 05	98 99 00 01 02 03 04 05
			Cooling		
			Transmission		
			Drive system		
			Fuel		
			Ignition		
			Electrical		
			AC		
			Suspension		
			Brakes		
			Exhaust		
			Paint/Trim		
			Body integrity		
			Power equip.		
			Body hardware		
			USED CAR VERDICTS		
	better than avg.	Better than average	NEW CAR PREDICTION	Better than average	Better than average

	Toyota Tacoma V6	Toyota Tundra V8	TROUBLE SPOTS	Volkswagen Golf 4-cyl.	Volkswagen Jetta Sedan 4-cyl.
	00 01 02 03 04 05	98 99 00 01 02 03 04 05	Engine	98 99 00 01 02 03 04 05	98 99 00 01 02 03 04 05
			Cooling		
			Transmission		
			Drive system		
			Fuel		
			Ignition		
			Electrical		
			AC		
			Suspension	Insufficient data	
			Brakes		
			Exhaust		
			Paint/Trim		
			Body integrity		
			Power equip.		
			Body hardware		
			USED CAR VERDICTS		
	Average	Much better than avg.	NEW CAR PREDICTION	New	NA

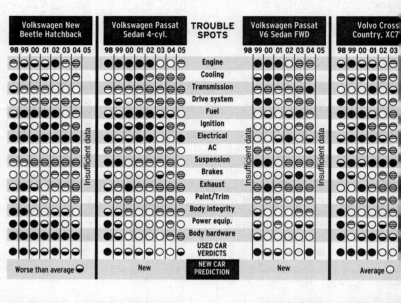

Volkswagen New Beetle Hatchback	Volkswagen Passat Sedan 4-cyl.	TROUBLE SPOTS	Volkswagen Passat V6 Sedan FWD	Volvo Cross Country, XC7
98 99 00 01 02 03 04 05	98 99 00 01 02 03 04 05		98 99 00 01 02 03 04 05	98 99 00 01 02 03
		Engine		
		Cooling		
		Transmission		
		Drive system		
		Fuel		
		Ignition		
		Electrical		
		AC		
		Suspension		
		Brakes		
		Exhaust		
		Paint/Trim		
		Body integrity		
		Power equip.		
		Body hardware		
		USED CAR VERDICTS		
Worse than average ⊖	New	NEW CAR PREDICTION	New	Average ○

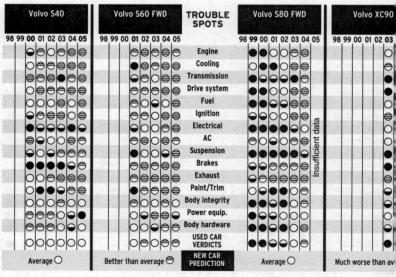

Volvo S40	Volvo S60 FWD	TROUBLE SPOTS	Volvo S80 FWD	Volvo XC90
98 99 00 01 02 03 04 05	98 99 00 01 02 03 04 05		98 99 00 01 02 03 04 05	98 99 00 01 02 03
		Engine		
		Cooling		
		Transmission		
		Drive system		
		Fuel		
		Ignition		
		Electrical		
		AC		
		Suspension		
		Brakes		
		Exhaust		
		Paint/Trim		
		Body integrity		
		Power equip.		
		Body hardware		
		USED CAR VERDICTS		
Average ○	Better than average ⊖	NEW CAR PREDICTION	Average ○	Much worse than av

Ratings and Reliability

CONTENTS

QUICK GUIDE

PRODUCT RATINGS AND BRAND RELIABILITY

The product rating and brand reliability information that follows is designed to help you zero in on the model you want to buy. Start by reading the general buying advice for the product you're interested in. The page numbers for these reports are noted on each Ratings page. Then turn to the Ratings chart to get the big picture in terms of performance.

The Quick Picks highlight the best models for most people plus models that may be especially suited to your family's needs. The Recommendations provide additional detail on features and performance for individual models. The key numbers helps you move between the charts and the other information. Products with equal scores are listed alphabetically.

CONSUMER REPORTS checked to make sure most of the products rated in this Buying Guide were still available when the book was published. However, depending on how long after publication you use this book, you may find a Rating for a product that is no longer available. Or, you may not find a Rating for a model that is available because it hadn't been tested as of publication. Models similar to the tested models, when they exist, are also listed. Such models differ in features, not essential performance, according to the manufacturers.

Besides checking for similar models, you can also refer to the brand repair history charts for some products. Most products today are pretty reliable, but some brands have been more reliable than others.

Every year we survey readers on repairs and other problems they encounter with household products. From their responses, we derive the percentage of a brand's products that have been repaired or had a serious problem. The reliability graphs that accompany the Ratings give brand repair rates for 13 product categories. Our findings have been consistent over the 30-plus years we've surveyed brand reliability, though they are not infallible predictors.

A brand's repair history includes data on many models, some of which may have been more or less reliable than others. And surveys of a brand's past models can't anticipate design or manufacturing changes in its new models. Still, you can improve your chances of getting a trouble-free product by getting a brand that has been reliable in the past.

Product categories include appliances such as washers and ranges, electronic products such as computers and digital cameras, and lawn mowers and tractors. Note that repair histories for different products are not directly comparable.

AIR CONDITIONERS

All the air conditioners in our tests should keep you cool. Top-scoring models perform the most efficiently and quietly.

The Ratings rank models by overall performance within size groups. Once you determine the right size, consider that the more off-center your window, the more it matters that the unit blow air where you need it. Buy the highest-rated model within your budget that meets this need and that has other attributes you may favor, such as a top score for noise.

Safety plugs are required by Underwriters Laboratories on units made after July 2004. In the Ratings, the following models have these plugs: GE AGM06LH, Frigidaire FAA067P7 (Lowe's), Goldstar WG6005R, Frigidaire FAA087P7 (Lowe's), GE AGM08LH, Goldstar WG8005R, LG LWHD8000R, Friedrich SS10L10-A, Frigidaire FAC107P1 (Lowe's), GE AGW10AH, GE AGM12AH, Fedders Y Series A6Y12F2A, LG LWHD1000R. The others, carryover models from recent tests, do not, though all similar models do.

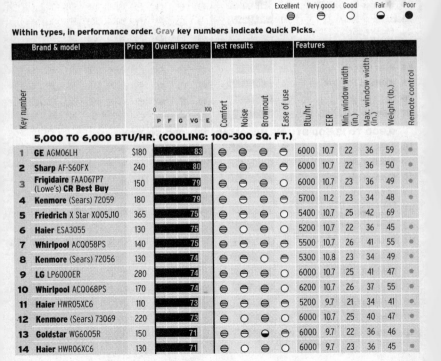

Excellent Very good Good Fair Poor

Within types, in performance order. Gray key numbers indicate Quick Picks.

Key number	Brand & model	Price	Overall score	Comfort	Noise	Brownout	Ease of use	Btu/hr.	EER	Min. window width (in.)	Max. window width (in.)	Weight (lb.)	Remote control
	5,000 TO 6,000 BTU/HR. (COOLING: 100-300 SQ. FT.)												
1	**GE** AGM06LH	$180	83	⊖	⊖	⊖	⊖	6000	10.7	22	36	59	●
2	**Sharp** AF-S60FX	240	80	⊖	⊖	⊖	⊖	6000	10.7	22	36	50	●
3	**Frigidaire** FAA067P7 (Lowe's) **CR Best Buy**	150	79	⊖	⊖	⊖	○	6000	10.7	23	36	49	●
4	**Kenmore** (Sears) 72059	180	79	⊖	⊖	⊖	○	5700	11.2	23	34	48	●
5	**Friedrich** X Star X005J10	365	75	⊖	⊖	⊖	○	5400	10.7	25	42	69	●
6	**Haier** ESA3055	130	75	⊖	○	⊖	⊖	5200	10.7	22	36	45	●
7	**Whirlpool** ACQ058PS	140	75	⊖	⊖	⊖	⊖	5500	10.7	26	41	55	●
8	**Kenmore** (Sears) 72056	130	74	⊖	⊖	○	⊖	5300	10.8	23	34	49	●
9	**LG** LP6000ER	280	74	⊖	⊖	⊖	○	6000	10.7	25	41	47	●
10	**Whirlpool** ACQ068PS	170	74	⊖	⊖	⊖	○	6200	10.7	26	37	55	●
11	**Haier** HWR05XC6	110	73	⊖	⊖	⊖	⊖	5200	9.7	21	34	41	●
12	**Kenmore** (Sears) 73069	220	73	⊖	○	⊖	○	6000	10.7	25	40	47	●
13	**Goldstar** WG6005R	150	71	⊖	⊖	◑	⊖	6000	9.7	22	36	46	●
14	**Haier** HWR06XC6	130	71	⊖	○	⊖	○	6000	9.7	23	36	45	●

Within types, in performance order. Gray key numbers indicate Quick Picks.

Key number	Brand & model	Price	Overall score (0–100 P F G VG E)	Comfort	Noise	Brownout	Ease of use	Btu/hr.	EER	Min. window width (in.)	Max. window width (in.)	Weight (lb.)	Remote control
5,000 TO 6,000 BTU/HR. (COOLING: 100-300 SQ. FT.)														
15	**Fedders** X Series A6X06F2	$180	69	⊖	○	⊖	⊖	6000 *continued* 9.7		24	38	48	●
16	**Fedders** X Series A6X05F2B	195	66	⊖	◐	⊖	⊖	5200	9.7	24	37	42	●
7,000 TO 8,200 BTU/HR. (COOLING: 250-550 SQ. FT.)														
17	**Frigidaire** FAA087P7 (Lowe's) **CR Best Buy**	180	79	⊖	⊖	⊖	○	8000	10.8	23	36	53	●
18	**GE** AGM08LH	240	79	⊖	⊖	⊖	⊖	8000	10.8	22	36	64	●
19	**LG** LW8000ER	260	78	⊖	⊖	⊖	⊖	8200	10.9	23	38	65	●
20	**Kenmore** (Sears) 76081	220	76	⊖	◐	⊖	⊖	8000	10.8	24	39	65	●
21	**Sharp** AF-S80FX	310	73	⊖	○	⊖	⊖	8000	10.8	22	36	54	●
22	**Fedders** Q Series A7008F2A	230	72	⊖	○	⊖	⊖	8000	10.8	24	36	66	●
23	**Goldstar** WG8005R	170	72	⊖	⊖	◐	⊖	8000	9.8	22	36	60	●
24	**Haier** ESA3085	220	70	⊖	○	⊖	○	8000	10.8	23	35	54	●
25	**Whirlpool** ACQ088MS	220	70	⊖	○	⊖	⊖	8000	10.8	26	39	62	●
26	**LG** LWHD8000R	170	69	⊖	⊖	◐	⊖	8000	9.8	22	36	58	●
27	**Friedrich** SS08J10R	590	66	⊖	◐	⊖	○	8200	11	26	43	100	●
9,800 TO 12,500 BTU/HR. (COOLING: 350-950 SQ. FT.)														
28	**Friedrich** SS10L10-A	700	84	⊖	⊖	⊖	○	10400	12.0	28	42	109	●
29	**Kenmore** (Sears) 74107	300	76	⊖	⊖	⊖	⊖	10000	10.8	27	39	80	●
30	**Kenmore** (Sears) 75121	330	76	⊖	⊖	⊖	⊖	12000	10.8	27	39	83	●
31	**LG** LW1000ER	300	76	⊖	⊖	⊖	○	10000	11	28	39	79	●
32	**Frigidaire** FAC107P1 (Lowe's) **CR Best Buy**	220	74	⊖	○	⊖	○	10000	10.8	23	36	78	●
33	**Kenmore** (Sears) 76129	370	73	⊖	○	⊖	⊖	12300	10.8	28	41	86	●
34	**LG** LB1200ER	330	73	⊖	⊖	⊖	◐	12300	10.8	27	42	83	●
35	**GE** AGW10AH	270	72	⊖	⊖	◐	⊖	10000	9.8	25	36	71	●
36	**Whirlpool** ACC108PS	290	72	⊖	⊖	⊖	⊖	10000	10.8	27	38	97	●
37	**GE** AGM12AH	350	71	⊖	○	○	⊖	12000	10.8	27	39	82	●
38	**Frigidaire** FAC127P1	250	70	⊖	○	⊖	⊖	12000	10.8	23	39	80	●
39	**Sharp** AF-S100FX	310	70	⊖	○	⊖	⊖	10000	10.8	23	38	79	●
40	**Sharp** AF-S125FX	350	69	⊖	○	○	⊖	12000	10.8	23	38	80	●

				Excellent	Very good	Good	Fair	Poor
				⊖	⊖	○	⊖	●

Key number	Brand & model	Price	Overall score	Test results				Features					
			0 100 P F G VG E	Comfort	Noise	Brownout	Ease of use	Btu/hr.	EER	Min. window width (in.)	Max. window width (in.)	Weight (lb.)	Remote control

9,800 TO 12,500 BTU/HR. (COOLING: 350-950 SQ. FT.) *continued*

Key number	Brand & model	Price	Overall score	Comfort	Noise	Brownout	Ease of use	Btu/hr.	EER	Min. window width (in.)	Max. window width (in.)	Weight (lb.)	Remote control
41	Goldstar WG1005R	$230	68	⊖	⊖	⊖	⊖	10000	9.8	22	36	70	●
42	Haier HWR10XC6	190	67	⊖	○	⊖	⊖	10000	9.8	23	33	64	●
43	LG LWHD1000R	230	65	⊖	⊖	⊖	⊖	10000	9.8	22	36	68	●
44	Fedders Y Series A6Y12F2A	345	64	⊖	⊖	○	⊖	12000	9.8	27	43	88	●
45	Fedders Q Series A6Q10F2A	300	59	⊖	●	⊖	⊖	10000	9.8	24	38	71	●

See report, page 83. Based on tests posted to Consumer Reports.org in June 2006, with updated prices and availability.

Guide to the Ratings

Overall score is based mainly on comfort, noise, and energy efficiency. **Comfort** is how well temperature and humidity are controlled at the low-cool setting. The best performers held temperatures to within 1½ degrees of the setpoint. **Noise** is a judgment of indoor noise at the low-cool setting and combines an objective measurement of noise level using a decibel meter with a subjective assessment of noise quality (how annoying or grating the particular sounds were). **Brownout** gauges the unit's ability to run and restart during extreme heat and low voltage. **Ease of use** reflects control-panel layout, including the clarity of its markings, as well as how easy and intuitive the controls were to operate. **Price** is approximate retail.

Quick Picks

Efficient, quiet, and CR Best Buys:
  3 Frigidaire FAA067P7 (Lowe's), $150
  17 Frigidaire FAA087P7 (Lowe's), $180
  32 Frigidaire FAC107P1 (Lowe's), $220
All do a better job directing air to the left.

If quiet is paramount:
  1 GE AGM06LH, $180

  18 GE AGM08LH, $240
  29 Kenmore (Sears) 74107, $300
Both GEs are difficult to install. The Kenmore (Sears) 74107 is somewhat louder than the Friedrich SS10L10-A but far less expensive. It's a good choice if you want air blown to the right, as is the LG LW8000ER.

Recommendations

5,000 TO 6,000 BTU/HR. (COOLING: 100-300 SQ. FT.)

1 **GE** AGM06LH Excellent cooling and extremely quiet. Easy to use, but you'll need to slide the machine out of its case to attach window baffles before the first installation. 6,000 Btu/hr., 10.7 EER. Discontinued, but similar model AGM06LJ may still be available.

2 **SHARP** AF-S60FX Excellent cooling, but lacks energy-saving mode. Not as quiet as top-rated model. 6,000 Btu/hr., 10.7 EER.

3 **FRIGIDAIRE** FAA067P7 (Lowe's) **A CR Best Buy** Very good; quiet, efficient. Continuously variable fan speeds are a plus. 6,000 Btu/hr., 10.7 EER. Similar model: FAA065P7A.

4 **KENMORE (SEARS)** 72059 Very good, and among the most energy-efficient models tested. 5,700 Btu/hr., 11.2 EER. Discontinued, but similar model 75052 may still be available.

5 **FRIEDRICH** X Star XQ05J10 Very good overall, but pricey. 5,400 Btu/hr., 10.7 EER. Discontinued, but similar model X Star XQ05L10 may still be available.

6 **HAIER** ESA3055 Very good overall, and a solid value. But the unit does not offer energy-saving mode or up/down louver control. Blows to the right. 5,200 Btu/hr., 10.7 EER.

7 **WHIRLPOOL** ACQ058PS Very good unit equipped with a dirty-filter indicator and autofan. 5,500 Btu/hr., 10.7 EER.

8 **KENMORE (SEARS)** 72056 Very good performer at a competitive price. But only has two fan speeds on cool. 5,300 Btu/hr., 10.8 EER. Discontinued, but similar model 75051 may still be available.

9 **LG** LP6000ER Low-profile design for this very good performer. Has handles to ease carrying. 6,000 Btu/hr., 10.7 EER. Discontinued, but similar model BP6000ER may still be available.

10 **WHIRLPOOL** ACQ068PS Very good performer that comes with a dirty-filter indicator and autofan. But it does not blow air to the left or right very well. 6,200 Btu/hr., 10.7 EER.

11 **HAIER** HWR05XC Very good performer at an attractive price. The unit has only two fan speeds and does not offer energy-saving mode or up/down louver control. 5,200 Btu/hr., 9.7 EER.

12 **KENMORE (SEARS)** 73069 Low-profile design for this very good performer. Has handles to ease carrying. 6,000 Btu/hr., 10.7 EER. Discontinued, but similar model 75062 may still be available.

13 **GOLDSTAR** WG6005R Very good overall, but did not compensate for brownout as well as most. 6,000 Btu/hr., 9.7 EER.

Recommendations

14 HAIER HWR06XC6 Very good performer at an attractive price. But it has only two fan speeds and lacks energy-saving mode. 6,000 Btu/hr., 9.7 EER.

15 FEDDERS X Series A6X06F2 Very good. But has only two fan speeds on cool. 6,000 Btu/hr., 9.7 EER. Discontinued, but similar models Maytag M6X06F2D, X Series A6X06F2E may still be available.

16 FEDDERS X Series A6X05F2B Well-priced air conditioner at a competitive price, but noisier than most. Has only two fan speeds on cool. 5,200 Btu/hr., 9.7 EER. Discontinued, but similar models Maytag M6X05F2D, X Series A6X05F2G may still be available.

7,000 TO 8,200 BTU/HR. (COOLING: 250-550 SQ. FT.)

17 FRIGIDAIRE FAA087P7 (Lowe's) **A CR Best Buy** Very good cooling overall. Continuously variable fan speeds a plus. 8,000 Btu/hr., 10.8 EER. Similar models: FAA085P7A, FAA086P7A.

18 GE AGM08LH Very good performance, and very quiet. Easy to use, but you'll need to slide the machine out of its case to attach window baffles before the first installation. 8,000 Btu/hr., 10.8 EER. Discontinued, but similar model AGM08LJ may still be available.

19 LG LW8000ER Very good overall, but harder to install than most. 8,200 Btu/hr., 10.9 EER. Similar model: LB8000ER.

20 KENMORE (Sears) 76081 Very good unit with a slide-out chassis and an exterior support bracket. 8,000 Btu/hr. 10.8 EER.

21 SHARP AF-S80FX Excellent cooling, but lacks energy-saving mode. Louder than some other lower-priced models. 8,000 Btu/hr., 10.8 EER. Similar model: AF-S85FX.

22 FEDDERS Q Series A7Q08F2A Very good performer, but harder to install than most. 8,000 Btu/hr., 10.8 EER. Discontinued, but similar models Maytag M7Q08F2B, Q Series A7Q08F2B may still be available.

23 GOLDSTAR WG8005R Very good air conditioner, especially if you need more air blown to the right. But did not compensate for brownout as well as most. 8,000 Btu/hr., 9.8 EER.

24 HAIER ESA3085 Very good, but there's no energy-saving mode. The unit blows to the right. 8,000 Btu/hr. 10.8 EER.

25 WHIRLPOOL ACQ088MS Very good, efficient unit that features a dirty-filter indicator and autofan. But it delivers only fair comfort on energy-saving mode, and the grill and associated clips appear fragile. 8,000 Btu/hr., 10.8 EER.

26 LG LWHD8000R Very good performance, but did not compensate for brownout as well as most. 8,000 Btu/hr., 9.8 EER.

27 FRIEDRICH SS08J10R Very good and among the most efficient. But it's pricey. It's also noisier and harder to install than most. It weighs 100 lbs., much heavier than most. 8,200 Btu/hr., 11.0 EER. Discontinued, but similar model SS08L1 may still be available.

9,800 TO 12,500 BTU/HR. (COOLING: 350-950 SQ. FT.)

28 FRIEDRICH SS10L10-A Excellent performer and extremely quiet, but pricey. Among the most energy-efficient air conditioners tested. But it weighs 109 lbs., much heavier than most. 10,400 Btu/hr., 12.0 EER.

29 KENMORE (SEARS) 74107 Very good performer, especially if you need more air blown to the right. It weighs 80 lbs., heavier than most. 10,000 Btu/hr., 10.8 EER. Discontinued, but similar model 75101 may still be available.

30 KENMORE (SEARS) 7512 Very good performer with a slide-out chassis and an exterior support bracket. 12,000 Btu/hr., 10.8 EER.

31 LG LW1000ER Very good, and among the most energy-efficient. 10,000 Btu/hr., 11.0 EER.

32 FRIGIDAIRE FAC107P1 (Lowe's) **A CR Best Buy** Very good performance at an attractive price. Continuously variable fan speeds are a plus. 10,000 Btu/hr., 10.8 EER. Similar models: FAC105P1, FAC106P1.

33 KENMORE (SEARS) 76129 A very good machine. It weighs 86 lbs., heavier than most. 12,300 Btu/hr., 10.8 EER. Discontinued, but similar model 75132 may still be available.

34 LG LB1200ER Very good, efficient unit with a slide-out chassis and an exterior support bracket. Blows to the right. 12,000 Btu/hr., 10.8 EER.

35 GE AGW10AH Very good performance. Easy to use, but you'll need to slide the machine out of its case to attach window baffles before the first installation. Did not compensate for brownout as well as most. 10,000 Btu/hr., 9.8 EER. Discontinued, but similar model AGH10AJ may still be available.

36 WHIRLPOOL ACC108PS Very good machine equipped with a dirty-filter indicator and autofan. It blows to the right. It provides only fair comfort on energy-saving mode, and the grill and associated clips appear fragile. 10,000 Btu/hr., 10.8 EER.

37 GE AGM12AH Very good overall, but you'll need to slide the machine out of its case to attach window baffles before the first installation. It weighs 82 lbs., heavier than most. 12,000 Btu/hr., 10.8 EER. Discontinued, but similar model AGM12AJ may still be available.

38 FRIGIDAIRE FAC127P1 Very good machine with continuously variable fan speeds—a plus. 12,000 Btu/hr., 10.8 EER. Similar models: FAC125P1, FAC126P1.

39 SHARP AF-S100FX Very good basic machine. No energy-saving mode. 10,000 Btu/hr., 10.8 EER.

40 SHARP AF-S125FX Very good basic unit—no bells or whistles. 12,000 Btu/hr., 10.8 EER. Similar model: AF-S120FX.

41 GOLDSTAR WG1005R Well-priced, very good performer overall. But did not compensate for brownout as well as most. 10,000 Btu/hr., 9.8 EER.

42 HAIER HWR10XC6 Very good unit and well-priced. Good if you need more air blown to the right. 10,000 Btu/hr., 9.8 EER.

43 LG LWHD1000R Well-priced, very good performer overall. But did not compensate for brownout as well as most. 10,000 Btu/hr., 9.8 EER.

44 FEDDERS Y Series A6Y12F2A Very good unit, especially if you need more air blown to the right. But noisier than most. You must manually turn machine back on when power has been interrupted. It weighs 88 lbs., heavier than most. 12,000 Btu/hr., 9.8 EER. Discontinued, but similar models Maytag M6Y12F2B, Y Series A6Y12F2B may still be available.

45 FEDDERS Q Series A6Q10F2A Good overall and well-priced, but harder to use than most, and very noisy. 10,000 Btu/hr., 9.8 EER. Discontinued, but similar models Maytag M6Q10F2B, Q Series A6Q10F2B may still be available.

CAMCORDERS

You can expect a digital camcorder to deliver very good video, as our Ratings scores demonstrate. Many of the digital camcorders that record directly onto small DVD discs were ranked at or near the top. However, that doesn't automatically make them the best choice. As the Ratings show, most DVD models were not markedly better than many camcorders that use MiniDV tape. The MiniDV camcorders win on price, making them the type that most people should consider first. The DVD models are for people who want ease of playback above all else.

Most camcorders weigh about a pound, give or take a few ounces. As camcorders get smaller and lighter, image-stabilization features become more important. A lightweight camcorder is harder to hold steady than a heavy one. Fortunately, most did an excellent job of minimizing the shakes.

Analog camcorders are a dying breed. Only one model, the Sony CCD-TRV138, at $235, remains in the Ratings, and it's not in the same league as the digitals.

Excellent	Very good	Good	Fair	Poor
⊖	⊖	○	⊖	●

Within types, in performance order. Gray key numbers indicate Quick Picks.

Key number	Brand & model	Price	Format	Overall score	Picture quality	Ease of use	Image stabilizer	Audio quality	Weight (lb.)	Digital-still capable	Optical zoom	LCD size (in.)	Battery life (min.)
					Test results				Features				
DIGITAL MODELS													
1	**Canon** DC40	$770	DVD-R/RW	69	⊖	○	⊖	⊖	1.2	●	10x	2.7	75
2	**Hitachi** Ultravision DZGX20A	570	DVD-RAM, DVD-R	68	⊖	○	⊖	⊖	1.3	●	10x	2.5	125
3	**Panasonic** VDR-M75	630	DVD-RAM, DVD-R	68	⊖	○	⊖	⊖	1.1	●	10x	2.5	125
4	**Canon** ZR200	315	MiniDV	65	⊖	⊖	⊖	⊖	1.1	●	20x	2.4	85
5	**Sony** DCR-DVD92	500	DVD-R, DVD-RW, DVD+RW	65	⊖	○	⊖	○	1.1		20x	2.5	80
6	**Sony** DCR-HC90	630	MiniDV	65	⊖	○	⊖	⊖	1.1	●	10x	2.7	80
7	**Canon** Optura 50	445	MiniDV	63	⊖	○	⊖	⊖	1.3	●	10x	2.5	75
8	**Hitachi** UltraVision DZGX3200A	585	DVD-RAM, DVD-R, DVD-RW, DVD+RW	63	⊖	⊖	⊖	⊖	1.2	●	10x	2.7	125
9	**Sony** DCR-HC96	640	MiniDV	63	⊖	○	⊖	⊖	1.2	●	10x	2.7	80
10	**Sony** DCR-PC55	500	MiniDV	62	⊖	○	⊖	⊖	0.8	●	10x	3	95
11	**Toshiba** GSC-R60	750	Hard Disk	62	⊖	○	○	⊖	1	●	10x	2.5	110
12	**Sony** DCR-PC1000	980	MiniDV	61	⊖	⊖	⊖	○	1.0	●	10x	2.7	80
13	**Sony** DCR-TRV280 **CR Best Buy**	275	D8	61	⊖	○	⊖	⊖	2		20x	2.5	80

Key number	Brand & model	Price	Format	Overall score	Picture quality	Ease of use	Image stabilizer	Audio quality	Weight (lb.)	Digital-still capable	Optical zoom	LCD size (in.)	Battery life (min.)
	DIGITAL MODELS continued												
14	**Hitachi** Ultravision DZMV730A	$370	DVD-RAM, DVD-R	60	○	○	⊖	○	1.1	●	16x	2.5	70
15	**Sony** DCR-DVD405	680	DVD-R/RW, DVD+RW	60	⊖	○	⊖	●	1.3	●	10x	2.7	85
16	**Sanyo** Xacti C6	495	External cMemory	59	⊖	○	○	●	0.4	●	5x	2	60
17	**Panasonic** PV-GS31	290	MiniDV	58	○	○	⊖	●	1	●	26x	2.5	85
18	**Sony** DCR-HC46	$440	MiniDV	58	○	○	⊖	●	1	●	12x	2.7	100
19	**Panasonic** VDR-D200	490	DVD-RAM, DVD-R, DVD-RW	57	⊖	○	○	●	1.2	●	30x	2.5	120
20	**Sony** DCR-DVD7	465	DVD-R, DVD-RW, DVD+RW	56	⊖	●	⊖	●	0.9		10x	2.5	90
21	**Canon** Elura 100	350	MiniDV	55	⊖	○	○	◐	0.9	●	20x	2.7	140
22	**Canon** ZR700	350	MiniDV	55	○	○	○	◐	0.9	●	25x	2.7	90
23	**JVC** Everio G Series GZ-MG77	765	Hard Disk	55	○	○	⊖	○	0.9	●	10x	2.7	90
24	**JVC** Ultra-Compact Series GR-DF550	365	MiniDV	55	○	○	○	●	1.1	●	15x	2.5	60
25	**JVC** GR-D395	330	MiniDV	53	⊖	●	○	●	1.2	●	32x	2.5	180
26	**Panasonic** PV-GS180	500	MiniDV	53	○	○	◐	●	1.1	●	10x	2.5	70
27	**Samsung** SC-D453	280	MiniDV	53	○	○	○	●	0.9	●	10x	2.5	80
28	**Panasonic** PV-GS39	315	MiniDV	50	○	○	◐	●	1	●	30x	2.7	80
29	**Sony** DCR-DVD305	545	DVD-R/RW, DVD+RW	50	○	○	○	●	1	●	12x	2.7	75
30	**Samsung** DuoCam SC-D6550	450	MiniDV	49	○	○	○	●	1.2	●	10x	2.5	90
31	**Sanyo** Xacti HD1	720	External Memory	34	◐	○	⊖	●	0.5	●	10x	2.2	60
32	**Samsung** SC-DC164	405	DVD-R/RW, DVD+RW	33	◐	○	◐	●	1.1	●	33x	2.7	65
33	**Samsung** SC-D365	300	MiniDV	30	◐	○	●	●	0.9	●	33x	2.7	80
	ANALOG MODELS												
34	**Sony** CCD-TRV138	235	Hi8	51	○	○	NA	⊖	2		20x	2.5	115

Overall score scale: 0 — 100, P F G VG E

See report, page 19. Based on posted on ConsumerReports.org in July 2006, with updated prices and availability.

Guide to the Ratings

Overall score mainly reflects picture quality and ease of use. **Picture quality** is based on the judgments of trained panelists who viewed static images shot in good light at standard speed (SP) for tape and "fine" mode for DVDs. **Ease of use** takes into account ergonomics, weight, how accurately the viewers reflected the scene being shot, and LCD contrast. **Image stabilizer** reflects how well the model reduces the shakes in a scene. Most stabilizers are electronic, and some of those are digital (digital stabilization is used on both analog and digital camcorders). Some camcorders have optical stabilization. All three types can be effective, though using a tripod is the surest way to get a steady image. **"NA"** indicates the model lacks this feature. **Audio quality** represents accuracy using the built-in microphone, plus freedom from noise and flutter. **Weight** is measured in pounds, and includes the battery and tape (or disc). **Digital still capable** concerns those camcorders that can take snapshots, much like a digital camera (though not necessarily of the same quality). The camcorder can then be plugged into a computer and the images downloaded from the memory. Using a removable memory card (such as MemoryStick, Compact Flash, Multimedia Card, or SmartMedia) you can transfer stills to a computer without having to connect the camcorder, but you need proper card-reader hardware. **Optical zoom** allows the camcorder to fill the frame with far-away objects at the touch of a button. An optical zoom rated at 16x means the camcorder can magnify the image up to 16 times the normal size. **LCD size,** measured diagonally, typically ranges from 2 to 4 inches. **Battery life** is the manufacturer's statement, in minutes, of how long the camcorder can record images continuously with the LCD viewer in use. **Price** is approximate retail.

Quick Picks

Best values in digital tape:
  4 Canon ZR200, $315
 13 Sony DCR-TRV280, $275, **CR Best Buy**
The Canon ZR200 lacks still-image capture. (A newer sibling, the Canon ZR700, and the similar Canon ZR500 and Canon ZR600 are lighter and smaller but scored lower overall.) The D8 Sony DCR-TRV280 is feature-laden but some thumb-activated buttons are not located well and it has mediocre sound quality. JVC also has some high-scoring, low-priced models, but Sony (D8 and MiniDV) has been the most reliable brand among digital camcorders.

Best value in a DVD camcorder:
  5 Sony DCR-DVD92, $500
The Sony DCR-DVD92 has very good picture quality, with an excellent image stabilizer and autofocus. It also has good picture quality in low light if manual settings are used. The location of its strap can make DVD access difficult. We don't have enough data to judge the reliability of DVD camcorders.

If small size is paramount:
 16 Sanyo Xacti C6, $495
This model is as small as a subcompact digital camera and provides much better video quality (albeit at a higher price than most subcompact cameras). It captures about 41 minutes of high-quality video onto a 1-GB SD memory card. It also takes 6.1-megapixel still images and has very good image stabilization.

Models that require no recording media:
 11 Toshiba GSC-R60, $750
 23 JVS Everio G Series GZ-MG77, $765
These camcorders resemble MiniDV models but capture and store video digitally onto a built-in, nonremovable hard drive. The Toshiba GSC-R60 and the similar GSC-R30 record 13.5 hours and 6.7 hours, respectively, of very good video to the drive, but audio quality was only fair. Images from the JVC GZ-MG77 were a little worse in quality than the Toshibas—merely good—but the JVC's audio was a little better and the unit has an excellent image stabilizer.

Recommendations

DIGITAL

1 CANON DC40 Very good overall. Excellent picture quality at standard speed and good low-light picture quality. VCR controls are very easy to use. Image stabilizer only slightly effective. Must use provided proprietary cable for S-video connection. Lacks FireWire port.

2 HITACHI Ultravision DZGX20A Very good picture quality and image stabilizer worked very well. Very good picture quality in low light. A relatively light model that didn't sit in the hand well. Fair audio quality. Uses proprietary A/V cable. Discontinued, but may still be available.

3 PANASONIC VDR-M75 Very good picture quality; image stabilizer worked very well. A relatively light model that didn't sit in the hand well. Fair audio quality. Uses proprietary A/V cable. Discontinued, but may still be available.

4 CANON ZR200 Easy to use and hold. Very good picture quality. Image stabilizer and autofocus are excellent. Fair audio quality. Similar model: ZR300.

5 SONY DCR-DVD92 Very good picture quality, with excellent image stabilizer and autofocus. Good picture quality in low light if manual settings are used. Strap location can make loading and unloading DVDs hard. Uses proprietary A/V cable.

6 SONY DCR-HC90 A relatively light, feature-laden model with very good picture quality, audio quality, and image stabilizer. Thumb-activated buttons were hard to use. Uses proprietary A/V cable. Among digital camcorders, Sony (D8 and MiniDV) has been the most reliable brand.

7 CANON Optura 50 Feature-laden model with very good picture quality. Image stabilizer is excellent, but autofocus failed to work in many situations. Fair audio quality. Sits awkwardly in hand.

8 HITACHI UltraVision DZGX3200A Very good overall. Easy to use overall. Determining how to load the disc or battery is obvious. Image stabilizer and autofocus worked very well, but recorded audio had noticeable background noise. Must use provided proprietary cable for S-video connection. Lacks FireWire port.

9 SONY DCR-HC96 Sony (D8 and MiniDV) has been the most reliable brand.

10 SONY DCR-PC55 Very good picture quality. Image stabilizer and autofocus are excellent. Fair audio quality. Uses proprietary A/V cable. Some connectors are not on camcorder, only on docking station. Strap design doesn't hold camcorder to hand. Among digital camcorders, Sony (D8 and MiniDV) has been the most reliable brand. Discontinued, but may still be available.

11 TOSHIBA GSC-R60 Very good overall but poor picture quality in low light. Determining how to load the tape or battery isn't obvious. Background noise is noticeable in recorded audio. Audio noise was also recorded during zooming. Uses proprietary A/V cable. Lacks manual aperture control, audio fade, video fade, and FireWire port. Similar model: GSC-R30.

12 SONY DCR-PC1000 Very good picture quality. Image stabilizer worked very well. A relatively light model that was hard to hold and use. Uses proprietary A/V cable. Among digital camcorders, Sony (D8 and MiniDV) has been the most reliable brand.

13 SONY DCR-TRV280 **A CR Best Buy** Feature-laden model with very good picture quality. Image stabilizer and autofocus are excellent. Fair audio quality. Some thumb-activated buttons not located well. Among digital camcorders, Sony (D8 and MiniDV) has been the most reliable brand.

14 HITACHI Ultravision DZMV730A Good picture quality, and image stabilizer worked very well. Good low-light picture quality in 'Auto' mode. A relatively light model that didn't sit in the hand well. Uses proprietary A/V cable. Similar model: Ultravision DZMV750A.

15 SONY DCR-DVD405 Good overall. Image stabilizer and autofocus worked well. But background noise is noticeable in recorded audio. Audio noise was also recorded during zooming. Uses propri-etary A/V cable. Lacks FireWire port.

16 SANYO Xacti C6 Good overall. Menu is very easy to use. A relatively light model. Included docking station or proprietary cable required for audio-video connections, including S-video output. Audio had noticeable background noise. Lacks backlight compensation switch, manual aperture control, audio fade, video fade, and FireWire port.

17 PANASONIC PV-GS31 Autofocus worked very well and menu is very easy to use. Fits hand well, but thumb activators are cramped due to larger battery pack. Fair audio quality. Similar model: PV-GS35.

18 SONY DCR-HC46 Sony (D8 and MiniDV) has been the most reliable brand.

19 PANASONIC VDR-D200 Good overall. Must use provided cable for S-video output. Background noise is noticeable in recorded audio. Audio noise was also recorded during zooming. Uses propri-etary audio-video cable. Lacks quick review and FireWire port. Similar model: VDR-D100.

20 SONY DCR-DVD7 Very good picture quality, and image stabilizer worked very well. A relatively light model that was hard to hold and use. Uses proprietary A/V cable. Lacks still-image digital capture.

21 CANON Elura 100 Good overall. Good low-light picture quality (in 'Auto' mode). But menu is hard to use. Audio had very noticeable background noise. Lacks backlight compensation switch.

22 CANON ZR700 Good overall. Menu is hard to use. Audio had noticeable background noise. Similar models: ZR500, ZR600.

23 JVC Everio G Series GZ-MG77 Good over-all. Image stabilizer and autofocus worked very well. Lacks manual aperture control, quick review, FireWire port, and viewfinder.

24 JVC Ultra-Compact Series GR-DF550 Feature-laden model with good picture quality and good low-light picture quality. A relatively light model that didn't sit in the hand well. Fair audio quality. Discontinued, but may still be available.

25 JVC GR-D395 Good overall, but some-what hard to use. Determining how to load the tape or battery isn't obvious. VCR controls are difficult to use, and menu is hard to navigate. Audio had noticeable background noise. Similar models: GR-D350, GR-D370, GR-D396.

26 PANASONIC PV-GS180 Good overall. Menu is very easy to use. Must use provided cable for S-video output. But image stabilizer only slightly effective. Audio had noticeable background noise.

27 SAMSUNG SC-D453 Good picture quality and image stabilizer. Sits in hand well, but record button is crowded. Fair audio quali-ty. Discontinued, but may still be available.

Recommendations

28 PANASONIC PV-GS39 Good overall. Autofocus worked very well. Menu is very easy to use. But image stabilizer is only slightly effective. Eyepiece was inaccurate at framing scenes. Audio had noticeable background noise. Similar model: PV-GS59.

29 SONY DCR-DVD305 Good overall. Audio had noticeable background noise. Uses proprietary audio-video cable. Lacks FireWire port. Similar model: DCR-DVD205.

30 SAMSUNG DuoCam SC-D6550 Duocam adds a separate lensing system for digital stills. Good picture quality and image stabilizer. Padded strap makes it comfortable to hold. Fair audio quality.

31 SANYO Xacti HD1 Fair overall. Menu is very easy to use. A relatively light model. Included docking station or proprietary cable required for audio-video connections, including S-video. But fair picture quality at standard speed. Audio had very noticeable background noise. Noise was in recorded audio when zooming. Lacks backlight compensation switch, audio fade, video fade, FireWire port, and viewfinder.

32 SAMSUNG SC-DC164 Fair overall. Must use provided cable for S-video output. But fair picture quality at standard speed. Image stabilizer only slightly effective. Audio had noticeable background noise. Uses proprietary audio-video cable. Lacks quick review and FireWire port.

33 SAMSUNG SC-D365 Fair overall. Must use provided cable for S-video output. Fair picture quality at standard speed. Image stabilizer not very effective. Tape or battery loading not obvious. Audio had noticeable background noise. Uses proprietary audio-video cable. Similar model: SC-D363.

ANALOG

34 SONY CCD-TRV138 Analog Hi8 model. Autofocus is excellent. Good low-light picture quality. Lacks image stabilizer and digital stills. Some thumb-activated buttons not located well.

Brand Repair History

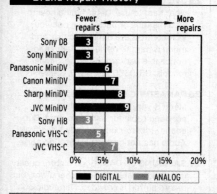

Readers report on 35,181 camcorders
This graph shows the percentage of these brands of digital and analog camcorders, bought new between 2002 and 2005, that have been repaired or developed a serious problem that wasn't repaired. Differences of less than 3 points aren't meaningful. We don't have enough reader data to judge the reliability of DVD camcorders. Models within a brand may vary, and design and manufacturing changes may affect reliability. Nevertheless, you can improve your chances of getting a trouble-free camcorder if you choose a brand that has been reliable in the past.

Data are based on readers responses about camcorders to the Annual Product Reliability Survey conducted by the Consumer Reports National Research Center. Data are adjusted to eliminate differences linked to age and use.

CELL PHONES

In the Ratings, we show approximate prices based on a two-year contract. Rebates or "instant savings" can reduce these prices substantially. Sprint Nextel and T-Mobile tend to rely more heavily on these supplemental discounts than other carriers. To find the best price on any phone, check with carriers and retailers, both online and in stores.

All but the Samsungs (21 and 27) and Palm (10) have voice dial for hands-free dialing. The Nokias (15 and 29) lack the convenience of side-mounted volume controls, which are available on all the other models we tested. The Motorolas (24, 28, 30) and the Sony Ericsson (26) are quad-band GSM phones that maximize coverage of the U.S., Europe, and Asia.

Excellent	Very good	Good	Fair	Poor
⊜	⊖	○	◐	●

Within types, in performance order. Gray **key numbers indicate Quick Picks.**

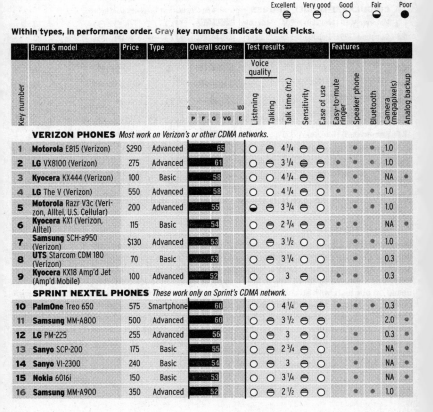

Key number	Brand & model	Price	Type	Overall score (0–100, P F G VG E)	Voice quality: Listening	Voice quality: Talking	Talk time (hr.)	Sensitivity	Ease of use	Easy-to-mute ringer	Speaker phone	Bluetooth	Camera (megapixels)	Analog backup
VERIZON PHONES *Most work on Verizon's or other CDMA networks.*														
1	**Motorola** E815 (Verizon)	$290	Advanced	65	○	○	4¼	⊖	⊖		●	●	1.0	
2	**LG** VX8100 (Verizon)	275	Advanced	61	○	⊖	3¼	⊖	⊖	●	●	●	1.0	
3	**Kyocera** KX444 (Verizon)	100	Basic	58	○	⊖	4¼	⊖	⊖		●		NA	●
4	**LG** The V (Verizon)	550	Advanced	58	○	⊖	4¼	⊖	⊖	●	●	●	1.0	
5	**Motorola** Razr V3c (Verizon, Alltel, U.S. Cellular)	200	Advanced	55	⊜	⊖	3¾	⊖	⊖		●	●	1.0	
6	**Kyocera** KX1 (Verizon, Alltel)	115	Basic	54	○	⊖	2¾	⊖	⊖	●	●		NA	●
7	**Samsung** SCH-a950 (Verizon)	$130	Advanced	53	○	⊖	3½	⊖	⊖		●	●	1.0	
8	**UTS** Starcom CDM 180 (Verizon)	70	Basic	53	○	⊖	3¼	○	○		●		0.3	
9	**Kyocera** KX18 Amp'd Jet (Amp'd Mobile)	100	Advanced	52	○	○	3	⊖	⊖		●	●	0.3	
SPRINT NEXTEL PHONES *These work only on Sprint's CDMA network.*														
10	**PalmOne** Treo 650	575	Smartphone	60	○	○	4¼	⊖	⊖	●	●	●	0.3	
11	**Samsung** MM-A800	500	Advanced	60	○	⊖	3½	⊖	⊖		●	●	2.0	●
12	**LG** PM-225	255	Advanced	56	○	⊖	3	⊖	⊖		●		0.3	●
13	**Sanyo** SCP-200	175	Basic	55	○	⊖	2¾	⊖	○		●		NA	●
14	**Sanyo** VI-2300	240	Basic	54	○	⊖	3	⊖	○		●		NA	●
15	**Nokia** 6016i	150	Basic	53	○	○	3¼	⊖	○		●		NA	●
16	**Samsung** MM-A900	350	Advanced	52	○	⊖	2½	○	○		●	●	1.0	

	Excellent	Very good	Good	Fair	Poor
	⊖	⊖	○	⊖	●

Within types, in performance order. Gray **key numbers indicate Quick Picks.**

Key number	Brand & model	Price	Type	Overall score (0 – 100) P F G VG E	Voice quality Listening	Voice quality Talking	Talk time (hr.)	Sensitivity	Ease of use	Easy-to-mute ringer	Speaker phone	Bluetooth	Camera (megapixels)	Analog backup
	SPRINT NEXTEL PHONES *These work only on Sprint's CDMA network.* continued													
17	**Sanyo** MM-8300	$335	Advanced	51	○	⊖	2¾	○	⊖		•		0.3	•
18	**Sanyo** MM-9000	550	Advanced	48	○	⊖	3	○	○		•		1.0	
19	**Nokia** 3155i	190	Basic	46	⊖	○	3¾	⊖	⊖		•		NA	•
	CINGULAR/T-MOBILE PHONES *These work on Cingular's or T-Mobile's GSM network.*													
20	**Motorola** V360 (T-Mobile)	200	Advanced	67	○	○	7	⊖	⊖	•	•	•	0.3	
21	**Samsung** e335 (T-Mobile)	535	Basic	66	○	⊖	6¾	⊖	⊖	•	•		0.3	
22	**Nokia** 6101 (T-Mobile)	150	Basic	64	⊖	○	6½	⊖	⊖		•		0.3	
23	**Samsung** SGH-d307 (Cingular)	200	Advanced	64	⊖	○	7	⊖	⊖	•	•	•	NA	
24	**Motorola** Razr V3 (Cingular, T-mobile)	265	Advanced	62	○	○	5¼	⊖	⊖	•	•	•	0.3	
25	**Motorola** ROKR E1 (Cingular)	300	Advanced	62	○	○	6¼	⊖	⊖	•	•	•	0.3	
26	**Sony** Ericsson W600i (Cingular)	300	Advanced	62	⊖	○	6½	⊖	⊖	•	•	•	1.0	
27	**Samsung** e635 (T-Mobile)	350	Basic	61	○	○	5½	⊖	⊖	•	•		0.3	
28	**Motorola** V220 (Cingular)	250	Basic	60	○	○	5¼	○	⊖		•		0.3	
29	**Nokia** 6682 (Cingular)	300	Advanced	56	○	○	5¼	⊖	○		•	•	1.0	
30	**Motorola** PEBL U6 (T-Mobile)	300	Advanced	54	○	○	3¼	○	⊖	•	•	•	0.3	

See report, page 121. Based on tests in Consumer Reports in April 2006, with updated prices and availaibility.

Guide to the Ratings

Overall score is based mainly on voice quality and talk time. **Listening** rates the voice quality you hear during a cell-phone conversation. **Talking** rates the voice quality heard by the person you call. Listening and talking tests were conducted in noisy and quiet environments using live phone calls. **Talk time,** in hours, is the average time for calls you should expect, based on our tests with strong and weak signals. **Sensitivity** is a measure of a phone's voice quality when a call is placed using a weak signal. The scores are applicable only within a Ratings group, not between groups. **Ease of use** takes in the design of the display and keypad and the ease with which you can send or receive text messages and the like. **Price** is approximate for a phone purchased from the carrier with a two-year contract in fall 2005. Prices shown are the manufacturer's standard, excluding rebates or special offers, which can be substantial but constantly change.

Quick Picks

Best for Verizon (CDMA):

1 Motorola E815, $290
3 Kyocera KX444, $100
4 LG The V, $550

The Motorola E815 is a top-performing, fully featured advanced phone. Its keypad is easy to read under most lighting conditions, though the display can be hard to see in bright light. It's compatible with Verizon's high-speed EV-DO network, which provides access to video programs and faster Web surfing than with regular cell service. LG's V phone is another EV-DO-ready model that doubles as an e-mail/messaging terminal. Turned on its side, this candy-bar phone flips open to reveal a QWERTY keyboard and larger display that's well-suited for text-based communication. But it's much thicker than most phones. The Kyocera KX444 is a very good basic phone with a simple display that was the easiest to read under any lighting conditions of all the phones we tested. But its bulky rectangular case is cumbersome. It's compatible with Verizon's push-to-talk service.

Best for Sprint (CDMA):

11 Samsung MM-A800, $500
13 Sanyo SCP-200, $175
16 Samsung MM-A900, $350

The Samsung MM-A800 has a high-resolution camera and removable memory card for storing pictures. Its PictBridge interface lets you connect compatible printers via cable to print pictures directly from the camera. But the sliding case is bulky. The Samsung MM-A900 competently stuffs high-speed network access, Bluetooth connectivity, and other advanced features into a stylishly thin case. It's the only CDMA phone we've seen that can swap photos, music, and other files with other Bluetooth devices. It's also one of the few phones that can download music from the new cell-phone music services. But battery life is relatively short and internal memory is a puny 48 megabytes. Also, there's no slot for an external memory card, and it lacks the analog backup offered by most CDMA phones. The Sanyo SCP-200 is a good, basic, no-frills phone for use with voice-only plans.

Best for Cingular (GSM):

24 Motorola Razr V3, $265
26 Sony Ericsson W600i, $300
28 Motorola V220, $250

All three phones can make and receive calls on international GSM networks, but unlike CDMA phones, they lack the analog backup that provides better coverage where a digital network is unavailable. The Motorola Razr V3 crams Bluetooth and other advanced phone features into an ultraslim case that slips easily into a tight pocket. Unlike its Verizon cousin, this Razr has a programmable jog dial for instant access to important features. The keypad and display are easy to see in low-light conditions, but just average in bright light. The Motorola V220 is a good, basic phone combining very good battery life with solid overall performance. But the display can be hard to read in bright light. The Sony Ericsson W600i has a well-integrated MP3 player that automatically pauses music playback when you answer an incoming call, then resumes it when the call ends. As with other Sony Ericsson models, the Bluetooth connection works well with headsets and when transferring pictures and files, but doesn't work with all hands-free speaker phones. Its 256 megabytes of internal storage can't be expanded with an external memory card, not ideal for a music-enabled phone.

Best for T-Mobile (GSM):

20 Motorola V360, $200

Like all GSM phones, this lacks analog back-up, but its 850/1900MHz capability expands domestic coverage. The V360 combines Bluetooth, international roaming, and other advanced features with excellent battery life. Its keypad and display are readable everywhere except in bright light.

DESKTOP COMPUTERS

Workhorse desktop computers cost more than budget models but also offer more. A workhorse paired with a $200 to $300 media receiver would be your best choice for creating a basic, computer-based home-entertainment center. Either type of desktop can handle most typical chores, including photo editing. If you need a new monitor, consider that LCD screens save desk space and use less power than CRT monitors. Serious photographers, designers, and gamers, however, may prefer the color rendition, response time, and viewing angle of a CRT.

All have memory-card slots except 6 and 11. S-video out available on 2, 7, 8, and 9. Remote control available on 6, 8, 10, and 11.

Ratings: Excellent ⊖ · Very good ⊖ · Good ○ · Fair ◐ · Poor ●

Key number	Brand & model	Processor	Video adapter	Price	Overall score	Test results						Features		
						Features	Ergonomics	Speed	3D gaming	Speakers	Expansion	FireWire port	DVI display port	Digital audio out
BUDGET MODELS Have 512MB of RAM, a 160GB hard drive, a DVD burner, and stereo speakers.														
1	**Compaq** Presario SR1900Z	Sempron 3400+	Nvidia 6150	$480	56	○	⊖	⊖	◐	○	⊖			•
2	**Compaq** Presario SR1930T	Celeron D 352	ATI 200	470	56	○	⊖	⊖	◐	○	⊖		•	•
3	**HP** Pavilion a1400e	Sempron 3400+	Nvidia 6150	490	56	○	⊖	⊖	◐	○	⊖			•
4	**HP** Pavilion a1400y	Celeron D 356	ATI 200	510	54	○	⊖	⊖	◐	○	⊖			•
5	**eMachines** T3508	Celeron D 356	ATI 200	430	52	○	○	⊖	◐	○	⊖			
6	**Apple** Mac Mini [1] [2] [3]	1.5GHz Core Solo	Intel 950	680	40	⊖	○	○	●	●	●	•	•	•
WORKHORSE MODELS Have 1GB of RAM, a 250GB hard drive, a DVD burner, a DVD-ROM drive, and speakers with a subwoofer.														
7	**Gateway** FX510S	Pentium D 930	128MB Nvidia 6600	1,255	72	⊖	⊖	⊖	⊖	⊖	⊖	•	•	•
8	**HP** Pavilion d4500e	Athlon 64 X2 4600+	256MB ATI X1600	1,475	72	⊖	⊖	⊖	⊖	⊖	⊖	•	•	•
9	**Gateway** DX310X	Pentium D 930	128MB Nvidia 6600	1,205	68	⊖	⊖	⊖	⊖	⊖	⊖	•	•	•
10	**Dell** Dimension E510 **CR Best Buy**	Pentium D 930	256MB ATI X600	1,020	67	⊖	⊖	⊖	⊖	⊖	⊖	•	•	•
11	**Apple** iMac 17" [2] [4]	1.83GHz Core Duo	128MB ATI X1600	01,200	64	⊖	⊖	⊖	○	○	○	•		•

[1] 60GB hard drive. [2] Integrated speakers [3] CD-RW/DVD combo drive. [4] Includes only DVD burner.

See report, page 128. Based on testing in Consumer Reports in November 2006.

Best basic desktops:
  2 Compaq Presario SR1930T, $470
  3 HP Pavilion a1400e, $490
Both of these desktop models offer a well-rounded feature set, very good speed, and excellent expandability at a budget price. However, tech support and reliability have been undistinguished for both brands, according to our surveys. The Compaq uses Intel chips; the HP is AMD-based.

If you need more power:
  7 Gateway FX510S, $1,255
  10 Dell Dimension E510, $1,020,
    CR Best Buy
The Gateway combines a full feature list and very good performance with a reason-able price. The Dell offers the most bang for the buck, especially because it includes a 17-inch monitor. However, both Gateway and Dell's tech support and reliability have been undistinguished.

If reliability and tech support are of paramount importance:
  11 Apple iMac 17-inch, $1,200
Apple's desktops have proven very reliable, and its tech support has been superior. The Mac operating system is also less vulnerable than Windows to viruses and other malware. Apple recently began equipping this Mac with a Core 2 Duo processor.

Guide to the Ratings

Overall score covers features, ergonomics, speed, and other factors. **Features** includes important items such as audio, video, and communications connections, storage devices, and software. **Ergonomics** evaluates keyboard, mouse, case design, and noise. **Speed** measures performance while running office productivity and content creation applications. **3D gaming** covers performance while playing 3D-intensive games. **Speakers** looks at speaker quality, including fidelity, bass response, and loudness. **Expansion** is expandability and ease of upgrades. **Price** is approximate retail and without a display, except for the Dell (10) and Apple iMac (11), which include a 17-inch LCD.

For Brand Reapir History information, see page 267.

DIGITAL CAMERAS

Based on our judgments of uncropped 8x10-inch prints, all the cameras produced images that were excellent. But if we had used only a small portion of the original image and enlarged it to 8x10, the higher-megapixel cameras would have produced better results than the others. The advanced compact and super-zoom models have features that demanding photographers will appreciate, such as manual controls, especially long battery life, and a next-shot delay no longer than two seconds. All rated excellent or very good for ease of use.

Ratings: Excellent ⊕ Very good ⊖ Good ○ Fair ◑ Poor ●

Within types, in performance order. Gray **key numbers indicate Quick Picks.**

Key number	Brand & model	Price	Overall score	Print quality	Megapixels	Weight (oz.)	Flash range (ft.)	Battery life (shots)	Next-shot delay (sec.)	Optical zoom	Manual controls	Charger	AA batteries	Wide angle	Image stabilizer
	COMPACT MODELS														
1	**Canon** PowerShot A620	$220	76	⊖	7	12	14	500	2	4X	•		•		
2	**Kodak** EasyShare Z700	250	76	⊖	4	10	12	200	2	5X	•	•	•		
3	**Olympus** Stylus 800	330	73	⊖	8	7	21	400	2	3X	•	•			•
4	**Hewlett-Packard** PhotoSmart R817	220	72	⊖	5.1	7	12	260	1	5X	•	•			
5	**Canon** PowerShot A520 **CR Best Buy**	160	71	⊖	4	8	11	300	2	4X	•		•		
6	**Hewlett-Packard** PhotoSmart R717	260	71	⊖	6.2	7	16	80	2	3X	•	•			
7	**Nikon** Coolpix S4	330	66	⊖	6	9	10	300	3	10X			•		•
8	**Kodak** EasyShare One	210	65	⊖	4	9	10	120	2	3X		•			
	SUBCOMPACT MODELS														
9	**Canon** PowerShot SD500 Digital ELPH	280	75	⊖	7.1	7	16	160	2	3X	•				
10	**Casio** Exilim Zoom EX-Z750	300	72	⊖	7.2	6	10	320	2	3X	•	•			•
11	**Kodak** EasyShare V550	240	72	⊖	5	6	8	120	1	3X	•				•
12	**Pentax** Optio SV	220	72	⊖	5	6	14	100	9	5X	•	•			
13	**Canon** PowerShot SD430	450	70	⊖	5	5	11	150	2	3X	•				
14	**Canon** PowerShot SD450	260	68	⊖	5	5	11	150	2	3X	•				
15	**Sony** Cyber-shot DSC-M1	430	66	⊖	5	8	6	160	4	3X	•				
16	**Kodak** EasyShare V570	350	65	⊖	5	5	10	140	1	3X	•			•	•
17	**Panasonic** Lumix DMC-FX8	240	64	⊖	5	5	6	300	2	3X	•				•
18	**Pentax** Optio S5z	240	64	⊖	5	4	11	180	3	3X	•				
19	**Fujifilm** FinePix Z1	270	62	⊖	5.1	5	10	170	2	3X	•				
20	**Sony** Cyber-shot DSC-T7	330	61	⊖	5.1	5	9	150	1	3X	•				
21	**Canon** PowerShot SD30	270	60	⊖	5	4	7	160	2	2.4X	•				

Consumer Reports®
EXPERT • INDEPENDENT • NONPROFIT

✓ **YES!** Start my subscription to **Consumer Reports.** I'll receive 13 issues including the year-end Buying Guide 2008 Issue for just $26. Plus, I'll receive the Buying Guide 2007 FREE!

Savings Coupon

Here's What You Get:

11 Regular Monthly Issues	$55.89
1 April Auto Issue	$ 5.99
1 Buying Guide 2008 Issue *(when published)*	$ 9.99
Buying Guide 2007 *(yours free)*	$ 9.99
TOTAL RETAIL VALUE	~~$81.86~~

SAVE $55⁸⁶   *You pay only $26*

KD6C13

SATISFACTION GUARANTEED

Cancel at any time and get a prompt refund for the remainder of your subscription while keeping all issues sent and the Buying Guide 2007. Please allow 4 to 8 weeks for delivery of your first issue and free guide. This rate is for U.S. only. All other countries, please add $6 per subscription.

NAME _____

ADDRESS _____ APT. # ___

CITY _____ STATE ____ ZIP ____

10% post consumer recycled paper.

FREE GIFT

FREE GIFT

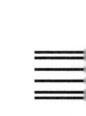

Within types, in performance order. Gray **key numbers indicate Quick Picks.**

Key number	Brand & model	Price	Overall score	Print quality	Megapixels	Weight (oz.)	Flash range (ft.)	Battery life (shots)	Next-shot delay (sec.)	Optical zoom	Manual controls	Charger	AA batteries	Wide angle
	ADVANCED COMPACT MODELS													
22	**Kodak** EasyShare P880	$450	73	⊜	8	21	13	260	2	5.8X	●	●		●
23	**Fujifilm** FinePix E900 **CR Bext Buy**	350	72	⊜	9	9	12	280	2	4X	●	●	●	
24	**Olympus** SP-350	290	70	⊜	8	8	12	200	7	3X	●	●		
25	**Panasonic** Lumix DMC-LX1	430	69	⊜	8.4	7	13	240	2	4X	●	●		●
26	**Sony** Cyber-shot DSC-R1	760	69	⊜	10	37	28	500	2	5X	●	●		●
27	**Leica** D-LUX 2	750	64	⊜	8.4	8	6	240	6	4X	●	●		●
	SUPER-ZOOM MODELS													
28	**Canon** PowerShot S2 IS	350	81	⊜	5	19	17	550	2	12X	●		●	
29	**Kodak** EasyShare P850	380	79	⊜	5.1	16	15	260	4	12X	●	●		
30	**Panasonic** Lumix DMC-FZ20S	410	78	⊜	5	22	23	280	1	12X	●	●		
31	**Fujifilm** FinePix S5200	260	77	⊜	5	17	13	500	1	10X	●		●	
32	**Kodak** EasyShare Z740	220	74	⊜	5	12	16	260	2	10X	●		●	
33	**Fujifilm** FinePix S9000	550	72	⊜	9	27	18	340	2	10.7X	●		●	●
34	**Samsung** Digimax Pro815	700	67	⊖	8	36	20	460	3	15X	●	●		●

See report, page 22. Based on tests posted on ConsumerReports.org in April 2006, with updated prices and availability.

Guide to the Ratings

Overall score is based largely on picture quality and convenience factors. **Print quality** is based on panelists' judgments of glossy 8x10-inch photos made on a high-quality inkjet printer. **Megapixels** shows how many million pixels the image sensor has. As a rule, with more megapixels, you can make larger prints or enlarge parts of an image without losing detail or image quality. **Weight**, in ounces, includes battery and memory card. **Flash range**, in feet, is the maximum claimed range for a well-lighted photo. **Battery life** reflects the number of high-resolution photos we could take with a fresh set of alkaline batteries (or, if included, with rechargeables that were fully charged). The LCD image display was turned off (if possible), the flash was used for half of the shots, and the zoom lens was racked in and out. **Next-shot delay** is the time, in seconds, the camera needs to ready itself for the next shot. **Optical zoom** magnifies the image using a real multifocal-length lens, whereas a digital zoom uses electronics to enlarge the center portion of the image using interpolation. **Manual controls** allow the user to set the aperture (f-stop), shutter speed, or (usually) both. This feature is used to override the automatic exposure settings when more control is needed. **Charger** indicates whether the camera comes with a charger. **AA batteries** indicates whether the camera accepts AA batteries. This options allows you to use disposable or rechargeable batteries. **Wide angle** shows which model has a lens that can zoom as wide as a 28-mm lens. **Price** is approximate retail.

Brand Repair History

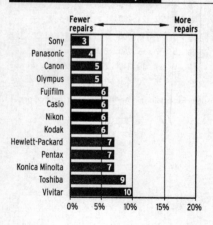

Brand	Repairs
Sony	3
Panasonic	4
Canon	5
Olympus	5
Fujifilm	6
Casio	6
Nikon	6
Kodak	6
Hewlett-Packard	7
Pentax	7
Konica Minolta	7
Toshiba	9
Vivitar	10

Fewer repairs ← → More repairs

0%   5%   10%   15%   20%

Readers report on 186,900 digital cameras

This graph shows the percentage of these brands of digital cameras that were purchased new between 2002 and 2005 that have been repaired or developed a serious problem that wasn't repaired. Digital cameras have been generally very reliable. Differences of less than 4 points aren't meaningful. The graph does not include digital SLR cameras. Models within a brand may vary, and design and manufacturing changes may affect the repair history.

Data are based on readers responses about digital cameras to the Annual Product Reliability Survey conducted by the Consumer Reports National Research Center. Data are adjusted to eliminate differences linked to age and usage.

Quick Picks

Best value for most people:

   5 Canon PowerShot A520, $160,
        CR Best Buy

This has excellent print quality and battery life, manual controls, and uses AA batteries. It also has 4-megapixel resolution and a 4X optical zoom, but has a small LCD and limited time for each video recording.

For additional flexibility:

   1 Canon PowerShot A620, $220
   4 Hewlett-Packard PhotoSmart R817, $220

These compacts have excellent print quality and battery life, plus manual controls. The Canon has 7-megapixel resolution, a flip-out movable LCD, and uses AA batteries, but doesn't include a charger. The Hewlett-Packard has 5-megapixel resolution, a 5X optical zoom, short next-shot delay, and includes a charger for its proprietary battery. It also has image advice, in-camera red-eye removal, panoramic shooting with in-camera stitching, and the ability to save as a still image and enhance any frame from a video.

For a camera that fits in a purse:

   10 Casio Exilim Zoom EX-Z750, $300
   11 Kodak EasyShare V550, $240
   14 Canon PowerShot SD450, $260
   17 Panasonic Lumix DMC-FX8, $240

All are small and light, with excellent or very good print quality, and include a charger. All except the Casio have 5-megapixel resolution. The Casio has 7-megapixel resolution, excellent battery life, manual controls, an optical viewfinder, and MPEG-4 video at 30 frames per second. But its image stabilizer is simulated (less effective than optical stabilization). The Kodak has good battery life, an optical viewfinder, short next-shot delay, and MPEG-4 video at 30 frames per second. But it lacks manual controls and its ISO 800 setting automatically reduces resolution. The Canon has good battery life, an optical viewfinder, and a mode that helps you align shots to stitch together later for panoramic photos. But it lacks manual

controls and its image stabilizer is for video only. The Panasonic has excellent battery life, an optical image stabilizer (the most effective type), and a "baby" mode for softer images. But it lacks manual controls.

For an advanced compact camera:

   22 Kodak EasyShare P880, $450
   23 Fujifilm FinePix E900, $350,
        CR Best Buy
   25 Panasonic Lumix DMC-LX1, $430

You can't go wrong with any of these advanced compacts. The priciest, the Kodak, offers a lot to the serious photographer. It has 8-megapixel resolution, a 5.8X optical zoom with wide-angle capability, in-camera red-eye removal, and it can make advanced adjustments to a RAW file and save it as a separate JPEG. But it weighs more than twice as much as the other two models, and its ISO 800 setting automatically reduces resolution. For the best value, the Fujifilm has 9-megapixel resolution, excellent battery life, an extremely sharp lens, and less-grainy images than other models at high ISO settings. The 8-megapixel Panasonic is well-suited for displaying photos on widescreen digital TVs if you use its 16:9 aspect mode. Its resolution drops if you use narrower aspect modes. It also has very good battery life, a 4X optical zoom with wide-angle capability, and an optical image stabilizer (the most effective type).

For a long zoom range:

   28 Canon PowerShot S2 IS, $390
   31 Fujifilm FinePix S5200, $260

These 5-megapixel super-zoom models are well-suited for shooting situations where distance is a major factor, such as sports and nature photography. Both use AA batteries, which are easily obtained in a pinch. The Canon has a 12X optical zoom, an optical image stabilizer (the most effective type), high-quality Motion JPEG video recording at 30 frames per second, and can zoom optically during video recording. But it has a small LCD.

DISHWASHERS

Almost all of the dishwashers we tested scored at least very good overall and are available with stainless-steel exterior styling. All are from historically reliable brands. While you'll typically pay more for folding racks and other flexible-loading features, some of the tested models offer them for far less than others. Indeed, several high-scoring models cost roughly $500, rather than $800 or more.

While all tested models have a heavy-duty or pots-and-pans cycle, special cycles such as the concentrated Turbo Zone and Pro-Scrub on some Kenmore and KitchenAid models come at a higher price. But as we found, the KitchenAid KUDP02CR[WH], KitchenAid KUDI02IR[WH], Asko D3122XL, Amana ADB1500AW[W], and GE Monogram ZBD0710K[SS] did especially well in our trial baked-on brownie-mix tests using their normal cycles.

You can also save money if you're willing to live without the eye appeal and stain resistance of a stainless-steel tub. Other features, such as fully hidden controls, can actually make using a dishwasher less convenient.

	Excellent	Very good	Good	Fair	Poor
	◖	◓	○	◒	●

In performance order. Gray key numbers indicate Quick Picks.

Key number	Brand & model	Price	Overall score (0–100 P F G VG E)	Washing	Energy use	Noise	Loading flexibility	Ease of use	Cycle time (mins.)	Sensor	Self-cleaning filter	Stainless-steel tub	Hidden controls	Ample flatware slots	Adjustable upper rack
1	**Bosch** SHU66C0[2]	$880	87	◓	◓	◓	◓	◓	105	•		•		•	•
2	**Bosch** SHU43C0[2]	580	86	◓	◓	◓	◓	○	105	•		•		•	•
3	**Kenmore** (Sears) 1603[2] **CR Best Buy**	520	86	◓	◓	◓	◓	◓	115	•	•			•	
4	**Kenmore** (Sears) Elite 1378[2] Elite 1379[ ] 1000	1000	83	◓	◓	◓	◓	◓	125	•	•	•		•	•
5	**Kenmore** (Sears) Elite 1630[2] Elite 1730[ ] 1020	800	83	◓	◓	◓	◓	◓	105	•		•		•	•
6	**KitchenAid** KUDP02CR[WH]	800	83	◓	◓	◓	◓	◓	120	•		•		•	•
7	**Kenmore** (Sears) Elite 1376[2]	800	82	◓	◓	◓	◓	◓	130	•		•		•	•
8	**KitchenAid** Superba KUDS02SR[WH]	1100	82	◓	◓	◓	◓	◓	125	•	•	•	•	•	•
9	**Asko** Encore D3531XLHD[SS]	1600	81	◓	◓	◓	◓	◓	145	•	•	•	•		•
10	**LG** LDF7810[WW]	800	81	◓	◓	◓	◓	◓	110	•	•	•		•	•
11	**Maytag** MDB4651AW[W] **CR Best Buy**	430	81	◓	○	○	○	◓	110	•	•				
12	**Miele** G894SCiG694SCi 1550	1550	81	◓	◓	◓	◓	◓	135			•	•		•
13	**Whirlpool** DU1055XTP[Q]	460	81	◓	◓	○	○	◓	115		•			•	

In performance order. Gray key numbers indicate Quick Picks.

Key number	Brand & model	Price	Overall score (P F G VG E)	Washing	Energy use	Noise	Loading flexibility	Ease of use	Cycle time (mins.)	Sensor	Self-cleaning filter	Stainless-steel tub	Hidden controls	Ample flatware slots	Adjustable upper rack
14	**Whirlpool** DU1100XTP[Q] **CR Best Buy**	$435	81	⊖	⊖	⊖	○	⊖	115	•	•			•	
15	**Whirlpool** Gold GU2400XTP[Q]	500	81	⊖	⊖	⊖	○	⊖	125	•	•			•	
16	**Asko** D3122XL	850	80	⊖	⊖	○	○	○	115			•		•	•
17	**KitchenAid** Architect KUDU02FR[WH]	1200	80	⊖	○	⊖	⊖	⊖	165	•	•	•	•	•	
18	**KitchenAid** KUDI02IR[WH]	600	80	⊖	⊖	⊖	⊖	⊖	125	•	•			•	•
19	**LG** LDS5811[W]	770	80	⊖	⊖	⊖	⊖	⊖	140	•		•		•	•
20	**GE** GLD4300L[WW]	380	78	⊖	⊖	○	⊖	⊖	110	•	•			•	
21	**GE** GLD6200L[WW]	450	78	⊖	⊖	○	⊖	⊖	125	•	•			•	
22	**Admiral** DDB1501AW[W] (Home Depot)	300	77	⊖	○	○	⊖	⊖	115	•	•				
23	**Amana** ADB1500AW[W] **CR Best Buy**	330	77	⊖	○	○	⊖	⊖	115	•	•				
24	**GE** GLD5800L[WW]	400	77	⊖	⊖	○	⊖	⊖	125		•			•	
25	**Fisher & Paykel** DD603[W]	1200	76	⊖	⊖	⊖	⊖	⊖	115			•		•	
26	**Maytag** MDB8951AW[W]	850	76	⊖	○	⊖	⊖	⊖	120	•		•	•	•	•
27	**Miele** Advanta G2020SC	1000	76	⊖	⊖	○	⊖	○	125		•				
28	**GE** Monogram ZBD0710K[SS]	1300	75	⊖	⊖	⊖	○	⊖	115	•	•	•	•	•	
29	**GE** Profile PDW9800L[WW]	1100	75	⊖	⊖	⊖	○	⊖	120	•	•		•	•	
30	**Maytag** MDB5601AW[W]	500	75	⊖	○	⊖	⊖	⊖	120	•					
31	**Maytag** MDB6601AW[W]	500	75	⊖	○	⊖	⊖	⊖	120	•			•	•	
32	**Maytag** MDB7601AW[W]	520	75	⊖	◐	⊖	⊖	⊖	130	•	•		•	•	•
33	**Whirlpool** DU945PWP[Q]	320	75	⊖	○	◐	⊖	⊖	115	•					
34	**Maytag** MDB9601AW[W]	600	74	⊖	◐	⊖	⊖	⊖	120	•			•	•	
35	**Jenn-Air** JDB2150AWP	1010	73	⊖	◐	⊖	⊖	⊖	150	•	•		•	•	
36	**Maytag** MDB8751AW[W]	750	73	⊖	◐	⊖	⊖	⊖	125	•		•		•	
37	**Frigidaire** Gallery GLD2440RE[S]	380	72	⊖	⊖	○	○	⊖	110	•	•				
38	**Frigidaire** FDB2410LD[S]	480	70	⊖	⊖	◐	⊖	⊖	110	•	•				
39	**GE** Profile PDW9900L[WW]	1200	67	○	⊖	⊖	⊖	⊖	120	•	•	•	•	•	•
40	**KitchenAid** Architect KUDD01DP[WH]	1400	65	⊖	⊖	◐	⊖	⊖	115		•			•	
41	**Hotpoint** HDA3700G[WW]	300	64	⊖	⊖	◐	⊖	⊖	95		•				
42	**Whirlpool** DU850SWP[Q]	300	61	○	⊖	○	◐	○	85		•				
43	**Haier** ESD200	420	55	◐	⊖	○	○	○	100			•		•	
44	**Frigidaire** FDB1250RE[S]	300	34	NA	⊖	○	○	⊖	110		•				

Guide to the Ratings

Overall score is based mainly on washing, but also factors in noise, energy and water use, loading, and more. **Washing** is tested using our standard, very dirty, full load. Because we switched to an enzyme-based detergent for our tests, Ratings for models that appear here and in archived reports may differ. **Energy use** is for a normal cycle. The largest portion is needed for heating water, both at the water heater and in the machine. **Noise** was judged during fill, wash, and drain, mainly by a listening panel. **Loading flexibility** reflects the ability to hold extra place settings and oversized items such as platters up to 13½ in. long and Pilsner-type glasses up to 10 in. high. **Ease of use** considers convenience of controls and other factors. **Cycle time (min.)** is based on a normal cycle including heated dry, where that feature is available. **Price** is approximate retail.

See report, page 52. Based on testing posted on ConsumerReports.org in August 2006, with updated prices and availability.

Quick Picks

Best for most; fine cleaning, flexible loading, quiet running:

2 Bosch SHU43C0[2], $580

3 Kenmore (Sears) 1603[2], $520,
CR Best Buy

15 Whirlpool Gold GU2400XTP[Q], $500

The Bosch, Kenmore, and Whirlpool Gold are all well-equipped and scored very good for energy efficiency. Consider the Bosch if you don't mind paying extra for its stainless tub and periodically cleaning its manual filter. The Kenmore is a quieter machine than the Whirlpool Gold, although the Whirlpool's remaining-time display is a nice feature.

If a low price is more important than flexible loading; all are CR Best Buys:

11 Maytag MDB4651AW[W], $430

14 Whirlpool DU1100XTP[Q], $435

23 Amana ADB1500AW[W], $330

The Maytag, Whirlpool, and Amana are all fine performers at a relatively modest price. The Whirlpool is a quieter and more energy-efficient dishwasher than the Maytag for roughly the same price. The Amana gives up some energy efficiency, but it costs $100 less, placing it among the least expensive models that we tested.

Recommendations

1 BOSCH SHU66C0[2] High-priced but excellent at washing dishes and very quiet, with a stainless-steel tub. It has a manual-clean filter, rather than the more common self-cleaning type. Uses roughly 7 gallons of water in the normal cycle, about average. Has an adjustable top rack, which makes it easier to fit tall items. Hidden or partly hidden controls are available on higher-priced similar models. Stainless-steel finish available at a higher price.

2 BOSCH SHU43C0[2] Excellent at washing dishes and very quiet. It has a manual-clean filter rather than the more common self-cleaning type. Uses roughly 7 gallons of water in the normal cycle, about average. Has an adjustable top rack, which makes it easier to fit tall items. Stainless-steel finish available at a higher price.

3 KENMORE (SEARS) 1603[2] **A CR Best Buy** A top choice for many consumers, this model was excellent at washing dishes and very quiet. Uses less water than most, about 6 gallons in the normal cycle. Has an adjustable top rack, which makes it easier to fit tall items. Stainless-steel finish available at a higher price. Similar models: 1601, 1602, 1701, 1702, 1703.

4 KENMORE (SEARS) Elite 1378[2] This model was excellent at washing dishes and very quiet. It is among the most flexible for loading. It has a stainless-steel tub and an adjustable top rack that makes it easier to fit tall items. It uses less water than most, about 6 gallons in the normal cycle. Stainless-steel finish available at a higher price. Similar model: Elite 1379.

5 KENMORE (SEARS) Elite 1630[2] Excellent at washing dishes, this quiet dishwasher (made by Bosch) has a stainless-steel tub, but it's pricey. It has a manual-clean filter rather than the more common self-cleaning type. Uses roughly 7 gallons of water in the normal cycle, about average. Stainless-steel finish available at a higher price. Similar model: Elite 1730.

6 KITCHENAID KUDP02CR[WH] Pricey. Excellent at washing dishes. Stainless-steel tub. Quiet. Uses roughly 7 gallons of water in the normal cycle, about average. Has an adjustable top rack, which makes it easier to fit tall items. Stainless-steel finish available at a higher price. Similar models: KUDP02IR, KUDP02SR.

7 KENMORE (SEARS) Elite 1376[2] This model was excellent at washing dishes and very quiet. It is among the most flexible for loading. It has a stainless-steel tub and an adjustable top rack that makes it easier to fit tall items. It uses less water than most, about 6 gallons in the normal cycle. Stainless-steel finish available at a higher price. Similar model: Elite 1386.

8 KITCHENAID Superba KUDS02SR[WH] Pricey. Excellent at washing dishes. Has partly hidden controls. Stainless-steel tub. Quiet. Uses roughly 7 gallons of water in the normal cycle, about average. Has an adjustable top rack, which makes it easier to fit tall items. Stainless-steel finish available at a higher price. Has a special zone for tough soil. Similar model: Superba KUDS02FR.

9 ASKO Encore D3531XLHD[SS] Pricey, and Asko has been among the most repair-prone brands. It is very good at washing dishes and is very quiet. It is equipped with a manual-clean filter rather than the more common self-cleaning type, and has hidden controls and a stainless-steel tub.

Recommendations

Its normal cycle time is long. Uses less water than most, roughly 3 gallons in the normal cycle.

10 LG LDF7810[WW] Excellent at washing dishes. It is among the most flexible for loading. It has a stainless-steel tub and an adjustable top rack that makes it easier to fit tall items. Uses less water than most, about 5 gallons in the normal cycle. Stainless-steel finish available at a higher price.

11 MAYTAG MDB4651AW[W] **A CR Best Buy** Excellent at washing dishes. A little noisy. Uses roughly 7 gallons of water in normal cycle, about average. Stainless-steel finish available at a higher price.

12 MIELE G894SCi Quiet and excellent at washing dishes, but among the highest-priced. Has a stainless-steel tub. Uses about 6 gallons of water in the normal cycle. Long cycle time. Top rack can be adjusted, which makes it easier to fit tall items. Stainless-steel finish available at a higher price. Similar model: G694SCi.

13 WHIRLPOOL DU1055XTP[Q] Excellent at washing dishes. A little noisy. Uses less water than most, roughly 5 gallons in the normal cycle. Stainless-steel finish available at a higher price.

14 WHIRLPOOL DU1100XTP[Q] **A CR Best Buy** Quiet and excellent at washing dishes, a top choice for consumers seeking competence and value. Uses less water than most, about 6 gallons in the normal cycle. Stainless-steel finish available at a higher price. Similar models: DU1145XTP, DU1148XTP, DUL240XTP.

15 WHIRLPOOL Gold GU2400XTP[Q] Quiet and excellent at washing dishes. Has an adjustable top rack, which makes it easier to fit tall items. Uses roughly 7 gallons of water in the normal cycle, about average. Stainless-steel finish available at a higher price. Similar models: Gold GU2500XTP, Gold GU2548XTP, Gold GU2600XTP.

16 ASKO D3122XL Pricey, and Asko has been among the most repair-prone brands. Excellent at washing dishes. Has partly hidden controls. Stainless-steel tub. Has a manual-clean filter rather than the more common self-cleaning type. A little noisy. Uses less water than most, roughly 6 gallons in the normal cycle. Stainless-steel finish available at a higher price.

17 KITCHENAID Architect KUDU02FR[WH] Pricey. Excellent at washing dishes. It is among the most flexible for loading and has hidden controls and a stainless-steel tub. Uses less water than most, roughly 5 gallons in the normal cycle. Stainless-steel finish available at a higher price.

18 KITCHENAID KUDI02IR[WH] Excellent at washing dishes. Stainless-steel tub. Quiet. Uses roughly 7 gallons of water in the normal cycle, about average. Stainless-steel finish available at a higher price. Similar models: KUDI02CR, KUDI02FR.

19 LG LDS5811[W] Excellent at washing dishes. Stainless-steel tub. Very quiet. Uses more water than most, about 9 gallons in the normal cycle. Normal cycle time is long. Has an adjustable top rack, which makes it easier to fit tall items. Stainless-steel finish available at a higher price.

20 GE GLD4300L[WW] Low-priced. Excellent at washing dishes. A little noisy. Uses less water than most, roughly 6 gallons in the normal cycle. Stainless-steel finish available at a higher price. Similar model: GLD4100L.

Recommendations

21 GE GLD6200L[WW] Excellent at washing dishes. Quiet. Uses roughly 7 gallons of water in the normal cycle, about average. Stainless-steel finish available at a higher price. Similar models: GLD6300L, GLD6500L.

22 ADMIRAL DDB1501AW[W] (Home Depot) Low-priced. Excellent at washing dishes. A little noisy. Uses roughly 8 gallons of water in the normal cycle, about average. Stainless-steel finish available at a higher price.

23 AMANA ADB1500AW[W] **A CR Best Buy** Excellent at washing dishes. A little noisy. Uses roughly 8 gallons of water in the normal cycle, about average. Stainless-steel finish available at a higher price.

24 GE GLD5800L[WW] Excellent at washing dishes. A little noisy. Uses less water than most, roughly 6 gallons in the normal cycle. Stainless-steel finish available at a higher price.

25 FISHER & PAYKEL DD603[W] Excellent at washing dishes but pricey, and Fisher & Paykel has been the most repair-prone brand. This uniquely styled model has two drawers that can be used together or separately. It has partly hidden controls and a manual-clean filter. Uses roughly 8 gallons of water in the normal cycle, about average. No heated-dry option. Stainless-steel finish available at a higher price.

26 MAYTAG MDB8951AW[W] Excellent at washing dishes but a little noisy. Among the most flexible for loading, it has hidden controls, a stainless-steel tub, and an adjustable top rack that makes it easier to fit tall items. It uses roughly 8 gallons of water in the normal cycle, about average. Stainless-steel finish available at a higher price.

27 MIELE Advanta G2020SC Excellent at washing dishes but a little noisy. It has a stainless-steel tub and an adjustable top rack that makes it easier to fit tall items. Uses roughly 6 gallons of water in the normal cycle, less than most.

28 GE MONOGRAM ZBD0710K[SS] Pricey. Very good at washing dishes. Has hidden controls and a stainless-steel tub. A little noisy. Uses roughly 7 gallons of water in the normal cycle, about average. Has a stainless-steel finish. Similar model: Monogram ZBD0700K.

29 GE PROFILE PDW9800L[WW] Pricey. Very good at washing dishes. Has hidden controls and a stainless-steel tub. Quiet. Uses roughly 7 gallons of water in the normal cycle, about average. Stainless-steel finish available at a higher price.

30 MAYTAG MDB5601AW[W] Excellent at washing dishes. It uses roughly 9 gallons of water in the normal cycle, more than most. Stainless-steel finish available at a higher price.

31 MAYTAG MDB6601AW[W] Excellent at washing dishes but a little noisy. It has an adjustable top rack that makes it easier to fit tall items. It uses roughly 9 gallons of water in the normal cycle, more than most. Stainless-steel finish available at a higher price.

32 MAYTAG MDB7601AW[W] Excellent at washing dishes. Has partly hidden controls. Quiet. Uses more energy than most. Uses more water than most, about 10 gallons in the normal cycle. Has an adjustable top rack, which makes it easier to fit tall items. Stainless-steel finish available at a higher price.

33 WHIRLPOOL DU945PWP[Q] Excellent at washing dishes and low-priced, but noisy and not the best choice if you want maximum loading flexibility. Uses more water than most, about 9 gallons of water in the normal cycle. Has an adjustable top rack, which makes it easier to fit tall items. Stainless-steel finish available at a higher price. Similar models: DU930PWP, DU948PWP, DUL140PP.

34 MAYTAG MDB9601AW[W] Excellent at washing dishes but a little noisy. It uses more water than most, about 10 gallons in the normal cycle. Stainless-steel finish available at a higher price.

35 JENN-AIR JDB2150AWP This pricey pro-style model has a stainless-steel finish and tub and was excellent at washing dishes, but it's a little noisy. Uses more energy and water than most, about 12 gallons in the normal cycle. Cycle time is longer than most.

36 MAYTAG MDB8751AW[W] Excellent at washing dishes. Has partly hidden controls. Stainless-steel tub. A little noisy. Uses more energy than most. Uses more water than most, about 10 gallons in the normal cycle. Stainless-steel finish available at a higher price.

37 FRIGIDAIRE Gallery GLD2440RE[S] Low-priced. Very good at washing dishes. A little noisy. Uses roughly 8 gallons of water in the normal cycle, about average. Stainless-steel finish available at a higher price.

38 FRIGIDAIRE FDB2410LD[S] Very good at washing dishes. Noisy. Uses roughly 7 gallons of water in the normal cycle, about average. Stainless-steel finish available at a higher price.

39 GE Profile PDW9900L[WW] Pricey, and rates only good at washing dishes. It has hidden controls and a stainless-steel tub.

Among the most flexible for loading. Uses roughly 7 gallons of water in the normal cycle, about average. Stainless-steel finish available at a higher price.

40 KITCHENAID Architect KUDD01DP[WH] Pricey, and rates only very good at washing dishes as well as a little noisy. It has partly hidden controls. Uses roughly 8 gallons of water in the normal cycle, about average. Stainless-steel finish available at a higher price.

41 HOTPOINT HDA3700G[WW] This basic, low-priced machine was very good at washing dishes but noisy. Uses roughly 7 gallons of water in the normal cycle, about average. Cycle time is shorter than most.

42 WHIRLPOOL DU850SWP[Q] Low-priced but just OK at washing dishes and a little noisy. You can get better performance for not much more money. Uses less water than most, about 6 gallons in the normal cycle. Cycle time is shorter than most. Stainless-steel finish available at a higher price.

43 HAIER ESD200 Low-priced for a model with a stainless-steel tub but only fair at washing dishes and a little noisy. You can get better performance for the same price or less. Uses less energy and water than most, about 4 gallons in the normal cycle. Cycle time is shorter than most. Has an adjustable top rack, which makes it easier to fit tall items.

44 FRIGIDAIRE FDB1250RE[S] Low-priced. Two tested samples had poor washing performance; a third had improved performance. A little noisy. Uses less water than most, roughly 6 gallons in the normal cycle. Stainless-steel finish available at a higher price.

Brand Repair History

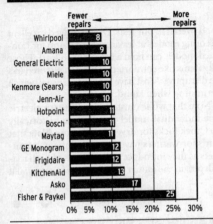

Fewer repairs ← → More repairs

Whirlpool	8
Amana	9
General Electric	10
Miele	10
Kenmore (Sears)	10
Jenn-Air	10
Hotpoint	11
Bosch	11
Maytag	11
GE Monogram	12
Frigidaire	12
KitchenAid	13
Asko	17
Fisher & Paykel	25

0% 5% 10% 15% 20% 25% 30%

Readers report on 110,000 dishwashers

The graph at left shows the percentage of these brands of dishwashers bought new between 2001 and 2005 that were ever repaired or had a serious problem. Differences of less than 4 points are not meaningful. While dishwashers are relatively reliable as a category, our data show that Asko and especially Fisher & Paykel have been the most repair-prone of those 14 brands. Remember that models within a brand may vary, and changes in design or manufacture may affect reliability. Still, choosing a reliable brand can minimize the likelihood of problems.

Data are based on readers responses about dishwashers to the Annual Product Reliability Survey conducted by the Consumer Reports National Research Center. Data are adjusted to eliminate differences linked to age and usage.

DRYERS

Most of these dryers scored at least a very good overall in our tests. Dryers judged excellent for drying were noticeably better than lower-scoring models at leaving a load damp for ironing and at drying delicates at low heat. All tested models can hold a typical wash load. Those judged excellent for capacity are best for bulky items like comforters. Those that scored less than excellent or very good for noise could be disruptive. Most have moisture sensors, which have proven better than thermostats at determining when laundry is dry.

Our Ratings rank dryers by overall score. Note that while our test scores are for electric dryers, equivalent gas models (listed on the individual model pages) have historically performed similarly in our tests. We have no Quick Picks for dryers at this time. Note that tougher new 2007 energy-efficiency standards for washers have prompted many manufacturers to discontinue previously tested dryers as they introduce new versions of both machines. You'll find additional test results for dryers in the January 2007 issue of CONSUMER REPORTS.

Within types, in performance order.

	Excellent	Very good	Good	Fair	Poor
	◓	◒	○	◒	●

Key number	Brand & model	Price	Overall score 0–100 (P F G VG E)	Drying performance	Capacity	Noise	Stainless-steel drum	Porcelain top	Removeable drying rack	Custom programs
1	**GE** Profile Harmony DPGT750EC[WW]	$800	84	◒	◒	◒	•		•	•
2	**LG** DLE5977[W]	850	84	◒	◒	◒	•	•	•	•
3	**Maytag** Neptune MCE8000AY[W]	1000	83	◒	◒	◒			•	
4	**Kenmore** (Sears) Elite Oasis 6706[2] Elite Oasis 7706[ ] $960, Elite Oasis 7707[ ] $1060, Elite Oasis 6707[ ] $1000	900	82	◒	◒	◒			•	
5	**Maytag** Neptune MDE9700AY[WW]	800	81	◒	◒	◒	•		•	
6	**Whirlpool** Duet GEW9250P[W]	800	81	◒	◒	◒			•	
7	**GE** DBVH512EF[WW] DBVH512GE[ ] $700, Adora DHDVH52GF[ ] (Home Depot) $680, Adora DHDVH52EF[ ] (Home Depot) $630	650	80	◒	◒	◒			•	
8	**KitchenAid** Superba Ensemble KEHS02R[MT] Superba Ensemble KGHS20R[ ] $1110	1050	80	◒	◒	◒			•	
9	**Maytag** Neptune MDE7500AY[W] Neptune MDG7500A[ ] $870	800	75	◒	◒	○		•		•
10	**Amana** NDE8805AY[W] NDG8805A[ ] $500	430	74	◒	◒	◒	•		•	
11	**Maytag** MDE4806AY[W] MDG4806A[ ] $450	400	74	◒	◒	◒				
12	**LG** DL-E2514[W] DL-G2524[ ] $650	600	70	◒	◒	◒			•	
13	**Frigidaire** LEQ2152E[S] (Lowes) GLEQ2152E[ ] $670, GLGQ2152E[ ] $660, LGQ2152E[ ] (Lowes) $650	600	68	◒	◒	◒			•	

Key number	Brand & model Small type: similar model(s)	Price	Overall score 0 ... 100 P F G VG E	Drying performance	Capacity	Noise	Stainless-steel drum	Porcelain top	Removeable drying rack	Custom programs
14	**Estate** by Whirlpool TEDS840J[Q] TEDS740P[ ] $370	$370	62	○	⊜	○				
15	**Admiral** ADE7005A[W] (Home Depot) ADG7005A[ ] $400	350	56	○	⊜	○			●	
16	**Speed Queen** CES68AWF[W] CGS68AWF[ ] $650	600	46	◐	⊜	○		●		

See report, page 55. Based on tests posted on ConsumerReports.org in June 2006, with updated prices and availability.

Guide to the Ratings

Overall score is based primarily on drying performance, drum volume and noise. **Drying performance** combines performance on four types of laundry loads of different sizes and fabric mixes: A 12-lb. load, predominantly cotton, representing a family's large weekly load; an 8-lb. load of all-cotton items; an 8-lb. load of cotton/polyester blends; and a 3-lb. load of synthetic delicates, women's pajamas, nightgowns, bras and underwear. **Capacity** measures drum volume, which varied from about 5 cu. ft. to 7.5 cu. ft. **Noise** score was determined by a panel of judges who listened while machines dried an 8-lb. load, measuring sound quality and volume. **Price** is approximate retail.

Brand Repair History

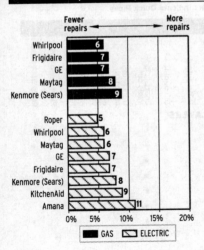

Fewer repairs ← → More repairs

Whirlpool	6
Frigidaire	7
GE	7
Maytag	8
Kenmore (Sears)	9
Roper	5
Whirlpool	6
Maytag	6
GE	7
Frigidaire	7
Kenmore (Sears)	8
KitchenAid	9
Amana	11

0%   5%   10%   15%   20%

■ GAS   ▨ ELECTRIC

Readers report on 94,050 dryers

The graph shows the percentage of these brands of dryers bought new between 2001 and 2005 that were ever repaired or had a serious problem. Differences of less than 3 points aren't meaningful. Amana was among the more repair-prone electric-dryer brands. Models within a brand may vary, however, and changes in design or manufacture may affect reliability. Still, choosing a reliable dryer brand can improve your odds of getting a reliable model.

Data are based on readers responses about clothes dryers to the Annual Product Reliability Survey conducted by the Consumer Reports National Research Center. Data are adjusted to eliminate differences linked to age and usage.

DVD PLAYERS

Excellent picture quality is a hallmark of DVD players. For typical use with a conventional (as in standard-definition) TV, most people can safely purchase by disc capacity, features, price, and brand reliability. The Ratings cover a representative sample of players from major brands, selected for value and a wide diversity of features and capabilities. We've listed models in the Ratings chart below not by overall performance but by price within types.

If you're buying a player for use with a high-definition or enhanced-definition TV, you should be choosier. You can use any DVD player with your HDTV. But as our Quick Picks reflect, some players are better than others at smoothing moving images on an HDTV. (On HD sets, DVD images appear in an enhanced-definition mode, known technically as "480p" for 480 lines using progressive-scan formatting. It looks better than conventional TV but falls a little short of true high-definition resolution.)

If you want to connect your DVD player to a digital receiver to get surround sound from a multispeaker setup, check that its outputs (as noted in the chart) match those of your audio receiver. Also, if you own an HDTV that has digital video input (HDMI or DVI), note that some models have a matching output. Our tests, however, found that a digital-video connection does not necessarily provide better picture quality than one between the component-video input of any HDTV and the matching output found on almost any DVD player or recorder.

	Excellent	Very good	Good	Fair	Poor
	⊖	⊖	○	◑	●

Within types, in performance order. Gray key numbers indicate Quick Picks.

Key number	Brand & model	Price	Well-suited for HDTVs	Plays DVD-audio discs	Plays SACD discs	HDMI output	DVI output	Coaxial digital audio out	Optical digital audio out	Six-channel decoder	Reads JPEG image files	Plays video CDs	Plays WMA-audio files
PROGRESSIVE-SCAN, SINGLE-DISC PLAYERS
1	**Toshiba** SD-3960	$50	•					•			•	•	•
2	**Toshiba** SD-3980	50	•					•			•	•	•
3	**Philips** DVP3500/37	60						•			•	•	
4	**JVC** XV-N310B	65	•					•			•		•
5	**Panasonic** DVD-S27	65	•					•			•	•	•
6	**Philips** DVP642	65						•	•		•	•	•
7	**Samsung** P241	65	•					•			•		•
8	**Kenwood** DVF-8100	70	•					•	•		•	•	•
9	**Panasonic** DVD-S29	70	•					•			•	•	•

Within types, in performance order. Gray key numbers indicate Quick Picks.

PROGRESSIVE-SCAN, SINGLE-DISC PLAYERS continued

Key number	Brand & model	Price	Well-suited for HDTVs	Plays DVD-audio discs	Plays SACD discs	HDMI output	DVI output	Coaxial digital audio out	Optical digital audio out	Six-channel decoder	Reads JPEG image files	Plays video CDs	Plays WMA-audio files
10	RCA DRC246N	70						•	•		•	•	•
11	JVC XV-N410B	75	•					•	•		•	•	
12	Sony DVP-NS50P	75	•					•			•	•	
13	JVC XV-N420B	80						•			•	•	•
14	RCA DRC240N	85	•					•	•		•	•	•
15	Kenwood Fineline DVF-3250	90	•					•	•		•		
16	Pioneer DV-578A	100	•	•	•			•	•		•	•	•
17	Samsung P341	100	•					•	•		•		
18	Pioneer DV-588A-S	120	•	•	•			•	•		•	•	•
19	JVC XV-N510B	$125	•	•				•	•		•	•	•
20	Toshiba SD-4960	125		•	•			•	•		•	•	•
21	Denon DVD-1710	130						•	•		•	•	•
22	Denon DVD-1720	130	•					•	•		•	•	•
23	Sony DVP-NS70H	135	•			•		•	•		•	•	
24	Toshiba SD-5980	140	•			•		•	•		•	•	•
25	Samsung DVD-HD841	145		•	•		•	•	•		•	•	•
26	Samsung DVD-HD850	145				•		•	•		•	•	•
27	Toshiba SD-5970	145	•			•		•	•		•	•	•
28	Toshiba SD-6980	170	•	•	•	•		•	•	•	•	•	•
29	LG LDA-511	175		•		•		•	•		•	•	•
30	Harman Kardon DVD 22	185						•	•		•	•	•
31	Samsung DVD-HD950	195		•	•	•		•	•		•	•	•
32	Panasonic DVD-S77	220	•	•				•	•		•	•	•
33	Yamaha DV-S5860SL	230	•	•	•			•	•		•	•	•
34	Onkyo DV-SP502	280	•	•	•			•	•		•	•	•
35	Denon DVD-1920	300	•	•	•			•	•		•	•	•
36	Yamaha DVD-S1500	310	•	•	•			•	•		•	•	

PROGRESSIVE-SCAN, MULTIDISC PLAYERS

Key number	Brand & model	Price	Well-suited for HDTVs	Plays DVD-audio discs	Plays SACD discs	HDMI output	DVI output	Coaxial digital audio out	Optical digital audio out	Six-channel decoder	Reads JPEG image files	Plays video CDs	Plays WMA-audio files
37	Toshiba SD-5915	90	•					•			•	•	•

Key number	Brand & model	Price	Well-suited for HDTVs	Plays DVD-audio discs	Plays SACD discs	HDMI output	DVI output	Coaxial digital audio out	Optical digital audio out	Six-channel decoder	Reads JPEG image files	Plays video CDs	Plays WMA-audio files
PROGRESSIVE-SCAN, MULTIDISC PLAYERS *continued*													
38	**Toshiba** SD-6915	100		•	•			•	•	•	•		•
39	**Panasonic** DVD-F86	110		•				•			•	•	•
40	**Panasonic** DVD-F87	115	•	•				•			•	•	•
41	**Sony** DVP-NC80V	125	•		•			•	•	•	•	•	
42	**Sony** DVP-CX995V	310			•	•		•	•	•	•	•	
43	**Onkyo** DV-CP802	410	•	•	•			•	•	•	•	•	

See report, page 25. Based on tests posted on ConsumerReports.org in March 2006, with updated prices and availability.

Guide to the Ratings

Features are important attributes that might affect your buying decision, such as whether a model is **well-suited for HDTVs.** Features for players indicate whether it plays **DVD-audio** or **SACD discs;** which have **HDMI output** or **DVI output;** and which inputs/outputs have **coaxial digital audio out** or **optical digital audio out.** We also note other features, such as **six-channel decoder,** whether the player reads **JPEG image files,** plays **video CDs,** and plays **WMA-audio files. Price** is approximate retail.

Quick Picks

For use with a standard-definition TV:
You could simply start with the lowest-priced models at the top of the category that best meets your needs, and work down to find a player with the features you want.

For use with a high-definition TV:
For widest selection and best value, most HDTV owners should choose among the many models we've identified in the chart column entitled "Well-suited for HDTVs." In our tests, those players yielded a smoother enhanced-definition (480p) picture with all DVDs. If you often play discs whose content was shot on video cameras, including DVDs of many TV programs and concert videos, consider narrowing your choice to a subset of those models that smoothed video-based

content more than others. Those players, listed from least to most expensive, are the Toshiba SD-3960, $50 (a bargain that's discontinued and may be hard to find); Toshiba SD-5970, $145; Panasonic DVD-S77, $220; and Yamaha DVD-S1500, $310 (also an older and scarce model.)

For a player that can accept a wide range of disc types:
All the players can play audio CDs, including CD-R or CD-RW discs (including those that carry MP3 files). If you expect to use other disc types, check the Ratings chart. Expect to pay a premium for players that can handle high-resolution audio formats such as DVD-Audio and Super Audio CD.

GAS GRILLS

Expect to spend between $200 and $500 for a grill that can handle most of your cooking needs. Spending more may get you more stainless styling and a few additional convenience features, but not necessarily better performance.

While most grills flare up momentarily when loaded with fatty foods, the key is whether they keep burning. Tested models that flared up more than others include Napoleon Ultra Chef UP405RBPSS, Ducane Standard Series 1605SHLPE, Jenn-Air 720-0163 (Lowe's), Ducane Standard Series 1305SHLPE, George Foreman GBQ440, Kirkland Signature (Costco) [Item 963157] 720-0193, Frigidaire Gallery GL30LKEC, Kenmore (Sears) 16329, Viking T Series VGBQ300-2RTL, Coleman Back Home Select 6000 994-7A726, and BBQ Grillware 720-0001 (Lowe's).

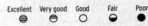

	Excellent	Very good	Good	Fair	Poor
	⊖	⊖	○	⊖	●

Within types, in performance order. Gray key numbers indicate Quick Picks.

Key number	Brand & model	Price	Overall score	Test results			Features				
	Small type: Similar model(s)		0 · · 100 P F G VG E	Evenness	Grilling	Convenience	Stainless-steel grates	Coated cast-iron grates	All or mostly stainless	Long-warranty burners	Side burner
	MEDIUM-SIZED MODELS										
1	**Vermont Castings** VM400XBP (Home Depot) **CR Best Buy**	$400	84	⊖	⊖	⊖		•			
2	**Broilmaster** P3[BL]	1000	83	⊖	⊖	⊖		•		•	
3	**Kenmore** (Sears) 16324	450	82	⊖	⊖	⊖			•	•	•
4	**Vermont Castings** VM450SSP (Home Depot)	630	82	⊖	⊖	⊖		•		•	•
5	**Weber** Genesis Silver B 6221411 (Home Depot) 🔟 Genesis Silver B 6721411 (Home Depot) $450	450	79	⊖	⊖	⊖		•		•	
6	**Fiesta** Optima Pro Series EZD555-B428 [Item # 209647] (Home Depot)	165	78	⊖	○	○		•			•
7	**TEC** Patio II	1500	78	⊖	⊖	⊖	•		•	•	
8	**Thermos** Stainless 461262006 (Target) **CR Best Buy**	300	77	⊖	⊖	⊖		•		•	•
9	**BBQ Grillware** GSF-2616 (Lowe's) **CR Best Buy**	200	76	⊖	⊖	⊖		•		•	•
10	**Kenmore** (Sears) 16211	200	75	⊖	⊖	⊖					•
11	**Napoleon** Ultra Chef UP405RBPSS	550	75	⊖	⊖	⊖				•	
12	**Ducane** Standard Series 1605SHLPE	750	74	⊖	⊖	⊖	•			•	
13	**Modern Home Products** WNK4P-OCOL	900	73	⊖	⊖	⊖	•			•	•

Within types, in performance order. Gray **key numbers indicate Quick Picks.**

Key number	Brand & model / Small type: Similar model(s)	Price	Overall score (0–100)	Evenness	Grilling	Convenience	Stainless-steel grates	Coated cast-iron grates	All or mostly stainless	Long-warranty burners	Side burner
MEDIUM-SIZED MODELS *continued*											
14	**Weber** Summit Gold B4 5720001 Summit Gold A4 5710001 $1000,Summit Gold D4 5740001 $1400	$1100	72	⊖	⊖	⊖				•	•
15	**Charmglow** 720-0036-HD-05 [sku #573005] (Home Depot)	350	71	⊖	⊖	⊖			•		•
16	**Holland** Tradition BH421SG4 ▣ Heritage BH421SG5 $480	675	71	⊖	○	○	•			•	
17	**Jenn-Air** 720-0163 (Lowe's)	700	71	⊖	⊖	⊖	•				•
18	**Char-Broil** Commercial Series 463268706 (Lowe's)	400	69	○	⊖	⊖		•	•	•	•
19	**Ducane** Standard Series 1305SHLPE	650	69	⊖	⊖	⊖	•			•	
20	**Brinkmann** Pro Series 6330 810-6330-W (Walmart) Pro Series 810-6345-0 (Target) $200	200	68	○	⊖	⊖		•	•	•	•
21	**George Foreman** GBQ440	450	64	⊖	⊖	⊖		•	•	•	•
22	**Kirkland Signature** (Costco) [Item 963157] 720-0193	800	64	⊖	●	⊖	•		•	•	•
23	**Ducane** Stainless Steel 24 30400040 (Home Depot)	700	60	○	⊖	⊖	•		•	•	
24	**Frigidaire** Gallery GL30LKEC	1100	58	○	⊖	⊖	•		•		•
25	**Superb** by BroilMaster 200 Series SBG200	700	58	○	⊖	⊖		•		•	
26	**Kenmore** (Sears) Quantum Series 16234	250	41	○	○	○					
27	**BBQ** Pro Deluxe 24" [item #116396] (K-Mart)	350	37	●	○	⊖		•	•	•	•
LARGE MODELS											
28	**Great Outdoors** Pinnacle TG-560 **CR Best Buy**	500	85	⊖	⊖	⊖	•		•	•	•
29	**Kenmore** (Sears) 16329	800	77	⊖	○	⊖	•		•	•	•
30	**Viking** T Series VGBQ300-2RTL	3200	76	⊖	⊖	⊖	•		•		
31	**Weber** Summit Gold D6 5790001 Summit Gold D6 5890001 $1650	1800	71	⊖	⊖	⊖	•		•	•	•
32	**Brinkmann** Pro Series 4400 810-4400-0 (Walmart) **CR Best Buy**	300	69	○	⊖	⊖		•	•		•
33	**Aussie** Bonza 4 7462 Bonza Deluxe 4 7462 $500	500	68	⊖	⊖	⊖		•	•		
34	**Igloo** BB10514A (Walmart)	380	64	○	⊖	⊖	•	•	•	•	•

	Excellent	Very good	Good	Fair	Poor
	⊖	⊖	○	⊖	●

Key number	Brand & model / Small type: Similar model(s)	Price	Overall score	Evenness	Grilling	Convenience	Stainless-steel grates	Coated cast-iron grates	All or mostly stainless	Long-warranty burners	Side burner
LARGE MODELS *continued*											
35	**Coleman** Back Home Select 6000 994-7A726	$720	58	○	○	⊖	●		●	●	●
36	**Perfect Flame** SLG-2006C (Lowe's)	400	58	○	⊖	⊖		●	●	●	●
37	**Jenn-Air** 720-165 [Item # 30082] (Lowe's)	1300	48	⊖	⊖	⊖	●		●	●	●
SMALL MODELS											
38	**Weber** Genesis Silver A 6711001	400	68	⊖	⊖	⊖				●	
39	**Char-Broil** Quickset 463631705 (Wal-Mart)	130	66	⊖	⊖	○					
40	**Fiesta** Advantis 1000 EZA30030	135	63	⊖	⊖	⊖					
41	**Char-Broil** Quickset Traditional 463731706 (Walmart) Quickset Traditional 463761606 (K-Mart) $150	140	59	○	⊖	○					●
42	**Aussie** Bushman Elite 7720 Bondi II Deluxe 7820 $130, Bushman Deluxe 7710 $130	130	49	○	⊖	○					●
PORTABLE MODELS											
43	**Weber** Q 396001	180	82	⊖	⊖	⊖		●			
44	**Weber** Baby Q 386001	130	58	○	○	○		●			
45	**BBQ Grillware** 720-0001 (Lowe's)	100	54	⊖	○	○	●				

D Discontinued, but similar model is available.
See report, page 90. Based on tests posted on ConsumerReports.org in June 2006, with updated prices and availability.

Guide to the Ratings

Overall score is based on performance, features, and convenience. We tested **evenness** of heating over the grill's surface at high and low settings using thermocouples, then combined the scores. Results were verified by searing 15 burgers on the worst and best grills' high settings for 1½ minutes. **Grilling** measures each model's ability to cook chicken and fish on a low setting. **Convenience** evaluates construction and materials, useful accessory burners and shelves, rack space, and ease of use, as well as propensity for flare-ups. **Price** is approximate retail.

Best for most; high-scoring midsized grills; all are CR Best Buys:

1 Vermont Castings VM400XBP (Home Depot), $400

8 Thermos Stainless 461262006 (Target), $300

9 BBQ Grillware GSF-2616 (Lowe's), $200

Top performance makes the Vermont Castings VM400XBP (Home Depot) a fine choice. Consider the Thermos Stainless 461262006 (Target) for its mostly stainless construction, fourth burner, and generous cooking area and shelf space, and the BBQ Grillware GSF-2616 (Lowe's) for its fine searing, long-warranty burners, and low price.

If you often cook for a crowd; both are CR Best Buys:

28 Great Outdoors Pinnacle TG-560, $500

32 Brinkmann Pro Series 4400 810-4400-0 (Wal-Mart), $300

Both deliver lots of cooking and shelf space for the money. The Great Outdoors Pinnacle TG-560 has mostly stainless construction, a fifth burner, and an infrared burner for better searing. The Brinkmann Pro Series 4400 810-4400-0 (Wal-Mart) trades stainless-steel styling and some performance for a much lower price that includes free assembly.

For smaller groups and tailgating:

43 Weber Q 396001, $180

The portable Weber Q 396001 offers better performance without sacrificing cooking space than many other small grills. You can take the grill off the cart for tailgating. Price is $265 with cart and adapter.

LAPTOPS

The Ratings rank models by performance and features. Quick Picks take into account not only performance but reliability, tech support, and value. All the major brands have had similar repair rates. Apple's tech support has been the best by far, followed by Lenovo (IBM).

All have FireWire ports except 3, 4, and 20. Fingerprint readers available on 2, 12, 16, 19, and 20. Built-in Webcam available on 5, 9, 11, 18, and 19. Remote control available on 5, 7, 11, 12, 13, 16, and 18.

Excellent	Very good	Good	Fair	Poor
⊖	⊖	○	⊖	●

Within types, in performance order. Gray key numbers indicate Quick Picks.

Key number	Brand & model	Processor	Price	Overall score (0–100)	Ergonomics	Display	Multimedia features	Speed	Speakers	Battery life (hr.)	Weight (lb.)	Memory-card slot	Built-in microphone
14.1-INCH BUDGET MODELS *Have 512MB of RAM, a 60GB to 80GB hard drive, and a CD-RW/DVD combo drive.*													
1	**Gateway** NX260X [1]	Core Duo T2050	$1,025	63	○	○	○	⊖	○	5½	5.8	•	
2	**Toshiba** Satellite M100	Core Duo T2300E	935	63	○	○	○	⊖	○	3¾	5.4		
3	**Dell** Inspiron E1405	Core Duo T2300E	830	57	⊖	○	○	⊖	○	5½	5.4		
4	**HP** Pavilion dv2000t / Compaq Presario V3000T	Core Duo T2050	940	55	⊖	○	⊖	⊖	○	3¼	5.5	•	•
5	**HP** Pavilion dv2000z / Compaq Presario V3000Z	Turion 64 X2 TL-52	1,010	53	⊖	○	⊖	⊖	○	2¾	5.5	•	•
15.4-INCH BUDGET MODELS *Same as above, but with a larger screen.*													
6	**Lenovo** 3000 N100 [2]	Core Duo T2300	950	53	○	○	○	⊖	○	3½	6.1	•	
7	**Dell** Inspiron B130 [2] **CR** **Best Buy**	Pentium M 735	560	51	○	○	○	○	⊖	2	6.6		
8	**Toshiba** Satellite A100	Celeron M 420	970	51	○	○	○	○	○	1¼	5.8		
15.4-INCH WORKHORSE MODELS *Have 1GB of RAM, an 80GB to 120GB hard drive, and a DVD burner.*													
9	**Apple** Macbook Pro 15" [2]	2.0GHz Core Duo	2,100	63	⊖	⊖	⊖	⊖	⊖	3¼	5.5		•
10	**Gateway** NX560XL	Core Duo T2500	1,510	59	○	⊖	⊖	⊖	⊖	4	6.5	•	•
11	**Dell** Inspiron E1505	Core Duo T2400	1,060	58	○	○	⊖	⊖	○	2½	6.6	•	•
12	**HP** Pavilion dv5000t / Compaq Presario V5000T	Core Duo T2400	1,060	58	○	○	⊖	⊖	○	3	6.8	•	•
13	**Lenovo** Thinkpad Z61m [2]	Core Duo T2500	1,665	58	○	⊖	⊖	⊖	⊖	2¾	7.0	•	•
14	**Sony** VAIO VGN-FE590G / VGN-FE690	Core Duo T2400	1,370	57	○	⊖	○	⊖	○	3	6.2	•	•
15	**HP** Pavilion dv6000z / Compaq Presario V6000Z	Turion 64 X2 TL-52	1,060	55	○	○	⊖	○	○	2¼	6.5	•	•
16	**HP** Pavilion dv5000z / Compaq Presario V5000Z	Turion 64 ML-37	955	53	○	○	○	○	○	2¼	6.7	•	

	Excellent	Very good	Good	Fair	Poor
	⊜	⊜	○	◐	●

Within types, in performance order. Gray key numbers indicate Quick Picks.

Key number	Brand & model	Processor	Price	Overall score (P F G VG E, 0–100)	Ergonomics	Display	Multimedia features	Speed	Speakers	Battery life (hr.)	Weight (lb.)	Memory-card slot	Built-in microphone
	17-INCH WORKHORSE MODELS *Same as above, but with a larger screen that makes these especially suitable as desktop replacements.*												
17	**Apple** Macbook Pro 17" [2]	2.16GHz Core Duo	2,800	70	Very good	Excellent	Very good	Very good	Very good	4	6.7		●
18	**Toshiba** Qosmio G35-AV600 [3]	Core Duo T2400	2,400	61	Good	Excellent	Excellent	Very good	Very good	2 3/4	10.0	●	●
19	**Dell** Inspiron E1705 [2]	Core Duo T2400	1,365	60	Very good	Good	Very good	Very good	Good	3 1/2	7.8		●
20	**HP** Pavilion dv8000t	Core Duo T2400	1,200	59	Very good	Good	Very good	Very good	Good	4 1/4	8.2		●
21	**Toshiba** Satellite P100	Core Duo T2400	1,335	57	Good	Good	Good	Very good	Good	1 3/4	7.4		●
22	**Gateway** NX860X [2]	Core Duo T2500	1,585	56	Good	Good	Good	Very good	Fair	2 3/4	7.9		
23	**Averatec** 7160-EC1	Turion 64 ML-32	1,100	35	Poor	Good	Good	Good	Poor	2 1/4	7.3		●
	12.1- TO 13.3-INCH SLIM AND LIGHT MODELS *Have 1GB of RAM, a 60GB to 80GB hard drive, and a CD-RW/DVD combo drive.*												
24	**Apple** Macbook 13.3"	Core Duo 1.83GHz	1,200	62	Good	Good	Very good	Very good	Poor	4	5.1		●
25	**Sony** VAIO VGN-SZ140 13.3" VGN-SZ240	Core Duo T2400	1,630	60	Good	Good	Very good	Very good	Fair	3 1/4	4.2		●
26	**Gateway** NX100X 12.1" [4]	Core Solo U1400	1,400	50	Fair	Good	Good	Good	Poor	2 3/4	3.2		●
27	**Toshiba** Portege R200 12.1" [5]	Pentium M 773	2,225	50	Fair	Good	Good	Good	Poor	4	2.8		
28	**Averatec** 2260-EY1 12.1" [4]	Turion 64 MT-32	1,000	43	Fair	Good	Good	Good	Good	2 1/2	4.2		●

[1] 1GB RAM. [2] Matte displays. [3] Has two 100GB hard drives. [4] DVD burner. [5] 512MB RAM.

Based on testing in Consumer Reports in November 2006.

Guide to the Ratings

Overall score is based on ergonomics, display quality, multimedia features, and other factors. **Ergonomics** represents the ease of using the keyboard, touchpad, and switches, as well as case design. **Display** covers screen quality, including clarity, contrast, and viewing angle. **Multimedia features** include hardware (memory-card slots and AV connections), and software (multimedia playback and editing programs). **Speed** measures performance while running office productivity and content creation applications. **Speakers** covers speaker fidelity, bass response, and loudness. **Battery life** is while running productivity applications. **Weight** includes optical drives and one battery (but no AC adapter). **Price** is approximate retail. All of the tested laptop models in the Ratings have Wi-Fi.

Quick Picks

Best inexpensive laptop:
  7 Dell $560, CR Best Buy
  great choice for a rudimentary laptop or a
  second PC.

Best if you want more features and performance in a laptop:
  1 Gateway $1,025
  2 Toshiba $935
  11 Dell $1,060
  12 HP $1,060

The Gateway and Toshiba were the best-performing budget systems in our tests. The Dell and HP machines performed equally well in the workhorse category, and both represent good values.

Best desktop replacements:
  17 Apple $2,800
  19 Dell $1,365
  20 HP $1,200

The Apple shines, with great design, display, and performance. The Dell's design and features were very good, while the HP is better for gaming.

Best lightweight laptop:
  25 Sony $1,630

Excellent performance and best features set of all the slim-and-light models. The Sony is a good choice for business travelers who want a lot of power in a very portable package.

Brand Repair History

Readers report on 127,800 computers.

These graphs show the percentage of the following brands of computers bought between 2002 and 2006 that have ever been repaired or had a serious problem. Differences of less than 4 points are not meaningful for desktops, less than 3 points for laptops. Models within a brand may vary, and changes in design or manufacture may affect reliability. Still, choosing a brand with a good repair history can improve your odds.

Desktops

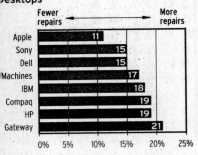

Laptops

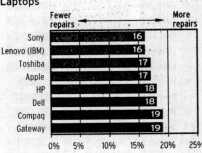

Data are based on more than 77,700 responses to our Annual Product Reliability Survey, conducted by the Consumer Reports National Research Center. Data have been adjusted to eliminate differences solely linked to the age and the usage of the product.

Data are based on more than 50,100 responses to our Annual Product Reliability Survey, conducted by the Consumer Reports National Research Center. Data have been adjusted to eliminate differences solely linked to the age and the usage of the product.

LAWN MOWERS

You needn't pay a premium for superb mowing. You'll find many capable, self-pro pelled, gasoline-powered mowers as brands like Craftsman, Honda, Lawn-Boy, and To create new designs with better decks and controls. The best of these mowers typically i clude easy mode changes and bag removal, and comfortable handlebars. For smaller lawn you'll find more top push mowers for less as retailers like Home Depot, Lowe's, and Sea compete for your business. Several capable models perform nearly as well as the best in th class for $200 or less.

	Excellent	Very good	Good	Fair	Po
	⊖	⊖	○	⊖	

Within types, in performance order. Gray key numbers indicate Quick Picks.

Key number	Brand & model	Price	Overall score (0–100)	Evenness	Mulching	Bagging	Side-discharging	Handling	Ease of use	Rear bag	Easy mode change	Deck size (in.)	Engine power (hp)
SELF-PROPELLED MOWERS
1	**Honda** HRX217HXA	$700	85	⊖	⊖	⊖	○	⊖	⊖	●	●	21	6.5
2	**Honda** HRR2163VXA	580	84	⊖	⊖	⊖	⊖	⊖	⊖	●	●	21	5.5
3	**Toro** Super Recycler 20055	520	84	⊖	⊖	⊖	⊖	⊖	⊖	●	●	21	Not stated
4	**John Deere** JX75	900	83	⊖	⊖	⊖	⊖	⊖	⊖	●	●	21	6.75
5	**Lawn-Boy** 10697	550	83	⊖	○	⊖	⊖	⊖	⊖	●	●	21	5.5
6	**Toro** Recycler 20070	400	80	⊖	○	⊖	⊖	⊖	⊖	●	●	22	6.5
7	**Lawn-Boy** 10685	380	79	⊖	○	⊖	⊖	⊖	⊖	●	●	21	6.5
8	**Lawn-Boy** 10695	460	79	⊖	○	⊖	⊖	⊖	⊖	●	●	21	5.5
9	**Honda** HRR2163TDA	480	75	⊖	⊖	⊖	⊖	⊖	⊖	●	●	21	5.5
10	**Lawn-Boy** 10684	340	75	⊖	○	⊖	⊖	⊖	⊖	●	●	21	6.5
11	**Husqvarna** 55R21HV	400	70	○	○	⊖	⊖	⊖	⊖	●	●	21	5.5
12	**John Deere** JS 20	400	66	⊖	○	○	⊖	⊖	⊖	●	●	21	6.75
13	**Husqvarna** 5521CHV	330	65	○	○	○	⊖	⊖	⊖	●	●	21	5.5
14	**Craftsman** (Sears) 37657	330	62	○	○	○	⊖	⊖	⊖	●	●	22	6.75
15	**Craftsman** (Sears) 37706	300	62	○	○	◑	⊖	⊖	⊖	●	●	21	6.5
16	**Troy-Bilt** 12AV834Q	350	61	○	○	○	⊖	⊖	⊖	●	●	21	5.5
17	**Toro** Recycler 20016	320	59	⊖	○	⊖	○	○	○	●	●	22	6.5
18	**Honda** Harmony II HRS216SDA	415	57	⊖	⊖	●	⊖	○	○		●	21	5.5
19	**Snapper** RP217018BV	550	54	○	○	⊖	○	○	○	●		21	7

Within types, in performance order. Gray **key numbers indicate Quick Picks.**

Key number	Brand & model	Price	Overall score (0–100, P F G VG E)	Evenness	Mulching	Bagging	Side-discharging	Handling	Ease of use	Rear bag	Easy mode change	Deck size (in.)	Engine power (hp)
	SELF-PROPELLED MOWERS *continued*												
20	**Craftsman** (Sears) 37071	$300	53	○	○	◐	○	⊖	○	•	•	21	6.5
21	**Craftsman** (Sears) 37605	250	53	○	○	◐	NA	○	○	•	•	22	6.75
22	**Yard-Man** 12A-5690	290	53	○	○	○	◐	○	○	•	•	21	5.5
23	**Yard-Man** 12A-26MB	215	51	○	○	NA	⊖	○	○		•	22	Not stated
	GAS-POWERED PUSH MODELS												
24	**Lawn-Boy** 10683	320	69	⊖	○	⊖	⊖	○	⊖	•	•	21	6.5
25	**Yard-Man** 11A-439Q **CR Best Buy**	200	61	○	○	○	○	⊖	○	•	•	21	5.5
26	**Craftsman** (Sears) 38885	230	59	○	⊖	◐	NA	⊖	○	•	•	21	6.5
27	**Bolens** 11A-414E	160	58	○	○	○	NA	⊖	○	•	•	21	4.5
28	**MTD** Pro 11A-588Q	200	58	○	○	○	NA	⊖	○	•	•	21	5.5
29	**Troy-Bilt** 11A-542Q	240	58	○	○	○	○	⊖	⊖	•	•	21	5.5
30	**Craftsman** (Sears) 38535	180	57	○	○	NA	○	⊖	○	•	•	22	6
31	**Craftsman** (Sears) 38895	200	57	○	○	◐	○	⊖	○	•	•	21	6.5
32	**Honda** Harmony II HRS216PDA	365	57	⊖	○	●	⊖	○	⊖			21	5.5
33	**Craftsman** (Sears) 38768	220	51	○	○	NA	○	○	○		•	22	6.5
	CORDED ELECTRIC PUSH MODELS												
34	**Black & Decker** MM875	230	48	⊖	○	●	○	○	⊖	•	•	19	12 amp
	CORDLESS ELECTRIC PUSH MODELS												
35	**Black & Decker** CMM 1000	430	61	○	⊖	●	⊖	○	⊖	•	•	19	24v

See report, page 95. Based on tests posted on ConsumerReports.org in June 2006, with updated prices and availability.

Guide to the Ratings

Overall score is based mainly on cutting performance, handling, and ease of use. **Evenness** shows cutting performance for two or three modes; scores notably better or worse in any mode are called out in the recommendations. **Mulching** reflects how completely the mower distributed the clippings over the lawn's surface. **Bagging** denotes how many clippings the bag held before it filled or the chute clogged. **Side-discharging** shows how evenly clippings were dispersed in this mode. **Handling** includes ease of operating the drive controls (for self-propelled), pushing and pulling, making U-turns, and maneuvering in tight spots. **Ease of use** measures ease of starting the engine, operating the blade-stopping controls, shifting speeds (for self-propelled), and adjusting the cutting height. Bag convenience and ease of changing modes are separate judgments that contribute to the overall score. **Price** is approximate retail.

Quick Picks

Best for most; versatile mowing:
  2 Honda HRR2163VXA, $580
  3 Toro Super Recycler 20055, $520
  6 Toro Recycler 20070, $400
  7 Lawn-Boy 10685, $380

Between the Honda and Toro Recycler, consider the Honda for its blade-brake clutch, the Toro for its electric start. Choose the Toro Super Recycler for its side-discharging, the Lawn-Boy if mulching is less of a priority.

For smaller, flatter lawns:
 24 Lawn-Boy 10683, $320
 25 Yard-Man 11A-439Q, $200,
     CR Best Buy

Between the gas Lawn-Boy and Yard-Man, paying more for the Lawn-Boy buys cleaner cutting. Lawn-Boy has been repair-prone for push mowers; we'll see whether a recent redesign changes that.

For greener choices, electric mowers that create no exhaust emissions:
 35 Black & Decker CMM 1000, $430
The cordless Black and Decker offers push-button starts and zero exhaust emissions, but it's pricey and provides limited run time per charge.

Recommendations

SELF-PROPELLED MOWERS

1 **HONDA** HRX217HXA Top performance and premium features, though pricey. A unique Versamow System allows partial bagging and mulching simultaneously. Has an infinitely variable hydrostatic transmission. Plastic deck.

2 **HONDA** HRR2163VXA Top performance and premium features at a reasonable price. Has a unique infinitely variable drive control system and tilt-up handlebar. Rear-mounted side-discharge attachment is $40 extra.

3 **TORO** Super Recycler 20055 A top-performing, well-rounded mower with a relatively long warranty. Aluminum deck. Five-year warranty.

4 **JOHN DEERE** JX75 Top performance and premium features, but pricey. Among the more repair-prone brands. Some key features cost extra. Blade-brake clutch. Aluminum deck.

5 **LAWN-BOY** 10697 Top performance and premium features at a reasonable price. Has unique, easy-to-use blade-brake clutch engagement and tilt-up handlebar.

Recommendations

Collection-bag interlock eliminates hinged inner flap.

6 TORO Recycler 20070 Fine performance and value. Has electric start. Similar model: Recycler 20017.

7 LAWN-BOY 10685 Fine performance and value with unique features. Has tilt-up handlebar. Collection-bag interlock eliminates hinged inner flap.

8 LAWN-BOY 10695 Fine performance with unique features. Has tilt-up handlebar. Collection-bag interlock eliminates the hinged inner flap.

9 HONDA HRR2163TDA Fine performance at a reasonable price. Rear-mounted side discharge attachment is $40 extra. Maximum cutting height is only 3".

10 LAWN-BOY 10684 Fine performance with unique features, but only one ground speed. Collection-bag interlock eliminates the hinged inner flap.

11 HUSQVARNA 55R21HV A fine choice if bagging is your mowing mode of choice.

12 JOHN DEERE JS 20 A fine choice for side-discharging, but among the more repair-prone brands. Has no-choke engine and fuel-preserving cap. Grass-collection bag is awkward to install.

13 HUSQVARNA 5521CHV A fine, relatively inexpensive mower, but basic. Only one ground speed. Front-drive makes this a dubious choice for steep slopes.

14 CRAFTSMAN (SEARS) 37657 A fine, relatively inexpensive choice. Has fuel-preserving cap.

15 CRAFTSMAN (SEARS) 37706 A good, inexpensive choice if bagging isn't a priority. Has fuel-preserving cap.

16 TROY-BILT 12AV834Q A good choice for bagging. Has no-choke engine.

17 TORO Recycler 20016 Good and relatively inexpensive, but front-drive makes this a dubious choice for steep slopes. Lap turns are difficult.

18 HONDA Harmony II HRS216SDA A good choice, provided bagging isn't a priority. Some attachments cost extra. Only one ground speed. Side bag. Bagging requires blade change.

19 SNAPPER RP217018BV A choice for bagging, but pricey and among the more repair-prone brands. Hard-to-use drive control. Discontinued, but similar model RP217017BV may still be available.

20 CRAFTSMAN (SEARS) 37071 A good choice, provided bagging isn't a priority.

21 CRAFTSMAN (SEARS) 37605 A good choice if mulching is your mowing mode of choice and bagging is not a priority. Does not side-discharge. Has no-choke engine and fuel-preserving cap.

22 YARD-MAN 12A-569Q A good choice if side-discharging is not a priority.

23 YARD-MAN 12A-26MB A good choice for mulching. Lacks a bagging mode.

GAS-POWERED PUSH MODELS

24 LAWN-BOY 10683 A top performer, but pricey for a push mower. Collection-bag interlock eliminates spring-loaded inner flap. While Lawn-Boy has been the most-repair-prone brand of push mowers, its mowers have been redesigned and are now built by Toro. We will monitor whether that affects Lawn-Boy's reliability.

25 YARD-MAN 11A-439Q **A CR Best Buy** A good, inexpensive choice. Uncomfortable handlebar grip.

Recommendations

26 CRAFTSMAN (SEARS) 38885 A good, inexpensive choice if bagging isn't a priority. Has fuel-preserving cap. Excessive play in handlebar. Uncomfortable handlebar grip.

27 BOLENS 11A-414E Inexpensive, but lacks a side-discharge mode—a potential problem in tall grass. Pushing and U-turns especially easy. Uncomfortable handlebar grip.

28 MTD Pro 11A-588Q Inexpensive, but lacks a side-discharge mode—a potential problem in tall grass. Uncomfortable handlebar grip. Available only at Sam's Club warehouse stores. Discontinued, but similar model Pro 11A-589B may be available.

29 TROY-BILT 11A-542Q A good, inexpensive choice.

30 CRAFTSMAN (SEARS) 38535 A good, inexpensive choice, but lacks a bagging mode. Has fuel-preserving cap. Excessive play in handlebar. Uncomfortable handlebar grip.

31 CRAFTSMAN (SEARS) 38895 A good, inexpensive choice if bagging isn't a priority. Has fuel-preserving cap. Excessive play in handlebar. Uncomfortable handlebar grip.

32 HONDA Harmony II HRS216PDA Top side-discharging performance, but you pay for it. Some attachments cost extra. Side bag. Bagging requires blade change.

33 CRAFTSMAN (SEARS) 38768 An unexceptional performer. Lacks a bagging mode. Excessive play in handlebar. Uncomfortable handlebar grip.

CORDED ELECTRIC PUSH MODELS
34 BLACK & DECKER MM87 A good corded electric choice for small properties where clippings are mostly mulched or side-discharged. Cord hard to keep out of the way while mowing.

CORDLESS ELECTRIC PUSH MODELS
35 BLACK & DECKER CMM 1000 A good, if pricey, cordless choice for small properties, provided bagging isn't a priority. Run time per battery charge is relatively short.

Brand Repair History

Readers report on nearly 62,000 lawn mowers

Self-propelled mowers continue to be more repair-prone than push types in our survey. The graphs show the percentage of these mower brands bought between 2000 and 2005 that have ever been repaired or had a serious problem. Differences of less than 4 points are not meaningful. John Deere and Snapper have been among the more repair-prone self-propelled mower brands. Lawn-Boy, historically the most repair-prone pushmower brand, has recently redesigned its mowers and now builds them in the same plant as Toro models. We will monitor whether that affects the brand's reliability. Models within a brand may vary, and changes in design or manufacture may affect reliability. Still, choosing a brand with a good repair history can improve your odds of getting a reliable model.

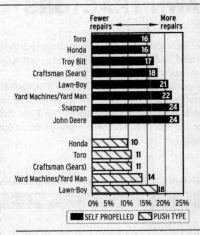

Data are based on reader responses about mowers to the Annual Product Reliability Survey conducted by the Consumer Reports National Research Center. Data are adjusted to eliminate differences linked solely to age and usage.

LAWN TRACTORS

All of these machines are at least adequate at side-discharging and mulching clippings. The best tend to distribute clippings more evenly, and add better bagging and easier handling for as little as $1,300.

Note that the tested Toro LX420 13AX60RH, Toro LX460 13AX60RG, and Troy-Bilt Super Bronco 13AX60TG tractors share the same design, parts, and manufacture with models from MTD's Cub Cadet, Yard Machines, and Yard-Man brands. While those three MTD brands have been repair-prone in our tractor surveys, we don't know about reliability for Toro and Troy-Bilt.

	Excellent	Very good	Good	Fair	Poor
	⊖	⊖	○	⊖	●

Within types, in performance order. Gray key numbers indicate Quick Picks.

Key number	Brand & model	Price	Overall score (0–100)	Evenness	Side-discharging	Mulching	Bagging	Handling	Ease of use	Deck size (in.)	Engine power (hp)
AUTOMATIC-DRIVE MODELS											
1	**John Deere** X304	$3500	84	⊖	⊖	⊖	⊖	⊖	⊖	42	17
2	**John Deere** 125 **CR Best Buy**	1800	76	⊖	⊖	○	⊖	⊖	⊖	42	20
3	**Craftsman** (Sears) 27690 **CR Best Buy**	2000	74	○	⊖	○	⊖	⊖	⊖	54	26
4	**Cub Cadet** LT1042 13AX11CG	1600	72	○	⊖	○	⊖	⊖	⊖	42	19
5	**Simplicity** Regent 16hp 44"	2800	71	○	○	⊖	⊖	⊖	⊖	44	16
6	**Toro** Wheel Horse 16-38 HXL	2200	71	○	○	⊖	○	⊖	⊖	38	16
7	**Toro** LX420 13AX60RH	1300	69	○	○	⊖	⊖	⊖	⊖	42	18
8	**John Deere** 155C145 $2300	2600	68	○	○	⊖	○	⊖	⊖	48	25
9	**Troy-Bilt** Super Bronco 13AX60TG	1300	68	○	⊖	○	○	⊖	⊖	42	19
10	**Yard-Man** 13AX605G	1300	68	○	⊖	○	○	⊖	⊖	42	19
11	**Husqvarna** YTH20F42T	1700	66	○	○	⊖	○	⊖	⊖	42	20
12	**Kubota** T1670 40"	3000	66	●	○	⊖	⊖	⊖	⊖	40	15
13	**Cub Cadet** LT1045 13AX11CH	1700	61	○	○	⊖	●	⊖	⊖	46	20
14	**Cub Cadet** LT1050 13AP11CP	2000	60	○	○	○	○	⊖	⊖	50	23
15	**Craftsman** (Sears) 27664	1400	59	○	○	⊖	⊖	⊖	⊖	42	20
16	**Husqvarna** YTH1542XP	2000	59	⊖	⊖	○	○	⊖	⊖	42	15

Within types, in performance order. Gray **key numbers indicate Quick Picks.**

Key number	Brand & model	Price	Overall score (0–100 P F G VG E)	Evenness	Side-discharging	Mulching	Bagging	Handling	Ease of use	Deck size (in.)	Engine power (hp)
	AUTOMATIC-DRIVE MODELS *continued*										
17	**Craftsman** (Sears) 27678	$1200	56	○	○	○	⊖	○	○	42	20
18	**Toro** LX460 13AX60RG	1500	55	○	⊖	○	⊖	⊖	⊖	46	20
	GEAR-DRIVE MODELS										
19	**John Deere** 102 CR Best Buy	1400	67	⊖	⊖	○	⊖	○	○	42	17
20	**Craftsman** (Sears) 27663	1300	55	○	○	○	⊖	○	○	42	20
21	**Yard Machines** 13AM762G	920	53	○	○	⊖	⊖	◒	○	42	15.5
	ZERO-TURN-RADIUS MODELS										
22	**Toro** TimeCutter ZX440	4200	76	○	⊖	⊖	⊖	⊖	⊖	44	Not stated
23	**Snapper** ZT18440KH	4000	71	○	⊖	⊖	⊖	⊖	⊖	44	18
24	**Lawn-Boy** 81245	3400	63	○	⊖	○	◒	⊖	⊖	42	16
25	**Cub Cadet** RZT50 17AA5D7P	3000	61	○	⊖	○	○	⊖	○	50	22
26	**Craftsman** (Sears) 27772	2700	60	○	○	○	⊖	⊖	○	44	20
27	**Ariens** 915065 1540	3100	59	○	○	⊖	◒	⊖	○	40	15
28	**Dixon** 918	3350	43	○	○	○	●	◐	⊖	42	16

See report, page 98. Based on tests posted on ConsumerReports.org in July 2006, with updated prices and availability.

Guide to the Ratings

Overall score is based on a combination of performance, handling, and ease of use. **Evenness** refers to how close the tractors came to even, carpet-like mowing. **Side-discharging** is how evenly clippings were dispersed from the side-discharge chute. **Mulching** is how finely and evenly clippings were cut and dispersed in this mode. **Bagging** measures effective capacity of the grass bag, determined when it was full or when the chute clogged and clippings weren't being collected. **Handling** includes clutching or drive engagement, braking, steering, turn radius, and stability. **Ease of use** is a composite score that includes leg room, seat and steering-wheel comfort, and ease of blade engagement, cut-height adjustment, parking brake engagement, bag removal, and cutting-mode changes. **Price** is approximate retail.

Quick Picks

Best for most; versatile mowing; both are CR Best Buys:

2 John Deere 125, $1,800
19 John Deere 102, $1,400

Both of these 42-inch lawn tractors mowed nearly as well as the John Deere X304. Between the two, the John Deere 102 trades automatic drive for a lower price.

For large, open spaces; a CR Best Buy:

3 Craftsman (Sears) 27690, $2,000

Wide-mowing tractors tend to cut less evenly. This 54-inch Craftsman (Sears) 27690 mows especially well for its width and offers comfortable seating and value, though it does require a blade change for mulching.

For lawns with lots of obstacles:

1 John Deere X304, $3,500
25 Cub Cadet RZT50 17AA5D7P, $3,000
26 Craftsman (Sears) 27772, $2,700

All three offer tight turning. The four-wheel-steer John Deere X304 tractor turns nearly as tightly as the Toro TimeCutter ZX440 zero-turn-radius mower and cuts more evenly for less money. Among zero-turn machines, the Cub Cadet RZT50 17AA5D7P won't cut in reverse, but consider it for its fine side-discharging and the Craftsman (Sears) 27772 for its mulching.

Recommendations

AUTOMATIC-DRIVE MODELS

1 **JOHN DEERE** X304 Excellent overall with very good evenness and excellent bagging. Kawaski twin-cylinder engine. Has cruise control and hour meter. Must change blades to mulch. Must engage override switch to cut in reverse. Bag, $400. Mulch kit, $77. Similar model: X300.

2 **JOHN DEERE** 125 **A CR Best Buy** Very good overall with very good evenness of cut. Briggs & Stratton twin-cylinder engine. Has cruise control and hour meter. Must engage override switch to cut in reverse. Bag, $400. Mulch cover included. Similar models: 115, 135.

3 **CRAFTSMAN (SEARS)** 27690 **A CR Best Buy** Very good overall with excellent bagging. Kohler twin-cylinder engine. Large 3-blade, 54-in. cutting deck. Has cruise control, hour meter, and electric blade engagement. Foot-operated hydrostatic drive. Comfortable seat. Must change blades to mulch. Has reverse-cut interlock. Bag, $400. Mulch kit, $50. Similar models: 27680, 27691, Husqvarna YTH2454T.

4 **CUB CADET** LT1042 13AX11CG Very good overall, but among the most repair-prone tractor brands. Kohler engine. Has cruise control and hour meter. Electric blade engagement and deck washout port. Has reverse-cut interlock. Bag, $320. Mulch cover included. Similar model: 13AL11CG.

5 **SIMPLICITY** Regent 16hp 44" Very good overall. Excellent bagging and handling. Kohler engine. Hydrostatic drive with foot-operated speed control. Electric blade engagement. Deck has a fan attachment to improve grass bagging, also useful for leaf pickup. Has reverse-cut interlock. Must change blade to mulch and bag. Bag with fan assist, $400. Mulch kit, $135.

6 **TORO** Wheel Horse 16-38 HXL A top pick for mulching. Smooth drive engagement. Precise steering and comfortable steering wheel. Briggs & Stratton engine. Deck washout port. High brake pedal awkward. Must engage override switch to cut in reverse. Bag. $340. Mulch kit included.

7 **TORO** LX420 13AX60RH Very good overall. This model shares the same design

Recommendations

and manufacture with models from Cub Cadet, Yard Machines, and Yard-Man. While those three brands have been repair-prone in our tractor surveys, we don't know the reliability for Toro. Kohler engine. Pedal drive (not a true hydrostatic—requires shifting from forward to reverse) with foot-operated speed control. Has cruise control and hour meter. Has reverse-cut interlock. Bag, $380. Mulch cover included. Similar model: Cub Cadet 13AX1OCG.

8 **JOHN DEERE** 155C Very good overall, with a 3-blade, 48-in. cutting width and excellent bagging. Cruise control. Electric blade engagement. Comfortable seat. Briggs & Stratton twin-cylinder engine. High brake pedal awkward. Must engage override switch to cut in reverse. Bag, $420. Mulch cover included. Similar model: 145.

9 **TROY-BILT** Super Bronco 13AX60TG Very good overall. This model shares the same design and manufacture with models from Cub Cadet, Yard Machines, and Yard-Man. While those three brands have been repair prone in our tractor surveys we don't know the reliability for Troy-Bilt. Kohler engine. Pedal drive (not a true hydrostatic—requires shifting from forward to reverse) with foot-operated speed control. Fuel level visible from seat. Cruise control. Must engage override switch to cut in reverse. Bag, $320. Mulch cover included. Similar model: White Outdoor 13AX605G.

10 **YARD-MAN** 13AX605G Very good overall, but among the most repair-prone tractor brands. Kohler engine. Pedal drive (not a true hydrostatic—requires shifting from forward to reverse) with foot-operated speed control. Cruise control. Must engage override switch to cut in reverse. Bag, $320. Mulch cover included.

11 **HUSQVARNA** YTH20F42T Very good overall. Kohler engine. New design with easier-to-use controls. Has cruise control, hour meter, and electric blade engagement. Comfortable seat. Has reverse-cut interlock. Bag, $270. Mulch kit, $50. Similar model: YHT2242T.

12 **KUBOTA** T1670 40" Very good overall, but evenness is only fair. Excellent bagging and handling. Kohler engine. Automatic drive with foot-operated speed control. Must change blade to mulch. Bag, $454. Mulch kit, $180.

13 **CUB CADET** LT1045 13AX11CH Very good overall, but among the most repair-prone tractor brands. Only fair for bagging. Cut evenness has a slight ridge, characteristic of 3-blade decks. Large 46-in. deck. Kohler engine. Hydrostatic drive with foot-operated speed control. Electric blade engagement. Comfortable steering wheel. Must engage override switch to cut in reverse. Hour meter and deck washout port. Bag, $400. Mulch cover included. Similar models: 13AP11CH, White Outdoor 13A4616H.

14 **CUB CADET** LT1050 13AP11CP Very good overall, but among the most repair-prone tractor rands. Cut evenness has a slight ridge, characteristic of 3-blade decks. Large 50-in. deck. Kohler engine. Hydrostatic drive with foot-operated speed control. Electric blade engagement. Comfortable steering wheel. Must change blades to bag. Has reverse-cut interlock. Hour meter and deck washout port. Bag, $500. Mulch cover included. Similar model: 13AQ11BP.

15 **CRAFTSMAN (SEARS)** 27664 Good overall. Briggs & Stratton engine. New design with easier-to-use controls. Hydrostatic drive with fender lever control. Must change blades to mulch. Has reverse cut interlock. Hour meter. Bag, $340. Mulch kit, $50. Similar models: 27662, 27668.

16 HUSQVARNA YTH1542XP Fine overall. Electric blade engagement. Kawasaki engine. Has reverse cut interlock. Bag kit, $270. Mulch cover included.

17 CRAFTSMAN (SEARS) 27678 Good overall. Briggs & Stratton engine. Hydrostatic drive with fender-lever control. Must change blades to mulch. Has reverse cut interlock. Hour meter. Bag, $340. Mulch kit, $50.

18 TORO LX460 13AX60RG Good overall. This model shares the same design and manufacture with models from Cub Cadet, Yard Machines, and Yard-Man. While those three brands have been repair-prone in our tractor surveys, we don't know the reliability for Toro. Only fair for side-discharge, leaving a noticeable row of clippings. Large 3-blade, 46-in. deck. Kohler engine. Pedal drive (not a true hydrostatic—requires shifting from forward to reverse) with foot-operated speed control Comfortable steering wheel. Has reverse-cut interlock. Hour meter. Must change blades to bag. Bag, $400. Mulch cover included. Similar model: MTD Pro 13AT605H.

GEAR-DRIVE MODELS

19 JOHN DEERE 102 **A CR Best Buy** Very good overall gear drive. Briggs & Stratton engine does not have full pressurized oil system. Lacks hour meter. Must engage override switch to cut in reverse. Bag, $400. Mulch cover included.

20 CRAFTSMAN (SEARS) 27663 Good overall. Briggs & Stratton engine. New design with easier to use controls. Gear drive. Must change blades to mulch. Has

reverse cut interlock. Hour meter. Bag, $340. Mulch kit, $50.

21 YARD MACHINES 13AM762G There are better choices. Among the most repair-prone tractor brands. Briggs & Stratton engine does not have full pressurized oil system. Not a gear-drive transmission but a continuously variable transmission with six manual positions. Does not cut in reverse. Bag, $320. Mulch cover included. Similar models: 13BN771G, Huskee 13AD771G.

ZERO-TURN-RADIUS MODELS

22 TORO TimeCutter ZX440 Highest-scoring zero-turn mower with excellent mulching and bagging, the latter courtesy of a fan-assist system. Kohler engine. Electric blade engagement. Must change blades to bag and mulch. Bag, $910. Mulch kit, $130.

23 SNAPPER ZT18440KH Very good overall; among the best of the zero-turn-radius models tested. Has separate hydraulic pump and motors for better steering control and balance. Excellent bagging due to fan assist. Kohler engine. Electric blade engagement. Must change blades to bag. Bag, $840. Mulch plate included. Similar model: Simplicity ZT1844.

24 LAWN-BOY 81245 Very good overall. Bagging only fair. Relatively small bag capacity. Honda twin-cylinder engine. Among the quietest tested. Electric blade engagement. Deck washout port. Bag, $460. Mulch kit, $80. Similar models: Toro Z420, 81240.

25 CUB CADET RZT50 17AA5D7P Very good overall. Does not cut in reverse. Electric blade engagement. Kawasaki twin-cylinder engine. Awkward parking brake and cut-height adjustment. Bag,

Recommendations

$500. Mulch cover included. Similar model: Troy-Bilt RZT50.

26 CRAFTSMAN (SEARS) 27772 Good overall. Kohler engine. Electric blade engagement. Awkward deck-height adjustment. Must change blades to mulch. Bag, $400. Mulch kit, $175.

27 ARIENS 915065 1540 Good overall. Bagging uses a fan assist, but is only fair.

Briggs & Stratton engine. Electric blade engagement. Must change blades to mulch. Bag, $750. Mulch kit, $80.

28 DIXON 918 There are better choices. Worst at bagging. Difficult to handle, with jerky motions when steering. Briggs & Stratton engine. Electric blade engagement. Bag, $525. Mulch kit, is $55.

Brand Repair History

Readers report on 17,322 tractors and riders

Tractors and riding mowers are among the most repair-prone products in our reliability surveys. The graph shows the percentage of these brands bought between 2001 and 2005 that have ever been repaired or had a serious problem. Differences of less than 5 points are not meaningful. Cub Cadet and Yard Machines/Yard-Man have been the most repair-prone tractor brands. Rider data include regular and zero-turn models; we lack sufficient data to comment specifically on zero-turn mowers. Models within a brand may vary, and changes in design or manufacture may affect reliability. Still, choosing a brand with a good repair history can improve your odds of getting a reliable model.

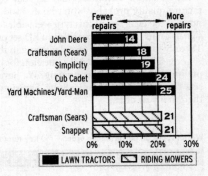

Data are based on reader responses about tractors and riders to the Annual Product Reliability Survey conducted by Consumer Reports National Research Center. Data are adjusted to eliminate differences linked solely to age and usage.

LCD TVs

On the best of the tested LCD TVs, picture quality was clear, crisp, and detailed, especially with HD content and progressive-scan DVD signals. Some of the newest LCD models are 1080p sets, with 1920x1080 resolution. They're capable of pushing the resolution limits of the HDTV format, displaying an unprecedented level of detail.

An LCD TV's antireflective surface helps reduce glare, which can be a problem with plasma TVs. The best LCD sets are making strides with color accuracy, the ability to display the deepest black, and wider viewing angles, but they haven't quite caught up with plasma TVs. Lower-priced sets with good picture quality could be fine if image quality isn't critical. (Scores for HD programming and DVD playback are held to higher standards than scores for regular TV.)

An enhanced-definition (ED) set may cost a bit less than an HD model, but the picture quality probably won't be as good. Unlike the plasma ED sets we've tested, none of the LCD sets of this type were able to display a down-converted version of HD signals on its own. We'd consider an ED set or a smaller-screen standard-definition LCD TV only for uses such as casual viewing in the kitchen.

Long-term reliability is still a question for newer TV technologies, including LCD, but preliminary data are encouraging. We have enough repair data to report that LCD sets from Sharp, Panasonic, Sony, Samsung, and Toshiba have been reliable during their first year of use.

	Excellent	Very good	Good	Fair	Poor
	⊖	⊖	○	◒	●

Within types, in performance order. Gray key numbers indicate Quick Picks.

Key number	Brand & model	Price	Overall score	HD	DVD	Standard-def.	Sound quality	Remote	Menu	ATSC	QAM	CableCard	Component	HDMI
	All tested models have a native resolution of 1366x768 except as noted.		0 — 100 (P F G VG E)	Picture quality				Ease of use		Digital tuners			HD-capable inputs	
40-INCH AND LARGER MODELS														
1	**Sony** Bravia KDL-V40XBR1 (40-in.) ②	$3,000	64	⊖	⊖	⊖①	○	⊖	⊖	●	●		3	1
2	**JVC** LT-40X787 (40-in.)	2,800	63	⊖	⊖	○	⊖	⊖	○	●	●		2	2
3	**Sony** Bravia KDL-40S2000 (40-in.)	2,300	59	⊖	⊖	○	⊖	⊖	○	●	●		2	1
4	**Westinghouse** LVM-42W2 (42-in.) ②	2,000	57	⊖	○	○	⊖	○	⊖				2	1
5	**LG** 42LB1DR (42-in.)	2,300	51	○	○	◒	⊖	⊖	○	●	●	●	2	2
6	**Sony** Bravia KLV-40U100M (40-in.)	2,200	51	○	○	○	⊖	⊖	○				1	1
7	**Sharp** Aquos LC-45D40U (45-in.)	3,300	44	○	◒	◒	⊖	⊖	○	●	●		2	2
8	**Samsung** LN-S4092D (40-in.)	2,600	39	○	◒	◒	⊖	⊖	○	●			1	2

Key number	Brand & model	Price	Overall score (0–100) P F G VG E	HD	DVD	Standard-def	Sound quality	Remote	Menu	ATSC	QAM	CableCard	Component	HDMI
	All tested models have a native resolution of 1366x768 except as noted.													
37-INCH MODELS														
9	**Sharp** Aquos LC-37D90U [2]	$2,500	68	⊖	⊖	○	⊖	⊖	○	•	•		1	2
10	**JVC** LT-37X787	2,300	62	⊖	⊖	○	○	⊖	○	•	•		2	2
11	**Toshiba** 37HLX95	2,800	60	⊖	○	⊖	○	⊖	◐	•	•	•	2	1
12	**LG** 37LC2D	1,700	58	⊖	⊖	○	⊖	⊖	○	•	•		2	1
13	**Sharp** Aquos LC-37D6U	2,000	49	○	○	○[1]	⊖	⊖	◐	•	•	•	2	1
14	**Sharp** Aquos LC-37SH20U	1,750	45	○	○	○	⊖	⊖	○	•	•		1	1
15	**Westinghouse** LTV-37W2	1,300	45	○	○	◐	○	⊖	○	•	•		2	1
16	**Kreisen** KR-370T	2,450	36	●	○	⊖[1]	⊖	○	◐				1	
32-INCH MODELS														
17	**Sony** Bravia KDL-V32XBR1	2,000	65	⊖	⊖	◐[1]	⊖	⊖	○	•	•	•	3	1
18	**JVC** LT-32X787	1,500	63	⊖	⊖	○	○	⊖	○	•	•		2	2
19	**Sony** Bravia KDL-32S2000	1,500	63	⊖	⊖	○	⊖	⊖	○	•	•		2	1
20	**Toshiba** 32HL66	1,200	62	⊖	⊖	○[1]	○	⊖	◐	•	•		2	1
21	**Panasonic** TC-32LX60	1,300	57	⊖	⊖	○	⊖	⊖	○	•	•		1	1
22	**Sharp** Aquos LC-32DA5U	1,600	57	○	○	⊖	⊖	⊖	◐				2	1
23	**Panasonic** TC-32LX600	1,400	56	⊖	⊖	○	○	⊖	◐	•	•		1	2
24	**Samsung** LN-S3251D	1,600	53	⊖	○	○	○	⊖	○	•			1	2
25	**Westinghouse** LTV-32W4 HDC	1,000	53	○	○	◐	○	⊖	⊖	•	•		2	1
26	**LG** 32LC2D	1,200	52	○	○	○	⊖	⊖	○	•	•		2	1
27	**Magnavox** 32MF231D/37	1,000	51	⊖	⊖	◐	○	○	◐	•	•		2	1
28	**Sharp** Aquos LC-32D40U	1,400	51	○	○	⊖	⊖	⊖	◐	•	•		2	2
29	**HP** Pavilion LC3200N [3]	1,300	49	○	○	○[1]	⊖	○	◐	•	•	•	2	1
30	**Samsung** LN-S3241D	1,400	46	○	○	◐	⊖	⊖	○	•			1	2
31	**HP** LC3260N	1,000	43	○	○	◐	⊖	⊖	◐	•	•		2	2

[1] Tested via the S-video input; quality should be comparable to that of the component-video results for the other sets. [2] 1080p, or 1920x1080 resolution. [3] Limited availability.

See report, page 140. Based on tests in Consumer Reports in November 2006.

Quick Picks

Good buys in a 32-inch set:
25 Westinghouse LTV-32W4HDC, $1,000
27 Magnavox 32MF231D/37, $1,000

The Westinghouse did well and has a built-in DVD player. The Magnavox had a very good picture, bright and punchy.

Best 32-inch models:
17 Sony Bravia KDL-V32XBR1, $2,000
18 JVC LT32X787, $1,500
19 Sony Bravia KDL-32S2000, $1,500
20 Toshiba 32HL66, $1,200
21 Panasonic TC-32LX60, $1,300

The two Sony sets are fine choices, like their 40-inch siblings. The JVC had the widest viewing angle, and the Toshiba had the best black levels and HD picture. The Panasonic did very nicely, too.

Top picks in 37-inch sets:
9 Sharp Aquos LC 37D90U, $2,500
12 LG 37LC2D, $1,700

One of the few 1080p sets of this size, the Sharp displayed very fine, clear detail. It's among the best LCD TVs we've tested, but it has a fairly narrow angle for optimal viewing, and black levels could be deeper. The LG is a fine set at a great price.

Best 40-inch sets:
1 Sony Bravia KDL-V40XBR1, $3,000
2 JVC LT-40X787, $2,800
3 Sony Bravia KDL-40S2000, $2,300

The Sony (1) had a sharp, clear, colorful picture, even with regular TV content. An older set, it could be scarce. Initial tests of the newer KDL-V40XBR2 show that it's at least as good, if not better. This 1080p set has three HDMI inputs, a wider viewing angle, and better sound than the XBR1. It costs $3,500. The lower-priced Sony (3) came close in picture quality to the XBR1. The JVC had fine picture quality and sound, and a wide viewing angle.

Good value for a 42-inch 1080p set:
4 Westinghouse LVM-42W2, $2,000

This 42-inch 1080p set displayed very fine detail and had very good HD picture quality, though color accuracy was off a bit. Also, quality of DVD images didn't match that of the best sets. One reason for the low price: It's a monitor with no built-in tuners, requiring an external tuner (such as a cable box) to receive any TV signals.

Guide to the Ratings

Overall score is based primarily on picture quality; sound quality and ease of use are also considered. Trained panelists evaluated picture quality for clarity and color accuracy. Under **picture quality, HD** reflects display of a high-definition (1080i) signal, such as that from a digital-cable box or satellite receiver (all tested sets were HD models). **DVD** reflects display of a 480p signal, such as the output from a progressive-scan DVD player. **Standard-def.** (SD) picture scores are for a standard-definition (480i) signal, such as that of a regular TV program. All signals were routed through a component-video input except where noted. Picture-quality scores for HD, DVD, and SD content aren't directly comparable across signal types because each is capable of a different level of quality. Thus, a very good score for HD indicates a better picture than a very good score for regular TV signals. **Sound quality** is for the set's built-in speakers. **Ease of use** is our assessment of the remote control and on-screen menus. Under **digital tuners,** an **ATSC** tuner allows a set to receive digital signals, including HD, via antenna; a **QAM** tuner can receive unscrambled digital signals from cable; a **CableCard**-ready set can receive scrambled (e.g., premium) and unscrambled digital channels on cable when equipped with a CableCard. Where no digital-tuning option is listed, models are HD-ready sets that require an external digital tuner, such as an HD-capable cable or satellite box. **Price** is approximate retail.

MICROWAVE OVENS

Most models will do a capable job of basic microwaving chores, such as reheating leftovers or making popcorn. First decide whether you want an over-the-range or countertop model. If you opt for a countertop, also consider how large a unit your kitchen counter or other available space will accommodate.

For better venting and microwave cooking, buy a range hood and a countertop microwave oven. Capable countertop models include the compact Emerson Professional Series MW8992[SB], $75, and the midsized Kenmore (Sears) 6325[2], $110; both are CR Best Buys. Also consider the large GE JE1460[B]F, $130, a CR Best Buy, and GE Profile JES2251SJ[SS], $220, which adds cooking capacity and a stainless finish.

	Excellent	Very good	Good	Fair	Poor
	⊖	⊖	○	⊖	●

Within types, in performance order. Gray **key numbers indicate Quick Picks.**

Key number	Brand & model	Price	Overall score	Heating evenness	Auto-defrost	Ease of use	Turntable diameter (in.)	Tested capacity (cu. ft.)	Claimed capacity (cu. ft.)	Watts	Convection mode	Sensor	Detailed prompts	Stainless/SS-look option
	Test results							**Features**						
	COMPACT COUNTERTOP MODELS													
1	**Emerson** Professional Series MW8992[SB] **CR Best Buy**	$75	61	⊖	⊖	⊖	11.6	0.6	0.9	900				●
2	**Westinghouse** Beyond WBYMW1	200	46	○	⊖	⊖	11.7	0.6	0.9	850				
	MIDSIZED COUNTERTOP MODELS													
3	**Kenmore** (Sears) 6325[2] **CR Best Buy**	110	67	○	⊖	⊖	13.5	0.9	1.2	1200		●	●	●
4	**Kenmore** (Sears) Elite 6428[9]	250	64	○	⊖	⊖	11.3	0.7	1.0	1000	●	●	●	●
5	**Amana** AMC5101AA[B]	110	62	○	⊖	⊖	12.0	0.7	1.0	1000				●
6	**Sharp** Carousel R-308H[K]	85	61	⊖	○	⊖	12.3	0.7	1.0	1100				●
7	**Sharp** Carousel R-320H[K]	100	60	⊖	⊖	○	12.2	0.8	1.2	1200		●	●	
8	**Daewoo** WM1010CC	150	54	⊖	⊖	○	11.9	0.7	1.0	1000	●			●
9	**Sunbeam** SMW978	90	49	○	○	⊖	11.7	0.7	1.1	1000				●
10	**Oster** OMW1199	130	46	○	○	○	11.7	0.6	1.1	1000				●
11	**Emerson** Professional Series MW8111[SS]	100	40	○	○	⊖	12.0	0.7	1.1	1000				●

Within types, in performance order. Gray key numbers indicate Quick Picks.

Key number	Brand & model	Price	Overall score	Heating evenness	Auto-defrost	Ease of use	Turntable diameter (in.)	Tested capacity (cu. ft.)	Claimed capacity (cu. ft.)	Watts	Convection mode	Sensor	Detailed prompts	Stainless/SS-look
LARGE COUNTERTOP MODELS															
12	**GE** Profile JES2251SJ[SS]	$220	80	⊖	⊖	⊖	15.8	1.5	2.2	1000		•	•	•
13	**GE** JE1860[W]H	165	72	⊖	⊖	⊖	13.5	1.2	1.8	1100		•	•	•
14	**GE** JE1460[B]F **CR Best Buy**	130	71	⊖	⊖	⊖	11.8	1.0	1.4	1150		•		•
15	**GE** Profile JE2160[B]F	170	69	⊖	⊖	⊖	15.3	1.5	2.1	1200		•	•	•
16	**Frigidaire** Professional PLMB209D[CA]	280	66	○	⊖	⊖	14.6	1.3	2.0	1200		•	•	•
17	**Panasonic** Genius Prestige NN-P794[S]F	170	66	⊖	◐	⊖	14.0	1.0	1.6	1250		•	•	•
18	**Panasonic** Genius NN-T995[S]F	180	62	⊖	⊖	○	15.8	1.5	2.2	1250		•	•	•
19	**Amana** AMC5143AA[B]	120	61	○	⊖	⊖	13.4	1.0	1.4	1100		•		
20	**Sharp** R-530EK[S]	140	59	○	⊖	◐	14.6	1.3	2.0	1200		•	•	•
21	**Daewoo** WM1310PM	170	48	⊖	○	○	11.8	0.9	1.3	1000				
22	**Haier** MWG100214T[WW]	100	42	○	◐	○	12.3	0.9	1.4	1000				
OVER-THE-RANGE MODELS															
23	**Kenmore** (Sears) Elite 8083[9]	530	81	⊖	⊖	⊖	15.2x13.2	1.6	2.0	1100		•	•	•
24	**Whirlpool** Gold GH4155XP[B] **CR Best Buy**	430	78	⊖	⊖	⊖	11.5	0.7	1.5	1000		•	•	•
25	**GE** Profile Spacemaker JVM2070[B]	525	77	⊖	⊖	⊖	13.5	1.1	2.0	1100		•	•	•
26	**LG** Glide n' Cook LMVM2055[ST]	430	77	○	⊖	⊖	14.8x12	1.5	2.0	1100		•	•	•
27	**Samsung** SMH7178[STD]	350	75	⊖	⊖	⊖	13.5	0.8	1.7	1100		•	•	•
28	**Samsung** SMH7177[STE] **CR Best Buy**	300	74	⊖	⊖	⊖	13.2	0.8	1.7	1100		•	•	•
29	**Whirlpool** Gold GH6177XP[B]	600	74	○	⊖	⊖	11.4	0.9	1.7	1100		•	•	•
30	**LG** Glide 'n Cook LMVM1945[SW] **CR Best Buy**	300	73	○	⊖	○	14.8x12	1.5	1.9	1100		•	•	•
31	**KitchenAid** Ultima Cook KHHS179L[BL]	800	72	⊖	⊖	⊖	11.4	0.9	1.7	1100		•	•	•
32	**Whirlpool** Gold GH5184XP[B]	450	72	○	⊖	⊖	11.5	0.9	1.8	1100		•		•
33	**Kenmore** (Sears) 8060[9]	430	71	⊖	⊖	○	11.3	0.9	2.0	1100		•	•	•
34	**Maytag** MMV5207BA[B]	450	71	◐	⊖	⊖	14.8x12	1.4	2.0	1100		•	•	•
35	**Whirlpool** Gold Velos GH6208XR[B]	750	69	○	○	⊖	15.0	1.1	2.0	1200		•	•	•
36	**Whirlpool** Gold Velos GH7208XR[Q]	870	69	○	○	⊖	15.0	1.1	2.0	1200	•	•	•	•

	Excellent	Very good	Good	Fair	Poor
	⊖	⊖	○	◑	●

Key number	Brand & model	Price	Overall score	Heating evenness	Auto-defrost	Ease of use	Turntable diameter (in.)	Tested capacity (cu. ft.)	Claimed capacity (cu. ft.)	Watts	Convection mode	Sensor	Detailed prompts	Stainless/SS-look option

OVER-THE-RANGE MODELS *continued*

Key number	Brand & model	Price	Overall score	Heating evenness	Auto-defrost	Ease of use	Turntable diameter (in.)	Tested capacity (cu. ft.)	Claimed capacity (cu. ft.)	Watts	Convection mode	Sensor	Detailed prompts	Stainless/SS-look option
37	Whirlpool MH3185XP[B]	$400	69	⊖	○	⊖	11.4	0.9	1.8	1000			●	●
38	Frigidaire Gallery GLMV169D[B]	330	68	⊖	⊖	⊖	11.7	0.8	1.6	1000			●	●
39	GE Profile Spacemaker JVM1790[B]K	650	67	○	⊖	⊖	12.9	0.8	1.7	1000	●		●	●
40	GE Profile Spacemaker JVM1850[B]F	375	67	⊖	⊖	⊖	13.5	0.9	1.8	1000			●	●
41	GE Spacemaker JVM1650[B]B	320	67	○	○	⊖	13.0	0.8	1.6	1000			●	●
42	Maytag MMV4205BA[B]	300	67	⊖	⊖	⊖	13.5	0.9	2.0	1150			●	●
43	Bosch HMV930[5]	630	66	○	⊖	⊖	11.3	0.8	1.8	1000			●	●
44	Jenn-Air JMV9169BA[B]	750	65	○	⊖	⊖	12.6	0.8	1.6	950	●		●	●
45	Panasonic Genius NN-H275[B]F	350	64	⊖	⊖	○	11.5	0.8	2.0	1200			●	●
46	Sharp R-187[0]	530	61	○	○	⊖	12.2	0.7	1.1	850	●		●	●
47	GE Advantium 120 SCA1001K[SS]	780	59	○	○	⊖	12.1	0.7	1.4	900	●		●	●
48	Magic Chef MCO153UB (Home Depot)	150	55	○	◐	⊖	12.0	0.8	1.5	1000			●	●

NOT RECOMMENDED MIDSIZED COUNTERTOP MODEL

Key number	Brand & model	Price	Overall score	Heating evenness	Auto-defrost	Ease of use	Turntable diameter (in.)	Tested capacity (cu. ft.)	Claimed capacity (cu. ft.)	Watts	Convection mode	Sensor	Detailed prompts	Stainless/SS-look option
49	Haier MWG10081T[W]	140	50	○	⊖	○	10.7	0.6	1.0	1000	●			

See report, page 62. Based on tests posted on ConsumerReports.org in August 2006, with updated prices and availability.

Guide to the Ratings

Overall score is based mainly on evenness of heating, ease of use, and auto-defrosting ability. **Heating evenness** reflects how evenly a model reheated a dish of cold mashed potatoes. **Auto-defrost** is based on how well the automatic-defrost program defrosted one pound of frozen ground chuck. **Ease of use** includes how easy it is to set the microwave without referring to the instructions. **Turntable diameter** is the measured diameter of the oven's turntable, rounded to the nearest tenth of an inch, not including rim. **Tested capacity** is the usable space, in cubic feet, based on our measurements, and excludes the corner spaces for models with rotating turntables. Note that most over-the-range models allow you to turn the rotation off to fit large dishes. A few countertop models offer this feature, as well. With the rotation off, measured capacity approximates claimed. However, food may require extra tending and stirring. **Claimed capacity,** in cubic feet, is the capacity as listed on the product or packaging. **Watts** is the manufacturer's figure of the microwave's power output. In general, the more watts an oven offers, the greater its cooking power and the faster your food will be cooked. That said, differences in claimed wattage of 100 watts or less are unlikely to result in significant differences in performance. **Price** is approximate retail.

Quick Picks

If you want a basic microwave oven for a dorm room, office, or other small space, consider a compact countertop model:

1   Emerson Professional Series MW8992[SB], $75, **CR Best Buy**

The Emerson is an inexpensive, basic model that performed well in all of our tests.

If counter space is scarce in your kitchen, consider a midsized countertop model:

3   Kenmore (Sears) 6325[2], $110, **CR Best Buy**

The modestly priced Kenmore was easy to use and excelled at our defrosting test.

If you have kitchen counter space to spare, consider a large countertop model:

12   GE Profile JES2251SJ[SS], $220
13   GE JE1860[W]H, $165
14   GE JE1460[B]F, $130, **CR Best Buy**

All three were relatively easy to use. The GE JE1860[W]H was one of only two countertop models with a turntable on/off switch, a useful feature. If you need a roomy microwave, the GE Profile has the largest capacity of the three.

Best for most people who want an over-the-range microwave oven; fine performance at a reasonable price:

24   Whirlpool Gold GH4155XP[B], $430, **CR Best Buy**
28   Samsung SMH7177[STE], $300, **CR Best Buy**
38   Frigidaire Gallery GLMV169D[B], $330

The Whirlpool Gold, Samsung, and Frigidaire Gallery heated evenly. Frigidaire, Kenmore, Maytag, and Whirlpool have been reliable in our surveys; we lack data for LG, Panasonic, and Samsung.

For added cooking space in an over-the-range microwave oven:

23   Kenmore (Sears) Elite 8083[9] , $530
30   LG Glide 'n Cook LMVM1945[SW], $300, **CR Best Buy**

The Kenmore Elite and LG Glide 'n Cook have trays that move from side to side for large plates. The pricier Kenmore has more-even heating and a known repair history.

Recommendations

COMPACT COUNTERTOP MODELS

1 EMERSON Professional Series MW8992[SB] **A CR Best Buy** Very good.

2 WESTINGHOUSE Beyond WBYMW1 Good. Has scanning wand to read bar codes on some foods to program cooking times. Manufacturer claims to have pre-programmed 4,000 foods. Many of the packages we scanned were not on the list. Also, it often required repeated swipes to get a readout. No auto-reheat. Discontinued, but similar model Beyond WBYMW2 may still be available.

MIDSIZED COUNTERTOP MODELS

3 KENMORE (SEARS) 6325[2] **A CR Best Buy** Very good.

4 KENMORE (SEARS) Elite 6428[9] Very good.

5 AMANA AMC5101AA[B] Very good.

6 SHARP Carousel R-308H[K] Very good. Discontinued, but similar model Carousel R-308J may still be available.

7 SHARP Carousel R-320H[K] Good.

8 DAEWOO WM1010CC Good. Has grilling feature, but no auto-reheat.

9 SUNBEAM SMW978 Good. Auto-reheat less effective than most.

10 OSTER OMW1199 Good. Has grilling feature.

11 EMERSON Professional Series MW8111[SS] Fair. Discontinued, but similar model Professional Series MW8115 may still be available.

LARGE COUNTERTOP MODELS

12 GE Profile JES2251SJ[SS] Very good. Turntable fits 9x15-inch dish.

13 GE JE1860[W]H Very good. Turntable fits 9x15-inch dish while rotating. Turntable on/off switch which may allow larger plates to fit. Optional kit allows wall or cabinet mount.

14 GE JE1460[B]F **A CR Best Buy** Very good.

15 GE Profile JE2160[B]F Very good. Turntable fits 9x15-inch dish. Auto-reheat less effective than most. Optional kit allows wall or cabinet mount.

16 FRIGIDAIRE Professional PLMB209D[CA] Very good. Turntable fits 9x15-inch dish. Optional kit allows wall or cabinet mount. Similar model: Gallery GLMB209D.

17 PANASONIC Genius Prestige NN-P794[S]F Very good. Relatively quiet. Turntable fits 9x15-inch dish. Optional kit allows wall or cabinet mount.

18 PANASONIC Genius NN-T995[S]F Very good. Relatively quiet. Turntable fits 9x15-inch dish. Auto-reheat less effective than most. Optional kit allows wall or cabinet mount.

19 AMANA AMC5143AA[B] Very good. Optional kit allows wall or cabinet mount.

20 SHARP R-530EK[S] Good. Turntable fits 9x15-inch dish. Optional kit allows wall or cabinet mount.

21 DAEWOO WM1310PM Good.

22 HAIER MWG100214T[WW] Good. Turntable fits 9x15-inch dish while rotating. Turntable on/off switch which may allow larger plates to fit.

OVER-THE-RANGE MODELS

23 KENMORE (Sears) Elite 8083[9] Excellent. Relatively quiet. Has side-to-side sliding glass tray and turntable within rectangular tray. Fits 9x15-inch dish.

24 WHIRLPOOL Gold GH4155XP[B] **A CR Best Buy** Very good. Turntable on/off switch may allow larger plates to fit.

25 GE Profile Spacemaker JVM2070[B]H Very good. Turntable on/off switch may allow larger plates to fit.

26 LG Glide n' Cook LMVM2055[ST] Very good. Has side-to-side sliding glass tray. Fits 9x15-inch dish.

27 SAMSUNG SMH7178[STD] Very good. Turntable on/off switch may allow larger plates to fit.

28 SAMSUNG SMH7177[STE] **A CR Best Buy** Very good. Relatively quiet. Turntable on/off switch may allow larger plates to fit.

29 WHIRLPOOL Gold GH6177XP[B] Very good. Turntable on/off switch may allow larger plates to fit. Has supplemental halogen or quartz bulbs for browning or crisping foods as part of speed-cook option. Performed well in speed-cooking tests for chicken, biscuits, and pizza.

30 LG Glide 'n Cook LMVM1945[SW] **A CR Best Buy** Very good. Relatively quiet. Has side-to-side sliding glass dish. Fits 9x15-inch dish. Auto-reheat less effective than most.

31 KITCHENAID Ultima Cook KHHS179L[BL] Very good. Turntable on/off switch may allow larger plates to fit. Has supplemental halogen or quartz bulbs for browning or crisping foods as part of speed-cook option. Performed well in speed-cooking tests for chicken and biscuits but unimpressive for pizza.

32 WHIRLPOOL Gold GH5184XP[B] Very good. Turntable on/off switch may allow larger plates to fit.

33 KENMORE (SEARS) 8060[9] Very good. Turntable on/off switch may allow for larger plates. Auto-reheat less effective than most.

34 MAYTAG MMV5207BA[B] Very good. Has side-to-side sliding glass tray. Fits 9x15-inch dish.

35 WHIRLPOOL Gold Velos GH6208XR[B] Very good. Relatively quiet. Turntable on/off switch may allow larger plates to fit. Turntable fits 9x15-inch dish while rotating. Has supplemental halogen or quartz bulbs for browning or crisping foods as part of speed-cook option. Performed well in speed-cooking tests for chicken, steaks, biscuits, and pizza. Auto-reheat less effective than most. Exhaust vent more effective than most.

36 WHIRLPOOL Gold Velos GH7208XR[Q] Very good. Quiet. Turntable on/off switch may allow larger plates to fit. Turntable fits 9x15-inch dish while rotating. Has supplemental halogen or quartz bulbs for browning or crisping foods as part of speed-cook option. Performed well in convection or speed-cooking tests for chicken, steaks, biscuits, and pizza. Auto-reheat less effective than most. Exhaust vent more effective than most.

37 WHIRLPOOL MH3185XP[B] Very good. Turntable on/off switch may allow larger plates to fit. Discontinued, but similar mode MH3184XP may still be available,

38 FRIGIDAIRE Gallery GLMV169D[B] Very good. Turntable on/off switch may allow larger plates to fit. Similar model: Professional PLMV169D.

39 SPACEMAKER JVM1790[B]K Very good. Turntable on/off switch may allow larger plates to fit. Has supplemental heating for browning or crisping foods as part of speed-cook option. Performed

Recommendations

well in convection tests for chicken and biscuits but unimpressive for pizza.

40 GE Profile Spacemaker JVM1850[B]F Very good. Turntable on/off switch may allow larger plates to fit. Discontinued, but similar models Profile Spacemaker JVM1870F and Spacemaker JVM1850H may still be available.

41 GE Spacemaker JVM1650[B]B Very good. Relatively quiet. Turntable on/off switch may allow larger plates to fit. Discontinued, but similar models Spacemaker JVM1640J and Spacemaker JVM1650H may still be available.

42 MAYTAG MMV4205BA[B] Very good. Turntable on/off switch may allow larger plates to fit.

43 BOSCH HMV930[5] Very good. Relatively quiet. Turntable on/off switch may allow larger plates to fit.

44 JENN-AIR JMV9169BA[B] Very good. Turntable on/off switch may allow larger plates to fit. Has supplemental halogen or quartz bulbs for browning or crisping foods as part of speed-cook option. Performed well in convection or speed-cooking tests on chicken and biscuits but unimpressive for steaks and pizza.

45 PANASONIC Genius NN-H275[B]F Very good. Turntable on/off switch may allow larger plates to fit. Auto-reheat less effective than most.

46 SHARP R-187[0] Very good, but Sharp has been the most repair-prone brand of OTR ovens. Turntable on/off switch may allow larger plates to fit. Has supplemental heating for browning or crisping foods as part of speed-cook option. Performed well in convection or speed-cooking tests for chicken, biscuits, and pizza but unimpressive for steaks.

47 GE Advantium 120 SCA1001K[SS] Good. Has supplemental halogen or quartz bulbs for browning or crisping foods as part of speed-cook option. Performed well in convection- or speed-cooking tests for chicken, steaks, and pizza but unimpressive for biscuits. Auto-reheat less effective than most.

48 MAGIC CHEF MCO153UB (Home Depot) Good. Turntable on/off which may allow larger plates to fit. Auto-reheat less effective than most.

NOT RECOMMENDED MIDSIZED COUNTERTOP MODEL

HAIER MWG10081T[W] Not recommended. All five units we purchased were defective. Has grilling feature.

Brand Repair History

Readers report on 18,000 microwave ovens

This graph shows the percentage of these brands of over-the-range ovens bought between 2001 and 2005 that have ever been repaired or had a serious problem that was not repaired. Differences of less than 4 points are not meaningful. Sharp was the most repair-prone brand. There was a major recall for Kenmore and Whirlpool models produced from 1998 to 2001, leading to uncharacteristically high repair rates. As a result, data for recalled models for all brands were removed to reflect the underlying historical reliability of this product. Some brands were not included because too few subscribers reported on

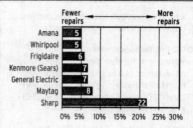

that brand to yield a meaningful finding. Models within a brand may vary, and changes in manufacturing and design may affect reliability. Still, choosing a brand with a good repair history improves your odds of getting a reliable microwave oven.

Data are based on readers responses about microwave ovens to the Annual Product Reliability Survey conducted by the Consumer Reports National Research Center. Data are adjusted to eliminate differences linked to age and usage.

MP3 PLAYERS

Like most digital devices, MP3 players perform very well at their key task. As the Ratings show, many MP3 players can produce near-audio-CD-quality sound out of the headphone jack, and the others were nearly as good. The headphones supplied with the players were a bit better on some models than others, though even the worst performed respectably.

Flash-memory players offer the smallest, lightest, and most affordable way to enjoy MP3 music on the go, and can typically run much longer than their hard-drive cousins on a single charge. But hard-disk players have much greater storage capacity, with larger LCD displays and controls. So-called microdrive players offer an appealing compromise between price and capacity, but perhaps not for long. Flash-memory-player capacities are steadily advancing into microdrive territory.

A growing number of players now have color displays. Most models allow you to display photos and other images, often in slideshow fashion and sometimes with the ability to listen to music at the same time. And an increasing number of color-display models also allow you to watch videos.

All players accept music you already own on CD, which you convert into digital music files and transfer to the player using supplied software. And all the players we've chosen can play copy-protected music purchased from online stores.

Many tested models have similar models that differ from the test unit mainly in capacity; consider these if the tested unit is larger, pricier, or smaller than you need.

	Excellent	Very good	Good	Fair	Poor
	⊖	⊖	○	◑	●

Within types, in performance order. Gray key numbers indicate Quick Picks.

Key number	Brand & model	Price	Overall score	Ease of use	Headphone quality	Audio quality	Picture quality	Audio-playback time (hr.)	Plays online music	Mac compatible	Color display	Video playback	Slideshow capability	FM radio	Built-in microphone
	Small type: similar models(s)		P F G VG E												
FLASH-MEMORY MP3 PLAYERS (128MB TO 4GB)															
1	**iRiver** U10 (1 GB) U10 (512 MB) $140	$200	72	⊖	⊖	⊖	⊖	28	•		•	•	•	•	•
2	**Cowon** iAudio U3 (2 GB) iAudio U3 (1 GB) $125	180	70	⊖	⊖	⊖	○	18	•		•	•	•	•	•
3	**Samsung** YP-T8Z (1 GB) YP-T8X (512 MB) $140	175	69	⊖	○	⊖	○	17	•		•	•	•	•	•
4	**Apple** iPod Nano (2 GB) iPod Nano (1 GB) $150, iPod Nano (4 GB) $250	200	66	⊖	⊖	⊖	○	15	•	•	•		•		
5	**iRiver** T10 (1 GB) T10 (512 MB) $100	155	66	○	○	⊖	NA	39	•		•		•	•	
6	**iRiver** iFP-799 (1 GB) iFP-790 (256 MB) $80, iFP-795 (512 MB) $100	130	65	○	○	⊖	NA	34	•		•			•	•
7	**iRiver** T30 (1 GB)	130	64	○	○	⊖	NA	15	•					•	

		Excellent	Very good	Good	Fair	Poor
		⊖	⊖	○	◑	●

Within types, in performance order. Gray key numbers indicate Quick Picks.

Key number	Brand & model Small type: similar models(s)	Price	Overall score 0 · · · 100 P F G VG E	Test results					Features						
				Ease of use	Headphone quality	Audio quality	Picture quality	Audio-playback time (hr.)	Plays online music	Mac compatible	Color display	Video playback	Slideshow capability	FM radio	Built-in microphone

FLASH-MEMORY MP3 PLAYERS (128MB TO 4GB) *continued*

Key number	Brand & model	Price	Overall score	Ease of use	Headphone quality	Audio quality	Picture quality	Audio-playback time (hr.)	Plays online music	Mac compatible	Color display	Video playback	Slideshow capability	FM radio	Built-in microphone
8	**RCA** Lyra RD2217 (1 GB) Lyra RD2212 (256 MB) $90, Lyra RD2215 (512 MB) $100	$125	64	○	○	⊖	NA	39	•	•				•	
9	**Samsung** YP-Z5 (2 GB) YP-Z5 (4 GB) $250	200	63	○	○	⊖	○	35	•	•	•	•		•	
10	**Creative** Zen Nano Plus (1 GB) Zen Nano Plus (512 MB) $60	70	62	○	○	⊖	NA	13	•					•	•
11	**Oregon** Scientific MP121 (1 GB)	170	62	⊖	⊖	⊖	NA	8	•						
12	**Philips** SA178 (512 MB)	100	61	○	○	⊖	NA	13	•					•	
13	**SanDisk** Sansa m240 (1 GB) Sansa m230 (512 MB) $60, Sansa m250 (2 GB) $125	85	61	○	○	⊖	NA	15	•					•	•
14	**Creative** MuVo TX FM (1 GB) MuVo TX FM (128 MB) $60, MuVo TX FM (256 MB) $70, MuVo TX FM (512 MB) $75	100	60	○	○	⊖	NA	14	•					•	
15	**JVC** XA-MP101 (1 GB) XA-MP51 (512 MB) $95	120	59	○	○	⊖	NA	13	•					•	
16	**Samsung** YP-F1 Z (1 GB) YP-F1 V (256 MB) $100,YP-F1 X (512 MB) $110	125	58	⊖	○	⊖	NA	7	•					•	
17	**Apple** iPod shuffle M9725LL/A (1 GB) iPod Shuffle M9724LL/A (512 MB) $70	100	57	○	⊖	⊖	NA	16	•	•					
18	**Dell** DJ Ditty (512 MB)	100	57	○	○	⊖	NA	7	•						
19	**Sony** Walkman Bean NW-307 (1 GB) Walkman Bean NW-305 (512 MB) $95	125	57	○	○	⊖	NA	52	•					•	
20	**MobiBLU** DAH-1500i (1 GB) DAH-1500i (512 MB) $100	130	56	○	○	⊖	NA	8	•					•	•
21	**SanDisk** Sansa e140 (1 GB) Sansa e130 (512 MB) $60	85	56	○	○	⊖	NA	11	•					•	
22	**Sony** Network Walkman NW-E107 (1 GB) Psyc Network Walkman NW-E103PS (256 MB) $80,Psyc Network Walkman NW-E105PS (512 MB) $90	95	56	○	○	⊖	NA	41	•					•	
23	**RiData** OLE 3000 (512 MB) OLE 3000 (128 MB) $70,OLE 3000 (256 MB) $100	130	51	○	○	⊖	NA	11	•					•	•
24	**Bang and Olufsen** Beosound 2	460	45	◑	⊖	⊖	NA	8	•		•				

Key number	Brand & model / Small type: similar models(s)	Price	Overall score (0–100, P F G VG E)	Ease of use	Headphone quality	Audio quality	Picture quality	Audio-playback time (hr.)	Plays online music	Mac compatible	Color display	Video playback	Slideshow capability	FM radio	Built-in microphone
MICRODRIVE HARD-DISK MP3 PLAYERS (3GB TO 8GB)															
25	**Creative** Zen Micro Photo (8 GB)	$225	64	○	⊖	⊖	○	16	•		•			•	•
26	**RCA** Lyra RD2765 (5 GB)	175	63	⊖	⊖	⊖	⊖	11	•	•	•				
27	**Archos** Gmini XS 100 (3 GB)	125	62	⊖	○	⊖	NA	11	•	•					
28	**iRiver** H10 (6 GB) H10 (5 GB) $250	270	61	⊖	○	⊖	⊖	6	•		•			•	•
29	**Creative** Zen Micro (6 GB) Zen Micro (4 GB) $150, Zen Micro (5 GB) $180	200	58	○	○	⊖	NA	13	•					•	•
30	**Samsung** YH-820 (5 GB)	230	56	○	○	⊖	⊖	9	•					•	•
HARD-DISK MP3 PLAYERS (10GB TO 60GB)															
31	**Cowon** iAudio X5L (30 GB)	300	68	⊖	⊖	⊖	⊖	30			•	•		•	•
32	**iRiver** H10 (20 GB)	200	68	⊖	⊖	⊖	⊖	15	•		•			•	•
33	**Cowon** iAudio X5 (20 GB) iAudio X5 (30 GB) $300	280	67	⊖	⊖	⊖	⊖	13			•	•		•	•
34	**Creative** Zen Vision M (30 GB)	300	66	⊖	○	⊖	⊖	18	•		•	•	•	•	•
35	**Archos** Gmini 402 Pocket Multimedia Center (20 GB)	340	65	⊖	○	⊖	○	12	•	•	•	•			
36	**Creative** Zen Sleek Photo (20 GB)	200	65	○	⊖	⊖	⊖	18	•		•			•	•
37	**Apple** iPod (30 GB)	300	63	⊖	○	⊖	⊖	15	•	•	•	•	•		
38	**Creative** Zen Sleek (20 GB)	250	63	⊖	○	⊖	NA	18	•					•	•
39	**Toshiba** gigabeat MEGF20 (20 GB) gigabeat MEGF10 (10 GB) $200, gigabeat MEGF40 (40 GB) $250, gigabeat MEGF60 (60 GB) $325	210	63	⊖	○	⊖	○	19	•		•		•		
40	**Archos** Gmini XS 202 (20 GB)	300	62	⊖	○	⊖	NA	16	•	•					
41	**Archos** Gmini XS 202s (20 GB)	250	62	○	○	⊖	NA	16	•	•					
42	**Samsung** YH-999 (20 GB)	340	62	○	○	⊖	○	14	•		•	•	•	•	•
43	**Philips** HDD6330 (30 GB)	250	61	○	○	⊖	○	17	•		•			•	•
44	**Creative** Zen Vision (30 GB)	400	59	⊖	○	⊖	○	15	•		•	•	•	•	•

See report, page 33. Based on tests posted on ConsumerReports.org in July 2006, with updated prices and availability.

Guide to the Ratings

The MP3 player market is dominated by three types: flash-memory, microdrive, and hard-disk. Flash-memory players are the smallest and lightest of the group. They're no bigger than a pack of gum and weigh no more than three ounces. They're solid-state, meaning they have no moving parts, and their storage capacities range from 128 megabytes to 6 gigabytes (about 30 to 1,500 songs). Palm-sized microdrive players have tiny hard drives with a storage capacity of 3 to 8 gigabytes (about 750 to 2,000 songs). They weigh about a quarter-pound. Hard-disk players are about the size of a deck of cards and have a storage capacity of 10 to 60 gigabytes (about 2,500 to 15,000 songs). Some hard-disk players with video capability have relatively larger displays, and as a result tend to be the bulkiest players. You can expect a player to hold about 250 songs per gigabyte of memory. **Overall score,** as MP3 players, is based primarily on ease of use, headphone quality, audio quality, damage resistance and audio-playback time. Video and picture quality are rated but not included in the overall score. **Ease of use** mainly covers player characteristics that aid in convenience, versatility, and portability. These primarily include navigation and scrolling features; the accessibility and readability of the controls; the readability and breadth of the information in the display; size and weight; and ease of use while walking or jogging. Some features and capabilities considered include the presence of an FM radio, built-in microphone, upgradable firmware, equalizer, data storage, software assessment, and the player's ability to be recognized as a hard drive by a computer without the installation of additional drivers. **Headphone quality** reflects judgments from a listening panel comparing the player and its supplied headphone with a test audio CD and a high-fidelity headphone. All uncompressed (audio CD or WAV) test music sources were ripped (encoded) to MP3 format (128, 192, and 256 kbps CBR rate) using a high-quality encoder. **Audio quality** reflects judgments from a listening panel comparing the player with a test audio CD, using the high-fidelity headphone for both. All uncompressed (audio CD or WAV) test music sources were ripped (encoded) to MP3 format (128, 192, and 256 kbps CBR rate) using a high-quality encoder. **Picture quality** reflects judgments based mainly on viewing angle, display size, and clarity and color in different lighting conditions, using the JPEG format. **Audio-playback time** reflects lab measurements of continuous playback time to the nearest hour, using a selection of music tracks encoded to MP3 format at a 128 kbps CBR rate; fully charged rechargeable batteries; backlight at the minimum setting; with included headphone; and volume set at a reasonable level. For players that can use standard batteries such as alkaline, expect a bit longer playback time. Our measurements should not be compared with those stated by the manufacturer, which may use different testing methods and criteria. **Price** is approximate retail.

Quick Picks

If low price, light weight, and small size are paramount:

   2 Cowon iAudio U3 (2GB), $180
   4 Apple iPod Nano (2GB), $200
   8 RCA Lyra RD2217 (1GB), $125
  13 SanDisk Sansa m240 (1GB), $85

The Cowon iAudio U3 and Apple iPod Nano combine fine performance and high capacity, albeit at a relatively high price. In their 2GB versions, these players hold about 500 songs—enough variety for any long weekend. There's also a 4GB Nano for $50 more. (A newer player that isn't in the Ratings, the Sansa e270, $270, has a 6GB capacity and performed well in our initial tests, and more high-capacity flash players are expected from other manufacturers.) The Cowon includes an FM radio (from which you can record programs), a built-in microphone, and a line input for recording from other sources. It's also one of the few flash units that plays video. But it doesn't work with Macintosh computers. The slightly bigger—but much thinner—Nano lacks these bells and whistles, but provides seamless access to one of the biggest legal sources for online music: the 2 million-song iTunes store. It adds volume-leveling, plus a volume limiter to protect your hearing. For both players, the AC charger is optional. The Cowon's costs $10; the Nano's $30.

The more-affordable RCA Lyra RD2217 and SanDisk Sansa m240 lack color displays and hold half the songs, but provide lots of features for the buck. The sports-oriented RCA has a stopwatch, and calorie and pulse-rate modes. It also has a relatively long playback time and an FM radio. The SanDisk also has an FM radio and stopwatch, plus a built-in microphone for personal memos. But it won't work with Macs. Both use standard batteries.

For fairly high capacity in a compact size:

25 Creative Zen Micro Photo
(8GB), $225

26 RCA Lyra RD2765 (5GB), $175

These models are larger than flash-memory players, though they still fit comfortably in your palm. And they hold many more songs than most flash players. Both have color displays and show slideshows, though neither allows you to play accompanying music. The 8GB Creative holds about 2,000 songs and features an FM radio, built-in microphone, and volume-leveling playback capability. But it doesn't work with Macs and the AC charger is a $40 option. The less expensive 5GB RCA is similarly sized, but has fewer features and holds 1,250 songs.

For the best combination of huge capacity and a fairly low price:

32 iRiver H10 (20GB), $200

34 Creative Zen Vision M (30GB),
$300

36 Creative Zen Sleek Photo
(20GB), $200

37 Apple iPod (30GB), $300

While these models are larger and heavier than flash-memory and microdrive players, they can hold more music—from 2,500 to 15,000 songs, depending on the model. The Apple iPod (30GB) should be the first choice in a high-capacity MP3 player for most people, given its palm-friendly dimensions. Video and photo quality was among the best of any model we tested. Like the Nano, it includes a volume leveler and limiter. Some quibbles: As with the Nano, the charger is a $30 option. It also lacks the proprietary cable ($20) needed for connecting the player to a TV set to view videos or photos on a larger screen.

Those who need a player with a radio or voice recorder must turn to other brands, some of which offer models that cost a little less than the iPod. The iRiver H10 (20GB) offers an FM radio (from which you can record programs) and built-in microphone. The Creative Zen Vision M (30GB) packs most of the features of the similarly priced iPod, including video playback and volume leveling, and adds an FM radio (from which you can record programs), built-in microphone, and line output. Video quality was as good as the iPod, though there's not as much top-tier content to download. The less expensive—and less capacious—Creative Zen Sleek Photo (20GB) has volume leveling but lacks video. All three models are thicker than the iPod and don't work with Macs.

PLASMA TVs

The best of the plasma sets we tested have fine picture quality, with good brightness and contrast from any angle. Most plasma sets have 42-inch screens, but you'll increasingly find more 50-inch and larger screens. These larger-screen plasma TVs cost considerably more than comparably sized microdisplay projection sets, but plasma sets are much slimmer and can be wall-mounted. You can get flat-screen LCD sets with bigger screens now, but plasma TVs typically cost less.

Less-familiar brands of plasma TVs being sold at big-box chains cost much less than major brands. While their prices are tempting, the sets we've tested have been middling to mediocre, so you'll sacrifice some picture quality.

If you watch a lot of DVDs, check out the DVD-playback scores, which indicate picture quality from a progressive-scan DVD player. Picture quality scores for HD, DVD, and SD content are not directly comparable across signal types, because each is capable of a different level of quality. Thus, a very good score for HD indicates a better picture than a very good score for regular TV signals.

Quick Picks

Best 50-inch sets:

 2 LG 50PC1DR, $3,300
 4 Panasonic TH-50PX60U, $3,100

The LG offers a lot for the money, including a built-in DVR. Picture quality was very good, though images were a bit soft, and it had very good sound. With its DVR and CableCard slot, you don't have to connect any boxes, a plus for wall-mounting. It has a 2-year warranty instead of the typical 1 year. The Panasonic displayed sharp, clear, colorful images, but its overall score was hurt by mediocre sound. Audio is OK for standard TV fare, but hook up speakers to get sound as good as the picture. The 50-inch Fujitsu (1) has a fine picture and excellent sound rivaling some bookshelf speakers, but it's hard to justify the $2,000-plus premium over other very good sets.

Value-priced 50-inch sets:

 3 HP PL5060N, $2,600
 5 Zenith Z50PX2D, $2,500

The HP is low-priced for a 50-incher and a solid performer. Exaggerated sharpness created slight graininess in images, though HD picture quality was still very good. The side-mounted speakers add a foot or so to the width but can be detached. The Zenith also had very good HD picture quality, though images were a tad soft, with slight graininess. (This is an older set that was available at press time, but it may be hard to find at this point.)

Top picks for a 42-inch TV:

 9 HP PL4260N, $1,700
 10 Panasonic TH-42PX60U, $2,100
 11 Hitachi Ultravision 42HDS69, $2,200

These three sets are all fine choices with pleasing picture quality. The HP is noteworthy for value and excellent sound. As with its 50-inch sibling, HD images were a bit grainy because of exaggerated sharpness, but still very good. The Panasonic was much like the larger model (4) recommended above. It's a good buy. The Hitachi, with a resolution of 1024x1080, has enough pixels vertically to display all 1,080 lines in an HD signal, but its horizontal resolution falls short of a 1080p set's. It displayed fine detail and very good HD picture quality, but it had minor flaws. Colors were slightly off and there were some jaggies along the edges of moving objects.

	Excellent	Very good	Good	Fair	Poor
	⊜	⊖	○	◒	●

Within types, in performance order. Gray **key numbers indicate Quick Picks.**

Key number	Brand & model	Price	Overall score (P F G VG E, 0–100)	Picture quality: HD	DVD	Standard-def.	Sound quality	Ease of use: Remote	Menu	ATSC	QAM	CableCard	Component	HDMI
	50-INCH MODELS *All tested models have a native resolution of 1366x768.*													
1	**Fujitsu** Plasmavision P50XTA51UB	$5,500	63	⊖	⊖	○	⊖	○	○	●	●	●	2	1
2	**LG** 50PC1DR	3,300	63	⊖	⊖	○	⊖	○	○	●	●	●	2	2
3	**HP** PL5060N	2,600	59	⊖	○	○	⊖	○	○	●	●		2	1
4	**Panasonic** TH-50PX60U	3,100	55	⊖	⊖	○	○	○	◒	●	●		2	2
5	**Zenith** Z50PX2D ③	2,500	55	⊖	⊖	○①	⊖	○	◒	●	●		2	1
6	**Samsung** HP-S5053	3,200	51	○	○	○	⊖	⊖	○				2	2
7	**Dell** W5001C	3,000	46	○	○	⊖①	⊖	⊖	◒	●			2	2
	42-INCH MODELS *All tested models have a native resolution of 1024x768 except as noted.*													
8	**Fujitsu** Plasmavision P42XTA51US	4,500	61	⊖	⊖	○	⊖	○	○	●	●	●	2	1
9	**HP** PL4260N	1,700	59	⊖	○	○	⊖	○	○	●	●		2	1
10	**Panasonic** TH-42PX60U	2,100	58	⊖	⊖	○	○	○	◒	●	●		2	2
11	**Hitachi** Ultravision 42HDS69 ②	2,200	55	⊖	⊖	○	⊖	◒	◒	●	●	●	3	2
12	**LG** 42PC3D	1,900	55	○	⊖	○	⊖	○	◒	●	●		2	1
13	**Samsung** HP-S4253	2,200	50	○	○	◒	⊖	⊖	○	●			2	2
14	**Toshiba** 42HP66	2,000	39	○	◒	◒	⊖	⊖	○	●	●		2	2
15	**Proview** MH-422HU ③	2,200	38	◒	◒	○①	⊖	◒	◒				2	

See report, page 140. Based on tests in Consumer Reports in November 2006.

Guide to the Ratings

Overall score is based primarily on picture quality; sound quality and ease of use are also considered. Under **picture quality, HD** reflects display of a high-definition (1080i) signal, such as that from a digital-cable box or satellite receiver (all tested sets were HD models). **DVD** reflects display of a 480p signal, such as the output from a progressive-scan DVD player. **Standard-def.** (SD) picture scores are for a standard-definition (480i) signal, such as that of a regular-TV program. All signals were routed via a component-video input except where noted. Picture-quality scores for HD, DVD, and SD content aren't directly comparable across signal types because each is capable of a different level of quality. Thus, a very good score for HD indicates a better picture than a very good score for regular TV signals. **Sound quality** is for the set's built-in speakers. **Ease of use** is our assessment of the remote control and onscreen menus. Under **digital tuners,** an ATSC tuner allows a set to receive digital signals, including HD, via antenna; a QAM tuner can receive unscrambled digital signals from cable; a CableCard-ready set can receive scrambled (e.g., premium) and unscrambled digital channels on cable when equipped with a CableCard. Where no digital-tuning option is listed, models are HD-ready sets that require an external digital tuner, such as an HD-capable cable or satellite box. **Price** is approximate retail.

PRINTERS, ALL-IN-ONE

If all you do is print, you can save money and space by purchasing a dedicated printer. But if there's any chance you might want to copy or scan, it's worth investigating an all-in-one. While most models are bigger than the typical new stand-alone printer, they take up less space and cost less than a separate printer, scanner, and copier. Having to hook up only one device to your computer simplifies setup as well. An all-in-one's scanning function should be fine for print originals. Some can also handle basic film and slide scanning, though for top quality we recommend a separate scanner. The copying function is fine for casual use. Some all-in-ones add fax, phone, and answering functions. As the Ratings show, paying more for a printer doesn't necessarily mean you'll get better photos. And don't consider only the purchase price of the printer itself. Per-print costs can make a cheaper model more expensive in the long run than a higher-priced printer with low per-copy costs.

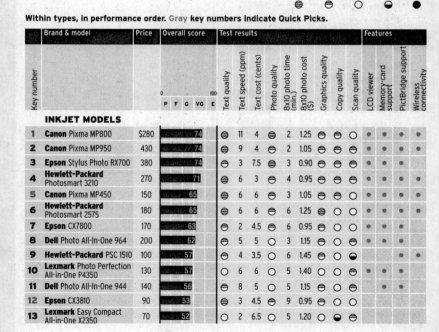

		Excellent	Very good	Good	Fair	Poor
		⊖	⊖	○	⊖	●

Within types, in performance order. Gray key numbers indicate Quick Picks.

Key number	Brand & model	Price	Overall score	Text quality	Text speed (ppm)	Text cost (cents)	Photo quality	8x10 photo time (min.)	8x10 photo cost ($)	Graphics quality	Copy quality	Scan quality	LCD viewer	Memory-card support	PictBridge support	Wireless connectivity
INKJET MODELS																
1	**Canon** Pixma MP800	$280	74	⊖	11	4	⊖	2	1.25	⊖	⊖	○	•	•	•	•
2	**Canon** Pixma MP950	430	74	⊖	9	4	⊖	2	1.05	⊖	⊖	⊖	•	•	•	•
3	**Epson** Stylus Photo RX700	380	74	⊖	3	7.5	⊖	3	0.90	⊖	⊖	⊖	•	•	•	
4	**Hewlett-Packard** Photosmart 3210	270	71	⊖	6	3	⊖	4	0.95	⊖	⊖	⊖	•	•	•	•
5	**Canon** Pixma MP450	150	65	⊖	6	6	⊖	3	1.05	⊖	○	○		•	•	
6	**Hewlett-Packard** Photosmart 2575	180	65	⊖	6	6	⊖	6	1.25	⊖	⊖	⊖	•	•	•	•
7	**Epson** CX7800	170	63	⊖	2	4.5	⊖	6	0.95	○	○	⊖	•	•	•	
8	**Dell** Photo All-In-One 964	200	62	⊖	5	5	○	3	1.15	⊖	○	⊖	•	•	•	
9	**Hewlett-Packard** PSC 1510	100	57	⊖	4	3.5	○	6	1.45	⊖	○	◒		•	•	
10	**Lexmark** Photo Perfection All-in-One P4350	130	57	○	6	6	⊖	5	1.40	⊖	○	⊖	•	•	•	
11	**Dell** Photo All-in-One 944	140	56	⊖	8	5	⊖	5	1.15	⊖	○	⊖		•	•	
12	**Epson** CX3810	90	53	⊖	3	4.5	⊖	9	0.95	⊖	○	○		•		
13	**Lexmark** Easy Compact All-in-One X2350	70	52	○	2	6.5	○	5	1.20	○	◒	⊖				

Key number	Brand & model	Price	Overall score	Test results									Features			
			0 100 P F G VG E	Text quality	Text speed (ppm)	Text cost (cents)	Photo quality	8x10 photo time (min.)	8x10 photo cost ($)	Graphics quality	Copy quality	Scan quality	LCD viewer	Memory-card support	PictBridge support	Wireless connectivity
	LASER MODELS															
14	**Brother** MFC-7420	$300	69	⊜	15	2	NA	NA	NA	○	○	○				
15	**Brother** DCP-7020	200	66	⊜	13	1.5	NA	NA	NA	○	○	○				
16	**Samsung** SCX-4521F	250	66	⊜	13	3	NA	NA	NA	⊖	○	○				●

See report, page 140. Based on tests posted on ConsumerReports.org in July 2006, with updated prices and availability.

Guide to the Ratings

Overall score is based on speed and quality of print, scan, and copy functions, plus ease of use. **Text quality** is an assessment of clarity and crispness of black text. **Text speed** measures pages per minute (ppm) for a five-page document at default settings. **Text cost** is for one black-text page (ink or toner plus plain paper) or one 8x10-inch color photo (ink and glossy 8½x11-inch paper). A borderless 4x6-inch print would cost about one-third as much. **Photo quality** reflects a color snapshot's appearance. **8x10-photo time** measures, to the nearest half-minute, the time to print an 8x10-inch color photo at the best-quality setting. **8x10 photo cost** is the estimated cost of the color ink and glossy photo paper needed to produce an 8x10 photo. **Graphics quality** assesses output such as Web pages, greeting cards, and charts; for laser models, we tested with black-and-white graphics. **Copy quality** is for photos, graphics, and text. **Scan quality** is for color photos, graphics, and text scanned at each model's default settings and judged on a high-quality monitor; scores can't be compared with those of the flatbed scanners, which were tested differently. **Price** is approximate retail. All tested models work with Windows XP and 2000; all but the Dell (8, 11) support Windows ME and 98. Most support Macs.

Quick Picks

Best choices among all-in-one inkjets:
1   Canon Pixma MP800, $280
5   Canon Pixma MP450, $150
12   Epson CX3810, $90

The Canon Pixma MP800 printed excellent photos and text and was among the fastest we tested, printing an 8x10 in 2 minutes, for $1.25. The other Canon did almost as well,

and its cost for an 8x10 was $1.05. Both have an LCD viewer, card reader, and PictBridge; the MP800 adds film-scanning. The Epson is low-priced, and it has fine photo and text quality. But it's slow (9 minutes for an 8x10) and lacks an LCD, card reader, and PictBridge. You can print only from a computer.

PRINTERS, SNAPSHOT

There are three reasons to choose a snapshot printer over a full-sized inkjet printer: convenience, speed, and portability. Ease of use is unequaled—this is as close to one-touch printing as you can get. Getting images to print is also a snap. You simply connect the printer to a PictBridge-enabled camera with a USB cable, choose a shot, and click "Print" on the camera's display. Speed is a plus; most snapshot printers can print a 4x6-inch photo in less than 2 minutes. (Dye-sub models are usually faster than inkjets.) And then there's the portability. Small and lightweight (3 to 7 pounds), these printers are easily toted on trips or to parties.

But you do sacrifice versatility. Snapshot printers can't print large photos, text, or graphics. If you want one device that can handle all of your printing, stick with a full-sized inkjet.

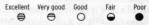

Excellent ⊖ Very good ⊖ Good ○ Fair ◐ Poor ●

Within types, in performance order. Gray **key numbers indicate Quick Picks.**

Key number	Brand & model	Price	Overall score (0-100)	Photo quality	4x6 photo time (min.)	4x6 photo cost ($)	Printing method	LCD viewer	Memory-card support	PictBridge support	Wireless connectivity
1	**Hewlett-Packard** PhotoSmart 475 GoGo Photo Printer	$250	67	Very good	2	.30	Inkjet	•	•	•	•
2	**Canon** Selphy CP600	200	66	Good	1.25	.28	Dye-sub			•	
3	**Hewlett-Packard** PhotoSmart 425 GoGo Photo Printer	280	65	Very good	2	.30	Inkjet	•	•	•	
4	**Hewlett-Packard** PhotoSmart 428 GoGo Photo Printer	300	65	Very good	2	.29	Inkjet	•	•	•	
5	**Samsung** SPP-2040	100	65	Very good	1.25	.42	Dye-sub	•	•	•	
6	**Hewlett-Packard** PhotoSmart 385 GoGo Photo Printer	170	63	Very good	2	.30	Inkjet	•	•	•	•
7	**Canon** Selphy CP710	140	62	Good	1.5	.28	Dye-sub			•	
8	**Canon** Selphy DS810	150	62	Good	2	.60	Inkjet			•	
9	**Hewlett-Packard** PhotoSmart 335 GoGo Photo Printer	130	62	Very good	2	.30	Inkjet	•	•	•	
10	**Samsung** SPP-2020	80	62	Very good	1.25	.42	Dye-sub			•	
11	**Canon** Selphy CP510	90	60	Good	1.5	.28	Dye-sub			•	
12	**Epson** PictureMate Deluxe Viewer Finder	200	59	Good	1.5	.23	Inkjet	•	•	•	
13	**Epson** PictureMate Express Edition	130	58	Good	1.75	.23	Inkjet		•	•	
14	**Sony** PictureStation DPP-FP50	150	58	Good	1	.40	Dye-sub	•	•	•	
15	**Kodak** EasyShare Photo Printer 500	190	56	Good	1.5	.29	Dye-sub	•	•	•	

Within types, in performance order. Gray key numbers indicate Quick Picks.

Key number	Brand & model	Price	Overall score	Photo quality	4x6 photo time (min.)	4x6 photo cost ($)	Printing method	LCD viewer	Memory-card support	PictBridge support	Wireless connectivity
16	**Kodak** EasyShare Printer Dock Plus Series 3	$160	56	○	1.5	.29	Dye-sub		●	●	●
17	**Kodak** EasyShare Printer Dock Plus	180	55	○	1.5	.29	Dye-sub		●	●	●
18	**Olympus** P-11 Digital Photo Printer	140	54	○	0.75	.39	Dye-sub			●	
19	**Lexmark** P450 Photo Printer	200	44	◒	2.75	.42	Inkjet	●	●	●	●
20	**Kodak** EasyShare Photo Printer 300	100	37	◒	1.75	.29	Dye-sub			●	
21	**Kodak** EasyShare Printer Dock	135	37	◒	1.75	.29	Dye-sub			●	
22	**Kodak** EasyShare Printer Dock Series 3	150	37	◒	1.75	.29	Dye-sub			●	

See report, page 140. Based on tests posted on ConsumerReports.org in July 2006, with updated prices and availability.

Guide to the Ratings

Overall score is based on speed, photo quality, and ease of use. **Photo quality** is our assessment of the appearance of photos. Models with higher scores produce more natural-looking photos, with smoother changes in shading and fewer problems with banding. **4x6 photo time** is our measurement, to the nearest half-minute, of how long it took each snapshot printer to output a 4x6 borderless photo directly from a digital camera. **4x6 photo cost** is the estimated cost of the color ink or ribbon (for dye-sublimation models) and glossy photo paper needed to produce a 4x6 photo. **Printing method** indicates which technology a printer uses to create an image onto paper or other media. Most printers use inkjet technology, though many snapshot printers use dye-sublimation. Printers intended primarily for text use laser technology. **LCD viewer** indicates whether the printer has a built-in LCD screen for viewing and editing images from a memory card. The screen is small, usually only 1 to 3.5 inches, and editing capability is very limited. **Price** is approximate retail.

Quick Picks

For the best quality and value:

- 7 Canon Selphy CP710, $140
- 9 Hewlett-Packard PhotoSmart 335 GoGo Photo Printer, $130
- 13 Epson PictureMate Express Edition, $130

All three models are strong performers. Photos from the HP inkjet were a bit sharper and richer than those from the Canon dye-sub and Epson inkjet. The Canon printed a 4x6 in 90 seconds; the HP and Epson in less than 2 minutes. Photo costs were 23 cents for the Epson, 30 cents for the HP, and 28 cents for the Canon. All three are PictBridge-enabled and have a card slot; the HP and Canon have an LCD viewer. The Canon is small and can run on a battery ($80). If you'll print only from the camera and don't need a card slot, consider the Canon Selphy CP510, similar to the CP710 but only $90.

Tops if you don't print many photos:

- 5 Samsung SPP-2040, $100

The Samsung dye-sub printer produced very good photos in 70 seconds, but its per-photo cost was high at 42 cents. If you don't print a lot, the quality and speed might be worth the cost. The SPP-2020, $80, offers comparable performance but lacks the card slot and LCD viewer of the SPP-2040. Both are PictBridge-enabled.

Great for portable use:

- 2 Canon Selphy CP600, $200

This printer includes a battery—a costly option for other models—and is among the smallest and lightest models. It's as good as its brand mates for photo quality and costs, but is faster, printing a 4x6 in just over 1 minute. It's PictBridge-enabled but has no card slot or viewer.

PRINTERS, REGULAR

Standard inkjets are the best all-purpose printers for most consumers who want to print both text and color photos. They offer versatility, top print quality, and low-cost enlargements. They can print almost anything, including photos 8x10 inches or larger, text, and graphics like greeting cards. You can use various types and sizes of paper, from business cards to banners.

Quality is another plus. The photos from the best inkjets are as good as those you get from a photofinisher. Larger prints also typically cost less than you'd pay a photofinisher—about $1 to $1.50 for an 8x10-inch photo, compared with $2 to $4 for professional processing. But inkjets aren't known for speed, so it could take a while to print a number of 8x10s.

Don't print photos or color graphics? Traditional black-and-white laser printers can't be beat for fast text printing at a good cost, especially if you print reams of black-and-white text documents.

As the Ratings show, paying more for a printer doesn't necessarily mean you'll get better photos. And don't consider only the purchase price of the printer itself. Per-print costs can make a cheaper model more expensive in the long run than a higher-priced printer with low per-copy costs.

			Excellent	Very good	Good	Fair	Poor
			⊖	⊖	○	⊖	●

Within types, in performance order. Gray **key numbers indicate Quick Picks.**

Key number	Brand & model	Price	Overall score	Text quality	Text speed (ppm)	Text cost (cents)	Photo quality	8x10 photo time (min.)	8x10 photo cost ($)	Graphics quality	LCD viewer	Memory-card support	Individual color tanks	PictBridge support	Wireless connectivity
	INKJET MODELS														
1	**Canon** Pixma iP5200R	$215	88	⊖	10	4	⊖	1.5	1.05	⊖			●	●	●
2	**Canon** Pixma iP5200	150	87	⊖	10	4	⊖	1.5	1.05	⊖			●	●	
3	**Canon** Pixma iP4200	100	83	⊖	8	4	⊖	3	1.05	⊖			●	●	
4	**Canon** Pixma iP6600D	195	82	○	4	55	⊖	1.5	1.05	○	●	●	●	●	
5	**Epson** Stylus Photo R340	175	77	⊖	2	35	⊖	4	1.00	⊖	●	●	●	●	
6	**Hewlett-Packard** PhotoSmart 8250	170	73	⊖	4	25	⊖	2.5	0.90	⊖	●	●	●	●	
7	**Canon** Pixma iP6220D	145	72	⊖	2	12	⊖	4	1.40	⊖	●	●	●	●	
8	**Epson** Stylus C88	80	72	⊖	5	4	⊖	5.5	0.90	⊖			●		
9	**Epson** Stylus Photo R320	180	72	⊖	2	35	⊖	4	1.00	⊖	●	●	●	●	
10	**Epson** Stylus Photo R220	100	71	○	2	35	⊖	3.5	0.85	⊖			●	●	

Excellent ⊖ Very good ⊖ Good ○ Fair ⊖ Poor ●

Within types, in performance order. Gray key numbers indicate Quick Picks.

Key number	Brand & model	Price	Overall score	Text quality	Text speed (ppm)	Text cost (cents)	Photo quality	8x10 photo time (min.)	8x10 photo cost ($)	Graphics quality	LCD viewer	Memory-card support	Individual color tanks	PictBridge support	Wireless connectivity
	INKJET MODELS *continued*														
11	**Canon** Pixma iP6210D	95	70	⊖	2	12	⊖	4	1.40	⊖	●	●			●
12	**Hewlett-Packard** Deskjet 5940	90	69	⊖	6	55	○	5.5	1.30	⊖					●
13	**Hewlett-Packard** Photosmart 8050 Photo Printer	130	69	⊖	7	5	⊖	5.5	1.30	⊖	●	●			●
14	**Hewlett-Packard** Deskjet 3940	50	59	⊖	2	12	○	11.5	1.00	⊖					

See report, page 140. Based on tests posted on ConsumerReports.org in July 2006, with updated prices and availability.

Guide to the Ratings

Overall score, for full-sized printers, is based primarily on print quality and speed for printing text and color photos. **Text quality** indicates how crisply and clearly a printer produced black text in a variety of faces, sizes, and styles. Models with higher scores produce more uniform type, with sharper edges and smoother curves. **Text speed** is our calculation of the printer's typical output in pages per minute (ppm) for a three-page document. Speeds generally range from 2 to 9 ppm. **Text cost** is the estimated cost of black ink and paper, in cents, to produce a single text page. **Photo quality** is our assessment of the appearance of each photo. Models with higher scores produce more natural-looking photos, with smoother changes in shading and fewer problems with banding. **8x10 photo time,** to the nearest half-minute, is our measure of how long it took each full-sized printer to output an 8x10 color print, at the printer's best setting, using a 2.8-GHz PC with 496 megabytes of RAM. **8x10 photo cost** is the estimated cost of the color ink and glossy photo paper needed to produce an 8x10 photo. **4x6 photo cost** is the estimated cost of the color ink or ribbon (for dye-sublimation models) and glossy photo paper needed to produce a 4x6 photo. **Graphics quality** is our assessment of the appearance of color graphics produced by the printer. Models with higher scores produce graphics whose colors are brighter, more uniform, and less prone to band or bleed into one another on the page. **Price** is approximate retail.

Quick Picks

The best all-around inkjets:

2 Canon Pixma iP5200, $150

5 Epson Stylus Photo R340, $175

The Canon stands out for quality, low print costs, and speed. Photos and text were excellent; costs were $1.05 for an 8x10 print, 35 cents for a 4x6 print, and 3 cents for a text page. It printed an 8x10 in a minute and a half and text at 8 pages per minute. It has a second paper tray, which you can use for 4x6 paper. It is PictBridge-enabled but has no card reader or LCD viewer. A sibling, the iP5200R, adds Wi-Fi, allowing wireless links to compatible computers and cameras, along with Ethernet for easy networking. It costs $225. The Epson produced very good photos and text but was much slower than the Canon, with speeds of 4 minutes for an 8x10 and 2 ppm for text. Print costs were comparable to the Canon's. It has an LCD viewer and card reader as well as PictBridge, but only one paper tray.

A bit slower but lower-priced:

3 Canon Pixma iP4200, $100

This model performed much like the newer iP5200, above, and has the same features. The main difference is slightly slower speed for photos: 3 minutes to print an 8x10.

RANGES

You can find a high-performing electric range without breaking the bank. As the Ratings show, several of the models we tested in the $450 to $1,000 price range outperformed ranges costing $1,500 or more. Many of those moderately priced models also offer stainless steel or stainless-steel trim, high-powered elements or burners, and other features. Spending more than $1,000 generally buys extras such as an additional oven or warming drawer and convection, and in gas ranges, burners rated at 15,000 Btu/hr. and higher, and a fifth burner. More money also gets you more stylish design.

But more high-heat elements or burners don't always translate into better cooking or better performance in the long run. For gas ranges, pro-style models such as DCS, Dacor, and Viking have been among the lower scorers in past tests.

Excellent Very good Good Fair Poor

Within types, in performance order. Gray key numbers indicate Quick Picks.

SMOOTHTOP MODELS

Key number	Brand & model (Small type: similar models)	Price	Overall score	High-power elements	Medium-power elements	Low-power elements
1	**Jenn-Air** JER8885QA[S]	$1400	81	2	None	2
2	**Kenmore** (Sears) 9641[2] **CR Best Buy** 9642[ ] $750	750	81	2	None	2
3	**Kenmore** (Sears) Elite 9912[2]	1400	80	1	2	1
4	**Maytag** MER5775RA[S]	1000	77	2	None	2
5	**Frigidaire** Gallery GLEF369D[S]	650	76	2	None	2
6	**GE** Profile JB968TK[WW]	1550	76	1	2	1
7	**Kenmore** (Sears) 9611[2] **CR Best Buy** 9612[ ]$580	580	76	2	None	2
8	**Maytag** Gemini MER6775AA[S]	1500	76	2	None	2
9	**Frigidaire** Professional PLEF398D[C] Professional PLEFZ398E[C]$1350	1400	75	2	2	None
10	**GE** JBP84TK[WW]	1100	74	1	2	1
11	**Maytag** MER5752BA[W]	600	74	2	None	2
12	**GE** JBP81TK[WW]	950	73	2	None	2
13	**GE** JSP42WK[WW]	1000	72	1	2	1
14	**Maytag** MES5775BA[S]	1550	71	2	None	2
15	**Bosch** HES25[2]	1500	69	1	1	2
16	**Frigidaire** Gallery GLES389E[S]	1550	69	2	2	None
17	**Hotpoint** RB787WH[WW]	450	69	None	2	2

Key number	Brand & model	Price	Overall score (P F G VG E)	Cooktop high	Cooktop low	Baking	Broiling	Oven capacity	Oven cleaning	High-power elements	Medium-power elements	Low-power elements	Convection oven	Stainless-steel available
	Small type: similar models													
SMOOTHTOP MODELS *continued*														
18	**Whirlpool** Gold GR448LXP[Q]	$750	67	⊖	⊖	⊖	○	○	⊖	2	None	2		●
19	**Jenn-Air** JES8850AA[W]	1600	66	⊖	⊖	⊖	○	○	⊖	2	None	2	●	●
20	**Whirlpool** Polara GR556LRK[P]	1700	64	⊖	⊖	○	○	○	⊖	2	1	1	●	●
21	**Whirlpool** RF364PXM[Q]	550	64	○	⊖	⊖	⊖	○	○	None	2	2		
22	**Whirlpool** RF368LXP[Q]	600	62	⊖	⊖	○	○	○	⊖	2	None	2		●
23	**Viking** VESC306-4B[SS]	4000	60	⊖	⊖	○	○	◒	◒	1	2	1	●	●
24	**Sharp** Insight KB-3300J[W]	1300	59	⊖	⊖	⊖	○	◒	⊖	1	1	2		●
COIL MODELS														
25	**Kenmore** (Sears) 9421[2]	530	82	⊖	⊖	⊖	⊖	⊖	⊖	2	None	2		●
26	**GE** JBP35WH[WW] **CR Best Buy**	450	78	⊖	⊖	○	⊖	⊖	⊖	2	None	2		
27	**Hotpoint** RB757WH[WW] **CR Best Buy**	350	73	⊖	⊖	⊖	⊖	⊖	⊖	2	None	2		
28	**Maytag** MER5555QA[W]	600	72	○	⊖	⊖	⊖	⊖	⊖	2	None	2		
29	**GE** JBP35WK[WW]	500	69	○	⊖	⊖	○	○	⊖	2	None	2		●
30-INCH GAS MODELS														
30	**Hotpoint** RGB745WEH[WW] **CR Best Buy**	550	72	○	⊖	⊖	⊖	⊖	⊖	1	2	1		
31	**Maytag** MGS5775BD[S]	1450	70	⊖	⊖	⊖	○	○	○	1	2	1		●
32	**Thermador** PG304BS	4100	70	⊖	⊖	○	⊖	⊖	○	4	None	None	●	●
33	**GE** Profile JGBP918WEK[WW]	1600	69	⊖	⊖	⊖	⊖	⊖	○	1	2	2	●	●
34	**GE** JGBP35WEJ[WW]	800	68	○	⊖	⊖	⊖	⊖	○	1	2	1		
35	**GE** JGBP85WEJ[WW]	850	68	⊖	⊖	⊖	⊖	⊖	○	1	2	1		●
36	**Jenn-Air** JGS8750AD[W]	1500	68	⊖	⊖	⊖	⊖	○	⊖	1	2	1		●
37	**Maytag** Gemini MGR6775AD[S]	1500	68	○	⊖	⊖	⊖	⊖	⊖	1	2	1		●
38	**Maytag** MGR5875QD[W]	900	68	○	⊖	⊖	⊖	⊖	⊖	2	2	1		●
39	**Whirlpool** Gold GS470LEM[Q]	1000	68	○	⊖	○	⊖	⊖	⊖	2	1	1		●
40	**Whirlpool** SF368LEP[Q]	600	68	○	⊖	○	⊖	⊖	⊖	1	2	1		●
41	**GE** JGBP88WEK[WW]	1000	67	⊖	⊖	⊖	⊖	⊖	○	1	2	2	●	●
42	**Maytag** MGR5751AD[W] MGR5751BD[ ]S550	550	66	○	⊖	⊖	⊖	⊖	⊖	1	3	None		●
43	**Frigidaire** FGF366D[S] FGF366E[S]S550	700	65	⊖	⊖	⊖	⊖	⊖	○	1	3	None		●
44	**Frigidaire** Gallery GLGF386D[S]	700	65	⊖	⊖	⊖	⊖	⊖	○	2	2	1		●
45	**GE** Profile JGB900WEF[WW]	1000	64	○	○	⊖	⊖	⊖	○	1	2	1	●	●
46	**Bosch** HGS25[2]	1550	62	○	○	⊖	⊖	⊖	⊖	2	1	1		●

	Excellent	Very good	Good	Fair	Poor
	⊖	⊖	○	◐	●

Within types, in performance order. Gray key numbers indicate Quick Picks.

Key number	Brand & model (Small type: similar models)	Price	Overall score (0–100, P F G VG E)	Cooktop high	Cooktop low	Baking	Broiling	Oven capacity	Oven cleaning	High-power elements	Medium-power elements	Low-power elements	Convection oven	Stainless-steel available
30-INCH GAS MODELS *continued*														
47	**DCS** RGSC-305	$3700	62	◐	⊖	⊖	⊖	○	◐	5	None	None	●	●
48	**Kenmore** (Sears) 7881[2]7882[ ]S950	950	62	○	⊖	⊖	⊖	○	⊖	2	2	1		●
49	**Kenmore** (Sears) Elite 7936[2]	1400	61	○	○	⊖	⊖	○	⊖	2	2	1	●	●
50	**GE** Profile JGS905TEK[WW]	1700	59	○	○	○	○	⊖	⊖	None	3	1		●
51	**GE** JGBP26WEH[WW]	750	52	○	●	⊖	⊖	○	○	None	4	None		
30-INCH DUAL-FUEL MODELS														
52	**Bosch** HDS25[5]	2000	69	⊖	⊖	⊖	⊖	⊖	○	2	1	1	●	●
53	**GE** Profile J2B912WEK[WW]	1400	69	⊖	⊖	⊖	◐	⊖	○	1	2	1	●	●
54	**GE** Profile J2B918WEK[WW]	1700	69	⊖	⊖	⊖	○	⊖	○	1	2	2	●	●
55	**Jenn-Air** JDS8850AA[S]	2150	68	○	⊖	⊖	⊖	⊖	⊖	1	2	1	●	●
56	**Wolf** DF304	5200	67	○	⊖	⊖	◐	○	◐	3	1	None	●	●
57	**Frigidaire** Professional PLCS389E[C]	1900	66	○	⊖	⊖	◐	◐	⊖	2	1	1	●	●
58	**Kenmore** (Sears) Elite 7938[2]	1550	66	⊖	○	⊖	⊖	⊖	⊖	2	2	1	●	●
59	**Jenn-Air** JDS9860AA[W]	2000	63	◐	⊖	⊖	⊖	○	⊖	None	4	None	●	●
60	**Dacor** ERD30SO6[BK]	3800	61	○	⊖	⊖	◐	○	○	4	None	None	●	●
61	**Viking** VDSC305-4B[SS]	3800	61	○	○	⊖	◐	⊖	○	4	None	None	●	●
62	**Viking** VDSC307-4B[SS]	4000	61	○	⊖	○	⊖	◐	◐	4	None	None	●	●
63	**KitchenAid** Architect Series KDRP707R[SS]	4100	49	○	●	⊖	⊖	◐	⊖	4	None	None	●	●
36-INCH GAS MODELS														
64	**Thermador** Pro Grand PG366BS Pro Grand PG364GEBS $6600, Pro Grand PG364GLBS $6600	5800	70	⊖	⊖	⊖	○	⊖	○	6	None	None	●	●
65	**Viking** Professional Series VGSC367-6B Professional Series VGSC367-4GS$6580, Professional Series VGSC367-4Q $6580	5950	57	⊖	⊖	○	○	⊖	○	6	None	None	●	●
36-INCH DUAL-FUEL MODELS														
66	**GE** Monogram ZDP36N6H[SS] Monogram ZDP36N4DH[SS] $5260, Monogram ZDP36N4RH[SS] $5260	5000	61	○	⊖	○	○	○	○	6	None	None	●	●
67	**KitchenAid** Architect Series KDRP462L[SS] Architect Series KDRP463L[SS] $5300, Architect Series KDRP467K[SS]$5200	5300	50	○	◐	◐	○	⊖	⊖	2	None	2	●	●

See report, page 64. Based on tests in Consumer Reports in November 2006.

Guide to the Ratings

Overall score is based on oven capacity, cooktop speed and simmer performance, and oven baking, broiling, and self-cleaning performance. **Cooktop high** reflects how quickly the most powerful element could raise a 6-liter (6⅓ quart) pot of water from room temperature to a near boil. **Cooktop low** reflects the ability of the lowest power element to melt and hold chocolate without scorching it. We also set the most powerful element to its lowest setting to test its ability to hold a large pot of tomato sauce below a boil. **Baking** reflects the evenness of cookies and cakes in multirack baking tests. **Broiling** denotes upper-element evenness as well as high-temperature searing using a broiler pan full of hamburgers. **Oven capacity** is our evaluation of usable space, including shelf area and vertical space for casseroles. For dual-oven models, the score includes both ovens. **Oven cleaning** is a gauge of the self-cleaning cycle's effectiveness after the oven is coated with a mixture of eggs, lard, cherry-pie filling, cheese, tomato purée, and tapioca. **Price** is approximate retail.

Quick Picks

ELECTRIC RANGES
Best for most; fine overall:
 2 Kenmore (Sears) 9641[2], $750, **CR Best Buy**
 5 Frigidaire Gallery GLEF369D[S], $650
 7 Kenmore (Sears) 9611[2], $580, **CR Best Buy**

All three are high-performing smoothtops with expandable elements that can accommodate pots of different sizes. Both Kenmore models offer excellent broiling and fine baking, and are available in stainless steel. The Kenmore adds a warming drawer and a warming element, and is very good at oven cleaning.

If you want convection:
 3 Kenmore (Sears) Elite 9912[2], $1,400
Paying more for the Kenmore buys you a convection oven, warming drawer, triple element, bridge element, and touchpad controls with a digital display.

If price is paramount; both are CR Best Buys:
 26 GE JBP35WH[WW], $450
 27 Hotpoint RB757WH[WW], $350
Among coil-tops, the GE offers a larger oven and excellent broiling and simmering, and is available in stainless steel. The Hotpoint offers slightly better baking, but

isn't as adept at broiling and isn't available in stainless steel.

GAS RANGES
Best for most; fine overall:
 30 Hotpoint RGB745WEH[WW], $550, **CR Best Buy**
 34 GE JGBP35WEJ[WW], $800
The no-frills Hotpoint is our highest-rated gas range, but it lacks cast-iron grates. Choose the GE for more stylish features.

If you want a gas cooktop and an electric oven:
 54 GE Profile J2B918WEK[WW], $1,700
 58 Kenmore (Sears) Elite 7938[2], $1,550
On average, dual-fuel ranges perform no better than single-fuel models. The GE has a second oven for cooking two dishes at different temperatures and was better at simmering, while the Kenmore was better at broiling in our tests.

If you want a 36-inch range:
 64 Thermador Pro Grand PG366BS, $5,800
The Thermador was the best of the big pro-style ranges we tested. But it costs $5,800, and data indicate the brand has been repair-prone.

ELECTRIC RANGES
Smoothtop Models

1 **JENN-AIR** JER8885QA[S] A very good, well-equipped range, though Jenn-Air has been among the more repair-prone electric-range brands. Has warming drawer and numeric keypad for entering oven temperatures and time. Has convection, which tests show may yield time savings when roasting. Has three oven racks, along with a split rack. Cooktop has rim or wells to contain spills. Has dual elements and separate warming element. Cooktop has rim or wells to contain spills.

2 **KENMORE (SEARS)** 9641[2] **A CR Best Buy** Excellent overall. Has warming drawer, dual cooktop elements, warming element, and "hot" light indicator for each element. But only small elements in rear of cooktop.

3 **KENMORE (SEARS)** Elite 9912[2] Excellent overall. Has warming drawer, numeric keypad for setting oven temperature and time, and convection option. Comes with a searing grill and three oven racks, including one split rack. Has a triple element, bridge element, warming element, and "hot" light indicator for each element. Has touch controls for cooktop elements with digital display.

4 **MAYTAG** MER5775RA[S] Very good overall. Has dual and triple elements and warming element.

5 **FRIGIDAIRE** Gallery GLEF369D[S] Very good overall. Dual cooktop elements. But has only small elements in rear and only one hot-surface indicator light.

6 **GE** Profile JB968TK[WW] Very good overall. Has convection option. Double oven (no storage drawer). Has warming element, bridge element and triple element. Comes with meat probe for

automatic shutoff. "Hot" light for each element. Did an excellent job in self-cleaning test.

7 **KENMORE (SEARS)** 9611[2] **A CR Best Buy** Very good overall. Dual cooktop elements, and "hot" light indicator for each element. But has only small elements in rear of cooktop.

8 **MAYTAG** Gemini MER6775AA[S] Very good overall. Has convection option and a double oven (no storage drawer). Has warming element, dual elements. Did an excellent job in self-cleaning test.

9 **FRIGIDAIRE** Professional PLEF398D[C] Very good overall. Has numeric keypad for setting oven temperature and time, warming drawer, and convection option. Comes with three oven racks. Cooktop elements have digital display. Has dual cooktop elements and "hot" light indicator for each element. But only small elements in rear of cooktop.

10 **GE** JBP84TK[WW] Very good overall. Has convection option. Has warming drawer, warming element, bridge element, dual cooktop elements.

11 **MAYTAG** MER5752BA[W] Very good overall. Did an excellent job in self-cleaning test.

12 **GE** JBP81TK[WW] Very good overall. Has warming drawer and separate warming element, dual cooktop elements.

13 **GE** JSP42WK[WW] A very good, slide-in model with no side panels or backsplash. Numeric keypad for entering oven temperatures and time. has dual elements, "hot" light indicator for each element.

14 **MAYTAG** MES5775BA[S] Very good overall. Slide-in with dual and triple elements and warming element. Has a split

Recommendations

rack for oven. Did an excellent job in self-cleaning test.

15 BOSCH HES25[2] Very good overall. Magnetic dial and touch-sensitive element controls on right-hand-side of cooktop with digital display of cooktop settings. Has meat probe for automatic shutoff. Has convection option. Comes with three oven racks. Cooktop elements also function as warming elements. "Hot" light for each element. Has one dual cooktop element, one triple cooktop element, and warming drawer.

16 FRIGIDAIRE Gallery GLES389E[S] Very good overall. Slide-in. Excellent window view. Warming drawer. Has convection feature. Has dual cooktop elements and "hot" light for each element. Numeric digital display of cooktop element settings.

17 HOTPOINT RB787WH[WW] Very good, basic smoothtop.

18 WHIRLPOOL Gold GR448LXP[Q] Very good overall. Dual elements, warming element, and "hot" light indicator for each element. But only small elements in rear of cooktop. Comes with split rack for oven.

19 JENN-AIR JES8850AA[W] A very good slide-in range, but Jenn-Air has been among the more repair-prone brands of electric ranges. Has numeric keypad for setting oven temperature and time, convection option, dual elements, meat probe for automatic oven shutoff, and "hot" light indicator for each element. But cooktop has no rim to contain spills.

20 WHIRLPOOL Polara GR556LRK[P] A very good smoothtop with a unique feature: a refrigeration mode that allows you to set the range to keep the food cool during the day, then cook it just before you return in the evening. Has convection option, "hot" light for each element and dual cooktop elements.

21 WHIRLPOOL RF364PXM[Q] Very good overall. Door and window less hot than most during self-cleaning.

22 WHIRLPOOL RF368LXP[Q] Very good overall. "Hot" light indicators for each element. But only small elements in rear of cooktop.

23 VIKING VESC306-4B[SS] Very good pro-style stainless steel model, but only fair in oven self-cleaning test. Door and window less hot than others during self-cleaning. Both oven and range controls on front panel. Oven dial instead of touchpad controls; lacks digital temperature display. Has convection option, and comes with three oven racks. Has dual cooktop elements, bridge element, and "hot" light indicator for each element. But cooktop has no rim to contain spills.

24 SHARP Insight KB-3300J[W] Very good model with microwave drawer at waist level and conventional oven below. Oven has only four rack positions. Comes with three oven racks. Both oven and cooktop controls on front panel; touchpads are easy to activate by mistake. Numeric keypad for setting oven temperature and time. Dual cooktop elements and "hot" light for each element. (Note that the price listed is for a white finish.)

Coil Models

25 KENMORE (SEARS) 9421[2] An excellent basic oven at a low price. Warming drawer. Cooktop has rim or wells to contain spills.

26 GE JBP35WH[WW] **A CR Best Buy** and a very good basic range.

27 HOTPOINT RB757WH[WW] **A CR Best Buy** Inexpensive and very good, though fairly basic.

28 MAYTAG MER5555QA[W] Very good basic model. Door and window less hot than most during self-cleaning.

29 GE JBP35WK[WW] Very good basic model.

GAS RANGES
30-inch Gas Models

30 HOTPOINT RGB745WEH[WW] **A CR Best Buy** Very good, fairly basic range at a good price. Has steel grates.

31 MAYTAG MGS5775BD[S] Very good overall. Slide-in. Has continuous grates.

32 THERMADOR PG304BS A very good pro-style range with all-stainless construction, but pricey. Has oven and cooktop controls on front control panel. Has convection, which tests show may yield time savings when roasting. Has three oven racks. Cooktop has rim or wells to contain spills. Continuous grates are sturdy, but heavy and unwieldy to clean. Sealed cooktop burners have auto-reignite.

33 GE Profile JGBP918WEK[WW] Very good overall, with dual ovens for cooking two meals at different temperatures. Numeric keypad for entering oven temperatures and time. Has meat probe for monitoring internal meat/food temperature. Has convection, which tests show may yield time savings when roasting. Has three oven racks. Cooktop has rim or wells to contain spills. Continuous grates are sturdy, but heavy and unwieldy to clean.

34 GE JGBP35WEJ[WW] Very good overall. Has continuous grates.

35 GE JGBP85WEJ[WW] Very good overall. Has numeric keypad for setting oven

temperature and time, warming drawer, and continuous grates.

36 JENN-AIR JGS8750AD[W] Very good slide-in range. Has numeric keypad for setting oven temperature and time, and continuous grates. Rangetop burners automatically reignite if they go out.

37 MAYTAG Gemini MGR6775AD[S] Very good overall. Double oven (no storage drawer). Has continuous grates.

38 MAYTAG MGR5875QD[W] Very good. Has numeric keypad for setting oven temperature and time, convection option, and continuous grates. One of its three oven racks can be split. Door and window less hot than most during self-cleaning. Has five cooktop burners; some burners that appear the same size actually have different maximum power ratings.

39 WHIRLPOOL Gold GS470LEM[Q] Very good. Has warming drawer and continuous grates. One of its two oven racks can be split.

40 WHIRLPOOL SF368LEP[Q] Very good overall.

41 GE JGBP88WEK[WW] Very good overall. Has warming drawer, five cooktop burners, and continuous grates.

42 MAYTAG MGR5751AD[W] Very good overall. Door and window less hot than most during self-cleaning. Some surface burners that appear the same size actually have different maximum power ratings.

43 FRIGIDAIRE FGF366D[S] Very good overall.

44 FRIGIDAIRE Gallery GLGF386D[S] Very good overall. Has convection option, five cooktop burners, and continuous grates.

Recommendations

45 GE Profile JGB900WEF[WW] Very good overall. Has numeric keypad for setting oven temperature and time, and continuous grates.

46 BOSCH HGS25[2] Very good overall. Has convection option, warming drawer, and continuous grates. Has meat probe for automatic shutoff. Comes with three oven racks.

47 DCS RGSC-305 A very good pro-style range. Has convection option, continuous grates, and burners that reignite if they go out. Cooktop and oven controls in front. Oven dial instead of touchpad controls; lacks digital temperature display. Only four rack positions and among the least effective at self-cleaning. Has five cooktop burners, but large fifth burner wasn't the fastest, despite its high heat.

48 KENMORE (Sears) 7881[2] Very good overall. Has warming drawer, five cooktop burners, and continuous grates.

49 KENMORE (Sears) Elite 7936[2] Very good overall. Has numeric keypad for setting oven temperature and time. Has warming drawer and convection option. Comes with a searing grill and three oven racks, including a split rack. Has five cooktop burners and continuous grates.

50 GE Profile JGS905TEK[WW] Good overall. Slide-in.

51 GE JGBP26WEH[WW] Good, basic model. Door and window less hot than most during self-cleaning. But unsealed burners and poor performance in cooktop low tests.

30-inch Dual-Fuel Models
52 BOSCH HDS25[5] Very good overall. Dual-fuel. Has convection option, warming drawer, and continuous grates. Has meat probe for automatic shutoff.

53 GE Profile J2B912WEK[WW] Very good overall. Dual-fuel (120V). Has warming drawer and continuous grates.

54 GE Profile J2B918WEK[WW] Fair in oven self-cleaning test. Dual ovens for cooking two meals at different temperatures. Numeric keypad for entering oven temperatures and time. Has meat probe for monitoring internal meat/food temperature. Has convection, which tests show may yield time savings when roasting. Has three oven racks. Cooktop has rim or wells to contain spills. Continuous grates are sturdy but heavy and unwieldy to clean.

55 JENN-AIR JDS8850AA[S] A very good dual-fuel range. Slide-in model; no side panels or backsplash. Burners reignite if they go out. Has convection option, continuous grates, and meat probe with automatic oven shutoff. Door and window less hot than most during self-cleaning.

56 WOLF DF304 Very good pro-style stainless-steel range, but only fair in oven self-cleaning test. Both oven and cooktop controls on front panel. Has convection option and meat probe with automatic shut-off. Comes with three oven racks. Has continuous grates. Burners automatically reignite if they go out.

57 FRIGIDAIRE Professional PLCS389E[C] Very good overall. Dual-fuel. Has convection option, warming drawer, and continuous grates.

58 KENMORE (SEARS) Elite 7938[2] Very good overall. Has numeric keypad for setting oven temperature and time. Has warming drawer and convection option. Comes with a searing grill and three oven racks, including a split rack. Has five cooktop burners and continuous grates. (Note that the price listed is for a white finish.)

59 JENN-AIR JDS9860AA[W] Very good slide-in range. Dual-fuel range has grill module and downdraft vent, convection option, and meat probe for auto-shutoff. But fairly slow cooktop speed.

60 DACOR ERD30S06[BK] Very good, dual-fuel stainless-steel model has convection option, simmer plate, and continuous grates. Cooktop burners auto-reignite. Baking performance very good in pure convection mode; results in regular bake mode were poor. Dacor dual-fuel ranges have been quite repair-prone.

61 VIKING VDSC305-4B[SS] Very good but very expensive stainless-steel dual-fuel range. Has convection option, continuous grates, and burners that reignite if they go out. Cooktop and oven controls in front. Oven dial instead of touchpad controls; lacks digital temperature display. Smallish oven and unsealed burners, and is among the least effective at self-cleaning.

62 VIKING VDSC307-4B[SS] A very good dual-fuel, pro-style range. Has convection option, continuous grates and burners that reignite if they go out. Cooktop and oven controls in front. Oven dial instead of touchpad controls; lacks digital temperature display. Door and window less hot than most during self-cleaning. Smallish oven, and among the least effective at self-cleaning.

63 KITCHENAID Architect Series KDRP707R[SS] Good overall. Dual-fuel. Has a traditional oven dial instead of touchpad. Comes with simmer plate and steam assist for oven cooking, though in our tests this feature failed to impress.

36-inch Gas Models

64 THERMADOR Pro Grand PG366BS A very good pro-style range with all-stainless construction, but pricey. Features oven and cooktop control dials on front panel, convection option, and three oven racks. The sealed cooktop burners have auto-reignite. Continuous grates are sturdy but heavy and unwieldy to clean. Door and window less hot than most during self-cleaning.

65 VIKING Professional Series VGSC367-6B A good pro-style range with all-stainless construction, but pricey. Has oven and cooktop dials on front control panel, convection option, and three oven racks. Sealed cooktop burners have auto-reignite. Door and window less hot than most during self-cleaning. Viking gas ranges have been quite repair-prone.

36-inch Dual-Fuel Models

66 GE Monogram ZDP36N6H[SS] A very good dual-fuel, pro-style range with all-stainless construction, but pricey. Has cooktop and oven control dials on front panel, three oven racks (but only four rack positions), reversible grates for wok cooking, and convection option. Burners reignite if they go out. Continuous grates are sturdy but heavy and unwieldy to clean.

67 KITCHENAID Architect Series KDRP462L[SS] A good dual-fuel, pro-style range with all-stainless construction, but pricey. Has cooktop and oven-control dials in front with digital temperature display, convection option, three oven racks, sealed burners, grille module, and a simmer plate. Continuous grates are sturdy but heavy and unwieldy to clean. Excellent in self-cleaning.

Brand Repair History

Gas and dual-fuel ranges

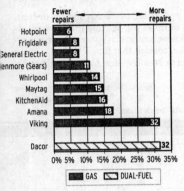

Fewer repairs ← → More repairs

Hotpoint	6
Frigidaire	8
General Electric	8
Kenmore (Sears)	11
Whirlpool	14
Maytag	15
KitchenAid	16
Amana	18
Viking	32
Dacor	32

0% 5% 10% 15% 20% 25% 30% 35%

GAS   DUAL-FUEL

Data are based on reader responses concerning gas and dual-fuel ranges to the Annual Product Reliability Survey conducted by the Consumer Reports National Research Center. Data have been adjusted to eliminate differences linked to age.

Electric ranges

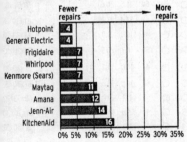

Fewer repairs ← → More repairs

Hotpoint	4
General Electric	4
Frigidaire	7
Whirlpool	7
Kenmore (Sears)	7
Maytag	11
Amana	12
Jenn-Air	14
KitchenAid	16

0% 5% 10% 15% 20% 25% 30% 35%

Data are based on reader responses concerning electric ranges to the Annual Product Reliability Survey conducted by the Consumer Reports National Research Center. Data have been adjusted to eliminate differences linked to age.

Readers report on 28,862 gas and dual-fuel ranges

This graph shows the percentage of these brands of gas and dual-fuel ranges bought new between 2000 and 2005 that were ever repaired or had a serious problem that was not repaired. Differences between brands of less than 3 points are not meaningful. Among gas ranges, Hotpoint, Frigidaire, and GE excelled, while Viking was the most trouble-prone, as were Dacor dual-fuel ranges. Though we don't have enough data to include Thermador in our gas range chart, the data we have indicate that it has been relatively repair-prone. While we lacked sufficient data to include them in the chart, Frigidaire, GE, Kenmore, Jenn-Air, and KitchenAid dual-fuel ranges don't appear to have been very repair-prone. Remember that models within a brand may vary, and changes in design and manufacture may affect reliability. Still, choosing a brand with a good repair history improves your odds of getting a reliable range.

Readers report on 53,830 electric ranges

This graph shows the percentage of these brands of electric ranges bought new between 2000 and 2005 that were ever repaired or had a serious problem that was not repaired. Differences between brands of less than 3 points are not meaningful. Among electric ranges, Hotpoint, General Electric, Frigidaire, Whirlpool, and Kenmore were most reliable. Remember that models within a brand may vary, and changes in design and manufacture may affect reliability. Still, choosing a brand with a good repair history improves your odds of getting a reliable range.

REFRIGERATORS

Most models we tested chill and freeze adequately and include pull-out shelves or bins, spill guards, and room on the door to hold a gallon of milk. Top-scoring models typically deliver more consistent temperatures. Once you know how much space you have, particularly the width, our Quick Picks will help you find models that fit.

Note on features: No top-freezers offer stainless-steel or stainless-steel look. All others do, except as noted.

	Excellent	Very good	Good	Fair	Poor
	⊖	⊖	○	⊖	●

Within types, in performance order. Gray key numbers indicate Quick Picks.

Key number	Brand & model	Price	Overall score	Temperature performance	Energy efficiency	Noise	Ease of use	Energy cost/yr.	Total usable capacity (cu. ft.)	Claimed capacity (cu. ft.)	Cabinet-depth	French door	Water dispenser	HxWxD (in.)
											Features			**Dimension**
TOP-FREEZERS														
1	**Kenmore** (Sears) 7425[2]	$720	76	⊖	⊖	⊖	○	44	16.8	21.6	•			66x33x31
2	**Kenmore** (Sears) 7495[2]	650	73	⊖	⊖	○	○	41	14.5	18.8	•			66x30x31
3	**Whirlpool** ET1FHTXM[Q]	750	72	⊖	⊖	⊖	○	43	16.7	20.9	•			66x33x30
4	**Hotpoint** HTS22GBP[WW] **CR Best Buy**	540	69	⊖	⊖	⊖	⊖	52	16.5	21.9				68x33x32
5	**Frigidaire** Gallery GLRT217TD[W]	730	68	⊖	⊖	⊖	⊖	50	16.8	20.6		•		70x30x33
6	**GE** GTH18KBR[WW]	725	67	⊖	⊖	⊖	⊖	40	14.4	17.9				67x30x31
7	**Maytag** MTF2195AE[W]	760	66	⊖	⊖	⊖	○	42	16.3	21.0		•		67x33x31
8	**Frigidaire** Gallery GLRT13TE[W]	630	65	⊖	⊖	⊖	⊖	50	16.7	20.5		•		70x30x33
9	**Frigidaire** Gallery GLRT183TD[W]	550	63	⊖	⊖	⊖	⊖	47	14.0	18.2				67x30x31
10	**Frigidaire** FRT18S6A[W]	550	62	⊖	⊖	⊖	⊖	47	14.5	18.2				67x30x31
11	**GE** GTS22KCP[WW]	750	62	○	⊖	⊖	⊖	52	17.1	21.7				68x33x32
12	**Maytag** MTB1891AR[W]	530	62	⊖	⊖	○	⊖	47	14.6	18.0				67x30x30
13	**Hotpoint** HTS18BCP[WW]	610	46	⊖	⊖	⊖	⊖	47	15.1	17.9				67x30x31
BOTTOM-FREEZERS														
14	**Amana** ABB1921DE[W] **CR Best Buy**	750	77	⊖	⊖	⊖	⊖	47	13.4	18.5				69x30x31
15	**Amana** AFD2535DE[W]	1650	77	⊖	⊖	⊖	⊖	50	17.5	25.1		•	•	70x36x32
16	**Maytag** Ice20 MFI2568AE[W]	2100	77	⊖	⊖	⊖	⊖	57	14.6	24.9		•	•	70x36x33
17	**Maytag** MFF2557HE[W]	1430	76	⊖	⊖	⊖	⊖	50	16.7	24.8		•		70x36x32
18	**GE** GDS20KBS[WW]	1100	75	⊖	⊖	○	⊖	44	14.0	19.5				68x30x32
19	**Kenmore** (Sears) 7500[2] **CR Best Buy**	750	75	⊖	⊖	⊖	⊖	51	15.2	19.7				68x30x32
20	**GE** GBS20KBR[WW]	895	74	⊖	⊖	○	⊖	44	13.3	19.5				68x30x32

thin types, in performance order. Gray **key numbers indicate Quick Picks.**

Brand & model	Price	Overall score	Temperature performance	Energy efficiency	Noise	Ease of use	Energy cost/yr.	Total usable capacity (cu. ft.)	Claimed capacity (cu. ft.)	Cabinet-depth	French door	Water dispenser	HxWxD (in.)
BOTTOM-FREEZERS													
Maytag MFC2061HE[W]	2100	72	◑	◑	○	○	47	14.2	19.6	•	•	•	71x36x27
LG LRFC22750[SW]	2000	70	◑	◑	○	◑	48	14.4	22.4		•		70x33x32
Liebherr CS1650[SS]	4200	70	◑	◑	◑	●	44	13.0	15.4	•			82x30x26
GE Profile PFS22MIS[WW]	1600	69	◑	◑	○	◑	49	15.0	22.2		•	•	69x33x32
KitchenAid KBFA20ER[WH]	2400	69	◑	○	○	◑	55	13.8	19.6	•	•	•	70x36x28
Whirlpool Gold GB9SHKXM[Q]	855	68	◑	◑	○	◑	47	13.1	18.5				67x30x31
Fisher & Paykel E522B	1050	53	○	○	◑	○	49	11.3	17.3	•			67x32x28
SIDE-BY-SIDES													
Samsung RM255BA[RB] RM255LA[ ] (Lowes) $3000	$3000	79	◑	◑	◑	◑	68	15.0				•	71x36x34
GE GSH25JFT[WW]	1100	75	◑	◑	○	◑	60	16.2				•	70x36x32
LG LRSC26941[SW]	1700	73	◑	◑	◑	◑	60	15.6				•	70x36x33
GE Profile PSS26NGP[WW]	2035	72	◑	◑	○	◑	61	16.2				•	70x36x33
Jenn-Air JCD2290HE[W]	1930	71	◑	◑	○	◑	53	12.8		•		•	71x36x27
Whirlpool Gold GC3SHEXN[Q]	2300	70	◑	◑	◑	◑	54	13.8		•		•	69x36x28
LG LSC27950[SW]	2200	68	◑	◑	◑	◑	60	16.0				•	70x36x33
GE Profile Arctica PSC25PSS[SS]	3450	66	◑	○	○	◑	60	13.3		•		•	72x36x28
GE Profile PSH25PST[SV]	4000	65	◑	◑	◑	◑	59	14.4		•		•	73x36x28
Whirlpool Gold GS6NBEXR[Q]	1900	65	○	◑	◑	◑	61	15.9				•	70x36x33
Admiral LSD2615HE[W]	800	63	○	◑	○	○	61	17.4				•	71x36x32
Frigidaire FRS6R5E[MB]	950	62	◑	○	○	○	71	16.7				•	70x36x33
Kenmore (Sears) Elite 4430[2]	2100	60	○	◑	◑	◑	57	13.3		•		•	70x36x28
Samsung RS269LA[RS]	1800	59	●	◑	◑	◑	60	18.5				•	70x36x33
Galaxy 5562[2] (Sears)	730	56	○	○	◑	◑	71	16.2				•	70x36x32
GE GSC23KGT[WW]	2000	53	○	○	○	◑	67	13.5		•		•	70x36x28

			Excellent	Very good	Good	Fair
			⊜	⊖	○	◒

Key number	Brand & model	Price	Overall score	Test results							Features			Dimensions
				Temperature performance	Energy efficiency	Noise	Ease of use	Energy cost/yr.	Total usable capacity (cu. ft.)	Claimed capacity (cu. ft.)	Cabinet-depth	French door	Water dispenser	HxWxD (in.)
	BUILT-INS													
44	**Sub-Zero** 650/F	4500	75	⊖	⊖	○	○	50	15.4	20.6	•			84x37x..
45	**KitchenAid** KSSC42QM[SS]	6000	71	⊖	⊖	⊖	⊖	55	17.6	25.3		•	•	84x42x..
46	**Viking** DFSB423	5300	71	⊖	⊖	⊖	⊖	64	16.6	24.0		•		83x43x..
47	**Jenn-Air** JS42FWD[W]	4650	69	⊖	○	⊖	⊖	71	14.5	26.0		•	•	84x42x
48	**Viking** DFBB363	4700	69	⊖	⊖	○	⊖	55	15.0	20.3	•			84x36x..
49	**Thermador** KBUDT4270A	5280	67	⊖	⊖	⊖	⊖	70	15.9	25.2		•	•	84x41x..
50	**GE** Monogram ZISS420DR[SS]	6500	65	⊖	○	⊖	⊖	61	14.9	26.1		•	•	85x43x..
51	**GE** Profile PSB42LSR[BV]	6200	65	○	⊖	⊖	⊖	60	16.6	25.2		•	•	84x42x..
52	**Sub-Zero** 650G	6000	65	⊖	⊖	⊖	◒	56	15.4	20.8	•			84x36x..
53	**Sub-Zero** 680	5600	61	⊖	⊖	○	⊖	68	16.9	23.7		•	•	84x43x..

See report, page 67. Based on tests posted on ConsumerReports.org in August 2006, with updated prices and availability.

Guide to the Ratings

Overall score gives the most weight to energy efficiency and temperature performance, then to noise and ease of use. **Temperature performance** combines results of tests measuring the accuracy of initial temperature settings along with how well a model 1) kept optimum temperatures in the refrigerator and freezer at the same time; 2) kept temperatures even throughout each compartment; 3) kept temperatures constant despite changes in room temperatures; and 4) maintained set temperatures even with very high room temperatures. **Energy efficiency** reflects electricity consumption (as stated on the Energy Guide) per cubic foot of measured usable storage space. For example, two refrigerators with the same energy cost per year may have different energy efficiencies (the unit with more storage space being more efficient). **Noise** was gauged by a sound meter and panelists. **Ease of use** assesses features and design including layout, controls, and lighting. **Energy cost/yr.** the cost in dollars, based on the 2004 average national electricity rate of 9.06 cents/kwh (kilowatt hours). Your cost will vary depending on the rate for electricity in your area. **Total usable capacity** the volume, in cubic feet, of usable interior space, based on our measurements. We included icemakers in the storage measurements for top-freezer and bottom-freezer models, but not for side-by-sides. **Claimed capacity** is the manufacturer's estimate of the volume, in cubic feet, of interior space. **Price** is approximate retail.

TOP FREEZERS
Small (30 inches wide):

5 Frigidaire Gallery GLRT217TD[W], $730
Among top-freezer models in this size, the Frigidaire Gallery costs hundreds less than comparable models, and offers stainless steel and more capacity.

Midsized (33 inches wide):
3 Whirlpool ET1FHTXM[Q], $750
4 Hotpoint HTS22GBP[WW], $540,
   CR Best Buy
Among the top-freezer models in this size, the Whirlpool and Hotpoint are good basic choices.

BOTTOM FREEZERS
Small (30 inches wide), both are CR Best Buys:
14 Amana ABB1921DE[W], $750
19 Kenmore (Sears) 7500[2], $750
Among the bottom freezers in this size, the Kenmore has slightly more fridge space.

Midsized (33 inches wide):
24 GE Profile PFS22MIS[WW], $1,600
Among the bottom-freezers in this size, the GE Profile offers French doors.

Large (36 inches wide):
15 Amana AFD2535DE[W], $1,650
16 Maytag Ice2O MFI2568AE[W], $2,100
17 Maytag MFF2557HE[W], $1,430
21 Maytag MFC2061HE[W], $2,100
Among the bottom-freezer, French-door models in this size, the Maytag MFF2557HE[W] costs less than the Amana but it lacks a water dispenser. Consider the French-door Maytag Ice2O if you're willing to pay extra for through-the-door ice and water. The cabinet-depth, French-door Maytag MFC2061HE[W] offers the built-in look for less and is an efficient appliance.

SIDE BY SIDES
Large (36 inches wide):
33 Whirlpool Gold GC3SHEXN[Q], $2,300
Among side-by-sides, the Whirlpool Gold offers the built-in look for less.

BUILT-INS
Large (36 inches wide or wider):
44 Sub-Zero 650/F, $4,500
47 Jenn-Air JS42FWD[W], $4,650
Built-in refrigerators have been repair-prone overall in our surveys. But if you prefer their style, among the built-ins in this size, consider the Sub-Zero and Jenn-Air for their performance and value compared with others.

TOP-FREEZERS

1 KENMORE (SEARS) 7425[2] Very good overall, with excellent energy efficiency. Has water filter and internal water dispenser. Similar model: 7426.

2 KENMORE (SEARS) 7495[2] Very good overall, with excellent energy efficiency. Has water filter and internal water dispenser. Similar models: 6495, 7496.

3 WHIRLPOOL ET1FHTXM[Q] A very good model with excellent energy efficiency. Has a water filter but no freezer light or pull-out shelves.

4 HOTPOINT HTS22GBP[WW] **A CR Best Buy** Very good overall and low-priced for this type of refrigerator. No spill-proof shelves, pull-out shelves, or light in freezer.

5 FRIGIDAIRE Gallery GLRT217TD[W] Very good with excellent energy efficiency, though controls are likely to be blocked by food.

6 GE GTH18KBR[WW] A very good model with excellent energy efficiency. Meat-keeper was too warm. No pull-out shelves.

7 MAYTAG MTF2195AE[W] Very good top freezer with excellent energy efficiency, but Maytag has been the most repair-prone brand of top-freezer refrigerators. Meat-keeper was too warm. Has a curved door.

8 FRIGIDAIRE Gallery GLRT13TE[W] Excellent energy efficiency in a stainless/stainless-look unit, but with a noise score of Fair. Offers freezer light, gallon storage on door, and icemaker. The flat-front door does not accept a panel, and there are pull-out shelves/bins in the refrigerator only.

9 FRIGIDAIRE Gallery GLRT183TD[W] Very good, low priced top-freezer.

10 FRIGIDAIRE FRT18S6A[W] This low-priced top-freezer does not offer a freezer light, the flat-front door does not accept a panel, and there are pull-out shelves/bins in the fridge only. It also has gallon storage on door and an icemaker.

11 GE GTS22KCP[WW] A very good model with excellent energy efficiency. No pull-out shelves.

12 MAYTAG MTB1891AR[W] A basic, inexpensive top-freezer. Tested model includes optional icemaker. Maytag has been the most repair-prone brand of top-freezer refrigerators.

13 HOTPOINT HTS18BCP[WW] Good overall. Manufacturer's recommended setting kept freezer too warm. Single control for both refrigerator and freezer. No spill-proof shelves, pull-out shelves, or light in freezer. Similar model: HTS18BBP.

BOTTOM-FREEZERS

14 AMANA ABB1921DE[W] **A CR Best Buy** Very good low-priced bottom-freezer with swing-open freezer door. Lacks spill-proof shelves. No stainless option.

15 AMANA AFD2535DE[W] A very good French door bottom-freezer with excellent energy efficiency. Water filter. Bottom-freezer with pull-out drawer freezer door.

16 MAYTAG Ice2O MFI2568AE[W] A pricey French-door bottom-freezer with a stainless/stainless-look option and smooth, curved front doors. Offers a range of features: door-open alarm; beverage chiller on door; crank-adjusting shelf; icemaker/dispenser and water dispenser/filter; freezer light; gallon storage on door; pull-out shelves/bins;

Recommendations

temperature-controlled meat/deli bin; digital displays and touchpad controls.

17 MAYTAG MFF2557HE[W] Though relatively noisy, this full-featured, French-door bottom-freezer offers excellent energy efficiency and temperature performance.

18 GE GDS20KBS[WW] Very good bottom-freezer with pull-out drawer. Has textured, curved front doors. No stainless option.

19 KENMORE (SEARS) 7500[2] **A CR Best Buy** A very good low-priced bottom-freezer. Curved front doors. Door-open alarm. No stainless option.

20 GE GBS20KBR[WW] Though basic, this fine-performing refrigerator is among the least-expensive bottom-freezer models and features a curved front and a swing-open freezer door. Tested with optional icemaker, which isn't reflected in the price. No stainless option.

21 MAYTAG MFC2061HE[W] Very good French-door/cabinet-depth bottom-freezer with pull-out freezer drawer. Has door-open alarm, digital display of temperature settings with actual compartment temperatures, built-in water filter, temperature controlled meat/deli bin, water dispenser.

22 LG LRFC22750[SW] A pricey French-door bottom-freezer with a stainless/stainless-look option and smooth, curved front doors. Features include: door-open alarm; freezer light; gallon storage on door; icemaker; pull-out shelves/bins; temperature-controlled meat/deli bin; digital display and touchpad controls.

23 LIEBHERR CS1650[SS] Pricey cabinet-depth bottom-freezer with smooth, curved front doors, stainless/stainless-look option, and excellent noise score.

Features include: icemaker; gallon storage on door; digital display; and pull-out shelves/bins.

24 GE PROFILE PFS22MIS[WW] Very good French-door bottom-freezer with pull-out freezer drawer. Has textured, curved front doors, built-in water filter, temperature-controlled meat/deli bin, and water dispenser.

25 KITCHENAID KBFA20ER[WH] A pricey French-door, cabinet-depth bottom-freezer with a stainless/stainless-look option and flat-front doors that do not accept panels. Features include: door-open alarm; freezer light; gallon storage on door; icemaker and built-in water filter and water dispenser; pull-out shelves/bins (freezer only); temperature-controlled meat/deli bin; digital display and touchpad controls.

26 WHIRLPOOL Gold GB9SHKXM[Q] While inexpensive for a bottom-freezer refrigerator, you'll find better performers at comparable lower prices. Features include a swing-open freezer door. Tested with optional icemaker, which isn't reflected in the price. No stainless option.

27 FISHER & PAYKEL E522B Low-priced, cabinet-depth bottom-freezer with swing-open freezer door, smooth, curved front doors, and stainless/stainless-look option. Has a door-open alarm but no freezer light or spill-proof shelves, and pull-out shelves/bins

SIDE-BY-SIDES

28 SAMSUNG RM255BA[RB] A pricey side-by-side with stainless/stainless-look option and excellent noise score. The flat-front doors do not accept a panel. Features include: door-open alarm; digital displays and touchpad controls; built-in water filter; freezer light; gallon storage on door; icemaker and dispenser; pull-out shelves/bins; temperature-controlled meat/deli bin; and specially adjustable shelves. Similar model: RM255LA[ ] (Lowe's).

29 GE GSH25JFT[WW] A flat-front model with stainless/stainless-look option. Features include: touchpad controls with digital display; built-in water dispenser and filter; freezer light; gallon storage on door; icemaker and dispenser; pull-out shelves/bins; and temperature-controlled meat/deli bin.

30 LG LRSC26941[SW] Very good side-by-side with excellent noise score. Has smooth, curved front doors. Has digital controls on door that display temperature setting and actual compartment temperatures. Built-in water filter. Temperature controlled meat/deli bin. Must scroll through temperatures to set.

31 GE Profile PSS26NGP[WW] Very good overall. Has water filter, curved doors, and door alarm. Discontinued, but similar model Profile PSS26NGS may still be available.

32 JENN-AIR JCD2290HE[W] Very good cabinet-depth side-by-side model. Beverage chiller on door. Crank adjusting shelf.

33 WHIRLPOOL Gold GC3SHEXN[Q] This cabinet-depth, side-by-side model offers solid performance and has an array of features. Major ones include through-the-door ice and water, temperature-controlled deli drawers, touchpad controls, and digital displays of temperature settings. It also makes lots of ice, and an ice bin on freezer door makes the ice easier to take out.

34 LG LSC27950[SW] A pricey side-by-side with flat-front doors, stainless/stainless-look option, and excellent noise score.

Features include: digital displays and touchpad controls; built-in water dispenser and filter; freezer light; gallon storage on door; icemaker and dispenser; pull-out shelves/bins; and uniquely adjustable shelves.

35 GE Profile Arctica PSC25PSS[SS] This pricey cabinet-depth side-by-side is available only in stainless steel and is relatively inefficient on energy. But its price buys an array of features that include a beverage chiller on door, digital temperature displays, and dual evaporators that help prevent odor migration between compartments. Discontinued, but similar model Profile Arctica PSC25PST may still be available.

36 GE Profile PSH25PST[SV] A pricey cabinet-depth side-by-side with flat-front doors and stainless/stainless-look option. Features include: digital displays and touchpad controls; built-in water dispenser and filter; freezer light; gallon storage on door; icemaker and dispenser; pull-out shelves/bins; temperature-controlled meat/deli bin; and uniquely adjustable shelves.

37 WHIRLPOOL Gold GS6NBEXR[Q] Very good side-by-side. Has curved front doors. Ice bin on freezer door for easy access and removal. Built-in water filter. Similar model: Gold GS6NFEXR.

38 ADMIRAL LSD2615HE[W] Though inexpensive and energy efficient, this basic side-by-side's temperature performance was unexceptional. No stainless option.

39 FRIGIDAIRE FRS6R5E[MB] A low-priced side-by-side with flat front and stainless/stainless-look option. Built-in water filter. Freezer light. Features include: freezer light; gallon storage on door; icemaker/dispenser; water dispenser; and pull-out shelves/bins.

Recommendations

40 KENMORE (SEARS) Elite 4430[2] A very good cabinet-depth side-by-side model. Digital display of temperature settings and actual compartment temperatures. Door-open, power-loss, and high-internal-temperature alarm indicator lights inside refrigerator. Crank adjusting shelf. Discontinued, but similar model Elite 4438 may still be available.

41 SAMSUNG RS269LA[RS] Excellent energy efficiency in a flat-front model with stainless/stainless-look option and excellent noise score but fair temperature performance. Features include: door-open alarm; digital displays; water dispenser and built-in water filter; freezer light; gallon storage on door; icemaker/dispenser; temperature-controlled meat/deli bin; and uniquely adjustable shelves.

42 GALAXY 5562[2] (Sears) Good, low-priced side-by-side. Digital display of actual compartment temperatures, temperature controlled meat/deli bin and built-in water filter. Lacks spillproof shelves. No stainless option.

43 GE GSC23KGT[WW] Pricey cabinet-depth side-by-side with flat front and stainless/stainless-look option. Features include: door-open alarm; digital displays and touchpad controls; water dispenser and built-in water filter; freezer light; gallon storage on door. Icemaker/dispenser; and uniquely adjustable shelves.

BUILT-INS

44 SUB-ZERO 650/F Very good built-in, bottom-freezer model. Bottom freezer pulls open like a drawer. Needs custom panels at extra cost. But Sub-Zero has been the most repair-prone brand of top- and bottom-freezer refrigerators.

45 KITCHENAID KSSC42QM[SS] This pricey, stainless-steel built-in is quiet and includes touchpad controls and digital temperature displays. Has many features, including an ice bin on the freezer door.

46 VIKING DFSB423 Very good built-in, side-by-side model. Has door alarm. Needs custom panels at extra cost. Similar models: DDSB423, VCSB423SS.

47 JENN-AIR JS42FWD[W] Very good built-in side-by-side model. Has water filter, door alarm, and crank-adjustable shelf. Needs custom panels at extra cost.

48 VIKING DFBB363 Very good model. Bottom-freezer opens like a drawer. Needs custom panels at extra cost. Stainless option costs about $700 more. Similar models: DDBB363, DTBB363, VCBB363.

49 THERMADOR KBUDT4270A Very good built-in side-by-side model. Has water filter, ice bin on door, and digital controls (actual temperature). No spillproof shelves. Needs custom panels at extra cost. Similar models: KBUDT4250A, KBUDT4260A, KBUIT4250A, KBUIT4260A, KBUIT4270A.

50 GE Monogram ZISS420DR[SS] Very good built-in side-by-side. Very quiet. Has water filter, door alarm and digital displays with temperature settings and actual compartment temperatures.

51 GE Profile PSB42LSR[BV] Pricey and fully featured, this built-in side-by-side delivered unexceptional temperature performance.

52 SUB-ZERO 650G This relatively narrow, 36-inch built-in bottom-freezer model is quiet and energy efficient, and has a pull-out drawer along with a glass-door refrigerator compartment. But Sub-Zero has been the most repair-prone brand of top- and bottom-freezer refrigerators. The

Recommendations

glass refrigerator door precludes door shelves. This model also lacks some features you'll find on lower-priced models, such as a temperature-controlled meat-keeper and humidity-controlled crispers.

53 SUB-ZERO 680 Very good built-in, side-by-side model. Has water filter. No spill-proof shelves. Storage compartment for meats too warm. Needs custom panels at extra cost. Discontinued, but similar model 685F may be available.

Brand Repair History

Side-by-sides with icemaker and dispenser

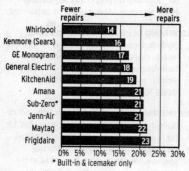

* Built-in & icemaker only

Readers report on more than 89,000 refrigerators

The graphs show the percentage of these brands of full-sized refrigerators bought between 2001 and 2005 that were ever repaired or had a serious problem. Differences of less than 4 points aren't meaningful. Maytag has been the most repair-prone among top-freezers, while Sub-Zero built-in bottom-freezers with icemakers were more repair-prone than other top- and bottom-freezer brands. Our data suggest that built-in bottom-freezer refrigerators are more repair-prone than freestanding types. Models within a brand may vary, and changes in design or manufacture may affect reliability. Still, choosing a reliable brand can minimize the likelihood of problems.

Top- and bottom-freezers without icemakers

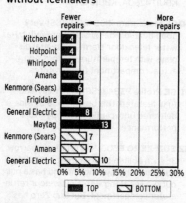

Top- and bottom-freezers with icemakers

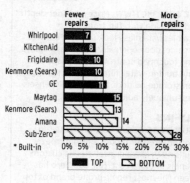

* Built-in

Data are based on readers responses about refrigerators to the Annual Product Reliability Survey conducted by the Consumer Reports National Research Center. Data are adjusted to eliminate differences linked to age.

VACUUM CLEANERS

Nearly all full-sized uprights cleaned bare floors quickly and neatly, but carpets remain the toughest challenge for most machines. Top-scoring models deep-cleaned impressively while providing strong airflow through the hose for use with tools.

Most full-sized uprights weigh about 20 pounds. The highest-scoring lightweight upright was the 9-pound Riccar SupraLite RSL3, but it has no tools and was noisy enough that we recommend you wear ear protection to prevent hearing loss. Another noisy upright for which you'll need earplugs or muffs is the Dirt Devil Vision Self-Propelled M087900. Pay particular attention to our noise Ratings if you have bare floors, which echo sound.

Our tests found one model, the Hoover Fusion U5180-900, that leaked dust or broke consistently enough to be judged Not Recommended. The Eureka Optima 431A released enough dust while vacuuming with tools to be judged Not Recommended.

Nearly all canisters do a fine job of cleaning bare floors and stairs, but carpets remain their toughest challenge. Top-scoring models combine impressive deep-cleaning with strong airflow through the hose for use with tools for cleaning upholstery and drapes. Most full-sized canisters tend to be heavier, bulkier, and more expensive than uprights. Pay particular attention to our noise ratings if you have bare floors, which echo sound.

	Excellent	Very good	Good	Fair	Poor
	⊖	⊖	○	◐	●

Within types, in performance order. Gray key numbers indicate Quick Picks.

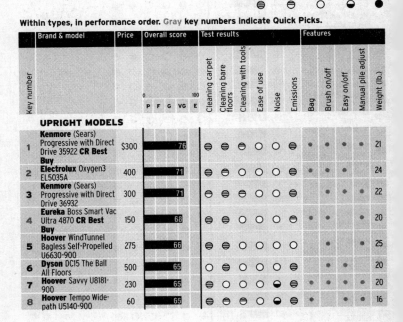

Key number	Brand & model	Price	Overall score	Cleaning carpet	Cleaning bare floors	Cleaning with tools	Ease of use	Noise	Emissions	Bag	Brush on/off	Easy on/off	Manual pile adjust	Weight (lb.)
	UPRIGHT MODELS													
1	**Kenmore** (Sears) Progressive with Direct Drive 35922 **CR Best Buy**	$300	76	⊖	⊖	⊖	○	○	⊖	•	•	•	•	21
2	**Electrolux** Oxygen3 EL5035A	400	71	⊖	⊖	○	○	○	⊖	•	•	•		24
3	**Kenmore** (Sears) Progressive with Direct Drive 36932	300	71	⊖	⊖	⊖	○	○	⊖	•	•	•		22
4	**Eureka** Boss Smart Vac Ultra 4870 **CR Best Buy**	150	68	⊖	⊖	○	○	○	⊖	•	•			20
5	**Hoover** WindTunnel Bagless Self-Propelled U6630-900	275	66	⊖	⊖	○	○	○	⊖		•		•	25
6	**Dyson** DC15 The Ball All Floors	500	65	○	⊖	○	○	○	⊖		•	•		20
7	**Hoover** Savvy U8181-900	230	65	⊖	○	○	○	◐	⊖	•	•			20
8	**Hoover** Tempo Wide-path U5140-900	60	65	⊖	⊖	○	○	◐	⊖	•	•		•	16

Within types, in performance order. Gray key numbers indicate Quick Picks.

UPRIGHT MODELS continued

Key number	Brand & model	Price	Overall score	Cleaning carpet	Cleaning bare floors	Cleaning with tools	Ease of use	Noise	Emissions	Bag	Brush on/off	Easy on/off	Manual pile adjust	Weight (lb.)
9	Hoover WindTunnel Self Propelled Ultra U6439-900	$230	65	⊖	○	⊖	⊖	○	⊖				•	22
10	Oreck XL21-700	700	65	○	⊖	●	⊖	⊖	⊖			•		11
11	Panasonic MC-V7720	250	65	○	⊖	○	○	○	⊖			•		20
12	Riccar SupraLite RSL3	350	65	⊖	⊖	⊖	⊖	●	⊖			•		9
13	Dyson DC07 All Floors	400	64	○	⊖	⊖	⊖	○	⊖		•			19
14	Dyson DC14 Complete	550	64	○	⊖	⊖	⊖	○	⊖		•			19
15	Hoover Z 700 U9145-900	500	64	⊖	⊖	○	⊖	○	○		•			28
16	Kenmore Progressive 36622	180	64	⊖	⊖	⊖	○	⊖	⊖	•	•		•	19
17	Riccar Radiance	900	64	⊖	⊖	⊖	⊖	⊖	⊖	•	•	•	•	21
18	Hoover EmPower U5262-910	100	63	⊖	⊖	○	⊖	○	⊖			•	•	17
19	Hoover WindTunnel Bagless U5753-900	160	63	⊖	⊖	○	○	○	⊖			•	•	22
20	Hoover WindTunnel Supreme U5458-900	130	63	⊖	⊖	○	⊖	○	⊖	•		•	•	17
21	Dirt Devil Vision Self-Propelled M087900	170	61	⊖	⊖	○	○	○	⊖			•	•	21
22	Aerus Lux Legacy	1000	60	⊖	⊖	⊖	○	○	⊖	•		•		17
23	Sebo Automatic X4	700	60	○	⊖	⊖	⊖	○	⊖	•	•	•		18
24	Bissell Lift-Off Revolution Turbo 3760-1	180	59	○	⊖	⊖	○	⊖	⊖			•	•	23
25	Electrolux Aptitude EL5010A	250	59	○	⊖	⊖	⊖	○	⊖			•	•	19
26	Bissell PowerForce 3522-6	40	57	⊖	⊖	○	○	○	⊖			•	•	14
27	Bissell CleanView Revolution Deluxe 3596	130	56	○	⊖	○	○	○	⊖			•	•	18
28	Bissell CleanView Revolution Plus 3595-1	100	56	⊖	⊖	○	⊖	⊖	⊖			•	•	17
29	Miele Powerhouse S184	380	56	○	⊖	○	○	⊖	⊖	•		•		15
30	Vax X5	285	56	○	○	●	○	⊖	⊖			•	•	19
31	Eureka Boss 4D 5892	150	55	○	●	⊖	⊖	○	⊖			•	•	24
32	Bissell PowerForce 6579-2	50	53	○	⊖	⊖	○	○	○			•	•	15
33	Hoover Foldaway Widepath U5170-900	70	53	○	⊖	●	○	⊖	⊖			•	•	16
34	Oreck XL Deluxe U3700HH	400	53	○	⊖	●	⊖	⊖	⊖	•		•		10
35	Sanyo Performax SC-A116	125	53	○	⊖	○	⊖	○	⊖			•	•	16
36	Panasonic Fold'N Go MC-V5485	120	52	○	○	⊖	○	○	⊖			•		17
37	Dirt Devil Reaction M110000	160	49	⊖	⊖	⊖	○	○	⊖			•	•	20

Excellent ◑	Very good ◑	Good ○	Fair ◔	Poor ●		

Key number	Brand & model	Price	Overall score (0 P F G VG E 100)	Cleaning carpet	Cleaning bare floors	Cleaning with tools	Ease of use	Noise	Emissions	Bag	Brush on/off	Easy on/off	Manual pile adjust	Weight (lb.)
UPRIGHT MODELS *continued*														
38	**Eureka** Altima 2981	$80	43	○	○	●	○	○	◑				•	20
NOT RECOMMENDED MODELS														
	Eureka Optima 431A	60	53	○	◑	○	○	○	◔			•		13
	Hoover Fusion U5180-900	130	50	○	◑	○	○	○	◔		•	•		19
CANISTER VACUUM CLEANERS														
39	**Electrolux** Oxygen3 Ultra EL7020A	500	72	◑	◑	○	◑	◑	◑	•	•	•	•	24
40	**Kenmore** (Sears) Progressive 25614	350	72	◑	◑	○	○	○	◑	•	•	•	•	23
41	**Kenmore** (Sears) **Progressive** 25914	500	72	◑	◑	○	○	○	◑	•	•	•	•	24
42	**Kenmore** (Sears) Progressive 25512 **CR Best Buy**	300	70	◑	◑	○	◑	○	◑	•	•	•	•	22
43	**Bosch** Premium Prestige Electro Duo H BSG 81360UC	800	69	◑	◑	◑	○	◑	◑	•	•	•		19
44	**Sebo** Air Belt C3.1	900	69	◑	◑	○	○	◑	◑	•		•		26
45	**Electrolux** Oxygen EL6988A	450	68	◑	◑	○	◑	◑	◑	•	•	•	•	21
46	**Oreck** Dutch Tech DTX1400B	900	68	◑	◑	◑	○	◑	◑	•	•	•		25
47	**Miele** Plus 1200W S251	500	67	○	◑	○	○	◑	○	•	•	•		19
48	**Riccar** 1700 Simplicity S36 $1000	1000	67	○	◑	◑	○	◑	○	•	•	•	•	27
49	**Aerus** Lux Guardian C154E	1500	64	○	◑	◔	○	◑	○	•	•	•		25
50	**Hoover** WindTunnel Bagless S3765-040	250	64	◑	◑	○	○	◔	○		•	•		22
51	**Hoover** WindTunnel Plus S3639	180	63	◑	◑	○	○	○	○		•	•		23
52	**Hoover** Duros S3590	160	61	○	◑	◑	◔	○	◑		•	•		22
53	**Aerus** Lux Legacy C153C	1000	60	◑	◑	●	○	○	◑		•	•		22
54	**Fantom** Falcon FC251	180	59	◑	◑	●	○	○	◑		•			22
55	**Sanyo** SC-X1000P	120	59	◑	◑	○	○	◔	◑		•	•		25
56	**TriStar** Mg2 A101N	1500	59	○	◑	◔	○	◑	◑	•	•	•		23
57	**Filter** Queen Majestic 360 AT1100	1900	56	◑	◔	○	○	○	○		•	•		25
58	**Rainbow** e-series E2	1500	56	○	◔	◑	○	○	○			•	•	32
59	**Airider** G1-9000-07-1US	400	53	●	◑	●	○	◑	◑		•	•		17

See report, page 115. Based on tests posted on ConsumerReports.org in August 2006.

Guide to the Ratings

Overall score is based mainly on cleaning performance and ease of use. **Cleaning carpet** shows how much embedded talc and sand a vacuum cleaner lifted from a medium-pile carpet. **Cleaning bare floors** shows how well a vacuum cleaner picked up sand without dispersing it on bare floors. **Cleaning with tools** indicates the strength of airflow through the hose. **Ease of use** evaluates dirt capacity and ease of pushing, cleaning under furniture, and carrying. **Noise** is based on measurements in decibels. **Emissions** is a measurement of the quantity of wood-flour particles that are released under two conditions: first, only when the motor is turned on, and second, while vacuuming. **Price** is approximate retail.

Quick Picks

Best uprights for most tasks:

1 Kenmore (Sears) Progressive with Direct Drive 35922, $300, **CR Best Buy**

2 Electrolux Oxygen3 EL5035A, $400

4 Eureka Boss Smart Vac Ultra 4870, $150, **CR Best Buy**

The Kenmore excels at cleaning carpets and bare floors, and vacuuming using tools. The Electrolux offers more features, but is a notch lower for bare floors and tools suction, and costs more. Both models are excellent when it comes to emissions. The Eureka trades some through-the-hose suction for a much lower price. But its carpet and bare floors cleaning are excellent.

If light weight and low cost are worth a few trade-offs:

8 Hoover Tempo Widepath U5140-900, $60

26 Bissell PowerForce 3522-6, $40

The 16-pound Hoover is among the best at cleaning carpets, a plus because you cannot switch off the brush. If you have more bare floors than carpet, seldom use the tools, and need a low-emissions model, you may prefer the 18-pound bagless Hoover EmPower U5262-910, which was otherwise judged similarly. For a quieter vacuum, the 14-pound Bissell PowerForce scored very good or better for carpets and bare floors, but is pretty basic.

Best canisters for most tasks:

40 Kenmore (Sears) Progressive 25614, $350

42 Kenmore (Sears) Progressive 25512 , $300, **CR Best Buy**

Both are best on bare floors, tops for emissions, and fine on carpets, but the Progressive 25512 is easier to use. If you have mostly carpeting, consider the Electrolux Oxygen3 Ultra EL7020A, which outperformed the Kenmores on carpets, but is noisier and more expensive.

Recommendations

UPRIGHT MODELS

1 **KENMORE (SEARS)** Progressive with Direct Drive 35922 **A CR Best Buy** Very good overall performance with many features, including on/off switch located on handle, full-bag indicator, brush on/off switch, manual carpet-height adjustment, suction control, overload protection for blower-fan motor and rotating-brush motor, and motor control with more than one speed. Hose is longer than most. A dirt sensor signals when no more dirt can be picked up in an area. Comes with small powered brush for stairs. Bags: $8/2;

Recommendations

$11/8 (microfilt.) Similar model: Progressive with Direct Drive 35923.

2 ELECTROLUX Oxygen3 EL5035A Very good performer. This bag-equipped upright is unstable on stairs while cleaning. Its hose is longer than most in its category but its retractable power cord is shorter than most in its category. Features: brush on/off switch, easy on/off switch, full-bag/bin indicator, suction control, overload protection for blower-fan motor, on/off switch located on handle, and high-efficiency particulate air (HEPA) filter.

3 KENMORE (SEARS) Progressive with Direct Drive 36932 Very good overall bagless vac. Has brush on/off switch, full-bin alert, manual carpet-height adjustment, HEPA filter, and overload protection for blower-fan motor and rotating-brush motor. Hose longer than most but is prone to tip over when hose is extended, and lacks suction control. Motor control with more than one speed. Dirt sensor signals when no more dirt can be picked up in an area. Comes with small powered brush for stairs. Filter: $8-11; $15/2. Similar model: Progressive with Direct Drive 36933.

4 EUREKA Boss Smart Vac Ultra 4870 **A CR Best Buy** Very good overall. This bag-equipped upright is prone to tip over when hose is extended and is unstable on stairs while cleaning. Features: brush on/off switch, suction control, overload protection for blower-fan motor, belt/brush indicator (window), manual carpet-height adjustment, high-efficiency particulate air (HEPA) filter.

5 HOOVER WindTunnel Bagless Self Propelled U6630-900 A very good overall vacuum. This bagless upright is prone to tip over when hose is extended and is

unstable on stairs while cleaning. It also lacks suction control and a headlamp. Its hose is longer than most in its category. Features: manual carpet-height adjustment, brush on/off switch, full-bag/bin indicator, overload protection for blower-fan motor, on/off switch located on handle, belt/brush indicator (window), high-efficiency particulate air (HEPA) filter. Dirt sensor signals when no more dirt can be picked up in an area. Similar models: WindTunnel Bagless Self Propelled U6618-900, WindTunnel Bagless Self Propelled U6634-900.

6 DYSON DC15 The Ball All Floors A very good, bagless vac. Brush on/off switch. Full bin alert. Overload protection for blower-fan and rotating-brush motors. Hose longer than most. Lacks suction control. Lacks headlamp. Similar model: DC15 The Ball Animal.

7 HOOVER Savvy U8181-900 Very good overall vac with on/off switch located on handle. Has full-bag indicator, manual carpet-height adjustment, HEPA filter, overload protection for blower-fan motor, small powered brush for stairs, and dirt sensor that signals when no more dirt can be picked up in an area. Hose is longer than most, but lacks suction control. Bags: $8/3; filter $30. Similar models: Savvy U8174-900, Savvy U8183-900.

8 HOOVER Tempo Widepath U5140-900 Very good overall vacuum. Has full-bag indicator, manual carpet-height adjustment, overload protection for blower-fan motor, and small powered brush for stairs. But not stable on stairs while stair cleaning. Hose shorter than most and prone to tip over when hose is extended. Lacks on/off switch for rotating brush, upholstery tool, and suction control. Power cord is shorter than most. Bags: $8/3.

Recommendations

9 HOOVER WindTunnel Self Propelled Ultra U6439-900 Very good performer. This bag-equipped upright is prone to tip over when hose is extended and is unstable on stairs while stair cleaning. Lacks suction control. Features: brush on/off switch, full-bag/bin indicator, overload protection for blower-fan motor, on/off switch located on handle, belt/brush indicator (window), manual carpet-height adjustment. Dirt sensor signals when no more dirt can be picked up in an area. Similar models: WindTunnel Self Propelled Ultra U6436-900, WindTunnel Self Propelled Ultra U6454-900.

10 ORECK XL21-700 Very good. Overload protection for blower-fan motor. Motor control with more than one speed. HEPA filter. Lacks on/off switch for rotating brush. Lacks suction control. Pusher configuration. Bags: $20/8. Bags for compact canister: $10/12 plus filter.

11 PANASONIC MC-V7720 Very good overall cleaning performance, but two of four samples of this bagless upright had inoperative release levers. Manufacturer says it has redesigned housing to remedy the problem. Has full-bin alert, HEPA filter, overload protection for blower-fan motor and rotating-brush motor, and motor control with more than one speed. Hose is longer than most. Dirt sensor signals when no more dirt can be picked up in an area. Filters: exhaust $12; Dirt cup $25. Similar models: MC-V7721.

12 RICCAR SupraLite RSL3 Very good overall. Overload protection for blower-fan motor. HEPA filter. Lacks on/off switch for rotating brush. Pusher configuration. Bags: $17/6. Similar model: Simplicity Freedom F3500.

13 DYSON DC07 All Floors A very good bagless vac, but has confusing controls. Hose longer than most. Noisy. Hard to push and pull. No headlamp. HEPA filter (washable): $17.50. Similar models: DC07 Animal, DC07 Full Gear, DC07 Full Kit, DC07 Low Reach.

14 DYSON DC14 Complete A very good bagless vac, but has confusing controls. Easier to use than the comparable Dyson DC07 when using wand with attachments. Hose longer than most. Noisy. Hard to push and pull. No headlamp. HEPA filter (washable): $17.50. Similar models: DC14 All Floors, DC14 Animal, DC14 Full Access (Best Buy), DC14 Full Gear, DC14 Full Kit, DC14 Low Reach.

15 HOOVER Z 700 U9145-900 Overall very good. This bagless upright is unstable on stairs while cleaning. Its cord is less convenient to wrap than others. It lacks suction control. Its hose is longer than most in its category. Features: brush on/off switch, full-bag/bin indicator, overload protection for blower-fan motor and rotating-brush moto, motor control with more than one speed, high-efficiency particulate air (HEPA) filte, telescopic wand. Similar model: Z 400 U9125-900.

16 KENMORE Progressive 36622 A very good overall vacuum. This bag-equipped upright is prone to tip over when hose is extended and is unstable on stairs while stair cleaning. Its power cord is shorter than most in its category, but its hose is longer than most in its category. Features: brush on/off switch, suction control, overload protection for blower-fan motor and rotating-brush motor, on/off switch located on handle, manual carpet-height adjustment, motor control with more than one speed, high-efficiency particulate air (HEPA) filter. Dirt sensor signals when no more dirt can be picked up in an area. Telescopic wand. Similar model: Progressive 36623.

Recommendations

17 RICCAR Radiance Very good overall. Brush on/off switch. Full-bag alert. Manual pile adjustment. Suction control. Overload protection for blower-fan motor. HEPA filter. Hose shorter than most. Not stable on stairs. Bags: $15/6. Similar model: Simplicity Synergy.

18 HOOVER EmPower U5262-910 Very good overall bagless vac with full-bin alert. Has manual carpet-height adjustment, HEPA filter, overload protection for blower-fan motor, and small, powered brush for stairs. Hose longer than most and motor control has more than one speed. But lacks independent on/off switch for rotating brush and suction control. Filter: $30. Similar models: EmPower Turbo U5268-970, EmPower U5265-900, EmPower U5269-900.

19 HOOVER WindTunnel Bagless U5753-900 Very good overall. This bagless upright is prone to tip over when hose is extended and unstable on stairs while stair cleaning. Lacks suction control and independent on/off switch for rotating brush. Features: Full-bag/bin indicator. Manual carpet-height adjustment. Overload protection for blower-fan motor. On/off switch located on handle. High-efficiency particulate air (HEPA) filter. Dirt sensor signals when no more dirt can be picked up in an area. Similar model: WindTunnel Bagless U5753-960, WindTunnel Bagless U5760-900.

20 HOOVER WindTunnel Supreme U5458-900 Very good overall vac with on/off switch located on handle. Has full-bag indicator, overload protection for blower-fan motor, manual carpet-height adjustment, and dirt sensor that signals when no more dirt can be picked up in an area. But lacks on/off switch for rotating-brush and suction control. This upright is prone to tipping over when hose is extended

and isn't stable on stairs while stair cleaning. Bags: $8/3. Discontinued, but similar model WindTunnel Supreme U5468-900 may be available.

21 DIRT DEVIL Vision Self-Propelled MO87900 A very good bagless vac, but noisy. Hose longer than most. Had to bend to adjust rug height. No upholstery tool. Filter: $25. Discontinued, but similar model Vision Self Propelled MO87400 may be available.

22 AERUS Lux Legacy A very good overall vacuum with full-bag alert. On/off switch located on handle. Has overload protection for rotating-brush motor. Comes with small, powered brush for stairs, but lacks independent on/off switch for rotating brush. Hose longer than most, but vac is prone to tip over when hose is extended. Tools not stowed on board. Hose not attached at suction end. Bag price set by dealer.

23 SEBO Automatic X4 Very good, but compromised by notable flaws. Brush on/off switch. Full-bag alert. Overload protection for blower-fan motor. Tippy with hose is extended. Unstable on stairs. Cord shorter than most. Lacks headlamp. Bags: $19/10.

24 BISSELL Lift-Off Revolution Turbo 3760-1 A good performer. This bagless upright is prone to tip over when hose is extended and is unstable on stairs while stair cleaning. Lacks suction control. Features: Brush on/off switch. Full-bag/bin indicator. Overload protection for blower-fan motor. Belt/brush indicator (window). Manual carpet-height adjustment. High-efficiency particulate air (HEPA) filter. Telescopic wand. Similar models: 3760-2, 3760-3, 3760-H, 4220, Turbo 6850.

25 ELECTROLUX Aptitude EL5010A Good, but pricey and noisy. Bag-equipped.

Tippy with hose extended. Hose longer than most. Motor control has more than one speed. Had to bend to adjust rug height. No upholstery tool. Bags: $11/5. Filter: $20.

26 BISSELL PowerForce 3522-6 Overall good performer. This bag-equipped upright is prone to tip over when hose is extended and is unstable on stairs while stair cleaning. Lacks independent on/off switch for rotating-brush and suction control. Its hose shorter than most in its category and its power cord is shorter than most in its category. Features: Full-bag/bin indicator. Manual carpet-height adjustment.

27 BISSELL CleanView Revolution Deluxe 3596 A good overall vacuum. This bagless upright is prone to tip over when hose is extended and is unstable on stairs while stair cleaning. Lacks independent on/off switch for rotating-brush and suction control. Features: Full-bag/bin indicator. Belt/brush indicator (window). Manual carpet-height adjustment. High-efficiency particulate air (HEPA) filter. Dirt sensor signals when no more dirt can be picked up in an area.

28 BISSELL CleanView Revolution Plus 3595-1 Good overall bagless vacuum, but one of three samples emitted dust. Has full-bag indicator, manual carpet-height adjustment, HEPA filter, and small powered brush for stairs. But lacks independent on/off switch for rotating brush. Hose longer than most, but prone to tip over when hose is extended. Lacks suction control. Not stable on stairs while stair cleaning. Need to bend to adjust rug height. Filters: $9-13.25. Similar models: CleanView Revolution 3595, CleanView Revolution 3595-2, CleanView Revolution Turbo 3595-6.

29 MIELE Powerhouse S184 A good vac with some notable flaws. Brush on/off switch. Full-bag alert. Hose longer than most. Motor control with more than one speed. HEPA filter. Prone to tip when hose is extended. Cord shorter than most. Lacks suction control. Unstable on stairs. Lacks upholstery tool. Bags: $15/5 Filter: $35.

30 VAX X5 Good overall cleaning is compromised by poor suction for cleaning with tools. This bagless vac has on/off switch located on handle, full bin alert, HEPA filter, brush on/off switch, retractable cord, and overload protection for blower-fan motor and rotating-brush motor. Hose longer than most. Comes with small powered brush for stairs, but not stable on stairs while stair cleaning. Power cord is shorter than most and lacks suction control. Similar model: X3.

31 EUREKA Boss 4D 5892 Poor bare-floor performance compromises this bagless vac. Brush on/off switch. Full bin alert. Manual pile adjustment. Overload protection for blower-fan motor. Hose longer than most. HEPA filter. Lacks suction control. Lacks headlamp. Filter: $20.

32 BISSELL PowerForce 6579-2 A good overall vacuum. This bagless upright is prone to tip over when hose is extended and is unstable on stairs while stair cleaning. Lacks independent on/off switch for rotating-brush and suction control. Its hose shorter than most in its category and its power cord is shorter than most in its category. Features: Easy on/off switch. Full-bag/bin indicator. On/off is by foot switch. Manual carpet-height adjustment.

33 HOOVER Foldaway Widepath U5170-900 Good overall cleaning performance is compromised by poor suction for cleaning with tools. This bagless vac has full-bin alert, overload protection for blower-fan motor, and manual carpet-height adjustment. But lacks on/off switch for rotating brush, suction control, and headlamp. Power cord is shorter than most. Filter: $15. Discontinued, but similar model Foldaway Widepath U5172-900 may be available.

34 ORECK XL Deluxe U3700HH Good overall cleaning is compromised by poor suction for cleaning with tools. The on/off switch is located on handle, but lacks on/off switch for rotating brush. Bags: $20/8.

35 SANYO Performax SC-A116 A good vac compromised by some notable flaws. Easy on/off switch. Lacks independent On/off switch for rotating brush. Tippy with hose extended. Lacks suction control. Bags: $12/6. Filter: $11/2.

36 PANASONIC Fold'N Go MC-V5485 Good overall cleaning with mediocre suction for cleaning with tools. This bagless vac has a full-bin alert, HEPA filter, and overload protection for blower-fan motor and rotating-brush motor. But lacks on/off switch for rotating brush, upholstery tool, headlamp, and suction control. Prone to tipping over when hose is extended and not stable on stairs while stair cleaning. Filters: exhaust $12; Dirt cup: $25.

37 DIRT DEVIL Reaction M110000 A good performer. This bagless upright is prone to tip over when hose is extended and is unstable on stairs while stair cleaning. Lacks independent on/off switch for rotating brush, suction control, and upholstery tool. Hose longer than most in its category. Features: Easy on/off switch. Full-bag/bin indicator. Overload protection for blower-fan motor. On/off is by foot switch. Belt/brush indicator (window). Manual carpet-height adjustment. High-efficiency particulate air (HEPA) filter.

38 EUREKA Altima 2981 A good upright. This bagless upright is prone to tip over when hose is extended and is unstable on stairs while stair cleaning. Lacks independent on/off switch for rotating brush, suction control, and upholstery tool. Its cord is less convenient to wrap than others. Features: Full-bag/bin indicator. Overload protection for blower-fan motor. Belt/brush indicator (window). Manual carpet-height adjustment. High-efficiency particulate air (HEPA) filter. Similar model: Altima 2991AVZ.

NOT RECOMMENDED MODELS

EUREKA Optima 431A Not recommended. The power cord on this bagless upright is shorter than most in its category. It lacks an upholstery tool. Features: Brush on/off switch. Full-bag/bin indicator. Suction control. Overload protection for blower-fan motor and rotating-brush motor.

HOOVER Fusion U5180-900 Not recommended: This bagless vac emits large quantities of dust. There are better choices.

CANISTERS

39 ELECTROLUX Oxygen3 Ultra EL7020A A very good overall canister. The power cord on this bag-equipped canister is shorter than most in its category. The wand is unstable when placed in upright position; it's more convenient to disconnect wand from powerhead. Features: Brush on/off switch. Retractable cord. Easy on/off switch. Full-bag/bin indicator. Suction control. Overload protection for blower-fan motor and rotating-brush motor. On/off switch located on handle. Belt/brush indicator (window). Manual carpet-height adjustment. Motor control with more than one speed. High-efficiency particulate air (HEPA) filter. Telescopic wand.

Recommendations

40 KENMORE (SEARS) Progressive 25614 Bag-equipped. Full-bag indication. Brush on/off switch. Retractable cord. Easy on/off switch. Manual pile-height adjustment. Suction control. Overload protection for blower-fan and rotating-brush motor. Hose longer than most. Retractable cord. On/off switch located Bags: $8/2. Similar model: Progressive 25615.

41 KENMORE (SEARS) Progressive 25914 A very good, bag-equipped canister. On/off brush switch. On/off switch on handle. Retractable cord. Full-bag alert. Suction control. Manual pile adjustment. Overload protection for blower-fan and rotating-brush motor. Hose longer than most. HEPA filter. Motor control with more than one speed. Dirt sensor. Bags: $8/2. Similar model: Progressive 25915.

42 KENMORE (SEARS) Progressive 25512 **CR Best Buy** Very good overall bag-equipped canister with on/off switch on handle. Has brush on/off switch, manual carpet-height adjustment, retractable cord, and full-bag indicator. Overload protection for rotating-brush motor. HEPA filter. Has small powered brush for stairs. Disconnecting the wand from the hose and the wand from the wand was difficult. Bags: $8/2; $11/8 (microfilt.) Similar model: Progressive 25513.

43 BOSCH Premium Prestige Electro Duo H BSG 81360UC Very good. Bag-equipped. Brush on/off switch. Retractable cord. Full-bag alert. Suction control. Overload protection for blower-fan motor. On/off switch on handle. Cord shorter than most. Lacks headlamp. Wand unstable in upright position.Bags: $15/5.

44 SEBO Air Belt C3.1 A very good, bag-equipped canister. Retractable cord. Full-bag alert. Overload protection for blower-fan motor and rotating brush. Motor control with more than one speed. HEPA filter. Lacks on/off switch for brush. Power cord shorter than most. Lacks suction control. Lacks headlamp. Bags: $19/10.

45 ELECTROLUX Oxygen EL6988A A very good canister with better-than-average cleaning on carpet. Bag-equipped. Hose longer than most. Cord shorter than most. Difficult to detach wand-to-wand connection and wand from hose. Bags: $9/5.

46 ORECK Dutch Tech DTX1400B Bag-equipped. Full-bag indication. Brush on/off switch. Retractable cord. Easy on/off switch. Overload protection for rotating-brush motor. Hose longer than most. On/off switch located on handle. On/off is by foot switch. Motor control with more than one speed. Bags: $14/5.

47 MIELE Plus 1200W S251 Very good. Less bulky, and heavy than most. Cord shorter than most. Bags: $15/5.

48 RICCAR 1700 Very good. Bag-equipped. Brush on/off switch. Retractable cord. Full-bag alert. Manual pile-height adjustment. Overload protection for blower-fan and rotating-brush motor. Hose longer than most. Motor control with more than one speed. HEPA filter. Lacks suction control. Wand felt heavy when using tools. Bags: $15/6. Similar model: Simplicity S36.

49 AERUS Lux Guardian C154E Very good. Bag-equipped. Brush on/off switch. Retractable cord. Full-bag alert. Suction control. Overload protection for blower-fan and rotating-brush motor. On/off switch on handle. HEPA filter. Lacks headlamp. Wand felt heavy when using tools. Bags: $22/12.

Recommendations

50 HOOVER WindTunnel Bagless S3765-040 A very good canister vac, with better cleaning than most on carpet. But relatively noisy, and released dust when we emptied the bin. Dirt cup filter: $17. HEPA: $15. Hoover canisters have been among the more repair-prone vacuum cleaners. Similar model: WindTunnel Bagless S3755.

51 HOOVER WindTunnel Plus S3639 A very good vacuum. It's less convenient to disconnect the wand from the powerhead and it's difficult to detach wand-to-wand connection on this bag-equipped canister. Features: Brush on/off switch. Retractable cord. Easy on/off switch. Full-bag/bin indicator. Suction control. Overload protection for blower-fan motor. On/off is by foot switch. Belt/brush indicator (window). High-efficiency particulate air (HEPA) filter.

52 HOOVER Duros S3590 A very good vacuum overall. But this bag-equipped canister lacks suction control, its wand felt heavy when using tools, and its hose and power cord are shorter than most in its category. Features: Brush on/off switch. Retractable cord. Easy on/off switch; on/off is by foot switch. Full-bag/bin indicator. Motor control with more than one speed.

53 AERUS Lux Legacy C153C A very good, bag-equipped canister. Brush on/off switch. Retractable cord. Full-bag alert. Overload protection for blower-fan and rotating-brush motor. Motor control with more than one speed. Power cord shorter than most. Lacks suction control. Wand felt heavy when using tools. Bags: $22/12.

54 FANTOM Falcon FC251 Good overall, with better-than-average cleaning on carpet. But disconnecting the power-head and wiring to change tools was very difficult. Vac also was relatively noisy, and released dust when bin was emptied. HEPA filter: $30.

55 SANYO SC-X1000P Brush on/off switch. Retractable cord. Easy on/off switch. Hose longer than most. Retractable cord. On/off is by foot switch. Bagless. Full-bin indication. HEPA filter. Power cord is shorter than most. Lacks suction control. Wand unstable when placed in upright position.

56 TRISTAR Mg2 A101N Very good. Bag-equipped. Brush on/off switch. Suction control. Overload protection for blower-fan motor and rotating-brush motor. Less convenient to wrap cord than others. Lacks headlamp. Wand felt heavy when using tools. Bags: $15/12.

57 FILTER Queen Majestic 360 AT1100 A good bagless vac with notable flaws. Brush on/off switch. Overload protection for blower-fan and rotating-brush motor. Hose longer than most. Full-bin indicator. Motor control with more than one speed. Less convenient than others to wrap cord. Cord shorter than most. Lacks suction control. Unstable on stairs. Lacks headlamp. Wand felt heavy when using tools. Filters: $14/6 paper cones, 1 cloth cone.

58 RAINBOW e-series E2 Extremely high price not justified by performance. Among the worst on bare floors, and relatively noisy. Unusual design uses water to retain dust and dirt that's been picked up, which makes the machine very heavy (32 lbs.) when filled with water. Special features include the ability to pick up wet spills (not tested), an inflator for toys, and a dusting brush for plants and animals.

59 AIRIDER G1-9000-07-1US A good overall vacuum. This bagless canister is not stable on stairs while cleaning. It lacks a headlamp and its wand is unstable when placed in upright position. Its power cord is shorter than most in its category but its hose is longer than most in its category. Features: Brush on/off switch. Retractable cord. Easy on/off switch. Full-bag/bin indicator. Suction control. Overload protection for blower-fan motor. On/off is by foot switch. Telescopic wand.

Brand Repair History

Readers report on 72,000 vacuum cleaners

The graph shows the percentages of these brands of upright and canister vacuums purchased new between 2001 and the first half of 2005 that have been repaired or had a serious problem. Differences of less than 4 points aren't meaningful. Belt repairs were excluded. Hoover canisters have been among the more repair-prone vacs. While Dyson hasn't been on the market long enough to gather data for our repair graphs, we've seen no unusual repair problems with its upright vacuums over the two years' worth of data we have. Models within a brand may vary, and changes in manufacturing and design may affect vacuum reliability. Still choosing a brand with a good repair history improves your odds of getting a reliable vacuum.

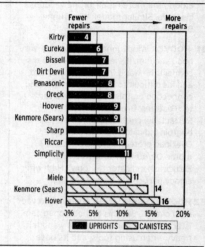

	Fewer repairs ← → More repairs
Kirby	4
Eureka	6
Bissell	7
Dirt Devil	7
Panasonic	8
Oreck	8
Hoover	9
Kenmore (Sears)	9
Sharp	10
Riccar	10
Simplicity	11
Miele	11
Kenmore (Sears)	14
Hover	16

0% 5% 10% 15% 20%

■ UPRIGHTS ▧ CANISTERS

Data are based on readers responses about vacuum cleaners to the Annual Product Reliability Survey conducted by the Consumer Reports National Research Center. Data are adjusted to eliminate differences linked to age and usage.

WASHING MACHINES

Lower prices have helped traditional top-loading washers outsell the more-efficient front-loaders; you'll find competent models that cost as little as $300 or so. But manufacturers are narrowing the gap with competent front-loaders priced well under $1,000. These less-expensive models tend to outperform high-efficiency top-loaders for the same price or less.

Compact machines and one-piece, stacked washer-dryer laundry centers are two alternatives for apartments and other tight spots. But the washers we tested, the Miele Touchtronic W1113 and Asko W6021, were relatively pricey. Laundry centers have also delivered mixed results. The $1,000 Frigidaire GLEH1642D we tested delivered fine drying, but washing was only fair. The reverse held for the $1,800 Maytag MLE2000AY version.

A better bet: Check our Ratings for dryers that can be stacked above compatible front-loading washers.

Note that tougher new energy-efficiency standards for washers take effect in January 2007. While front-loading washers and a handful of high-efficiency top-loaders already meet this latest standard, most traditional top-loading models do not and are no longer sold. You'll find additional test results for high-efficiency front-loading washers in the January 2007 issue of CONSUMER REPORTS.

The **Ratings** rank washers by overall score. **Quick Picks** lists high-value models from reliable brands.

Excellent	⊖	
Very good	⊖	
Good	○	
Fair	⊖	
Poor	●	

Within types, in performance order. Gray **key numbers indicate Quick Picks.**

Key number	Brand & model	Price	Overall score 0 — 100 P F G VG E	Washing performance	Energy efficiency	Water efficiency	Capacity	Gentleness	Noise	Cycle time (min.)	Stainless-steel tub	Porcelain top/lid	Auto temp. control	Auto bleach dispenser
HIGH-EFFICIENCY TOP-LOADING MODELS														
1	**Kenmore** (Sears) Elite Oasis HE 2708[2]	$1000	72	⊖	⊖	○	⊖	○	⊖	60	•	•	•	•
2	**GE** Profile Harmony WPGT9360E[WW]	890	65	⊖	○	○	⊖	⊖	⊖	55	•		•	•
FRONT-LOADING MODELS (HIGH-EFFICIENCY)														
3	**LG** Tromm SteamWasher WM2688H[N]M	1600	83	⊖	⊖	⊖	⊖	⊖	⊖	70	•	•	•	•
4	**Kenmore** (Sears) Elite HE4t 4508[1]	1500	79	⊖	⊖	⊖	⊖	⊖	⊖	95	•	•	•	•
5	**Whirlpool** Duet HT GHW9400P[W]	1300	79	⊖	⊖	⊖	⊖	⊖	⊖	65	•	•	•	•
6	**Frigidaire** LTF2940E[S] (Lowes) Gallery	750	78	○	⊖	⊖	⊖	⊖	⊖	55	•	•	•	•
7	**Maytag** Neptune MAH8700A[WW]	1100	77	⊖	⊖	⊖	⊖	⊖	⊖	85	•	•	•	•

FRONT-LOADING MODELS (HIGH-EFFICIENCY) *continued*

Key number	Brand & model	Price	Overall score	Washing performance	Energy efficiency	Water efficiency	Capacity	Gentleness	Noise	Cycle time (min.)	Stainless-steel tub	Porcelain top/lid	Auto temp. control	Auto bleach dispenser
8	**Samsung** SilverCare WF316LA[W]	$1200	77	⊖	⊖	⊖	⊖	⊖	⊖	75	•		•	•
9	**LG** WM1814C[W]	800	76	○	⊖	⊖	⊖	⊖	⊖	80	•		•	•
10	**Whirlpool** Duet GHW9150P[W]	1100	76	⊖	⊖	⊖	⊖	⊖	⊖	65	•		•	•
11	**LG** WM2277H[W]	1100	75	○	⊖	⊖	⊖	⊖	○	75	•	•	•	•
12	**Maytag** Neptune MAH9700S[W]	1300	75	⊖	⊖	⊖	⊖	⊖	⊖	90	•		•	•
13	**Frigidaire** FTF2140E[S]	700	72	○	⊖	⊖	⊖	⊖	○	45	•			•
14	**GE** WBVH6240F[WW]	900	72	⊖	⊖	⊖	○	○	⊖	105	•		•	•
15	**Frigidaire** Gallery GLTR1670A[S]	620	66	○	⊖	○	○	○	⊖	60	•			•
16	**Maytag** Neptune MAH6500A[WW]	900	64	⊖	○	○	○	○	○	70	•	•	•	•
17	**Miele** Touchtronic W1113	1600	63	⊖	⊖	⊖	●	⊖	⊖	90	•		•	
18	**Asko** W6021	1000	61	⊖	⊖	⊖	●	⊖	⊖	120	•		•	

Overall score scale: 0 — 100, P F G VG E

See report, page 75. Based on tests posted to ConsumerReports.org in July 2006, with updated prices and availability.

Guide to the Ratings

Overall score is based primarily on washing ability, efficiency, capacity, and noise. **Washing performance** reflects the degree of color change to swatches of fabric that were included in an 8-lb. test load of mixed cotton items using the machine's most aggressive normal cycle. (We do not use special cycle or option buttons.) **Energy efficiency** is based on the energy needed to heat the water for 8-lb. and maximum loads using a warm wash and cold rinse. We consider both gas and electric water heaters, and include electricity needed to run the washer and energy needed for drying. Washers that extract more water are scored higher. **Water efficiency** denotes how much water it took to wash our 8-lb. load and each machine's maximum load. On models that didn't set the fill level automatically, we used the lowest fill setting that sufficed for the 8-lb. load. We then calculated water used per pound of clothing. **Capacity** for top-loaders is based on how well the washer agitates increasingly large loads. For front-loaders, the score is based on our judgment of the maximum sized load that the washer holds. Models that earned lower scores for **gentleness** are more likely to treat your clothes roughly, causing wear and tear. **Noise** reflects judgments by panelists during the fill, agitate, and spin cycles. **Cycle time** is our measurement of the time, rounded to the nearest five minutes, to complete the most aggressive normal cycle with our 8-lb. load. (We do not use special cycle or option buttons.) **Price** is approximate retail.

Quick Picks

For more performance and efficiency:
  10 Whirlpool Duet GHW9150P[W], $1,100
This front-loader costs less than most, with

good capacity. Matching dryer: Whirlpool
Duet GEW9250P, $800.

Recommendations

HIGH-EFFICIENCY TOP-LOADING MODELS

1   KENMORE (SEARS) Elite Oasis HE 2708[2] This unconventional top-loader replaces the usual vertical agitator with a single, large wash plate that moves the laundry around the tub. It has an especially large capacity and did a very good job washing our loads. It's among the quieter, more energy-efficient top-loading washers we've tested. But it had a tendency with some loads to ball up clothing, sometimes unbalancing the machine and requiring readjustment of the clothing. High-efficiency, low-sudsing detergent is recommended for best results and washer performance. Reliability data for Kenmore high-efficiency washers may not apply to the new Oasis, which uses different technology than other Kenmore high-efficiency models. We have no repair data for this new model. The lid has a glass pane that lets you view the laundry while it's being washed. Similar model: Elite Oasis HE 2709.

2   GE Profile Harmony WPGT9360E[WW] This unconventional top-loader uses a washing disk instead of a center agitator post, and it can hold relatively large loads. It did a very good job washing clothing, but the spin cycle did not extract water as well as most washers we tested, which can lengthen drying time. It has touch-screen controls with a digital display of menus. The washer electronically signals the matching dryer to indicate which

wash cycle was used, and the dryer automatically chooses a corresponding setting—a unique but not especially helpful feature. Low-sudsing detergent is recommended for the best results and washer performance. Although GE top-loaders have been about average in reliability, that may not apply to this washer because it uses different technology.

FRONT-LOADING MODELS (HIGH-EFFICIENCY)

3   LG Tromm SteamWasher WM2688H[N]M Overall, an excellent high-capacity washer with outstanding energy and water efficiency. It offers two optional steam settings: a cycle to moisten clothing to make ironing easier, and another that adds steam to boost cleaning performance. This was among the best machines tested at extracting water from clothes, with spin speeds up to 1,320 rpm. It has an internal water heater. Still, you'll find competent front-loading washers without that feature for as little as half the SteamWasher's $1,600 price. We don't have enough survey data to establish a track record for reliability.

4   KENMORE (SEARS) Elite HE4t 4508[1] This front-loader has a very large capacity and is among the most frugal with both energy and water. It did a very good job washing clothes. As with all front-loaders, low-sudsing detergent is recommended for the best results and washer performance. It was among the quietest models tested, but it had a rather long cycle time and is high-priced even for a front-loader. An optional 13-inch-high pedestal with a storage drawer raises the washer for easier unloading. This washer can be stacked with a companion dryer. Similar model: Elite HE4t 4509.

5 WHIRLPOOL Duet HT GHW9400P[W] This front-loader has a very large capacity and it did a very good job washing clothes. Low-sudsing detergent is recommended for the best results and washer performance. Like many front-loaders, it's very efficient with both water and energy and is among the quietest washers tested. An optional 13-inch-high pedestal with a storage drawer raises the washer for easier unloading.

6 FRIGIDAIRE LTF2940E[S] (Lowes) A moderate-capacity front-loading washer, this machine did a good job cleaning clothes, which would be fine for all but very soiled laundry. Like many front-loaders, it's very efficient with both water and energy, and is among the quietest washers we've tested. Low-sudsing detergent is recommended for the best results and washer performance. Similar model: Gallery GLTF2940E.

7 MAYTAG Neptune MAH8700A[WW] A high-capacity front-loading washer, this machine was very good at washing. Like many front-loaders, it's very efficient with both water and energy, and is among the quietest washers tested. Low-sudsing detergent is recommended for the best results and washer performance. However, reliability is a concern. Maytag front-loaders have been the most repair-prone brand of front-loaders and were more repair-prone than most brands of washers.

8 SAMSUNG SilverCare WF316LA[W] Overall, a very good high-capacity washer with excellent energy and water efficiency but less-than-stellar washing performance. It could be better at extracting water in its final spin. It has an internal water heater. This model has a feature the maker says will sterilize your wash by releasing a trace amount of silver when you choose the SilverCare setting. We're also concerned about what happens with the silver when it leaves your machine; the EPA is currently investigating. You'll find better front-loading washers for as little as $800 or so and able top-loaders for even less. We don't have enough survey data to establish a track record for reliability.

9 LG WM1814C[W] This low-priced front-loader holds very large loads and did a good job getting clothes clean, which would be fine for all but the most soiled laundry. It's frugal with water and energy, and very quiet. Low-sudsing detergent is recommended for the best results and washer performance. We don't have enough survey data to establish a track record for reliability

10 WHIRLPOOL Duet GHW9150P[W] This competent, well-priced front-loader did well on all counts. Very quiet and efficient with both water and energy, it did a very good job getting clothes clean and has a very large capacity. An optional 13-inch-high pedestal with a storage drawer raises the height for easier unloading. Low-sudsing detergent is recommended for the best results and washer performance.

11 LG WM2277H[W] This front-loader holds very large loads and did a good job getting clothes clean. It's frugal with water and energy. It was among the best at extracting water from clothes, which

Recommendations

speeds drying. Low-sudsing detergent is recommended for the best results and washer performance. We don't have enough survey data to establish a track record for reliability.

12 MAYTAG Neptune MAH9700S[W] A high-capacity front-loading washer, this machine was very good at washing. However, Maytag front-loaders have been the most repair-prone brand of front-loaders and were more repair-prone than most brands of washers. Like many front-loaders, it's very efficient with both water and energy, and it's among the quietest washers tested. Low-sudsing detergent is recommended for the best results and washer performance.

13 FRIGIDAIRE FTF2140E[S] A lower-priced, moderate-capacity front-loading washer, this machine did a good job cleaning clothes, which would be fine for all but very soiled laundry. Like many front-loaders, it's very efficient with both water and energy. Low-sudsing detergent is recommended for the best results and washer performance. Similar model: LTF2140E (Lowes).

14 GE WBVH6240F[WW] This lower-priced front-loading washer did a very good job cleaning clothes. Like many front-loaders, it's very efficient with both water and energy, and is among the quietest washers we've tested. Low-sudsing detergent is recommended for the best results and washer performance. Similar model: WHDVH626F (Home Depot).

15 FRIGIDAIRE Gallery GLTR1670A[S] Among the lowest-priced front-loaders, this capable model did a good job cleaning clothes, which would be fine for all but very soiled laundry. Its capacity isn't as large as some front-loaders, but it

holds a decent-sized load—as much as many top-loaders. It's very quiet and frugal with energy. Low-sudsing detergent is recommended for the best results and washer performance. Similar model: Gallery GLTF1670A.

16 MAYTAG Neptune MAH6500A[WW] This low-priced front-loader did a good job cleaning clothing, which would be fine for all but very soiled laundry. Its capacity isn't as large as some front-loaders, but it holds a decent-sized load—as much as many top-loaders—and it's frugal with water. Low-sudsing detergent is recommended for the best results and washer performance. However, reliability is a concern. Maytag front-loaders have been the most repair-prone brand of front-loaders and were more repair-prone than most brands of washers. Similar model: Neptune MAH5500B.

17 MIELE Touchtronic W1113 This compact front-loader holds only small loads but fits into tight spaces. It did a very good job getting clothes clean. It's very quiet and frugal with water and energy, and requires a dedicated 240-volt outlet. It has a long wash cycle but was among the best at extracting water from clothes, which speeds drying. It's pricey even for a front-loader. Low-sudsing detergent is recommended for the best results and washer performance. We have no repair data for this brand.

18 ASKO W6021 This compact front-loader holds only small loads but fits into tight spaces. It did a very good job getting clothes clean. It's very quiet and frugal with water and energy, and requires a dedicated 240-volt outlet. It has a long wash cycle but was among the best at extracting water from clothes, which

Recommendations

speeds drying. Low-sudsing detergent is recommended for the best results and washer performance. We don't have enough survey data to establish a track record for reliability.

Brand Repair History

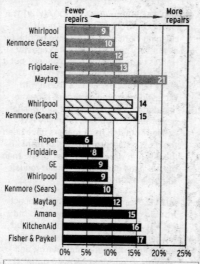

Fewer repairs → More repairs

Whirlpool	9
Kenmore (Sears)	10
GE	12
Frigidaire	13
Maytag	21
Whirlpool	14
Kenmore (Sears)	15
Roper	6
Frigidaire	8
GE	9
Whirlpool	9
Kenmore (Sears)	10
Maytag	12
Amana	15
KitchenAid	16
Fisher & Paykel	17

0% 5% 10% 15% 20% 25%

■ FRONT-LOADERS ◩ HIGH-EFFICIENCY TOP-LOADERS
■ CONVENTIONAL TOP-LOADERS

Readers report on 93,995 washing machines

The graph shows the percentage of these brands of washers bought new between 2001 and 2005 that were ever repaired or had a serious problem. Differences of less than 4 points aren't meaningful. Amana, KitchenAid, and Fisher & Paykel top-loading washers and Kenmore and Whirlpool high-efficiency top-loaders had more repairs than most conventional top-loading washers. The reliability data shown in the graph for Kenmore high-efficiency washers may not apply to the new Kenmore Oasis model. The Oasis uses a technology that differs from other Kenmore high-efficiency models and we have no repair data for this newly introduced model. Maytag front-loaders were the least-reliable washers. Models within a brand may vary, however, and changes in design or manufacture may affect reliability. Still, choosing a reliable washer brand can improve your odds of getting a reliable model.

Data are based on readers responses about washing machines to the Annual Product Reliability Survey conducted by the Consumer Reports National Research Center. Data are adjusted to eliminate differences linked to age and usage.

PRODUCT RECALLS

Products ranging from child safety seats to chain saws are recalled when there are safety defects. Various federal agencies—such as the Consumer Product Safety Commission (CPSC), the National Highway Traffic Safety Administration (NHTSA), the U.S. Coast Guard, and the Food and Drug Administration (FDA)—monitor consumer complaints and injuries and, when there's a problem, issue a recall.

But the odds of hearing about an unsafe product are slim. Manufacturers are usually reluctant to issue a recall in the first place because they can be costly. And getting the word out to consumers can be haphazard. If you return the warranty card that comes with a product, however, you're more likely to receive notification of a recall.

A selection of the most far-reaching recalls appears monthly in CONSUMER REPORTS. What follows is a list of products recalled from December 2005 through November 2006, as reported in issues of the magazine. For details on these products and hundreds more, go to our Web site, *www.ConsumerReports.org*, to access our free, comprehensive list of product recalls.

If you wish to report an unsafe product or get recall information, call the CPSC's hotline, 800-638-2772, or go to its Web site, *www.cpsc.gov*. Recall notices about automobiles can be obtained from a new-car dealer or by contacting NHTSA at 888-327-4236 or *www.nhtsa.dot.gov*. Questions about food and drugs are handled by the FDA's Office of Consumer Affairs, 888-463-6332 or *www.fda.gov*.

VEHICLES AND EQUIPMENT

'89-98 Toyota pickups and SUVs
'99-02 Chevrolet and GMC pickup trucks and SUVs
'05 Chrysler, Dodge, and Jeep SUVs, pickups, and passenger cars
'04-05 Hyundai Elantra and Kia Spectra
'04-05 Toyota Prius
'05-06 Scion TC with sunroof assembly
'05 Kawasaki Brute Force ATV
'03-06 Chevrolet Express and GMC Savana
'06 Dodge Durango
'06 Honda Civic
'03-05 Kia Rio
'06 Ford F-150 and Lincoln Mark LT
'05-06 Ford Freestar and Mercury
'04-06 Chevrolet, GMC, and Isuzu pickup trucks
'03-04 Jeep Grand Cherokee
'04-06 Toyota Prius
'04-06 Lexus and Toyota (various models)
'02-06 Jeep Liberty
'03 Nissan Altima and Sentra

CHILDREN'S PRODUCTS

Safety 1st and Kid Trax by Safety 1st battery-powered ride-on toy vehicles
Children's metal necklaces and zipper pulls
Graco "Aspen 3-in-1" wood crib with wood mattress support
Mead Johnson GENTLEASE powdered infant formula
The First Years liquid-filled baby teethers
Mood necklace and ring, glow-in-the-dark necklace and ring, and UV necklace and ring sold at dollar-type stores
Wood cordless toy telephones
Children's necklaces sold at Dollar General Stores
Schwinn Deluxe Bicycle Child Carriers

ELECTRONICS

HP and Compaq notebook computer batteries
Sony PlayStation 2 (Slim Version)
Nikon digital SLR camera battery packs
Dell notebook computer batteries
Olympus compact 35mm film cameras
Disney personal DVD players
HP Photosmart R707 digital cameras
Lexar JumpDrive FireFly and 1GB Secure II

FOOD

"Wolfgang Puck" and various other beverages and soups in self-heating containers

HOUSEHOLD PRODUCTS

Haier Oscillating Electric Tower Fan
Lasko, General Electric, Galaxy, and Air King box and pivoting floor fans

Mainstays "Love Seat" and "Porch" wood rockers sold at Wal-Mart stores
First Alert OneLink smoke and combination smoke/carbon-monoxide alarms
RedMax and Shindaiwa gas-powered back-pack blowers
Black & Decker automatic coffeemakers models TCM800 and TCM805
Bunn 10-cup automatic drip coffeemakers, "Power Xtension" extension cords
"Mainstays Associate" office chair sold at Wal-Mart

RECREATION

Back Trails Jr. bicycle helmets sold at Target stores
Hoist free-weight exercise benches

BRAND LOCATOR

Phone numbers and Web site addresses of selected manufacturers.

A
Acura	800-382-2238	www.acura.com
ACD Systems	250-544-6201	www.acdsee.com
Adobe	800-833-6687	www.adobe.com
Admiral	800-688-9900	www.maytag.com
Aerus (Electrolux)	800-243-9078	www.aerusonline.com
Aiwa	800-289-2492	www.us.aiwa.com
Akai	800-726-4405	www.akaiusa.com
Amana	800-843-0304	www.amana.com
AMD	800-222-9323	www.amd.com
America Online	800-827-6364	www.aol.com
Apex	866-427-3946	www.apexdigitalinc.com
Apple	800-692-7753	www.apple.com
ArcSoft	510-440-9901	www.arcsoft.com
Ariens	920-756-4688	www.ariens.com
Asko	800-898-1879	www.askousa.com
Asus	502-995-0883	usa.asus.com
AT&T	800-222-3111	www.att.com
Audi	800-822-2834	www.audiusa.com
Audiovox	800-645-4994	www.audiovox.com

B
B&W	800-370-3740	www.bwspeakers.com
BellSouth	888-757-6500	www.bellsouth.com
BIC	888-461-4628	www.bicamerica.com
Bionaire	800-788-5350	www.bionaire.com
Bissell	800-237-7691	www.bissell.com
Black & Decker	800-544-6986	www.blackanddecker.com
BMW	800-831-1117	www.bmwusa.com
Bosch	800-921-9622	www.boschappliances.com
Bose	800-999-2673	www.bose.com
Boston Acoustics	800-246-7767	www.bostonacoustics.com
Broilmaster	800-851-3153	www.broilmaster.com
Brother	800-276-7746	www.brother-usa.com
Buick	800-422-8425	www.buick.com

C
Cadillac	800-333-4223	www.cadillac.com
Cambridge Soundworks	800-367-4434	www.hifi.com
Canon	800-828-4040	www.usa.canon.com
Carrier	800-227-7437	www.carrier.com
Casio	800-706-2534	www.casio.com
Cerwin-Vega	818-534-1500	www.cerwinvega.com
Char-Broil	800-241-7548	www.charbroil.com

Chevrolet .... 800-222-1020 .... www.chevrolet.com
Chrysler .... 800-992-1997 .... www.chrysler.com
Cingular........................... 800-331-0500 .... www.cingular.com
Coleman .... 800-356-3612 .... www.coleman.com
Compaq .... 800-752-0900 .... www.compaq.com
CompuServe .... 800-336-6823 .... www.compuserve.com
Corel.............................. 800-772-6735 .... www.corel.com
Craftsman .... Call local Sears store....... www.sears.com
Creative Labs..................... 800-998-1000 .... us.creative.com
Cub Cadet .... 877-282-8684 .... www.cubcadet.com
Cuisinart .... 800-726-0190 .... www.cuisinart.com

D

Dacor .... 800-793-0093 .... www.dacor.com
Daewoo .... 800-323-9668 .... www.daewoous.com
Dell .... 800-624-9897 .... www.dell.com
DeLonghi.......................... 800-322-3848 .... www.delonghiusa.com
Denon. .... 800-497-8921 .... www.usa.denon.com
DeWalt .... 800-433-9258 .... www.dewalt.com
DirecTV .... 888-238-7177 .... www.directv.com
DirecWay.......................... 866-347-3292. .... www.hughesnet.com
Dirt Devil. .... 800-321-1134. .... www.dirtdevil.com
Dish Network (EchoStar).......... 800-825-2557 .... www.dishnetwork.com
Disney Interactive................. 800-328-0368. .... disney.go.com/disneyinteractive
Dodge............................. 800-992-1997 .... www.dodge.com
Ducane. .... 800-382-2637 .... www.ducane.com
Dynamic Cooking Systems (DCS).. 800-433-8466. .... www.dcsappliances.com
Dyson............................. 866-693-9766 .... www.dyson.com

E

EarthLink .... 800-327-8454 .... www.earthlink.net
Echo.............................. 800-673-1558 .... www.echo-usa.com
Electrolux .... 800-243-9078 .... www.electroluxusa.com
EMachines......................... 877-566-3463 .... www.e4me.com
Emerson .... 800-909-1240 .... www.emersonradio.com
Envision........................... 888-838-6388. .... www.envisiondisplay.com
Epson .... 800-463-7766 .... www.epson.com
Ericsson .... 800-374-2776. .... www.ericsson.com
Eureka .... 800-282-2886 .... www.eureka.com

F

Fantom .... 800-668-9600 .... www.fantom.com
Fedders .... 217-347-6459 .... www.fedders.com
Fiesta .... 800-396-3838 .... www.fiestagasgrills.com
Fisher. .... 818-998-7322. .... www.fisherav.com
Fisher & Paykel .... 888-936-7872 .... www.usa.fisherpaykel.com
Ford .... 800-392-3673 .... www.fordvehicles.com
Franklin .... 800-266-5626 .... www.franklin.com
Friedrich .... 800-541-6645 .... www.friedrich.com
Frigidaire .... 800-374-4432 .... www.frigidaire.com
Fujifilm .... 800-800-3854. .... www.fujifilm.com
Fujitsu .... 800-838-5487. .... www.fujitsupc.com

G

Garmin............................ 800-800-1020 .... www.garmin.com
Gateway .... 800-369-1409 .... www.gateway.com
GE (appliances).................... 800-626-2005 .... www.geappliances.com
GE (electronics).................... 800-447-1700 .... www.home-electronics.net
GMC.............................. 800-462-8782 .... www.gmc.com

Goldstar	800-243-0000	www.lgeus.com
Grizzly	570-546-9663	www.grizzly.com

H

Haier	877-337-3639	www.haieramerica.com
Hamilton Beach	800-851-8900	www.hamiltonbeach.com
Harman/Kardon	516-255-4545	www.harmankardon.com
Hewlett-Packard	800-752-0900	www.hp.com
Hitachi	800-448-2244	www.hitachi.com
Holland	800-880-9766	www.hollandgrill.com
Holmes	800-284-3267	www.holmesproducts.com
Homelite	800-242-4672	www.homelite.com
Honda (autos)	800-999-1009	www.hondacars.com
Honda (mowers)	770-497-6400	www.hondapowerequipment.com
Hoover	800-944-9200	www.hoover.com
Hotpoint	800-626-2005	www.hotpoint.com
Hughes	800-347-3288	www.hughes.com
Husqvarna	800-487-5962	www.usa.husqvarna.com
Hyundai	800-633-5151	www.hyundaiusa.com

I

IBM	800-426-4968	www.ibm.com
Infiniti	800-662-6200	www.infiniti.com
Infinity	516-674-4463	www.infinitysystems.com
Intel	800-538-3373	www.intel.com
Iomega	888-516-8467	www.iomega.com
Isuzu	800-255-6727	www.isuzu.com

J

Jaguar	800-452-4827	www.jaguarusa.com
JBL	516-255-4525	www.jbl.com
Jeep	800-925-5337	www.jeep.com
Jenn-Air	800-688-1100	www.jennair.com
John Deere	800-537-8233	www.deere.com
Jonsered	877-693-7729	www.usa.jonsered.com
JVC	800-252-5722	www.jvc.com

K

KDS	800-283-1311	www.kdsusa.com
Kenmore	Call local Sears store	www.sears.com
Kenwood	800-536-9663	www.kenwoodusa.com
Kia	800-333-4542	www.kia.com
Kirby	800-437-7170	www.kirby.com
KitchenAid	800-422-1230	www.kitchenaid.com
KLH	818-767-2843	www.klhaudio.com
Kodak	800-235-6325	www.kodak.com
Konica	800-523-2696	www.konicaminolta.us
Kyocera	800-421-5735	americas.kyocera.com

L

Land Rover	800-346-3493	www.landroverusa.com
Lawn-Boy	800-526-6937	www.lawnboy.com
LearningCo.com	800-395-0277	www.learningcompany.com
Lexmark	800-539-6275	www.lexmark.com
Lexus	800-255-3987	www.lexus.com
LG	800-243-0000	www.lgeus.com
Lincoln	800-521-4140	www.lincoln.com
Lotus	800-746-7426	www.lotus.com
Lucent	866-582-3688	www.lucent.com

M

Magic Chef	800-688-9900	www.magicchef.com
Magnavox	800-705-2000	www.magnavox.com
Makita	800-462-5482	www.makita.com
Maxim	800-233-9054	www.esalton.com
Maytag	800-688-9900	www.maytag.com
Mazda	800-222-5500	www.mazdausa.com
McCulloch	800-521-8559	www.mccullochpower.com
Mercedes-Benz	800-367-6372	www.mbusa.com
Mercury	800-521-4140	www.mercuryvehicles.com
Micron PC	888-719-5031	www.buympc.com
Microsoft	800-642-7676	www.microsoft.com
Microsoft Network	800-373-3676	www.msn.com
Microtek	310-687-5940	www.microtekusa.com
Miele	800-843-7231	www.mieleusa.com
Milwaukee	800-729-3878	www.milwaukeetool.com
Minolta	800-523-2696	www.konicaminolta.us
Mintek	866-709-9500	www.mintekdigital.com
Mitsubishi	888-648-7820	www.mitsubishicars.com
Motorola	800-331-6456	www.motorola.com/us
MTD	800-269-6215	www.mtdproducts.com
Murray	800-224-8940	www.murray.com

N

NEC	800-338-9549	www.necus.com
Network Associates (McAfee VirusScan)	800-338-8754	www.mcafee.com/us
Nextel	800-777-4681	www.nextel.com
Nikon	800-645-6689	www.nikonusa.com
Nintendo	800-255-3700	www.nintendo.com
Nissan	800-647-7261	www.nissanusa.com
Nokia	888-665-4228	www.nokiausa.com

O

Oki	800-654-3282	www.okidata.com
Oldsmobile	800-442-6537	www.oldsmobile.com
Olympus	888-553-4448	www.olympusamerica.com
Onkyo	800-229-1687	www.onkyousa.com
Optimus	800-843-7422	www.radioshack.com
Oreck	800-289-5888	www.oreck.com
Oster	800-334-0759	www.oster.com

P

PalmOne	800-881-7256	www.palm.com/us
Panasonic	800-211-7262	www.panasonic.com
Pentax	800-877-0155	www.pentaxusa.com
Philips	800-531-0039	www.philipsusa.com
Pioneer	800-421-1404	www.pioneerelectronics.com
Polaroid	800-432-5355	www.polaroid.com/us
Polk Audio	800-377-7655	www.polkaudio.com
Pontiac	800-762-2737	www.pontiac.com
Porsche	800-767-7243	www.porsche.com/usa
Porter-Cable	800-487-8665	www.porter-cable.com
Poulan	800-554-6723	www.poulan.com
Precor	800-477-3267	www.precor.com
Precisionaire	800-800-2210	www.precisionaire.com
Proctor-Silex	800-851-8900	www.proctorsilex.com
PSB	888-772-0000	www.psbspeakers.com

Q

Quasar	800-405-0632	www.panasonic.com

R

RadioShack	800-843-7422	www.radioshack.com
RCA	800-336-1900	www.rca.com
Regal	262-626-2121	www.regalware.com
Regina	228-867-8507	www.reginavac.com
Remington	888-917-2244	www.remingtonchainsaw.com
ReplayTV	254-299-2705	www.replaytv.com
Research Products	800-334-6011	www.resprod.com
Rival	800-323-9519	www.rivalproducts.com
Riverdeep	800-825-4420	www.riverdeep.net
Roper	800-447-6737	www.roperappliances.com
Rowenta	781-396-0600	www.rowentausa.com
Royal	800-321-1134	wwww.dirtdevil.com
Ryobi	800-525-2579	www.ryobitools.com

S

Saab	800-722-2872	www.saabusa.com
Sabre by John Deere	800-537-8233	www.deere.com
Salton	800-233-9054	www.esalton.com
Sampo	888-373-4368	www.sampoamericas.com
Samsung	800-726-7864	www.samsungusa.com
Sanyo	800-877-5032	www.sanyo.com
Saturn	800-553-6000	www.saturn.com
Sega	800-872-7342	www.sega.com
Sharp	800-237-4277	www.sharpusa.com
Siemens	888-777-0211	www.icm.siemens.com
Simplicity (yard equipment)	262-284-8669	www.simplicitymfg.com
Simplicity (vacuum cleaners)	888-974-6759	www.simplicityvac.com
Skil	877-754-5999	www.skiltools.com
Snapper	800-935-2967	www.snapper.com
Solo	757-245-4228	www.solousa.com
Sony	800-222-7669	www.sony.com
Southwestern Bell	800-222-0300	www.sbc.com
Sprint PCS	800-777-4681	www.sprint.com
Stanley	800-788-7766	www.stanleytools.com
Stihl	800-467-8445	www.stihlusa.com
Subaru	800-782-2783	www.subaru.com
Sub-Zero	800-222-7820	www.subzero.com
Sunbeam	800-458-8407	www.sunbeam.com
Suzuki	800-934-0934	www.suzukiauto.com
Symantec (Norton Antivirus)	800-441-7234	www.symantec.com

T

Tappan	800-374-4432	www.frigidaire.com
TEC	800-331-0097	www.tecgasgrills.com
Technics	800-211-7262	www.panasonic.com
Thermador	800-656-9226	www.thermador.com
TiVo	877-289-8486	www.tivo.com
T-Mobile	800-937-8997	www.t-mobile.com
Toastmaster	800-233-9054	www.esalton.com
Toro	800-348-2424	www.toro.com
Toshiba	800-867-4422	www.toshiba.com
Toyota	800-331-4331	www.toyota.com
Trion	800-884-0002	www.trioninc.com
Troy-Bilt	888-848-6083	www.troybilt.com

U

Umax	214-342-9799	www.umax.com
Uniden	800-297-1023	www.uniden.com

V

Verizon Wireless	800-922-0204	www.verizonwireless.com
ViewSonic	800-688-6688	www.viewsonic.com
Viking	888-845-4641	www.vikingrange.com
Visioneer	925-251-6398	www.visioneer.com
Vivitar	805-998-0463	www.vivitar.com
Volkswagen	800-822-8987	www.vw.com
Volvo	800-458-1552	www.volvocars.us
VTech	800-595-9511	www.vtech.com

W

Walker	800-843-7422	www.radioshack.com
Waring	800-492-7464	www.waringproducts.com
Weber	800-446-1071	www.weber.com
Weed Eater	800-554-6723	www.weedeater.com
West Bend	262-334-6949	www.westbend.com
Whirlpool	800-253-1301	www.whirlpool.com
White Outdoor	800-269-6215	www.whiteoutdoor.com
White-Westinghouse	800-374-4432	www.frigidaire.com
WinBook	800-254-7806	www.winbook.com

X

Xerox	800-275-9376	www.xerox.com

Y

Yamaha	800-492-6242	www.yamaha.com
Yard Machines by MTD	800-800-7310	www.mtdproducts.com
Yashica	800-421-5735	www.yashica.com

Z

Zenith	877-993-6484	www.zenith.com
Zone Labs	415-633-4500	www.zonealarm.com

4-YEAR INDEX TO CONSUMER REPORTS

This index indicates when the last full report on a given subject was published in CONSUMER REPORTS. The index goes back four years.

In text below, **bold type** indicates Ratings reports or brand-name discussions; *italic type* indicates corrections, followups, or Updates.

BUYING GUIDE INDEX

Statement of Ownership, Management, and Circulation

(Required by 39 U.S.C. 3685)

1. Publication Title: Consumer Reports. 2. Publication No: 0010-7174. 3. Filing Date: September 18, 2006. 4. Issue Frequency: Monthly, except two issues in December. 5. No. of Issues Published Annually: 13. 6. Annual Subscription Price: $26.00. 7. Complete Mailing Address of Known Office of Publication: Consumers Union of United States, Inc., 101 Truman Avenue, Yonkers, New York 10703-1057. 8. Complete Mailing Address of Headquarters or General Business Office of Publisher: Consumers Union of United States, Inc., 101 Truman Avenue, Yonkers, New York 10703-1057. 9. Full Names and Complete Mailing Addresses of Publisher, Editor, and Managing Editor. Publisher: Consumers Union of United States, Inc., 101 Truman Avenue, Yonkers, New York 10703-1057. President:

James A. Guest; Sr. Director/Editor: Margot Slade; Managing Editor: Robert Tiernan. 10. Owner: (If the publication is published by a nonprofit organization, its name and address must be stated.) Full Name: Consumers Union of United States, Inc., a nonprofit organization. Complete Mailing Address: 101 Truman Avenue, Yonkers, New York 10703-1057. 11. Known Bondholders, Mortgagees, and Other Security Holders Owning or Holding 1 Percent or More of Total Amount of Bonds, Mortgages, or Other Securities. If none, so state: None. 12. For Completion by Nonprofit Organizations Authorized to Mail at Special Rates: The purpose, function, and nonprofit status of this organization and the exempt status for federal income tax purposes has not changed during preceding 12 months.

15. Extent and Nature of Circulation:	Average no. copies each issue during past 12 mo.	Actual no. copies of single issue published nearest to filing date
A. Total no. of copies (net press run)	4,845,677	4,780,565
B. Paid and/or requested circulation		
1. Paid/requested outside-county mail subscriptions stated on Form 3541	4,397,636	4,327,389
2. Paid in-county subscriptions stated on Form 3541	NA	NA
3. Sales through dealers, carriers, street vendors, counter sales, and other non-USPS paid distribution	138,180	98,500
4. Other classes mailed through the USPS	0	0
C. Total paid and/or requested circulation (sum of 15b(1), (2), (3), and (4))	4,535,816	4,425,889
D. Free distribution by mail (samples, complimentary, and other free)	28,717	28,948
E. Free distribution outside the mail	14,712	13,641
F. Total free distribution (sum of 15d and 15e)	43,429	42,589
G. Total distribution (sum of 15c and 15f)	4,579,245	4,468,478
H. Copies not distributed	266,432	312,087
I. TOTAL (sum of 15g and 15h)	4,845,677	4,780,565
J. Percent paid and/or requested circulation	99.05%	99.05%

17. I certify that the statements made by me above are correct and complete.
Louis J. Milani, Senior Director, Publishing Operations

5 tips for buying that new car

Expert advice from David Champion, Director of Auto Testing, and The Consumer Reports New Car Price Service

1 Learn the lowest cost
Get the Consumer Reports Wholesale Price

Here's the real key to your deal: you must find out what the dealer paid for the car so you can negotiate the price you'll pay for it. You have to find out this information for yourself and you have to be sure it's up-to-date and correct!

The best way to do this is to make a quick call to the Consumer Reports New Car Price Service. You'll be glad you did. New car buyers who use the service save $1,900 on average. For a fee of just $14, you receive a report by fax or mail that includes:

- The Consumer Reports Bottom Line Price, including current national rebates, unadvertised incentives, and holdbacks.

- The "invoice" price (provided by the manufacturer to the dealer).

- The "sticker" price (what the dealer wants you to pay).

- Invoice and sticker prices of all factory-installed options and packages; CONSUMER REPORTS equipment recommendations.

- Plus solid advice on buying or leasing your new car.

2 Get ready to bargain
Your homework's done. It's all there in plain English with easy-to-follow information. The Consumer Reports Bottom Line Price, along with the invoice and sticker price comparisons, give you a clear understanding of your negotiating room. You're ready.

3 Start bargaining
Always bargain up from the Consumer Reports Bottom Line Price, never down from the sticker price. If the car you want is in tight supply, you may have to pay the full sticker price.

4 Play the game
The advice you receive with your report takes you through the hard part, negotiating a fair price. It takes you step-by-step through the rest of the negotiating game with professional new-car buying advice, such as...*Be wary. The dealer may try*

to sell you undercoating, rustproofing, fabric protection, extended warranty, windshield etching, etc. They're generally worthless or overpriced.

5 If you have a trade-in
Don't even mention it u you've agreed on a pric for your new car. But when it's time to talk trade-in, you shoul know what your trade-in is wor whether you sell it privately or a dealership. You can get that information from us too and it costs just an additional $12.

Detailed price information fro Consumer Reports New Car Pr Service, an organized plan an advice on playing the game. That's how to buy a new car. Y best source for all that help is near as your phone.

Just call the number below:

▼ **1-800-269-11**

For quick results please have th following ready when you call:
- Year, make, and model of the new minivan, van, sport-utility vehicle, pickup truck you want to buy (suc as 2007 Toyota Camry).
- Year, make, model, and trim line of your trade-in, if you have one (e. 1996 Nissan Pathfinder 4WD LE)
- Your credit card (Visa, MasterCar Discover, or American Express).

Consumer Reports NEW CAR PRICE SERVICE

Can buying a new car be less of an ordeal for you? We think so. If you arm yourself with knowledge and an organized plan, you'll get the car you want, equipped to your liking, at a fair price.

David Champion, about to a car through its paces at o state-of-the-art test facility.

BG0